THE SOCIAL HISTORY OF IDEAS IN QUEBEC,
1760–1896

McGILL-QUEEN'S STUDIES IN THE HISTORY OF IDEAS
Series Editor: Philip J. Cercone

THE SOCIAL HISTORY OF IDEAS
IN QUEBEC, 1760–1896

Yvan Lamonde

Translated by
Phyllis Aronoff and Howard Scott

McGill-Queen's University Press
Montreal & Kingston • London • Ithaca

© McGill-Queen's University Press 2013
ISBN 978-0-7735-4106-1 (cloth)
ISBN 978-0-7735-4107-8 (paper)

Legal deposit second quarter 2013
Bibliothèque nationale du Québec

Printed in Canada on acid-free paper that is 100% ancient forest free
(100% post-consumer recycled), processed chlorine free

This book has been published with the help of a grant from the Canadian
Federation for the Humanities and Social Sciences, through the Awards to
Scholarly Publications Program, using funds provided by the Social Sciences
and Humanities Research Council of Canada. We acknowledge the financial
support of the Government of Canada, through the National Translation
Program for Book Publishing for our translation activities.

McGill-Queen's University Press acknowledges the support of the Canada
Council for the Arts for our publishing program. We also acknowledge the
financial support of the Government of Canada through the Canada Book
Fund for our publishing activities.

Library and Archives Canada Cataloguing in Publication

Lamonde, Yvan, 1944–
    The social history of ideas in Quebec / Yvan Lamonde; translated
by Phyllis Aronoff and Howard Scott.

(McGill-Queen's studies in the history of ideas, ISSN 0711-0995; 58)
Translation of: Histoire sociale des idées au Québec.
Includes bibliographical references and indexes.
Contents: v. 1. 1760-1896.
ISBN 978-0-7735-4106-1 (bound: v. 1). – ISBN 978-0-7735-4107-8 (pbk.: v. 1)

1. Political science – Québec (Province) – Philosophy – History. 2. Political
culture – Québec (Province) – History. 3. Québec (Province) – Civilization.
4. Québec (Province) – Social conditions. I. Title. II. Series: McGill-Queen's
studies in the history of ideas; 58

FC2919.L34713 2013   320.509714   C2012-907566-3

This book was typeset by Interscript in 10/12 New Baskerville.

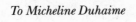

To Micheline Duhaime

Contents

Acknowledgments

I WOULD LIKE TO THANK THE KILLAM FOUNDATION, which gave me a grant that permitted me for two years to make great strides toward the clearing. I am grateful to the archivists, librarians, and Interlibrary Loan Service of McGill University's McLennan Library for a thousand and one signposts on my long hike. I also wish to thank my colleague Jean-Paul Bernard and the evaluator of the Aid to Scholarly Publications Program for their illuminating comments. As usual, Phyllis Aronoff and Howard Scott did impeccable translation work. I am also grateful to the staff at McGill-Queen's University Press, Jonathan Crago, Jessica Howarth, Elena Goranescu, Ryan Van Huijstee, and Joanne Muzak.

On a personal note, I would like to express to Philip J. Cercone, the executive director of McGill-Queen's University Press, my gratitude for the ongoing efforts that have made this translation possible. That was all I needed to make my scholarly and McGillian happiness complete.

The Quest for a Clearing:
Preface to the French Edition

IN AMERICA, AND IN QUEBEC, the challenge of pushing back the forest was faced not only by the seventeenth-century explorers, but also by colonists and settlers up to the nineteenth century, when the Abitibi region was opened up to settlement. The forest was the site of the first fundamental confrontation, the first resistance, the first struggle. The newcomers discovered it, ventured into it, looked for landmarks, got lost in it, searched for themselves in it as in a rite of initiation, and found themselves again in a clearing that soon opened out onto a horizon.

Thirty years ago, when I asked myself where I was coming from intellectually and began searching for beaten paths, roads, avenues, I had the feeling of being in the position of an explorer facing more or less virgin forest. Throughout the process of intellectual discovery and research, one image stood out for me and sustained me: that of the clearing. My project was to find my way out of the woods I had entered – to come upon a little clearing, make my way to a larger clearing, and begin to see things clearly. I went from clearing to clearing, and now I am standing here gazing at a horizon, remembering the dense forest and its paths. This book is the story of the path taken, with landmarks and beacons placed so that readers and other explorers can also find their way to the horizon.

This is a *social* history in that it aims to describe the complete circuit of ideas, their production, dissemination, and reception. It looks at the social background of the individuals who formulated the ideas (the French-speaking middle class in the liberal professions, the clergy, the English-speaking merchant bourgeoisie, the colonial and metropolitan authorities, the citizens), the networks and media that disseminated the currents of opinion, and the social penetration of the ideas. Chapters 2, 5, 13, and 15, in particular, analyze the network of cultural institutions and instruments that disseminated the ideas, debates, and arguments.

The ideas in this social history are civic rather than strictly political, ideas that are found in the discourse of public figures both civil and religious. These civic ideas refer to the major currents of thought and opinion that cut across the two centuries considered – monarchism, republicanism, democracy, revolution and counter-revolution, loyalism, colonialism, liberalism, conservatism, ultramontanism, "nationalism," "philosophism," anticlericalism – and it is the strands formed by these currents of ideas that I follow over two centuries. Although I occasionally refer to literature, painting, and the sciences, I do not claim to offer an archeology of Quebec thought at given periods or to identify a unique intellectual thread that runs through a particular era. That would be an interesting project, but it was not mine.

This social history of ideas in Quebec begins in 1760 and ends, in a second volume, in 1960. Of course, the history of ideas in New France is still to be written – that forest is there for other interests, other clearings – but it is obvious that in choosing to begin with the British colonial regime, I am using the advent of parliamentary government and the development of print to trace the emergence of public opinion. In so doing, I am focusing on bourgeois culture, that of educated people who talk, write, and leave traces in correspondence, the press, or pamphlets. Readers will not find here a history of popular culture, rural or urban, as expressed in stories and legends and in material culture, the culture of objects, dress, food, and decorative patterns. Those are areas of the forest still awaiting the axe.

This social history of ideas in Quebec, from the Conquest and the cession to the Quiet Revolution, is that of French-speaking Quebecers. This is a pragmatic choice because, while I give a lot of space to the culture and cultural institutions of the English-speaking community, I will leave for others the pleasure of finding those clearings.

I also examine the intellectual history of francophone Quebec in relation to the international situation over two centuries, in particular its relationships to its former mother countries and its political and cultural "metropolises": France, England, the United States, and Rome. I feel that this history, with its comparison of both cultural forms and institutions and their content, could serve as a model for other intellectual histories of regions of Canada, if not for an intellectual history of Canada itself.

I often let the contemporaries speak for themselves, because, even if history is always a construction by a historian, it is still of interest to readers to have some idea of the materials that were used in that construction. The quotations and translations from the original texts also provide a sense of the culture of a period through its spoken and written

language. Readers who would like to consult some of the texts themselves, the original documents, may see the anthology I compiled with
Claude Corbo, entitled *Le rouge et le bleu* (PUM, 1999). I have used quan-
titative analysis to establish long-term trends, and rather than include
large numbers of statistical tables in this volume, I refer to the tables
published in Yvan Lamonde and Claude Beauchamp, *Données statistiques
sur l'histoire culturelle du Québec, 1760–1900* (Chicoutimi: Institut interuniversitaire de recherches sur les populations [IREP], 1996). This book,
which is no longer readily available in the print version, is now accessible
in a digitized version on the Internet at http://classiques.uqac.ca/
contemporains/lamonde_yvan/donnes_stats_hist_culture/donnes_
stats_hist_culture.html.

I refer the reader first of all to the manuscript and print sources described in the endnotes. Wherever possible, I also give the reference
to the microfiche collection of the Canadian Institute for Historical
Microreproductions (CIHM), so that Quebec, Canadian, and international readers will be able to have access to the documents through this
valuable collection of the print heritage.

Studies of the cultural and intellectual history of Quebec have been
catalogued over the past three decades in the following bibliographies.

Lamonde, Yvan. *L'histoire des idées au Québec (1760–1960)*. Bibliographie des
études. Montreal: BNQ, 1989.
– "L'histoire culturelle et intellectuelle du Québec (1960–1990): bibliographie
des études." *Littératures* 4 (1989): 155–89.
– "L'histoire des idées au Québec (1760–1993). Premier supplément bibliographique et tendances de la recherche (1re partie)." *Cahiers d'histoire du
Québec au xxe siècle* 3 (Winter 1995): 163–76.
– "L'histoire des idées … (2e partie)." *Cahiers d'histoire du Québec au xxe siècle* 4
(Summer 1995): 152–67.
– "L'histoire des idées et de la culture au Québec (1760–1997): deuxième supplément bibliographique (1993–97) et tendances de la recherche." *Bulletin
d'histoire politique* 9, no. 3 (Summer 2001): 159–61. www.unites.uqam.ca/bhp/
biblio1.htm.
– and Éric Leroux. "L'histoire des idées et de la culture au Québec (1760–
2003): troisième supplément bibliographique (1998–2003)." *Mens* 6 (2005–
2006): 159–61. http://www.revuemens.ca/bibliographies.html.

A series of overviews of the socio-cultural history of Quebec have made
it possible to define the evolution and methodological challenges of this
area of historical research. The latest one, which provides references

to previous overviews, is Yvan Lamonde, "L'histoire culturelle comme domaine historiographique au Québec," *Revue d'histoire de l'Amérique française* 51, no. 2 (Fall 1997): 285–99.

Yvan Lamonde
Montreal, Saint-Ours-sur-Richelieu,
Baie-Saint-Paul, Orleans (Cape Cod)

Introduction to the English Edition

AFTER TEN YEARS OF REVIEWS AND DISCUSSIONS of this book, which was first published in 2000, English-language readers will have the benefit of clarifications and perspective in relation to work published more recently in the field of intellectual history.

A SOCIAL HISTORY

Journals of social history vary in how explicit and how consistent they are in their editorial approach, but over the past thirty years, there have been practically as many definitions of social history as there have been historians practising it. In the early 1970s, at Université Laval, when I was beginning to conceive of this history of ideas, the trend was shifting from economic history (Albert Faucher, Fernand Ouellet, Yves Roby) to social history (Ouellet, Jean Hamelin). Social history then covered both labour and capital, and with a more or less latent Marxism circulating in the history community, it was making more room for working conditions and union organization, causing students' vocabulary to waver between "social classes" and "social groups." The key word was *bourgeoisie*, divided into the "merchant bourgeoisie" and the "bourgeoisie of the liberal professions"; even the clergy was sometimes presented as belonging in its way to the latter variant of the bourgeoisie.

It was also, on both sides of the Atlantic, the period of the *Annales* school in its "economy and society" version, which neglected "civilizations" – including the "history of mentalities" (Claude Galarneau) – and had to constantly prove its seriousness by relating things to the economic and social spheres, whether or not it was using a Marxist model. At a conference in September 1975, Fernand Ouellet and Robert Mandrou explained their conception of "socio-cultural history."[1]

At the same time, cultural history was closely identified with the history of the book (Galarneau, Jean-Pierre Wallot, John Hare); at Laval, frequent visits by Mandrou, the author of a study of French popular culture in the seventeenth and eighteenth centuries (*De la culture populaire en France aux XVIIᵉ et XVIIIᵉ siècles*, 1964) and an important book on *La Bibliothèque bleue de Troyes* (1964), and Roger Chartier contributed to keeping research on Quebec current in this field. Now, if it wanted to earn historiographic credentials, the nascent cultural and intellectual history had to be social, the history of social groups or social classes. Among other things, the history of the book raised the economic and social issues of the conditions of production, distribution, and consumption or reception of printed matter, just as Galarneau's history of classical education shed light on the education and "mental tools" of the elites, the bourgeoisie of the liberal professions and the clergy.

In tackling the history of philosophy and its teaching in the classical colleges for my master's degree and my doctorate, I was moving more explicitly toward the history of content, the history of ideas and the intellectual strands that run through the history of Quebec. I was approaching, by another path, the work of Philippe Sylvain on ultramontanism and liberalism in French Canada and Europe, that of Jean-Paul Bernard on the Rouges (1971) and that of Nadia Fahmy Eid on the ultramontanists (1978). The syllogism went this way: cultural history had to be social, and intellectual history had to be part of cultural history. Taking into account the socioeconomic context guaranteed the intelligibility of the analysis of ideas, currents of opinion, and public debate. There could be no cultural history that was not social. It was necessary, at any rate, to do intellectual history and cultural history together, given that knowledge in these two areas of history was so incomplete.

THE HISTORY OF WHOSE IDEAS?

The ideas I focused on were not those of thermodynamics or the conception of nature in French Canadian society, but, rather, civic ideas, ideas at work, much like the phrase "tax dollars at work." While these civic ideas concerned politics, they went beyond, insofar as they involved civil society in general much more than the political elite. Today, I consider the fact that I took such an interest in liberalism in its doctrinal and political forms, and that the theme of democracy was such a constant concern, as indicative of this. These ideas were not obscure: they were expressed in the public sphere, in debates and controversies, and they had emerged with parliamentarism, the press, printed matter, and painting. And if they were at work, they sooner or later involved power.

The postulate of the social and power was instilled during this time as a result of the attention given to ideologies in an interdisciplinary context. An indication of this is the first works on ideologies in French Canada (1850–1900), first published in *Recherches sociographiques* (1969) and then reprinted in book form in a series that took the study of ideologies up to 1960. The list of participants in this first seminar on history and sociology speaks for itself: Fernand Dumont, Jean Hamelin, Yves Roby, René Hardy, N.F. Eid, and Gérard Bouchard, to mention only a few. Ideology being a position of a group or class presented as universal in a given society in order to buttress a power structure, one could search only for the ideologies of social groups and think only about the ideas that were associated with power, that sought power or justified it.

The categorical imperative "ideas–social group–power" had become rather imperialistic. My approach was going to be social in two ways: the ideas (intellectual history) would be inscribed in a socioeconomic context (cultural history), and they would be those of the bourgeoisie of the liberal (and religious) professions. This was at the time when Ouellet had just shown how the rise of the liberal professions in the period 1760–1840 had occurred at the expense of the clergy, which decreased in numbers. In the French Canadian community, the bourgeoisie of the liberal professions and the Catholic clergy personified the ideas of social groups seeking power. In addition, these two social groups had knowledge, power, and assets, and they expressed themselves publicly in writing, speeches, and sermons. The traces of their ideas were the medium of their messages.

A social history of ideas could have been the history of *all* social groups, as much the so-called popular classes as the anglophone bourgeoisie of the liberal professions or business. With two students, Lucia Ferretti and Daniel Leblanc, I explored the concept of popular culture in a historiographic review of working-class culture in Montreal, *La culture ouvrière à Montréal (1880–1920)* (1982), and argued in favour of a history of mass culture ("Pour une histoire de la culture de masse et des médias") in the UNESCO journal *Cultures* (1981). My social history of ideas included the charivaris during the Rebellions, the social makeup of the membership of the Institut canadien de Montréal – which combined elements of a debating society and of the Mechanics' Institutes – and the positions of the union movement on questions such as the standardization of textbooks and compulsory schooling. This interest focused on popular culture in the urban context, but there was also the popular culture of the rural and pre-industrial context. I became convinced of two things: first, that it was necessary to begin to identify and understand the culture of people with power before attempting to identify differences between popular culture and bourgeois culture, and second, that the forms of social expression of the common people – oral culture (stories, legends, proverbs), material culture (clothing, artifacts produced on farms), the culture of physical movement (work in the fields, in the forest or at sea, charivari, strikes) – required documentation and a specific method. The existence of the folklore archives at Université Laval was a daily reminder to me of the wealth of material and the requirements. I even called on an ethnologist so that we could work jointly on the two social forms of culture. There is still work to be done in order to create a history of popular culture in rural and urban contexts and the arrival of mass culture in Quebec, which is closely associated with industrialization and the mass media, as Leonard B. Kuffert has done in *A Great Duty: Canadian Responses to Modern Life and Mass Culture in Canada, 1939–1967* (2003). Knowing the demands of a study of popular culture, I did not venture there; that is another history.

A SOCIAL HISTORY OF THE IDEAS OF FRANCOPHONES

The same type of demands exist for a social history of the ideas of the anglophone population of Quebec. Critics have talked about the "exclusion" of anglophones from my study. That is not accurate. Wherever it was necessary to take into account the leadership of the anglophone community in the cultural sphere, I did so – and this was quite a new approach – in print culture (print shops, newspapers, libraries, bookstores, associations) and the culture of the middle classes (shows and sports, following the work of Alan Metcalfe). It was not possible to understand the cultural dynamics of francophones without addressing this. But that is not the same as simultaneously writing an intellectual history of the anglophones of Montreal, Quebec City, and the Eastern Townships. To know, understand, and explain the history of the ideas of a cultural community requires a longstanding knowledge and familiarity with the words, concepts, and discussions – which I did not have. That remains to be done – I have always hoped it would be done in my university – and the comparison developed. The question, then, is more one of respect for the scholarly requirements than merely of "exclusion."

In the same ideological vein as the idea of "exclusion," critics have spoken of a "heroic nationalist history"; not doing at the same time – in a work that required some thirty years – the history of the ideas of the anglophone community thus necessarily meant doing a "heroic nationalist history." It is not easy to enter into a historiography other than one's own; we have to get away from the cliché of nationalist Quebec history and understand that we can and should address the construction of a society and the constitution of a "nationality," to use a term from the mid-nineteenth century.

When James Stuart was about to go to London as the spokesperson for the second plan for union, that of 1822, he wrote: "The unreasonable extent of political rights conceded to this population ... with a sense of their growing strength, has already had the effect of realising in the imagination of many of them their fancied existence as a separate nation under the name of NATION CANADIENNE ... a system of Gov. which in its ulterior consequences must expose G[reat] B[ritain] to the mortification and disgrace of having at immense expense reared to the maturity of independence a foreign conquered country." Here Stuart grasped the dynamics of the colonial situation, at the same time as Lord Bathurst, Sir James Mackintosh, and Louis-Joseph Papineau were dealing with the question of the possible emancipation of the colony. Recognizing in the historical narrative the fact that in the 1830s, a first expression – in the negative – of the principle of nationality ("no nation is willing to obey another, for the simple reason that no nation knows how to command another") was already circulating in Lower Canada, and recognizing the debate in 1848 between liberalism and nationality indicates only one thing: the awakening of nationalities is not a "nationalist" fixation, but a historical phenomenon that marked Europe and the Americas during the nineteenth century. It is understandable that my recognition of the appeal to the principle of nationality is regarded as doing "heroic nationalist history": anglophones in Lower Canada and Upper Canada tended not to think in these terms of emancipation, since they wished to maintain the connection with the mother country and extend its culture to the whole of the colony.

Finally, is it doing nationalist history to point out that, in 1840, the metropolis abolished the democratic principle of representation by population when this strategy served its imperial plan, and then, after the census of 1851, re-established it when the plan had a better chance of success in demographic terms? The issue here, if it must be stated, has more to do with the development of democracy in the colony than with any militant nationalist history.

A SOCIAL HISTORY OF IDEAS
IN AN INTERNATIONAL CONTEXT

In 1995, in the *Canadian Historical Review*, Allan Greer made a strong appeal for a comparative history of the Rebellions that would reopen the subject, providing a more systematic analysis of the demands and strategies of Lower and Upper Canada in order to get a true sense of the similarities in the views of Papineau and William Lyon Mackenzie. This still remains to be done. A contribution made by this book, however, was placing the political situation of the 1830s in the international context, examining the knowledge the Patriotes had of the awakening of nationalities and nationalist affirmation in Italy, Greece, Belgium, Ireland, Poland, and South America. It then became a little clearer that the evolution of the colonial demands was part of a broader Romantic and emancipatory spirit.

It is this same concern for linking the local and the international in the historical long term that motivated me in addressing the intellectual and political legacies of the successive metropolises. The formula I finally made up from these components of the *external* legacies to French Canada ($Q = - F + GB + USA^2 - R$) and developed in *Allégeances et dépendances: Histoire d'une ambivalence identitaire* (2001) clearly expressed a desire to recall the colonial situation of society in Lower Canada and Quebec and to draw the intellectual and geopolitical conclusions. Knowledge and recognition of this situation were necessary, and they made it possible to see the American (not only in the sense of the United States) strand in French Canada from the American invasion of 1774 to the idea of a spiritual and religious vocation of the French race *in America* in the years 1859 to 1945. The approach used – which would be continued by a McGill student, Damien-Claude Bélanger – was a further development, with regard to Quebec, of the work of my former colleagues Stephen J. Randall and John H. Thompson, and with regard to Canada, of the work of Allan Smith, and it opened two windows: on the "Americanity" of Quebec, defined as a consciousness of belonging to the American continent, and on the urgency of inscribing the cultural and intellectual history of Lower Canada and Quebec in a North American framework. Carl Bode's *The American Lyceum: Town Meeting of the Mind* (1968) helped me see a culture of America that did not reproduce the culture of Europe in every respect, and taught me not to look for French cultural institutions – Académies de province, for example – in Lower Canada. The culture studied in this book is a colonial and American culture and the local "lyceum" is a voluntary cultural and civic association such as the Institut canadien de Montréal, which I have examined in depth; this is similar to what Jeffrey McNairn did in 2000 in his way with respect to Upper Canada in *The Capacity to Judge: Public Opinion and Deliberative Democracy in Upper Canada (1791–1854)*.

APPROACHES TO THE CULTURAL AND INTELLECTUAL HISTORY OF CANADA IN THE PAST TEN YEARS

Since the publication of this history of ideas in Quebec in the eighteenth and nineteenth centuries, there have been a number of new orientations in the cultural and intellectual history of English-speaking Canada. Without claiming to be systematic, I will mention a few historiographic approaches, focusing on the debate around the idea of Canada as a liberal project.

The *History of the Book in Canada / Histoire du livre et de l'imprimé au Canada* (University of Toronto Press / Presses de l'Université de Montréal), the national projects on the history of the book in France, the United States, England, Scotland, Australia, and New Zealand, and the work of Roger Chartier and Robert Darnton attest to the organic link between cultural history and print culture for about the past forty years. While these projects were mainly concerned with what cultural and intellectual history has contributed to the history of printed matter, what the history of printed matter has contributed to the cultural history of Canada should also be noted. The table of contents of the three volumes of the *History of the Book in Canada / Histoire du livre et de l'imprimé au Canada* already reveals a periodization of the cultural development of Canada, and in particular, the takeoff of Canadian culture in the 1880s. It further shows the decisive importance of literacy, personal libraries, and reading in the intellectual and cultural education of citizens. Perhaps the most important contribution of the history of print in Canada involves the history of the public library and the emergence of a public culture in Canada between 1840 and 1880, which was followed by a commercialization of culture, as is illustrated by the history of bookstores and copyright, for example.[2] At the end of that immense project, we were better able to see how and why we need to argue in favour of histories of other media, such as those (radio, television, digital) that followed the domination of print culture, in the wake of work by Asa Briggs in England, Eric Barnouw in the United States, and Mary Vipond, Howard Fink, Renée Legris, and Pierre Pagé in Canada and Quebec.[3]

Since the pioneering collection edited by Allan Greer and Ian Radforth, *Colonial Leviathan: State Formation in Mid-Nineteenth-Century Canada* (1992), the approach of analyzing the construction of the state has taken many forms, such as in the work of the historical sociologist Bruce Curtis.[4] Whether the focus is state involvement in the introduction of national statistics and school statistics,[5] or the governmentality of Lower Canada or the school system,[6] the concern is the same: to see the construction of the state under way before the existence of the welfare state.

At a time when the culture of spectacle meets the culture of politics, and the history of historians takes the form, for citizens, of still-evident traces of the past, traces, and memory that are co-opted for many purposes, we are able to revisit and review their previous forms through commemorations, festivities, and civil rituals in the public space. Whether it be the third centenary of Quebec City,[7] the pomp of a royal visit,[8] the "political theatre" of Lord Durham,[9] or the demonstrations at the time of the law on compensation of 1849,[10] the power of a queen or a king or their representatives is seen again by Canadian historians through the lens of public actions. In a society dominated by representation, memory has places, special moments, and heroes that extend history in an unprecedented way, from the dawn of time to the present.

ABOUT LIBERALISM AS "PROJECT"
AND AS "GENERAL LOGIC"

With the publication of the proceedings of a conference held at McGill University (Montreal) in 2006 to discuss a text by Ian McKay and a book by Michel Ducharme, liberalism gained an unexpected historiographic visibility.[11]

The initial reference in Ian McKay's text to a book by Fernande Roy is doubly revealing: the reflection starts from an examination of the liberalism of the French Canadian "business people" of the last quarter of the nineteenth century and from a book published after almost two decades of debate in Quebec historiography on liberalism and ultramontanism. It is understandable that McKay started with this book: it allowed him to introduce the two components of liberalism, economic and political, turning his attention first to the former, and it suggested the choice of 1840 as a starting point. For Quebec historians, the question of liberalism as a statement of principle and as a civic and political theme is not new, and the reminder of this makes it possible to weigh the importance accorded to the programmatic scope of this text, which is also promisingly ambitious in its project of bringing consistency to the concept of liberalism. The discussion has all the more resonance given that this book follows liberalism as a fundamental strand in the intellectual history of Quebec of the eighteenth and nineteenth centuries.

There are two reasons for the difficulty of defining or characterizing liberalism: the meaning of this "value" cuts across all human experience, individual and collective, and belonging to a given political culture can shift the meaning or the emphasis placed on one or another of its dimensions. Indeed, depending on whether one is familiar with John Locke or John Stuart Mill or the French Enlightenment philosophers, one will tend to emphasize the right to property, the radical affirmation of the individual or the citizen, or the great freedoms (of expression, the press, association, religion). This means that the intellectual background of "liberals" in Canada is particularly important, and because it was sometimes difficult to find Locke and Mill in the classical colleges and even the universities of Quebec before 1960, it is therefore difficult to identify a single "liberal project" in Canada.

In the case of Quebec, one cannot easily begin the periodization of the liberal strand in 1837 or 1840. From this perspective, my research leads me to share Jerry Bannister's view that it is difficult not to begin the history of liberalism in Canada in the eighteenth century.[12] This choice leads to another one: to address political liberalism as much as economic liberalism. This is the basic choice I made, to focus first on liberalism conceived in terms of its etymology –freedom, liberties – and in accordance with its importance in Europe and in the Americas of the period. Without losing sight of the fact that England had its revolution a century before France and that its Parliament already included a democratic component, it must be recognized that the American War of Independence (1776) and the French Revolution of 1789 sparked a debate around the rights of the individual citizen, property, and the great freedoms. With the rise of the liberal professions in Lower Canada after 1815, liberal ideas found defenders and promoters.

We must begin the history of liberalism in the eighteenth century if we want to understand the emergence of the dimensions that marked its evolution in the eighteenth and nineteenth centuries – if only to know to what extent French Canadians opted for English-, French-, or American-style liberalism, or what blend of the three. The Parti canadien (1805) and Papineau were admirers of the "English liberties" until the second plan for union in 1822; they wanted those liberties for themselves and discovered that the metropolis was conceding them very sparingly. While in 1774–75 the French Canadians showed a "benevolent neutrality" toward the "Bastonnois" (Bostonians), after 1823, the Parti patriote (1826) looked beyond England for its orientations. It found them to the south, in the United States, an example of successful emancipation where the citizens elected their senators as it would have liked the members of the Legislative Council to be elected. Liberalism then took on a new accent. Louis-Georges Harvey has made an excellent study of this American and republican strand in the Patriotes' liberalism.[13]

In 1848, the liberals of the Institut canadien de Montréal were enthusiastic about the revolutions occurring in France, Italy, and Hungary, seeing the principle of nationality as a liberal application of the right, not of individuals, but of peoples, to self-determination. I mention this because when Wilfrid Laurier, who was to leave the Institut, gave his famous speech of 26 June 1877 on "political liberalism," he reconfigured the history of French Canadian liberalism for philosophical and electoralist reasons, presenting it as English-style liberalism rather than French-style liberalism; 1848 was thus a youthful indiscretion of liberalism, and the

Introduction

history of liberties in France was written "in letters of blood," while in England it was one of gradual adjustment through reform after reform.[14] This little-known and underrated speech by Laurier is the clearest possible reminder of how French and British liberal traditions intermingled in the French Canada of the time.

Laurier's views undoubtedly drew from what had been the "liberalism" of Louis-Hippolyte La Fontaine and George-Étienne Cartier, who had distanced themselves from the democratic liberalism of Papineau at the beginning of the Union.[15] The term "liberal conservative," which was used at this time, clearly indicates a reorientation of liberal thought with the Reformers.[16]

From Papineau and Étienne Parent to Maurice Duplessis, Quebec had a tradition of economic liberalism in free trade and laissez-faire capitalism. The free trade that followed the repeal of the Corn Laws might have pleased people such as Papineau, who was a continentalist and was in favour of increased trade with the United States, but in 1849 it did not please the Tories in Montreal, who lost trade protection at a time when, in addition, the victims of the Rebellions were receiving compensation. Papineau's often paradoxical position on the seigneurial system suggests a view of liberal capitalism that was, to say the least, different from that of the merchant bourgeoisie of Montreal. As for Duplessis's liberalism, we can understood the title of Gilles Bourque, Jules Duchastel, and Jacques Beauchemin's *La société libérale duplessiste, 1944–1960* (1994) as referring essentially to economic liberalism. These few examples suggest that there are significant differences between the tradition of economic liberalism of French Canada and that of English Canada.

Another dimension of liberalism, that of radical individualism, may be seen to have a different orientation in intellectual history when we consider, for example, the place of the individual and individuality in the Protestant tradition and in the Catholic tradition. Individual examination has a very different meaning in these two mentalities. We can also look at the question of the individual from the perspective of philosophical modernity and the Cartesian tradition of "*I* think, therefore *I* am," and see how the subject has been constructed in the culture of a given society.[17] I would claim is that this is still part of the question of liberalism.

Liberalism is integral to any intellectual history – still to be written – of the liberal women, such as the wife of Louis-Joseph Papineau, Julie Bruneau-Papineau, and his sister, Rosalie Papineau-Dessaulles;[18] the daughter of Louis-Antoine Dessaulles, Caroline Dessaulles-Béique;[19] the daughter Henriette, known as Fadette,[20] of Georges-Casimir Dessaulles, and his second wife, Fanny Leman;[21] the daughter of Premier

Félix-Gabriel Marchand, Joséphine Marchand-Dandurand;[22] and the groundbreaking Éva Circé-Côté.[23]

Finally, as Bannister suggests in the collection *Liberalism and Hegemony*, there is a "conservative framework" that is the counterpart of the "liberal framework" in Canada. In the case of Quebec, this conservatism has not always been omnipresent. We need to recognize the historiographic work of Fernand Ouellet, who showed the rise and strong presence of people in the liberal professions with liberal ideas between 1815 and 1840, and that of Philippe Sylvain and Jean-Paul Bernard, who clearly identified the struggle between liberalism and conservatism from 1840 to 1880. If there was a political conservatism that was dominant until 1897 and a religious conservatism until the Depression, we clearly see which strand of conservatism ran parallel to that of liberalism.

This book, covering a long historical period, can be read as an experience of changing one's scenery, as on a continental journey. The constant question of the traveller boils down to this: why are the inhabitants of the country the way they are? And it is often on their return that travellers search more zealously for answers to that question. Here the reader will travel in place through a history that offers answers to the question.

For this change of scenery to be a pleasant experience, travellers can spend a day or two in a chapter. They don't have to see the whole country in five days. Better to have a pied-à-terre – at home, in a café, in an apartment – and tour one chapter one day and another one the next.

The history recounted here has much in common with the experience of a geographic change of scenery. It increases in interest with the pleasure of discovering something that intrigues or enlightens at each street corner, in each neighbourhood, on each page. It is a history that seeks to show the reasons and the circumstances in which the inhabitants of a space have over time established their ways of thinking and doing things. Set out now on the journey, following the current: "In May each year, the people living along the shores of the St Lawrence ..."

Yvan Lamonde
17 December 2011

PART ONE

1760–1815

1

French, English, American, or Canadian?
(1760–1815)

IN MAY EACH YEAR, the people living along the shores of the St Lawrence were in the habit of paying close attention to the first ships to sail up the river after the break-up of the ice. The appearance of the first sails was a sign of a new beginning.

"THE YEAR OF THE ENGLISH" (1759)

On 19 May 1759, the inhabitants of Le Bic, east of Quebec City on the south shore, were intrigued by the first vessels that appeared on the horizon; gradually they realized that the ships were not flying the French flag. On 25 May, witnesses confirmed that they had seen "fifty sails at Le Bic and ten at L'Isle-Verte." It was the vanguard of an English flotilla under the command of Vice-Admiral Durrell, and it was joined on 18 June by the fleet, which came from Halifax and was commanded by Admiral Charles Saunders.

During the night of 18–19 June, signal fires on the shore transmitted the news to Rivière-Ouelle and a courier was dispatched to Quebec City. On 20 June, the fleet was at Tadoussac, and on 21 June, it was facing Kamouraska, where "147 enemy sails [were seen] ... from Île aux Basques to the end of Île aux Lièvres, 14 of them [with] 60 to 80 cannon, 16 frigates [with] 26 to 50 cannon, and the rest various ships, try-sails, brigantines, schooners and boats." This small armada dropped anchor off Île-aux-Coudres on 23 June, and north of the Montmagny archipelago on Saint-Jean-Baptiste Day. There was a constant stream of ships through the islands; they sailed along the Charlevoix coast, steered toward the south of Île d'Orléans and turned to port and entered the narrow strait known as the Traverse, between Île d'Orléans and Île Madame. The fleet then entered the North Channel and dropped anchor across from Saint-Laurent-de-l'Île-d'Orléans. Detachments landed on Île d'Orléans, at Beaumont on the south shore, and at Pointe-Lévy across from Quebec City.

Evacuation of the inhabitants of the south shore had already begun and men were being enlisted. General Wolfe issued a proclamation in Saint-Laurent-de-l'Île-d'Orléans on 28 June, in which he stated that this "formidable ... armament" was intended to "check the insolence of France." The antagonism between the two great powers could not have been expressed more bluntly. Wolfe assured the population of "royal clemency," but "if, by a vain obstinacy and misguided valour, [the Canadians] presume to appear in arms, they must expect the most fatal consequences; their habitations destroyed, their sacred temples exposed to an exasperated soldiery, their harvest utterly ruined, and the only passage for relief stopped up by a most formidable fleet."[1]

On 12 July, the bombardment of Quebec City began. Three months later, on 13 September 1759, the English defeated the Canadians and the French on the Plains of Abraham. On 18 September, Quebec City surrendered. Montreal fell a year later, on 8 September 1760. New France was no longer.

The public opinion, ideas, currents of thought, and debates on ideas that emerged in the colony of British North America were influenced by three determining factors: the presence of interlocutors from various cultures and communities; the establishment, through debate, of political forms that were new – as much so in the Western world as in the colony – and the creation of media, printing, and newspapers, which encouraged debate and enabled a record to be left of this nascent public opinion.

The military conquest of New France by England, the succession of political regimes (the Treaty of 1763, the Quebec Act of 1774, the Constitutional Act of 1791) during a time when America (1776) and Europe (1789) were experiencing revolutions, the clash of political cultures, and the divergent interests of social groups stimulated remarkable intellectual activity, with the House of Assembly, pamphlets, "gazettes," and coffee shops becoming forums. It was within this constellation that the ideas of religious tolerance, loyalism, and "English liberties" were formulated. Public opinion came into being in Quebec with democratic aspirations, parliamentarism, religious and civil eloquence, and print.

This period, which began with a military conquest and saw two revolutions – not to mention the revolutions in Spain's and Portugal's American colonies – finally came to a close with the end of the Napoleonic Wars and the Continental Blockade and the signature of the Treaty of Vienna of 1815.

REACTIONS TO THE CESSION

New France was no longer. But would Canada be another New England? Would Great Britain keep or negotiate away its new colony? If it kept it, what measures would it employ to make British subjects of the Canadians?

After the destruction of a third of the buildings in Quebec City, as well as several villages along the St Lawrence, the conquerors had every interest in treating the vanquished well in order to gain their loyalty. In fact, the conquerors showed "marks of humanity" toward the vanquished: donations from their pay by some soldiers; the obligation to declare wheat; regulation of the price of firewood to prevent speculation. In spite of this, the concerns of the conquered people about their property, their language, their laws, and their religion remained; there were hesitations, disappointments, and expectations. Reactions were expressed.

Although after the dispersion of the Acadians in 1755, the Catholic Church had warned the people that the advance of the English could mean the introduction of the "detestable errors of Luther and Calvin" into the colony and said that it was essential to "preserve this vast country from heresy," it very early showed signs of gratitude toward Governor Murray, that "charitable and generous benefactor."[2] The coronation and marriage of George III were greeted with expressions of submission and celebration. The religious authorities asked parish priests to sing a "Te Deum" and remind parishioners that "The God of armies, who disposes crowns as he wishes and extends or restricts at his pleasure the boundaries of empires, having by his eternal decrees put us under the domination of his Britannic Majesty, it is our duty, based on natural law, to be interested in all that concerns him. We order you to submit to the king and to all those who share his authority."[3] The bishop of Quebec City, Mgr Briand, thanked the king for his protection of the Catholic religion and said of the English, "They are our masters, and we owe them what we owed the French when they were our masters." He was a man and a priest of his time, that of the ancien régime: he preached in favour of an alliance between throne and altar, between political power and religious power. He wrote to Major Abercrombie that secular power "must lend itself to the support of religion, as the ecclesiastical power [must lend itself] to making peoples render the respect and obedience that they owe princes and superiors."[4] The position of the Church with regard to political power had been established for two centuries.

Probably at the time the news came of the Treaty of Paris (signed on 10 February 1763), the bishop of Quebec City asked all the priests to sing a "Te Deum" in thanksgiving for the blessing of peace. On the

Sunday following the reception of his pastoral letter, all the priests read the bishop's directive to their parishioners: "Be rigorous in fulfilling the duties of subjects who are faithful and loyal to their prince; and you will have the consolation of finding a kind-hearted, benevolent king devoted to making you happy, and favourable to your religion ... Nothing can exempt you from perfect obedience, scrupulous and strict loyalty, and inviolable and genuine attachment to your new Monarch and to the interests of the nation with which we have been joined."[5] A few days later, a Récollet priest wrote to the Bishop: "I sang the 'Te Deum' according to your pastoral letter, *oculis lacrymantibus*," that is, with tears in his eyes.[6] Submission, then, did not occur without regret. But French feeling had to give way to Catholic feeling. Responding to the favourable first provisions of the English with respect to religion, Cardinal Castelli wrote from Rome to Abbé de l'Isle-Dieu: "For their part, priests and bishop must ... sincerely forget that they are French."[7] In the mind and the interest of the Church, religion took priority over language and culture. This would be the pattern of the history of the Catholic Church in French Canada: alliance of state and Church, loyalty to the established authorities, primacy of religion over other cultural characteristics.

The notables were a little less quick to take a position with respect to the conquerors. In June 1762, the "principal" inhabitants of Quebec City assured the governor and the king of their loyalty, recognizing the sovereign who was "so necessary to his peoples and whose government is so gentle for his new subjects that they form, so to speak, a single nation."[8] Following the signature of the Treaty of Paris, the bourgeoisie of Quebec City addressed the governor and the king, who they said had treated them as a father would, and as he did his old subjects: "Here come down from Heaven is this peace so much desired ... We are irrevocably incorporated into the body of the subjects of the Crown of England. Such are the edicts of the Supreme Being. It is up to us to conform to them and to be as faithful subjects of our new monarch as we were, or should have been, to the King of France."[9]

In spite of these expressions of submission, there were still individual and collective expectations. Governor Haldimand considered, in April 1763, that half the population did not believe that peace had really been established,[10] but it was felt that the treaties would change this. A nun from the Hôpital général de Québec told a member of the French Court: "We cannot, Monseigneur, describe plainly the pain and bitterness that has gripped every heart at the news of this change of domination; we like to think that some revolution that Providence will bring about will return to us our rights."[11] Mother d'Youville had difficulty accepting the loss of France: "We had persuaded ourselves that France would not abandon us, but we were mistaken in our expectations." She would be further disappointed in 1765, when France reimbursed the old payment orders at only 25 per cent of their value; she said, "After having been treated harshly in that, we are once again [being treated harshly], in this."[12]

The reactions to the military conquest of the country by the English revealed a mentality that belonged to the ancien régime. The civil and religious population had always lived under absolute monarchy, and now it was experiencing a change of the monarch "so necessary to his peoples." The notables saw in this the "decrees of the Supreme Being," while the Church saw the action of Providence or the "God of armies" in the changes of "crown," "empires," or "masters," and made the alliance of throne and altar and obedience to the prince its political credo. But as the notables had guessed, the challenge was to know if the "new subjects" (the *Canadiens*) and the old ones (the British immigrants) "form, so to speak, a single nation." What political institutions could the British Protestant metropolis, the enemy of Paris and Rome, offer or concede to this new colony of North America, the vast majority of which was French and Catholic?

Initially, the colony was governed by a military treaty, the Treaty of Paris; significantly, only article 4 was related to Canada, and it concerned religion: "that his new Roman Catholic subjects may profess the worship of their religion according to the rites of the Romish church, as far as the laws of Great Britain permit." This religious tolerance was reiterated in other documents, which, however, noted that it would be advisable to watch the French priests for possible intrusion into political matters and that there could not be any form of foreign, papal, religious authority in the colony. The Royal Proclamation of 7 October 1763 provided for the administration of the colony, entrusted power to the governor and his Council and suggested, for the benefit of future British settlers, that "assemblies" could be called when circumstances permitted. Instructions to Governor Murray imposed the obligation to take the Test Oath (non-recognition of the pope, the Virgin, saints, and transubstantiation) in order to be eligible for public office, the magistrature, juries, or other functions. This requirement was obviously an obstacle for Catholics.[13]

WHAT FORM OF GOVERNMENT? THE QUEBEC ACT (1774)

Pressures from within and outside the colony were soon felt in London, which had to consider the best form of government to give to its American colonies, which were governed by a simple military treaty. In the colonies to the south, the Sugar Act of 1764 raised the question of the legitimacy of the metropolis taxing the colonies and revealed a fundamental issue for believers in "English liberties": "no taxation without representation." The Stamp Act of 1765, although it was repealed in 1766, nevertheless contributed to the formation of the "Sons of Liberty" in the colonies to the south.

In 1768, Governor Carleton, untouched by the spirit of English liberties and wanting to maintain the support of the seigneurs of the colony, devised a "feudal plan," observing that the landed aristocracy of Canada would never be the British landed aristocracy.

On the other Hand the better Sort of Canadians fear nothing more than popular Assemblies, which, they conceive, tend to render the people refractory and insolent. Enquiring what they thought of them, they said, they understood some of our Colonies had fallen under the King's Displeasure, owing to the Misconduct of their Assemblies, and that they should think themselves unhappy, if a like Misfortune befell them. It may not be improper here to observe, that the British form of government, transplanted into this continent, never will produce the same fruits as at home, chiefly because it is impossible for the dignity of the Throne and Peerage to be represented in the American forests.

Conscious of the specific characteristics of America, Carleton was not very favourable to granting parliamentary democracy.

A popular Assembly, which preserves its full Vigor, and in a Country where all Men appear nearly upon a Level, must give a strong Bias to Republican Principles. Whether the independent Spirit of a Democracy is well adapted to a subordinate Government of the British Monarchy, or their uncontrollable Notions, ought to be encouraged in a Province, so lately Conquered, and Circumstanced as this is, I with great Humility submit to the Superior Wisdom of His Majesty's Councils.[14]

The colonial authorities therefore relied on support from the Catholic Church and the seigneurs to delay granting the colony certain liberties of the metropolis. This was all the more the case because there was no landed aristocracy that could, like the British House of Lords, serve as a counterbalance to "the crown and the country." They thus had to be careful about granting institutions that might take an unexpected direction in America. In London, this was seen as a major challenge: should they give the recently conquered Americans, who were French and Catholic to boot, those liberties of which England was so proud?

Petitions then began to be presented to the governor of the colony. Some English-speaking merchants asked for the establishment of a house of assembly to which only Protestants subjects could be elected. This paradoxical proposal had little chance of success: it would have meant that a minority could impose its decisions on a majority, diminishing the primary meaning of the English liberties. Political plans proliferated between the Boston Massacre of March 1770 and the Boston Tea Party of December 1773. In October 1773, about forty Englishmen organized a committee, and in November, they circulated a petition in favour of a house of assembly.

As you appear to have the true Interests of this Country at heart, We take the liberty to trouble you with the Draught of a Petition which the English Inhabitants of the province have determined to present to the Governor and Council. It is now the general opinion of the people (French and English) that an Assembly would be of the utmost advantage to the colony though they cannot agree as to the constitution of it. The British inhabitants, of whom we are appointed a committee, are of very moderate principles. They wish for an Assembly as they know that to be the only sure means of conciliating the New Subjects to the British Government as well as of promoting the Interests of the Colony and securing to its Inhabitants the peaceable possession of their rights and propertys. They would not presume to dictate.[15]

Unlike the British immigrants, who had already experienced English liberties, the *Canadiens* had only known the monarchy of divine right, but they constituted the great majority of the population. In addition to their unfamiliarity with British institutions, there were other reasons for their hesitation regarding the plans of the "old subjects."

Mr. McCord endeavoured all this Summer, and again since the appointment of the Committee, to persuade the Canadians to join the old Subjects in petitioning for an Assembly, used every Argument he could think of for that Purpose, and carried the first Draft set on Foot for it to a Canadian Gentleman of this Town to translate into French; the Canadians suspecting their only View was to push them forward to ask, without really intending their Participation of the Privilege, declined joining them here or at Montreal.[16]

In late December 1773 and early January 1774, one hundred and fifty petitioners, seven or eight of whom were French-speaking Canadians, including Pierre du Calvet, reminded the king of the intention stated in the Royal Proclamation of 1763 to call assemblies "so soon as the state and circumstances of the said Colonies will admit thereof." Without giving an opinion on the composition of such a body, they expressed the belief that it was time to establish an assembly.

Your Petitioners being fully convinced from their Residence in the Province, and their Experience in the Affairs of it, that a general Assembly would very much contribute to encourage and promote Industry, Agriculture and Commerce and (as they hope) to create Harmony and good Understanding between your Majesty's new and old Subjects.[17]

Council member Francis Maseres, who sent the petition to Lord Dartmouth, Secretary of State for the Colonies, favoured an expanded council rather than a house of assembly, which he felt would be appropriate when the colony was more anglicized and "Protestantized."[18] Dartmouth, who introduced a bill in the House of Lords on 2 May 1774, said he was convinced that "the Arrangements for the Government of Quebec should be no longer delayed," and that his bill would "remove those difficulties [that had] so greatly embarrassed" the colonial authority,[19] in particular since the traumatic Boston Tea Party of December 1773, which had accelerated a process that had been developing for about ten years in one of the northern colonies.

The Quebec Act was given royal assent on 22 June 1774 and was to come into force on 1 May 1775. French and English texts of the act were printed by William Brown, and the French text was published on 8 December 1774 in the *Quebec Gazette / Gazette de Québec*, which Brown and Thomas Gilmore had founded in 1764. The relative numbers made this a necessity: this first constitutional law governed approximately eighty thousand new subjects and two thousand old subjects.

Power remained in the hands of the governor, with an executive appointed by him. The metropolis retained control of the colony and considered the establishment of a house of assembly premature. It is clear that in maintaining the seigneurial system, the "Coutume de Paris" (the customary law of Paris) and the French laws, the political authorities intended to rely on the support of the seigneurs, seven of whom were on the first Council. The seigneurs and the local and metropolitan authorities shared the same values and interests: belief in monarchy, loyalty to the king, support for the aristocracy, and belief in the union of state and church.

The constitutional law recognized freedom of religion for the Catholic Church, "subject to the King's Supremacy," and the right to collect the tithes that ensured the survival of the parishes and priests, and only required an oath of allegiance rather than the Test Oath. But the Church lost its legal recognition as an institution: "Canadian Subjects ... the religious orders and Communities only excepted, may also hold and enjoy their Property and Possessions." This was a way for the political authorities to ensure the loyalty of the Church, whose properties and institutions such as hospitals, colleges, and convents, but especially its numerous huge seigneuries, had become vulnerable.[20] As a legal person, the Church was tolerated, but it was still subject to confiscation of its property.

Exemption from the Test Oath made public office accessible in principle to the merchant and professional bourgeoisie, which was small in number. The peasants continued to be taxed (seigneurial rents, tithes) without having the right to any form of representation.

The most disappointed group was the British merchants: as merchants, with the implementation of French civil law and English criminal law, they lost the advantages of having only a single body of law, English law; as British subjects familiar with English liberties, they found in the Quebec Act no promise of a house of assembly, no guarantee of habeas corpus (the right not to be detained without trial), and no right to trial by jury.[21] In London, in the House of Lords and the House of Commons, this had been keenly debated during the deliberations on the bill in 1774. It was a major issue: how to take into account the heritage of the Glorious Revolution of 1688 and to make room for another culture in the imperial system without alienating all its subjects, both the old subjects, a minority but a powerful one, and the new subjects, very much in the majority but newly conquered and unfamiliar with British institutions? How could these new Catholic French-speaking subjects be made British? Could one be British without being English and Protestant? Barely a century after 1688, the question of religion had caused a storm in the Commons, breaking party lines and giving rise to opposition to the bill. The British political class and the press found it hard to understand this recognition of "papist" Catholicism in a colony of England, which was used to the dominance of the Anglican Church. Charles Fox, the great orator of the Whig party, had hoped to see them "growing wise enough, growing Christian enough, growing philosophic enough to hold principles of toleration."[22] Peter Wedderburn, the solicitor general, went to the heart of the matter; to him, tolerance was always less risky politically than intolerance.

The safety of the state can be the only just motive for imposing any restraint upon men on account of their religious tenets. The principle is just but has seldom been justly applied; for experience demonstrates that the public safety has been often endangered by these restraints, and there is no instance of any state that has been overturned by toleration. True policy dictates then that inhabitants of Canada should be permitted freely to profess the worship of their religion.[23]

It was clear, then, to both the English and the Catholic Church in the colony, but for different reasons, that the issue was primarily religious, and secondarily cultural or linguistic.

Governor Carleton, when consulted by the House of Commons, expressed the view that Canadians did not want a house of assembly or trial by jury, but he was systematically contradicted on this by Maseres, who felt that they would want to have these institutions sooner rather than later. The seigneur Michel Chartier de Lotbinière felt that Canadians wanted a house of assembly and that they should be part of it, but it was too much at once to raise the question of a house of assembly in a British colony, a house that, moreover, could be made up mostly of French-speaking Catholics.

The opposition in Parliament made much of the fact that French law was being maintained, which would complicate life in the colony, and also of the question of the borders, which could displease the colonies to the south and favour the settlement of "papists" in North America. The law was adopted, but the *London Evening Post* of 15 October 1774, with a view to the British general election, went so far as to publish a "black list" of the members who had voted for the Quebec Act. The number of Canadians of the Catholic religion had obliged the metropolis to be conciliatory; but the fact remained that obvious constitutional concessions were made to the imperial policy and that neither English nor Irish Catholics benefited from such a policy of emancipation of Catholics.

The end of the Seven Years' War had created hopes for peace between London and the colonies to the south, and Protestantism had proven successful against "papism," and the metropolis and the colonies to the south seemed to be in perfect agreement on the religious question; sermons and demonstrations by the radical American Protestants constantly repeated, "No popery." The colonies to the south, which had expressed their opposition to monopolies created by London with the Boston Tea Party in December 1773, took a dim view of the passage of the Quebec Act in June 1774. They were displeased not only with its recognition of the Catholic religion, but also with its failure to grant a house of assembly and the return to the old borders, cutting into the territory of the colonies to the south. It was thus not surprising that the first Continental Congress, which met in Philadelphia in September and October 1774 to propose the formation of a militia and an association that would apply economic sanctions against Great Britain, had a sometimes paradoxical attitude to the Province of Quebec, especially since Canada could provide a base for an invasion of these colonies by the British army.

THE YEAR OF THE "BASTONNOIS" (1775)

Having experienced certain advantages of the Glorious Revolution of 1688 in its first constitution, the British colony in North America again found itself in the middle of a war of independence, another revolution, this time a continental one, which would be followed by the revolution in France. It could not have been more deeply immersed in the maelstrom of Atlantic revolutions.

In 1774, the colonies to the south chose to address the British of the metropolis and the Canadians directly through messages and emissaries; but their reservations about the Quebec Act explain why the messages to the Canadians and to the British of the metropolis were different. And this difference, if not to say this duplicity, was very revealing of their true intentions.

Their first address was sent "to the People of Great Britain" (21 October 1774), reminding them of the importance of English liberties and rights, which had to be maintained even "three thousand miles from the royal palace." It again criticized the Stamp Act, the symbol of an "unconstitutional and unjust scheme of taxation." But the letter particularly attacked the Quebec Act, saying that it was harmful for British immigrants because of the loss of trial by jury and habeas corpus and because their religion was threatened by "papism"; they feared that the Canadians would "be fit instruments in the hands of power, to reduce the ancient free Protestant Colonies to the same state of slavery."[24] The messages from the southern colonies to the Canadians did not include the fawning criticisms expressed in those to the British.

Before invading Canada on 5 September 1775, the colonies meeting in Philadelphia sent four messages to the Canadians. The first Continental Congress put its policy into practice and hired a French printer in Philadelphia, Fleury Mesplet, to print a French version of the letter "To the Inhabitants of the Province of Quebec" (26 October 1774). The letter insisted on the legitimate right of Canadians to a democratic government: "of the people having a share in their own government by their representatives chosen by themselves, and, in consequence, of being ruled by laws, which they themselves approve, not by edicts of men over whom they have no control." The letter listed other legitimate rights – trial by jury, habeas corpus, ownership of land, freedom of the press, a house of assembly, power to tax, separation of powers – and it invited the Canadians to unite with them, "as our cause is just" and "your province is the only link wanting, to compleat the bright and strong chain of union."[25] The appeal was repeated in a message (21 February 1775) from Samuel Adams on behalf of the Massachusetts Provincial Congress, in a second letter printed by Mesplet, "Letter to the Oppressed Inhabitants of Canada" (29 May 1775), which raised the possibility of intervention by France on the side of the Americans and expressed the hope that they would not have to deal with the Canadians as enemies.

A letter (2 June 1775) from the Committee of Correspondence of the New York Provincial Congress gave reassurances about military manoeuvres taking place around Lake Champlain, when Governor Carleton issued a proclamation (9 June 1775) ordering the establishment of militias. The letters from the Americans were read in private or out loud, for people who were illiterate, in coffee houses and inns, in public markets, on church steps, and at parish meetings, and the message was passed on in the countryside by English merchants in favour of rights and liberties.[26]

The Catholic Church was worried about these machinations. On 22 May 1775, Mgr Briand published a pastoral letter "on the American invasion of Canada," which, after stressing the kindness of the king and the beneficence of the governor with regard to the Quebec Act, ordered parishioners as follows:

Your oaths and your religion impose on you an indispensable obligation to defend your country and your king with all your power. Close your ears, therefore, dear Canadians, and do not listen to those seditious men who seek to make you unhappy, to smother in your hearts the sentiments of submission to your legitimate superiors that your education and religion have engraved there ... The voice of religion and that of your interests are joined here, and assure us of your zeal to defend our borders and our possessions.[27]

Étienne Montgolfier, a Sulpician priest and vicar general in Montreal, also published a circular letter, on 13 June, on the meaning that should be given to the "re-establishment of the militias."

Always careful to provide the province entrusted to him with honours and benefits, His Excellency General Carleton today adds a new favour to his previous benefits, in the re-establishment of the militia in this province. This is an efficacious means of maintaining order in our parishes and polity among your habitants; and it is at the same time a mark of esteem and confidence with which he honours every individual of the Province, and above all, those whom he appoints to military duties, whom he only wishes to choose insofar as his choice may be agreeable to the public. I do not doubt that this occasion will imprint on every heart a gratitude proportional to this benefit.[28]

The military invasion began in September 1775 by way of Lake Champlain and the Richelieu River under the command of General Schuyler, and led to the surrender (on 12 November) of Montreal, which would remain under American occupation for the next eight months. Meanwhile, General Arnold went down the Chaudière River and took up a position across from Quebec City, where he was joined by General Montgomery in December. The siege was difficult and the arrival of the English fleet on 6 May 1776 saved the capital and the colony, and the American army withdrew to Ticonderoga on 18 June.

During the ten months of the occupation, there were more and more political messages from the Americans: General Schuyler urged the Canadians not to take up arms against the Americans; General Washington suggested that the Canadians join the Americans "under the standard of general Liberty"; General Montgomery assured the people of Montreal, at the time of the surrender, that their religion was not threatened; Mesplet published another letter "to the Inhabitants of the Province of Canada" (24 January 1776) from the Congress explaining "that your liberty, your honour, and your happiness, are essentially and necessarily connected with the unhappy contest which we have been forced into for the defence of our dearest privileges."[29] Benjamin Franklin even came to Montreal for a brief visit on 29 April 1776.

Arms had sealed the fate of the armies of the "Yankees," but words had also warned the people against their ideas. The *Quebec Gazette / La Gazette de Québec*, owned by the American Brown, but dependent on the government, had remained faithful to the Crown during the war. Mgr Briand and Father Montgolfier had made it clear that rebels would be considered unworthy of the sacraments or church burial if they were to die with arms in their hands.[30] A pastoral letter from the bishop of Quebec City dated 31 December 1775 "on the subject of rebels during the American war" provided a summary of the political theology of the Catholic Church in the colony at that time and later.

Your rebellion, as contrary to religion as it is to good sense and reason, already merited exemplary and rigorous punishments from the prince from whom you have until now received only marks of a generosity that is extraordinarily rare in a powerful conqueror, and that none of us expected, a generosity that allowed you to experience the change of domination only as increased well-being ...

They [the rebels] have thus represented [the Quebec Act] to you as an attack on your freedom, as tending to return you to slavery, at the mercy of your Seigneurs and the nobility; they have promised you exemption from seigneurial rents, and you loved that injustice; and that you would no longer pay tithes, and you were not horrified at that impious, sacrilegious ingratitude toward God, without whose blessing neither would your fields be fertile nor your work successful ...

Had you held out for a long time against seduction, you who could be said without insult to know your religion very little and to be in crass ignorance of almost all the points of your faith and all the evidence that proves it certain, and who, moreover, like fanatics and miserable madmen and deplorable blind men, have made it a principle to no longer listen to the voices of those who were given to you by God to be your leaders, your guides, your light and the defenders of your faith ...

Jesus Christ, who said positively that whoever did not listen to the ministers he sent to teach the world and govern his Church did not listen to him; that resisting and scorning the priests resisted and scorned him.[31]

This pastoral letter, read in all the churches of the colony, clearly expressed what was feared in the propaganda of the Americans: the loss of power of the established authorities and the loss of the resources of this power: submission, seigneurial rents, and church tithes. After the god of war, it appealed to the god of the fields and the authority of the priest, who was by analogy of the same nature as Jesus Christ: to resist the priests was to resist Jesus Christ.

The tone of this pastoral letter is understandable when we know to what extent religious authority had been challenged. Mgr Briand wrote to a parish priest: "My authority is not respected any more than yours: they say of me, as they say of you, that I am English."[32] Thirty years later, Mgr Plessis liked to think that "Lord Dorchester publicly recognized that it was the Catholic clergy that had preserved the Province of Quebec for the King ... This conduct fortified the Governor's trust in the Bishop and the Clergy and strengthened the bonds that already united them."[33]

The American propaganda had found receptive individuals. Some peasants had complained about priests who were too involved in political matters; others had interrupted preachers, objecting to their preaching in favour of the English; some had taken over the presbytery of a parish priest who was considered too loyalist.[34] In Montreal, forty signatories had expressed their support for the actions and ideas of the Americans.[35] Aid given by Canadians to the American troops had taken many forms: provisions, wheat, flour, ladders, corvées, transport, guard duty, hiding of spies, transmission of messages by signal fires along the rivers. But as shown by a survey carried out by Messrs Baby, Taschereau, and Williams in fifty-four parishes from Trois-Rivières to Kamouraska from May to July 1776, there were more volunteer militiamen (2,000) than "bad subjects" (approximately 500). A total of 2,500 adults out of a population of 90,000 inhabitants of both sexes and all ages is not a lot, but it is sufficient to show the neutrality, at best the "benevolent neutrality," of the Canadians toward the invaders.

But for eighteen months, new ideas had been circulating: representative government, taxation – but taxation imposed by representatives of the people – abolition of seigneurial rents and church tithes, freedom of the press. These ideas were familiar to the English of the colony but were less so to the French Canadians; they were their introduction to something other than monarchy by divine right or even constitutional monarchy. Overall, the *Canadiens* had remained ambivalent with regard to the Americans' appeals. What indeed could these former Frenchmen newly conquered by England expect from the "Bastonnois" – or "people of Boston," as the *Canadiens* called the Americans – who talked to them about new ideas and who could become their second conquerors?

But the democratic ideas had an impact. Governor Carleton wrote in 1777: "These People had been governed with too loose a Rein for many years, and had imbibed too much of the American Spirit of Licentiousness and Independence administered by a numerous and turbulent Faction here, to be suddenly restored to a proper and desirable Subordination."[36]

The bishop's account in 1790 corroborated the governor's perception: "If, since 1775, this ardour has dimmed in certain places of the Province, if one does not always find the same eagerness, the same submission to public authority, do we not have the right to blame the progress made among our *Canadiens* of the spirit of freedom and independence first brought by the circulation of the manifestos of the Anglo-Americans at the beginning of the last war, and since spread by the proliferation and the licence of our gazettes and the freedom of conversations on political matters?"[37]

PETITIONS IN FAVOUR OF A HOUSE OF ASSEMBLY (1774–1789)

The English-speaking merchants of the colony did not delay in asking again for the repeal of the Quebec Act, to which they were strongly opposed. In November 1774, they submitted a petition to the House of Commons and the House of Lords, bemoaning the absence of habeas corpus and trial by jury in the colony. In 1778, they stated that there was such "general discontent" that they proposed "to change their present form of government" for a "free government, by an assembly or representation of the people."[38] Governor Haldimand took a dim view of the proposal; to him, granting a house of assembly would be the first step toward annexation to the United States, which had just gained independence. A pragmatic man, he instead prepared orders to establish habeas corpus (1784) and trial by jury (1785), as he knew of the injustice of certain arbitrary situations, including one denounced by Pierre du Calvet in his *Appel à la justice de l'État* (Appeal to the justice of the state) in 1784.[39]

The pressure mounted in 1784 when French-speaking merchants and professionals joined the English-speaking subjects in demanding rights.

The ministers must not take it into their heads to try to divert us with palliatives and lenitives. We will be content only when parliament has responded to our claims by giving us the same rights and privileges as the English; and why not? We are English subjects just as they are. The ministers will fancy perhaps that ours is not the voice of Canada but only talk from a few factious partisan hotheads. Well then, we shall be charmed to be tested so that we may enlighten them. During the summer we shall be at work in order to have the petition signed by the generality of the parishes of Canada, except for a few nobles and ambitious individuals who crave office and the pay and perquisites thereof, and to that end grovel before the great, but by whom we will not be duped ... Freedom, Gentlemen, Freedom at all cost.[40]

Committees were formed in Montreal and Quebec City, bringing together old and new subjects. On 24 November 1784, a petition was sent to the King with 2,291 signatories – 855 old subjects and 1,436 new subjects, including 384 from Quebec City – asking for a house of assembly elected by the old and new subjects, and various other rights. Among the signatories from Quebec City and Montreal were Pierre-Stanislas Bédard, the father of Pierre Bédard; merchant and notary Jean-Guillaume Delisle; businessman Pierre Foretier; teacher Louis Labadie; the printer of the *Montreal Gazette/Gazette de Montréal*, Fleury Mesplet; Joseph Papineau, the father of Louis-Joseph, who would be born two years later; the playwright Joseph Quesnel; Denis Viger, the father of Denis-Benjamin; and Jacques Viger, the father of Jacques Viger, the future first mayor of Montreal.[41]

There was not unanimity, however. The seigneurs, advantaged by the Quebec Act, had Fleury Mesplet print two hundred copies of their objections to the petition of November 1784, with 2,400 signatures – which they had obtained by brandishing the possibility that an eventual house of assembly could impose taxes that would be "useless and prejudicial to the colony."[42] The Catholic hierarchy joined with them in their opposition.

A nascent Colony, a People very imperfectly instructed in British Laws and constitutions, does not believe it should rashly ask for the application of Laws and Customs unknown to it; it must on the contrary ... rely entirely on the Benevolence of His August Sovereign, who better knows the Government that suits his Subjects and the most proper Means to make them happy. May we only be permitted to ensure Your Majesty that we do not participate in any Manner in the Actions of Your Old Subjects, jointly with a few of the New, the Number of whom, with Respect to those in our Province, cannot have a great deal of Influence.[43]

The Canadian reformers – notaries, lawyers, merchants, and shopkeepers – were delighted with the effects of Pierre du Calvet's *Appel à la*

Justice de l'État (1784), which appealed to public opinion and denounced the arbitrary nature of the regime put in place by the Quebec Act from the point of view of rights and liberties; they congratulated themselves on the "perfect Unity" of the members of the various committees.[44] Mesplet supported the plan for a constitution and gave the petitioners access to the pages of his *Gazette*, which had begun to publish again in August 1785. But members of the governor's Executive Council were developing other scenarios. This was the case for Hugh Finlay, the deputy postmaster, who said, "the mass of Canadians are still incapable of judging this affair," and described them as people whose happiness depended on their religion and the absence of taxes. He further stated, "We might make the people entirely English by introducing the English language. This is to be done by free schools, and by ordaining that all suits in our Courts shall be carried on in English after a certain number of years."[45] This scenario would have quite a future.

On 20 October 1789, a few months after the storming of the Bastille in Paris, Lord Grenville, the home secretary, secretly told the governor of the colony, Lord Dorchester: "I am persuaded that it is a point of true Policy to make these Concessions at a time when they may be received as matter of favour, and when it is in Our own power to regulate and direct the manner of applying them, rather than to wait 'till they shall be extorted from us."[46] In an official dispatch dated the same day, he took a position on a question that had been left unresolved, the composition of the future house of assembly: "Every consideration of policy seemed to render it desirable that the great preponderance possessed in the Upper Districts by the King's antient [*sic*] Subjects, and in the lower by the French Canadians should have their effect and operation in separate legislatures, rather than that these two bodies of People should be blended together."[47]

Numbers were thus the determining factor. The landed aristocracy of seigneurs was quantitatively negligible, and representation based on a poll tax and land ownership would necessarily involve the majority of the landowners, that is, the *Canadiens*.[48] But the plan for a new constitution that Grenville had been working on since the summer of 1789 would only be submitted to the British Parliament in the spring of 1791.

THE YEAR OF THE FRENCH (1789)

Having been exposed to the Revolution of 1688 through its metropolis and to the American Revolution by appeals from the colonies to the south in 1774 and 1775, Canada once again heard the call of revolution, this time from its former mother country. While exchanges between

Canada and France had become less frequent since the Conquest, they had not broken off altogether. Correspondence by families, clergy, and religious institutions and communities enabled Canadians to keep up with affairs in France. But above all, the three newspapers published in the colony, the bilingual *Gazettes* of Quebec City and Montreal and the *Quebec Herald*, kept their readers informed on international affairs, with a delay of three months.

In April of 1789, the newspapers informed the colony of the meeting of the Estates-General in France; the storming of the Bastille on 14 July 1789 was made known at the beginning of October.[49] The press was favourable to the events in France, and continued to be so until the end of 1792. The *Quebec Gazette/La Gazette de Québec*, which was close to the colonial government and used material from the British press, congratulated itself on the fact that France was finally adopting a constitution, as England had done a century before. From January to March 1792, *La Gazette de Québec* even published the text of the new French constitution. The newspaper made a point of suggesting that the king of France, who had aided the Americans in 1776, perhaps deserved his fate. It occasionally published texts on the spirit of the Enlightenment (19 August 1790) or the abolition of the feudal system (20 and 27 January 1791), and its general approach was clearly shown on 31 March 1791: "It has now been sixteen months that the French have been living under a free government and enjoying freedom of the press, and in this short space, reason has made more progress and minds have become more enlightened than they probably would have done during a century before the Revolution."

La Gazette de Montréal was more radical, and its publisher, Mesplet, showed remarkable inventiveness in suggesting similarities between the situations in France and Canada and proposing for the colony the solutions found by the Revolution. Every week it filled columns with praise for the Enlightenment and the benefits of reason ("let them examine everything") and the exercise of freedom and rights: "Come, Sir, courage and perseverance. Think that we are no longer in 1779, and that to breathe it is no longer required today as it was then to feign ignorance, flatter the Nobility and praise the Clergy; to act the adulating, grovelling hypocrite. No: the man required in 1790 should know the rights granted him by nature, know how to enjoy them, and defend them."[50] Mesplet and his editor, Valentin Jautard, above all denounced religion and the clergy and called for the separation of temporal and spiritual.

The priests have their particular duties, and they should keep to them, and they will not expose themselves to being ridiculed by the entire public … We are ourselves duped by our clergy. Often they try to deceive us in a thousand things that hardly come from farther than their mouths; they make for themselves among the ignorant ... a holy reputation. Give yourselves to your priests with regard to the spiritual, it is only just; it is your duty, as well as theirs. But for the temporal, do not let yourselves be led blindly by their counsel. Let us encourage the study of great writing, and this feigned supremacy of the clergy will vanish.[51]

On 16 September 1790, the *Gazette* published the decree nationalizing the property of the clergy and expressed its approval. It also denounced the feudal system and the *Canadien* seigneurs who were opposing by every means the plan for a house of assembly for the colony.

The Catholic Church followed the course of events, but for the time being kept its opposition to the Revolution private. Vicar General Brassier, a Sulpician, wrote to Mgr Hubert, the bishop of Quebec City: "The gazettes of Europe have much influence on the minds of the citizens of Montreal; they preach freedom and independence everywhere. Sirs, our churchwardens want today to govern the Church not only for the temporal but for the spiritual, already they have put their hands on the censer."[52] From Paris, a priest informed Mgr Briand:

You are no doubt aware, dear respectable uncle, of the revolution that has taken place in France through philosophy, and the anarchy, trouble and division that have ravaged it for the past three years. It is totally changed ... it has been turned completely upside down ... it is no longer recognizable ... Without going into detail about crimes and abominations the recitation of which would horrify you, without mentioning the attacks committed against the sacred person of the king and his respectable family, without speaking of the streams of the purest blood of the French that our inhumane philosophers have caused to flow, I will only tell you briefly the story of our sorrows that will ever be the shame and opprobrium of the French nation.[53]

The perception of the Revolution began to change at the end of 1792; a correspondent wrote to *La Gazette de Québec*: "There then are the worthy fruits of modern Philosophy, as well as the Spirit of innovation or rather of vertigo that instead of attempting prudently the Reform of abuses when it encounters them, destroys everything indiscriminately and overturns the social and Religious State to its ancient and still respectable foundations."[54]

THE YEAR OF THE CANADIANS (1791)

By October 1789, the position of the home secretary, Lord Grenville, on the demands for a house of assembly had been communicated to

Governor Dorchester. London then feared new appeals by the Americans to the Canadians, if not new attacks, and the best guarantee against republican propaganda seemed to be to grant the representative body that was lacking in the colony, a body like the one France had just established in an even more radical way than the United States. In the House of Commons, government and opposition both recognized that a colonial house of assembly with taxation powers would also relieve the metropolis of annual expenses of £100,000, not to mention the funds allocated to the military government. Internal requests from the *Canadiens* and British, external pressures from America and France, and the political and economic interests of the metropolis explain London's decision after thirty years of observation and concessions.

A new constitutional act was introduced in Parliament in the spring of 1791, was given royal assent on 10 June, and came into force on 26 December. It provided that the colony should be divided into two parts, Lower and Upper Canada, each with a house of assembly, and thus that in the house of assembly of Lower Canada, "the great preponderance possessed ... in the lower [districts] by the French Canadians should have [its] effect and operation." As early as 1789, Grenville had seen that this house of assembly could one day have a majority of French-speaking Catholic members, representatives of a different culture, and had wanted this to be. Numbers, democracy, and political wisdom made this a necessity.

London would certainly remain the metropolis, with the right to disallow any colonial law up to two years after its passage by the colonial parliament. The governor, the symbol of the monarchy, would be assisted by an executive council of nine members appointed by him. A legislative council of fifteen members appointed by the governor would continue to represent the aristocratic element, with some English-speaking members. From 1792 to 1814, anglophones occupied 68 per cent of the seats and controlled 78 per cent of the Council's budget. The House of Assembly, the symbol of the democratic branch, had fifty members; it was the beginning of parliamentary democracy in the colony, thirty years after the Treaty of Paris had suggested that "assemblies" could be called "so soon as ... circumstances ... will admit thereof."[55]

The seigneurs and the Catholic clergy were not pleased with this law, which seriously undermined the aristocratic power of the landowners and suggested that power, at least in part, did not come from God but from the people. The law had barely received royal assent when a priest at the Séminaire de Québec wrote to a colleague in Paris: "Those who in my view think a little are very angry over this change, because there are many of our vain *Canadiens* and many English admirers of the national assembly who are already talking about establishing human rights as a principle of law."[56]

The proponents of a house of assembly now had to prepare for its establishment and operation and plan a first election in a country that had no familiarity with this tradition. In January 1792, citizens meeting in Frank's Tavern in Quebec City founded the Constitutional Club to spread knowledge of the British Constitution and help citizens learn the rules of deliberative assemblies. There was debate and discussion. Alexandre Dumas, a businessman and lawyer, made a "speech" that was reassuring with respect to religion and taxes and denounced the seigneurs, who, by "condition, fortune, or chimerical nature," wanted to deceive the habitants. He observed that an "ignorant people ... can be subjected to extortion without resistance" and invited "those who want to be educated" to read or have read to them the Constitution and newspapers. In the spirit of the objectives of the Constitutional Club, "Solon" published an analysis of the new constitution in *La Gazette de Québec* and *La Gazette de Montréal*, which printer John Neilson then distributed in the form of a pamphlet. "Solon" insisted, "We consider it to be the duty of Priests, Seigneurs, Notaries, Schoolmasters and educated Merchants to diffuse our productions among the people, to read them and explain them, so that, enjoying a free constitution, they will not be ignorant of its value and nature."[57]

Foremen and pressmen in the Neilson and Mesplet print shops went to work: the newspapers no longer lacked local news. In Quebec City, Neilson had in his forms excerpts of the rules and procedures of the House of Commons of Great Britain. Already, orders for election broadsheets and pamphlets were coming in.

The first election of "representatives" was to take place in the summer of 1792. Suffrage was not universal, but was very broad: voters had to be Canadians by birth or naturalization, at least twenty-one years of age, owners of real estate worth a minimum of two pounds, in the country, or, in the cities, owners of goods worth five pounds, or tenants paying an annual rent of ten pounds. Few heads of families – the vast majority male – were thus excluded, and the rural electorate carried a lot of weight in the election of members. Canadians of twenty-one years of age who were members of the Legislative Council, ministers of the Church of England or the Roman Catholic Church, or had been found guilty of treason or a felony did not have the right to vote.[58]

The election campaign of 1792 established a public space through debates on the "public interest" and "public happiness." Public opinion was born of this public discussion in publications and the candidates' advertising in the newspapers or the fifteen or so broadsheets and pamphlets that circulated during the campaign. These publications explained what "representation" was, described the qualities required of a representative and the functioning of an election, and emphasized the necessity of voting and the need to exercise prudence with regard to candidates' promises. The social stakes quickly became evident. Who could claim to merit the power delegated by the sovereign people? The seigneurs, with their rights and privileges, who had made laws that were advantageous to them? The merchants, who were always speculating rather at random and who would do the same with regard to public affairs, but whose "interest in union" with the people was more evident than that of the seigneurs? Lawyers, who made their fortune from the ruin of their clients? "Mechanics" or artisans, whose skills would allow them to make laws as well as "machines"? The labourer who fed humankind and was "the spirit of the state"? Such was the thread of a *Dialogue sur l'Intérêt du Jour entre plusieurs Candidats et un électeur libre et indépendant* (Dialogue on the Interest of the Day among several Candidates and a free and independent voter), which came out in May 1792, and which ended with these words: "He who seeks to deceive you with politeness, favours and other means not commonly used prior to the era of the new Constitution wants to buy you in order to sell you." In Charlesbourg, the election was even contested, and it gave rise to a "conversation" between a candidate and a voter ill-informed about the new political rules who thought the election was a party where people drank and a vote was an item of exchange. The candidate ended by persuading the voter: "The country is not worth our trouble to defend by force of arms if we do not properly abide by its laws. You see that if you give a place in the House in return for money, that is no less a betrayal of the country than if you were to give up your post to the enemy in time of war."[59]

In the first election, fifty-one candidates were elected in eleven urban constituencies and thirty-nine rural constituencies (there was one by-election). There were sixteen candidates of British origin elected, eight of them in urban constituencies and eight in the country; they made up 31 per cent of the House of Assembly although they constituted less than 10 per cent of the population of the colony. Of the thirty-five *Canadiens* elected, thirty-two were in rural constituencies and three in urban constituencies. There were thirty merchants, mostly in the fur trade, who made up 58 per cent of the members, which also included nine seigneurs, nine members of the liberal professions, and three artisans. More than 50 per cent of the members were owners of seigneuries, an indication of the importance of land ownership for the rural population. But it is also clear that, from the first election, the numerical preponderance of *Canadiens* had an impact, as Grenville had predicted and wished.[60]

This situation determined the orientation of a question that had been left unresolved, that of language, which arose in December 1792 with regard to the choice of the speaker and the working language and the language of publication of the debates of the House. In these first hours of parliamentary democracy, the discussion on the choice of speaker was very lively. Those who were opposed to the proposition that Jean-Antoine Panet be chosen put forward the idea that the speaker had to speak the language of the king and be familiar with the British Constitution. The supporters of Panet argued that the king signed treaties in all languages, that Jersey and Guernsey were French-speaking, and that Panet, a lawyer, knew the British Constitution. After a good deal of strategizing, Panet was finally elected by twenty-eight votes to eighteen. The speaker immediately reassured the English-speaking members by declaring to the lieutenant-governor on behalf of the House, "It is a very great satisfaction for us to have the opportunity to join our eulogy and our admiration for the system of Government of Great Britain, which gives it such a decisive superiority and advantage over other Nations."[61]

The debate on the working language of the House was more stormy. Speaking in favour of the unity of language in the Empire, member John Richardson proposed that only English be considered legal. Joseph Papineau made a counter-proposal for the recognition of both languages, while Pierre-Amable de Bonne proposed that motions be translated into the other language, but that bills on criminal law be presented in English and those on civil law, in French, since in either case, they would have to be translated before discussion. In the House, Seigneur Taschereau joked that Richardson had made the members travel through the Empire, going on "a tour of the world without being able to disembark anywhere, because they only speak English." Seigneur de Lotbinière pointed out that unity of language in the Empire was no guarantee of loyalty to the king. The press also took up the issue and the debate became quite heated. On 23 January 1793, the law was finally voted (twenty for, fourteen against): The texts of motions would be "put in both languages" and any member could present a bill in his own language, with translation of the texts being required before any debate.[62] From then on, language, as much as religion, would be at the forefront of the public stage. Having been Catholic since 1763, the colony was also becoming clearly francophone. While some dreamed of Protestantizing it, others would dream of anglicizing it.

THE REIGN OF TERROR (1793) AND
THE COUNTER-REVOLUTIONARY TRADITION

Alarming news came to Quebec just when the law on the language of the Assembly was being passed: Louis XVI had been beheaded on 21 January 1793, and France had declared war on England on 1 February. The tensions between the old and the new mother countries would affect the colony until they eased in 1815, while a current of ideas that strengthened the colony's, and in particular, the *Canadiens'*, support for the monarchy was becoming established.

Very early, the colonial authorities made known their opposition to the enemy France and the regicidal Revolution. It was fine to put an end to absolute monarchy, but not to monarchy altogether. On 25 April, the lieutenant-governor called for every means to be taken to "harass" French vessels and ruin France's trade. Two days later, the House of Assembly unanimously voted to send the following letter to the lieutenant-governor and the king.

We His Majesty's dutiful and Loyal Subjects the Representatives of the People of Lower Canada … assure Your Excellency, that it is with horror we have heard that the most atrocious Act which ever disgraced society has been perpetrated in France: and it is with concern and indignation we now learn, that the persons exercising supreme authority there, have declared War against His Majesty.

The Legislative Council followed suit, as did Chief Justice William Smith, who observed:

This enemy is the band of Democrats who under the pretext of giving liberty to France, have found the means to lead their King to the scaffold, and flooded his Kingdom with the blood of many thousands of their fellow citizens.

It is nevertheless possible that the seductions of our enemies will find the means to place here instruments capable of acting successfully against the ignorant. That is why our fellow citizens, and especially the great jurymen, will do well to watch over the words of various people, in order to better discover the dissemination of this poison, which has converted one of the most beautiful kingdoms of Europe into one of the most miserable countries on earth.[63]

Suspicion took hold. The authorities began circulating counter-revolutionary propaganda: from 1793 to 1812, eight books or pamphlets were distributed describing the sufferings of the King and the Church and the "horrible effects of anarchism and impiety." In 1793, the government had 150 copies printed of *Vue de la Guillotine, Mort tragique du roi de*

France (*View of the Guillotine, The Tragic Death of the King of France*), which fuelled people's imagination.[64]

Nothing was left to chance. In addition to the old French-English rivalries and the growing suspicion, a garrison mentality developed that saw agents and spies for France everywhere. There were not many of them, but it took just one case, that of "Citizen" Genet, to exacerbate the fears. Minister to the United States for the French Revolution, Genet succeeded, in June 1793, in distributing in Lower Canada 350 copies of a letter from "the free French to their Canadian brothers," in which he offered to "make [Canadians] as free as we are." It was time, he said, "to overthrow a throne on which hypocrisy and imposture have too long been seated." The letter was relayed to Montreal by Mesplet and his friends at *La Gazette de Montréal*, distributed in the countryside, and read aloud on church steps and in taverns. But the colonial authorities quickly got wind of the matter.[65] In November, the governor ordered a search for perpetrators of sedition: "Whereas divers evil disposed Persons have lately manifested seditious and wicked Attempts, to alienate the Affections of His Majesty's Loyal Subjects, by false Representations of the Cause and Conduct of the Persons at present exercising the supreme Authority in France, and particularly certain Frenchmen being alien Enemies who are lurking and lie concealed in various parts of this province."[66] The Alien Act, passed in 1793 and extended until 1814, was intended primarily to identify French nationals entering the colony.

In June 1794, the government and the Church encouraged the formation of "loyal associations" on the model of those established in England and Scotland during the American War of Independence. The mostly English-speaking members of these associations, in Quebec City, Montreal, Sorel, Trois-Rivières, Saint-Ours, Berthier, and L'Assomption, helped maintain vigilance with regard to possible French emissaries or seditious activities associated with specific events or laws poorly received by the population.[67]

Popular discontent was most often expressed at compulsory corvées or military exercises: between 1779 and 1789, more than 40 per cent of the fines imposed by justices of the peace were related to charges arising from this. In January 1794, *censitaires* (tenant farmers of seigneurs) and peasants in Berthier rebelled against their treatment by the English seigneur Cuthbert and militia officers. Between April and July, in Montreal, there was a situation in which a man was sentenced to the pillory and citizens freed the prisoner and threw the pillory into the river.

Dissatisfaction and disturbances became widespread in May 1794, when because of the fear of war with the United States, the government passed a militia law. People were opposed to the law, according to one witness, because they believed that its real purpose was not to defend the country, but to send people away until it was eventually depopulated. The memory of the deportation of the Acadians was still fresh. The opposition to enlistment was real: in the district of Quebec City, thirty-four out of forty-two parishes said no to the law. Resistance was organized in Charlesbourg, where Genet's letter was being circulated; likewise in Montreal, in Côte des Neiges, where a crowd of five hundred people protested. In September, seven people were arrested in Montreal, six for seditious language and one for publishing seditious and libelous writing against the government.

Again in 1796, a law was passed that obliged the inhabitants to build and maintain the king's roads and bridges. The population refused to comply with the law. Violent behaviour led to arrests; road inspectors had to resign because of threats. In March 1797, there were eleven Montreal residents and twenty-three Quebec City residents found guilty of incitement, treason, assault, or seditious words.

In the La Malbaie seigneurie, new corvée obligations and the seigneur's plans to appropriate the most profitable fisheries of porpoise and salmon suggest that, without necessarily subscribing to the letter of the revolutionary propaganda, the people were becoming economically and socially receptive to the spirit of traditional revolutionary demands regarding taxation, corvées, and militia obligations.

The hysteria about revolutionary agents reached a climax in 1797 during the trial of David McLane, who was accused of high treason and conspiracy. In what was a parody of a trial, before a French-speaking judge and twelve English-speaking jurors, McLane, who was simple-minded rather than a conspirator, was condemned to death. He was hanged on 21 July in front of a huge crowd, and then beheaded and disembowelled. The colonial authorities wanted to make an example of him, and they succeeded. Once again, printed matter served a cause: Chief Justice Sewell had two thousand copies of the testimony in the trial printed; *La Gazette de Québec*, which had reported on the trial, published a summary in two pamphlets, one in English and the other in French.[68]

The Catholic Church, which had been rather quiet since 1789, committed itself fully to denouncing the Revolution. In 1793, the Bishop of Léon published a letter to French priests who were refugees in England, emphasizing the generosity of the "English Nation" and the King, calling for heaven's blessings on this people chosen by heaven to "vindicate the violated laws of nature and humanity." This document became a handbook of the wrongdoings of the Revolution: religion violated, altars stripped, the Church heritage usurped, vessels desecrated.[69] The bishop of Quebec City, Mgr Hubert, warned his priests:

The spirit of religion, of submission and attachment to one's king which was once the glory of the Kingdom of France, has given way over the last few years to a spirit of irreligion, independence, anarchy and parricide which has not only resulted in the death or exile of honourable French citizens but has taken their virtuous king to the scaffold and justly incurred the indignation of all the European powers; and ... the most unfortunate occurrence that could happen in Canada would be to welcome these revolutionaries.

The events in France reinforced the bishop's belief in a holy alliance between throne and altar.

The respect that we owe to the representatives of His Majesty cannot be taken too far, since they are sufficiently reserved to demand nothing contrary to our conscience. Add to this that the surprising agitation into which the revolution of France has thrown the Spirits of peoples makes agreement between the empire and the priesthood more necessary.[70]

THE BEGINNING OF THE NAPOLEONIC SAGA (1798–1805)

The denunciation of the "bloody" Revolution continued with the construction of a discourse against Napoleon, using the English victories over the "monstrous tyrant" as a pretext. Four months after the victory of Vice-Admiral Nelson at Aboukir, Egypt, Mgr Denaut wrote to the faithful: "God Almighty, who holds in his hands the fate of Kings and Empires, has again given unequivocal signs of that enduring protection He has deigned to grant to the arms of Our Gracious Sovereign." The bishop urged the priests "to make their parishioners keenly aware of the obligations they have to heaven for having placed them under the influence and protection of His British Majesty, and to exhort them once again to remain there in loyalty and gratitude." His successor, Mgr Plessis, went even further in this vein on 10 January 1799, in a speech "on the occasion of the victory won by the naval forces of His British Majesty in the Mediterranean on 1 and 2 August 1798 over the French fleet," in which he stated that it "is glorious for Vice-Admiral Horatio Nelson to have been the instrument that the Almighty used to humiliate an unjust and arrogant power." He took up the Bishop of Léon's theme and applied it to "Buonaparte": "There are no excesses of this kind that he has spared. Places of piety proscribed; monuments of religion smashed; Priests' throats slit at their Altars; ... the Divine faith destroyed; the sacrosanct Mysteries trampled underfoot; the solemn days abolished; the idol placed in the temple of the true God, the Holy Virgins driven from their cherished refuges; the leader of the Catholic Church ... cruelly expelled from his see." And he asked, "What return, Sirs, is required of us for so many benefits?"[71]

Inspired by the English press, the local newspapers celebrated "the invincible navy" that had defeated the French Jacobins. Local rhymesters, composing verses as if they were in school, wrote poems favourable to the monarchy, singing loyalty and the English victory:

Let us sing Nelson's courage,
Let us crown his head with laurels,
He tames the rage of the French,
Nothing resists our warriors.
Let us respect the thrones of Kings,
Let us despise the awful anarchy
That reduces France to desperate straits.
Let us keep our monarchy.

The rhymesters also devoted themselves to exposing Napoleon's contradictions ("Sovereign for life / Though Republican") and imagining the scenario of him reconquering Canada and selling it to the highest bidder, as he had just done with Louisiana.[72]

A TURNING POINT: THE *QUEBEC MERCURY* (1805)
AND *LE CANADIEN* (1806)

Since 1760, social groups had affirmed their identity through events that revealed both their material interests and their intellectual positions. The colonial authorities, following the example of London and feeling the pressure of the Atlantic revolutions, had shown a forced liberality that had angered the British colonials, especially the merchants. It had taken these people some time to obtain English liberties in the colony, and now they found themselves in the minority in a House of Assembly numerically dominated by the *Canadiens*.

The seigneurs, traditional supporters of the colonial authorities and the personification of monarchist ideas, found themselves becoming marginalized by the implementation of parliamentary democracy. Indeed, Joseph Quesnel, in 1803, in a play that was never staged, entitled *L'anglomanie*, had ridiculed the zealous loyalism of the seigneurs. The Catholic Church, whose legal status had been suspended since the Quebec Act, had already declared its allegiance: monarchism and anti-democracy, alliance of throne and altar, defence of the established authority, loyalism by conviction and by interest.

Between 1760 and 1789, public life had been lethargic and discussions of ideas had been reduced to their simplest expression, but since the revolution in France, the granting of a house of assembly and the beginning of parliamentary democracy in 1791, public opinion was solicited. This is shown symbolically in a long poem by Seigneur Ross Cuthbert entitled *L'aréopage* (1803), a critical depiction of debates in the House of Assembly. The denunciation of the Terror in France, the counter-revolutionary propaganda of the political and religious authorities, and the garrison mentality inspired by the fear of spies and the possibility of the return of the French led by "Buonaparte" shaped the debates on ideas and the true stakes of those ideas.

From 1805 on, the press and parliamentarism together created public opinion, the vitality of which would be irreversible. The founding of the *Quebec Mercury* and then of *Le Canadien*, the disagreement about prisons, the consolidation of the Parti canadien under Pierre-Stanislas Bédard, and the crisis under Governor Craig contributed to the identification of currents of ideas and the beginning of real intellectual debate.

English merchants, whose political frustrations had been accumulating for close to half a century, founded the *Quebec Mercury* (5 January 1805) as a means of expression and self-affirmation. Proclaiming the primacy of commerce ("certain it is that private interest is public good"), the *Quebec Mercury* denounced the seigneurial system that shackled it, sought ways to ensure that the English colonials maintained control of the political institutions and became for years to come the advocate of a policy of assimilation of the *Canadiens* through legislative union, schools, religion, and language: "This province is already too much a French province for an English colony. To unfrenchify it as much as possible ... should be a primary object, particularly in these times when our archenemy [Napoleon] is straining every nerve to Frenchify the universe ... After forty-seven years possession of Quebec it is time the province should be English."[73]

Once again, after the parliamentary battle of 1792 on the choice of a francophone or anglophone speaker and the debate on the language of publication of the debates of the house, French became the focus of a strategy that would raise the *Canadiens*' awareness of their linguistic and cultural difference and increase their determination to maintain it.

The *Mercury* had nothing but contempt for the *Canadiens*, conventional in their type of agriculture, influenced by "parish despots" – priests – and avowed ignoramuses or "knights of the cross," that is, illiterates, whose signature was an X. To the merchants and the *Mercury*, who saw commerce as the engine of economic development, the argument about prisons in 1805 revealed two different visions of the colony's future. The issue was whether the construction and repair of prisons would be funded by property tax or by a tax on exports, which were controlled by the English-speaking merchants of the colony. The law that was passed in the House of Assembly by a majority of French-speaking Canadians imposed a tax on imports and exports, demonstrating, if that was still needed, that a house of assembly, contrary to what the seigneurs had so often told the peasants, did not always tax the less wealthy.

Almost two years after the launch of the *Mercury*, on 13 November 1806, a prospectus was published for a French-language newspaper that would be called *Le Canadien*. Its name indicated the paper's program, it being understood that "the freedom of an Englishman" was also that of a *Canadien*. The prospectus expressed support for freedom of the press, describing it as an essential condition of a constitution, which would otherwise be despotic. According to the future *Le Canadien*, the press made the people's opinions known to the political authorities, who were sometimes tempted to rely solely on a limited circle of interested parties. *Le Canadien* also intended to refute "the dark insinuations of a paper published in English," "to dissipate the misunderstandings" maintained by it, and "to avenge the loyalty" of the *Canadiens*.

The weekly publication, the first issue of which came off the presses on 22 November, was an ongoing reply to the positions and allegations of the *Mercury*. It was the organ of the francophone members of the House of Assembly, since four of its founding editors were members (Pierre-Stanislas Bédard, the leader of the francophone members; Jean-Antoine Panet, speaker of the house; Jean-Thomas Taschereau; and Joseph-Bernard Planté) and two others would become members (Joseph LeVasseur Borgia and François Blanchet). The name *Le Canadien* was doubly meaningful: the paper promoted the British Constitution and the application of its democratic principles to the Canadian colony, and it sought precisely to define Canadians in relation to the French, the British, and the "Americans."

The Assembly members/editors formulated their understanding or their vision of the British Constitution in *Le Canadien,* showing how quickly and thoroughly they had learned the British political system since 1791. *Le Canadien* expressed almost unreserved admiration for the British Constitution, that "rare treasure." It quoted Fox and referred to British laws, regulations, and precedents in the House of Commons, as the editors were familiar with the four volumes of John Hatsell's *Precedents of Proceedings of the House of Commons* (1796).[74] Very quickly, based on Blackstone, DeLolme, and Locke, *Le Canadien* sought to draw the consequences of the sovereignty of the people and the power of the majority by establishing the independence and primacy of the House of Assembly in the balance of constitutional powers; this was necessary because the Constitution of 1791 was silent on this subject, and the primacy of the elected House favoured their power.[75]

The same was true for the idea of a ministry and ministerial responsibility, which was absent from the Constitution of 1791 but operated in the British Parliament, because, for *Le Canadien*, and for Bédard and Louis Bourdages in particular, it was necessary to be able to criticize the governor, the representative of the king, without necessarily calling into question the monarchy itself. The way to achieve this was to ensure that the governor's counsellors were chosen from the House of Assembly, so that, at least in part, the governor would be "responsible" to the House, and therefore to the people. Bédard had a clear understanding of this constitutional way of functioning; he wrote in *Le Canadien* on 24 January 1807:

The Ministry necessarily has to have a majority in the House of Commons. As soon as it loses the influence this gives it, or as soon as its system no longer seems good, it is removed. It sometimes also occurs that when the king wishes to know which of two systems, that of the ministry or that of an opposition, the nation wants to adopt, he dissolves Parliament. Then the nation exercises its judgment by electing those whose system and conduct it approves of.

For Bourdages, whose comments in the House were reported in *Le Canadien* of 26 April 1809, "this idea of a ministry was not an empty word; [it was] essential for the conservation of our constitution." The edition of 9 March 1808 stated, "there is a ministry in the province," and already in 1807, the recently arrived Governor Craig was ready to believe it: "They either believe, or affect to believe, that there exists a Ministry here and that, in imitation of the Constitution in Britain, that Ministry is responsible to them for the conduct of Government. It is not necessary to point out to your Lordship the steps to which such an Idea may lead them."[76] These reflections on ministerial responsibility by *Le Canadien* and the members were not theoretical; they were part of everyday parliamentary activity in which the governor's counsellors were appointed and were not members of the Assembly. They were often, as noted by *Le Canadien* of 30 December 1809 and 5 January 1810, "émigrés" who were more concerned about what they would take away than what they would leave and who had the attention of the governor of the colony and the authorities of the metropolis. And for the francophone *Le Canadien*, it was this "Ministry constantly in opposition" that created "discord between the representative of the King and the House of Assembly" and provoked "this odious division between Englishmen and *Canadiens* ... Because since the entire ministry is made up of Englishmen, all the

Englishmen in the House of Assembly unite with them ... and the House
... is divided into Englishmen on one side and *Canadiens* on the other."77
This was a decisive perception of the main flaw in the colonial political
system, which would be the source of future problems and the interpre-
tations made of them.

Le Canadien could not reply to the *Mercury* and defend the *Canadiens'*
loyalty without at the same time identifying these "new Subjects" of His
Majesty who were admirers of the Constitution and wished to draw all
the consequences of the "English liberties" for themselves. *Le Canadien's*
pro-Britishism, its suggestion that 1791 was a more significant date than
1760, may seem surprising. The first issue, that of 22 November 1806,
presented Canadians as "British Americans." In the issue of 4 November
1809, Bédard spoke of "those unhappy times that preceded the Conquest
of the country, when a Governor was an idol before which it was not
permitted to raise one's head," whereas since that period, "the rule of
law has gradually established its Empire" and the colony enjoyed a
Constitution "in which a man is something."

The lawyer Denis-Benjamin Viger, who had articled with Bédard and
Panet and who wrote for *Le Canadien*, published a pamphlet in 1809 in
which he explained the reciprocal interests of the colony and Great
Britain. Denouncing the "revolutionary madness" of 1789 and the "too
illustrious tyrant who governs France," he felt that the Conquest was "a
blessing from heaven," because France had attached so little importance
to its colony; he felt the mores of the *Canadiens* were no longer those of
the old French and that this difference was already pronounced before
the Conquest. He recalled that in 1775, the *Canadiens* had been loyal.
He clearly distinguished the Englishmen of the colony – the "émigrés"
– from the Englishmen of London, and placed his hopes on those of the
metropolis. To him, the *Canadiens* were "destined to form a people entirely different from the French and from our neighbours."78

There are both upstream and downstream reasons for this pro-
Britishism. The *Canadiens* had learned to appreciate the real advantages
of the House of Assembly granted by London; they were aware that they
had known nothing like it under the French Regime. Their pro-Britishism
was also a reminder of their loyalty, directed at London at a time when
they were demanding the expansion of the powers of the Constitution
and when they needed to distinguish themselves from both Napoleonic
France and the Americans, whom an active minority of English colonials
was counting on to increase the anglophone population of the Eastern
Townships. In these circumstances, neither France nor the United States
could be used as a model: for "the new subjects," the "rare treasure" was
the British Constitution.

LE CANADIEN AND THE HOUSE OF ASSEMBLY VS. GOVERNOR CRAIG (1810)

The demands and the influence of *Le Canadien* were quite disturbing in certain quarters. Seigneur Pierre-René de Saint-Ours reported to Craig's secretary, H.W. Ryland, that a few people, even in Montreal, where the paper was received as enthusiastically as in Quebec City and its *faubourgs*, had gone so far as to say that if such abuses continued, it would take a revolution to remedy them. Mgr Plessis wrote to the Sulpician priest Roux: "*Le Canadien* has just risen from its ashes through a great many new subscriptions. You cannot imagine the ravages caused by this miserable paper among the people and the clergy. It aims to destroy all principles of subordination, and start a fire in the province." A few editors from the former *Courier de Québec* (3 January 1807–31 December 1808) even founded *Le Vrai-Canadien* (10 March 1810–6 March 1811), a paper favourable to the Executive, to counteract "the poisoned breath of certain seditious papers that have been circulating in this Province" for a few years; its format and typeface imitated those of *Le Canadien*, and its motto was "Ever faithful to the King."[79]

Tensions had clearly mounted in the colony since Governor Craig's arrival in October 1807. Craig believed the French would be there sooner or later and would begin their attack from the south. In spite of the loyalist feelings expressed after Nelson's victory (21 October 1805) over Napoleon at Trafalgar ("Yes, proud Englishmen, never doubt / To vanquish, you will have our bodies / For you, for us, we will fight"), he felt the *Canadiens* were still French at heart and that they would join an American army commanded by a French officer and would willingly return to the domination of France.[80]

In the House, the French-speaking members made the ineligibility of judges their new key issue; they were all the more in favour of separation of the legislature and the judiciary because when judges – who were often English-speaking – were elected, they took a strongly pro-government stance. The House therefore passed a law making judges ineligible. But, like so many other laws passed by the elected House, it was rejected by the Legislative Council.[81] In the middle of an election campaign, the question of the civil list (the salaries of civil servants and the pensions granted by the governor from funds not controlled by the House) continued to be contentious in the House. It planned to vote on all spending in the colony on the basis of the principle of "no taxation without representation"; the electoral platform of Pierre-Stanislas Bédard, the leader of the Parti canadien, for example, was explicit on this point. But Craig refused to transmit a letter from the House on this question to the king.[82]

The tension was such that the governor had *Le Canadien*'s presses seized on 17 March 1810 and its editors, including Bédard, jailed. On 21 March, a proclamation from the governor appeared in the newspapers and was posted on the doors of parish churches.

Whereas divers wicked, seditious and treasonable writings have been printed, published and dispersed in this Province, with the care and government of which I am entrusted; and whereas such writings have been expressly calculated to mislead His Majesty's good Subjects, to impress their minds with distrust and jealously of his Majesty's Government, to alienate their affections from His Majesty's Person, and to bring into contempt and vilify the Administration of Justice, and of the Government of the Country; and whereas, in the prosecution of these wicked and traitorous purposes, their authors and abettors have not scrupled audaciously to advance the most gross and daring falsehoods, while the industry that has been employed, in dispersing and disseminating them at a very great expense, but the source of which is not known, strongly evinces the perseverance and implacability with which it is intended that these purposes should be pursued … it is impossible for me any longer to disregard or suffer practices so directly tending to subvert the Government.

The governor was clearly counting on the loyalism inspired by religion: "Have you in any one instance, or under any one circumstance, been disturbed in the free and uncontrolled enjoyment of your Religion?" He exhorted

all His Majesty's subjects, to be on their guard … and to be cautious how they listen to the artful suggestions of designing and wicked men, who by spreading false reports, and by seditious and traitorous writings, ascribe to His Majesty's government evil and malevolent purposes, seeking only thereby to alienate their affections, and lead them into acts of Treason and Rebellion, calling upon all well disposed Persons, and particularly upon all the Curates and the Ministers of God's Holy Religion, to use their best endeavours to prevent the evil effects of such incendiary and traitorous acts, to undeceive, to set right, such as may have been misled them, and to inculcate in all, the true principles of loyalty to the king, and obedience to the Laws. And I do hereby further strictly charge and command all Magistrates, in and throughout this Province, all Captains of Militia, Peace Officers and others, His Majesty's good subjects, that they do severally make diligent enquiry and search, to discover as well the authors as the publishers of all wicked, seditious and traitorous writings as aforesaid, and of false news in any way derogatory to his Majesty's government, or in any way tending to inflame the Public Mind, and to disturb the public peace and tranquility.[83]

The proclamation was transmitted to the priests in a circular letter from Bishop Plessis.

His Excellency the Governor-in-Chief has charged us with notifying you of his positive intention, that you yourselves all publish this proclamation to the people in your respective parishes ...

His Excellency expects, moreover, that, in your public instructions as well as in your individual conversations, you not miss any opportunity to make the people prudently understand that its future happiness depends on the affection, respect and trust it will show to the government; that it cannot, without running the gravest risks, give in to the deceptive ideas of an unconstitutional freedom that certain ambitious characters are attempting to insinuate to it, and this in contempt for a government under which divine Providence has placed this colony only through the effect of a predilection for which we cannot bless the heavens enough.

We need not add here that you yourselves have a very great interest in maintaining the faithful in the respect and submission they owe to their Sovereign and those who represent him, because we know that, independently of any interest, the clergy of this Diocese has always made strong profession of those principles which have the most solid of foundations, knowledge of the maxims of the holy religion that we preach to the people, which is essentially the enemy of independence and of all reckless reflection on the conduct of the persons whom God has established to govern us.

The next day, the bishop sent the archpriests another circular letter on the loyalty of the clergy.

A few persons are seeking to make the loyalty of the clergy suspect to the government. It is the duty and interest of everyone to banish this suspicion, which would do honour neither to your religion nor to your prudence. The time is critical. All eyes are upon you. The Governor-in-Chief must send to England a report on the manner in which you have conducted yourselves in the present crisis. This report can only be advantageous insofar as you will keep yourselves apart from the supposed friends of the people and bind yourselves invariably to the interests of the executive power. Take this notice seriously and communicate it as soon as possible to the priests of your jurisdictions.[84]

Mgr Plessis took all necessary precautions against "the spirit of democracy [that] is wreaking havoc among us."

Craig reported to Liverpool, Secretary of State for the Colonies:

The most false and scandalous reports were assiduously propagated, & the most seditious and inflammatory publications were universally spread thro' the province which were read & commented upon by their Agents in every Parish. In these Government was grossly represented and verified ["vilified" probably intended], the administration of Justice brought into Contempt, and a spirit of dissatisfaction, distrust and alienation excited tending to the most alarming consequences. Such as it became at last impossible any longer to disregard, and imperiously to call for the intervention of the Executive power.[85]

The governor delayed no longer. Hardly had the presses of *Le Canadien* been seized and its editors imprisoned when he dissolved the House of Assembly on the pretext that it had denied Judge de Bonne the right to sit in it. Bishop Plessis, in a sermon that was exceptionally widely distributed, associated the altar with the throne in denouncing the very basis of the work of the House and of *Le Canadien*: "Let us admit, my brothers, that of all the sophisms which have been abused in these recent times to deceive and mislead nations and dispose them to revolt, this one is perhaps the most wicked ... the most false and the most absurd, I mean, the system of sovereignty of the people." Abbé de Calonne, who was the brother of one of Louis XVI's ministers and had been "driven" from France by the Revolution, wrote:

I have put aside the idea that the Governor had been overly alarmed. In truth, Monseigneur, it is more violent than is commonly thought. He is right to say that these are all French principles. Writings have been spread in my parish, and that is nothing, but some people have been indoctrinated to become completely corrupted. There is one among them who has spoken the most inflammatory words, even talking of rebellion and of going in force to remove those who have been arrested unless they are released from prison.[86]

The results of the election around 21 April 1810, proved the governor's manoeuvering vain. The Parti canadien, which had elected thirty-three members in 1804, and thirty-six in 1808, and thirty-seven in 1809, elected thirty-eight members in 1810 compared to twelve members for the British Party. This caused panic for the governor and his circle of advisors and senior civil servants. Disappointed with the outcome of the election, Craig wrote to the Secretary of State for the Colonies in London expressing his grievances: his lack of control over the House of Assembly, the claim of the existence of a ministry and a nation. He wrote:

The House has ever been as it is now, in great proportion as to the Canadian part, filled up with Avocats, and Notaries, shop-keepers, and with the Common Habitants, as they are called, that is, the most ignorant of Labouring farmer, some of these, can neither read nor write ...

In such a house of assembly as I have described, Your Lordship will easily perceive that it is impossible that Government can possess any influence, they are certainly the most independent Assembly that exists, in any known Government in the world, for a Governor cannot obtain among them even that sort of influence that might arise from personal intercourse ...

The great vehicle of communications between the leader & the people has been a paper called *Le Canadien*, which has published & industriously circulated in the Country for these three or four years past; the avowed object of this paper has been to vilify and degrate the officers of Government under the title of *Gens en place*, and to bring into contempt His Majesty's Government itself, under of affection of the supposed existence of a Ministere; The conduct of which was as open to their animadversions as is that of His Majesty's Ministers at Home ...

Indeed it seems to be a favourite object with them to be considered as [a] separate Nation; La *Nation Canadienne* is their constant expression, and with regard to their having been hitherto quiet & faithful subjects, it need only be observed that no opportunity has presented them an encouragement to shew themselves otherwise.[87]

While Craig shared the garrison mentality and feared Napoleon's successes in Europe, his words and actions – the seizure of *Le Canadien* and imprisonment of its editors, and the dissolution of the House – show an accurate sense of the new consciousness the *Canadiens* had of their destiny and their power. The dispute about prisons, the use of the title *Le Canadien*, and the name Parti canadien were small but real indications of this new collective consciousness, which would be fed by the scenarios put in place by the governor, his advisors, and some of his English-speaking fellow citizens.

Craig's letter to Liverpool also included possible solutions to counteract the actions of the *Canadiens*: abrogation of the Constitution of 1791, considered to have been granted prematurely, and a new electoral division of the province with more constituencies in the English-speaking "townships." The governor's report was based on a brief by Chief Justice Sewell on the situation in the province, in which he proposed the assimilation of the *Canadiens* through heavy British immigration, changes to suffrage, and the poll tax for eligibility for election to the House and, especially, the union of Upper and Lower Canada.[88] This first plan for union was one of several such proposals in 1810, including one from a spy, John Henry, who envisaged a poll tax based on high incomes, increased power for the governor to create new English-speaking counties, the obligation that members be able to read, write, and translate from English, the establishment of English schools in the parishes, and the imposition of English in the courts in five years and in the House of Assembly in seven years.[89] These plans for control and assimilation testified to the existence of a new consciousness among the *Canadiens* regarding their destiny, and at the same time intensified that consciousness.

THE CLERGY AND THE BOURGEOISIE
IN THE LIBERAL PROFESSIONS

Until the departure of Governor Craig in June 1811, the bishop of Quebec City, Mgr Plessis, said he agreed with him regarding the dissolution of the House and the seizure of *Le Canadien*.

It is true that the members of the Assembly have conducted themselves badly toward the government and that it was right to dissolve their House. It is also true that the paper entitled *Le Canadien* was a wicked sheet whose editors criticized the public administration with far too much licence and it acted wisely in incarcerating them, the only way to calm their itch to write.

I was called to the council along with Abbé de Calonne to second the views of the Government and serve in the maintenance of good order in the province.[90]

This appointment of the only bishop and one of the most monarchist priests in the colony to the Legislative Council consummated the alliance of throne and altar. Both powers had an interest in forming an alliance: the throne increasingly needed the support of the altar, which itself was in a position of vulnerability. In fact, the Roman Catholic Church had not had legal recognition since 1791, and the confiscation of the Jesuits' estates in 1800 was a reminder of the reality of the threat. In 1810, as it had had to do since the Conquest, the Church had to demonstrate its loyalty to the British colonial power, and it would have to continue to do so. In addition, as the Bishop wrote to a priest, "when the fabric is so short, it is very difficult to fill all the holes."[91] Indeed, the numbers of clergy were not sufficient: there were 148 priests in 1791, and 168 in 1805, and 182 in 1812.[92] The Church could no longer officially recruit in France, and the seminary-colleges in Quebec City (1765), Montreal (1767), Nicolet (1803), and Saint-Hyacinthe (1811) were too new to supply the numbers needed. Still, the British authorities allowed some fifty immigrant priests into Montreal and the "little France" on the shores of Lac Saint-Pierre between 1791 and 1802, including many Sulpicians and priests "driven out" by the Revolution, who showed a profound loyalty. Abbé de Calonne was one of them.

In contrast, the liberal professions – lawyers, notaries, judges, doctors, and surveyors – saw their numbers grow, going from 150 in 1791 to 224

in 1805, to 273 in 1810, and 331 in 1815,[93] with *Canadiens* making up
59 per cent of them in 1791 and 66 per cent in 1815. This growth, which
was especially marked in the legal professions, meant also that *Canadiens*
were in the majority in all the professions except medicine, and were
particularly numerous among notaries. It was these professionals, along
with merchants, who made up the members of the House of Assembly,
the Parti canadien, and the editors of *Le Canadien,* and who promoted
liberties, liberal ideas, and the vision of the "nation canadienne" disparaged by Governor Craig.

It became clear to the Church that the "clergy of Canada could expect
nothing from Catholic laymen for its general interests and for those of
religion" and that "after God, the Catholic religion in this country offers
protection to its ministers only through the Government. The most zealous of the faithful are among the lower classes of the people. The upper
class of Catholics, Council members, judges, lawyers, merchants of any
credit, are in general no friends of the clergy."[94]

A SECOND WAR WITH THE AMERICANS (1812)

The conflict between Great Britain and the United States that arose out
Napoleon's blockade on English trade with Europe awakened a loyalty
that was markedly different from the Canadians' attitude of "benevolent neutrality" in 1774 and 1775. The arrival of Governor Prevost in
September 1811, which ended the garrison mentality and the antagonistic strategy the colony had known under Craig, facilitated the recruitment of Canadians and the House's voting of the funds required for the
war. For the old aristocracy, the conflict between the United States and
Canada was an opportunity both to defend monarchist values against
the Republic and to restore its military honour.[95] The Catholic Church
reaffirmed its loyalty to the monarchy and its rejection of republicanism: "In this important crisis, let us recall ... that while America has long
had an attitude of ingratitude and rebellion, we for our part have always
resisted the contagion of its pernicious examples." When there was a
riot – an isolated one – against recruitment in Lachine in June 1812,
Abbé Lartigue, who had studied law before being ordained, proclaimed
without hesitation:

For it is no longer the time to say that your Pastors should preach the Gospel to
you without becoming involved in political affairs. No, my brothers, when we
speak to you of your obligations as subjects and as citizens, it is nothing other
than the Gospel, and the pure Gospel, that we are preaching to you. Since
when are the duties of subjects toward their sovereigns no longer a dogma of

religion? ... Render unto Caesar the things which are Caesar's: may every soul submit to the powers established by God; for those who resist this power resist God himself. Have you forgotten these words of the prince of the apostles: submit to all those who are above you, whether to the king as head of state or to governors or those who command you on his behalf. And also submit to all those who govern you, even when they are unjust to you. For that is God's will. It is not politics that inspires these maxims; it is the very word of your God that we proclaim on his behalf.

The Abbé found his politics in the Gospels, in the "very word" of God or in St Paul's precepts of submission and loyalty. But what was new was that this future bishop of Montreal, who had adopted as his own the new sense of destiny of his "compatriots," called himself "*Canadien* too" and spoke of the "nation canadienne." That nation would owe its future to its tradition of loyalty going back to 1774–75.[96]

The French Canadian professionals and merchants, who for years had been seeing the anglophones of the colony rely on the arrival of Loyalists to populate the Eastern Townships, thus seemed less attracted by the republican democracy of the United States. Their salvation remained in the hands of England, which since the Conquest seemed more reliable to them than the political authorities of the colony; although they were both English-speaking, the metropolis and the colony differed from the point of view of constitutional credibility. And these *Canadiens*, who were already calling for the "conservation of our institutions and customs," felt that it was this very difference that constituted a bulwark against invasion by the United States.

And when Colonel Michel de Salaberry won the Battle of Châteauguay on 26 October 1813, people were quick to see and to say that the loyalty of the *Canadiens* had helped save the colony.[97]

A VIEW OF THE CONSTITUTION AND OF POWER (1814)

Beginning in 1807, *Le Canadien* and the Parti canadien had attempted to identify the reason for the deadlock and dysfunction of powers in the colony. *Le Canadien* had quite explicitly referred to the idea of a ministry such as existed in the metropolis, which would make the government "responsible" or accountable.

The battle over the eligibility of judges that took place in 1808 and was reignited in 1814, the crisis of 1810 and the assimilation scenarios that were formulated then, the strategy of total control of the colony's spending, the abortive plan to appoint an agent of the House of Assembly in London who could present the reality in the colony differently than the governors or the "émigrés" did, and Governor Craig's recognition in 1807 and 1810 of their desire for a ministry all justified the Canadians pointing out the problems in the colony in 1814. Whether it was by Bédard, Bourdages, or Blanchet, the *Mémoire au soutien de la requête des habitans du Bas-Canada* (Brief in support of the petition of the inhabitants of Lower Canada) summed up the understanding the Canadians then had of the Constitution and the direction of their demands.

The brief reiterated the Canadians' loyalty to London, while clearly identifying the flaw in the colonial institutions. The distortion of the balance of powers was said to arise from the fact that the "people in place," the ones who sat on the Legislative Council and the Executive Council and shaped the opinion of the successive governors, were all English-speaking. In contrast to these people, who were more or less temporary residents, the *Canadiens*, "more attached to their country," formed the majority in the House of Assembly but "could not be Council members, which is the cause of all the disorder that appears in the exercise of our constitution." The brief stated that if "the Governor had the power to call to the Council the principal members of the majority of the House of Assembly, he would thus have a means to hear both parties, and not be obliged to know one only through the information received from the other." Without this "responsibility" of the Council and the Executive, the *Canadiens*, "incapable of defending themselves, have no resources other than the protection of the mother country." But Bédard was no fool: the strategy of the metropolis was to divide and rule, as he said to John Neilson on 16 January 1815: "How could one imagine ... that the constitution could go with the positions as they are placed? How is it conceivable that one of the parties be in possession of one of the branches of the legislature and the other party be in possession of the other branch? Does it not seem that things have been arranged expressly to cause a division in the Legislature?"[98] Hence the *Canadiens*' expectations with respect to London rather than to the colonial authorities in Quebec.

With the flaw identified in this way, the antagonism between old and new subjects, between Englishmen and *Canadiens*, was explained and the *Canadiens* were not considered to be solely responsible – any more than *Le Canadien* could be understood without reference to the *Quebec Mercury*.

The brief on the constitutional and political evolution of the colony arrived in London at the end of Napoleon's rule and the economic blockade he had set up. A priest with the Missions étrangères wrote from London to a colleague in the Séminaire de Québec:

How we must bless divine Providence for the happy changes that have occurred in Europe! Divine Providence has finally cast its merciful eyes on us! The Holy

Father has returned to Rome and his domains have been given back to him! The Bourbons will again ascend to the throne of their ancestors! We will finally be able to breathe again! God blinded Buonaparte. He refused conditions of peace that, strengthening him on the throne of France, would have prolonged our sorrows and placed the Church in the greatest danger.[99]

The end of the blockade pleased the Church for obvious reasons. It would also restore the regular circulation of people and goods between Europe and America, in particular the exchange of cultural goods between Canada and France.

A LOOK AT THE AFFAIRS OF EUROPE AND AMERICA

While *La Gazette de Québec* and *La Gazette de Montréal* gave space to international news, the attention *Le Canadien* gave to foreign affairs was revealing of the interest of the rising *Canadien* bourgeoisie in colonial and imperial political affairs. Drawing on the *Courrier* from Glasgow, the *Royal Gazette,* also from Scotland, or newspapers from London or Kingston, Jamaica, *Le Canadien* used extracts from news or articles that, between 1808 and 1810, mostly concerned Napoleon's campaigns in Spain and Portugal. The point of view was very British, but certain vocabulary tended to recur: "Spanish nation," "great nation," "nations of Europe," Spanish "patriots."

Le Canadien hoped that Napoleon would be beaten and that his defeat would be the glory "of His Majesty's armies." There was little mention, until *Le Canadien* stopped publishing in March 1810, of Latin America, which was breaking ties with Madrid and Lisbon precisely because of Napoleon's actions in that part of Europe. The newspaper recognized that "without peace with France, Bonaparte ... cannot expect to prevent the separation of the Spanish colonies from their mother country; a separation which already appears to have begun"; but *Le Canadien* insisted on "comparing our happy fate with the divided and desperate condition of the States of America that are our neighbours." On the question of relationships between colonies and empires, the newspaper pointed out that "*Canadiens* have never celebrated human rights" and "are content with their government and have no desire to change it."[100]

CONCLUSION

A whole ideological vocabulary and an ideological activism was and would continue to be drawn from England's conquest of Canada. But one fact remains: traumatic or not, it would permeate every aspect of the individual and collective experience of the *Canadiens*: their language, religion, customs, and political system.

The two major events in the history of Quebec – the military conquest of 1760 and France's cession of its colony to England, and the Rebellions of 1837 and 1838 – were not a war of independence or a successful democratic revolution, but defeats. The defeat of 1760 was a defeat for France in one of its colonies, the degree of "Canadianization" of which is still not recognized. In a sense, and without equivocation, it was France that was defeated, but the colonists who had been building New France for a century and a half, of whom there were close to seventy thousand around 1760, continued building Canada, not France. The fact that these colonists were called, and called themselves, *Canadiens* and designated their political party and their newspaper with the same name is a sign of an identity in construction. In fact, in 1760, what is in question is the dual identity of the *Canadiens* already, *before* the cession, these French colonists who had become *Canadiens* and whose relationship with France was gradually changing: either France lost its meaning in terms of identity or that French identity was revived by the cession, but in many directions: regret, nostalgia, a feeling of abandonment, of being forgotten. Whether radical or partial, a break occurred, the results of which became a central thread in the history and the imagination of Quebec.

If France was fading in imagination and reality, England was becoming clearer, stroke by stroke, to the point that the *Canadiens* expected from the metropolis what they could not hope for from its colonial representatives or immigrants. The appeal of America, the continent and even the hemisphere, came from the "Yankees," who were perceived in two main ways. First, they were the republicans who in 1774 had proposed to the *Canadiens* that they separate from the king and the country with which they had been trying to identify for only fifteen years. We can thus understand the ambivalence of the *Canadiens* toward these "Bastonnois." And then around 1810, "Americans" were the Loyalists that the editors of the *Quebec Mercury* and those people devising plans for assimilating the *Canadiens* welcomed to the Eastern Townships in order to swell the ranks of anglophone Protestants and finally obtain a majority in the House of Assembly. The ambivalence was also fed by this image.

Along with this fragmentation of identity, there was a shared experience of life and politics: the society of Lower Canada had gone from absolute monarchy to constitutional monarchy. The *Canadiens* thus served their apprenticeship in liberalism in a colonial context: how should the colony be governed; how could liberties be institutionalized; what sort of representation should be established; how broad should be the suffrage that goes with the sovereignty of the people in a colony whose metropolis is a constitutional monarchy?

The British Constitution was attractive because it enabled the *Canadiens* to demand the rights and liberties of the British. Starting in 1784, the *Canadiens* joined with the Englishmen of the colony in demanding a house of assembly, which they quickly learned to use, and in which they formed the majority by the turn of the nineteenth century, after obtaining a francophone speaker and bilingual debate. For the *Canadiens*, London – for which this was a real challenge – had been consistent with regard to the English liberties, permitting representation to operate normally, that is, according to population. London and the British Constitution became an object of admiration, a means and a source of great expectations, while the English of the colony were disappointed and began to seek other ways to change the democratic game.

But it was still a monarchy, and not a republic like the United States or France. The monarchist feeling had a tradition: it was what the *Canadiens* had known since 1608. The British constitutional monarchy found support in the colony from seigneurs, who had every interest in perpetuating this political system, and from the Church, which, out of principle and interest, constantly allied itself with the state. Even the notables in 1762 spoke of the sovereign as being necessary to his peoples, and after 1810, the very idea of a ministry or of responsible government may be seen as a way to challenge power without touching the power of the king. This monarchist feeling was cultivated by the colonial authorities and in the press in 1789: as long as the revolution was not regicidal, it was acceptable, insofar as France appeared only to be repeating 1688. With the Terror in 1793, the Church added its imprecations to those of the state. The pro-revolutionary work of Mesplet and Jautard's *La Gazette de Montréal* should certainly be taken into account, while recalling that the plan for a house of assembly, already conceived by Grenville in 1789 but granted in 1791, had satisfied some *Canadiens*, who appreciated this parliamentarism all the more because it would soon give them decisive political leverage. The granting of a house of assembly relieved the pressure created by the situation in 1776 and in 1789. The conflict between the House, on the one hand, and the governor and the Legislative Council, on the other hand, would dampen their enthusiasm, but for the time being, the institution was remarkable, it was a model. In this period, Lower Canada was more reformist than revolutionary, more favourable to constitutional monarchy than to republicanism.

For the people of Lower Canada, the challenge was to know how to be Canadian in an America without France but with Great Britain.

2

The Emergence of Public Opinion
in the Colony (1760–1815)

COLONIAL LOWER CANADA was at this time largely a rural, agrarian society in which oral culture and communication dominated. Life followed the rhythm of the seasons and the religious calendar, and sociability – the social relationships among people – was deeply marked by rurality and orality. The habitants, isolated by work, distance, and seasons, could come together on Sunday at church, to listen to the priests' sermons and chat on the church steps or in the parish hall. This oral culture, in which legends and stories were transmitted through the spoken word, benefited the Catholic Church, which had a network for transmitting the religious and political word. The priest's sermon, the pastoral letter from the bishop of Quebec City that was read from the pulpit in every parish in Lower Canada, the major printed sermons of Bishop Plessis, which were sometimes read out loud for the illiterate, clearly show the privileged position of the Church in this rural and oral society. In the country, there were various places for socializing: the family, the church, the general store, and the inn if the village was big enough. Oral culture was predominant; the literacy rate in Lower Canada is estimated at 16 per cent on average between 1760 and 1820. This figure, which is an indication more than hard evidence, since it is based on an analysis of the capacity of spouses to sign their names on marriage certificates, was lowest during the decade 1770–79, after a period of decline that began not with the British conquest but with the decade 1730–39. The literacy rate fluctuated until the decade 1810–19, and then grew slowly but steadily.[1]

SOCIABILITY, ASSOCIATIONS, AND LITERACY

Urban sociability, that of the places and forms of mediation among citizens, was more intense. The salon and the café, for example, provided interfamily sociability and occupational (merchants, lawyers) sociability.

The variety of concerns and interests gave rise to many different places and forms of assembly. Some of these voluntary associations that fuelled community life were thus based on the most symbolic of these "assemblies": the House of Assembly.

Political concerns were prominent in most of the associations, such as the Constitutional Club of 1791, which was organized to familiarize citizens with British institutions, or the Loyal Associations established in 1794 to counter the ideas associated with the Reign of Terror. The Académie de Montréal seems to have been so closely connected with the "gazettes," which "advertised" the associations, that it may have existed only in the columns of Fleury Mesplet's *Gazette du commerce et littéraire*. Various subjects were debated in the pages of this publication, which was founded on 21 October 1778, and members replied to one another as if the Académie in fact held meetings in Montreal during the period. The Société des Patriotes, whose motto was "Humanity, tolerance and liberty," and which Mesplet also took an interest in, celebrated the Revolution of 1789, called for a house of assembly and denounced the clergy. This is shown in the toasts, veritable summaries of public opinion, at a Société des Patriotes dinner: "To the generous La Fayette!," "To the patriotic Mirabeau!," "To the abolition of abbots!," "To the destruction of the Récollets!," "To the felicity of the people!," "To a house of assembly in this province!" In contrast, the short-lived Société littéraire de Québec (Quebec literary society) met on 3 June 1809 to celebrate the birthday of George III.

The English-speaking Montreal Society United for Free Debate, which met at Dillon's Hotel and had a few French-speaking members, including a friend of Mesplet, Henri Mézière, seems to have been the association most focused on sociability and discussion of subjects peripheral to politics: the superiority of commerce or agriculture, public or private education, marriage or celibacy. This debating society, more than any other, anticipated subsequent associations, which would also include public lectures. Little is known about Masonic lodges other than the fact that they existed and that some of them had francophone members.[2]

Urban sociability relied more than rural on printed matter and writing, and the literacy rate was much higher in the city. Between 1760 and 1820, in Quebec City, 41 per cent of the population knew how to read and write, almost three times the average for Lower Canada. People in colonial Lower Canada were more likely to be literate if they lived in the city – where there were more schools – and if they were Protestant, English-speaking, male, and practised a trade that required literacy. Anglophone Protestants were twice as literate as francophone

Catholics, but they were a small minority concentrated in the cities (Quebec City and Montreal), they had most often been educated in the metropolis, and the Protestant tradition, with its emphasis on individual reading of the Bible, favoured learning to read. Of the men in Lower Canada, 18.6 per cent were literate, compared to 14.3 per cent of women, and the proportion in Quebec City was 47.6 per cent, compared to 34.5 per cent. Also in Quebec City, 88 per cent of people in the liberal professions, businessmen, and officers were literate, compared to 56 per cent of shopkeepers, self-employed artisans, non-commissioned officers, and civil servants and 31 per cent of artisans, skilled workers, soldiers, and small merchants.[3]

THE "GAZETTES" AND COMMUNICATIONS

While rural sociability was based on oral culture, urban sociability and community life drew on print culture. Clubs and societies published pamphlets and announced their meetings in the newspapers, which sometimes reported on them. These forms and places of assembly created interest groups, "publics" that in turn gave rise to a broader public, and a public life where opinion was shaped. Nothing did more than the gazettes – which were also called *papiers publics*, from the English "public papers" – to shape this nascent public opinion. *Public, publication, publicity* all have the same root, and this public of readers who informed, addressed, and responded to each other, shaped a more abstract and urban sociability that was as much that of the "Voltairian" Académie de Montréal, which had a paper existence, as of the new public that cut across the foundation and dialogue of the *Mercury* and *Le Canadien*.[4]

As early as 1764, as we have seen, the colonial authorities encouraged the foundation of a "gazette" in Quebec City to disseminate information and ordinances, and the granting of a parliament in 1791 conveyed the idea that the "English liberties" could exist and survive only through freedom of the press.

In America, a printer of the period could only survive by publishing a "gazette." Newspapers were quite rare in the colony from 1764 to 1814; there were fourteen of them, nine in Quebec City and five in Montreal. The two cities had about the same population, around 6,500 residents in 1784 and 15,000 in 1815.[5] Of the fourteen papers published weekly, five were English, five were bilingual, and four were French. Significantly, the anglophone population, less numerous but more urban, richer, and better educated, had greater means in terms of culture and communications. In Quebec City, the main newspapers were the *Quebec Gazette /*

La Gazette de Québec, the *Mercury*, and *Le Canadien*, and in Montreal, Mesplet's *La Gazette du commerce et littéraire*, whose name and language varied over the years, *The Canadian Current*, and *The Canadian Spectator/ Le Spectateur canadien*.[6]

While the *Quebec Gazette/La Gazette de Québec* was seen as a place for the publication of ordinances, and priests had to subscribe to it and "read to their congregations on Sunday, immediately after the church service, all the ordinances and orders that will be published from time to time," the Church did not frown on this print competitor with the oral messages of its own teachings. This changed with the publication of Mesplet's *Gazette* in Montreal, which disseminated Enlightenment ideas in the subtle manner of the philosophers of the *Encyclopedia*. Étienne Montgolfier, the Superior of the Sulpicians in Montreal, complained to the bishop of Quebec City, "I had always hoped that this gazette, by giving it the contempt it deserves, would collapse on its own: but since it has appeared that it is spared through the protection of the government." He also appealed directly to the governor, who assured him that he would permit nothing to be published there that could "foment discord among the Peoples who for all sorts of reasons must support the Interests of a government that has protected them."[7] In fact, Mesplet had promised, in May 1778, to "steer clear of anything that might could cause umbrage to the government and to religion" and not to discuss "current affairs." He would not hold to that: when he was forced to sell his newspaper and print shop, *La Gazette*, in its first incarnation, stopped publishing in June 1779, and Mesplet and his editor Valentin Jautard were imprisoned for three years. The struggle for freedom of the press had begun.[8]

The battle would be continued by *Le Canadien*, which felt that the "English liberties" could not be exercised without the fundamental liberty of freedom of the press: "Freedom of the Press ... must respect only religion and wise Government ... it must repudiate the Rich and the Great if they are vicious, and protect the poor and the small if they are virtuous; it must continually be on its guard, in order not to personally offend any individual; but it can, and it even must, discuss boldly and generally all that is contrary to society and harmful to the people."[9]

After the closing of the *Gazette* in 1779, another francophone newspaper, *Le Canadien*, would be seized in 1810, and its journalists imprisoned.

The publication of newspapers and the presence of printers in the only "cities," Quebec City and Montreal, like the decisive importance of the urban environment for the literacy rate, clearly indicates the close relationship of the level of cultural development to population density in colonial North America. Lower Canada in this period, which was limited to the St Lawrence Valley and the shores of the river, saw its population quintuple from 1763 to 1814, going from 70,000 to 335,000 inhabitants. A half-century after the conquest of the country, there were 300,000 French Canadians and 25,000 Anglo-Americans, and this linguistic split corresponds quite closely to the religious division between Catholics and Protestants.

The concentration of the colony's population in towns and villages was minimal: in 1765, there were only eight villages with more than one thousand inhabitants, compared to forty-one in 1790, and the majority of the population still lived in villages of less than a thousand. There were, however, six towns or cities with more than two thousand inhabitants in 1790: L'Assomption, Berthier-en-Haut, Saint-Eustache, Varennes, Quebec City, and Montreal. At the turn of the nineteenth century, the population of Montreal would surpass that of Quebec City.[10]

This degree of population concentration could hardly permit the establishment of institutions and resources capable of stimulating and sustaining a certain intellectual life in a New World colony. Associations, print shops, the press, theatres, and even inns require a certain demographic threshold to be economically profitable. The circulation of goods and people was slow: inland and Atlantic navigation was essentially by sail, and only possible when the St Lawrence was not frozen, that is, from May to December. Even with the first steamboat, the *Accommodation*, launched by the Molsons in 1809 and followed by the *Swiftsure* in 1812, it took thirty-six hours to travel the distance between Montreal and Quebec City. The "chemin du Roy" (King's road) on the north shore was the only land route, and it was not easily passable during the spring thaw. It was the road used around 1810 by the postmaster, who was responsible for carrying the mail twice a week between Quebec City and Montreal. There were post houses in Trois-Rivières, Berthier-en-Haut, and L'Assomption. Starting in 1797, there was a mail coach between Montreal and Burlington, Vermont; this route, which started in the Atlantic ports of the United States, sped up communication with Halifax and Saint John, and made it possible from December to May, when the ice prevented navigation.[11]

PRINTERS AND PRINTED MATTER

Printers in this period were versatile: if a printer in Quebec City or Montreal made his living or subsisted by publishing a newspaper, he would also do job printing, sell books and stationery, and bind newspapers, pamphlets, and books, and he was sometimes responsible for the "post office" or even made paper, as was the case for James Brown. Printers often had English names and came from the United States: this was true of Brown, Gilmore, Mower, and Mesplet, a Frenchman who had come by way of Philadelphia.

Printed matter in the colony dates from 1764. The number of titles printed (1,115 from 1764 to 1820) grew continuously, and close to 50 per cent of the titles published during this period came out between 1811 and 1820; 71 per cent of them came out between 1801 and 1820. This printed matter, which was mostly French (52 per cent), was published in Quebec City (77 per cent) and Montreal (23 per cent). A third of the titles consisted of only a single page, a quarter were two to four pages long, and another quarter could be called books and were more than fifty pages long.[12]

Printed matter in Lower Canada was primarily government-related (proclamations; documents of the militia, the House of Assembly and the Legislative Council; police, city, and port regulations) or political (election leaflets, political pamphlets). Next came religious titles (prayer books, pastoral letters, sermons, catechisms), commercial catalogues, trial transcripts, almanacs and calendars, the annual "New-Year's verses" for newspaper carriers, and a few poems, primers, and school books.[13] While it was political, printed matter primarily had practical and social functions.[14]

LIBRARIES

While local printing focused on practical material, reading took place in "libraries," often rudimentary, socially limited places. As early as 1778, the very "enlightened" printer Fleury Mesplet saw the value of libraries. He wrote in his *Gazette littéraire et du commerce*:

Already emulation is beginning to make its stimulus felt; already the love of good taste that pierces the darkness of prejudices, is awaking us from the lethargic sleep in which we have been immersed; we are starting to feel the effects of reading chosen books, of which a few particular ones enrich the Country; but in too small numbers to be compared to the utility that could be drawn from the Public Libraries that should be found in our towns.[15]

Governor Haldimand had other reasons of think about the establishment of a library in Quebec City.

The few resources here, and the reason I have every day for perceiving that the ignorance of the people is one of the greatest obstacles that must be conquered to make them acquainted with their duties and their own interest, have given me the idea of establishing a public Library. I have led the Bishop and the Superior of the Seminary to see the advantage which would result from it. They have entered into my ideas, and I have had a subscription opened, which they have signed with me, as have several priests, almost all the British merchants and several Canadians.[16]

The support of the clergy was more reserved than the governor suggested.

I confess to you, monseigneur, that if I contribute to this establishment [the library], it would only be grudgingly and by the pure motive of Christian policy. I am profoundly convinced that in all the establishments of Printing and Public Libraries, although they have themselves something of good, there is always more bad than good, and that they do more harm than good, even in places in which there is a certain policy for the conservation of faith and good morals.[17]

Because of delays and difficulties in obtaining French-language books, the Quebec Library / Bibliothèque de Québec opened its doors in November 1783 as a subscription library rather than a real public library funded by public monies and accessible to the entire literate public. In January and February 1779, the *Quebec Gazette / La Gazette de Québec* and Mesplet's *Gazette* in Montreal spoke of interest in a library in Montreal. Meeting at Dillon's tavern, subscribers-shareholders founded the Montreal Library / Bibliothèque de Montréal in 1796.[18]

The subscribers of the two libraries learned of the titles available in the rare catalogues that they published. The French content of the Quebec Library went from 1,209 volumes in 1792 to 1,245 in 1801 to 1,425 in 1808 and to 1,535 in 1813. Most of the books offered were history books, biographies, memoirs, and travel narratives: histories by Bossuet, Raynal, and Charlevoix, histories of various countries, books on France and the Revolution, memoirs by Thomas Paine and Calonne. Next in number came works on science, art, and literature: the *Encyclopedia* in thirty-five volumes, Buffon in twenty-seven volumes, Rousseau's *Confessions*, Locke's *Essay Concerning Human Understanding*, Fénelon, and books on agriculture and horticulture. Among the sets of complete works were those of Voltaire (forty volumes), Rousseau (twenty-three volumes), Helvétius, Hume, Montesquieu, Corneille, Racine, Molière, Boileau, and La Fontaine. Next were poetry, theatre, and novels: Ariosto, Tasso, Milton in French translation, Beaumarchais, Madame de Genlis, Chateaubriand (*Atala, l'Itinéraire de Paris à Jérusalem*), the Nouvelle bibliothèque de romans in thirty-two volumes, the *Tableau de la littérature française du xviiiᵉ siècle.* There were also political works: Blackstone on English law and criminal procedure, the British Constitution, Locke's essay on civil government, and law books on the "coutume de Paris," and *Les Causes célèbres* in sixty-four volumes. The few religious books in the library had a clearly apologetic function: the *Anti-dictionnaire philosophique, Les Erreurs de Voltaire* by Abbé Nonnotte, Pascal's *Pensées,* Fénelon on the evidence for the existence of God.

In 1797, the Montreal library offered 1,558 volumes, 830 in English and 728 in French; it emphasized the eighteenth century, with Voltaire, Helvétius, Mirabeau, Condorcet, and Volney, as well as Locke and Bayle. It goes without saying that in both libraries, French-speaking borrowers could borrow books in English on British politics, the constitution and parliamentarism.[19]

The clergy was not absolutely against books; it was against printed matter that it did not control – "bad" books. Members of the clergy sometimes possessed large libraries, consisting mostly of theology, religion and belles-lettres.[20] There were also books in the presbyteries and, of course, the seminaries in Quebec City, Montreal, Nicolet, and Saint-Hyacinthe. In 1782, the library of the new Séminaire de Québec, used for training both clergy and other students, contained mostly books on theology and religion, textbooks, belles-lettres, and history.[21]

The members of the Assembly, who urgently needed to consult books on constitutional law, procedure, and subjects they had to legislate on, could find useful documentation in the House of Assembly library starting in 1802. In this library, which in 1811 still had only 137 titles, two out of three titles were on law.[22]

It was therefore possible for subscribers, priests, college students, and Assembly members to have access to books in both semi-public and private institutions. But individuals also had libraries or, to be more precise, books. We know this from inventories of estates after death. In Montreal, in the city and on the island, from 1765 to 1790, a sampling of inventories after death shows that 12 per cent of them included books. The book owners, who were mostly francophones, were merchants and members of the elite, and they mainly owned religious books and belles-lettres (dictionaries, theatre, poetry, correspondence, and memoirs).[23] Again in Montreal, another sampling of inventories after death, from 1800 to 1820, reveals the presence of books in 38 per cent of them, with a total of 11,512 books, an average of fifty-six volumes or sixteen titles per owner. Two thirds of these book owners were Protestants, therefore anglophones; it was anglophones who owned the largest private libraries. The "libraries" were, in fact, simply shelves in the dining room or bedroom:

28 per cent of them contained one to five volumes, and 27 per cent contained six to nineteen volumes; the majority of the libraries thus contained one to nineteen volumes. Only 13 per cent of private libraries counted more than one hundred volumes, and those were usually belles-lettres (poetry, dictionaries, grammars), books on science and art, secular history or law, or devotional books.[24]

In Quebec City, 26.1 per cent of the inventories after death from 1760 to 1799 and 36.6 per cent of those from 1800 to 1819 included books, for an average of 31.3 per cent, one third of the inventories. The number of "libraries" identified increased from 127 to 190, and the number of volumes inventoried went from 2,584 to 11,330, that is, an average of twenty volumes and sixty volumes per "library" respectively. People who owned books in their homes were mostly civil servants, merchants, members of the liberal professions, and tradesmen. Peasants owned less than 1 per cent of the books inventoried. Of the private "libraries," 63 per cent contained one to twenty volumes, and 10.7 per cent more than one hundred volumes. As in Montreal, these books included belles-lettres, science and art, history, law, and liturgical and devotional books.[25]

As well as borrowing books or owning them, one could, in the eighteenth century, rent books from commercial lending libraries called "circulating libraries." For a fee, the mode of payment and amount of which varied, one could rent a book for a week, undertaking to meet the costs of any damage to it. Some of these libraries, which could have more than a thousand titles, published catalogues of their collections, which consisted mostly of fiction. We know of three of these circulating libraries: in Quebec City, that of Germain Langlois, which opened in November 1764, and that of Thomas Cary, which opened in September 1797; in Montreal, the first one was that of William Manson, which first advertised in the *Gazette de Montréal* on 20 October 1806. Only Cary's circulating library combined renting books with the possibility of reading newspapers in a "news room," a reading room for periodicals and newspapers.[26]

THE COLONIAL BOOK TRADE

Specialized trade in books began only at the turn of the nineteenth century with two anglophone booksellers, John Neilson in Quebec City and H.H. Cunningham in Montreal. Books could be purchased from printers or from merchants, who advertised the titles they had in inventory or that had arrived in recent shipments by sea. They could also be bought at estate auctions.

In Quebec City, from 1764 to 1819, there were 563 advertisements in newspapers for books for sale. These advertisements, by John Neilson,

William Brown, John Jones, Samuel Neilson, and Thomas Cary, generally included fewer than five titles and offered, in order of importance, books on science and art, belles-lettres, history, law, and religion. The most-advertised authors were Walter Scott, Fénelon, O. Goldsmith, Samuel Johnson, and Voltaire, and other French authors included Montesquieu, Lesage, Bossuet, Racine, La Fontaine, Rousseau, Molière, and Chateaubriand.[27]

The Neilsons were the first to specialize in selling books from their print shop. From 1792 to 1812, the Neilson "bookstore" sold close to fifty thousand volumes, an annual average of close to 2,500 volumes. These were mostly French books – religious and school books.[28] However, it was English titles that dominated the three catalogues published by Neilson in 1802, 1803, and 1811, and once again, the titles offered were in belles-lettres, science and art, history, religion, and law.[29]

In Montreal, from 1776 to 1815, about sixty auctions, which were held in auction houses or in the Teasdale, Gillis, Sullivan, or Clamp café, included lots of books that were sometimes quite large. These books came from estates or import, and were occasionally described in catalogues available before the auctions.[30] There was no French bookstore in Montreal until 1815, and the only bookseller and stationery shop was that of H.H. Cunningham. In this context, it is understandable that the priests of the Missions étrangères (foreign missions society) at the Séminaire de Québec and the Sulpicians at the Collège de Montréal called on their colleagues in Paris, London, and Baltimore in order to acquire books. This was necessary after the cession of 1760, and especially during Napoleon's blockade, which closed English ports in the metropolis and the colony to French trade. It was possible to get around this situation by calling on the French priests in exile in London or the American Sulpicians in Baltimore, who had maintained contact with Europe through the Atlantic ports of the United States, which managed to maintain some trade with England and France.[31]

PUBLIC EDUCATION AND CLASSICAL
SECONDARY EDUCATION

Education was the key to cultural and intellectual development in the colony. It led to literacy, reading, symbolic creation, and the creation of institutions capable of ensuring and perpetuating the society's cultural development. The challenge was considerable: the average literacy rate in the colony was about 16 per cent (in Quebec City, 41 per cent), and Protestant anglophones, the urban population, and males tended to be more literate.

Travellers and the *Quebec Mercury* polemicists often said there were not even ten literate *Canadiens*. Recent immigrants or visitors, they did not take into account the concentration of the anglophone population in the cities and their American schooling. In response to these attacks, *Le Canadien* of 20 January 1810 stated that "the sciences are never encouraged in colonies; they find encouragement only in the metropolises"; the editor of the newspaper added that it "would be curious to see a colony composed entirely of nobles and philosophers."

But the accounts do agree in deploring the poor quality of education in the colony from 1760 to 1815. There were no universities in 1760, no colleges until 1765, after the shelling of the Collège des Jésuites in Quebec City in 1759, and only a few private schools mostly in the urban centres. It is estimated that in 1790, Montreal, Quebec, and Trois-Rivières, with a total population of 33,200, had twenty schools, that is, one school for 1,660 inhabitants, while in the rural areas, with a population of 128,100, there were thirty schools, or one school for 4,270 inhabitants. The 10,000 Protestants of the colony had access to seventeen schools (one school per 588 inhabitants), and the 160,000 Catholics, to a mere forty schools (1/4,000). In Quebec City, the average school teacher was a Protestant man and taught in the Upper Town. Like literacy rates, education levels grew proportionally with religious affiliation, sex, and residence in an urban setting. This latter factor is easily explained: demographic density made possible the creation and maintenance of schools.[32]

The Catholic Church had, since New France, carried out a traditional role in education, and it had been given significant land endowments to help it fulfill this role as well as that of organizing hospitals and charitable work. In 1760, the regular and lay clergy, male and female, had large seigneuries that could generate income.[33] The colonial government realized the extent of the problem, and in 1787 and 1790, it created committees of inquiry on the state of education, which identified the positions of the Church and the merchants.[34]

The first real initiative came in 1801 with the Act for the Establishment of Free Schools, a result of the efforts of the Anglican Bishop of Quebec City, Reverend Jacob Mountain, who in 1799 urged Governor Milnes to act. According to Reverend Mountain, everything possible had to be done to make sure the English colonial families would not be forced to send their children to study in the United States, because they "are not likely to imbibe that attachment to our constitution in Church and State, that veneration for the Government of their country, and that loyalty to their King, to which it is so peculiarly necessary in the present times ... to fix them deeply both in the understanding and the heart." In addition

. to this anti-republican objective, Mountain voiced his concern for the "lower orders": "it is notorious that they have hitherto made no progress toward the attainment of the language of the country under which government they have the happiness to live." And the remedy for this "want of a community of language" was "facilitating as much as possible the means of acquiring the English language to the children of the Canadians."[35] This political and cultural aim was repeatedly expressed in the school law of 1801; in 1808 Governor Craig's secretary – who was even surprised that the law was passed in 1801 – recalled that the purpose of the "royal schools" was to "gradually improv[e] the political and religious sentiments of the French Canadians."[36]

The 1801 law was the first expression of the desire that the state should be responsible for education. It makes no mention of the religious and linguistic aspects; article 4 stipulated that private confessional schools were not subject to the law, and regulations 20 and 23 stipulated that religious denominations had authority over the choice of textbooks. Article 8 stated that the foundation of a "royal school" was to be decided by the majority of the inhabitants of a place. During this period, the success of the law was limited: the number of schools was fewer than ten until 1807, and it reached its maximum in 1815, when the colony had twenty-nine schools. In 1818, of thirty-five "royal schools," only eleven were French-speaking.

While the state of education improved somewhat, it was still dismal in 1815. While the Roman Catholic clergy certainly took a dim view of the "royal schools," which were designed in part to Protestantize and anglicize the *Canadiens*, there were also other factors that explain this slowness of the expansion of education: the dispersion of the population, the harshness of the climate, the scarcity of textbooks, the lack of teachers and, of course, the poverty and apathy of mostly illiterate parents who, as Mgr Hubert suggested before the Education Committee in 1790, did not see the usefulness of the liberal arts to agriculture and needed labour for clearing land and harvesting crops.[37]

The Catholic Church was clearly more interested in classical secondary education, which was more likely to lead to local recruitment of clergy to make up for the shortage and the obstacles to recruiting in Europe, and in France in particular. Four college seminaries, which would train both candidates for the priesthood and students in law and medicine, were founded before 1815: the Petit Séminaire de Québec in 1765, the Collège sulpicien de Montréal in 1767, the Séminaire de Nicolet in 1803, and the Séminaire de Saint-Hyacinthe in 1811, with the latter two designed to promote vocations for the priesthood in rural areas. With the necessary adaptations, the instruction given was that of the Greco-Latin humanities fashionable in Europe and in France, where religion, Latin, belles-lettres, and rhetoric were the core of the curriculum. In addition, there were two final years of philosophy, the teaching of which aimed to train citizens more than scholars, and was based on the pedagogical bible of the period, the *Traité des études* (Treatise on studies) by Charles Rollin: "In fact, this study, when it is well conducted and done with care, can contribute a great deal to regulating morals, perfecting reason and judgment, enriching the mind with an infinity of knowledge … and what I consider infinitely greater, inspiring in young people a great respect for religion, and forearming them with solid principles against the false and dangerous reasoning of unbelief, which every day makes all too rapid progress among us."[38]

Knowledge of this instruction in philosophy is crucial for understanding the intellectual and civic training of the future religious and civil elites and the major currents of ideas in society: monarchism, liberalism, democracy, republicanism, rationalism, anticlericalism. Philosophy, which was taught in Latin, had three parts, aspects of which were revealing. In Logic, to counter Greek scepticism and, especially, Cartesian doubt and the authority of Cartesian proof, one sought criteria of certainty in common sense, the consent of peoples and authority. In Metaphysics, the emphasis was on the immortality of the soul and, particularly, the evidence of the existence of God, against agnosticism and atheism, which were considered a threat to individual morality and the foundation of authority. Finally, Ethics provided the civic and political training of the students. The ethics taught was normative, with more emphasis on duties than on rights. These duties were toward God, to whom inner and outer worship was required, in order to counteract the Protestantism of individual examination and the "religious indifference" that would soon be denounced by Félicité de Lamennais. It was the duties toward civil society that best showed the intersection of philosophy and culture. The philosophy textbooks taught that the best form of government was the monarchy of divine right, with a minimal tolerance for the constitutional monarchy under which the colony had lived since 1763. *Omnis potestas a Deo* (All power comes from God) was the expression the students learned, and subsequently believed in or rejected. Power came from God and was transmitted to a Sovereign, and it was thus not the people who were sovereign. Rebellion against legitimate authority was prohibited. This loyalist teaching of a loyalist Church once again endorsed the alliance of the throne and the college seminary.

CONCLUSION

Public opinion was born of the press and printing in 1764 and grew remarkably with parliamentary democracy, starting with the election of 1792. It really began to take off in 1805 and 1806, when a rivalry developed between the *Quebec Mercury* and *Le Canadien* that was both political and cultural. A public space different from that of the French colonial period was created. The body of opinion of the francophone middle class of professionals and merchants took form and became coherent: admiration and use of the liberties of British subjects and the constitution; struggle for the primacy of the elected House over the other components of political power; and consequently, promotion of a certain responsibility on the part of the government and identification of the fundamental political flaw of the colony as the recruitment of Council members only among anglophone immigrants; separation of legislative and judicial powers; control of public spending and of the civil list.

This escalation of demands would culminate in a political crisis under Governor Craig, who was supported by the Catholic Church. The plans for assimilation conceived by Craig, Sewell, and others – including a first plan to unite Lower and Upper Canada in 1810 – contributed to identifying cultural values (language, religion) that would play out in various ways and heightening the group consciousness of the *Canadiens*.

In a sense, the cultural system was established according to a split in values. The Protestant anglophones, concentrated in Quebec City and Montreal, were more literate. Coming from the metropolis, they were familiar with cultural institutions, and they provided Quebec City and Montreal with print shops, newspapers, associations, "public" libraries, and bookstores. Even the initiative of the "royal schools," conceived by Bishop Mountain as anti-republican and pro-British, could only please the Catholic clergy because of the first characteristic, especially since in their colleges, the clergy were training the future priests and practitioners of the liberal professions to denounce Cartesian reason, the sovereignty of the people and the Revolution – which, of course, did not mean that once out of college, lawyers, and doctors could not think the opposite. But the alliance of the trinity of throne, altar, and college seminary was sealed.

While the *Canadiens* had had some experience with associations and the benefits of print shops and, especially, freedom of the press before 1810, it was after that date that the growth of literacy, although still weak, became irreversible, the amount of printed matter increased and the library of the House of Assembly was established as a cultural instrument. This urban culture in which public opinion was forged through the spoken and written word, however, was still part of a culture that was mostly rural, oral, and material, which explains the paucity of improvements in public education.

PART TWO

1815–1840

3

Questions of Democracy and the Development of Consciousness in the Colony (1815–1834)

OBTAINING A HOUSE OF ASSEMBLY based on representation by population had been a turning point in the public life of the new British colony: the French-speaking population, which recognized the logical consistency of the metropolis's attitude regarding respect for "English liberties," formed the demographic and democratic majority, and the English-speaking population necessarily found this situation disadvantageous. The demographic ratio very rapidly fuelled an institutional and constitutional crisis in which the House of Assembly, the democratic branch of the colonial political system, which depended on rights and liberties, sought to affirm its primacy over the "aristocratic," non-elected branch, the Legislative Council. From the beginning, the strategy of the House of Assembly was to try to gain control of revenues and the budget, and to contest the composition of the Legislative Council and its strategy of blocking bills voted by the House; the members drew the logical conclusions of the British system, aiming for the separation of executive, legislative, and judicial powers and challenging the eligibility of judges to sit in the House of Assembly and their presence on the Legislative Council. These tensions in the colonial political system necessarily led to appeals to the metropolis, either to modify the system or to oppose colonial plans for constitutional change, such as the first proposal for union in 1810.

After a period of relative calm under Governor Prevost (1811–15), the unresolved issues – tensions between the House of Assembly and the Legislative Council, confusion of legislative and judicial powers, the budget and the civil list, strategies of assimilation – surfaced again and intensified because of the conflicts they produced, but, above all, also because of the existence of a rising social group, members of the liberal professions, who, along with the merchants, would demand and propose solutions to these unresolved issues; Louis-Joseph Papineau would become the leading figure of this group. The work of the House of Assembly and the contents of *La Gazette de Québec*, *Le Canadien*, and *La Minerve* involved a few major questions that were the real stakes at issue in the debates, conflicts, and plans: the advancement of the cause of democracy, the resolution of constitutional and institutional problems, the resulting re-evaluation of colonial ties, and the development of a "Canadian" identity, which also included relationships between church and state.

A RISING MIDDLE CLASS

The affirmation of liberalism and patriotism was based on the growth of a bourgeoisie in the liberal professions, which tripled in numbers from 1815 to 1838; lawyers, notaries, doctors, and surveyors increased from 331 at the beginning of the period to 939 at the time of the Rebellions, with a strong surge after 1821.[1] In 1831, for example, most members of the liberal professions were French-speaking and lived in Quebec City or rural areas. These francophones, who were mainly notaries and lawyers, gradually developed a culture of the legal professions that was marked by eloquence in speaking and writing.

These francophone middle-class members of the liberal professions also dominated the political culture of the colony: they made up on average during the period 74 per cent of the members of the House of Assembly.[2] Men in the liberal professions, mostly lawyers and notaries, slightly exceeded merchants in number, making up almost half of the members during the crucial decade of the 1830s. They formed the nucleus of the Parti canadien and later the Parti patriote (1826), which, while acting as the standard bearer for the aspirations of lower-class French Canadians and depending on their support, aimed to shape a society in keeping with its visions and its interests as a group.

This new middle class did not lack social visibility: luxurious residences, consumption of imported goods such as those offered by Fabre's bookstore, attendance at the (mostly English-speaking) theatre, portraits of public figures, such as the Papineaus, father and son, John Neilson, Vallières de Saint-Réal, Elzéard Bédard, Louis Bourdages, Ludger Duvernay, Mgr Plessis, Mgr Lartigue, and Mgr Signay, by artists Louis Dulongpré, Jean-Baptiste Roy-Audy, Antoine Plamondon, and Théophile Hamel, and miniature portraits and silhouettes of Berthelot, Mondelet, Saint-Ours, and de Salaberry.[3]

The rise of this middle class had effects on enrolments in the colleges, and the number of colleges increased from four to seven with the founding of new ones in Sainte-Thérèse (1825), La Pocatière (1829), and L'Assomption (1832), not to mention the Collège de Chambly (1825–44). With this new situation in mind, Mgr Plessis wrote to the superior of the Collège de Saint-Hyacinthe.

Our colleges in the cities of Quebec and Montreal will never provide us with a number of priests proportional to that we may expect from our colleges in the country. The students in the cities are usually supported in their studies by the plans of their parents, who intend them to become notaries, lawyers, members of the legislature and a few priests; but indifferent to that condition, when they have to decide, they naturally choose those [professions] whose appearance and freedom are more pleasing to them. This is not the case for the students of our colleges in the country; belonging to families whose most ambitious aims are to see their children become priests, in which their parents support and encourage them at every opportunity, they lead in their families a routine, quiet life before going to college and during their holidays, so that they want to return to their studies; which is not the case for the students in our cities.[4]

The founding of more colleges by diocesan and regular clergy was intended to make up for the departure of Jesuits and Récollets from the colony and the fact that it was no longer possible to legally recruit priests in France. "The material continued to be short," wrote Mgr Plessis: in Lower Canada, in 1830, a priest had to tend, on average, 1,834 faithful, compared to 1,080 twenty years later. In Montreal, a priest was responsible for one thousand faithful in 1815, and for 1,260 in 1831. Montreal then accounted for 48 per cent of the total number of clergy in Lower Canada, but only in 1836 would Mgr Jean-Jacques Lartigue, the suffragan in Montreal since 1821, be given a new diocese.

Although the numbers in the Catholic Church were "suffering" in comparison with those of the "triumphant" middle class, Notre-Dame, the new (1829) Sulpician church in Montreal, with its 1,500 pews and a capacity of ten thousand faithful, was a powerful symbol of the hopes of the Church. In fact, religious practice was declining in the diocese and in Notre-Dame itself, if we take as an indication attendance at Easter services, given the "Easter duty" to take communion at least once a year at Easter time. Between 1836 and 1840, the rate of non-attendance at Easter fluctuated between 6.8 per cent and 61.6 per cent depending on whether the parish was very urban or in a Patriote community. In the Montreal parish of Notre-Dame, which accounted for 10 per cent of the Catholics in the diocese, only one third of parishioners did their "Easter duty" in 1839. In the nine parishes of the diocese the same year, an average of 37 per cent of parishioners did not do their "Easter duty."[5]

The number of anglophone members of the liberal professions in the cities of Quebec and Montreal was a sign of a more global phenomenon: immigration from the British Isles after the Napoleonic Wars. On average, 8,041 British immigrants landed annually in the port of Quebec City from 1818 to 1822; 10,867 from 1823 to 1827; 31,541 from 1828 to 1832; and 22,444 from 1833 to 1837, with increasing numbers from Ireland toward the end of the period.[6] This influx, which made Montreal a majority anglophone city starting in 1835, aroused fears of assimilation among the *Canadiens*. The population of Lower Canada, which passed the half-million mark at the start of the 1830s, was mostly concentrated in Quebec City and Montreal, with the two cities closely matching each other in population at the end of the 1830s.[7]

QUESTIONS OF DEMOCRACY AND IDENTITY

Earlier political crises had not been forgotten, as shown by the creation, in 1812, of a committee on the Craig administration, which included Louis-Joseph Papineau (1786–1871). The son of the notary and seigneur Joseph Papineau (1752–1841), who had been a member of the House of Assembly since 1792, Louis-Joseph Papineau was a lawyer and a member of the House of Assembly since 1809. He was elected speaker of the House in 1815, after the departure of Antoine Panet, who had fulfilled that function since 1792. The position of leader of the Parti canadien opened up with the departure of Pierre Bédard, who was imprisoned in 1810; until 1817, there was no clear leader of the party, while Papineau familiarized himself with his duties as speaker of the House.

The absence of leadership in the Parti canadien was illustrated by the initiative taken in 1813 by member James Stuart, a candidate for leader of the party, to have the House of Assembly lay charges against Jonathan Sewell, the chief justice of Lower Canada, speaker of the Legislative Council, and a former advisor to Governor Craig, and James Monk, the chief justice of the district of Montreal. Stuart's initiative had the triple appeal of being a democratic move in favour of the separation of legislative and judicial powers, an attack on the people remaining from the time of Craig's policy and a settling of accounts between Stuart himself and Sewell. The saga was at the forefront of the public scene for some time, long enough at least for Governor Prevost to transmit the accusation to London, without, however, suspending the judges, who were acquitted by the Privy Council in 1816. Ironically though rather predictably, the Legislative Council, with Sewell as speaker, refused to allocate funds for Stuart to go present the case in London. It was with regard to another case of confusion between legislative and judicial powers – that of Judge Foucher – that

Papineau, who was also a candidate for leader of the party, first drew attention, making speeches on the impartial administration of justice and showing his democratic concern for the separation of powers.[8]

The refusal of the Legislative Council to allocate funds so that James Stuart, who was then practically the leader of the Parti canadien, could present the accusations against the judges in London, was only one episode in a longstanding endeavour to appoint an agent or delegate of the House of Assembly in London to promote the Canadians' point of view. The issue was serious because the members of the Parti canadien were convinced that only the British colonials who sat on the Executive and Legislative Councils had London's ear. The plan for a London agent had been unsuccessful since 1807 because of prorogations by the government or, most often, refusals by the Legislative Council to vote funds for it. The Assembly of Lower Canada would indeed find defenders of its position among the members of the Whig opposition in London, but only in 1831 would they be able to choose an agent and pass a resolution allocating the appropriate funding, bypassing the approval of the Legislative Council. The time it took to achieve this and the importance the delegate had in the 1830s clearly show the increasingly conflictual relationship between the colony and the metropolis and the emergence of a new awareness of the limitations of a colonial situation.[9] Disputes and manoeuvering made it necessary to have such an intermediary between a House of Assembly that was asking more and more insistently for reforms and a Colonial Office that had to play for time between a mainly anglophone Executive and a mainly francophone House.

The democratic fervour of the Parti canadien and Papineau, increasingly its confirmed leader and the new seigneur of the family seigneury of La Petite Nation, made the question of revenues and the civil list a recurring issue. The issue was simple but fundamental: "no taxation without representation," no real democracy without control of public spending by the representatives of the people. The parliamentary battle for control of public spending also revealed a colonial dimension in that its aim was to limit the governor's "arbitrary" spending power. In targeting the Executive, the House of Assembly was also challenging the power of the metropolis and seeking greater autonomy for the colony. From 1818 to 1822, the situation escalated, resulting in a serious parliamentary imbroglio. When London demanded that the colonial House of Assembly vote on revenues, the House countered with demands that were revealing of the tensions with the metropolis. The members of the Parti canadien refused to vote on the budget and the civil list globally or to vote on them for "the life of the King," deciding instead to study them and vote on them annually, and article by article.[10]

Papineau led the struggle on revenues: he explicitly denounced the sinecures maintained by the colonial government and opposed a permanent civil list because of the necessity of a budget that varied according to the needs of the country and as a precaution against excessive increases in the civil list, as occurred in 1819 and 1820. He insisted that the House of Assembly should have a role of monitoring public spending in the colonies and stated that the reasons for voting for the civil list "for the life of the King" had "no application and had never been applicable in the colonies, since there can be no analogy between the situation there and in England."[11]

THE SECOND AND THIRD PLANS FOR UNION (1822 AND 1824)

To add to this crisis in parliamentary institutions and relations with the metropolis, a new dispute began in 1817 over the division of customs duties on goods from Upper Canada passing through the ports of Lower Canada. Because of the parliamentary crisis, the agreement between the two provinces was not renewed in 1819, and Upper Canada petitioned the Imperial Parliament in 1822. Political conflict and a trade disagreement were thus at the source of this new major crisis that struck Lower Canada in 1822 and led to a new plan for union during the troubled term of Governor Dalhousie (1820–28).

The Canada Trade Act, presented to the House of Commons in June 1822 as a trade bill and also as having other purposes, became, the following month, a bill on the customs issue between Upper and Lower Canada, accompanied by a plan for the union of the two provinces. This union would be administered by a single house of assembly and a single legislative council, and the governor would have the right to create new counties in the Townships of Lower Canada and thus increase the number of English-speaking members in the united assembly; the financial criterion for the eligibility of candidates would be increased to £500 sterling; debates would take place only in English; and the king would have the right to veto laws voted by the new House of Assembly.[12]

The plan for union, which the colony learned of in September, led to assembly after assembly, speech after speech, for or against union. The main promoter of the plan for union and the unionists' agent in London was none other than James Stuart, who had once been a candidate for the leadership of the Parti canadien and the accuser of judges Sewell and Monk. His reversal was a surprise. Stuart's *Observations on the Proposed Union of the Provinces of Upper and Lower Canada* took the view that the existence of two houses of assembly in the colony was the result of an artificial division and deprived Upper Canada of access to the sea and the mother country. Stuart stated that the House of Assembly of Lower Canada was in the hands of "foreign people" and that with two legislatures, "the country is destined to remain perpetually French" and that, in a such a scenario, "it will become necessary, not for the French to assume an English character, but for the English to assume a French character; and both parties will be led to believe, that the French Canadians have not, without reason, designated themselves as the *Nation Canadienne*, in anticipation of the future national character they are to bear, and the high destinies that await them as a separate and independent people."

Since, according to Stuart, mechanisms for their assimilation had been neglected, a union urgently needed to be achieved in order to extinguish the "national prejudices and peculiarities" of the French Canadians, who opposed it because they were illiterate and had no concept of government and even less of the political framework of a union system; they also believed that union would dispossess them of their language, their religion, and their laws. Stuart attached to his *Observations* petitions from unionists in the Townships and Montreal; they stated: "And your Petitioners cannot omit to notice that the unreasonable extent of political rights which [have] been conceded to this population, to the prejudice of their fellow-subjects of British origin, together with a sense of their growing strength, has already the effect of realising, in the imagination of many of them, their fancied existence as a separate nation, under the name of '*Nation Canadienne*'; implying pretensions, not more irreconcilable with the rights of their fellow-subjects, than with a just subordination to the parent state."[13]

Petitions against union proliferated, and Papineau, the leader of the Parti canadien, took it upon himself to act as the spokesperson for the opposition to the bill. He reiterated his admiration for the British Constitution and denounced those "Pygmies [who in 1822] have dared to attack the magnificent works raised in 1791 by the hands of Giants." He saw the plan for union as an act of oppression that had "fortified among us a spirit of union that nothing will be able to weaken now." He reaffirmed that the *Canadiens* were "born English subjects just like those who come to us from the banks of the Thames" and that the legislators of 1791 "gave us the only effective way by which we can preserve [all our rights]: a majority in representation as long as we have a majority of the population." In December 1822, he wrote to R.J. Wilmot Horton, undersecretary of state for the colonies, to inform him of the opposition both in Lower and Upper Canada to the plan for union and the presentation of petitions against that plan. Against the "calumny" spread by the unionists, including their "supposed attachment to France," he recalled the "uniform conduct" and the loyalty of the French Canadians in 1774 and 1812. For Papineau, anglicization, or to use his term, Anglifying, had two different meanings: "By what they [the unionists] call Anglifying the country is meant the depriving the great majority of the people of this Province of all that is dear to men; their laws, usages, institutions and religion ... Great Britain wants no other Anglifying in this Colony, than that which is to be found in the loyalty and affection of its Inhabitants, no other British race than that of natural born subjects, loyal and affectionate. Such are the inhabitants of both Provinces."

Delegated to London with John Neilson in early 1823 to present the petition of sixty thousand signatures against the plan for union and put forward Lower Canada's point of view, Papineau expressed indignation that people in the colony had learned of the existence of the plan late and that London had not consulted those primarily concerned, and he emphasized that the opposition to the plan was general and extended "to all classes." The two delegates argued that this union, which would be equivalent in terms of territory to seven American states, would make it very difficult for members to participate in the work of the House because of the distances and climate. They added an argument on the fundamental difference in the legal systems of the two provinces and replied point by point to the unionists' arguments. First of all, union would not result in any reduction in spending. In terms of democracy, the Imperial Parliament could not decide in place of the colonial House of Assembly to create new electoral constituencies in order to favour one political position. The delegates were concerned about the fact that although Upper Canada (120,000 inhabitants) was much less populous than Lower Canada (550,000 inhabitants), it had recently seen a change in the number of representatives it was entitled to (forty), while the House of Assembly of Lower Canada had consistently seen its bills to increase the number of members (fifty), including those from the Townships, blocked by the Legislative Council. Papineau and Neilson saw clearly that an increase in the eligibility criterion for members to £500 sterling was being proposed to hinder French Canadian candidates, and they considered the plan to have members of the Legislative Council sit in the future House of Assembly unconstitutional. As for the elimination of French from the deliberations of the House, they regretted that it had been forgotten that this language and this culture had helped to maintain the British colony in North America since the American War of Independence.[14]

John Neilson, who was delegated to London with Papineau, also opposed union in his newspaper, *La Gazette de Québec / The Quebec Gazette*, which he had recently passed on to his son,[15] while the young Étienne Parent, who joined the editorial staff of *Le Canadien* in March 1822, was, next to Papineau, the strongest voice against union. The old *Le Canadien* of 1806, which had been seized by Craig in 1810 and had published from 1817 to 1819, came out again from 1820 to 1825, and in it, Parent stated that it "is not so much a union that is being sought, but a majority in representation in order to obey the wishes of the executive." He considered that union "would only increase the friction of a machine in which there is already too much" and used an equally mechanical metaphor to characterize the problem of the relationship between the Legislative Council and the Executive: "Not numerous enough, in relation to the population, to be able to dominate by itself, [the Anti-*Canadien* faction] has always used the Governors as a lever to multiply its force." In response to the declarations of the unionists, Parent defined French Canadians as descendants of the French but "inhabitants of America," and stated that in 1763, "the king of France abandoned the right he had to the loyalty of the *Canadiens* in favour of the King of England."[16]

Thanks to speeches by liberal members, in particular Sir James Mackintosh and the member for Bristol, Henry Bright, the British government did not have the unanimity it had counted on and gave up "for the present" on introducing the union bill, "of the policy and propriety of which, in the abstract they still retain their original opinion."[17]

The plan for a union between Upper and Lower Canada was discussed again when Chief Justice Jonathan Sewell and John Robinson proposed "A plan for the federal union of British provinces in North America." Craig's spirit was still alive in anglophone Lower Canada. Taking as a pretext the loyalism of the inhabitants of the different colonies (Upper and Lower Canada, Nova Scotia, New Brunswick, and Prince Edward Island) and their desire for protection by the mother country, this plan argued that the French Canadians must not be tempted to ally themselves with the United States; it stated that, for the French Canadians as well as the clergy, annexation to the United States would mean the end of their customs, their language, their religion, and their "feudal system." Sewell, the colonial champion of the assimilation of the French Canadians, felt that the merging of the provinces would increase the military strength of the colony and, above all, that a single legislative assembly for all the colonies, rather than five, would be easier for London to control, as would a house of assembly of thirty members, in which the majority would be reduced to sixteen. With the House of Assembly of Lower Canada in mind, the authors of the plan added: "In a general united parliament, the representation of any single province would not constitute a majority; and, therefore, mere local prejudices or attachments would be sunk, and the interests of the empire and the provinces would be considered as a whole."[18]

The plan for a legislative union was not adopted. Not for the time being. But the two plans for union showed clearly that for both sides, francophone and anglophone, control of the House of Assembly was the key
issue. The francophones of Lower Canada constituted the majority in it
because of their demographic weight and the very low economic threshold of eligibility for representatives; the anglophones sought to become
the majority in an assembly of the united provinces, even if they had to
bend the principle of "rep by pop." The plans for union were clearly
aimed at strengthening executive power and, at the same time, metropolitan power; the royal veto, already in place since 1791, confirmed
this. The elimination of the French language from parliamentary
debates seems to be connected with a fear of seeing the "nation canadienne" become consolidated. Papineau, who had sat in the House since
the time of Craig and the first plan for union of 1810, noted that these
second and third projects had instead strengthened "the spirit of union"
of French Canadians, at least of the sixty thousand of them who had
signed the petition against the plan. The lawyer for the unionists and the
unionists themselves were also aware of the plan for a "nation canadienne," as if, through adversity, a patriotic consciousness had been established and had attained a new level when the Parti canadien of 1805
became the Parti patriote (1826) and the lexicon of the *patrie*, the homeland, became more common.

LOYALISM AND DISSIDENCE IN THE CATHOLIC CHURCH

The plan for union of 1822 had caused an outcry and produced a rare
consensus among French Canadians – as they were beginning to be
called – including members of the Catholic clergy who had signed the
petitions. The stakes for the Church were clear: its political loyalism
stopped where its raison d'être began. Its true interest lay in maintaining
the rights of the Roman Catholic religion. Mgr Lartigue in 1827 drew all
the conclusions from the experience of 1822: "I see only one or two circumstances in which we would be obliged to involve ourselves in political
affairs if they occurred: this would be in the case in which the British
government wanted to decree something contrary to religion, as it had
done with the plan for the first union bill that failed on the remonstrances
of the province; or if it was again a question of the union of the two provinces ... but then it would be necessary to separate any political matter
and express ourselves only on questions related closely or distantly to
religion."[19]

Opposition to the plan for union was certainly the Church's only dissidence in an unfailing tradition of loyalism. The Secretary of State for

the Colonies, Lord Bathurst, understood the importance of this loyalism and told the governor of Lower Canada: "Our great object must be not to let the demagogues make the Roman Catholics the instruments of mischief ... and for this purpose you will I hope be able to establish a good understanding with the Roman Catholic Bishop. The power which he has over the clergy is very great, and must therefore be very great also through the Clergy over the people ... and there is no so effectual (I believe no effectual) way of conciliating the Roman Catholic laity, as by the clergy. There will be no indisposition here to attend to their Interests and wishes even tho' this should be unfavourable to the Protestants."[20]

The "zeal and loyalty" of Mgr Plessis and his "services rendered" since the period of Governor Craig were rewarded by his appointment to the Legislative Council in April 1817. Two years later, Mgr Plessis told Lord Bathurst: "I persist in believing, Milord, that in fostering the Catholic religion in H.M. provinces of North America your Lordship is working effectively for the support of the government of H.M. and that our altars protect the throne as the Throne protects them."[21] The alliance of state and church could not have been more explicit. In Montreal, the Sulpicians, whose seigneurial properties were threatened because of the absence of legal status for the Catholic Church, rallied to support the government, presenting themselves as "most agreeable to the Government" and as "the headquarters" and "the boulevard" of loyalty.[22]

The clergy, which was weak in numbers and had been without legal status since 1791, took note of the rise of the bourgeoisie and liberal ideas. Mgr Plessis, a bishop since 1806, evaluated the evolution of religious practice: "However, during the period when [Mgr Briand] governed, we could take on much more that it would be prudent to do today. There was more respect for the clergy and fewer open eyes to observe its actions. The faithful were more docile and still sheltered from the frightening progress made in their minds by the principles of liberty and democracy propagated by our new constitution and by the contagious example of the French revolution." The bishop of Quebec City noted the decline of religious fervour in the towns and villages; he felt that "the spirit of independence and democracy which, thanks to our *liberal* constitution, prevails in the people," had even won over the clergy.[23] And the parish priest of Baie-du-Febvre observed to a correspondent in 1817: "Dear Madam, do not believe that morals here and religion are not suffering any decline ... As the colony becomes prosperous through trade, industry, and even the sciences, which are taught brilliantly in all our colleges as philosophy spreads even as far as our

Canadian people, we see this spirit of impiety, of vertigo, which over-
threw France, the throne and the altars ... In the House of Assembly,
some *Canadiens* have shown impious principles, they wanted nothing less
than to remove from the priests the education of the youth and from the
nuns the administration of the sick."[24]

The shortage of priests when the population was increasing and was
widely dispersed, the decline in religious practice, and the rise of liberal
ideas were all indications of what the Church was beginning to call "indifference to matters of salvation." The Superior of the Séminaire de
Nicolet suggested his colleagues show a little more zeal: "There would be
some malcontents, no doubt, but there would be fewer lukewarm and
indifferent people." A correspondent of a priest at the Séminaire de
Québec noted the same spirit in Paris: "Everywhere we see discouragement, indifference."[25] In response to this growing indifference with respect to religion, a small nucleus of priests sought a restoration of
religion, a new Christian inspiration. They were mostly French priests –
abbés Raimbault, Fournier, Orfroy – who had been "driven out" by the
Terror and come to Canada with the approval of the British authorities
at the end of the eighteenth century. These priests, like Abbé de Calonne
in Trois-Rivières, had already publicly supported the initiatives of
Governor Craig in 1810. They had settled on the shores of Lac Saint-
Pierre, and their presence was so noticeable that people spoke of the
region as a "Little France." Abbé de Calonne (1743–1822), who was the
brother of Louis XVI's minister and had "once lived at the court of
Versailles," was fully informed by his relatives and correspondents of the
evolution of the political and religious situation in France. He received
current publications and subscribed to *L'Ambigu*, an anti-Bonapartist
paper published in London, and *L'Ami de la Religion et du Roi* (The friend
of religion and the king), edited by M. Picot, a former colleague, at the
Séminaire d'Orléans, of abbés Raimbault, in Nicolet, and Fournier, in
Baie-du-Febvre. He read those newspapers and circulated them. It was
through Abbé de Calonne that Félicité de Lamennais became known in
Canada. On 16 March 1819, a relative wrote to him from Paris: "A year
ago a book entitled sur l'indifférence de la religion [*sic*] by Abbé de
Lamennais was published. It is in its fourth edition. This book is unquestionably the most beautiful of this century." Abbé de Calonne's agent
sent it to him the following month, and on 9 November, Calonne quoted
Lamennais for the first time in an article sent to *La Gazette des Trois-
Rivières*, which immediately started a long debate on the orientations of
public education and, in the medium term, the possibility of a tradition
of liberalism, but a Catholic one.[26]

A NEW CRISIS IN THE COLONY (1827)

The two crises of the plans for union of 1822 and of 1824 had barely faded when tensions once again mounted between Lower Canada and England, the bone of contention this time being the Legislative Council and the vote on the colony's budget.

In 1824, François Blanchet, a doctor and member of the House of Assembly who had long been active in public life, published a lengthy appeal to the Imperial Parliament denouncing the anti-democratic machinations of the unionists with regard to representation, but above all, putting a new issue on the political agenda, that of the non-elected nature of the Legislative Council. He initiated a tradition that would be taken up by Papineau and Parent, among others, denouncing British attempts to establish an aristocracy in Lower Canada, in America, and legitimize a Legislative Council like the House of Lords.

The American continent is fundamentally different from the Old Continent in almost all respects. The climate, the soil, the natural products, the vegetation, the animals, everything is different. The people there have also been modified differently, and to want them to find good in America what they find good in Europe is completely absurd. The result is that despite all the efforts of despotism, both civil and religious, to maintain European institutions in South America, nothing has succeeded, and a system of government is going to be established there that is very different from that of Europe. The very people who were raised in Europe are the most opposed to its institutions; we could cite, for example, Bolivar, the liberator, the current president of the Republic of Colombia. Does one believe that when public opinion in the whole vast Continent of America is in favour of representative governments, that it would be very easy to establish and maintain a degenerate nobility in Canada. The idea is really most ridiculous.

And to add weight to the republican idea of "representative governments," Blanchet referred to the testimony of Charles Fox during the debates on the Constitution of 1791: "Fox said Canadians should be given a Constitution that would leave them nothing to envy their neighbours. Make the members of the Legislative Council elected, and you will have everything."

Blanchet also presented a damning account of how members of the Legislative Council were appointed, of people holding multiple functions and receiving inordinate salaries, and of the scandalous fact that four judges in Quebec City who were members of the Council could,

because of the quorum required, paralyze political life in the colony by
blocking the bills of the House of Assembly. As for the claim by "the
Governors and their dependents" that "Canadians of French descent
were more French in their dispositions than English," he opposed it,
declaring: "The *Canadiens* have tasted the benefits of liberty, and nothing
will be able to destroyed that sentiment in them ... The French Canadians
are therefore attached to their government by principles that nothing
will be able to destroy, we mean by that, *English principles, liberal principles,*
and not principles of monopolization and distinction."[27]

The issue of revenues reached such a point of no return that in March
1827, Governor Dalhousie prorogued the House and accused the members of failing to fulfill their responsibilities, questioning their loyalty to
their country and their king. Papineau and seven other members signed
a "Declaration from members of the assembly to our constituents," a
response to the governor who "wanted to destroy us in public opinion
and that of our constituents." In it, the members explained once again
their refusal to vote globally, "for the life of the King," on a colonial
budget that was constantly growing and was being used, by means of the
civil list, to enrich privileged individuals at the discretion of the
Executive. To the accusations of disloyalty, the members retorted in uni-
son: "Home! Home! that single word is enough" as "the oath of fidelity
to the Country."[28]

The candidate Papineau took up this theme in an important speech
on 11 August 1827, during the election campaign, in the West Ward of
the City of Montreal. To him, the rules that applied in England "for the
life of the King" had "never had any application, nor can have any ratio-
nal application" in its colonies, marking a new sensibility that was republican and akin to that of the United States. He showed how the civil list
had gone from £20,000 to £40,000 sterling in 1810, and then to £60,000
in 1818. Papineau, speaker of the House and leader of the Parti patriote,
showed that the governor was contradicting himself, reminding him that
when he was governor of Nova Scotia, he had accepted an annual vote
on the budget, which was also the practice in Upper Canada. Very well-
informed on constitutional practices in other British colonies, Papineau
reiterated the importance of the House of Assembly – which had just
been prorogued and which was prorogued more frequently than elsewhere – as a bulwark against abuse: "In no other part of the British
Empire is it so necessary and essential as in this Province, to find great
independence and energy in the Representative Body, because in that
body alone can be found a counterpoise to the excesses of power concentrated in a small number of persons having for the most part no link
of permanent interests with the country."

Papineau found a formulation that clearly explained to the voters the democratic dimension of his refusal to vote blindly for a budget that was used, among other things, to pay judges who were also appointed to the Legislative Council: "Let them not be all at once judges, and legislators, and administrators; let there be no chance for them to earn more, by the trade of fawning courtiers, than by that of impregnable expounders and interpreters of the laws, and we shall make them independent of the annual votes of our Assemblies." Papineau did not talk a lot about religion, but he did so when explaining why the House had passed a law – which was once again blocked by the Legislative Council – to give the same rights to the Protestant Dissenters from the Church of England and the Church of Scotland: "I recall these circumstances only to declare my unalterable creed that men are accountable for their faith and worship to their maker only, and not to the civil powers; that diversity of religious opinions which creates no resistance to the laws, ought not to be submitted to the oppression of laws enacted merely to prohibit and punish it; that the same freedom in that respect, which I claim for myself, for my countrymen, for those who have the same belief with them, I allow to those whose belief is different."[29]

Freedom for us, freedom for them: the formulation had a promising future in that time of the awakening of nationalities.

The resounding victory of the Parti patriote in the election of 1827 put Governor Dalhousie in a delicate position at the opening of the new Parliament. The conflict reached new heights in November when he refused to approve the choice of Papineau as speaker and again prorogued the legislature.[30] It was the last straw. Assemblies in Quebec City and in Montreal formulated resolutions – there would eventually be a total of ninety-two – that summarized the many grievances and abuses: the composition and financial dependence of the Legislative Council, excessive spending on salaries and sinecures that were not controlled by the elected House, repeated blocking by the Legislative Council of modifications to the parliamentary representation of the Townships and the appointment of an agent in London, the financial scandal of the misappropriation of £96,000 by receiver general Caldwell, discretionary distribution of lands in the public domain, the ineffectiveness of the laws on education, which was underfinanced because of the failure to restore Jesuit property that could be used for that purpose, and the blocking of bills on education while taking pleasure in deploring the "ignorance" of the *Canadiens*.[31]

At other assemblies, in Vaudreuil and Saint-Benoît, Dr Jacques Labrie, the author of a recently published introduction to the British Constitution, invited people to sign the petitions to the king and the two houses of the Imperial Parliament. He reaffirmed his loyalty to the Constitution, comparing the British colonial regime favourably with the French colonial regime and rejoicing that "arbitrariness has ceased to be our lot *legally*." According to him, "Canadians will obtain justice, without altering their allegiance, without deviating from their duties," because "Canadians have never asked for anything from the metropolis without obtaining it."[32] He was right: London had granted Canadians representation by population in 1791, and London had listened to the colony on the plans for union in 1810, 1822, and 1824. But ten years before the Rebellions, Labrie was taking a chance on the future: would London listen to the Canadians, and would the Canadians obtain justice "without altering their allegiance"? One thing was certain, as a correspondent of D.-B. Viger wrote, "All our inhabitants now take part in public affairs, know them and discuss them. This unfortunate crisis in which we find ourselves will at least have the effect of opening their eyes."[33]

THE COMMITTEE OF THE HOUSE OF COMMONS ON THE AFFAIRS OF CANADA (1828)

The same Viger was then in London, where he would be joined in March by John Neilson and Augustin Cuvillier, to convey the complaints and demands of the Canadians and present their petition of eighty-seven thousand signatures against the plan for union. This was not new to Neilson; he had been a delegate in 1822 during the crisis of the plan for union. If the Canadians' expectations with regard to London were increasing, it was because the problems in the colony had persisted so long that they had become structural. The Canadians had had London's ear in 1822, but six years later, the same problems had got worse and reforms were slow in coming.

The Tory government of England was known for its positive bias toward the anglophones of Lower Canada and its position in favour of the assimilation of the French Canadians. The Whig opposition favoured equal rights and local control in the colonies. William Huskisson, secretary of state for the colonies, presented to the House on 2 May 1828 a plan to set up a select committee on the situation in Canada. In addition to speeches in the House, there was testimony before the committee from 8 May to 15 July; the main speakers, in addition to Huskisson, were Wilmot and Stephen for the Colonial Office; the Tory Labouchere; Sir James Mackintosh for the Whig opposition; Samuel Gale; Lord Edward Ellice; Gillespie, McGillivray, and Merritt, three leading merchants from Montreal, for the "British part" of the colony; and Neilson, Viger, and Cuvillier, delegates of the House of Assembly.

In the House, Huskisson recalled England's right to modify the constitution of any of its colonies. He perceived Lower Canada as being like feudal France of the thirteenth century and intended to imbue the *Canadiens* "with English feelings" and British superiority, whatever the future of the colony. His undersecretary, Edward Stanley, who visited North America in 1824, explained that the division of the colony into two Canadas had obliged the governor to rule with a minority against the majority. According to him, the Legislative Council had not played its role and the members "were the means of keeping up a continual system of jarring and contention between the government and the people." Before the committee of the House, Wilmot, the former undersecretary of state for the colonies, went back to the plan for union and persisted in thinking that "all our colonies should be Anglicised rather than preserved in their original form." James Stephen, legal advisor to the Colonial Office, presented the committee with a more global vision of the situation and of the future. He noted the obstinacy with which "the French Population look forward to the establishment of the *Nation Canadienne* as a great counterpoise to the English authority on the North American Continent" and wrote to Huskisson's successor as secretary of state for the colonies, Sir George Murray, that "the Canadian Constitution is already so essentially republican, that it is too late to think of imparting a monarchical spirit and character to that Government." The coexistence of a plan for a "nation canadienne" and a republican tendency appeared to worry Stephen. Moreover, it was clear to him that control of the House of Assembly over the colony's budget and having an elected Legislative Council would diminish the power of the Executive. While he saw the Americanization of colonial institutions and already foresaw – a sign of the pressure from the colony – the possibility of granting responsible government, he also envisaged the possibility of union. After all, Upper Canada was located between Lower Canada and the St Lawrence on the east, and the United States and the Hudson River on the south, with no access to the Atlantic. Uncertainty in Lower Canada could lead in the future to attempts by the United States to annex Upper Canada.

As conservative as he was, the member of Parliament Labouchere, who was of French descent, felt that the Constitution of 1791 had not yielded all its benefits quite simply because it had not provided administratively for the the independence of the Legislative Council.

On the side of the Whig opposition, Sir James Mackintosh, who was well-informed about the situation in Lower Canada by the delegates of the House of Assembly, replied to Huskisson by criticizing him for putting more emphasis on hypothetical injustices suffered by the English colonials than on the well-founded demands of the authors of the petition. He felt that London should not intervene in the internal affairs of the colony, especially not on the pretext that the cause of the conflicts was the maintenance of French customs and laws. He pointed out the consequences of the obstruction of the parliamentary process by the Legislative Council and showed how the councillors, who were financially dependent on the Executive, were instruments of the governor. With regard to the idea of modifying the rules of representation in favour of a minority, he felt that a true liberal would consider it "a very bad symptom if the House were disposed to treat as a favoured race, as a ruling caste, any body of men, and to look on them as placed in one of our colonies to watch over the rest of the inhabitants. Shall we have an English colony in Canada separate from the rest of the inhabitants? Shall ... we deal out to them six hundred years of misery, as we dealt out in Ireland?"

The member Hume wondered about the structure of the legislative powers conceded to the colony by London, and its real meaning "if all the legislative power was to be lodged in the hands of the executive." What, indeed, had become the real power of the House of Assembly when it was constantly hampered by the Legislative Council and the Executive? Could this power structure lead to anything other than a build-up of frustrations in the colony? It was more than time, Hume said, that London "conciliate the population of Canada, instead of driving them to despair by acts of severity and oppression."[34]

The contribution of the delegates from Lower Canada consisted of denouncing the seigneurial system, and defending the maintenance of the laws and religion of the *Canadiens* and their "distinct condition from the people of America." Of the three delegates of the House of Assembly, Neilson, the most experienced, seems to have been the most convincing. He presented a number of bills that had been passed by the House of Assembly to modify the representation of the seigneuries and the townships or ensure the independence of the judiciary, for example, but that were all blocked by the Legislative Council or the governor. He pleaded in favour of taxation rights for the House – "no taxation without representation" – and presented a great deal of evidence of bad faith, abuse of power, and dishonesty: the constant refusal of the governors to accept a civil list that, while including the salaries of the principal civil servants, would exclude sinecures and other forms of patronage; huge amounts of discretionary spending by Governor Dalhousie without the agreement of the Assembly and without accountability; misappropriation of £96,000 in public funds by the receiver general. This pragmatic approach, backed up by constant reference to the liberal and democratic stakes involved in these actions, would bring results.[35]

The parliamentary committee submitted its report and its recommendations on 22 July. With respect to revenues and the civil list, London granted the House of Assembly control over income and spending with regard to all public revenues, while recommending "rendering the Governor, the Members of the Executive Council, and the Judges, independent of the annual votes of the House of Assembly for their respective salaries." It expressed regret that the Assembly of the colony had not informed the British Parliament earlier of Governor Dalhousie's having spent £140,000 sterling without the House of Assembly's approval, and urged the colonial administration to take measures to ensure that such misappropriation did not reoccur. Concerning the contentious recurring issue of the Legislative Council, the committee recommended "that a more independent character should be given to these bodies" and "that the majority of their Members should not consist of persons holding offices at the pleasure of the Crown." Judges should no longer sit on the Legislative Council nor be eligible for election to the House of Assembly. With regard to the representation of the "townships," the committee suggested that the population and size of areas be taken into account. To correct the problem of the distribution of public lands, it accepted that "a small annual duty [could be levied] on lands remaining unimproved and unoccupied." The tenure of land under the seigneurial system was maintained, with the possibility of changing this type of land ownership. The committee expressed the desire that "the proceeds" from the estates of the Jesuits "be applied to the purposes of general education." As for the proposal for a union of the two Canada, the committee was "not prepared, under present circumstances, to recommend that measure," given "the state of public feeling that appears to prevail in these Colonies."[36]

The colony breathed more easily. The House of Assembly's resolutions on the report on 6 December 1828 show strong satisfaction, but also caution, in particular with regard to the civil list, the possibility of an increase in the budget and the eventual composition of the Legislative Council. There was indeed a great deal of good will and hope expressed in these "administrative" recommendations, and they led to a reduction of pressure from the colony.[37]

THE ELECTIVE PRINCIPLE AND THE LEGISLATIVE
COUNCIL (1830–1834)

The Whig government elected in 1830 in England was in principle favourable to the appeals of Lower Canada, but Lord Grey was absorbed in domestic questions – the Reform Bill – and the issue of slavery in certain colonies, and he had little room to manoeuvre. London did not really follow up on the recommendations of the committee of 1828.

At the same time, there was a radicalization of the Parti patriote under pressure from the common people, who were sensitive to the fiscal demands of the seigneurs and the tithes of the priests, but worried about the massive immigration and the fate of unoccupied Crown land. The press, the increasingly frequent use of petitions, and elections contributed to politicizing the population. In addition, there was a new generation of members of the Assembly, young and more radical: Louis-Hippolyte La Fontaine, Augustin-Norbert Morin, Charles-Ovide Perrault, Étienne Rodier, Dr Cyrille Côté, Dr Edmund O'Callaghan, and the Nelson brothers, Robert and Wolfred, both doctors.[38]

Very quickly, the Legislative Council again became a bone of parliamentary contention. The idea of an elected Legislative Council that member François Blanchet had proposed in 1824 had made progress, becoming the new cause celebre. In the 1830s, there was also a desire to extend the principle of responsibility of elected officials to civic institutions such as the Legislative Council, the fabrique (the body administering parish property), and the education system. Lord Howick, parliamentary undersecretary for the colonies, was somewhat open to certain forms of an elected council, but Lord Goderich, secretary of state for the colonies, was opposed: it would pave the way for acceptance of the principle of responsible government.

The governor of the colony made an effort to appoint *Canadiens* to the Council, whether or not they were members of the House of Assembly. Papineau and Neilson, however, rejected the invitation, citing the regulation that prohibited a citizen from sitting in the House if he was receiving remuneration from the Crown. Papineau did not believe, or no longer believed, that this was the solution, either for himself or for the eight *Canadiens*, including four members of the Assembly, appointed to the Council in 1831, who in fact would not be very active in the Council. The Parti patriote maintained this position and demanded the expulsion of Assembly member Mondelet, who had been appointed to the Council. It finally saw a motive in the Governor's strategy of appointing *Canadien* members to the Council just before the sessions, with the possibility of then appointing an equal number who were favourable to the administration.[39]

The persistent conflict around the Legislative Council is of interest and significance for the history of ideas only in that it was revealing of the hidden stakes in terms of democracy and emancipation. The political crisis in the colony raised the stakes and would continue to do so for years to come. Papineau, the voice of the Parti patriote and speaker of the House, had already expressed reservations with respect to London in the early 1830s; as admiring as he had been of it until then, he asked whether the magnificent British Constitution was really suited to Canada, which was a colony and not an independent government. His criticism of the Legislative Council led him to an overall critique of the colonial institutions, including looking at the Constitution of 1791 from a historical perspective: "The government was embittered toward the colonies by the recent stain resulting from the triumph of the United States, and Pitt was in agony over the efforts of the French to reconquer their liberty ... At the same time as it wanted chains for the old France, did it want liberty for the new one? If it did want it, it did not take the measures to procure it."

Lower Canada, Upper Canada, and the Atlantic colonies were now the only British colonies with this type of executive and legislative bodies. And as Papineau stated in the House: "Consequently they have only been constituted, I think, according to the maxim of the tyrants: 'divide and reign.'"[40] The colonial dimension of the problem had surfaced again.

Papineau intended to further undermine the credibility of the Legislative Council by arguing that it differed from the House of Lords in that it was not a court of review or appeal, an elegant reminder that judges had no place there.[41] But his fundamental argument against the Legislative Council, which indicated the republican orientation of the Parti patriote and its leader, was the absurdity of such a governing body in America, where it could not be based on any form of aristocracy. An "aristocracy in the middle of the forest" was a ridiculous idea to him, all the more so since the one they wanted to establish in the colony was a "beggars' aristocracy," a parasite of the Executive. He declared, "The good old policy of England not to sanction the principle of aristocracy in its other colonies has therefore been wise, and that of introducing it here, a work either of madness or spite or servile, ill-considered imitation of what existed at home, of which it could not provide the reality but only a hideous simulacrum." He added, to clearly show that he belonged to the American hemisphere, "But there was nothing here of that blind deference they have in Europe for titles and birth, which give rise to such arrogance and pride on the part of those who come among us from the old continent and who think that they should be compensated here for the humiliation they have been subjected to there by demanding the same servility toward them." By that logic, the answer to his own question was obvious: "Is it in the customs and practices of England, or in those of the neighbouring provinces and the states of America, that we must search for examples to guide us?"[42]

For a moment, Papineau hesitated to follow the model of elected institutions; was not an elected Council less attractive than the House, which
took the real legislative initiatives? He opted for the principle of election
on the basis of this overall consideration: "Maintaining the current form
with its flaws would mean perpetuating national distinctions. Whoever
has renounced those narrow feelings becomes a useful member of a society in which the interest of all should be the common interest, and it
is only in a general system of elections that everyone is placed on a perfectly equal footing and has the degree of influence that belongs to
him in the country, and that he does not borrow from outside."[43] This
was another way of saying that the polarization between *Canadiens* and
English was created and maintained by and in the structure of colonial
power perpetuated by the metropolis.

It was therefore necessary to put an end to the current Council that
"smother[ed] the voice of the people" and distorted the representative
system; it was necessary to put an end to the excessive power of eight or
ten men called to the Council "by blind fate, or by an even more blind
favouritism" and that blocked laws on education, hospitals, and roads.
The time of the "ringing words" of the "loyal people" was over, the "men-
dacious phrases will no longer deceive any but fools." Papineau made
this radical statement in the House in April 1833: "Every day of this session has proven to us that we could not place any trust in the administration, neither in the leader, nor in his council members."[44]

What, then, was to be done? While Papineau maintained that he did
not want a "forced separation," he demanded that it be "permitted to
discuss the reasons and causes that will lead to it, although it is assuredly
not desirable." The Parti patriote demanded nothing "more now than
what is granted purely by royal charters to many of the former colonies.
A republican constitution." Papineau demanded nothing less than that
England "authorize the country to reform its constitution itself, it would
be the only equitable and prudent decision that it could adopt." And,
as a good republican, he proposed, in early 1833, that a convention be
held to discuss the creation of a new constitution.[45]

Parent wrote in favour of an elected Legislative Council that would
be responsible to its constituents for its actions, and demanded that the
Executive also answer for its actions. In 1832, as editor of *Le Canadien*, he
demanded nothing less than a "regular ministerial organization," a "provincial ministry," responsible government.[46] The situation had reached
the point of no return.

This radicalization of the Parti patriote line cost it the support of John
Neilson, who, along with Parent, had been a pillar of the party in Quebec
City and the surrounding region. Neilson had opposed a motion in the

House by Bourdages to make the Legislative Council an elected body, and had won the vote, calling for administrative rather than constitutional reform.[47] The bill finally passed in the House (fifty-one for, twelve against), but it was, of course, rejected by the Council. This was the first split in the Parti patriote, and it was hardly trivial; it alienated from the party a liberal anglophone who had been very useful to the *Canadiens'* cause in the House and as a delegate in London in 1822 and 1828, and it made the difference in sensibility between the liberals of Quebec City and those of Montreal more evident.

THE REPRESENTATION OF THE NOTABLES IN THE FABRIQUES (1831)

The issue of the elected nature of public office had already been raised in 1829 with the Assembly Schools Act, which allowed for the creation of "Assembly schools" administered by local trustees elected by the landowners.

An indication of the rise of the liberal professions, the public debate on the presence of the notables in the assemblies of the fabriques again raised the issue of democratic representation and for the first time explicitly raised the question of the distinction to be made between the spiritual mission of the Church and its administrative or temporal affairs.

Petitions, trials, and debates in the press and the House, as well as various bills, centred on two questions: whether the material property of parish churches belonged to the Church or to the parishioners who had contributed to it, and who should administer that property, the old and new church wardens or also the tax-paying notables, who had the right to representation?

The bill presented by Bourdages, a Patriote member of the Assembly, gave the notables the right to vote in elections for church wardens, to be present during the presentation of the accounts of the parish and to take part in the temporal government of churches. It worried Mgr Lartigue, who was saddened to see his "poor homeland" treat "religion and its ministers this way." The leader of the Parti patriote was conscious of how delicate the situation was, since it concerned the rights of all Catholic parishioners in relation to the majority of the clergy. Papineau reminded the Church that it was no longer under the French regime or a monarchist regime, that the people had a right to know what was done with the contributions to the Church, and that the administration of the parish was a place to learn about democratic participation. Papineau, a seigneur himself, proposed defining the notables not by tithes paid but according to land holdings. Using pseudonyms in all his journalistic

writing, Bishop Lartigue rejected the idea of introducing the democratic principle of the House of Assembly – "no taxation without representation" – into the running of the fabriques. To him, the wardens were
auxiliaries of the Church, administrators of property, and not representatives of the people, and tradition should be taken into account: administration was the responsibility of the church wardens, old and new.
He scoffed at Papineau – "the speaker who wants so much to spiritualize
us that soon we will have nothing temporal" – and expressed surprise
that Catholic members did not subject Protestant ministers to the same
red tape.

The petitions and briefs of the clergy had so little effect that Abbé
Painchaud wrote, under the pseudonym "Raison," in *La Gazette de Québec*
of 10 December 1831: "Since the Canadian clergy has nothing more to
hope for from the House of Assembly, it would be wise for it to untie the
cord of its hopes and attach them to the Executive."

The bill was adopted, but postponed indefinitely by the Legislative
Council, all of whose members, except James Cuthbert, were English
Protestants. Once again, the radicalization of the Parti patriote had been
doubly costly to it: by promoting the principle of election in the administration of parishes, it had alienated a large part of the clergy and it had
had another confrontation in the House with John Neilson, who maintained that the funds of the fabriques were not a form of taxation, but
rather voluntary contributions. The perspicacious Abbé Jacques Paquin,
who had a strong sense of history, lived and written, pressed his bishop
to "let the clergy organize, become accustomed to being involved in public and government affairs, devote itself to the study of its rights and defend them as a group, en masse and of one mind."[48]

THE ELECTION RIOT OF 21 MAY 1832

As much as the question of the Legislative Council, the problem of the
civil list in Lower and Upper Canada kept alive the tensions with the
metropolis. For London, the issue involved requiring a civil list that
would maintain the independence of the Executive, but there was no
agreement on the size of that list, which had been contentious for almost
twenty years. For Papineau and the Parti patriote, "the refusal of revenues is a constitutional means of counterbalancing abuses of power,"
and the granting of those revenues, "the boulevard to political freedom,"
the "great political lever." They pointed out that there was no such civil
list in other colonies such as Jamaica. In 1831, Papineau and Neilson
were once again opposed on this subject, with Neilson proposing

acceptance of a civil list of 5,900 Louis d'or, which the House refused. In 1833, another refusal to vote the revenues would once again say to London that reform could no longer be deferred.[49]

A riot in 1832 added fuel to the still-glowing embers of the conflicts regarding the Legislative Council and the voting of the budget. The election in the West Ward of Montreal, in which Stanley Bagg ran against Daniel Tracey, went on for twenty-three days, in accordance with the practice of the time to close a polling station only when an hour had passed with no voters. After some suspense, the result was a slim majority of four votes for Tracey. With brawls between "boulés" (bullies) from the two sides, the election degenerated into a riot that led to the intervention of the army, which had orders to shoot; three *Canadiens* were killed.

This event was a symbolic recapitulation of the tensions of the time. Tracey, an Irish patriot and editor of the pro-Patriote newspaper *The Vindicator*, was in favour of the refusal to vote on the budget, supported an elected Legislative Council, and favoured rescinding the privileges of a London company that had its sights on land in the colony, while Bagg promised many reforms without ever carrying them out. The vote was extremely polarized ethnically (French Canadians and the majority of the Irish vs. English and Americans), socially (majority of the common people vs. merchants and civil servants), and politically (Patriotes vs. local administration). The election, inquiry, and trial reinforced the feeling of inequality before the justice system and the judiciary (Grand Jury recruited in a biased way, dismissal of charges, enumeration of the events without attribution of responsibility, unilingual English-speaking judges). There was a polarization and breaking off of relations between Papineau and Governor Aylmer, who had written to the military to congratulate them for their actions. The *Canadiens* were puzzled when the king invited Colonel Mackintosh and Captain Temple to dinner and decorated them for their actions, but they excused the King as wrongly informed and badly advised, and Papineau stated in spite of everything, "It is England that we ask for a remedy for our ills."

With its spectacular aspects, the event also released the tensions and gave them a new visibility. The public acclamation for Tracey and Duvernay before the election and when they were released from prison, where they had been incarcerated for "libel" against the Legislative Council; the "Canadian Marseillaise," adapted to celebrate their actions; the twenty-three days of the election and tensions in the city; the intervention of the army; and the solemn funerals of the three *Canadiens* killed, which were marked by demonstrations and violence – all this showed that a new level of conflict had been reached.[50]

CONCLUSION

The political and intellectual path from 1815 to 1834 followed two main curves: the appeal to democratic principles and the development of consciousness in the colony.

The social explanation for this evolution lies in the rise of a middle class of merchants and members of the liberal professions who believed as much in the great idea of liberty (sovereignty of the people; freedom of expression, of the press, of association) as in the legitimacy of its political power as a group. This liberal middle class found in the House of Assembly and certain newspapers the ideal places and means for its action. It also had, during this period, a rallying point in a political party that had become the party of the "patriots," and a new and impressive voice in the speaker of the House and leader of the Parti patriote, Louis-Joseph Papineau. The combination of these places, these means, and this voice explains the new visibility of this middle class and the force of its demands.

The democratic conviction of these liberals, the Parti patriote, and Papineau was manifested in many ways. The struggle to ensure the primacy of the House of Assembly over other political bodies (Legislative Council and Executive Council) provided a first example of this conviction throughout the debates on the refusal to vote on the budget and the civil list. The democratic argument (the superiority of elected representatives to appointed ones) served here as the basis of the power of this middle class, but it was truly democratic and was not limited only to French Canadians. It included people such as John Neilson, Edmund O'Callaghan, Daniel Tracey, and a broad segment of the Irish community, and it was open to all English-speaking liberals as well as to the recognition of the rights of all religious denominations, not only the Church of England and Scotland or the Roman Catholic Church.

This democratic conviction was also the focal point of the central political and ideological battle of this period in favour of elected public institutions, in particular the Legislative Council and the fabriques. In the case of the fabriques, it was considered that the material contribution of Catholics to their Church was a form of taxation, and that there should therefore be some kind of representation, some kind of oversight of the administration of this temporal property by the contributors. The obligation to be accountable for public money would again be Papineau's argument for rejecting or consenting to grants by the House to Catholic hospitals and charities.

In the case of the Legislative Council, it was obvious that if it were made an elected body, it would, in all likelihood, become majority

French Canadian, like the House of Assembly. But how could anyone contest the democratic legitimacy of the argument put forward by Papineau and the Parti patriote, that "only in a general elective system is each person on a perfectly equal footing with another, and does each one have his rightful degree of influence in the country that he does not borrow from outside"? The adoption of a model that was clearly more republican than previous models claimed to resolve the persistent problem of the colony: on one hand, an elected body, the House of Assembly, that expressed the will and aspirations of the strongly French Canadian majority but was not reducible to that group; on the other hand, a non-elected body, the Legislative Council, that expressed the will and aspirations of an essentially English-speaking minority and was an obstacle and systematic obstruction in the constitutional mechanism of the colony. The problem had been clearly identified since Bédard's Brief of 1814. It was this issue of the non-elected nature of the Legislative Council that had created the colonial crisis of 1827, had led to the creation of the Committee of the House of Commons on the Affairs of Canada, and was now the symbol of the democratic and republican radicalization of the House, the Parti patriote, Papineau, Parent's *Le Canadien*, and Duvernay's *La Minerve*.

The radicalization around the question of elected representation and, secondarily, the civil list also contributed to the radicalization of relations between the colony and the metropolis. There was more than one sign of the new consciousness in the colony. First, it was shown in the unilateral decision of the House of Assembly to appoint a delegate to London in 1831. Affairs in Lower Canada were reaching such a degree of intensity and urgency that a lobby in London with the colonial secretary, the members of Parliament, and the press was needed. The plans for union of 1822 and 1824 had revealed a clear malaise among the British and Americans in the colony, while contributing to increased polarization and negative images on both sides. It was becoming clear that the main issue of these plans for union was control of an eventual single House of Assembly in the colony and, indirectly, the consolidation of the executive power and that of the metropolis. And in their own way, the unionists reinforced this by naming and repeating the idea that there was a plan in the air for a "Canadian nation" that was identified with the French Canadians. But for the time being, union did not seem to be the solution in London's view.

The addresses and petitions to the king and to Parliament with thousands of signatures, the plans for union and the sending of delegates, the presence of agents for Upper and Lower Canada, the correspondence of the governors with the Secretary of State for the Colonies, the Commons

Committee, and the speeches in Parliament by members of the opposition were concrete indications of the increased tensions in the colony. The issues were becoming increasingly clear and radical, and the slowness of reform, increasingly apparent and intolerable. And the issues of the civil list and the non-elected nature of the Legislative Council touched the nerve of imperial relations: overly limiting the civil list or eliminating it entirely would reduce the power of the Executive and the governor, and therefore of the metropolis, and accepting an elected legislative council would be equivalent to giving the French Canadians a majority and thus isolating and weakening the power of the Executive and the governor in relation to a house of assembly and a legislative council strongly focused on the needs and the future of the colony. This was the constitutional knot that had been tightening for close to twenty years and had to be untied.

London recognized the structural problems in the colony in the report of the committee in 1828, but the solutions proposed, which were administrative in nature and depended on good will, were not really followed up in England; in the colony, the few efforts of the governor to appoint French Canadians to the Legislative Council satisfied neither the House of Assembly nor the French Canadians.

By the beginning of the 1830s, Papineau and the Parti patriote had become less enthusiastic about the Constitution of 1791, in particular the articles related to the Legislative Council. This was a turning point because, since 1810, the recurring message of the Parti canadien, its leader Bédard, and *Le Canadien* had been the recognition of British institutions. Bédard had even spoken in 1808 of the "poison of equality" in the United States. Papineau had also praised the British Constitution and institutions in 1791. But it had become exceedingly clear that the political and constitutional structure in which the Legislative Council was charged, at the price of distortions to democracy, with ensuring power for the British minority in the colony had created, supported, and polarized "national distinctions" and seemed to have been designed by England to divide and rule in its colony. The traditional pro-Britishism of the French Canadians and their respect and expectations with regard to London were put to the test.

Radicalization in the colony was fuelled first by the intensity of the debates that separated French Canadians and British colonials, and colony and metropolis, and even divided the Parti patriote. John Neilson had become alienated from the party and it had antagonized the Catholic clergy with the bill on the fabriques. The Catholic Church, apart from the episode of its "spiritual" opposition to union, continually expressed its desire for a "temporal" alliance with British colonial political power against the rise of liberalism.

The tensions between the colony and the metropolis had also changed the *Canadiens'* perception of themselves. They continued to see themselves as British subjects, as individuals capable and desirous of English liberties. This was the distinction Papineau made: yes to political anglicization, but no to cultural anglicization. To Pierre Blanchet, the attachment to English principles – liberal principles – showed that the *Canadiens* were more English than French.

But the French Canadians' new perception of themselves at the beginning of the 1830s involved their recent attraction to the American experience, essentially that of the United States, as well as the expression and affirmation of their identity as *Canadiens*. The emergence of a consciousness of belonging to the American hemisphere was, of course, based on the memory of 1774 and 1812 and the presence of Loyalists from the United States in Montreal and the Townships. Papineau and others had travelled in the United States, and they read American newspapers, including *Le Courrier des États-Unis*, which was published in New York since 1826 by the French colony that had immigrated there. In addition to these geographic and cultural facts, there was a fundamental political dimension: the comparison between England and the United States with regard to the elected nature of public institutions contributed first and foremost to this new view of the neighbouring republic and former British colony. If, from around 1830, the example had to come from the south, it was because the United States Senate was elected and could provide a model for Lower Canada that would cut the Gordian knot that was tying up constitutional and political life in the colony.

A corollary of the admiration for the republican system was the denunciation and refusal of any "aristocracy in the middle of the forest" and a change in the attitude to monarchy – a change, and not a demand for its abolition: the Assembly refused to vote on the civil list "for the life of the King" because such a proposition made no sense in America, but the king remained a symbol, and the people of Lower Canada continued to send letters to him while the moderate Parent wrote in *Le Canadien* of 21 June 1833 "that the Kings of Europe with their hundred thousand bayonets, with their brilliant courts are small compared to this man of a free and sovereign people."

Looking toward the United States thus did not involve any plan for annexation to that great republic; on the contrary, in *Le Canadien* of 22 February 1832, Parent said he did not believe that "a people of six hundred thousand and a few souls can maintain its independence and its nationality, especially with such a powerful and enterprising nation a neighbour … It is for this reason that we have always maintained that it was in the interest … of England and Lower Canada that the nationality of the *Canadien* people be preserved and encouraged until it is capable of defending itself against the encroachments of its neighbours." And until then, the French language was precisely the barrier that permitted Great Britain to keep its colonies in North America.

As for the unionist Sewell, he had clearly seen in 1824 that the integration of the *Canadiens* into the United States would threaten their language, their religion, and their "feudal system." Replying to *La Gazette de Québec*, Parent agreed that this was a danger. Although for him there was no question of annexation, he felt that French Louisiana, which had entered the American union in 1812, prefigured the fate of a French culture in America, and that "our institutions, our language and our laws" would be threatened, French would certainly not be tolerated in Congress, and the massive arrival of American citizens in the new state of Quebec would cause French Canadians to lose their predominance as a "distinct people."[51]

As for the Canadian – that is, French Canadian – consciousness of the majority of people in Lower Canada, it had developed through the democratic struggles of the middle class during the period. The definition of the aspirations of French Canadians, the opposition to the plans for union by the "nation canadienne" and the determination of French Canadians to be British subjects in a Canadian colony whose metropolis would respect the democratic will rather than divide it were gradually shaping a group representation. In 1827, *La Minerve* asked its readers the question, "What are *Canadiens*?" The editor replied by pointing to the *Canadiens'* loyalty to Great Britain, "out of love and duty," but he emphasized that, in contrast, the "adventurers" of the colony could not claim to be *Canadiens*. The declaration of loyalty to the mother country was unequivocal: "Is the mother country guilty of these attacks against the most peaceful of peoples? It is easy to say no, that all the plans and projects with which we have been threatened have had their origin on this side of the sea and in our midst." It was oligarchy that the *Canadiens* did not welcome: "If the mother country needed us for its defence, if it asked our lives, we have already demonstrated it, we would not waver; but to believe that the influence the people must have in our government should be the prerogative of a small number of inhabitants only because they have abandoned their country; to think that this small number of people without a mission should have the right to use the name of the mother country as a bogey, Jean-Baptiste cannot accept that." The consciousness of the *Canadiens* was not directed against the English but against exploiters: "The French Canadians do not seek an exclusive power; they have no national hatred against the English; and as soon as an inhabitant of the country shows that he is really a citizen, no distinction is made any more. But those who view Canada as but an exclusive trading post, a place where one can live from the public purse or enrich oneself and return to live somewhere else; those who speculate on the properties of the country; they cannot reasonably be recognized as citizens of a country that they do not recognize as their own and that they would abandon if necessary, shaking the dust from their feet." From the perspective of their identity, *Canadiens* were not French either: "Moreover, we will see how wrong we would be to attribute the names *Canadiens* and *English* to the exclusive claims of the old inhabitants of the country, given that this distinction preceded the Conquest, and that in all the documents of the time we find that the *Canadiens* and the *French* were not the same thing." "Genealogically," the *Canadiens* were "those whose ancestors lived in the country before 1759"; "politically," they were "all those who make common cause with the inhabitants of the country, whatever their origin; those who do not seek to destroy the religion or rights of the mass of the people; those who have a real and lasting interest in the country; those in whom the name of this country stirs the sentiment of the homeland."[52]

Le Canadien, which began publishing again on 7 May 1831 under Parent, adopted a title and a motto – "Our institutions, our language and our laws" – that were emblematic: they expressed the cultural characteristics of the *Canadiens* as a group, summarized their evolution, and looked forward to a promising future. In that first issue of the fourth series of *Le Canadien*, Parent wrote: "Our watchword ... we will take it from the hearts of all those for whom love of country is not just a word empty of meaning; from those who in life cast their eyes beyond their individual existence, who have a national sentiment, that beautiful virtue without which societies will never be anything but assemblages of isolated creatures incapable of those great and noble actions that make great peoples, and that make nations a spectacle worthy of the divine gaze ... For it is the destiny of the *Canadien* people to have not only to preserve its civil liberty, but also to struggle for its existence as a people."[53] Moreover, the vocabulary of the "homeland" and the name of the Parti patriote referred to the political dimension of the larger project of this group.

When they were preparing for the drafting and voting on the 92 Resolutions, it was clear to the House of Assembly, the Parti patriote, and Papineau that the time for "ringing words" was over. After the election riot of 21 May 1832, Papineau's very republican proposal of convening a congress – like the Americans – to draft a new constitution was indicative of the progress of people's views. But it was "constitutionalism" that dominated the period, the desire that the metropolis would entrench liberties and the patience of the colony in waiting for the process to take place.

British reformist liberalism, which the *Canadiens* admired until around 1830, and which, out of impatience, they began to question, served as the liberal model in Europe at the same time. Its permanent reformism, combining liberalism and conservatism, stood up quite well to the test of the question of representation and suffrage (Reform Bill of 1832). Nevertheless, in British colonies such as Lower Canada, this temporizing reformism gave rise to impatience, as was the case with regard to the Report of the Committee of the House of Commons on the Affairs of Canada in 1828.

In these colonies, the liberalism of the Empire was confronted with the question of extending democracy and the principle of elected representation not only to local reforms – making the Legislative Council and the fabriques elected bodies – but also beyond individual liberties to the collective liberty of a people, a nation. After 1830, liberalism intersected with the question of nationality and the right of peoples to self-determination. It is important, in this regard, to point out that in Lower Canada, just as in Europe and the Americas, the liberal current had come ahead of the current of nationality.

The ultimate consequence of the extension of the principle of elected representation, which involved rights but also duties, was progress toward greater responsibility and toward the demand for responsible government for the colonies. Autonomy of the colonies could result from either the more radical appeal to the principle of nationality or the more reformist demand for responsible government.[54] Lower Canada was now faced with this choice.

4

Tensions in the Colony
(1834–1837)

THE STRONGEST INDICATION that the colonial situation had not been resolved is that the causes of the 1827 crisis remained unchanged in 1834: the dysfunction and composition of the Legislative Council, the demand that it be made an elected body, and the lack of agreement over the civil list and the vote on the annual budget. While the committee of the House of Commons had recommended in 1828 that the Legislative Council have "a more independent character" and that the salaries of the governor, the members of the Executive Council, and judges be made independent of the annual votes of the House of Assembly, the conflict had not abated and had even intensified after the riot of 21 May 1832. Another indication was the 92 Resolutions proposed in the House of Assembly on 17 February 1834, resolutions that recapitulated the French Canadians' grievances and demands of the past two decades. It would take three years for London to respond to them with the Russell Resolutions of March 1837, three years that were part of a period when nationalism was on the rise in Europe. There were lengthy negotiations between Lower Canada and London through agents, a royal commission of investigation, and debates on the subject at Westminster. Tensions in the colony, already constant and serious, mounted further, culminating in an impasse. The content of the demands and the heightened rhetoric in the House, the press, and public assemblies showed that Lower Canada was waking up to nationalism.

THE 92 RESOLUTIONS (FEBRUARY 1834): A TURNING POINT

Drafted by Papineau, revised by Augustin-Norbert Morin, and presented to the House of Assembly by Elzéar Bédard, a member from the Quebec City region who was an ally of the Parti patriote, the 92 Resolutions resembled the lists of grievances at the time of the French Revolution and formed a tight knot, the untying of which – or the failure to untie it – was a crucial issue and a turning point in the colonial destiny of Lower Canada.

The 92 Resolutions opened by reiterating the loyalty and attachment of French Canadians to the British Empire and the Imperial Parliament and stated that the authors were inspired by the Constitution and rights of Great Britain and called for the same powers of control as the British Parliament because nothing had changed since the report of the Committee in 1828 (Resolutions 1, 2, 5–8, 52, 69, 72, 79).[1] The overriding power of the House of Assembly, the expression of "the public will," was reaffirmed, as well as its right to control all revenues in the colony (Resolutions 23, 32, 39).

While the grievances involved the whole colonial political system, Resolutions 9 through 40 concerned a single entity: the Legislative Council. For the Parti patriote and the parliamentary majority, here lay the fundamental flaw in a colonial system based on the unrealistic pretention of establishing an authentic aristocracy in America, on the arbitrary and excessive power of a governor to control one of the bodies of government and to appoint to it only individuals supporting his views, and on the obstruction of political life in the colony by a body that had rejected 302 bills approved by the House of Assembly from 1822 to 1836. Because of the system of appointment to the Council, it had become the symbol of "monopoly and despotism in the executive, judicial and administrative departments of government," the means "to protect one class of His Majesty's subjects" and an "alarming character of strife and national antipathy" that was "of a nature to excite and perpetuate among the several classes of the inhabitants of this province, mutual distrust and national distinctions and animosities." According to the 92 Resolutions, confidence in the Legislative Council would be established only when it became an elected body.

There were also many grievances regarding the colonial power structure, from top to bottom. The resolutions denounced the attitude of the colonial secretary, who supported the system of appointment to the Legislative Council and whose "insulting" dispatches were "incompatible with the rights and privileges" of the House (Resolutions 49, 51). The governors were said to have gradually lost their credibility as a result of their appropriations of land sales revenues without the authority of the House, their too frequent reservation (blocking) of bills, and accusations made to the Colonial Office regarding one of them (Aylmer) (Resolutions 65, 66, 84.10, 85). The colonial administration was also scrutinized in detail. The unequal distribution of public offices was cited: in 1832, the seventy-five thousand people of British origin in the colony were given 157 public positions, compared to forty-seven for the 525,000 *Canadiens*, so that 12 per cent of the population received 77 per cent of the positions while 88 per cent received 23 per cent. Moreover, the British recipients had obtained "the higher and more lucrative offices." The Resolutions condemned the practice of allowing individuals to hold more than one office concurrently, the family compact, the appointment of judges to the Executive and the political opinions of those judges, the misappropriations of funds by the Receiver General, and refusals to proceed in cases of "flagrant acts of malversation" by judges (74, 84).

These grievances did not irrevocably destroy confidence in Great Britain; they did, however, undermine it enough that allusions to "the neighbouring States" were frequent. The United States was presented as a model for preventing the abuse of power, as a reminder of the social difference between the Americas and Europe, and thus as the paradise of elected public office. And in the opinion of the "resolutionaries," the British colonies of North America might even one day do what the colonies to the south had done in 1776 (Resolutions 31, 41, 43, 45, 46, 48, 50, 56).

On the very day of the debate in the House, Parent published the 92 Resolutions in *Le Canadien*, presenting Lower Canada as "the advance guard of Colonial Rights." Papineau, who rose in the House to speak in favour of the Resolutions, was well aware that Neilson and a few other members would not support the position of the majority. He reviewed the situation: "We have to examine whether today we have reached a time when it is necessary that the first authority of the government [the House of Assembly] recover the respect it has lost, and that the honour, fortune, liberty and existence of the people be secured, or else resolve to see the one fall to the lowest level of debasement, and the other give itself over to excesses. Yes, I believe it, we have arrived at that day." He declared that "each of us must today be the accuser, if love of country moves us," and that the history of recent years must lead the citizens to decide. He became more vehement as his exasperation and determination increased. He scoffed at the Governor, "supported by one branch of the Legislature, [who] can always do well by his favourites, men who themselves can make the fortune of the governors." "It seems to me," he continued, "that there is nothing baser than the English nobility who come to us in this country, so eager they are to place themselves and to enrich themselves." He took aim at the Duke of Richmond, who had come to "repair the ruins of his fortune" in the colony, and his successor, who had come to "earn something to repair his dilapidated old mansion." A caustic allusion to the big landowners presented them as people whose opinions, but "not their conscience, for they have none," could be bought by the governor, who dipped into the public coffers.

To Papineau, it was now clear that it was "only a matter of knowing that we are living in America, and knowing how we have lived here." The society and political institutions he envisaged for Lower Canada were oriented toward the destiny of the rest of the Americas: "It is certain that, not very long from now, all America must be republican." An avowed republican since the beginning of the 1830s, he was also a democrat, who saw the Legislative Council as the source of "national distinctions" and anticipated that an elected Council would put an end to ethnic antagonism. He hoped that a "handful of men of power" would not be able "to prevent remedies that will put an end to our ills, and will make all the people of the colony brothers and give them the reasons to join together. The national distinctions, privileges, hatred and antipathies will all be destroyed." Before taking his seat again, he summarized: "There is in these resolutions as much force in the truth of the facts as circumspection in the expression."[2]

The House voted on 21 February, and the 92 Resolutions were passed with fifty-six votes to twenty-three. The English-language press saw this as a call for secession. Parent, who was able to express indignation while keeping his composure and who had a natural reflex to place Lower Canada in the context of international events, responded in *Le Canadien* of 26 February:

If the representatives sincerely desired a prompt split between this colony and England, the surest way of seeing it carried out would certainly be to let the government advance more and more down the slope of the abyss toward which it is heading, to let it fill the cup of abuse, to give it free rein on the race-course of arbitrariness, to the point where the people could not tolerate the weight of the chains, would shake them off spontaneously and knock down their tyrants with them. And in this case, they would not have to fear as European peoples, as Spain before, as Italy today, that legions of soldiers would come running from their neighbours to raise up again the altar of despotism that had just been overturned. That would be the surest policy to follow for enemies of British allegiance.

Parent supported the continental views of Papineau, denouncing the colonial ministers who persisted "in making Americans live under a European regime."

When the session adjourned on 18 March, the moderate Neilson's *La Gazette de Québec* declared that it was "a revolution in the full force of the

term that the authors of the 92 Resolutions are asking for and fomenting." In *Le Canadien* of 4 April, Parent, who was just as moderate, replied
by simply demanding a responsible government in lieu of an irresponsible oligarchy. He wrote: "Let all classes, all origins that make up our
population be placed on an equal footing; let none have more privileges
than the others; then and only then will the special interests that create
trouble and confusion everywhere disappear; then we will no longer see
a Legislative Council that calls for speculation on our lands and supports
all the misdeeds of an inimical and imbecilic administration. If that is a
revolution, then a revolution is what is desired by the authors and supporters of the 92 Resolutions."

THE "PLAGUE" OF LIBERALISM

The English-language press were not the only ones to detect the odour of
sulphur floating over Lower Canada. The Catholic Church, which had
been loyal since 1791 and remained steadfast at the time of the bill on the
representation of notables in the fabriques in 1831, spread the word
through Father Paquin, who would himself preach by example in 1837–
38: "Let the clergy organize, become accustomed to being involved in
public and government affairs, devote itself to the study of its rights and
defend them as a group, en masse and of one mind." And Paquin, the parish priest from Saint-Laurent, near Montreal, described to his bishop the
mood of the population at the time of the 92 Resolutions: "Since the sad
affairs of the last Session of Our Provincial Parliament, our countrysides
are flooded with a mob of young supposed Patriotes who are overturning
the ideas of our good, honest and religious habitants, and harassing them
to make them sign petitions in support of the 92 Resolutions ... They
choose for this the days devoted to God and to gathering the faithful; they
wait for them at the exits of the Churches to tell them that these petitions
are to preserve Religion and drive away the English; that the priests who
show opposition to this are not for the *Canadiens*, that they are their enemies ... What they have done here, they have done elsewhere; they are
doing it almost everywhere."

Father Saint-Germain, who later reported on the effects of cholera,
confessed to Mgr Lartigue: "I cannot refrain from speaking to you of
another kind of disease that is tormenting the social body, making extremely rapid progress, and the results of which are all the more disturbing since it is morality that is being attacked. This plague that I wish to
speak about is liberalism, of which we can say with the Apostle: Serguit ut
cancer. It goes quickly ... very quickly!"[3]

After so many years of hopes and disappointments, the 92 Resolutions did not receive any response from the governor, the Executive, or the Legislative Council. They were really intended for the Imperial Parliament, to which they were transmitted on 1 March by A.-N. Morin, who had gone to London to join the agent of the House of Assembly, Denis-Benjamin Viger. The Resolutions were accompanied by a letter from the House, written by Papineau, which started by recalling that the report of the Committee in 1828 had not been "followed by any effective measures." The contents of the 92 Resolutions were repeated, with occasional emphatic references to such matters as the power of the House of Assembly to revise the Constitution of 1791 to make the Legislative Council an elected body. For Papineau, such a liberal measure would lead to "a noble Rivalry with the United States of America" and "preserve a friendly intercourse between Great Britain and this Province, as her Colony, so long as the tie between us shall continue, and as her ally whenever the course of events shall change our relative position." The letter ended on an allusive note, urging Parliament to ensure "that the people of this Province may not be forced by oppression to regret their dependence on the British Empire and to seek elsewhere a remedy for their afflictions."[4]

The discussion of the 92 Resolutions began at Westminster on 15 April 1834. The radical member of Parliament for Bath, John Arthur S. Roebuck, spoke for the opposition, warning the government that Lower Canada "is actually in a state of revolution." This was indicated, according to him, by the breakdown of relations between the governor and the House of Assembly, the lack of constitutional responsibility of the Legislative Council and an Executive of which he said: "I solemnly charge the Executive for the last twenty years with disgracefully and most corruptly endeavouring to create and perpetuate national and religious hatred among a large body of His Majesty's subjects." According to Roebuck, the French Canadian reformers no longer believed the promises of change; they instead were convinced "that a trick was played upon them." To those who were fanning the flames by comparing the convention proposed by Papineau to the Convention of the Reign of Terror, he suggested they consider "that the people of Canada were not copying revolutionary France, but quiet and well-governed America." Roebuck finally proposed to the House "the appointment of a Select Committee to inquire into the means of remedying the evils which exist in the form of the Governments now existing in Upper and Lower Canada."

While the member of Parliament Stewart proposed dealing with the situation by returning to the plan for union, the Secretary of State for the Colonies, Lord Stanley, supported by O'Connell, who was in favour of an elected Legislative Council, proposed instead "that a Select Committee be appointed to inquire and report, whether the grievances complained of in 1828 ... had been redressed ... and also to inquire into other grievances now set forth in the Resolutions of the House of Assembly in Lower Canada."[5] Roebuck's motion was defeated and in February 1835 the House appointed a royal commission on the Canadian situation, headed by Lord Gosford, who was appointed governor at the same time, replacing Aylmer.

With the approach of an election, the press, the House, and extra-parliamentary assemblies were all drumming up support. Parent, who showed a keen awareness of history, attacked Lord Stanley, "the great schemer," for wanting to maintain the current Legislative Council in order to protect "the British interest"; Parent wrote in *Le Canadien* of 6 June 1834:

This word comes from here, and we know what it means. This is the *interest* that shouted loudly when the Imperial Parliament passed the act of the 14th year, that re-established the old laws of the country that this *interest* had had abolished on the cession; it is this *interest* that since the first parliament has tried to banish the French language; ... it is this *interest* that in the time of 1810 opposed the exclusion of Judges from the House and control by the representatives of the people over spending by the government; it is this *interest* ... that dragged into the dungeons the most worthy, the most deserving citizens; it is this *interest* ... that in 1822 wanted to bury the *Canadien* population.

Papineau denounced Governor Aylmer's positions and his influence over Lord Stanley, whose speech in the House on 15 April he described as "deceitful." He scoffed at the Legislative Council and the "trading-post aristocracy that lives in Opulence and dies in Bankruptcy." To break the stalemate of the political situation in which the House of Assembly was refusing to vote on the revenues, living under the threat of prorogation, and waiting for London to respond to the 92 Resolutions, Papineau adopted a new strategy, the one that had been used by the Americans in 1774: airing grievances in public assemblies, associations, and Assembly members' committees of correspondence, and boycotting imported products in order to reduce revenues from the colony. Papineau urged people to wear clothes made of domestic fabric and consume alcohol produced in local breweries and distilleries. And once again, he warned London to "understand that the reforms desired by the peoples of Continental America should be graciously granted to them, if they do not want them a little later to be taken by force."[6]

A correspondent of *Le Canadien* on 27 June 1834, with accents borrowed from Lamennais, made St John the Baptist, the patron saint of the French Canadians, a liberator: "It bodes well for the patriots to have as their patron saint the Precursor of the Man-God who came to preach the Equality of men in the eyes of the Creator and deliver the world from slavery to powerful enemies from another world."

The election of October and November 1834 was mostly about the 92 Resolutions, which had been written in part as the election program of the Parti patriote. The party obtained 77 per cent of the vote, and forty-one Patriote members out of eighty-eight were elected by acclamation. The policies of the party formulated in the 92 Resolutions were supported by the vast majority of the population, including English reformists from the Townships and the Irish.

Papineau and the parliamentary majority were now in a position of strength to take their grievances to London and expect a response to the 92 Resolutions. The language of the warnings was becoming stronger: "One nation can never govern another. The affection of the British for Ireland and the Colonies has never been any thing else than the love of the pillage of Ireland and the Colonies, abandoned to the cutting and carving of the British Aristocracy and its creatures." The vision of the manifest destiny of Lower Canada was becoming more specific: "A local, responsible and national Government for each part of the Empire as far as the regulation of local interests, with a superintending authority in the Imperial Government to decide on peace and war and commercial relations with the stranger – that is what Ireland and British American demand."[7]

CHAPMAN AND ROEBUCK, THE VOICES OF THE HOUSE
OF ASSEMBLY IN LONDON

The tabling of the 92 Resolutions in the House of Commons in London and the appointment of a new commission of investigation on Canadian matters led the House of Assembly to give itself a voice in London, someone to explain Lower Canada's point of view to politicians and the press. After the return of D.-B. Viger and A.-N. Morin at the end of 1834, it relied on Henry S. Chapman, the publisher and owner of the *Daily Advertiser* in Montreal, who, since the 92 Resolutions, had shared the views of the Parti patriote. Favourable to the British radicals, and convinced that the conflict in the colony was social and not ethnic, he went as an emissary to London in December 1834, with Robert Nelson. He brought copies of his recent pamphlet *What is the Result of the Canadian Election?* in which he interpreted the massive vote for the Parti patriote as a vote in favour of an elected Legislative Council. In September 1835, he replied to an article in the *Monthly Repository* of London by presenting the Legislative Council and the oligarchy as the result of a plan "to manufacture an Aristocracy out of the salaried officials" and "a perfectly irresponsible body." He pointed out that the other British provinces of North America were making the same demand as Lower Canada.[8]

John Arthur Roebuck was appointed the agent of the House of Assembly on 28 February 1835 and Chapman became his secretary. Roebuck, the member of Parliament for Bath, was a correspondent of Papineau and defender of the 92 Resolutions in the House of Commons in April 1834; he was part of the radical opposition, who were proponents of the ideas of Jeremy Bentham. The Radical Party, which was favourable to the emancipation of the colonies in those difficult times when they were incurring costs for the metropolis, also denounced the patronage that maintained the aristocracy. The spokesman for the House of Assembly was thus in the opposition – unless, obviously, it could form the government – and in the Radical Party opposition, not the Whig opposition; the Whigs' recent term in power had hardly changed anything in the area of colonial policy. This shows how marginal Lower Canada's spokesman in London was, although he had the support of some members of Parliament (the moderate Radical Joseph Hume, Papineau's friend; the Irish leader Daniel O'Connell; John Temple Leader and a few others), Lord Brougham, and the journalists Thomas Falconer and John and Samuel Revans.

Roebuck quickly made his voice heard in the House. On 9 March 1835, he rose to denounce the irresponsibility of the Legislative Council, to declare that the recommendations of the 1828 Committee had never been followed up, and above all, to refute the false claims that there were in the colony of Lower Canada a French Party and an English Party. If that were the case, he asked, how could one explain the fact that, of the twenty-one Assembly members of British origin, ten had joined their French-speaking colleagues in signing the petition of the .Montreal Convention that he had just submitted to the House? He reiterated this idea in an article in the *London Review* of July 1835, reprinted in a pamphlet under the title *The Canadas and Their Grievances,* in which he analyzed what he considered to be the "evils" of the colony, in addition to. the questions of the civil list and the non-elected nature of the Legislative Council.[9]

The objective of these speeches and writings was to lay the groundwork for the results of the Gosford Commission, the members of which arrived in Quebec City on 23 August 1835. An unforeseen event, the disclosure of the Colonial Office's directive to the Gosford Commission by

the governor of Upper Canada, Sir Francis Bond Head, seemed to pres-
age the future of the saga between the metropolis and the colony. It was
clear from this directive that London had no intention of granting
changes to the Constitution of Lower Canada with respect to the status
of the Legislative Council. To Papineau, this "offensive and usurping"
Commission had received the minister's instructions in England and
was there to follow them; "all commitments of trust are released and
broken." The member Louis-Hippolyte La Fontaine went further:
the directive was "the first indirect response we have been given to the
92 Resolutions."[10] On 13 March, Papineau confessed to Roebuck that
there had been a moral separation from England and that England had
lost the trust of the Canadian people.[11] It was a turning point: the image
of Great Britain had taken a blow. It was not clear where the disappointed expectations would lead.

THE GOSFORD COMMISSION AND REPORT
(2 MARCH 1837)

The Commission was carrying out its inquiry while being targeted by the
reformers. Papineau observed that it was obtaining its information only
from "fanatical newspapers." In London, Chapman published another
pamphlet, *Recent Occurrences*, in which he sought to undermine the credibility of Governor Gosford and the Commission.

But it was Roebuck's speech in the House on 16 May 1836 that was
the culmination of the colony's campaign in the metropolis. After once
again lambasting the Legislative Council – "nothing more than a clique
holding power for their own particular purposes" – he presented the
creation of the Gosford Commission as a strategy "to gain time," while
the grievances involved had existed for thirty years. To clearly illustrate
the question of principle that was at stake and the prevarications of the
government, he repeated the observation Papineau had made in his
speech on the situation of the province a month earlier: "One pretends
to believe that our complaints are the fruit of our differences of origin
and Catholicism, when it is constant that the ranks of liberals include a
majority of men of every belief and every origin. But what can be said of
the support for this assertion when we see Upper Canada, where there
are only few Catholics and where almost all the inhabitants are of English
origin, denounce the same ills and demand the same reforms?"

The responses, a veritable barrage, all aimed to undermine Roebuck's
credibility. The undersecretary of state for the colonies, Sir George
Grey, provided a well-documented history of the resolutions of the House
of Assembly of Lower Canada regarding the demand for an elected

Legislative Council since the Bourdages motion of January 1832 in order to show that this demand, which had been absent from the concerns
of the 1828 Committee, justified the creation of the Gosford Commission.
Grey even tried to destabilize Roebuck by reminding him of a letter from
1835 in which he had said that the question of an elected Legislative
Council was an "illusion," forcing Roebuck to make an awkward distinction between his own views and those of the House of Assembly. The
member of Parliament Robinson, a shareholder in a company that
owned land in Canada, said that Roebuck only represented Papineau's
party, and that making the Legislative Council an elected body would
be a prelude to the loss of the colony. Regarding the members of the
Assembly from Papineau's party who were hostile "to the colonization of
British subjects," he observed: "[I] did not blame them for endeavouring
to maintain their own nationality, and their own interests; but, having
conquered that colony, were the people of Great Britain to deal with it
only in reference to the Canadian people and their interests? Why call
themselves exclusively Canadians, as if they wished to be considered a
distinct people?"

Joseph Hume responded by asking whether the people of Canada –
Upper and Lower – were to be treated as a conquered people. The debate became more heated when Sir John Hanmer challenged Roebuck's
right to be the agent of Lower Canada because of the fees he received for
it. The member of Parliament Worburton did not appreciate the comment and urged Hanmer to make a proper motion if he wished to discuss the question, for which he said there were precedents. Sir Robert
Peel, the former prime minister, said sarcastically that Roebuck had
made a motion only to withdraw it, so that he would have time to speak.
Lord John Russell, the home secretary, said he would wait for the report
of the Commission before taking a position.[12]

The House of Assembly continued to attend to its affairs. The
Grievance Committee, chaired by Dr O'Callaghan, submitted its report
on the conduct of Governor Aylmer.[13] In various "addresses," the House
reiterated the political position and demands of the 92 Resolutions. It
maintained the position that it would vote on revenues after obtaining
the reforms demanded until 30 September 1836, when it decided to
adjourn until it obtained a new constitution. It was a deadlock.

Meanwhile, in London, Roebuck and Chapman presented the issues
of the colonial situation in Lower Canada, emphasizing the lack of credibility of a commission in which the dice were loaded, as the disclosure
of the minister's directive had revealed.[14]

The report of the Gosford Commission was signed and dated on
15 November 1836 and presented to the House of Commons on 2 March

1837. The commissioners observed with regard to the Legislative Council that after 1791, because the British population had grown more slowly than predicted, the government, "instead of shaping its policy so as to gain the confidence of the House," had "adopted the unfortunate course of resting for support exclusively on the Legislative Council," and that the French Canadian majority in the House of Assembly "seems to have been thought a sufficient reason that there should be a majority of English in the Council," thus creating a power structure based on "antagonist principles almost from the commencement." The report recommended an elected Legislative Council with a very high financial threshold for eligibility, but stated, "we cannot advise the experiment now." The commissioners felt that with an elected Legislative Council, the Parti patriote would go further in its demands, and that the state of the colony would not permit such a change. What was meant by the "state of the colony" was that it was in danger of becoming too much like the United States and that, in any case, the French Canadians needed British protection as a minority not only in North America but even in the British colonies of North America. The idea of a general union of the colonies of North America, which had been formulated in 1824 and discussed again in 1828, was making progress.

With regard to the question of ministerial responsibility and responsible government, which had been demanded more and more explicitly since 1814, the signatories of the report recognized that "the means by which a colony can be advantageously released from its state of dependence, and started into being a nation by the voluntary act of the parent state, is an unresolved problem in colonial history"; they maintained that conditions in the British colonies were the best of all the colonial situations. Accordingly, responsible government was "incompatible with the unity of the Empire," and if it were granted, "the relation of dependence ... would be destroyed." The Executive was to be responsible only to the Imperial Parliament.

With respect to the control of revenues and expenditures, the Commission endorsed Goderich's recommendations of 1831: control of the colonial budget except for a civil list of £19,000 for "the life of the King" or at least seven years.[15]

CONCLUSION

There was no lack of signs of mounting political tension in the colony: the systematic formulation of grievances in the 92 Resolutions, the massive electoral support for the demands, the appointment of a new agent of the House of Assembly in London – who was, moreover, a member of

Parliament of the Radical Party – the establishment of a new commission of inquiry, the adjournment of the session of the House of Assembly in September 1836 until it obtained a new constitution, after Papineau had already stated that a "moral separation" from England was a fait accompli.

The 92 Resolutions, which reaffirmed, albeit half-heartedly, loyalty to the British Crown, described the failings of the Legislative Council and essentially demanded an elected council, and showed unequivocal admiration for the institutions of the United States, constituted a clear line of demarcation in opinion. While the document appeared radical to a liberal reformer such as John Neilson, it was an indication of both determination and flexibility to Papineau and the moderate Parent. Supported by fourteen of the twenty-one members of British origin in the House of Assembly after the decisive election of 1834,[16] the 92 Resolutions expressed demands identical to those of Upper Canada, a sign that the grievances could not be reduced to "national distinctions" or belonging to a particular cultural or religious group.

The young member Louis-Hippolyte La Fontaine had been right, in March 1836, in seeing the creation of the Gosford Commission as a first response by London to the 92 Resolutions. The Gosford recommendations recognized the dysfunction of the Legislative Council while differing on whether it should be reformed and made an elected body, out of fear of US-style republicanism and concern for the "protection" of the *Canadiens*, who were a minority everywhere. The Commission considered responsible government incompatible with the colonial status of Lower Canada. It viewed the rights of the Crown over ungranted land as inalienable. While London agreed to a reform of the Canada Tenures Act, it maintained a civil list of £19,000 voted "for the life of the King" or – a concession – a minimum of seven years.

On 6 March 1837, four days after the tabling of the Gosford report, Lord John Russell proposed ten resolutions to the House of Commons in response to the 92 Resolutions of the House of Assembly. Would they repeat the recommendations of the Gosford Commission?

5

A Politicized Liberal Culture Marked
by the English-Speaking Population
(1815–1840)

THE POPULATION OF LOWER CANADA more than doubled in three decades, going from 335,000 in 1814 to 697,084 in 1844.[1] This is explained by both a high birth rate and an increase in immigration from the British Isles after the end of the Napoleonic Wars. The numbers of immigrants arriving in the port of Quebec City, by five-year periods, were as follows: 8,041 immigrants per year on average from 1818 to 1822; 10,867 from 1823 to 1827; 31,541 from 1828 to 1832; and 22,444 from 1833 to 1837.[2] Up to 1833, the immigrants came mainly from England; after that date, they came mostly from Ireland. The Irish thread was beginning to be woven into the history of Lower Canada, and at a time when O'Connell had obtained the political emancipation of Catholics in Ireland, the mostly Catholic Irish of Lower Canada were making their presence felt in political and electoral life as well as in cultural spheres such as the press and associations.

DEMOGRAPHY AND CULTURE

Immigration of English-speaking people, which, since Sewell's plans in 1811, had been seen as a means of assimilation of the French Canadians, would have decisive effects both politically and culturally; for example, Montreal would become a majority English-speaking city in 1835, and the anglophone merchant bourgeoisie would leave its mark on the city's cultural institutions – voluntary associations, semi-public libraries, museums, bookstores – institutions that francophones would adopt and adapt, especially after 1840.

The size of the cities would also ensure the viability of certain institutions or cultural forms in the colony. The populations of Montreal and Quebec City were comparable until 1830, when that of Montreal surpassed that of the capital, reaching 45,000 in 1844, compared to 33,000 for Quebec City.[3] Centres with 1,001 to 2,000 inhabitants went from one quarter of all centres in 1822 to one third in 1825; one quarter of them had between 2,001 and 3,000 inhabitants during the period. Centres of 3,001 inhabitants or more accounted for one quarter of centres in 1825, and then one fifth in 1831.[4] In colonial North America, population density determined whether institutions such as a church, a school, an inn, a post office, a newspaper, a library, or a bookstore could exist.

THE CIRCULATION OF PEOPLE, GOODS, AND IDEAS

Domestic transportation and communication took place mostly by ship or boat. Navigation began between 8 April and 2 May and ended in late November or early December. Sailing ships were mostly used, although there were seven steamboats travelling between Quebec City and Montreal in 1819. Coach companies, which used the "chemin du Roy" on the North Shore, provided land transportation, with some difficulty in the spring; winter coaches, which began in 1825 between Montreal and Quebec City, and in 1828 between Saint-Jean-sur-Richelieu and New York City, went three times a week. The "Red Line" and then the "Green Line" carried the royal mail by way of post houses in Trois-Rivières, Berthier-en-Haut, and L'Assomption. The number of post offices quadrupled during the period, going from ten in 1816 to forty-two in 1827, to 117 in 1834, while revenue from letters doubled and revenue from newspapers tripled, indicating an increase in correspondence and a growing press.[5]

The lifting of the Napoleonic blockade in 1815 and the development of maritime technology led to an increase in the international circulation of people, goods, and ideas. Since navigation by sail to Europe was only possible from May to December, there was a lag of three months in the arrival of news and goods in the colony. The *Royal William*, the first steamboat built in Quebec City to cross the Atlantic (1833), took twenty days to travel from Quebec City to Liverpool in 1836. In winter, the Atlantic ports (Halifax, Portland, Boston, New York) took over, and the New York–Albany–Troy–Saint-Jean–La Prairie coach carried travellers and mail to Lower Canada. Non-winter transportation and communication with the United States also took place by water, by way of the Hudson and Richelieu rivers, Lake Champlain, and the Chambly Canal, which was opened in 1835. This corridor was soon being used by "tourists," as shown by the twenty-six travel guides published between 1824 and 1840 on the Canada–United States "tour." These guides were published in New York City; only the three editions of *The Picture of Quebec and its Vicinity*, by Bourne, were published in Lower Canada.[6]

The railway, which made a modest (twenty-six kilometre) appearance in 1836, linked Saint-Jean-sur-Richelieu and La Prairie on the south shore of the St Lawrence across from Montreal. Victoria Bridge was inaugurated only in 1860. But already, the existence of the north-south railway axis indicated the importance of continental transportation.

Transportation from Europe brought immigrants, soldiers, and travellers who crossed the Atlantic for various reasons. The immigrants, as we have seen, were mostly British, and among the soldiers were painters and watercolourists, such as James Pattison Cockburn and Thomas Davies.

Between 1815 and 1840, there was very little French immigration: it is estimated that there were some 325 persons between 1815 and 1860. Motivated by wars or coups d'état, these immigrants included teachers or journalists, such as Leblanc de Marconnay and Alfred Rambaud, who went to the St Lawrence Valley. Six Brothers of the Christian Schools arrived in Montreal via New York between 1837 and 1839.[7]

The young student Théodore Pavie, who travelled in Lower Canada in 1829–30, was a romantic traveller attracted by the exoticism of nature and the Indians of the New World and nostalgic for the colonial past of Lower Canada. He observed in Quebec City, "I heard men in the heat of a memory cry out with enthusiasm, 'And in spite of everything, we are French.'" Pavie was followed by Alexis de Tocqueville and Gustave de Beaumont, who stayed in Montreal and Quebec City from 24 August to 2 September 1831. During this brief visit, Tocqueville came to share the views of John Neilson, with whom he visited the countryside, L'Ancienne-Lorette and Saint-Thomas-de-Montmagny. Neilson was then still close to the Parti patriote, although he had recently distanced himself from it on the question of the notables. If he had heard of Papineau, Tocqueville did not meet him. He even wrote, "The man who will awaken the French population, and incite it to rise up against the English is not yet born," and said that nowhere did he see "a man of genius who would understand, feel and be capable of developing the national passions of the people." In addition to Neilson's account, Tocqueville drew on those of the Mondelet brothers, one of whom had just been appointed an honorary member of the Legislative Council, an anglophone merchant, Denis-Benjamin Viger and the Sulpician Quiblier, a loyalist seigneur, of whose monarchist views Tocqueville said: "One must either deny the usefulness of clergy, or have such as are in Canada." As he was about to leave the St Lawrence Valley, the man who had already pondered democracy in America observed in his journal: "All in all, this race of men seemed to us inferior to the Americans in knowledge, but superior in qualities of the heart. One had no sense here of that mercantile spirit which obtrudes in all the actions and sayings of an American."

The French Canadians "have in them all that is needed to create a great memory of France in the New World."[8]

There were, however, more *Canadiens* travelling to France. It is estimated that 265 of them went there between 1815 and 1850, including 168 between 1815 and 1844. There were clergy: Sulpician priests going to further their studies at la Solitude d'Issy-les-Moulineaux, parish priests making "cultural pilgrimages," and bishops going for various reasons. Mgr Plessis, Mgr Lartigue, and the future Mgr Turgeon travelled to England, France, and Rome in 1819–20. The bishop of Quebec City visited and carefully described the churches of France, including Saint-Joseph-des-Carmes in Paris, which led him to remember the *Histoire du clergé de France pendant la Révolution*, by Abbé Barruel, whom he met, and in Turin, he visited Joseph de Maistre, whose works, *Considérations sur la France* and *Du pape*, he was familiar with. Confronted daily with the irreligiousness of the people and the "dangerous minds" that lurked around the throne, Mgr Plessis delighted in Abbé Frayssinous's lectures at Saint-Sulpice church. Mgr Lartigue was equally struck by this "degraded and degenerate nation"; to him, the Parisians "think they know best about everything, even draymen and people of the lowest class, and simply believe that there is nothing good except in their country." When he left France, he wrote in his journal, "I have left with pleasure the volcano of impious France, to enter the peaceful land of England," even though the latter was Protestant.[9]

There were as many students – mostly in medicine – and businessmen who travelled to France. Booksellers such as Reiffenstein and Germain went to buy merchandise. Édouard-Raymond Fabre went to visit the family of Hector Bossange, who had come from Paris to open a bookstore in Montreal (which he ran from 1816 to 1819) and had gone back there married to Fabre's sister Julie. Fabre stayed in Paris in 1822–23, learning from the great bookseller Martin Bossange, on Quai Voltaire, in order to open his own bookstore in Montreal, the back room of which would become a meeting place for the Patriotes after 1830. Martin Bossange in 1821 published one of the first books on Canada, *Beautés de l'histoire du Canada* (Beauties of the history of Canada), by Philarète Chasles, under the pseudonym D. Dainville. When he was in exile in Paris after the Rebellions of 1837 and 1838, Papineau would be a friend of the Bossanges, as would other French Canadians.[10]

Other men of letters were finally able to see old France. Abbé Holmes from the Séminaire de Québec travelled there with three students, Amable Berthelot visited there, and Joseph-Isidore Bédard died there. The future historian François-Xavier Garneau was in England and France from 1831 to 1833, visiting France twice. His pro-Britishism won out over his discovery of revolutionary France, "which had just thrown a third throne to the four winds of heaven." The account of his voyage, written in 1854, provides a panoramic view of French geopolitics.

> But while France was not a completely constitutional country like the one [England] I had just left, neither was it a country fundamentally, essentially of freedom like the United States, in spite of the revolutions that had stirred its soil periodically in the past half-century ... France was not yet ready for a system of checks and balances, the fruit of time and reciprocal concessions in England, and of a calculation of imaginary probabilities in France, since the monarchy and aristocracy had been overturned there so many times that they no longer had any roots in the soil. However, while monarchy no longer had roots there, freedom was hardly more firmly established.[11]

Viger was one of the first politicians who went first to England and then to France, making the voyage in 1828; in 1831, he became the first delegate of the House of Assembly to the British government. The young Louis-Hippolyte La Fontaine hurriedly left Lower Canada for England and France in December 1837 to explain the situation in the colony. He frequently visited the Bossanges and he met Thiers, Lord Brougham, and several journalists. Papineau would leave his exile in the United States for Paris in 1839, where he would write and publish his *Histoire de l'insurrection du Canada en réponse au rapport de Lord Durham* (History of the insurrection in Canada in response to the report of Lord Durham).[12]

The circulation of books and newspapers between France and Lower Canada intensified. Hector Bossange contributed to this through his Montreal bookstore, followed by his brother-in-law Fabre and other exporters of printed matter. Books by prominent figures in the Catholic restoration quickly arrived in the former French colony through networks such as that of the French priests (for example, Abbés de Calonne and Raimbault) who had arrived in 1796 and settled on the shores of Lac Saint-Pierre, who read Lamennais, *L'Avenir*, and *L'Ami de la religion*. National religious paintings confiscated by the Revolution were purchased by Abbé Desjardins and shipped to Quebec City.[13]

France, which had been absent from Canada since 1763, was again beginning to show some interest in it. In 1831, when Tocqueville was travelling in Lower Canada, the new *Revue des Deux Mondes* published a long article on Canada by "Barker"; the author had gathered his information from several accounts of journeys and, especially, from British Parliament documents, in particular the report of the Committee of Inquiry in 1828. Without even having set foot in Lower Canada, the author declared, "The French Canadians are still, in terms of civilization, in the time of Louis XV. The same laws, the same customs, the same habits, the same ideas; the feudal system and church of that time subsists still among them in its entirety, and, a curious thing, they do not show the least desire to better their condition. Alone on the American continent, they have remained impassive and as if numb in the midst of the revolutions that have freed the New World." And repeating the thoughts of an English former merchant from the colony, Barker suggested that the French Canadians "are the best colonials of England"; in all likelihood, in his view, they had little nostalgia for France.

Better informed through his relationships in Lower Canada (N. Lemoult, A. Berthelot, D.-B. Viger, F.-X. Garneau, J.-I. Bédard, L. Duvernay, E. Parent, and A.-N. Morin) and his reading of *La Minerve* and *Le Canadien*, Isidore Lebrun published his *Tableau statistique et politique des deux Canadas* (Statistical and political portrait of the two Canadas) in Paris in 1833, and it was sold by Fabre in Montreal and Neilson and Cowan in Quebec City. Unhappy that Canada was "forgotten by some and despised by others" and calling for a renewal of French efforts in America, Lebrun drew a portrait of Lower Canada – with its tithes, its notables, its seigneurial regime, its clergy reserves, and its colleges – that was much more objective than Barker's, but was tinged with the republican views of the author. The clergy reacted immediately: Abbé Thomas Maguire, under the pseudonym Vindex, suggested that Lebrun wanted to import into Lower Canada "the poison of *irreligious liberalism*, and with it revolutionary fanaticism."[14]

In turn, Alfred de Vigny took an interest in the fate of this "dying nationality" when he attended a session of the House of Lords on 16 March 1839: "The question being coldly discussed before me was that of the absolute necessity of smothering a French nation of four hundred and fifty thousand souls. The operation was easy, one could be assured that France would not upset itself about it, that it would not even extend an idle hand to ask for some map of the world in order to enquire in what corner of North America cowered that sorry tribe." Vigny, nostalgic and somewhat blinded by ignorance, wrote in this text, which was never published: "Abandoned by us, those peaceful labourers no longer have past or present; neither history nor newspapers."[15] During the same period, another document, the Durham Report, would also pronounce itself on this absence of a history and a literature. France mourned Canada, evaluated it by the standard of 1789 or looked at it through the lens of the British metropolis or that of "America." In all cases, the signs of attachment were paradoxical.

Canadiens often travelled to the United States to board ships to cross the Atlantic to London or Le Havre. The New England states would be a refuge for the exiled Patriotes of 1837 and 1838, who knew more than one road to reach the border, Highgate and Swanton. Étienne Parent was very familiar with the US press; he read and cited the *New York Star*, the *New York Sunday News*, and the *New York Daily News*, in which the Patriote Thomas Storrow Brown published; he also knew New Orleans newspapers such as *L'Abeille* and New York City's *Le Courrier des États-Unis* (1826), published for the city's French community, which quickly become one of the main sources in Lower Canada for information and literature from France.[16]

AGAINST THE LIBERAL PRESS,
A "PULPIT IN A GOOD PUBLIC PAPER"

The rise of the bourgeoisie of the liberal professions and the gradual polarization of political life explain the rapid development of the press from 1815 to 1840. There were forty-two newspapers that lasted at least six months published in Lower Canada, half of them French, half English, at a time when the anglophone community made up only about 15 per cent of the population. Of these papers, twenty-four were published in Montreal, nineteen of which were French; eight in Quebec City, five of which were French; and ten elsewhere in the province, such as in Trois-Rivières or the large village of Saint-Charles-sur-Richelieu.[17]

Le Canadien of 1806 had been established to respond to the *Quebec Mercury*, but the francophone press of the 1830s, while continuing to wage war with anglophone papers such as the *Montreal Herald*, considered itself first and foremost the voice of the House of Assembly. Pierre Bédard, who had just resigned as leader of the Parti canadien, wrote to John Neilson, the owner of the bilingual *Gazette de Québec*, "The House will not go well as long as there is no press that publishes all that happens there, and which removes it from the influence of the gallery and charlatans and places it under that of the entire Province." Neilson was convinced of this, and said to Papineau, "*Canadiens* are good Englishmen at heart, but you need language to be heard, and you have it in the press. We have to make it work everywhere." *Le Canadien*, which had stopped publishing in 1810, came out again from 1817 to 1819 and from 1820 to 1825, and Étienne Parent undertook to publish the debates of the House to ensure that things would be "chewed over for the rest of the year." When *La Minerve* of Montreal put out its prospectus on 9 November 1826, it also emphasized the importance of publishing the parliamentary debates. After three years of journalism, the young Parent was already convinced "that nothing escapes opinion, the queen of the world. It is she who allows kings to reign and she who dethrones them."[18]

The political polarization of the press was not limited to exchanges between francophone and anglophone newspapers. In this time of the rise of the Parti patriote (1826), there was just as much rivalry between Duvernay's *La Minerve* and Tracey and O'Callaghan's *Irish Vindicator*, on one hand, and Parent's *Le Canadien* and Neilson's *La Gazette de Québec*, on the other hand, or between *Le Libéral* of Quebec City and *La Quotidienne* of Montreal, on one hand, and *Le Populaire* and *L'Ami du peuple, de l'ordre et des lois*, on the other. Even the newspaper carrier's "New Year's verses," which conveyed the newspaper's New Year's wishes in the form of a poem or song, were filled with allusions to anglicization, the civil list, favouritism, or misappropriations.

While the raison d'être and orientations of the newspapers were primarily political, people also attributed a cultural and patriotic dimension to them. Michel Bibaud, whose periodicals published poems that would be compiled in the first poetry collection, *Épîtres, satires, chansons, épigrammes et autres pièces de vers* (1830), and historical narratives that would be the basis of the first book on history by a French Canadian, *Histoire du Canada sous la domination française* (1837), said in the aptly named *Bibliothèque canadienne* (Canadian library), "A newspaper is the least expensive book one can find; because it can take the place of many books." Parent called the periodical press "the only library of the people." This idea was often repeated in the prospectuses for publications. *Le Courrier du Bas-Canada* formulated it as follows: "It is through newspapers alone that we can begin to spread education to all branches of Society, and inspire a desire to extend its sphere. In a country where there are not a large number of citizens who have enough leisure or fortune to routinely obtain or read books." *L'Écho du pays*, in Saint-Charles-sur-Richelieu, announced its colours: "We will embrace everything that can be useful to our country, everything that can serve to accelerate intellectual progress in this province that is unfortunately too isolated, and to enlighten a too long neglected people on its rights ... [Our newspaper], as its name announces, will be the echo of the feelings of the nation; its ever-sincere voice will be ready to constantly oppose any violations of the rights of the people."[19]

These four-page newspapers were weeklies or biweeklies, except for the two English-language dailies, the *Daily Advertiser* (1833–34) and the *Daily News* (1835–74). While their circulation was limited – *La Minerve* printed 1,200 to 1,500 copies from 1832 to 1837 – their readership was multiplied through reading out loud for people who were illiterate. The Patriote Boucher-Belleville observed in his journal: "Every Sunday, after Divine Office, [enlightened men] made speeches to the people, instructing them on their position and forming reading rooms where people read and commented on the newspapers," in particular *La Minerve*, *Le Populaire*, and *The Vindicator*, which was sometimes translated.[20]

The journalists of the period paid personally for their defence of freedom of the press. Duvernay and Tracey were imprisoned in 1831 for libel against the Legislative Council and were acclaimed by the public on their release. Parent, who considered the press "the last bastion of the British Constitution, and not the least formidable," was imprisoned for "seditious practices," though he was a moderate and a conciliator. On the pretext that he was the owner of presses or buildings where "seditious" newspapers were printed, Denis-Benjamin Viger was jailed in 1838. Many printers, newspaper editors, and booksellers joined the ranks of the Patriotes: Duvernay of *La Minerve*; François Cinq-Mars, who founded *L'Aurore des Canadas* and printed *L'Abeille canadienne* and *Le Diable bleu*; François Lemaître, who printed *Le Libéral*, *La Quotidienne*, the short-lived *Gazette patriotique*, the *Quebec Commercial List*, and *Le Journal de médecine de Québec*; Louis Perrault, printer of *The Vindicator*; Hiram-F. Blanchard, in Stanstead, who produced the *Canadian Patriot* in his print shop; Silas H. Dickerson, who published the *British Colonist and St Francis Gazette*; Napoléon Aubin and Adolphe Jacquies of *Le Fantasque*; Jean-Baptiste Fréchette, owner of *Le Canadien*; Robert Bouchette, editor of *Le Libéral*; Boucher-Belleville of *L'Écho du pays*, in Saint-Charles; the bookseller Édouard-Raymond Fabre, financial backer of *La Minerve* and *The Vindicator*; and his colleague the bookseller Théophile Dufort.[21]

This dynamic and crusading press of the middle class of the liberal professions and the Parti patriote was intensely disliked by the clergy, who saw the power of the pulpit being challenged. The bishop of Quebec City told his Montreal counterpart in 1824: "Contempt is all one can give these sorts of publications. *Le Canadien* is a paper that I read only rarely and that I have never encouraged because it has constantly been bad, in one aspect or another, since it has existed." Priests wrote to Duvernay to criticize his newspaper; as Father Brassard said, "God preserve me from approving its principles." His awareness of the power of the press and his denunciation of the principles of certain "gazettes" did not persuade the bishop of Quebec City to found a church newspaper. However, at the time of the July Revolution in France in 1830, his Montreal counterpart saw the need to do so, a sign that cultural leadership was moving from Quebec City to Montreal.

This is perhaps the most urgent time ever for the Province to establish a Church Newspaper on a solid footing in order to counter the revolutionary diatribes that will resound, and that have already started to appear in all your papers: we already see but horrors of this kind; and unfortunately our Catholics, Irish as well as *Canadiens*, generally give themselves over wholeheartedly to these follies ... If we give the democratic newspapers, which abound in this country, time to pour the poison of their errors among our peoples without giving them the antidote, there will no longer be time to try to return the public mind to the right path once it has been led astray.

Think about it, Monsignor, for the need seems urgent to me: it is without doubt a beautiful thing to build a house of religious education; but I believe that in this period forming the public mind is even more urgent. Moreover, one will not harm the other.

In 1831, the "notables bill" increased the clergy's awareness of "the need to have a Church press and newspaper"; *L'Avenir*, published in Paris by Lamennais and the liberal Catholics, was even occasionally used as a model.

With the rise of liberal ideas and what he perceived as their radicalization, Mgr Lartigue became insistent.

Here are our Canadian papers becoming more revolutionary than ever: *La Minerve* of the 16th of this month published an article signed S****** [Sicotte], in which the *Revolution* is highly proclaimed, and in which high treason not disguised under any veil.

Believe now that if we had an independent press ... it would not be necessary to gag this rabble; for such is freedom of the press ... as they understand it, when they refuse to print what is contrary to their opinions ... For me, after having made all my efforts, I wash my hands with respect to the results I dread; and I would be angry should anyone say subsequently that the clergy did not want to prevent evil when it could have.[22]

From 1832, Mgr Lartigue saw clearly that it was necessary to "form and control public opinion and to turn it in favour of the Church"; he was perfectly conscious of the fact that "the Bishop must not be content with preaching in his cathedral, but must establish his pulpit in a good public paper ... : so that it would be better to leave a parish or some other post vacant in order to use a priest suited to the writing of this work under the authority of the Bishop."[23] This would not happen officially until 1840. It would be done unofficially by the loyal Sulpicians of Montreal, who, as seigneurs of the island of Montreal, were then negotiating the recognition of their property rights in London. The Sulpicians funded *L'Ami du peuple, de l'ordre et des lois*, which was founded officially by Pierre-Édouard Leclerc, the chief of the Montreal police, and John Jones, the King's Printer.[24] The response to *La Minerve* and *The Vindicator* would come from the Sulpicians' newspaper.

HELP YOURSELF AND THE ASSOCIATION
WILL HELP YOU

Mgr Lartigue understood that the political and cultural community had made a qualitative leap attributable to a number of factors. Public opinion had been consolidated through thoughtful reporting on the affairs of the Assembly by the liberal press, fuelling public debate. In Quebec City, Montreal, and a few other towns, population density made possible schools or newspapers; the British immigrants, who were concentrated in Quebec City, Montreal, and the Townships, had economic resources, knowledge, and cultural experience in the metropolis. It is thus not surprising that the colonial middle class established a diverse and enduring press and adopted the cultural institutions of the metropolis and adapted them to the colony.

While sociability occurred through the nuclear and extended family and professional corporations such as the Bar, it was constructed mostly in associations organized around needs or interests. Such associations first developed in Quebec City and Montreal in the 1820s through initiatives by the British population of the colony. In the following decade, francophones would give a political and patriotic orientation to associations, and after 1840, a cultural orientation.

The anglophones of the colony first developed their social life in family and government contexts and then externalized it in athletic clubs.[25] And just as their curiosity had been piqued by an Amerindian physical activity, lacrosse, which they had then adopted, the flora and fauna and geology of the colony and the history of this North American society soon brought them together in associations such as the Literary and Historical Society of Quebec (1824–) and the Montreal Natural History Society (1825–).[26] At a time when major projects such as the Lachine Canal and shipbuilding were beginning, the merchant bourgeoisie immediately adopted the Scottish model of the Mechanics' Institute, founding one in Montreal (1828) and one in Quebec City (1831) to train artisans in new trades through evening classes, lectures, and a library.[27]

In the francophone community, the Société littéraire de Montréal (1817), founded to "make the name *Canadien* illustrious in literature," did not last long. A correspondent of *L'Aurore*, without realizing it, explained the ephemeral nature of the organization: "We also have a politics and economics society. What is it? one may ask. It is our House of Assembly. In my opinion, that institution is just as worthy as an academy of sciences or a literary society." In 1827, the aptly named Société pour l'encouragement des arts et des sciences au Canada (Society for the encouragement of the arts and sciences in Canada), organized to "bring out of obscurity those of our fellow citizens whom nature has endowed with necessary talents," barely survived until it merged with the Literary and Historical Society of Quebec in 1829.[28] Several *Canadiens* learned about metropolitan models of associations in Europe. François-Xavier Garneau, who travelled in England and France in 1831, became familiar with the clubs in London, the literary and scientific societies in Birmingham, and the news rooms in Paris. A correspondent of Denis-Benjamin Viger and an admirer of the public institutions of Paris, Pierre de Sales Laterrière proposed that these institutions be adopted in Lower Canada "to get Canadian youth out of the woods."[29]

But it was politics that awakened the *Canadiens* to the advantages of associations. Through the Parti patriote and elections, public assemblies starting in the summer of 1833, and the members' committees of correspondence (1834), which kept in touch with each other or with allies in the Radical Party in the House of Commons in London, the *Canadiens* discovered their patriotic sense; they celebrated the day of their "national" patron saint, St John the Baptist, for the first time on 24 June 1834. Swelled by immigration, the Irish community of Montreal founded two associations: St Patrick's Society, which was in favour of the constitutional movement, that is, of the status quo, and the Hibernian Benevolent Society, which was pro-Patriote and in favour of the 92 Resolutions. The following year, the English community founded St George's Society, the Scots gathered under the banner of St Andrew's Society, and the small German community created the German Society; these associations, along with St Patrick's Society, formed a federation, the Montreal Constitutional Association, in December 1835.[30] Demographically, Montreal was at this time a majority anglophone city.

It was in this context that the Aide-toi et le ciel t'aidera (Help yourself and heaven will help you) society was founded on 6 March 1834, on the model of the organization of the same name around the liberal newspaper *Le Globe* in France, which took part in the July Revolution of 1830. The notice convening the founding meeting at the Nelson Hotel in Montreal appealed to "your patriotism and your desire to advance everything related to your Country" and defined the objective of the association: "Our young *Canadiens* will be able there to become accustomed to writing and develop a taste for study." It was stipulated that "each member in turn will provide an essay on politics or literature," and "will discuss some subject orally." Ludger Duvernay, the moving force behind the patriotic holiday of 24 June and the owner of *La Minerve*, wrote in his newspaper on 24 April 1834:

Let us form patriotic societies that will be like the hearth from which the light will shine that should guide our compatriots. May true patriots gather in a designated place in each city, may they there in the calm of reflection discuss the best means to remedy the ills that we anticipate; may the most enlightened members come to each meeting with a speech, a piece of verse of their inspiration suited for maintaining or rekindling the sacred fire of love of the homeland, either by illuminating the conduct of our rulers or by giving just tribute of praise to the eloquent and courageous defenders of our rights, Papineau, Bourdages, Viger, etc. May this patriotic association spread into the villages, may many branches extend into the countryside, carrying to it the precious sap of love of independence.[31]

The clergy took a dim view of these "so-called clubs," where liberal plans were fomented and notaries and doctors gathered who "wanted to run everything." One of these, Dr Côté, a member of the Assembly, informed his constituents: "I was warned by several respectable people of the parish of Saint-Valentin that the priest of that parish had taken the liberty in the pulpit of giving political sermons against patriotic associations, and that he had promised them a big fuss about politics on the 16th." On 2 July 1834, *L'Ami du peuple, de l'ordre et des lois*, the Sulpicians' paper, identified Aide-toi et le ciel t'aidera with the Patriote Thomas Storrow Brown and "the old revolutionary clubs."[32]

The intensification of political debate and of this patriotism through associations, and the example of secret societies in Europe, explain the virulent exchange that occurred in 1837 with respect to associations, although not much is known about the Aide-toi et le ciel t'aidera society between 1834 and 1837. A speech on education to the members of the society in March 1837 sparked the debate. Referring to Lamennais's *Words of a Believer*, a pirate edition of which Duvernay had published in May 1836, the speaker lamented "the stasis" that was "the secret disease of our society"; he claimed that "industrial and scientific life … is missing from our lives, making them ephemeral and without force. We barely survive. There is not enough warmth and sun to fertilize the seeds of growth thrown sparsely upon our soil." He attributed this absence of industry and science to the priests, who "cannot be capable of educating the masses" and expressed the wish that "our numbing education would be improved."

In *L'Ami du peuple*, "A Trifluvian" (a resident of Trois-Rivières), an alias of Mgr Lartigue, expressed his lack of appreciation of this "tirade against education," this "liberal charlatanism." He demanded: "Stop, above all, stop dominating civil society, which does not call you to it and has no need of your services; return to the underground of your secret

Association, if the government cares so little about its own preservation as to allow you with impunity to undermine the Throne and the Altar." "A young Canadian," an alias of Abbé Joseph-Sabin Raymond of the Séminaire de Saint-Hyacinthe, took up the torch; recognizing that "today the writer's pen and the speaker's words are the highest social powers," the young admirer of Lamennais also sought to associate the Aide-toi et le ciel t'aidera society with the secret societies: "For what is the relationship of principles and morals between it and the Carbonari of Italy, the 'descamisadas' of Spain and those clubs in France?" Taking care to point out that nationality was "an electric word that causes a violent shock to the deepest fibres of our hearts," he expressed the view that the people "will not be able to ensure its life as a people, its existence as a nation," and that "it will be in the light of true science put in a state of lucidity by the sun of Christianity that we will know the means of social improvement." The "fibres" of nationality would have to be reheated by the "sun of Christianity," according to Abbé Raymond, a rising figure of Quebec Catholicism.

While the skirmish of 6 November 1837 between the Doric Club and the Fils de la liberté (Sons of liberty), the founding of the secret society Les Frères chasseurs (The hunters' lodge) in the summer of 1838, and more generally, the Rebellions of 1837 and 1838 would delay the consolidation of the association movement, the basis had been established for its continuing growth: in Le Fantasque of Quebec City, Napoléon Aubin anticipated the interest of young people in associations created so that they could help each other in their future careers; he felt that "the only way to shake off the yoke of fear, apprehensions, and especially ennui, is to join together to learn to know ourselves. Literature, music, theatre performances, the arts, the sciences and politics offer wonderful areas for the intelligence."[33] A public culture shaped by sociability was born; it would assert itself after 1840, and the associations would continue to be viewed with suspicion by the clergy as secret societies because of Aide-toi et le ciel t'aidera and the Frères chasseurs.

TAKING CONTROL OF EDUCATION

La Gazette des Trois-Rivières of 23 February 1819 published an anecdote about a bishop whose carriage was blocked by the cart of a rotund carter. When the carter refused to move aside, the bishop grew impatient and said, "My friend, you appear to be better fed than educated." "I say, Monsignor," replied the carter, "it is we who feed ourselves, and it is you who educate us." This exchange suggests the tensions around public education between 1815 and 1840. Four different systems existed, one after the other – "royal schools," schools of mutual instruction, parish fabrique schools, and Assembly schools – which conferred responsibility either on the government or on the Church, and which were the outcome of debates in the education committee of the House and controversies in the press. Responsibility for schools was clearly a social issue, the target of interests and powers that wanted to use the schools to transmit their own values.

The "royal schools," which were established in 1801, had by 1818 increased from four to thirty-five, of which eleven were in the francophone community; they went from thirty-seven in 1819 to forty-one in 1824, and then to sixty-six in 1831, reaching their peak – eighty-four – in 1829, mainly in the Townships, which had been settled by Loyalists from the United States and British immigrants. Their aim of anglicization was feared by the clergy, not without reason, and they began to decline in 1832, following the passage of a law on schools in 1829, dropping from sixty-nine in 1832 to three in 1846.[34]

In 1815, the idea was proposed of establishing schools based on "mutual instruction," a method developed by the Englishman Joseph Lancaster, in which the teacher was assisted by the more advanced students – "monitors" – who would teach certain subject to the younger students; the idea slowly made progress in spite of controversy and fierce opposition. *L'Aurore*, which published many articles on education in 1817 and 1818, questioned Lancaster's system. Very quickly, the Catholic clergy came to fear this system. A French priest who had been "driven out" by the Revolution and settled in "little France" on the shores of Lac Saint-Pierre wrote to a correspondent: "Since I am not a Lancastrian and I am not at all liberal, and my ideas are therefore not liberal, I have just given chase to a liberal man who had come here to teach in the liberal way; I purchased the location he had rented, and immediately bought another one close to the Church, where there is now a school for boys." About a petition to the House of Assembly that had not been acted upon, Abbé Fournier observed to Madame de Loynes de Morett: "The storm is already beginning to form, already people are shouting about fanaticism. In the House of Assembly, *Canadiens* have shown impious principles, they wanted nothing less than to remove from the priests the education of the youth and from the nuns the administration of the sick."[35]

His work against the Lancaster schools was carried on by his colleague in Trois-Rivières, Abbé de Calonne, who had been a staunch supporter of Governor Craig in 1810 and had been appointed by him to the Legislative Council; Abbé de Calonne drew on Félicité de Lamennais's *Essay on Indifference in Matters of Religion* to oppose the liberal approach of the House of Assembly: "Let us never forget it, religion is the sole education of the common people. Without religion it would know nothing, nothing especially of that which it is most important to society that it should know, and for itself to know." In addition to the fact that this is the first reference to an author who was destined for a certain renown in French Canada, Abbé de Calonne's position – "there can be no good education if religion is not its basis" – expressed the education dimension of ultramontanism, a religious philosophy that supported the primacy of religion over every other aspect of instruction. Abbé de Calonne's views led to a debate that continued from September 1819 to March 1820 in *La Gazette des Trois-Rivières, La Gazette de Québec, Le Canadien, La Gazette de Montréal, Le Spectateur,* and *Le Courrier du Bas-Canada.* The liberal contributions – for example, "Those who grow fat from the substance of the people and whose pleasures have been due in part to their misery thus had an interest in their being ignorant to the point of blindness" – were followed by contributions such as that of Abbé Painchaud of Sainte-Anne-de-la-Pocatière – "I wonder if the ignorance of the country has not always been the place of happiness, rather than the science and fine arts of the cities."[36] Public education remained a controversial subject. *La Gazette de Québec* debated education in the countryside again in 1821 when Joseph-François Perrault published his *Cours d'éducation élémentaire,* which was based on the Lancaster method. *Le Canadien* also argued in favour of this method, while the education committee of the House proposed in 1824 that schools be established by the fabriques – the first, albeit temporary, recognition of confessional responsibility in the area of schools. In parishes of less than two hundred families, the law permitted the fabrique (the body that administered the material property of the Catholic parish) – and therefore the priests and church wardens – to found schools and apply one quarter of the parish revenues to them. The results of the law were real but limited: forty-eight fabrique schools in 1828, and sixty-eight in 1830. The new law did not satisfy everyone; "Franc-parleur" ["Outspoken"] declared: "Let no one therefore come and tell us any more that education must be put in the hands of the clergy, that it is their property. Firstly, I do not see what wonders it has worked in this way, if not to bring down establishments [Royal Institution schools] that were not to its taste. Secondly, I do not see why we must necessarily entrust the civil education of laymen to priests. It seems to me that such an important thing should, as much as possible, be entrusted to the entire community, especially after the indifference and apathy that have neglected such an easy, simple means of education."

Mgr Lartigue read *Le Canadien* and observed the next day that the Parti patriote members of the Assembly had not lost hope of seeing an increase in the number of schools using the Lancaster method. He wrote to his Quebec City counterpart: "Your Quebec City philosophers have, it seems, resolved to destroy the principle of the education law passed last year to introduce the biblical system in the House of Assembly, veiled under the name of Lancaster. The prothonotary Perrault, who is delighted with it, does not see that the Borgias and Co. want to use it to ruin the influence of the clergy, which has not put enough zeal into having schools built in the countryside in accordance with that law. We must foil this new plan of impiety."

Mgr Plessis reassured him: "Many parish priests take pains to have schools on the principle of the Law of last year; but it takes time to establish them. Let us have patience. I have not yet seen the Bill on Lancaster Schools and do not know what one wants to do with them. Believe that the members of the Assembly are not easy to lead. I find in them a little too much liberality in the matter of religion, witness their address to the King in the previous session, in which they considered teaching by the Ministers of any sect as tending to give morality to the people."[37]

In addition to these objectives and practices with regard to the social control of public education, there were other factors involved in access to knowledge.[38] Research on the schools on the Island of Montreal in 1825 and in 1835 shows that school attendance was a function of environment (city dwellers were advantaged over country people), sex (more boys attended school), linguistic group (anglophones founded twice as many schools, which had more students), and income.[39] With respect to the anglophone community of the colony, these variables applied not only to schools, but also to the press, associations, and all cultural institutions. Property gave and took the means of knowledge.

The law on fabrique schools of 1824 did not last long. The French Canadian bourgeoisie in the liberal professions, which was on the rise, and which, with French-speaking merchants, gave the Parti patriote a majority in the House, succeeded in getting a law on so-called Assembly schools passed in 1829. The clergy was apprehensive about these schools: "The horizon is growing alarmingly dark here as in Europe," said Abbé Painchaud. "A spirit of insubordination and irreligion is plotting a system of general subversion in the shadows ... They are seeking to do here what has been done in too unhappy France, to remove education from Church control, that is, to deal a mortal blow to the sanctuary ... Let us hasten to wisely and at the appropriate time seize the strongholds before the enemy grows stronger there."[40]

The new law was based on the election of five school trustees by the landowners; the members of the Assembly were thus able to express a principle that was increasingly dear to them: the elected nature of civic functions. The government funded the construction of a schoolhouse in the amount of £50, paid the salary of the schoolmaster (£20 a year) and provided assistance to poor families by adding ten shillings to the teacher's salary for each poor student enrolled for free, provided that there were at least twenty but not more than fifty of them. A new element was that the government appointed school inspectors and, starting in 1832, required that teachers obtain a certificate of competency. When the Education Committee of the House also became permanent, the law led to a first takeoff in the number of schools, from 325 in 1828 to 1,372 in 1835; the number of students went from 11,679 to 53,377, and the number of teachers from 468 in 1829 to 1,305 in 1831.[41]

The enrolment rate had a clear effect on the literacy rate, which rose from 19.2 per cent between 1810 and 1819, to 25.4 per cent between 1830 and 1839.[42] The effect was different in Quebec City, where the enrolment rate was higher than in the countryside, as is usual in larger centres; Quebec City had a literacy rate of 39 per cent in 1830 as in 1800, despite an increase to 43 per cent between 1810 and 1830. A quarter of the population of Lower Canada was thus literate, and more than a third of the residents of Quebec City were literate. Men were more literate than women in the first half of the nineteenth century;[43] Protestant anglophones were twice as literate as Catholic francophones,[44] with the former living mostly in cities and towns, earning higher incomes, possibly being recent immigrants, and being motivated by intensive individual reading of the Bible.[45]

Once again, the takeoff of education was not lasting. Political tensions after the 92 Resolutions of 1834 and, especially, conflict between the House and the Legislative Council led the Council in 1836 not to extend the law of 1829 and to block the passage of the law that had been passed by the elected majority in the House of Assembly. Those in the English-language colonial press and the Legislative Council who stigmatized French Canadians as ignorant, calling them "knights of the cross" because, being illiterate, they signed their names with an X, and making fun of their refusal to return the property of the Jesuits and apply it to the needs of education, were the same people who in 1836 blocked a school law that had finally produced results. Parent, who, in *Le Canadien*, promoted schools as a means of teaching political rights, said of the Legislative Council on 6 April 1836: "Its misdeeds can no longer be counted. Through its rejection of the elementary schools bill alone, approximately forty thousand children will be deprived of education. The Council will continue to weigh on the country like a nightmare on a sick stomach, and to prolong its destructive rule, it wants to leave the people in ignorance. It is right: if the mass of the people could feel what is tyrannical, oppressive and even degrading in the existence of this body, public indignation would long ago have made the pernicious old men answer for their terrible misdeeds."

It was the moment for the clergy, which had been watchful since 1815, to try to take control "as by right, of the education of the People" and undertake a process of re-establishing the fabrique schools: "In addition to the fact that it [a new law] would do honour to the Church, it is the only means of tearing the future generation away from a detestable education; and I saw recently in the newspapers that the laymen would as early as possible renew their bad law of 1829 if we neglected this valuable, and maybe unique, opportunity to take control of the education of youth."[46]

Parent, who was lucid and capable, acknowledged in *Le Canadien* of 20 June 1838 this "prosperous and vigorous people of a half-million men that lacks only schools to be the most beautiful in the world." The failure to extend the law of 1829 and the Rebellions would leave scars and jeopardize a takeoff in education that had been singularly welcome.

The plan to found normal schools to remedy the glaring lack of teachers suffered the same fate. The Rebellions and the time spent looking for professors in Europe meant that the normal school in Quebec City did not open, and the one in Montreal had only about twenty students from 1837 to 1842. The Church had the same suspicion of the normal schools as of the Assembly schools; Mgr Lartigue stated to his colleague in Quebec City, "What the act of 1829 has done to debase our primary schools and remove them from the hands of the clergy and place them in those of lay persons, the new normal schools will do with respect to the training and education of our schoolmasters throughout the province."[47]

The failure of the schools to take off before 1840 was without doubt attributable to political conflicts, in particular the antagonism between the House of Assembly and the Legislative Council, and the conflict between the liberals of the Parti canadien / patriote and the Roman Catholic Church. These tensions clearly divided forces and efforts. The inability of the parliamentary majority to obtain the restitution of the property of the Jesuits for education also explains this failure. Finally, there were also material factors: the winter weather; the geographic dispersion of schools and the distances to be travelled; the poverty of parents, most often illiterate, who relied on the manpower available; the lack of satisfactorily trained teachers; and the scarcity of textbooks before 1830.

LAMENNAIS AND CATHOLIC LIBERALISM: A CONTROVERSY IN THE COLLEGES

The clergy did not show the same fear of classical secondary education, for which it retained responsibility. Five new colleges were added to the four founded before 1815: two that were short-lived, Saint-Roch, in Quebec City (1818), and Chambly (1825), and three that lasted, Sainte-Thérèse, north of Montreal (1825), Sainte-Anne-de-la-Pocatière (1829), east of Quebec City on the south shore, and L'Assomption (1832), founded by a layman, Dr Jean-Baptiste Meilleur, a major promoter of public education.

The colleges were not, however, immune to criticism or political events. A correspondent of *Le Canadien* wrote in 1823: "We have, it is true, many seminaries, but we believe that everyone is fully convinced of their ineffectiveness; we know that their goal is less to make citizens or to prepare youth to play a positive role in the world than to train students for the religious life. What a sad figure, most of the time, our young gentleman makes who after his course of study enters the world ... The world is a land completely foreign to him."[48]

While in some respects that was no doubt true, in others, the world outside made itself felt in the life of the colleges. In November of 1830, the year of the July Revolution in France and a time of rising popularity of the Parti patriote, the Collège des Sulpiciens on Saint-Paul Street experienced "a small Revolution in the French manner," in the words of Mgr Lartigue. Copying the students of the École Polytechnique in Paris who had taken part in the overthrow of Prince de Polignac's ministry, the exile of Charles X, and the ascent of Louis-Philippe d'Orléans to the throne, those of the Collège de Montréal attacked the well-known loyalism of the Sulpicians. The students, who may have included the Papineau sons Amédée and Lactance, posted calls for revolt, raised the tricolour flag and decorated the façade of the college with the effigy of Monsieur Séry – a.k.a. Polignac – who had too often called the *Canadiens* ignorant. They sang "La Collégiade," which denounced the Sulpicians: "We are sons of citizens, / Children of the homeland; / Let us be stout supports / Against tyranny, / Let us raise our voices / Against the *Frenchman* / Who is a despot to us. / May he follow the laws, / Respect our rights. / If not – REVOLT." But quickly, "the terror ceased to hang over the Masters" and everything "went back under the ancien régime," as Mgr Lartigue said.[49]

If the number of colleges / seminaries increased, it was to make up for the lack of Church personnel and at the same time to counter the rise of liberalism and "indifference in the area of religion," about which Lamennais had published a noted book in 1817, which had been quoted during a famous debate on public education in 1819.

The Catholic hierarchy in Lower Canada also caught up with the religious renewal, the religious restoration that, with Frayssinous, Lamennais, de Bonald, de Maistre, and Chateaubriand, was fighting against unbelief and trying to restore the image of the "apostolic tribune." Mgr Plessis, his future successor Abbé Turgeon and the future bishop of Montreal, Mgr Lartigue, travelled in Europe from July 1819 to August 1820, spending time with royalist and counter-revolutionary priests, and meeting Frayssinous, de Maistre, and Barruel. Mgr Lartigue subscribed to the *Drapeau blanc*, one of the contributors to which was Lamennais, about whom he wrote: "What a terrible man against impiety is this Mr. de La Mennais, whose book against indifference toward Religion I am reading! This book, through the energy of its thoughts, the depth of its reasoning, the intensity of its eloquence, is worthy of marking its time in the annals of Christianity."[50]

Ten years later, Lamennais was known to a large proportion of the French Canadian clergy. Vicar General Viau wrote to Mgr Lartigue: "Lamennais instills love of religion and its visible leader on earth. They [Lamennais and Muzarelli] have made me completely ultramontanist, and I am grateful to them." His bishop replied: "Lamennais has the double merit of both originality of thought and beauty of expression ... I believe, moreover, that all those who examine these great questions without prejudices, will very quickly be Ultramontanists."[51] This failed to take into account the Sulpicians, who already disapproved of Lamennais's ideas: "The general of the Jesuits has expressly forbidden teaching his philosophical system in all the Society's colleges. He has just published a book on the power of the Pope in relations with the civil government, and two letters addressed to the archbishop of Paris, which have done him much harm and have even displeased Rome."[52]

The term *ultramontanist* was thus introduced in Lower Canada. Used in France, it referred to Rome, "beyond the mountains" (the Alps), and to the recognition of the jurisdiction of Rome and the pope over national churches, in particular the Church of France, which was traditionally Gallican, submissive to the monarch or subject to the Revolution and civil power. The ultramontanists not only challenged the spirit of the Revolution, which had declared the separation of church and state, and the predominance of civil power over religious power, but they promoted the alliance of church and state, the religious and the political.

The enthusiasm for Lamennais and the young French priests who were giving new inspiration to Christianity was combined in Lower Canada with a recent interest in Romanticism, Chateaubriand in particular. While Bernardin de Saint-Pierre had paved the way at the turn of the century, it was the Catholic Romanticism of *The Genius of Christianity* and *Les Martyrs*, by Chateaubriand – found in the 1816 catalogue of the Bossange bookstore – that attracted certain French Canadians.

The letter of the future superior of the Collège de Sainte-Anne-de-la-Pocatière, Abbé Charles-François Painchaud, to Chateaubriand on 19 January 1826, gives a sense of this enthusiasm. Painchaud said that he devoured the books of Chateaubriand, who had travelled in America, and confessed to sometimes having to set them down in order to "dry the abundant tears of religion and admiration." He was delighted that "this kind of defence" of Christianity had been formulated: "Thus, in these recent times, after the destructive storm of the French revolution that shook the physical and moral world, it took nothing less than a Bonald, a de Maistre and especially a Chateaubriand to cover with their impenetrable shields the reconstruction of the old temple." Saluting "the man of nature and the man of religion," he said: "The irresistible force of your arguments all the better closes the mouths of the philosophists, since they have not even the opportunity to criticize you, like the Church authors, for the controlled exercise of the trade, if we may express ourselves thus." Abbé Joseph-Sabin Raymond confessed to Chateaubriand on 4 April 1834: "At barely thirteen years of age, I began to read your books. *The Genius of Christianity* from then on accustomed my soul to sweet, tender feelings, to love and admiration for this religion of whose charms you told us ... A thousand times have I blessed my rhetoric teacher who put it in my hands ... I saw myself falling into your arms ... I consoled myself by going to draw new emotions from your books."[53] The alliance of clergy and laymen working to restore the genius of the Christian religion was welcome. The religious renewal in Lower Canada found its inspiration, its first breath, here, about 1820, around a nucleus of French counter-revolutionary priests – Mgr Plessis, Mgr Lartigue, and a few others.

In 1830, the Sulpicians were no longer the only ones to question the orthodoxy of the thought and writings of Lamennais, who had gone from an ultramontanist to seeking to reconcile the Catholic tradition with the liberties acquired in 1789, and in particular with the idea of the sovereignty of the people. Mgr Lartigue had to come to Lamennais's defence, supported by *La Minerve*, which quoted Lamennais and *Le Mémorial catholique*, for which he wrote, to defend Catholicism and liberty.[54] Priests in Lower Canada who read and circulated *Le Mémorial catholique* were soon subscribers to *L'Avenir* (16 October 1830), from Paris, which represented French liberal Catholics and took positions in favour of Italian liberals and, especially, patriotic Polish liberal Catholics, who were fighting for emancipation from Czarist Russia. Subjected to attacks, criticisms, and vigilance by Rome, *L'Avenir* suspended publication on 15 November 1831, and "the pilgrims of liberty" went to Rome

to make themselves heard by the pope (13 March 1832) at a time when
Lamennais had just published his *Essai d'un système de philosophie catholique*
(Essay on a Catholic system of philosophy). The suspension of *L'Avenir*
worried the admirers of Lamennais in Lower Canada; Mgr Lartigue
wrote to the future Cardinal Wiseman in Rome, asking him "what authority and disinterested individuals think and say to Rome about his
principles, for which we feel here no repugnance, and in which we see
nothing that is not Catholic, but that have been much reviled in the
Gallican Church." On 25 February, the superior of the Collège de Saint-
Hyacinthe, Abbé Prince, was confident that "Rome will pronounce no
condemnation, nor will show any disapproval with respect to doctrines
supported by *L'Avenir* ... But the Papal States are in a situation that gives
such alarms that it is difficult to obtain an examination and an explicit
judgment."[55] These people became prudent when *Le Canadien* published an article presenting the critical examination the Jesuit Rozaven
had made of Lamennais's writings.[56]

The encyclical *Mirari Vos* of 15 August 1832 condemned the doctrines
of *L'Avenir* – sovereignty of the people, freedom of conscience, freedom
of the press – reiterating the Church's position on the submission due
to princes, in this case, the submission of the Catholic Polish patriots to
the Czar of all the Russias. *Le Canadien* of 9 November 1832 published
the text of the encyclical, while *La Minerve* of 12 November made public the
letter of submission from the editors of *L'Avenir*, dated 10 September.
For Mgr Lartigue, the papal condemnation of the political positions of
L'Avenir did not undermine Lamennais's philosophical system, which
had been taught in Saint-Hyacinthe since 1830 and which the teachers
had learned during their studies at the Séminaire de Nicolet, in "Little
France," the homeland of the "French" priests. But for his colleague in
Quebec City, the encyclical should do "inexpressible good, especially
among priests attracted by La Mennais, and even to the misguided mind
of that learned priest."[57]

Lamennais's thought had been imported in 1819, during a first controversy on public education, and interest in it reached a new peak during another controversy, this one on the teaching of philosophy at the
Collège de Saint-Hyacinthe. During "public exercises" in August 1833,
during which philosophy students defended "two new theses," one on
the origin of ideas and the other on the basis of certainty, the philosophy
teacher, Abbé Raymond, had to intervene to defend students who were
being energetically questioned by Abbé Jacques Odelin. A Cartesian,
Abbé Odelin maintained that the basis of knowledge was individual reason, private sense, and the obvious authority of "Cogito ergo sum," while
the students and their teacher maintained, with Lamennais, that it was

general reason, common sense, and established authority. Two weeks after this public session at the college, the controversy moved to the newspapers, where it was hotly debated from August 1833 to September 1834. The stakes were clear: it was a matter of opposing the Protestant Reformation of individual examination, Cartesianism, the "philosophical century," and the contemporary antireligious schools in favour of "the greatest visible authority, the Catholic Church." The superior of the college explained clearly that the two different philosophies led to two different societies: "So in this struggle from which must result the fate of society, there are only two really opposed principles ... Two philosophies represent the expression of these principles as the basis of their teaching. One says to man: all that infallible reason presents as true to your mind, believe it, it is the truth. The other says to him: man, defy your reason, the weakness of which so many errors and prejudices have shown, yet an invincible propensity directs you to the search for truth; well, then, what the generality of your fellows admit, that is what you must believe to be true; individual reason can only be correct if it conforms to general reason."[58]

The most Mennaisian of the teachers at Saint-Hyacinthe, Abbé Raymond, informed the editor of *L'Avenir* of the intricacies of the controversy in April 1834, when Lamennais published *Paroles d'un croyant* (*Words of a Believer*), the testimony of a democratic priest who had recently quit all priestly functions and for whom the Gospels were the founding text of a social Christianity. In it, Lamennais celebrated "the holy cause of peoples" crushed by kings, and the "martyrs who die for the safety of the human family," while condemning "the kings of that day [who] nailed to a cross ... one whom they called seditious." He declared: "Liberty is no placard which one reads at the corners of streets. She is a living power which a man feels within himself and round about him." The tone of the book was that of a messianic epic poem: "And that day there shall be great terrors ... Kings will scream on their thrones"; "the heaven hath never before been so serene, nor the earth so green and fertile." It was also an incantation: "If, then, you remember not the instructions of Christ, at least remember the catacombs." Lamennais blessed the weapons of the soldier who would fight "so that all may have in heaven a God, and on earth a country." These words were well received in a Catholic society in which the Parti patriote was beginning to talk about a country and would publish a pirated edition of *Words* in 1836.[59]

Rome did not take as long to condemn this book as it had *L'Avenir*. The encyclical *Singulari Nos* of 24 June 1834 called it "the wicked fruit of impiety and daring," which contained "empty doctrines, futile and uncertain doctrines."[60] Rome had spoken, and submission by the

Lamennaisian clergy in Lower Canada followed. Mgr Lartigue said: "We have received from the Pope a Bull dated [24] June of this year and which formally condemns the book entitled *Words of a Believer*, although the system of La Mennais on certainty was not specifically designated, nevertheless, his philosophical ideas in general having been condemned, I forbid that in future at Collège de St-Hyacinthe anything be taught of the books, systems or doctrine of that Author, taken from his writings; and I even desire that his name or his authority not be mentioned in any way in teaching."

Abbé Prince, the superior of the college, also submitted publicly, invoking against Lamennais precisely the anti-Cartesian argument of the fallibility of individual reason. As for Abbé Raymond, in a single night, he wrote a "Mennaisian memorial," the publication of which was refused by Mgr Lartigue; he had wanted to explain "the wretched apostasy" of this "Napoleon of thought," "excessive genius in everything," of whom he said, "He has changed, that is his glory," while noting, "Our faith knows no metamorphoses." Mgr Lartigue went about collecting issues of *L'Avenir* that might still remain in the colleges and presbyteries, checking the catalogue of the library of the Collège de Saint-Hyacinthe and warning Abbé Prince and the Mennaisians: "Be on your guard against the bishop of Quebec City ... who speaks of nothing less than eliminating you from the Collège de St-Hyacinthe ... Behave yourselves with him and offend as little as possible the prejudices of other educational institutions, for we are threatened with a storm and we must bring back the diocesan bishop through consideration, respect and politeness."[61]

Shaken by this double political and doctrinal storm around the ideas of Lamennais, the teaching of philosophy soon returned to orthodoxy. On the same day that Abbé Raymond put behind him the Mennaisian current that had been so admired until 1834, Abbé Holmes of the Séminaire de Québec announced to the superior of the Collège de Saint-Hyacinthe that the philosophy textbook by Abbé Demers was about to be published: "In it, no system on the origin of ideas is embraced – the doctrines of the more famous philosophers on this subject, as on the means of Metaphysical and Moral certainty, are presented ... The demonstrations will be supported by principles admitted by all parties (I can hear you saying very softly that they will *therefore be based on* common sense). The origin of political power is the most thorny question, especially in these times. I hope that the Roman Curia will not be angered when we establish that civil power comes neither from princes nor from the people, but from God. *Non est potestas nisi a Deo.*"

Rome was not angered, and the *Institutiones philosophicae ad usum studiosae juventutis*, by Abbé Jérôme Demers, the first philosophy textbook published in Quebec, came out in early 1835. It presented proofs of the immortality of the soul and the existence of God, against the "systems of atheism."[62] The Collège de Saint-Hyacinthe would inherit this intellectual life, this indelible enthusiasm of youth; it was watched for possible Patriote tendencies in 1838, and in the middle of the century, it would become a centre spreading opposition to radical liberals such as Louis-Antoine Dessaulles.[63]

ENGLISH-LANGUAGE LIBRARIES

The development of the French Canadian press, associations, schools, and colleges shows that these cultural institutions were deeply affected by politics and the quest for power. Apart from a few magazines owned by Michel Bibaud, the press was political, if not partisan, and the English-language press was larger in proportion to the population than the French-language press. There were no lasting French Canadian associations created out of scientific, historical, or literary interest; the associations were patriotic, and they were involved in creating orators and writers until the Rebellions interrupted these endeavours. The literacy rate and the school enrolment rate were also higher in the English-speaking population, and this was also the case for cultural institutions, such as libraries and bookstores, that required a certain amount of capital in addition to education.

The libraries in Lower Canada were mostly English-language, sometimes bilingual, rarely French-language. There were no real public libraries despite certain of their names: Quebec Public Library / Bibliothèque publique de Québec and Montreal Public Library / Bibliothèque publique de Montréal. Rather, they were the libraries of various communities or groups – members of the House of Assembly or of the Legislature Council, college students, lawyers, or doctors, or associations with various interests. A "mutual" library envisaged by the residents of Saint-Charles-sur-Richelieu never saw the light of day.

The Quebec Public Library was owned by its subscribers, who numbered fifty-five in 1821 and 142 in 1832. Only 10 per cent of these owners were French-speaking, and in the catalogues of 1821 and 1832, one third and one quarter of the pages respectively were devoted to French-language books. When the Montreal Public Library was incorporated in 1819, one fifth of the petitioners were French-speaking. The collection included approximately 10 per cent French titles in 1824, hardly more in 1833, and 20 per cent when the library was merged with the Mercantile Library in 1843. Borrowers in Montreal in 1824 could choose from among classical French authors such as Corneille and Racine; translated novels by Sir Walter Scott; Chateaubriand's *Itinéraire de Paris à Jérusalem* and *Génie du christianisme*, counter-revolutionary works by Barruel, Berryer, and Fleury; and studies by Blackstone, Lolme, Bentham, Malthus, Ricardo, and Adam Smith. In Quebec City in 1832, the library offered, in its "Sciences, arts and literature" section, educational books for young people by Madame de Genlis and Madame Le Prince de Beaumont, the complete works of Madame de Staël, the *Confessions* of Rousseau, *The Wealth of Nations* by Adam Smith in French translation, and the *Encyclopédie* in thirty-five volumes. The most recent book in the *Catalogue* dated from 1829, and in the "Sciences, arts and literature" section, one title out of five was published after 1800.[64]

The library of the House of Assembly (1802–) and that of the Legislative Council (1802–) in Quebec City were open to the members of the assembly and the council, and other citizens on request. The library of the House had 137 titles in 1811; 1,151 in 1831; and 1,955 in 1841; the collection consisted mostly of law books – constitutional, English, French, and colonial law – general and American history, and literature.[65] One of the librarians, Georges-Barthélémy Faribault, put together a collection of books on America and Canada, which he described in a catalogue published in 1837. The library of the House of Assembly would play a primary role in furthering learning about parliamentary democracy by French Canadians, in historical research by people such as Dr Labrie and François-Xavier Garneau, and in the design of major canal and road construction projects undertaken by the colonial government.[66]

Members of the bourgeoisie in the liberal professions, soldiers, and associations with various interests established libraries for themselves: the libraries of lawyers and of the Quebec City and Montreal Bars, the Garrison Library in Quebec City, the libraries of the Société médicale de Québec and the McGill Medical School, the libraries of the Literary and Historical Society of Quebec and the Montreal Natural History Society, as well as the libraries of the colleges / seminaries in Quebec City, Montreal, Saint-Hyacinthe, Nicolet, and Sainte-Anne-de-la-Pocatière. The anglophone community very quickly adopted the model of the Scottish and English Mechanics' Institute, which included a library, and opened such institutes in Montreal (1828) and Quebec City (1831).[67] These libraries often had limited collections; they met the specific needs of their owners and reached a limited public.

If you were not an owner / subscriber of a public library, a member of the Assembly, a lawyer or a member of an association, you could rent books from a "circulating library." Once again, these libraries were the initiatives, or rather, the businesses, of anglophones, except in the case of Germain Langlois in Quebec City. In Montreal, circulating libraries were opened by Laughlin (1818), Nickless and McDonald (1819), and Miller (1828); in Quebec City, Thomas Cary ran a circulating library as of 1797, and the subscriber of 1830 who wanted to read French books had a choice of eight hundred titles in the catalogue – out of a total of 5,314 – including books by Corneille, Racine, Fénelon, Molière, La Fontaine, Bossuet, Rousseau, and *Gil Blas, Don Quixote, Paul et Virginie, Les liaisons dangereuses,* Madame de Staël's *De la littérature, Robinson Crusoe,* the French translation of *Gulliver's Travels,* and the *Tableau de Paris* by Mercier in four volumes.[68]

When Alexis de Tocqueville visited a reading room in Quebec City in 1831, the tradition of this place for reading newspapers and magazines had already been in existence in Lower Canada for about fifteen years. The names – the Montreal News Room (1817 and 1829), the News Room and Exchange (1820), the Quebec Exchange and Library (1821), the News Room and Library in Montreal (1833) – clearly indicate the relationship between the newspaper and the stock exchange, between the need to read the press and the need to follow the market by means of business papers. What Tocqueville did spontaneously in Quebec City, French Canadian travellers also did abroad. A correspondent of *L'Écho du pays* mentioned the city of Ogdensburg and "the news rooms where you read two newspapers published in the village or those from other parts of the United States," while, in exile, Amédée Papineau went to the news room in Albany, New York. These news rooms, which were private businesses, show the growing importance of the press.[69]

The final place for reading was at home, in the privacy of a personal library, which could belong to a lawyer, a military officer, or a priest, and which could contain a few dozen or a few hundred books. It could also be the "library" of a more humble person, information on which is provided in an inventory after death. In Quebec City, from 1820 to 1829, for example, ninety private "libraries" have been identified in this way. They belonged mostly to members of the liberal professions, civil servants, and merchants; one third of the inventories after death of tradesmen contained books, and one fifth of those of farmers.[70] Of these "libraries," 62 per cent contained thirty or fewer titles, 30 per cent between thirty-one and three hundred titles and 8 per cent between 301 and 2,166 titles.[71] The owners were merchants, who possessed the most books (29 per cent of the total), then civil servants (22 per cent), members of the liberal professions (13 per cent), tradesmen (4 per cent), and farmers (0.65 per cent).[72] The books were mostly in English, although the owners were almost equally francophones (43 per cent) and anglophones (47 per cent). These "libraries" were very varied in content, in accordance with their owners; but novels, secular history, and civil law accounted for more than one third of the books, which were kept in the living room or on a simple shelf.[73]

FABRE, A MONTREAL BOOKSELLER

The retail book trade started to develop and become more specialized in the francophone community after 1815. Bossange, Fabre, and Dufort in Montreal and Fréchette in Quebec City benefited from the lifting of the European blockade and the resumption of normal circulation of goods across the Atlantic. But the specialization was relative: auctioneers were still very active in Quebec City and Montreal, with twenty-six book auctions in the period from 1816 to 1820 alone, ten of which offered lots of more than five hundred books. During the 1830s, printed catalogues for auctions show that some dozen lawyers, doctors, and merchants or their heirs disposed of their libraries. There were also books among the merchandise of peddlers who travelled the coast and the country.[74] The "booksellers" themselves had several occupations, such as printer, newspaper publisher, stationer, bookbinder, and the inventory of their businesses was quite diverse. Bossange offered a variety of imported products: mahogany night tables, French tapestries, glassware, fabrics, clothes, shoes, perfume and related items, and fine foods and wines. Fabre had paper, feathers, ink and pocketknives, as well as "a wide Assortment of silverware for Churches" and images of the Way of the Cross.[75] But the fact remains that in Montreal, for example, there were more anglophone bookstores, such as those of Lovell, McKay, Armour, Mower, and Merrifield.[76]

Books and bookstores were becoming more visible through catalogues and advertising. Doige's list (1819) and McKay's and then Lovell's annual directories allow us to identify and locate businesses selling books in Montreal. There were more and more advertisements for books in the press. In Quebec City, from 1820 to 1839, in the *Gazette de Québec / Quebec Gazette* and, especially, *Le Canadien*, there were 8,961 book titles mentioned in 631 advertisements, a third of which included more than five titles. The Neilson bookstore (later called Neilson and Cowan) alone accounted for half of all book advertising from 1764 to 1839.[77] In Montreal, from 1816 to 1822, Bossange published nearly sixty advertisements in *L'Aurore*, *Le Spectateur*, the *Montreal Gazette*, the *Herald*, and the *Canadian Courant*.[78]

Booksellers and customers mostly used catalogues to promote or select books. We know of at least a dozen from 1815 to 1840, and Fabre published five, including three that were more than a hundred pages long. Catalogues and advertisements provide information on the supply of books, but not on the demand or on actual reading. The titles in newspaper advertisements were mostly in belles-lettres, law, and history.[79] Among the titles advertised from 1764 to 1839, the authors most represented (thirty titles or more) were Sir Walter Scott, François Fénelon, Oliver Goldsmith, Samuel Johnson, Voltaire, Cicero, Montesquieu, Alain-René Lesage, Bossuet, and Shakespeare.[80]

The June 1837 catalogue of the Fabre bookshop in Montreal provides a good overview of the reading material offered in the store, which belonged to a rich Patriote and was a meeting place for the Patriotes' permanent central committee. In the catalogue, fifty-seven pages describe titles in literature and history; forty pages, titles in religion and piety; ten pages, titles in law and jurisprudence; and eight pages, titles in medicine. Colleges and students could find the classics of humanities courses: *Traité des études* by Rollin; *Principes de belles lettres et de littérature* by Batteux; *Cours de littérature ancienne et moderne* by Laharpe; literary histories by Villemain and by Guizot, the latter published in 1830; Fénelon; La Bruyère; La Fontaine; Montaigne; and Sir Walter Scott in seventy-three volumes. Mothers could find works by Madame de Genlis, Madame Le Prince de Beaumont, and Madame de Renneville on maternal love or child rearing. Customers interested in discussions of ideas had many choices. Those interested in the counter-revolutionary movement could find books by Abbés Fleury, Gaume, Bergier (*Le déisme réfuté*), Barruel (*Les Helviennes*), Count de Maistre, or Viscount de Bonald. Those interested in Romanticism could find *Paul et Virginie* by Bernardin de Saint-Pierre; *Itinéraire de Paris à Jérusalem, Les Natchez*, and *Voyages en Italie et en Amérique* by Chateaubriand; and *Corinne, Delphine*, and *Lettres sur l'Angleterre* by Madame de Staël. The Lamennais section included *La religion considérée dans ses rapports avec l'ordre politique et civil* and *Imitation de Jésus-Christ*, which he translated, but more books about Lamennais – by Rozaven, Guillon (*Histoire de la Nouvelle Hérésie du xixe siècle, ou réfutation complète des ouvrages de l'abbé de LaMennais*), Mgr Tharin (on *Words of a Believer*), and Vidal (*Paroles d'un catholique, ou défense de l'ordre social*). Montesquieu, Benjamin Constant, John Stuart Mill, and Simondi were also in the catalogue. Titles on America included *Democracy in America* by Tocqueville; *System pénitentiaire aux États-Unis* by Tocqueville and Gustave de Beaumont; the novel *Marie, ou de l'esclavage aux États-Unis* by Beaumont; the works of Pradt; travel accounts by Mackenzie and by Weld; as well as *Le Réveil*, a French newspaper from New York. Among the titles from Lower Canada, there were textbooks: an arithmetic book by Bibaud and one by Ladreyt; *Abrégé de géographie* by Abbé Holmes; a French grammar book by Lemoult, one by Potel, and an English one by Meilleur; a textbook on rhetoric from the Collège de Montréal; *Institutiones philosophicae* by Abbé Demers; a *Petit Catéchisme de Québec* and a *Grand Catéchisme de Québec*; a book by Abbé Maguire, published in Paris, on parish administration; a history of Canada by Perrault and one by Smith; *Épîtres, satires et poèmes* by Bibaud; and *Hawkins' Picture of Quebec*. And finally, the new social presence of artisans was shown in the variety of manuals: for bookbinders, foundry workers, turners, coachbuilders, milliners and hosiers, brewers, bootmakers, gunsmiths, saddlers, and tailors.[81]

Francophone bookstores got their stock mainly from France after the end of the economic blockade, and these imports were significant: for example, twenty-five tonnes of books from 1824 to 1827, a third imported by Fabre from Bossange in Paris, one fifth by Augustin Germain in Quebec City, who shipped them himself from Paris. The Church continued to compete with bookstores by importing books directly. The Sulpicians relied on their colleagues in Paris, Abbé Holmes bought for the Séminaire de Québec and other educational institutions during a trip to Europe in 1836, and Abbé Maguire ordered titles from the bookseller-publisher Gaume.[82]

Between 1815 and 1844, progress was made toward the establishment of a publishing system in Lower Canada. Since 1764, the date when the first book was printed in the colony, books had been produced by printers, but around 1830, printer-bookseller alliances were established, of which the two leading figures were Neilson in Quebec City and Duvernay-Fabre in Montreal. Duvernay had solid finances: he printed and published *La Minerve*, and his shops produced one quarter of the titles published in Montreal from 1827 to 1837 – about thirty out of a total of 123, of which forty-six were in French – mostly school books and books on politics and religion, as well as calendars and almanacs.

Duvernay formed a decisive relationship with Fabre: a dozen of the titles he printed were sold in the Fabre bookstore. This was made possible by the growth of public education as a result of the Assembly Schools Act of 1829 and the new market for textbooks, both original and adapted from foreign books. Duvernay and Fabre published titles such as *Le maître français* and *Traité abrégé de la sphère* in 1829, *Nouvel Alphabet* in 1830, and *Abrégé de géographie du Canada* and *Histoire abrégée de l'Ancien Testament* in 1831. The associates also published religious books: *La Confrérie de Notre-Dame auxiliaire* in 1829, a prayer book in the Nipissing language in 1830 and *Exercices de piété* in 1832, the year of the cholera epidemic. Both Patriotes, Duvernay and Fabre distributed pamphlets by Papineau, Viger, Bourdages, Mailhot, and La Fontaine, which were also sold in the Fabre bookstore.[83] In 1836, Duvernay even printed a pirate edition of *Paroles d'un croyant* (*Words of a Believer*) by Lamennais, which was distributed under the counter, but two dozen copies of which were acquired by the library of the House of Assembly. For Mgr Lartigue, this book condemned by Rome constituted a "rebellion against the Church" and the clergy had to appear not to know about this edition. "I believe," he wrote to the bishop of Quebec City, "that, indeed, religion would only lose by it and the Clergy would be compromised; but by temporizing, we will have our turn." In September 1838, while Duvernay was in exile in Vermont, the forms for *Paroles d'un croyant* were even stolen from his shop.[84]

Fabre did not limit his publishing activity to his initiatives with Duvernay. He printed, or had printed by Louis Perrault, *Treatise on Agriculture, Chemin de la Croix, Syllabaire des écoles chrétiennes,* and *Cours d'histoire,* the latter for the Brothers of the Christian Doctrine, who arrived in Montreal in 1837. At Workman and Bowman, he had the *Catholic School Book* printed, which he sold in his bookstore.

THE LEVEL OF CULTURAL ADVANCEMENT OF LOWER CANADA ON THE EVE OF THE REBELLIONS

In a social history of ideas that combines culture and civic life, a question arises: on the eve of the first rebellion in November 1837, what was the level of cultural advancement of Lower Canada, and how could culture be the vehicle for a project of national emancipation? How did cultural, material, and symbolic communication make possible – or not – a shared consciousness and a national project for the people of Lower Canada if not for French Canadians?[85]

Material communication was provided by the St Lawrence, the "chemin du Roy," and twenty-six kilometres of railway between Saint-Jean-sur-Richelieu and La Prairie. In the case of the railway and that of navigation on the river, the new technology of steam had led to advances. The climate was a factor that both hindered and facilitated transportation: while the freeze-up put a halt to river navigation from late November to May and made coach transportation difficult in the spring, it also made it possible for sleighs, carioles, and carriages on runners to move quickly on the watercourses in winter. The Patriotes would take this into consideration, relying on the ice upstream in the river to prevent the arrival of British troop reinforcements. This type of communication provided links in an essentially rural society; only one in four localities at the time had from two thousand to three thousand inhabitants. Montreal, with a population of about forty thousand in 1837 and an anglophone majority – although a very slim majority – would be deserted by the Patriotes and their leader. As for Quebec City, with some thirty thousand inhabitants, the Patriotes would be less present there than reformists such as Étienne Parent and John Neilson, but above all, the colonial administration and the garrison occupied both the physical and the social space.

Material communication was also based on printed matter and oral communication. On the eve of the Rebellion of 1837, the press was well-established in Montreal (*La Minerve*, *The Vindicator*, and *L'Ami du peuple, de l'ordre et des lois*) and Quebec City (*Le Canadien* and *La Gazette de Québec*) and less so in Trois-Rivières and Saint-Charles-sur-Richelieu (*L'Écho du pays*). A sign of the times was an increase in the number of newspapers in 1837, with *La Quotidienne* and *Le Populaire* in Montreal and *Le Libéral* in Quebec City. The outbreak of the Rebellions would lead to the closure of Duvernay's crucial *La Minerve*, and while in exile, he would attempt to set up newspapers in Burlington and elsewhere in New England. While it was possible to publish in Montreal and Quebec City then, most publishing, other than political pamphlets, consisted of school books, as shown by the 1837 catalogue of the Fabre bookstore in Montreal in its Canadian section. There were histories of France, England, and the United States and inspirational books such as those by Chateaubriand, Lamennais, and the first Romantics in bookstores in Montreal and Quebec City, but libraries in Lower Canada were anglophone, with the exception of those of the House of Assembly and the Bar.

In a rural society, the oral communication network was varied: it included domestic and village sociability, the sociability of inns, which would play a significant role in organization in 1837, and the Catholic Church, whether outside the church, on the front steps, or inside, in the pulpit, which the two bishops frequently used for communicating their pastoral letters and circulars. There was also the network of voluntary associations. Among francophones, associations were then essentially patriotic and still not much concerned with scientific or literary matters. Duvernay, the owner of *La Minerve*, was the founder of the Association Saint-Jean-Baptiste, which he fervently hoped would spread "the precious sap of love of independence." The founding of the Aide-toi et le ciel t'aidera society in 1834, modelled on the French organization of the same name that came into being with the revolution of 1830, suggests that a new dynamic existed in francophone Lower Canada. This new reality was perceived by the Sulpicians, who likened it to the "old revolutionary clubs," and by Abbé Raymond, who identified it with Italian and Spanish secret societies. A few months before the Rebellion, which disrupted all cultural institutions and resources, a speaker declared to the society: "I believe that there is not enough intelligence and industry in all the classes of the people to be national. Nationality is the daughter of industry and science. And in our country, there is neither industry nor science." He thus marked the beginning, if not the limits, of the cultural and intellectual development of his society on the eve of the Rebellions. The same type of interrupted takeoff is seen in the world of education. Since the resistance to the "royal schools" plan in 1801, there was increasing controversy around education bills aiming to establish fabrique schools (1824) or Assembly schools (1829). The latter, however, had begun to show results in 1836, when the Legislative Council refused to extend the 1829 law; the number of schools, teachers, and students had grown remarkably, but it would be necessary to start over again after 1840. The literacy rate of the population of Lower Canada was then about 25 per cent; it was about 33 per cent in Quebec City and probably the same in Montreal. While they could count on seven classical colleges in 1837, French Canadians did not yet have a university, a place of potential erudition.

From a strictly territorial point of view, culture in Lower Canada in 1837 was, for francophones, essentially limited to Quebec City and Montreal, except, of course, for public education, which, until 1836, had been spreading somewhat to the countryside. Newspapers, associations, libraries, and bookstores were concentrated in the cities, but it should be realized that newspapers reached even illiterate rural inhabitants through reading out loud.

This state of affairs was reflected in intellectual production of novels, histories, and poetry. While the first two French Canadian novels were published in 1837, the interest in fiction began around 1820 and solidified after 1830 with Romanticism. Sir Walter Scott was known in francophone Lower Canada from 1818, Chateaubriand from 1812, and Lamartine from 1826. This pre-Romanticism was above all Catholic and was understood as a way to promote the "genius of Christianity"; it was also in this intellectual current that interest developed, here and elsewhere, for the ideas of the "second" Lamennais, who was beginning to support liberal values. The Romantic novel, a genre that was not yet very popular in Lower Canada, was marked by a new attraction to nature, exoticism, the gothic, and Indians. From 1827 to 1837, there were many short narratives about Indians. Exoticism was made popular by Chateaubriand and also by James Fenimore Cooper, the "American Walter Scott," as he was called in an article in *La Minerve*. But tellingly, it was the French writers Isidore Lebrun and Philarète Chasles who encouraged Canadian writers to draw inspiration from the "American muse."[86]

After 1830, the literate public in Lower Canada became familiar with French literature through bookstores and libraries, but above all, through serials. *L'Ami du peuple* published Balzac in serial form starting in 1835 and the prospectus of a newspaper with the revealing title *Le Glaneur* (the gleaner) proposed: "we would reproduce a few selected pieces from Chateaubriand, Lamennais, Dumas, Janins, Victor Hugo and many other writers that illustrate France today." *Le Populaire* of 10 April 1837 described areas that could be exploited by an epic or picaresque "national literature": "a new, original, heroic, attractive, piquant, brilliant and sublime nature that would be appreciated and sought after in old Europe, where the literary merit of each people of the world does not lack enlightened admirers." This, in part, is what was featured in the first two – short – novels published in Lower Canada: *Le Chercheur de trésors, ou de l'influence d'un livre* (*The Influence of a Book*) by Philippe Aubert de Gaspé *fils*, which took its subject from the oral tradition, and *Les révélations du Crime, ou Cambray et ses complices* by François-Réal Angers, which was based on social and judicial chronicles of the time. It is telling that both "novelists" were parliamentary reporters of the House of Assembly debates for the newspapers. But this advance had its limits: critics condemned de Gaspé for not representing "Canadian mores," and when Napoléon Aubin published a prospectus in *Le Canadien* of 17 December 1838 for the *Répertoire de la littérature canadienne*, a publication that would permit Canadian literature to take its place "with honour in the brilliant legion of contemporary literatures," the initiative did not attract enough subscribers.[87]

Political life and the development of the press, publishing, and schools made possible the existence of the first publishers and authors. Those producing school books included Lemoult and Potel, editors of the *Nouveau cours complet de grammaire* (1830) and *L'Enseignement universel* (1831), J.-B. Boucher de Belleville, author of the *Nouvelle grammaire française* (1831), and J.-B. Meilleur, author of the *Cours abrégé de leçons de chymie* (1833). Those producing political pamphlets or fiction included Firmin Prudhomme, author of *Napoléon à Sainte-Hélène: Scènes historiques* (1831), and Michel Bibaud, author of *Épîtres, satires, chansons, épigrammes et autres pièces en vers* (1830).

Bibaud, an author who came out of anonymity, exemplifies the emergence of the figure of "the writer." He created a tradition of collections or "miscellanea"; he wrote or published the *Bibliothèque canadienne* (1825–30) and *Le magasin du Bas-Canada* (1832), followed, after the Union, by *Les mélanges religieux* (1840–52), *L'Encyclopédie canadienne* (1842–43), the "albums" of *La Revue canadienne* (1846–48), and *La Minerve* (1849–51). Over the issues and the years, his periodicals "collected" his poetic and historical "works," and Bibaud the author developed a way of doing things that became established with time: typesetting and publication first in instalments and then as a book.

The fact is that it was not easy for an author of fiction to get published. The novel as a genre had a bad reputation unless it was moralistic. And when Aubert de Gaspé *fils* wanted to publish his *Influence d'un livre* in September 1837, he used a dual approach, publishing excerpts in a periodical and also soliciting subscriptions. De Gaspé wrote to his friend L.-T. Drummond in February 1837: "Here I am, an author. And as you might have expected, I am asking for your patronage while awaiting your opinion on the little book I am going to publish ... You would do me a great service if you would circulate a subscription list for me in Montreal." To cover the printing cost of £64, de Gaspé needed 256 subscriptions of five shillings per copy. *Le Télégraphe* of 14 April, in Quebec City, and *Le Populaire* of 21 April, in Montreal, advertised the opening of the subscription campaign, which was also posted in the offices of various newspapers, in the Albion Hotel and in C.-P. Leprohon's Librairie canadienne, in Montreal, which would sell the novel.[88]

Authors had to have subscribers because publishing activity was still minimal, and, consequently, they had no legal existence or economic rights before the Act for the Protection of Copy Rights was passed by the House of Assembly in 1832. And still, it took some time before the law was applied. It recognized for authors of "literary publications," engravings, maps, and works of music, as well as their "executors, administrators or legal assigns," a property right of twenty-eight years starting from the date of registration of the work with the clerk of the Superior Court of their district. This right, which could be extended for fourteen years, was recognized as long as the registration was mentioned in the published book.[89]

Publishing of books on history was also in its infancy, at a time when people were still referring to the *Histoire et description générale de la Nouvelle-France* (1744), by the Jesuit Charlevoix. Bibaud published his articles on history in his magazines, along with others by Dr Jacques Labrie and Jacques Viger. These texts and the calls for a history of the country may have been inspired by *Beautés de l'histoire du Canada* by Philarète Chasles under the name of Dainville, which was published in 1821 by Bossange in Paris. Dr Labrie completed a voluminous manuscript on the history of Canada in 1831, but it went unread during the Rebellion of 1837. The notary and teacher Joseph-François Perrault published his *Abrégé d'histoire du Canada* in five parts between 1832 and 1836, at the same time as his column, "Histoire du Canada," was appearing in *L'Écho du pays*. Bibaud collected his history writings and in 1837 published *Histoire du Canada sous la domination française*, which was very political and descriptive but rather uninspired. François-Xavier Garneau, who is considered the first national historian, had copied historical documents in London during a stay in Europe from 1831 to 1833. While the first volume of his *Histoire du Canada* was only published in 1845, he announced in 1837 that he intended to write a proper history of his country, and between February and August, he published some twenty texts on "battles waged in Canada" in *Le Canadien*, which belonged to his friend Parent. His friend Georges-Barthélémy Faribault, librarian of the House of Assembly library, published the *Catalogue d'ouvrages sur l'histoire de l'Amérique*, listing some thirty titles after 1800. While the political struggle of the Parti canadien and then the Parti patriote had revived memories of the constitutional battles fought since 1763 and contributed to defining the elements of a national identity, the epic celebration of those battles and of French Canadian nationality had not yet, on the eve of the Rebellions, found true historical expression.[90]

The quest for national identity and its celebration may be seen especially in poetry, by authors who were often anonymous, scattered in the press of the period. Along with studiously constructed poetry in verse, based on the pantheon of Greek and Latin mythology or unabashedly partisan, there were expressions of indignation, ringing appeals to patriotism and moving declarations for the oppressed and against tyrants. Poets wrote about specific issues or events, such as the civil list or the election riot of May 1832; they celebrated the "liberator" Papineau, asking people to understand "That arms can take back / Rights won by arms." Napoléon Aubin prophesied: "Perhaps one day, our peaceful habitant / Will grow weary of the heavy yoke of a king." Duvernay pronounced: "My last wishes will be against tyranny / And my last cry FREEDOM!" George-Étienne Cartier proclaimed his country and his loves and declared, "Above all, I am a Canadian": "Originally from France, / Today subjects of Albion, / To which to give preference / One or the other nation? / But have we not, I pray you, / Still more powerful bonds? / To everything, we prefer the Homeland, / Above all, let us be Canadians." Viger and Aubin took up the refrain of the homeland, while Joseph-Isidore Bédard recognized that while "proud Albion" was keeping watch, there were "tyrants" in the colony. Bibaud, who published the first poetry collection in 1830, described the place of the poet in the chorus of emerging nations: "If orators are needed to maintain my laws, / Valiant warriors to defend my rights; / I have no less need of poets, / To sing my successes and publish my celebrations! / Without them, I could not claim, / To associate myself, by right, among the nations."[91]

Before 1837, consciousness of identity among French Canadians found its fullest expression in the motto of the "new" *Le Canadien* of 1831: "Our institutions, our language and our laws." This motto recalled that French laws still applied in many areas, that the seigneurial regime and the Catholic religion were still among "our" institutions, and that the French language had been constitutionally maintained in the House of Assembly. With the ploughman in its masthead, *Le Canadien*, a symbol of resistance and affirmation since 1810, summed up French Canadian identity in its motto: the francophone Canadian lived in a Catholic society with seigneurial land tenure and a French legal system. Could this consciousness of identity have been found before 1837 in a popular or national song? The press clearly paid attention to the national and popular anthems of different peoples and the patriotic songs of Spain ("El Himno de Riego") or Greece ("Navarino"); but before the famous "Le Canadien errant," which came after the Rebellions, can it really be said that the "patriotic songs of Canada" – with lyrics such as "dream of freeing yourself," "Form a nation," and "Oh, land of America, everything makes you sovereign" – were a rallying point?[92]

There was a marked emergence of national symbols after 1832: the 24 June banquets that, at the initiative of the Association Saint-Jean-Baptiste, were decorated with maple leaves and laden with meats and products of the country, the banners at Patriote demonstrations – "Papineau, source of freedom," "Flee, tyrants, for the people are awakening" – the decorations of maple boughs and the "freedom columns." All these symbols converged in the Patriote flag, which was often flown but whose meaning was indeterminate because it was multiple. There was no argument about the choice of the horizontal colours – red, white, green – of this Canadian "tricolour" that Upper Canada would also have adopted, but there is no agreement today on the multiple meanings of those colours: green for the Irish, white for the French, red for the British; or Liberty, Equality, Fraternity for the republicans; or Faith, Hope, Charity for the Christian Patriotes? Does anyone remember that some descriptions of the flag include two stars on the white band, which are said to have been added during the first days of combat? What should we make of the description given in *La Gazette de Québec* on the occasion of the public assembly in the county of Deux-Montagnes on 1 June 1837 – "the *national flag of Canada*, a tricolour, (red, white and green); emblems, a beaver, a maple branch and a fish (muskellunge)" – a copy of which is in the Château Ramezay Museum?[93]

CONCLUSION

The cultural development of Lower Canada came about through the affirmation of new social actors, the bourgeoisie in the liberal professions, and the new situation did not go unnoticed by the Catholic and Protestant clergy.

This new bourgeoisie, which came together in the Parti canadien and then in the Parti patriote, soon, along with French-speaking merchants, provided the majority of members in the House of Assembly. This rising bourgeoisie and its occupation of the political stage contributed to the politicization of public life, in particular its cultural dynamics.

The press, which often served as the organ of the House of Assembly and the Parti patriote, was the forum for debates between francophones and anglophones, between Patriotes and Constitutionalists, between the bourgeoisie and the Catholic clergy, which was seeing the power of the pulpit disputed by the new network of newspapers yet failed to establish an official press for the Church. The clergy did, however, have the unofficial newspaper of the Sulpicians, *L'Ami du peuple, de l'ordre et des lois*, which would play a decisive role in the Montreal opposition to the Patriotes' views. The presence of journalists among the Patriotes and the extensive use of the press and printed matter (pamphlets, arrest warrants, posters, proclamations, circulars to the clergy, episcopal pastoral letters) by the Patriotes, the Loyalists, the political authorities, and the clergy would again confirm, if need be, the politicization of print culture.

This politicization of the public sphere also affected associations, which were often the origin of community libraries and future public libraries. While anglophone associations were cultural (the Literary and Historical Society of Quebec, the Montreal Natural History Society) or national (the St George's, St Andrew's, and St Patrick's societies), francophone associations were essentially patriotic before 1840. The same was true for the schools question, where the political objective was social control of the education system. The stakes are summed up perfectly in the names of the school laws passed in 1824 and in 1829: the Fabrique Schools Act and the Assembly Schools Act, respectively.

From the point of view of the history of printed matter, it is precisely this combination of politics and education that made publishing – or rather, printing – possible and viable: printer and bookseller worked together to publish school texts and political pamphlets. The author also came into being in this context, as the writer of grammars or pamphlets, while the poet (Bibaud) and the novelists (de Gaspé and Angers) were, each in his own sphere, unique cases before 1840.

Censure by the Church was aimed at politics, as is shown by the condemnation of the liberal press and *L'Avenir* of Paris in the encyclical *Mirari Vos* of 1832, the attack on the liberal ideas of Lamennais's *Words of a Believer* in *Singulari Nos* in 1834, and the bishops' vigilance regarding the pirate edition of *Words of a Believer* published by Duvernay in 1836.

The second important factor marking the development of culture in the colony was the international situation after the signature of the Treaty of Vienna in 1815. The general effect of the treaty was to normalize the circulation of people, goods, and ideas after the lifting of the economic blockade put in place by Napoleon. Specific effects were the expansion of British immigration, with its impact on the population in Lower Canada, and the resumption of cultural imports such as books and luxury goods between Lower Canada and France.

British immigration and the natural growth of the population led to an increase in population density, which was reflected in the development of the press: of the forty-two newspapers published in Lower Canada from 1815 to 1840, there were twenty-four published in Montreal, eight in Quebec City, and ten in a few towns big enough to ensure their viability. However, before 1840, the density of the francophone community was not sufficient to permit the establishment of cultural voluntary associations, libraries, or bookstores outside of Quebec City and Montreal.

But in those cities, the anglophone community applied all its resources in the area of culture. Several factors explain the preponderance of the anglophone community in culture. The merchants had the means to carry out cultural initiatives; originally from the metropolis, they were educated and familiar with its cultural institutions and its economic corridors. The British immigrants settled mainly in the cities, where cultural institutions could be set up more easily and quickly.

The cultural presence of anglophones was visible in the press: 50 per cent of the titles published from 1815 to 1840 were in English, when anglophones made up only about 15 per cent of the total population of Lower Canada. The cultural (historical, literary, scientific) associations were also anglophone; they would be adopted and adapted by francophones after 1840. The libraries of the different communities or interest groups were mostly anglophone or, sometimes, bilingual – as in the case of those of the liberal professions – but rarely francophone, except for those of the classical colleges. The vast majority of the members of subscription libraries – the Quebec Library and the Montreal Library – were anglophones. This was also the case for circulating libraries and reading rooms, or news rooms. While inventories after death reveal that owners of personal libraries were both anglophone and francophone, these libraries overall contained more books in English. The bookstores in Montreal and Quebec City were also mostly anglophone, although the lifting of the economic blockade made it possible to establish lasting francophone bookstores in those cities after 1815.

It is not surprising, finally, that the anglophones of Lower Canada had higher levels of education and literacy than the francophones. They lived in urban centres by choice and by professional status; they were Protestants and read the Bible.

Furthermore, during this period, there was no connection established between liberalism and Catholicism. It was a decisive time. The hopes created in Poland and Belgium by Lamennais and his friends at *L'Avenir* were dashed by the two papal encyclicals of 1832 and 1834 condemning Lamennais's philosophical ideas and politics. In Montreal and Saint-Hyacinthe, young clerics who had been enthusiastic about Lamennais's ideas submitted to the authority of bishop and pope, leaving to the Patriotes the pirate publication of *Words of a Believer*, to Papineau a friendship to be established with Lamennais (1839), and to Papineau's Dessaulles nephews an enduring admiration (1839) for the author of *Les Affaires de Rome*. This was a turning point that would have a profound impact on the history of French Canadian liberalism, which was not going to be able to rely on Catholicism to establish a regime of liberties suited to the various currents of thought. From 1835 on, liberalism was on its guard, and the political future would belong to those who would find a regime other than that of "a free Church in a free State" or that of "separation."

To what extent was the culture a vehicle for a national project in 1837? How advanced culturally was this project? While the culture of the French Canadians imitated that of the anglophones, it clearly had its own dynamics. Except for schools, cultural institutions were concentrated in two cities, Quebec City and Montreal, which, tellingly, and for different reasons, would not play an important role in the actual rebellions. These cultural institutions also had limitations: there were seven classical colleges but no French-language university, and very few libraries or bookstores outside Quebec City and Montreal. The press was the most dynamic means of communication, and it should be emphasized that in opposition to the pro-Patriote papers such as *La Minerve* and *The Vindicator*, there were the Neilson family's *La Gazette de Québec*, Parent's *Le Canadien*, and the Sulpicians' *L'Ami du peuple*, the vitality of which has been underestimated.

Except for poetry, symbolic production was in its early stages: the first novel appeared in 1837, as did the first history, which Garneau tackled after a few attempts by Bibaud, Viger, and Labrie. Authors were still teachers preparing textbooks or politicians writing pamphlets; true writers were yet to come, and they would rely on subscriptions to establish a readership. The first signs of the promotion of a "national literature" coincided with a project to create a directory of Canadian literature, which would not see the light of day until ten years later.

A symbolic and historical consciousness was beginning to be articulated, finding its main impetus in patriotic poetry inspired by contemporary Romanticism, with much of the Catholic accent of Chateaubriand. Patriotism permeated the press, poetry, and associations, whether the Aide-toi et le ciel t'aidera society or the Association Saint-Jean-Baptiste. There were more and more national symbols, but none was really established yet. Were the Patriote flag and the motto of *Le Canadien* – "Our institutions, our language and our laws" – the most advanced symbols of the national consciousness on the eve of the Rebellions? If so, they were still rather indeterminate: the flag had a variable heraldry, and the "nationality" of *Le Canadien* was still not explicit.

6

Lower Canada and the Colonial
and National Liberation Movements
in Europe and the Americas
(1815–1837)

WHILE LOWER CANADA waited for a response to the 92 Resolutions, a perceptible cultural breakthrough was taking place against the backdrop of rising political and constitutional tensions, with rapid growth of schools, the press, associations, and patriotic poetry. These rising tensions and cultural development were combined with the international ferment that followed the end of the Napoleonic Wars and the Treaty of Vienna of 1815, which in the 1830s took the form of movements for colonial and national liberation. To understand the Rebellions of 1837 and 1838, we must take into account these three key elements: colonial politics, colonial cultural development, and liberation movements in Europe and the Americas.

In this regard, three questions arise about the Patriotes and their political leaders: What did they know about the liberation movements in Europe (Italy, Greece, Belgium, Poland, Ireland) and America (Argentina, Chile, Colombia, Mexico)? What ideological and political use did they make of that knowledge? Finally, did they formulate the principle of nationality, that is, the right of peoples to self-determination, for Lower Canada? There are numerous sources to help answer these questions. There are newspapers, first and foremost: sixteen weeklies or biweeklies, including one bilingual one, the Neilson family's *Quebec Gazette / La Gazette de Québec*, and one English-language one, *The Vindicator*, the voice of the pro-Patriote Irish. Of these, eleven were published in Montreal, four in Quebec City, and one, *L'Écho du pays*, in Saint-Charles-sur-Richelieu.[1] We can also draw on the writings of journalists and public figures – Papineau, Parent, Garneau, Viger – including those of the Patriotes (resolutions, declarations, addresses, memoirs, personal papers, correspondence). The Church's point of view on the international situation was expressed in pastoral letters, correspondence, pamphlets, and one newspaper, *L'Ami du peuple*, the voice of the Sulpicians in Montreal. Finally, the travel journals of Mgr Plessis, Mgr Lartigue, Pierre-Jean de Sales Laterrière, and especially François-Xavier Garneau show how travellers perceived Europe after the Treaty of Vienna.

One question arises at the outset: how did information on the Catholic Emancipation in Ireland or the November Uprising in Warsaw reach the ordinary country or city dweller in Lower Canada? The same question can be asked about the social penetration of the ideas of Papineau, Parent, or Mgr Lartigue, or the ideas of the Greek or Argentine revolution. This has to do with the place of printed matter in a rural society with an oral culture, where the majority of the population was not literate. Access to newspapers – which were increasing in number – was limited, but not only to subscribers or to literate people. Journalistic information circulated among those who knew how to read – 25.4 per cent between 1830 and 1839 – but it also reached the non-literate through being read aloud on church steps or in inns. Conscious of their peasant readership, the editors of newspapers even created dialogues between ordinary people to discuss issues such as the Irish question in vivid, simple terms. And printed matter was also transmitted by the bishop, who sent pastoral letters to priests, who would read them from the pulpit and refer to them during their homilies or in the confessional.

INTERNATIONAL INFORMATION
IN THE LOWER CANADA PRESS

"The steamer *Columbia,* which arrived in New York City last week, brought newspapers from England up to 2 July," *Le Spectateur canadien* of 17 August 1822 told its readers. This is the leitmotif that marks the beginning of "foreign correspondence" for the press of Lower Canada. The distance, the ocean, storms and lulls were all constraints to the transmission of news before the telegraph and the Atlantic cable. The editors of newspapers went from abundance to shortage of news, which delighted or dismayed them, the latter especially between parliamentary sessions, when material to fill their pages could be scarce.

The Lower Canada press thus relied on the arrivals of ships, and usually specified the sources of news and excerpts. The main source for *Le Canadien* and *La Minerve* was the American press: often the *Commercial Advertiser* or other newspapers from New York City (the *New York Columbian, New York Journal,* and *New York Evening Post*), Boston (the *Boston Palladium, Sentinel,* and *Pilot*), or Baltimore (the *Federal Gazette,*

Republican, and *Baltimore American*), or French-language American newspapers such as *L'Abeille américaine* from New Orleans, and *Le Courrier des États-Unis* from New York City. They also quoted newspapers from Chile, Bogotá, and Caracas, as well as *El Noticioso* of Havana. The British newspapers most used were the *London Morning Chronicle, Bell's Messenger*, and *Bell's Weekly Dispatch*. French news most often came from *Le Constitutionnel, Le Moniteur de Paris, L'Ami des lois*, and the French *La Minerve*.

Newspapers also published excerpts from books: *Le cri des peuples* by Crevel, *Le droit des gens* by Vattel, *Histoire de la révolution actuelle de la Grèce* by Blaquières, *Des trois derniers mois de l'Amérique méridionale et du Brésil* by Pradt, *Voyage au Mexique, au Chili et au Pérou* (*Extracts From a Journal Written on the Coasts of Chili, Peru, and Mexico in the years 1820, 1821, 1822*) by Hall, *De l'Amérique* by Azaïs, *De la révolution piémontaise* by Santarosa, and *L'histoire constitutionnelle de l'Angleterre* (*Constitutional History of England*) by Hallam. The editors were concerned with the history and statistics of countries; they borrowed from Avenel's *Annuaire historique universel* for 1824 and published statistics on the countries of Europe and on Turkey.[2]

Because of the uncertainties of the supply, sources of news had to be diversified: the foreign press, books, yearbooks. How many texts on the international situation began with the phrase "It appears that"? The editor of *Le Spectateur canadien* admitted that there was "nothing more obscure, more uncertain and more contradictory" than the possibility of intervention by Russia in Turkey. During the Greco-Turkish conflict, *La Minerve* expressed doubt about the London Protocol signed by Great Britain, France, and Russia, as published by an Augsburg newspaper, "a newspaper, it is true, that is one of the most justly respected in Europe" but whose information, "it seems to us, is not yet endowed with an official nature which would permit us to acknowledge its truth without examination. We also wished to call into doubt the existence of this document, which has defeated so much hope, smashed so many noble illusions. Unfortunately, we are forced today to recognize the authenticity of this document, which re-imposed on Greece a part of the yoke it had itself just thrown off, and with pain we place it before the eyes of our readers." Nor were the correspondents of certain French Canadians fooled by the particular reading the English press could make of the situation of France at the time of the Holy Alliance; one of them wrote to Abbé de Calonne: "I warn you, however, not to believe everything that is said in the English papers about our situation; because that would alarm you too much. The fact is that it is improving every day, that the spirit is getting better and that we are beginning to appreciate the paternal kindness of our dear King." After the Austrian victory over the Kingdom of Naples, the editor of *Le Spectateur canadien* wrote: "Meanwhile, everything that will come off the presses of Naples will have to be considered as the expression of the sentiments of Austria and not those of the Neapolitan nation."[3]

Newspaper editors sought to establish the credibility of information by reproducing "official" documents: declarations from the courts of Austria, Prussia, or Russia; the declarations of independence of South American countries; proclamations by Santander or Santa Anna; speeches by Ypsilantis to the Greek patriots or by Ferdinand VII to the Spanish Cortes; an abridged version of the Spanish constitution; a letter by San Martín; the oath of the Mexican members of the legislature; the capitulation of Spain in Mexico. In a few cases, the reproduction of the same document in two or three newspapers indicates a shared perception of its importance, or a common source or borrowing from each other.

Thus, international news in the press of Lower Canada took three forms: news of events, most often military and political; analyses or studies of varying length excerpted from different sources; anonymous opinion pieces from newspapers the main writers of which were sometimes known.

FRANCE IN 1815

Taking advantage of popular discontent over the return of the Bourbons, Napoleon returned from the island of Elba, landing at Golfe-Juan on 1 March 1815. The adventure of the Hundred Days would end at Waterloo on 18 June.

The news arrived in Canada in the second half of March, and Mgr Plessis told the Sulpician Roux: "The new revolution has stupefied minds as it has chilled hearts." Pierre-Jean de Sales Laterrière, who arrived in Bordeaux in May 1815, found himself in the midst of the events. He noted in his *Journal de voyage* that he "very quickly entered the lodgings, seeing that the weather was not good outside, the cannon encountered in the streets and the tumult that seemed to be there did not give me very favourable ideas about my situation." The cannon were there, Laterrière said, to force the inhabitants to recognize the emperor, and he considered it advisable to identify himself as an American rather than a citizen of a British colony.

It was obvious to the priests of "Little France" on the shores of Lac Saint-Pierre that there would be no peace in Europe until Napoleon was "destroyed." *Le Spectateur canadien* shared the view that without a navy, Napoleon would still disrupt peace in Europe. The clergy was worried about how the situation was developing, in particular about what might happen to their gains from the Bourbon Restoration; a correspondent of Abbé de Calonne wrote to him on 20 March: "Things are not going marvellously in France and neither the choice of the men in place nor the

institutions are reassuring for the future existence of the legitimate monarchy, morality and religion." Three years later, with the Restoration assured, the nephew of Abbé Raimbault hailed "the reign that gives us
back to ourselves." But the young Étienne Parent, who had just joined *Le
Canadien*, quickly asked the right questions: "Long live liberty, long live
the King, but long live the Ministry?"[4]

NAPLES AGAINST THE BOURBONS AND AUSTRIA

Beginning in May 1820, the press of Lower Canada covered the insurrec-
tion in the Kingdom of Naples, where the king was replaced by his son.
Readers were informed that the revolution was spreading to Sicily and
Piedmont.[5]

For *Le Spectateur canadien*, not only might the Romans and the
Sardinians want to imitate the Neapolitans, but the Lombards and the
Venetians could also rise up against Austria. A victory in Naples could
mobilize the other peoples of Italy and Sicily and "set things in motion
in the rest of Italy." For *Le Canadien*, the events in Naples constituted a
"revolution very pleasing to the friends of freedom."[6]

The Holy Alliance did not get very good press: the events related to
the attempted unification of Italy "revealed the previously hidden
thoughts and intentions of the absolute sovereigns," that "league of
Despots" who had displeased the peoples of Europe by imposing tyrannical reigns on them by arms, against their wishes. Austria was especially
targeted; *Le Spectateur canadien* recalled that subjects were not "solely
made for the pleasure of sovereigns, and nations to be the pastures of
governments." Despite the fact that "Metternich seems to be suggesting
that a free constitution in a state is like a monster in nature" and the view
"that despotism only is in keeping with order, reason and religion," the
paper felt that it might be "conjectured that that constitutional obsession
will spread in spite of all the efforts of the despotic sovereigns of Austria,
Prussia and Russia."[7]

GREECE AGAINST TURKEY

International tension shifted to Greece in 1821. The press of Lower
Canada followed the events: the non-recognition of the independence
of the Ionian Islands by the Ottoman Porte, Ypsilantis's call to arms, the
occupation of the Acropolis by the Turks, fighting on Chios, intervention in the conflict by Russia in 1825. Then the conflict intensified: the
massacre in Missolonghi, the presidency of Kapodistrias, the capitulation of Athens, the defeat of the Greek fleet at Navarino, the massacre of

the Cretans, and the reversal of the situation, until the recognition of Greek independence by the Turks and the choice of Otto, prince of Bavaria, as king of Greece.[8]

Canadiens who had gone to seminary and classical college had an exceptional familiarity with Ancient Greece and were interested in modern Greece. *Le Spectateur canadien* reminded the countries of Europe of their obligation to recognize Greece: "Enlightened nations! Enlightened governments! The time has come to pay your debts to our homeland Greece." Parent, who had just graduated from college, wrote in *Le Canadien* of 27 March 1822: "The friend of humanity will view with pleasure the ruins of the most flourishing nation that perhaps ever was, rise up on their own, and the descendants of the victors of Marathon and Salamis shake off the Ottoman yoke after eight hundred years of servitude. The ruins of the people of Lycurgus and Solon are certainly worthy of our rejoicing when we see them emerge from darkness."

As British subjects, the *Canadiens* were also concerned about the actions of Great Britain on the international stage. *La Gazette de Québec* wondered "if, as protector of the Greeks of the Ionian Islands, the honour of England did not require the intervention of its government to protect the states of Greece in their emancipation from the abominable tyranny of the Crescent." *Le Canadien*, which deplored the Christian powers' indifference to the Greco-Turkish conflict, acknowledged that "everywhere where the freedom of peoples is at stake, the English always make their presence felt."[9]

The long conflict in the Mediterranean provided an excellent lesson on issues related to nationalism. The responsibility of political leaders such as Ypsilantis was questioned: "He finds himself charged with a very great responsibility if he is the primary cause of all the ills that have befallen his nation." And it was said that the Greek resistance depended on external support: how long would they resist if they were not "aided from the outside"? But there was an awareness that interference by a foreign country in a nation's internal affairs could pose problems: one could want England to intervene in Greece without having wanted France to intervene in Spain. *La Gazette de Québec* pointed out the costs of independence and expressed the wish to "see the Greeks enjoy this independence that they have so nobly deserved by their perseverance, their sacrifices and their heroism."[10]

THREE GLORIOUS DAYS IN FRANCE (1830)

The July Revolution of 1830 in France was announced in Lower Canada with the special publication of a separate sheet in *La Minerve* of

Wednesday, 8 September. *La Minerve* borrowed the text from the *Montreal Gazette* of the Friday before, a text taken from the *Journal of Commerce* of New York City of the previous Friday morning, brought by the *Hibernia,* which had arrived from Liverpool on 4 August. The newspapers had already reported the dissolution of the Chamber and the impending election in France, as well as publishing Charles X's ordinance and his speech on the dissolution.

After the news of the "Three Glorious Days" of 27, 28, and 29 July, the press published many documents informing readers of subsequent events of the new revolution: addresses to the French people by the deputies and by Louis-Philippe d'Orléans, La Fayette's proclamation, the ordinances of Charles X to which the French refused to submit, the speech of Louis-Philippe d'Orléans at the opening of the Chambers, and the news of the court proceedings against the former ministers of Charles X. The events caught people's imagination, and the press published many articles on the adoption of the Marseillaise, comments by Chateaubriand and Lamartine, and the poem "À la jeune France" (To young France) by Victor Hugo.[11]

In a memoir written after the Rebellions of 1837 and 1838, Amédée Papineau referred to 1830 and the little revolution "à la Française" that took place at the Collège des Sulpiciens in Montreal: "The revolution of 1830 in France had an immense impact in Canada. Mondelet, La Fontaine, Vallée and Rodier paraded in the streets of Montreal with tricolour ribbons in their lapels. It even had repercussions in the colleges. And when classes started in the autumn, we almost had an insurrection at the Collège de Montréal. To tease our teachers, who we saw were not happy about the fall of the Bourbons, we sang verses from 'La Marseillaise' and 'La Parisienne' and displayed pieces of ribbon in the three colours."[12]

While *The Vindicator,* in January 1830, had predicted that France "will soon be the theatre of a 2nd revolution," *La Minerve* reported some ominous signs in June: "The men of the past waited in silence in the shadows, and as soon as a pernicious coincidence of events permitted them to show themselves, they came arrogantly to demand their vanished lives back, renouncing the lessons of experience and closing their eyes to the huge progress that has taken place during their sleep. Hence the movement that Prime Minister Polignac tried to impart to France." When the days of July were reported, Duvernay's newspaper wrote, regarding the dissolution of the parliament and the abolition of freedom of the press: "It must be admitted that a government is in a very extreme situation when it believes it necessary to turn to expedients of this nature." It was clear for the voice of the Patriotes that "one no longer trifles with impunity with peoples, who dispose of crowns at will."[13]

Very early, the press of Lower Canada provided a view of the constitutional confusion that reigned in France. *L'Observateur* took an excerpt from the *Tableau historique des progrès de la civilisation en France* that stated: "We are today composed of various alloys; the charter is the great solvent that tends to form, from all the various substances, one simple element, a homogeneous whole. The political chemist who would analyze all these substances would say to you, showing them to you one after the other: these are the dreams of the ancien régime; here, the republican utopias; there, the madness of the Empire; farther away, the delirium of military glory." *The Vindicator* of 10 September 1830 asked what form of government could suit France, expressing doubt that an American-style republic would be appropriate. Neilson's *La Gazette de Québec* looked at the successive revolutions that had occurred in France: "France has obviously made huge progress in the knowledge required to establish and maintain a free government," it stated; it commented that recent events provided "hope that the last revolution will be more fortunate than the one that preceded it," and translated a text from the *London Courier* that warned that if the French moved toward a republic, "they should not leave home, and they should not work to revolutionize other countries." Napoleon was still in the minds and memories of many. The position of *La Minerve*, the Patriote newspaper, on the July Revolution is a good indication of the importance it placed on both liberties and constitutionalism: 1830 "will be viewed as characteristic, in the history of empires, and in particular in the history of man, of man considered in society and viewed not as a slave subject to the whims of a few crowned individuals, but as a reasonable being, endowed with intelligence, capable of improvement and consumed with the pressing need for freedom." The paper added: "The governments that are called constitutional are therefore actual governments much more than governments of principles and theories ... but the republic is not popular in France, that name still brings back memories of the terror of 1793. We will no doubt for a long time still prefer a tempered monarchy, because it is part of the customs, because it is the final link in a chain to which are attached all the other institutions, which would otherwise have to be renewed in their entirety; because, finally, it offers more guarantees than a republic for external security and peaceful relations with the other states of Europe."[14]

Once again, the French situation was an opportunity to think about England and its institutions. *The Vindicator* observed "how far the nation is behind in the enjoyment of those civil rights to which Englishmen lay claim"; *La Gazette de Québec* hastened to point out what France had borrowed constitutionally from Great Britain: "In the amendments made to the Charter, the chamber introduced many counterparts to the English constitution; indeed, that great model appears generally to be its guide, and it did not deviate from it essentially on any point"; still favourable to the Patriotes, it observed: "One of the advantages of the English constitution is always being able to be amended."[15] The empathy with France was such that a subscription campaign was organized by *La Minerve*, but not without some people expressing surprise and others seeing it as primarily a symbolic gesture.[16]

One month after its launch, *L'Ami du peuple, de l'ordre et des lois*, which was the ultra-loyalist voice of the Sulpicians, who were in the process of negotiating their seigneurial rights with London, undertook to give another meaning to the July Revolution, denouncing "the democratic ambition, the popular violence." Referring in 1834 to the wars and revolutions on "the old continent," editor Pierre-Édouard Leclère or editor Michel Bibaud wrote: "At the sight of so many evils, so much misfortune, what voice will dare again to shout for revolution, what man will be enemy enough of his country to want to plunge Canada into the abyss of so much misery, there are none, we dare to believe, but if there are a few, may the people close their ears to their mad voices; may they learn from the history of nations to preserve themselves from so many evils and may they mistrust in particular the ambitious ones who seek to rush them into revolt. We do not believe that revolution is possible in this country; but if it came, we would see all the promoters of unrest hide from danger in the daytime, and reappear only if the triumph of their party offered them complete safety." Starting in April 1837, *Le Populaire* added its voice to denounce the "Three Glorious Days," which Papineau would cite as an example.[17]

BELGIUM SEPARATES FROM THE NETHERLANDS

One month after the July Revolution in France, a revolutionary movement took form in the United Kingdom of the Netherlands and became established in Brussels; the press of Lower Canada reported on this, starting in mid-October 1830. In November, the newspapers announced that the provisional government in Brussels was ready to declare the independence of Belgium. Further events quickly followed: the occupation of Antwerp, a proclamation by the Central Committee, the opening of a National Congress, the recognition of Belgium by the major powers, a search, as in Greece, for a royal family capable of establishing a constitutional monarchy.[18]

La Minerve stressed the tensions between the communities, arguing that the Walloons needed "boldly constitutional institutions" and that there was "too much disparity in all relationships between the Belgians and the Dutch for a government to function with facility between those two major divisions of the Kingdom of the Netherlands." In November 1830, *La Gazette de Québec* expressed the hope that the Belgians would "consent to nothing less than a separation from Holland and the establishment of a constitutional and liberal government." But a series of articles by Denis-Benjamin Viger entitled "Reflections on Belgium," published in *La Minerve* in May 1831 and then reprinted in a pamphlet, best expressed French Canadians' perception of Belgium's nationalist demands. While he was aware that there was little or no relation between Belgium and Lower Canada, Viger nevertheless considered the events in the Netherlands "a source of reflection eminently useful to the people of Lower Canada." Reviewing the history of Belgium, Viger, who was very well-informed on the political demands of Lower Canada, observed that "before turning to open resistance, the Belgians had for a long time made their complaints heard." He recognized that the Constitution "involved two peoples driven by ancient rivalries with each other, hatreds that have been, so to speak, hereditary for centuries," and listed the political ills of the Netherlands: unequal parliamentary representation between the Dutch and the Belgians, appointment of mostly Dutchmen to the upper house and the public service, a poorly advised monarch. He asked: "What situation would we be in today if the small minority that has had enough influence here to paralyze both the intentions of the government itself ... and the wishes of the country had been able to exercise limitless power over the majority and treat us as the Dutch have treated the peoples of Belgium?" Describing the restrictions placed by the Protestants on Catholic colleges with the intent of "gradually causing a merger of the two peoples, bringing the Belgians to analogous feelings on the subject of religion," Viger spoke of the history of the Royal Institution schools, the property of the Jesuits and of the Séminaire de Montréal, and the lands reserved for the Protestant clergy.

There was no lack of material for comparisons with Lower Canada: after political institutions and religion, Viger discussed the question of language, recalling that the Belgians had been forced to use Dutch before the courts, in legal documents and contracts and alluding to the "cold, insulting arrogance of that army of Dutch civil servants." With the struggles of the French Canadians in mind, he wrote: "Such are always the necessary consequences of attempts to establish a regime exclusively in favour of a particular class of men in a society, instead of placing all citizens without distinction under equal laws."

The memory of the plan for union of 1822 reminded Viger that something similar to the Belgian case could have happened: sharing of the debt – "It was to make them pay the price of the yoke that had been imposed on them when they were united with Holland"; equal rather than proportional representation – "The representation of Lower Canada would have been, so to speak, drowned"; abolition of the use of French and the jurisdiction of the Catholic bishop. Viger understood 1830 in light of 1815, the Treaty of Vienna and the Holy Alliance that had divided up the nations: "In the middle of the camps, they were divided up among the sovereigns as is done with the spoils of war taken from the enemy"; as a result, "the seeds were planted for new revolutions that would necessarily break out when these peoples had an opportunity to shake off the chains they had received only with trembling." In 1830, Viger cited the formulation of the principle of nationality that would become a leitmotif for Parent and Papineau: "No nation is willing to obey another, for the simple reason that no nation knows how to command another." He was glad, nevertheless, that Canada was a British colony: "It is by leaving to the inhabitants of most of its colonies the supervision and conduct of their interests, the use of the taxes raised by them and internal legislation, finally, that England has laid the foundations of their prosperity." He stated that in the British colonies, "the peoples are not constantly tormented by the fear of seeing the caprices of an individual, the whims of the power of the day, the greed of employees who change from one moment to the next shake the edifice of their rights; on the contrary, they have in this respect the surest of all possible guarantees: their fate is in their own hands." Viger concluded his reflections by declaring that "our cause is that of our metropolis itself."[19]

"WARSAW IS NO LONGER OURS"

The news of the Warsaw Uprising of 29 November 1830 appeared in *La Minerve* on 7 February 1831, taken from the *Journal de Paris* of 14 December 1830, which arrived in New York City on 30 January on board the *Sovereign*, the ship having left London on 20 December. The press published various official documents – the manifesto to the nation, the address from the government to the people of Poland and the Lithuanians, the text of Warsaw's capitulation, the letter of January 1832 from the Minister of Foreign Affairs recognizing that "Warsaw is no longer ours" – and historical or biographical sketches of Polish leaders.[20]

The press of Lower Canada was well aware of the presence of France on the side of the Poles; it stressed the grandeur of the white flag of Poland and the tricolour of France in the insurrection, informed readers of the subscriptions raised in France in aid of the Poles, published the manifesto of the French Central Committee in support of Poland and La Fayette's address assuring Poland of France's assistance: "Dombrowski, Kosciusko, Poniatowski are names that belong to France as much as to Poland; your compatriots have called for our help, and it will be granted to them." To make clear France's contribution to freedom, La Fayette added: "Already the Greeks bless you; may Poland recognize that it is indebted in part to you for its independence and its freedom."[21]

The press also expressed approval of the developments in the situation in Poland. *La Minerve* translated a text from *Bell's Messenger* declaring that every man of any sensitivity must rejoice in the Poles' attempt to regain their freedom and pointing out that, while France and Belgium had liberal forms of government, the Poles had been almost the only unemancipated slaves in Europe. *La Gazette de Québec* opined that it "appears even likely that Nicolas will permit the separation of Poland and grant the Poles a rather free constitution. The Poles deserve that. Never has a people shown itself to be more combative and enthusiastic for freedom." An analysis entitled "On Polish Nationality," which *La Minerve* reprinted from the *Journal des Débats* of Paris, stated, "Nowhere better than Poland can one study what nationality is, what this mysterious and powerful principle of the life of peoples is." Nationality, it said, could be recognized by two signs: rebellion and "the power that peoples have to produce great characters." It ended with a question: "What then will be the fate of this great and remarkable nation for which it seems as impossible to live as to die?" A text in *Le Canadien* translated from *The Times* of London proposed one last hope for the disenchanted Poles – America: "Poles! let us leave that wretched country, now no more our own, though soaked with the best blood of her defenders – let us leave Europe, a heartless spectator of our struggle and our despair. America is the only country worthy of affording an asylum to men who have sacrificed every thing for freedom; there Poland will be enshrined in our hearts."[22]

The Polish case quickly became a hobbyhorse for the Sulpicians' *L'Ami du peuple*, and soon also for *Le Populaire*. The former, which reproduced counter-revolutionary ideas and opposed the Patriotes, considered that the ills suffered by Poland, Spain, and Portugal should convince the *Canadiens* to be satisfied with the system that was the best and that had "the fewest imperfections." Again in 1838, *Le Populaire* contrasted Poland and Lower Canada: "The *Canadiens* should in no way be compared with the peoples we have cited [the Greeks, Poles, and Belgians], and sympathies should be based on their real political situation, not on the declarations of a few of their discontented children. The *Canadiens* never formed an independent nation, they have no nationality to lay claim to, no freedom to regain." *Le Populaire* in these matters followed the position of Mgr Lartigue, who, in his pastoral letter of 24 October 1837, referred to the papal brief to the Polish bishops condemning the revolutionary ideas of the liberal Polish Catholics.[23]

The repression of the Polish revolution by the Czar led the newspapers of Lower Canada to look for an explanation for the Polish patriots' lack of success. In addition to their military weakness, the disagreements among the military leaders, the fury of the parties, and the "fever of discord," *La Minerve* noted the persistence of feudalism: "If the different revolutions of Poland have not presented these characteristics and these triumphs, it is the fault of those who call themselves patriots and who were not patriots enough, or at least who did not fulfill all the obligations imposed by that beautiful title. Poland is a country still imbued with feudal principles: only two classes of individuals are recognized: nobles, who are rich and proud; peasants, who are poor and serfs."[24]

LOWER CANADA AND IRELAND: THE SAME STRUGGLE, THE SAME STRATEGY?

As part of the British Empire, Ireland was of interest to people in Lower Canada long before the July Revolution in France and the awakening of nationalism in Belgium and Poland. Already before 1830, Irish immigration to Lower Canada and the question of the political emancipation of Catholics were attracting attention in the British colony of North America. From the first petitions of the Catholics to obtain their full political and civic rights in 1824 to the repeal of the union in 1833 and the creation of the Catholic Association, to the issue of the admission of Catholics to the House of Lords, to the arrest and trial of Daniel O'Connell, and then his election and his first speech in the House of Commons, the events in Ireland were closely followed by the Canadian press, in particular *The Spectator*, which later became *The Irish Vindicator* and then *The Vindicator*.

Until the founding of *The Spectator* in 1823, the situation in Ireland served mainly to fuel the local rivalry of the press. *La Gazette de Québec* attacked the *Quebec Mercury* and its allies who "clamoured for this policy of fire and sword that has successively crushed and consumed Ireland." *Le Canadien* considered the situation of the *Canadiens* better than that of the Irish, but felt that the question of the lands reserved for the Protestant clergy in Lower Canada and that of the abolition of the seigneurial regime, which would leave the Catholic clergy financially destitute, were sensitive issues. An analyst of the Irish situation blamed it on "the negligence, stupidity, recklessness, insufferable pride and despotism of the men in authority in that country," and "the race of petty tyrants who were the first authors of the horrible condition of that society." As for the remedies proposed, *Le Spectateur canadien* doubted that they would be effective: "As usual, what is proposed against the ills is not remedies that cut them at the root, but that numb them temporarily, such as the suspension of *habeas corpus* and the renewal of what is known as the Insurrection Bill." Already in 1822, when there was a new plan for union, *Le Canadien* considered the consequences of such an initiative in light of the case of Ireland: "Who knows what will happen in this country if our enemies ever obtain a majority in our chamber? Can we expect a fate better than that of the Irish?"[25]

The new *Spectator* was quick to observe that "a faction will make the province a second Ireland." Viger, who continued his reflection on the situation in the colony and internationally, took the view that there had "never been more constancy in the execution of a plan as in that of anglicizing Ireland." *La Minerve* presented an imaginary dialogue between "Pierrot Campagnard [Countryman]" and "Jean-Baptiste Bourgeois" to raise awareness among its readers on the issue of Catholic emancipation. Pierrot wonders "if those people are as miserable as they say"; Bourgeois explains, "Indeed, my good friend, those Catholics are deprived of the right to send Catholic representatives to the Parliament of England, they are forced to choose Protestants; they are made to pay a real tithe (not one twentieth like you fortunate habitants!), and to whom? to Protestant ministers who hate them, abhor them and continually shout that the Irish Catholics are fine as they are." Pierrot, thinking of Lower Canada, asks: "But tell me then, all these Englishmen who live here, are they on the side of those men?" Bourgeois replies that a large part of them are on the side of the oppressors and that it is necessary to be vigilant: "They praise us for being good Catholics, but when they speak of the Catholics of Ireland, they are rabid dogs." With regard to the king, who had chosen Canning, a supporter of emancipation, as a minister, Pierrot acknowledges: "But our King, I can't believe it, he must have a heart bigger than our presbytery to have chosen a man he didn't like." At the same time, O'Connell supported the Catholics of Lower Canada on the issues of revenues and the civil list.[26]

From September 1828, support for Ireland was consolidated; it was expressed in the formation of Irish friendship societies in Montreal, Quebec City, and Trois-Rivières. Major figures such as Dr O'Callaghan and Cassidy spoke at some of their meetings. In Trois-Rivières, Dominique Mondelet read a draft of a letter to O'Connell describing the position of the friends of Ireland there: "Moved by a feeling for the unhappy condition of the Irish people, compelled to sympathize by the voice of humanity, guided by the voice of reason, and driven by the interest they take in the well-being and prosperity of the British Empire," the people of Lower Canada were said to admire the strategy of the Catholic Association in Ireland, which "did without difficulty what proclamations, threats and cannon could not even begin to do. It was thus patriotism against intolerance, reason against prejudices, that gave birth to the Association." Mondelet took up the leitmotif of nationalities – "no man has coercive jurisdiction over us" – and was critical of the metropolis: "There is England at the level of Spain and Constantinople, and receiving from Catholic countries the example of liberality, and from Protestant countries the most scathing criticisms of the obstinacy of those that govern its councils." Dr Wolfred Nelson rose, declaring himself Protestant, but stating that he did not feel Protestants were superior to Catholics. Dr Kimber sought to understand England's persistence in Ireland: "Glorious England has suffered all the disasters resulting from revolutions, civil wars to obtain its great charter, the sacred palladium of national freedom; it has shed its blood, spent its treasures to deliver Europe from the servitude to which the most powerful of its enemies was going to reduce it, it has determined in its councils to abolish the traffic of slaves in Africa, it has promoted the independence of the Greeks, recognized that of part of the Spanish colonies," but with respect to Ireland, "it still nourishes in its bosom a slavery that is as senseless as it is impolitic?"

At a time when a committee of the House of Commons was investigating affairs in Canada, the member of the Assembly Vallières de Saint-Réal expressed his concerns in *La Gazette de Québec*: "As long as Irish Catholics are persecuted because of their religion, there will be no safety for any Catholic anywhere in the Empire." He compared Canada and Ireland, two dependencies of the British Empire, two conquered countries; but he felt that, in contrast to Ireland, in Lower Canada, it was not religion, but rather the language, laws, and institutions that were under attack – and less by the metropolis than by the colonial administration: "Why are we not like unhappy Ireland? There is only one reason: we possess the majority in the representation of the country." As long as French Canadians retained the parliamentary majority, Lower Canada would not become "the Ireland of the New World."[27]

The *Canadian Spectator* became *The Irish Vindicator* on 12 December 1828, four months before the beginning of the last round of demands in favour of Catholic emancipation in the House of Commons, in April 1829. In March, the majority in the House of Commons voted in favour of emancipation and the House of Lords finally gave its consent in May, making it possible for O'Connell to take his seat in the House of

Commons. He then began a new campaign for the repeal of the union between Great Britain and Ireland.[28]

Irish immigration and a local organization gave Irish immigrants a new visibility in Lower Canada and made their presence felt as a new factor in Patriote politics and strategy. *The Irish Vindicator* was sold to French Canadian interests in July 1829, after emancipation had been achieved; it became *The Vindicator* in November 1832. The arrest and imprisonment of Duvernay of *La Minerve* and Tracey of *The Vindicator* strengthened the relationship between French Canadians and that part of the Irish in Lower Canada who were also fighting for an elected Legislative Council – only a part, because the result of the bloody by-election in Montreal in May 1832, a four-vote majority for Tracey, clearly indicates the division of the Irish vote and the tensions that existed at this time of a cholera outbreak.[29]

Tracey's *The Vindicator* put up a good fight; it warned the metropolis that "the governing must be just, if the governed are to be obedient." The paper, which was the voice of the Irish Patriotes, felt that the Emancipation Act had not gone far enough and said it knew by experience how the metropolis worked: "Never there was a concession yet made by the dominant authority of Great Britain to Ireland but when under the convincing power of absolute necessity." It observed that England "is still leaning to the old Machiavellian maxim *divide et impera.*"

Comparisons between Papineau and O'Connell were inevitable after 1833; a correspondent of Duvernay wrote: "If Mr. Papineau ... were to address a few little lessons to the country folk occasionally on the affairs of the province, as O'Connell has done in Ireland, great benefit would result, and before long our country districts would be prepared for anything." O'Callaghan, who was made editor of *The Vindicator* in March 1833 by the new French Canadian owners, wrote of Papineau: "God has marked this man to be a Political Chief, the regenerator of a nation," like O'Connell. Roebuck, the agent of the House of Assembly in London, declared, "The persecutions of Ireland have produced O'Connell, the misgovernment of Canada ... has produced its O'Connell also in the person of Mr. Papineau." And during the first public assembly in Saint-Ours-sur-Richelieu, there were calls to rally around "the Canadian O'Connell."[30]

Symbols were used, including the feast day of the French Canadians' patron saint, John the Baptist, which was associated with St Patrick's Day. In 1834, there were toasts to the health of Papineau and O'Connell, Duvernay and O'Callaghan, and to the union between the Irish and the *Canadiens*, and the 92 Resolutions. In 1835, they raised their glasses to

Bourdages, Bédard, Waller, Tracey, and the Aide-toi et le ciel t'aidera society, and Viger gave a speech on "strength through unity." Rodier spoke on "the people, the legitimate source of all political power," stating, "No one was created to exercise arbitrary power over others." The man of the hour at the celebration of July 1830, he referred to *Words of a Believer* and maintained that "the doctrine of passive obedience is as vile as it is ridiculous." De Bleury spoke of the king of England, saying, "He was at the edge of the precipice; the people saved him." C.-O. Perrault said a few words on "elected institutions," Colonel de Boucherville spoke on "the Canadian militia," Girod, another admirer of 1830, spoke "in praise of Daniel O'Connell" and de Marconnay in praise of freedom of the press. A letter from O'Callaghan was read that compared St John the Baptist and St Patrick, and their "lives of devotion to the cause of reform."[31]

But the Sulpicians, *L'Ami du peuple*, the *Irish Advocate* (1835–36) – the voice of the Tories and the local Orangemen – and *Le Populaire* took a different view of the Irish situation and Daniel O'Connell. For *L'Ami du peuple*, the situation in Ireland could be explained by the excessive generosity of the Whig government. It frequently published speeches by the king expressing the intention to repress all dissidence in Ireland, and it commented as follows: "This recommendation seems to us to augur unfavourably for the malcontents of Lower Canada." *La Gazette de Québec* did not miss the opportunity to point out that O'Connell did not agree with an elected intermediate branch of the legislature – the Legislative Council – under a monarchy, while raising a few questions on the uses made of the "O'Connell tribute" and on the possible creation of a similar "Papineau tribute."

In April 1837, at a time when O'Connell's rallying cry – "Hurrah for Agitation," "Agitate! Agitate!" – was taken up by O'Callaghan in Lower Canada and Roebuck declared in the Commons that "if our dominion reaches beyond the broad Atlantic, so also does our justice," *Le Populaire* claimed that the yoke was not intolerable, while raising the question of preparation for the struggle and the availability of leaders. *L'Ami du peuple* rejected any analogy between Lower Canada and Ireland, denying the existence of any form of religious or political domination in Lower Canada: "Would this be political domination? But it would be completely ridiculous. There is no party domination here; any more than there is an aristocracy; nowhere in the world is there a republic that can offer a picture of such equality."[32]

The campaign of *L'Ami du peuple* and *Le Populaire* against the identification of Lower Canada with Ireland and the comparison of Papineau with O'Connell intensified when public assemblies were organized in the spring of 1837. *L'Ami du peuple* maintained that "The *Canadiens* have nothing of such scourges to fight," and waxed ironic on "our little big men [who] constantly present Papineau as the O'Connell of Canada, and yet Papineau is doing for his country the complete opposite of what O'Connell is doing for Ireland." It was thus important for the Sulpicians' newspaper to convince the Irish of Lower Canada to dissociate their country of origin and their adopted country: "We will ask only of the children of Ireland what that can have to do with what is happening in Canada. While it may be true that the government has done great wrongs to Ireland, would that be a reason for the Irish to rise up here, if they find here a government that is just, protective and kind, and perfectly equal rights."

Le Populaire denounced Papineau as "the head agitator" and declared that "the cause of the Irish in Canada must forever be detached from the leader of the Canadian contrabandists," an allusion to a recent strategy of the Parti patriote. Pointing out the contradiction in the Patriotes' opposition to immigration, the newspaper condemned "our revolutionaries who want to topple the throne and the altar, who despise the Irish because that brave people is loyal, as the great O'Connell desires."[33]

The Sulpicians did not only concern themselves with the Irish in their newspaper; they combined words with action and, with the clergy, saw to it that Father MacMahon denounced the Irish supporters of the Patriotes and asked Abbé Phelan to "counter the propaganda of O'Callaghan and his *Vindicator* among the Irish of Montreal." Three months after the destruction of *The Vindicator*'s print shop by loyalists of the Doric Club, Abbé Maguire published in *La Gazette de Québec,* and soon after in the form of a pamphlet, the *Doctrine de l'Église d'Irlande et de celle du Canada sur la révolte* (The doctrine of the Church of Ireland and that of Canada on revolt), which argued in favour of the Church's right of intervention in the affairs of the civil government.[34]

THE AMERICAS: THE UNITED STATES (1776) AND THE TEXAS QUESTION (1836)

The reality and the image of the War of 1812 between Canada and the United States gradually faded after 1815, although the victory in Châteauguay was still mentioned occasionally. Familiarity with the great neighbour that had won its independence was such that, starting in 1830, the press of Lower Canada published the State of the Union messages of its presidents, from Monroe to Jackson to Van Buren.[35] And it was not unusual for *The Vindicator* or *La Minerve* to reprint the text of the Declaration of Independence or publish excerpts from a history of the American Revolution, especially in 1837.[36]

After 1830, the success of the Great Republic was cited as an example by Papineau and the Patriotes, but starting in 1833, the newspapers also mentioned the reality of slavery in the South and the initiatives of the abolitionists. Again imagining a conversation between two "Canadian habitants," *Le Populaire*, seeking to temper the pro-American enthusiasm of the Patriotes, said: "I cannot bear hearing a country where slavery reigns being called FREE."[37]

The press's constant interest in the United States is also evident in the reproduction of travel accounts and observations on the American situation. Papers published excerpts from the examination of the prison system by Tocqueville and Beaumont, long passages from Tocqueville's *Democracy in America* and a few pages from *Lettres sur l'Amérique* by Michel Chevalier and *Marie, ou de l'esclavage aux États-Unis* by Beaumont.[38]

But it was Texas's declaration of independence from Mexico in March 1836 that focused attention on events in the United States at the time when Lower Canada was still waiting for a response to the 92 Resolutions. *L'Ami du peuple* quickly saw that Texas could become a model for the relationship between Lower Canada and the United States, in particular for the Patriotes, who saw the United States "as the rainbow of liberty." Alluding to the Patriotes' expectations with respect to the United States, the paper emphasized the fact that the American government had paid little attention to the initiatives of Texas until "recognition by the former masters legitimized the rebellion." Addressing the "supposed patriots" who opposed immigration while Texas was calling for immigration, the paper recalled that the republic of Mexico had been "no match for the United States." And always vigilant with regard to *La Minerve* and *Le Libéral* in Quebec City, which had compared the situation in Lower Canada to the American Revolution, *Le Populaire* wrote on 4 October 1837: "For a long time, we have taken pains to demonstrate the pointlessness of an expectation of sympathy from the United States. We have proven overwhelmingly that neither the interests nor the affections of our neighbours could compensate for the risks, the losses and the huge consequences that militate against such cooperation." The anti-Papineau paper, the editor of which was Leblanc de Marconnay, who had gone from *La Minerve* to *Le Populaire*, and then went on to *L'Ami du peuple*, emphasized the "huge difference" between Texas and Canada: "The Texans belonged to one of those strange new republics that carry all the seeds of a revolution within them," a reminder that they had not had to deal with Great Britain. And in Canada, things were very different: "The Texans have pushed out the Mexicans, they are masters of their territory, they have declared their independence, they have waged violent struggles to obtain it and consolidate it. In Canada, everything remains to be done."[39]

THE "PATRIOTES" OF SOUTH AMERICA

"Some half a century ago, Europe was about the only part of the world that provided material for periodicals; journalists hardly talked about Asia, Africa or America, except occasionally upon the arrival of a vessel of discovery or a celebrated traveller; today the amount of material and the task have doubled because of the appearance of the American continent on the political horizon." This comment in *Le Spectateur canadien* of 6 July 1822 shows the place given by the press of Lower Canada to the events buffeting the colonies of South America and their métropolises after 1808, the beginning of the colonial liberation movements. From 1815 to 1837, the newspapers were filled with information on the military and political situation, in particular in Argentina, Chile, Peru, Venezuela, Colombia, Ecuador, and Mexico. The names of the major figures – Bolivar, San Martín, O'Donnell, O'Higgins – circulated, and there were biographies and speeches of Bolivar, information on decisive events such as the Congress of Tucuman on 9 July 1816, which declared the independence of the provinces of Rio de la Plata, and numerous proclamations by military and political leaders.[40]

Readers could appreciate the repercussions of the Napoleonic Wars on Spain and understand how the internal problems of Spain and Portugal in part explained the initiatives and success of colonial emancipation in their colonies in South and Central America. *La Gazette de Québec* considered that, given Spain's internal repression, it was not yet ready for a liberal system of government, and Parent's *Le Canadien* was not in favour of French intervention in Spain for at least two reasons: the memory of Napoleon's campaigns was still very much alive, and the principle of the autonomy of nations was clearly at stake.[41]

Given the internal situation in Spain, the recurring message of the press of Lower Canada was that it should not persist in trying to hold on to its colonies, and that the "unworthy country" could not "hope ever to regain possession of all it has lost," because within the year, "the last vestiges of Spanish power" would have been "erased from the Southern Continent." The papers emphasized the despotism of the governments of Spain and Portugal, the tyranny of old Spain and the "feudalism that we can hardly imagine on this side of the Atlantic."[42]

The crisis in both the metropolises and the colonies once again revealed the scheming of the Holy Alliance, and *Le Canadien* was pleased that Lower Canada was not subject to the pressures of this alliance of absolute monarchies: "We do not know what would be our fate if now we fell into the hands of the Holy Allies (how can one so profane the word *holy*!), but what we are very certain of is that we would never be at pains henceforth to profess such an evil doctrine. Let us therefore bless heaven for allowing us be born in an empire where one can proclaim loudly all that is just. We were born on the soil of liberty, we to whom liberty was so liberally given, let us pay the keenest interest to those who will soon be seen fighting to preserve it." Once again, the Holy Alliance did not receive very good press: it was called an "instrument of despotism," a league of crowned heads opposed to the republic and in favour of slavery, a "hideous head" of despotism, a group of monarchs "who arrogate to themselves the right to regulate the internal affairs of foreign nations, and even to punish them for what they do in their own countries"; *Le Spectateur canadien* added: "This seems to us to be an extraordinary thing in the annals of ancient and modern history."[43]

Like the members of the Holy Alliance, the other powers of the period had to react to these "extraordinary things" and "strange new republics" – first and foremost, the United States of America, which as early as 1819 was said to be beginning to think about recognizing the new independent states to the south. President Monroe still upheld the neutrality of his country at the beginning of 1822, while acknowledging that independence had been achieved in Argentina, Colombia and Mexico – with which *Le Spectateur canadien* expressed agreement. Then the United States recognized the independence of Spanish America in 1822 and 1823, before Monroe declared his well-known "doctrine" of noninterference by the countries of Europe in the affairs of the Americas in 1825. Great Britain would recognize the independence of Mexico, Argentina, and Colombia in 1825, to the displeasure of the Holy Alliance, and France would support Mexico in 1827.[44]

International recognition was also delayed because of the relative confusion in South America. *La Gazette de Québec* wrote in 1818: "As for southern America, confusion and all kinds of atrocities have reigned there these last ten years, and will probably continue still to reign for many years." It explained this confusion as follows: "A people made up of different races and different nations, without education or public virtue, aspires to govern itself, led by leaders many of whom seem without character or principles, driven by every motive other than that of the general well-being." *Le Canadien* declared that it had no illusions about the motives or behaviour of certain new countries: the fact that Chile had shaken off the Spanish yoke did not mean it was "the most free, most enlightened and most philanthropic people in the world."[45]

These "strange new republics" appeared as such because the question of independence and that of the most appropriate form of government arose at the same time: "While all or almost all the peoples of Europe tend toward constitutional monarchies and representative government, those of southern America are leaning toward republican regimes. It is not, however, love of liberty, but love of independence, that drives the Spanish Americans. Independence is, no doubt, an invaluable possession for a people, but one must know how to use it: if all the peoples of Spanish America were to conduct themselves as the people of Buenos Ayres did a few years ago, it would be infinitely more advantageous for them to remain subject to the constitutional King of old Spain." Similar reservations were expressed about Paraguay, which, though republican, seemed to behave like France after 1789, with its policy of deportations, exiles, and banishments, and about Mexico, whose "consecration" of "Emperor" Iturbide was called a "solemn farce." *Le Spectateur canadien* defined what it meant by "true liberty": "Whatever becomes of liberty in European Spain, the independence of Spanish America is assured; true liberty, that is, the liberty that is accompanied by wisdom, moderation and justice, will perhaps not be established forthwith; but it should not be believed that the example of the United States will be lost to it; Mexico in truth appears to want to differ from the political regimes of the other provinces that have shaken off the yoke of Spain; but whether this state be a republic, a kingdom or an empire, whether it be governed by a single man or many, the number of proponents of liberty is too considerable there, as it appeared in the first revolution, for despotism to be maintained for very long, even if Iturbide and his proponents were for that kind of government, as a few have believed."

The particular case of Brazil, which acquired its independence from Portugal in an unprecedented way, led to further reflections: "Brazil still preserves an appearance of dependency; it only remains now to determine whether the Brazilians will be happier as republicans than as subjects of a monarchist government as moderate as that of the metropolis is currently." *Le Spectateur canadien* took the opportunity to explain its predilection for constitutional monarchy, including in the Americas: "It would be desirable that Brazil remain a kingdom, not only so that there would be variety in the new states of America, but because it is known that constitutional and representative monarchic government is more favourable than republican government to public tranquility and true liberty in a big country where customs are not very simple and very pure." And once again, the model was Great Britain. *Le Spectateur canadien* proposed to Ferdinand of Spain: "May he exercise British liberality toward his colonies; may he protect religion instead of persecuting it in his name, and like England, he will see his colonials rally to his government to be its most certain supports."[46]

In a British colony in which, after 1830, the dominant discourse favoured the United States model and insisted that the colony belonged to the New World, American examples other than that of the United States were of great interest to political leaders. While Ludger Duvernay, the owner of *La Minerve*, found important information on the Americas in his newspaper, he was also reminded by one of his French correspondents: "Cast your eyes on the map of the Americas and you will see that you are the only people of this vast continent who have remained the very humble subjects of a European power." Finally, references to the continental American experience abounded in the resolutions and addresses of the Patriotes. At the Sainte-Scholastique assembly, they said they would rely on "the cooperation of our brothers in the neighbouring colonies for our disinterested views of colonial liberty and independence ... and on the support of the neighbouring republics, which, more fortunate than we, have traversed with such happiness the struggle against the despotism of the metropolis." The address of the Fils de la liberté described the time as "a favourable opportunity to take our place among the independent sovereignties of America," while that of the Confédération des Six Comtés (L'Acadie, Chambly, Richelieu, Rouville, Saint-Hyacinthe, Verchères) recognized that it was in a community of spirit "with the various nations of North and South America that have adopted the principles contained in this declaration."[47]

PAPINEAU, PARENT, GARNEAU, AND COLONIAL AND NATIONAL EMANCIPATION

A study of the geopolitics of Papineau, Parent, and Garneau between 1815 and 1837 gives a good idea of the representation French Canadians had of the state and the possible destiny of Lower Canada. Papineau had a political, partisan, parliamentary view of things; he had to deal with reality and the responsibility of power as the leader of the Parti canadien and then the Parti patriote. His public discourse reflected a constant spirit of personal and political strategy that was imposed on him by his responsibilities.

Parent, the editor of *Le Canadien* of Quebec City, was a man of public opinion. His work obliged him to read as broadly as possible in the foreign press, if only to select the news and articles he would use in his newspaper. He had an acute awareness of what Europe had become after the Treaty of Vienna; he wrote in 1834: "But it is especially in America that political reform has taken giant strides, not having found in simple, moral, religious American societies the vices and obstacles it has encountered in the luxury and corruption of European societies. The new ideas have, however, also made surprising progress in Europe, progress such that the ancient despotism has everywhere been obliged to come to terms with liberty; [the ancient despotism] has seen [liberty] overturn an ancient dynasty, tearing from it today two kingdoms, Spain and Portugal; overturning in Belgium its work of 1815; threatening it in Italy; muttering on the Rhine; gnawing at its chains in Poland; it sees it in Great Britain knocking down one by one the colonies of the gothic edifice of aristocracy; it sees it in Paris and in Lyon, testing itself against quasi-legitimacy."[48]

Garneau, also in the Quebec City region, was a traveller, a poet who had become a historian. A contemporary of the Romantics, he travelled in Europe at the time of the Congress of Vienna, the attempts to restore monarchies, and the awakening of nationalities. He started writing his *Histoire du Canada* at the time of the first rebellion in 1837; the first of three volumes was published in 1845, the last in 1852. Garneau spent time in England and France between 1831 and 1833, and published an account of this voyage in 1854. The last volume of his history of the country, which covered the period from 1791 to 1840, included an analysis of the 1830s and the Rebellions in light of the adoption, in 1840, of the constitutional regime of union.

The perception of England was necessarily the focus of the geopolitics of any public figure in the Lower Canada of the period, given the colonial situation. The new British metropolis encouraged French Canadians to see themselves incidentally in relation to their first metropolis, France, but first to take into consideration the future of former colonies that had become independent, such as the United States, or parts of the United Kingdom, particularly Ireland and Scotland. French Canadians of the period also often compared the colonial condition of Lower Canada with the situation of dependency or emancipation of other societies, such as those of Poland, Italy, Belgium, Greece, and countries in South America.

Papineau, Parent, and Garneau shared the same pro-Britishism, the same admiration for the British Constitution and the rights and liberties of British subjects. Since they could not expect significant reform from the colonial authorities, all three of them counted on a justice that would be established by the metropolis, which did not disappoint them with the plans for union of 1811, 1822, and 1824, but which worried them with the Gosford Commission and, finally, disillusioned them with the Russell Resolutions of February 1837. Like Papineau, whose pro-Britishism was tempered after 1830 in favour of a growing admiration for the neighbouring republic, Parent and Garneau were sensitive to political issues that were beginning to make French Canadians doubt London's goodwill: the essentially anglophone composition of the Legislative Council, whose members were appointed and not elected; the financial dependence of the Council members on the executive; the Council's blocking of dozens of laws that had been passed by the elected House of Assembly. Parent and Garneau were in agreement with the Parti patriote with regard to the 92 Resolutions in 1834, but they parted ways with Papineau on the initiative of the public assemblies in the spring of 1837, after the Russell Resolutions.

Garneau would speak of Parent's *Le Canadien* as the "last fighter of old England." Parent would say in January 1838 that "the idea of a separation from England did not have deep roots either in the masses of the colonial populations or in thoughtful minds"; he thought then of acting as the spokesperson at least of the citizens in the Quebec City region.[49]

While Papineau and the Patriotes envisaged liberty with the American Union, Parent sought it with England: "In the interest of [their] national existence, the *Canadiens* must remain united with the British Empire; in the interest of its domination on the American continent, Great Britain must protect the *Canadiens* in their national rights." This is the same man who had the courage to write that Great Britain had not been afraid of Napoleon and would not be afraid either of Canada or Lower Canada.[50]

Papineau, Parent, and Garneau also had their representations of historical and contemporary France. For Papineau, the military conquest of Canada by England in 1760 and its cession by France in 1763 corresponded to the transition from the reign of absolutist violence to the rule of law and justice. He wrote in 1820: "Let us remember that under the French government (arbitrary and oppressive, internally and externally) the interests of this colony had been more often neglected and poorly administered than in any other part of its dependencies ... But see the change. George III, a sovereign revered for his moral character, his application to his royal duties and his love of his subjects, succeeded Louis XV, a prince rightly despised for his debauchery, his indifference to the needs of the people, his extravagances with the public treasury for the benefit of his favourites and his mistresses. From that day, the rule of law has replaced that of violence." It was clear for Parent that in 1760, "the king of France lost the right he had to the loyalty of the *Canadiens* in favour of the king of England." Those francophone colonials and British subjects who were familiar with the English revolution of 1688 and the War of Independence of 1776 could decide between the pros and cons of 1789 and especially of 1793. Papineau could in all honesty deny "any supposed attachment to France and French principles" and insist that the "Convention" he often referred to was the American example and not the French one.[51]

Neither the Patriote leader, the editor of *Le Canadien*, nor the budding historian was much impressed by the France of 1830, which gave its impetus to the European nationalist movements. Papineau did not speak publicly of the July Revolution, and it should be noted that the 92 Resolutions, which he helped write, made no reference to it. An admirer of the English form of constitutional monarchy, which had just been adopted by France, Garneau, as a formerly French British subject in North America, felt that the monarchy and liberty were not assured in France: "In a word, it was a copy of the British Constitution adapted to France ... It follows from what I am saying here that if the monarchy was not well-established in France, liberty was not well-established either, and that it has many more battles to fight before it is as firmly rooted as it is on this side of the Channel and the Atlantic." For Parent, France had promised so much to Poland in 1830 and 1831, and had failed to keep its promises. Observing this in July 1837, he suggested that the "Americanomaniac" Patriotes not count too much on "elsewhere," the United States.[52]

Until the summer of 1837, Papineau, Parent, and Garneau shared an admiration for the neighbouring great republic, which, unlike France, had achieved its independence without Terror. They especially envied certain of its elected institutions such as the Senate, which served as the model for their demand to London for an elected Legislative Council. But their Americanity, their sense of belonging to America, was broader than this institutional question. Papineau took the view that it was "in the state of customs and practices" of the United States "that we should look for examples to guide us." He added: "There must necessarily be a king in Europe, where he is surrounded by monarchies ... The same is not true here; we do not have, we cannot have an aristocracy; we do not need those magnificent attributes. We need a simple government, like that of the United States ... We will not for a long time have the strength to support royal splendour and aristocracy, the prerogative of a brilliant Canadian empire." He observed that there was "nothing here of that blind deference they have in Europe for titles and birth, which bring out so much arrogance and pride in those who come among us from the old continent and who think they should be compensated here for the humiliation to which they have been subjected there by exacting the same servility." There was no doubt about his republicanism: "It is certain that before a very long time, all America must be republican ... It is simply a matter of knowing that we are living in America, and knowing how we have lived."[53]

For Parent, America was "the hemisphere where liberty was born," and Garneau the poet, who considered liberty to be achieved and well-established in America, also found in it the Romantic inspiration of the New World and nature. But the imminence of a confrontation in 1837 divided their allegiances to this American-style republicanism.

In the 92 Resolutions, Papineau and the Patriotes had abundantly reminded Great Britain of the exemplary nature and the attraction of
American institutions. They would imitate the American patriots, creating committees of correspondence, proposing the use of a convention,
organizing the Fils de la liberté on the model of the Sons of Liberty of
1775, and adopting the Yankee strategy of boycotting products imported
from Great Britain. For Papineau, the United States was an example of a
British colony that had successfully sought and won its independence.

The geopolitics of Parent and Garneau limited their republicanism.
For Parent, the United States could represent salvation only if England's
policy became threatening to the French Canadian nation. While recognizing that the inhabitants of Lower Canada needed "other institutions
than those of Europe," he used the following figure of speech: "The lion
has its claws, it is true; but does not the eagle have its talons?" Once
again, Parent had a sense of the constraints and the relevant questions:
who could Lower Canada truly count on internationally? He expected
nothing from France, nothing from the Yankees: to him, the Americans'
feeling "could result [only] from an arithmetic rule." A realist, he considered, in July 1837, that the Americans and the English "would be
foolish to cross swords over us." While Papineau made no public reference to the example of Louisiana, Parent set forth and recalled the case,
which "makes one tremble." He saw the case of Poland as another example of "honourable submission," because for him as for Garneau,
the annexation of Lower Canada to the United States would place the
French Canadians in a situation that would be perilous for their nationality, their language, their religion, and their legal system. To the
"Americanomaniac" Patriotes, he suggested that they "study the history
of Louisiana instead of parodying that of Poland or Ireland."

The debate on the Louisiana syndrome more broadly revealed the
knowledge and perceptions Patriotes and reformists had of the American
political system. Papineau had a particular view of the relationship between the states and the federal government. First of all, he explained at
the Saint-Laurent assembly of 15 May 1837, "the United States cannot
have colonies. Their constitution provides that a territory, as soon as it
has 60,000 inhabitants, can form a free and independent state. It becomes the master and absolute arbiter of its fate." From this he concluded that the twenty-six states that then constituted the United States
formed "twenty-six independent sovereignties," which enjoyed a prosperity they would not have known "if they had remained in dependency
and colonial servitude." In contrast, Parent felt that a Lower Canada annexed to the United States would only be one state among all the states

of the union, and that its representatives in Congress and the Senate would speak English.[54]

Consistently with their Americanity, Papineau, Parent, and Garneau saw Europe as an Old World, as the continent of dependency, characterized by a different social orientation. Conscious that America needed institutions different from those of Europe, Parent warned England against wanting "to make Americans live under a European regime."

Papineau's international references were twofold: one, American, that of a British colony that had achieved its independence, the United States; the other, European, that of Ireland, part of Great Britain, on the way to obtaining the reforms that Lower Canada was also demanding. This was the approach of a parliamentarian: to constantly compare the colonial situation of Lower Canada only with that of the other British colonies, such as Jamaica, Malta, and the British colonies of North America. According to him, the Colonial Office had the same plans for Ireland and Lower Canada: "Because there is no doubt that the petulant, haughty man who is at the head of the Colonial Office, Mr. Stanley, who subjugated Ireland, his homeland, by a barbaric and inhumane law, would like to give us something similar." Consistently with his view of a certain European aristocracy, he wrote: "When I think that the Duke of Richmond, who as viceroy had ruled Ireland, where a feeling of national pride surrounded him every day in the middle of Dublin and the pomp and splendour of the Monarchy, and that this man, after having abandoned that brilliant theatre, came here to repair the ruins of his fortune."

Papineau presented O'Connell's strategy and his achievement as a model of what could also be obtained for Lower Canada: "That, since days of peace and justice are promised to Ireland, the pillage and oppression of which have for centuries surfeited and dishonoured the British Aristocracy, from whom the liberator of his country and the friend of ours, O'Connell, is finally tearing this prey so rich, this victim so fat, they will also be given to the Canadas. O'Connell has already brought down Stanley, the Oppressor, he would likewise bring down his successor if he too wanted a government that had full power and authority over the people, and not a government that drew its authority from the people. It is such a government that the colony should have; from now on, it must no longer, can no longer tolerate any other." The reforms O'Connell had promised and obtained could serve as a guide for the Parti patriote: "That they had the guarantee of this friend of the human race, O'Connell, that they would have a reform, and that the promises of such a man should be of considerable weight. O'Connell promised emancipation to 7,000,000 of his compatriots and did he not win it for them? ... He guaranteed the abolition of titles, and they are on the verge of being abolished. He gave them his word that the union would be repealed and he will succeed … The promises of such a man, who has already delivered his homeland from the shackles that had been imposed on it and who has swept before him ministries after ministries, are an assurance that Canada too will soon receive the reform it had asked for in the institutions and its government." After the announcement of the Russell Resolutions in March 1837, Papineau would harden his tone somewhat with regard to the history of the colonial secretaries: "The inconsistent contradiction there is in their policy, which in the end, and after centuries of oppression against unfortunate Ireland, becomes liberal, because Ireland has made itself feared; which is so base and so cringing toward Russia, which has also made itself feared; and which is so unjust, arrogant and disdainful toward Canada, which they do not fear at all."[55]

Garneau met O'Connell in London and was impressed by his speech on the ills of oppression: "His gestures, the tone of his voice, the language, everything bespoke a powerful orator. He affected Irish pronunciation. His speech was applauded. The occasion did not require a great display of eloquence, but when he spoke of the ills of oppression, his voice had an almost trembling timbre and his eyes had an expression of pain and vengeance that I will never forget." But a comparison of the use of the example of Ireland by Papineau and Parent is more revealing of their views of the situation and the destiny of Lower Canada at a time when the Irish community of Quebec City and Montreal was becoming a significant part of political life. Papineau rejoiced in the reforms already obtained by O'Connell, who had gotten the better of Stanley the oppressor. After the Russell Resolutions, Papineau would become somewhat more radical, suggesting that Lower Canada should make itself feared as Ireland had. Parent instead advised England not to repeat in America the errors made in Ireland: "We cannot believe that England deludes itself with the mad hope of governing American colonies as it governs Ireland, with regiments of soldiers. If it wanted to, it would not have the means." He rejected the comparison between O'Connell and Papineau, because the latter no longer enjoyed unanimous support in Lower Canada as the former did in Ireland. Parent called himself reformist, like O'Connell, and not revolutionary, like the Americans. He opted for the Irish way over the American way, while Papineau sought a course between the successful experience of the United States and the soon-to-be-successful experience of O'Connell, between reformism and a reformism that was always subject to radicalization in an American context.[56]

The most Polish of the French Canadians of the nineteenth century was no doubt Garneau, who found himself in the small colony of Polish refugees in London between 1831 and 1833, and who published a few poems on "the cruel fate" of Poland. The young poet found many similarities then between the grievances of the Poles and those of his fellow citizens: "The same iron fist has always weighed on ancient and modern colonies ... Foreign domination is the greatest evil that can strike a people. Many of our grievances resemble those of which the brave and unhappy Poles complained. But be of good courage! The cause of justice and liberty is too healthy not to triumph." But neither in 1834 nor in 1837 would Garneau believe enough in the similarity of their grievances to mention the case of Poland in the context of his own national studies or demands. His Poland was more poetic and Romantic than political.

In contrast, Parent's Poland was very political, and it inspired in him a decisive attitude: "A weak people can resign itself to an unhappy fate without dishonour; there is honourable submission, just as there is dishonourable domination. Do you know where your beautiful, too hot zeal would lead you ...? To the state Poland has reached today. We would be thrown a few vain words of sympathy from afar, but make no mistake, the yoke of oppression would be left on our necks without anyone making the least effort toward our deliverance ... We have no sympathy to expect from any quarter; our sole recourse is ourselves." Parent was thinking of Poland having been ill-treated by France, which had not kept its promises of support. It was an opportunity for him to raise a fundamental question: who could Lower Canada count on internationally in its plans and demands for emancipation – France, the United States, Louisiana, Upper Canada? And for Parent, reference to the Polish or Belgian experiences certainly did not mean acceptance of the principle of nationality.[57]

Although he was a reader of Lamennais before 1837 and his friend after 1839, and Lamennais had, in *L'Avenir* of Paris, risked his intellectual and spiritual life with regard to the Polish insurrection of 1830, Papineau said nothing about Poland in his public writings. This is surprising, as is Papineau's persistent silence on the experiences of emancipation occurring in Belgium, Italy, Greece, and the America of the Rio de la Plata. Rather than confront the Colonial Office with more radical examples, Papineau, as a responsible parliamentarian and strategist aware of the positions and methods of his metropolitan interlocutors, chose to carry out his colonial struggle using only references to British colonies: the United States to illustrate excess, and Ireland as an example of moderation.

To explain Papineau's public silence on the nationalist decade of the 1830s, we need to take into account the fact that his republican radicalization began in 1830, gradually grew stronger with the election riot of 22 May 1832 and the writing of the 92 Resolutions in February 1834, and was consolidated, after the resolutions were rejected, with the ten Russell Resolutions in February 1837. It should also be noted that from the time of Papineau the father to that of Papineau the son, Lower Canada had gone from absolute monarchy (1759) to constitutional monarchy (1763) and then to a gradual attraction, in the last decade (1830), to American-style republican institutions. In seventy years, this was no small feat. One might also explain Papineau's silence on Belgium, Poland, Italy, and Greece by a simple reformism that led him to call for a partial emancipation somewhere between that of the United States and that of Ireland. This hypothesis, however, is not consistent with the little emphasis placed on responsible government in his political thought and action before 1837 in comparison to that placed on demands related to the civil list and an elected Legislative Council. If Papineau had been first and foremost a reformist, he would have focused on responsible government, as Parent did starting in 1832.

A Patriote-reformist split between Montreal and Quebec City emerges clearly from the analysis of the positions of Papineau, on the one hand, and Parent and Garneau, on the other. While Papineau's pro-Britishism could not withstand the constitutional stalemate of the 1830s, that of Parent and Garneau remained constant, even under criticism. While Parent was conscious of the rising power of the British Empire, Papineau continued to defy that empire.

The silence of these three individuals regarding the July Revolution of 1830 is surprising in view of the impact of those events on the nationalist movement of the decade. Unlike Papineau, Garneau and Parent used the Polish case: Garneau to express his poetic and Romantic attraction to the Polish cause, Parent as an example of a nation whose expectations had been disappointed and abused and to reject any recourse to the principle of nationality.

In thus comparing the points of view of three public figures of Lower Canada of the period, we realize that neither Parent nor Garneau, unlike Papineau, looked up to the independence of the United States. On the contrary, while Papineau was silent on Louisiana, Parent rubbed salt in the wound, pointing out the risks of any comparison between Lower Canada and the American union. This look at the contemporary international situation thus situates Papineau, Parent, and Garneau in their own society, but with different visions of the future of Lower Canada. Papineau saw its future as linked in some way to the United States; Parent and Garneau did not see it involving a union of Upper and Lower Canada; for Parent, such a union would be a federation.

The most surprising aspect of this comparison is that the one who, in light of the international situation, dealt most with the question of nationality and most clearly formulated the type of nationality apparently desired by half of the population, was Parent, the journalist from Quebec City. Papineau was not as explicit on the issue, and both were facing the same challenge: to ensure freedom without risking nationality. But it appears that this nationality, as summed up in the motto of *Le Canadien* of 1831, "Our institutions, our language and our laws" – to which Parent added, in the summer of 1837, an alliance of the flag and the cross – was a cultural and not a political project, that there was a refusal to appeal to the principle of nationality so that this project could be fulfilled through English liberties and liberalism.

THE PATRIOTIC AND NATIONALIST LEXICON

The political debates, the information on the international situation, and the reading and publication of certain poetry introduced citizens to a contemporary vocabulary that the names of the newspaper *Le Canadien* and the Parti patriote sum up very well. While the actual origin of the name "Parti patriote" is not really known, it can be safely attributed to the knowledge people in Lower Canada had of the American Patriots of 1776, as well as the use of the term in South America, which was referred to in the press of Lower Canada as early as 1818. In any case, the word comes from *patrie* ("homeland"), which was quite common in the vocabulary of the period, as was *patriotisme*. The semantic constellation of these words was thus familiar and common, as attested by the name of the political party.[58]

The term *nationalisme* would appear only at the end of the nineteenth century, but the adjective *national* was common, as was the noun *nationalité*, which Parent used frequently starting in 1831, in the restrictive sense he gave it. The word *nationalité* had been used a great deal at the time of the revolution in Belgium, and it was added to the *Dictionnaire de l'Académie française* in 1835. In a text entitled "De la manière dont se forment les nations" (On the manner in which nations are formed), *La Minerve* provided an enthusiastic definition: "Nationality is the regenerating baptism of peoples, it is the lustral water that washes away stain and servitude, it is the God who clothes them in a sublime vocation, it is the seal that imprints them with a sacred nature, it is the pact that unbinds their limbs, that breaks their chains, that opens the doors of their prison, that gives them participation in sovereignty, that makes them equal to their ancestors, to their neighbours, that puts them in charge of the exploitation of their own property, of their own affairs."[59]

Papineau used a minimal nationalist vocabulary: there are few references to tyrants or tyranny in his vocabulary. As he said himself, "The homeland! The homeland! That word alone suffices" as an "oath of loyalty to one's native land." Another time, he said, "Love of one's native or adoptive country is the first of the duties, the most beautiful of the virtues of the citizen." And he said the control of revenues was "the boulevard to national liberty." At the time of the Gosford Commission, he would state, "We represent a people."[60]

If Papineau's nationalist vocabulary was minimal it was because he was a sworn enemy of "national distinctions." Ideologically and politically, he could not and did not want to stir up national differences. He felt that "national antipathies" were "a degrading feeling when one has travelled." Papineau frequently objected to those "national distinctions"; and to the anglophone press and the likes of Adam Thom, who constantly expressed national prejudices, Papineau replied: "They pretend to believe that our demands are the fruit of our different origin and our Catholicism, when it is a constant that the ranks of liberals count a majority of men of every belief and every origin. But what can be said in support of that view when we see Upper Canada, where there are few Catholics and where almost all the inhabitants are of English origin, denouncing the same ills and demanding the same reforms?"

While refusing to provoke or maintain those "national distinctions," Papineau pointed a finger at the institutions responsible for doing so: the system of allocating positions, the system of clergy reserves that favoured the Anglican and Presbyterian clergy – the Roman Catholic clergy had seigneuries – but above all, the Legislative Council, which, through the years and the appointments, had established itself in an unacceptable role: "its unjust claim to have no mission but to provide security to a particular class of the Subjects of His Majesty in this Province as having interests that could not be sufficiently represented in this Assembly ... A claim of this nature is a violation of the Constitution, and can only arouse and perpetuate, among the various classes of the inhabitants of the Province, national suspicions, distinctions and animosities, and tend to give one part of the People an unjust and artificial superiority over the other in the hope of domination and undue preference." In August 1837, Papineau would again point to this major flaw in the colonial situation, one that Lord Durham would not address: "It is the Council itself that ... revealed the baseness of its predilections and its antipathies, that declared itself the organ and passive instrument of one faction, devoted itself to fomenting and protecting national distinctions as an element to be preserved and according to which the government was to be constituted, as if the ills of Ireland and the opprobrium of England had not sufficiently warned them that this principle was an inspiration from hell."[61]

CONCLUSION

Foreign news circulated in the press of Lower Canada after the Congress of Vienna, especially because of the rapid development of events in Europe and America. The newspapers quite often took positions and tried to ensure the accuracy of information by publishing "official" documents.

When the bad news of the Russell Resolutions came in April 1837, people in Lower Canada had at best learned a certain number of things about successful and unsuccessful attempts at national and colonial emancipation. Those who read the papers and those to whom they were read were familiar with a few of the major fighters for independence and emancipation: O'Connell in Ireland, Bolivar and San Martín in South America, Ypsilantis and Kapodistrias in Greece; they also knew about the responsibility taken by these liberators and the attacks "these great characters" could be subjected to. They were aware, through the examples of France in Spain, and England in Greece, that intervention by a country in the internal affairs of another country was a two-edged sword. What country, in the context of the Holy Alliance, would want to risk its peace for the benefit of an oppressed possession? Moreover, people were aware that external help was often needed for emancipation to be achieved; the experience of Poland waiting for support from France had struck their imagination. They had also observed that the emancipation and independence of a country could not be won without recognition, if not by the metropolis, at least by the major powers of the time, Great Britain, France and the United States. The experience of the Netherlands and Belgium in 1830 with regard to two languages and two religions was informative for Viger, his friends, and his readers; they saw the same political problems as those of the French Canadians – conflict between upper and lower houses, council members exercising undue influence over the local authority, the French language at risk – or those that could result from an eventual union after the fears of 1822 – equal rather than proportional representation, sharing of the debt, rights of Catholics threatened.

They had also observed "the fever of discord" in Poland, whose failed revolution had led the press of Lower Canada to seek the causes. Poland had quickly become a favourite example, for *L'Ami du peuple*, for Mgr Lartigue in his pastoral letter of 1837, and for Abbé Maguire in his *Doctrine de l'Église d'Irlande et de celle du Canada sur la révolte* (Doctrine of the Church of Ireland and that of Canada on revolt), leading Parent to feel that there was an "honourable submission" and that they must not count on "elsewhere," whether it be France or the United States.

Papineau was not wrong, in his parliamentarian's logic, to compare Lower Canada first with the British colonies. He was not the only one to use the case of Ireland, with which the similarities and parallels were clear. Moreover, there was much debate about the validity of the comparison of Lower Canada / Ireland, Papineau / O'Connell, and Saint-Jean-Baptiste / St Patrick. Ireland was doubly a mirror: for what took place there – the tensions between Catholics and Protestants, the strategy of repeal of the union, starting in 1830 – and for England's policies – the concessions made out of necessity. The fact that Papineau and Parent did not perceive the same Ireland and the same O'Connell says a lot about the two men, who embodied two different visions of the destiny of Lower Canada. One opted for the Irish way, keeping in reserve the possibility of appealing to the United States, and the other tried to hold together two examples of colonial demands, those that were in the process of being won in Ireland and those that had already been won in the United States.

The American model for the Patriotes was well-known, but the use of Texas as an example was less familiar. In fact, in 1836, the anti-Patriote newspaper *L'Ami du peuple* sought to show that Texas could not serve as a model for Lower Canada to join the American union. The paper maintained that the situation of Lower Canada in relation to Great Britain was in no way comparable to that of Texas in relation to Mexico, and warned that the Patriotes would have to wait as long as the Texans had waited for support and recognition from the United States. Besides, Mexico was one of those "strange new republics" where there was political and constitutional confusion, countries about which the press of Lower Canada wondered whether they should opt for a republican form of government or a constitutional monarchy, even in America.

While the European and American experiences of emancipation from tyranny and metropolis and the independence achieved in Greece, Belgium, and certain countries of South America were followed with interest in Lower Canada; while Austria in particular and the Holy Alliance in general were viewed unfavourably except perhaps by *L'Ami du peuple*; and while some papers showed a clear republicanism, it is striking to see the recurring references in the press to what one newspaper called "the constitutional mania." It was a "mania" that was seen as positive and that consisted of wanting countries that gained independence in one way or another, such as Greece, Belgium, and Poland, to have a "free constitution" – a free constitution that was more like a regime of constitutional monarchy based on the example of Great Britain and the place in the international situation accorded to it in the Lower Canada press.

The British Constitution was the basis France drew on – rather clum-
sily – after the July Revolution; its great strength lay in the possibility of
amendment, and it provided the best guarantees for civil rights. Using
different arguments, people in Lower Canada looked up to England until the Russell Resolutions, while denigrating the colonial authority before, during, and after those Resolutions. They desired the intervention
of British power in Greece; they recognized that the British monarchy
was not one "that trifles with peoples," they suggested that Ferdinand of
Spain show to the colonies of South America the same liberality England
showed to its colonies. There was criticism of the metropolis after 1830,
and at the time of the 92 Resolutions, Ireland of 1830 provided a pretext
for the Patriotes to ask why Great Britain, which was so liberal in Greece
and elsewhere, so resembled Spain and Turkey when it came to the
homeland of O'Connell – and by implication, Lower Canada and
Canada. But overall, in the context of the Treaty of Vienna of 1815 and
the decade of the 1830s, Great Britain was presented as a valid, credible
international arbiter, and its constitution as a model that could be applied to more than one emancipated country.

What, then, was the meaning of the July Revolution of 1830 and the
decade that followed in Lower Canada? First, that France continued to
be unstable politically and constitutionally, that it was hoped that the current revolution would turn out better than the previous one, and that the
best someone like Garneau could wish for it was a monarchy or improved
assurances of liberty. Second, 1830 was used by the anti-Patriote press, in
particular *L'Ami du peuple*, to denounce "the democratic ambition."
Finally, the "Three Glorious Days" of July 1830, despite what was suggested by Amédée Papineau, were not a source of strong and ongoing
inspiration. We may take as an indication of this the dominant vocabulary of *homeland* and *nationality*, and the important but secondary vocabulary of *tyranny* and *liberty*. The most advanced expressions of the claim of
nationhood in Lower Canada on the eve of the Rebellions were those of
Viger, Mondelet, Papineau, Parent, and Rodier, each of whom repeated
the same formulation: "No nation is willing to obey another, for the simple reason that no nation knows how to command another." The words
were far from commonplace, but they were still limited to the expression
of reservations or refusal, rather than what they would soon become: a
demand for the right to self-determination, the principle of nationality.

7

1837

THE CONSTITUTIONAL STRUGGLE that would culminate in the Rebellions of 1837 and 1838 heated up with the passing of the Russell Resolutions by London and the holding of popular assemblies starting in May 1837.

From the point of view of intellectual history, the Rebellions were first and foremost a decisive stage in the evolution of a certain number of ideas. Now that the nationalist component that inspired the Rebellions has been analyzed, there are four causes or dimensions that explain the Rebellions of 1837 and 1838 from the perspective of a social history of ideas: the anti-metropolis dimension (were the Rebellions against the metropolis, and were they triggered by the Russell Resolutions and the disillusionment resulting from London's position?); the anti-government dimension (were they against the colonial oligarchy and the British population whose interests it was protecting – and if so, how?); the anticlerical dimension (were the Patriotes who had to pay the tithe rejecting the principles and political positions of the Church?); the anti-seigneurial dimension (did this social regime impede republican aspirations to equality?).

I will analyze the positions, texts, actions, and events of 1837 and 1838 in light of these questions, documenting and assessing these four causes of the Rebellions.

THE RUSSELL RESOLUTIONS (MARCH 1837)
AND THE CONTEXT OF THEIR RELEASE

Home Secretary Lord John Russell was aware of the gravity of the situation when he rose in the House of Commons in London on 6 March 1837 to state the position of the Imperial Parliament on the 92 Resolutions of 1834 and follow-up the Gosford Commission's recommendations, which had been submitted four days earlier. He took the view that the recommendations of the 1828 Committee on the Affairs of Canada had been carried out; to him, there was no question of modifying the Constitution of 1791 since that would be inconsistent with the colonial status of Lower Canada.

The ten Russell Resolutions constituted a categorical refusal of the demands of the House of Assembly and the vast majority of the population of Lower Canada. No to an elected Legislative Council, which, according to Russell, would simply ratify the laws passed by the House of Assembly, and above all, would exclude the British of the colony, an admission that the appointed Legislative Council was indeed a power structure desired and perpetuated by the metropolis. At best, judges would – once again – be excluded from the Council, to which British and *Canadiens* would be appointed alternately, but the latter was not a procedural rule, only "a matter of discretion."

No to responsible government, which was incompatible with the colonial status of Lower Canada. For a monarchic metropolis, the king could not be represented in the colony by a person who could be replaced by the House of Assembly. The governor was responsible to the king who appointed him, and a responsible government was not conceivable except in an imperial government. If it was proposed that members of the Legislative Council and the House of Assembly be appointed to the Executive, the governor would have to be assured complete freedom to act against the wishes of the Executive.

No to the colonial claims with regard to the ownership of Crown lands, over which the Crown had an inalienable right.

No to the control of revenues, and the governor would be able, with or without the authorization of the House of Assembly, to levy the sum of £142,160 to pay the arrears in the administration of the colonial government since 1832.

Two members of Parliament from the Radical Party, John Temple Leader and Roebuck, who was the agent of the House of Assembly, opposed the proposal. For Leader, it was an arbitrary measure, a coercive law, a provocation: "And what would that amount to but to send troops to the country, and provoke the people by threats and the fear of slavery?" Leader disputed the interpretation of a "contest of races": "no, it was a contest between the people and a nominated council, it was a contest between the oligarchy and the democracy," and the fundamental question, according to him, was whether to side with the majority or the minority. Equating the struggle of Ireland and that of Lower Canada, Roebuck appealed to the sense of imperial justice as he saw it: "I call, then, upon all those who have fought the good fight for our suffering fellow citizens across the Irish Channel, to extend the range of their benevolence, and prove, that if our dominion reaches beyond the broad Atlantic, so also does our justice, and that our desire for good government is co-extensive with our empire."

The appeal to the Irish members of Parliament found a sympathetic ear in O'Connell, who denounced Lord Russell's resolutions: "They contained some of the very worst principles of the worst Tory times. They involved principles that had been the fruitful source of civil war, and dissension, and distraction in Ireland, for centuries. The analogy between Canada and Ireland was greater than the hon. Gentleman was willing to admit. In fact it was complete." And to clearly show how deep the analogy went and the fact that the political imbalance in Lower Canada was identical to that in Ireland, O'Connell added: "The Irish nation was opposed by the Orange party, and that party called the nation a party." The great Irish orator then proposed to the House: "Give the Canadians further constitutional privileges."[1]

The plea fell on deaf ears: the House adopted the Russell Resolutions by 318 votes to fifty-six. Although intended to put an end to the question, they did not achieve that goal. The crisis that had been building since 1810 over issues that had poisoned the political life of the colony since the time of Governor Craig persisted. The central question of an elected Legislative Council was not resolved, nor were those of the revenues and the control of public spending by the House of Assembly or that of responsible government. The Gordian knot had been tightened in order to maintain imperial power. In refusing to relinquish control of the Legislative Council, its voice in the colony, and acknowledging at the outset that responsible government was incompatible with the colonial status of Lower Canada, London was now stating more clearly its refusal to grant greater autonomy to the colony and its desire to prevent democratic power from turning into republicanism. Empire and monarchy stood together. For the French Canadians, it was the end of something – the end of the hope they had placed in the metropolis, a hope that had gone unrewarded for the past two decades. If London had given signs of listening during the plans for union of 1811, 1822, and 1824, if the House of Commons had seemed willing to hear another voice during the Committee on the Affairs of Canada in 1828, and the Gosford Commission from 1835 to 1837, it had finally taken a position under the increased pressure. The Empire had made its bed. It was a dead end, as Alexis de Tocqueville, who had spent a few days in Lower Canada in 1831 and had followed the colonial situation from afar, would observe in January 1838: "At the time of my visit, the *Canadiens* were full of prejudices against the English who lived among them, but they seemed genuinely attached to the English government, which they regarded as a

disinterested arbiter placed between them and this English population
that they feared. How is it that they have became the enemies of that
same government?"[2]

What was to be done, facing this wall: knock it down or continue to hope
that those who had erected it would knock it down? The bad news of the
Resolutions, which became known in Lower Canada about 10 or 11 April
1837, reached a community that was experiencing many pressures.

Since at least 1815, there had been agricultural crises caused by
weather conditions and weevil infestations, resulting in decreased production. This affected the peasants, who were increasingly concerned
about the situation.[3] As a result, the seigneurs and the priests were troubled about the possible loss of revenue from their *cens* (payments to seigneurs by their tenants) and their tithes. The financial crisis that struck
England at the end of 1836 affected the banks in the United States,
which stopped their payments in May 1837.

Along with the economic uncertainty, there were perceptible demographic pressures, with the population doubling every twenty-five years,
creating overpopulation in the seigneuries, for which the future outlet
would be the colonization of new regions or emigration to the United
States. This demographic challenge exacerbated the problem of land
ownership in the Townships and speculation by the British American
Land Company, which was created in 1831. The effects of British immigration following the end of the Napoleonic Wars were visible in the
cities; in 1835, Montreal became a majority anglophone city. Two cholera epidemics, in 1832 and 1834, contributed to social fear and the perception that Irish immigration, in particular, was a questionable policy
on the part of England. The demographic pressure stirred up social and
ethnic tensions, which were no longer limited to complaints about the
disproportionate number of people of British origin in public office: the
anglophone merchant bourgeoisie, which relied on imports and exports
and the imperial tie, opposed the seigneurial regime increasingly firmly;
in working-class Montreal and Quebec, the influx of immigrants created
new competition in the labour force. The election riot of 21 May 1832,
in the middle of a cholera epidemic, was a reflection of the new Irish
presence in the political situation between the Patriotes and the British.[4]

The most palpable pressure was political. Not only had the francophone community been waiting since February 1834 for a response to
the 92 Resolutions, which finally came with the report of the Gosford
Commission on 2 March 1837 and the Russell Resolutions on 6 March,
but the Parti patriote, whose parliamentary initiatives had been deferred
until the question of revenues was settled, had since February 1834 been
organizing committees of correspondence and a permanent central

committee for the district of Montreal (May 1834) to maintain contact
with Viger, Hume, and O'Connell in London, with the sister colonies,
with the members of the Assembly and with other counties. Patriotism
was intensified by the inauguration of Saint-Jean-Baptiste day, the feast
day of the patron saint, on 24 June 1834, and the establishment of the
Union patriotique de Montréal (2 May 1835), a means "of resistance
against abuses of power" according to *Le Canadien* of 1 June; even the
Irish who were in favour of the 92 Resolutions formed the Hibernian
Benevolent Society in March 1834.[5]

The most unprecedented political activity, however, was that of the
anglophones; a sign of the times was that their initiatives now went beyond those of the oligarchy represented by the Executive Council and
the Legislative Council. The Loyalists, who were in favour of maintaining
the Constitution, formed associations starting in November 1834; the
Quebec Constitutional Association and the Montreal Constitutional
Association were founded to "look after the interests of people of British
and Irish origin." The Montreal Constitutional Association soon included at least four patriotic societies – Saint Patrick's Society for the pro-
Constitution Irish, Saint George's Society for the English, Saint Andrew's
Society for the Scots, and the German Society – and in the spring of 1835
it founded the *Morning Courier*. In December 1834, the Doric Club,
which was more radical than the Montreal Constitutional Association
and more secretive, was founded; it published its only manifesto in the
Morning Courier of 22 March 1836. The patriotic determination of the
anglophones was heightened with the creation of the British Rifle Corps,
an organization of "British legionnaires," the dissolution of which
Governor Gosford decreed as a precaution in January 1836, and some
members of which then joined the Doric Club. The activities of patriotic
and political associations and the periodical press indicate that the
Loyalists were organized and had a public discourse that was just as
articulate and just as present as that of the Patriotes. The Loyalists took
a dim view of the national claims of the French Canadians and the
Patriotes, whom they saw as disloyal to the monarch and the Empire.
The British colony had to become and be British, through either assimilation of the French-speaking inhabitants, the union of Upper and
Lower Canada, or a union of the British colonies of North America.[6]

THE RESOLUTIONS OF THE POPULAR ASSEMBLIES
(MAY TO AUGUST 1837)

Because they had decided in 1836 to adjourn their deliberations as
long as they had not obtained satisfaction from London with respect to

revenues and the 92 Resolutions, and because the governor did not convene the House, the members of the Assembly for the Parti patriote adopted an extra-parliamentary strategy, organizing popular assemblies where ideas and demands were debated and expressed in the form of resolutions that were sent to Patriote newspapers such as *La Minerve*. About forty such popular assemblies were held, some thirty in the region of Montreal and six in Quebec City, La Malbaie, Saint-François-du-Lac, Yamachiche, and the counties of Bellechasse and Portneuf. Governor Gosford saw potential danger in these meetings and declared them illegal on 15 June 1837, which did not prevent the Patriotes from attending the vast majority of those held after that date.[7] A line had been crossed: the House of Assembly was now meeting with its electorate, and the popular assemblies attracted enough people that it felt justified in defying the law.

The resolutions expressed the positions and aspirations of the Patriote electorate, which had given the party a majority for ten years; they stated who were the targets of the opposition to the Russell Resolutions – London, the colonial Executive, the clergy, or the seigneurs.

Lower Canada's disappointment with the metropolis after the Russell Resolutions was proportional to its expectations in 1822, in 1828, and with the 92 Resolutions in 1834: it was profound and disturbing. The proliferation of resolutions, which began in 1831 (Goderich) and intensified in 1834 (the 92) and then in 1837 (Russell), continued with those of the popular assemblies. The fact that the recurring demands always took the constitutional or parliamentary form of resolutions is a clear indication of the movement's moderation.

For the people assembled in Saint-Ours-sur-Richelieu, the effect of the Russell Resolutions was to "take from us all guarantees of liberty and good government for the future in this province," and "this last disappointed hope has made us renounce forever the idea of seeking justice on the other side of the sea." Those in Sainte-Scholastique declared that the appropriation of £140,000 without the agreement of the House of Assembly to pay the arrears of the administration was done "against the will of the representation of the country in order to pay off the faction of colonial civil servants who are embezzlers, corrupt and allied against the people," and that it was "a flagrant violation of the essential rights of the People of this Province."[8] The Patriotes of Saint-François-du-Lac considered "that this government should no longer be recognized except as a government of force and oppression, and that it is toward us what it was toward the former colonies of America at the time of the Stamp Act and the tea tax." In La Malbaie, they went further: "We consider as broken and void the social contract that tied us to the British

Empire, which in ceasing to fulfill its commitments relieved us of the obligations treaties impose on us." In Saint-Constant, the possibility of resorting to arms was not excluded: "Given the despicable conduct of power toward this country, [the inhabitants] will view with pleasure the opportunity that will give them the means to shake off the tyrannical yoke that weighs on them, and ... if they ever take up arms, it will not be to save an inch of land in North America for the government."9

With the disappointment of the *Canadiens'* expectations with respect to England, there was a corresponding hope placed in the United States and in the fact of Lower Canada's belonging to America. The inhabitants of Saint-Laurent, near Montreal, considered that reforms such as an elected Legislative Council were the "only ones that suit the state of our society." Those of Saint-Marc-sur-Richelieu supported the strategy of boycotting imported goods and trading in contraband between Lower Canada and the United States. The Patriotes at the Montreal assembly resolved to rely "only on ourselves, our own energy and the sympathy of our neighbours on the American continent."10 New expectations were created that dispelled the old ones with respect to London.

While, as Tocqueville had perceived, the disillusionment with the metropolitan government was new and radical, French Canadians had no more illusions regarding the colonial government. The resolutions of the popular assemblies reiterated the essential demands for an elected Legislative Council and responsible government, demands that were ten years old; they had despaired of a solution ever coming from Quebec City and hoped for a settlement from London – one that in the end did not come.11 We must, however, distinguish the anti-government dimension of the resolutions from an anti-anglophone attitude. The fundamental flaw of colonial power indeed lay in the fact that the Legislative Council and Executive were made up essentially of anglophones; the Patriotes saw this as creating and fuelling the "national distinctions," for which they also blamed those British people in the colony who kept harping on them with the governors and the Colonial Office. At the same time, the Parti patriote was determined to refute accusations that it was anti-anglophone; it had anglophone members who had been elected to the Assembly in francophone counties – Neilson in Quebec City, Wolfred Nelson in Richelieu, O'Callaghan in Yamaska, W.H. Scott in Deux-Montagnes – or in mixed or anglophone counties – Robert Nelson in Montreal, E. Knight in Missisquoi, M. Child in Stanstead; since 1830, it had strengthened its ties with the Irish community of Montreal and Quebec City, and *The Irish Vindicator* had even been bought by French Canadian interests. There were resolutions rejecting such national distinctions; thinking about a possible convention to draft a new constitution, the Patriotes of

Saint-Marc-sur-Richelieu endorsed the "principle" of "the equality of all citizens, without distinction as to origin, language or religion." Despite the memory of the political and constitutional past, despite government favouritism, despite the tone of the anglophone press or the prose of Adam Thom, the Patriotes of Sainte-Scholastique called for "union among the inhabitants of this Province of all beliefs, languages and origins"; they pointed out:

That we have never maintained and that we have on the contrary always condemned the unfortunate national distinctions that our common enemies have sought and seek wickedly to foment among us, and we must proclaim loudly that the point alleged in the reports transmitted to His Majesty's government that the struggle here was between the inhabitants of British origin and those of *Canadien* origin is a malicious suggestion and is contradicted by the well-known character of the *Canadien* inhabitants; and that for our part, whatever the fate of the Country, we will work fearlessly and willingly, as in the past, to ensure for the entire people without distinction the same rights, equal justice and shared freedom.[12]

In spite of this recurrent discourse, it should not be forgotten that when tensions mounted, the first harassment by Patriotes would be against anglophones.[13]

While it was not very frequent in the resolutions of the popular assemblies, an anticlerical thrust was nevertheless evident in those of Vaudreuil and Saint-Ignace: "That religion was not established by its divine creator with the intention to make it an engine of political intrigues, nor an instrument of a party or opposition to the moral needs of peoples." These words and this tone had their origin in the declaration of Mgr Lartigue on 25 July 1837 during the consecration of his coadjutor, Mgr Ignace Bourget. Before the entire clergy of the diocese of Montreal at a banquet that ended with a toast to the king, the bishop reiterated the political doctrine of the Roman Catholic Church: it was forbidden to rebel against legitimate authority or to absolve those who preached such rebellion.[14] The liberal press in Montreal and Quebec City reacted strongly to the directive. *La Minerve* said it feared that "the tribunal of penitence" would be "converted into a political bogeyman" and reminded readers that "the alliance of church and state is a dangerous union," that "theocratic government is the most dangerous and most intolerable of all powers" and that "history demonstrates [that the alliance of the two powers] ended by disrupting all the nations where it had existed." More incisively, *Le Libéral* wrote: "They [the priests] would much better quietly receive their tithes and the thousand other contributions exacted through the ignorance of the people, as long as they preach in return the moral doctrines of Christianity to their flocks, than come down into the political arena, prompted as they always are in these questions by their private interests."[15] When the Patriotes of Vaudreuil passed their resolution, *La Minerve* went on the offensive again, stating what liberals meant by "legitimate authority": "to preach respect for legitimate authority is to preach respect for the people, the only legitimate source of authority." The people was sovereign and "*Omnis potestas [non est] a Deo.*"

The warnings about church taxes (tithes) could be coupled with others about seigneurial taxes (rents). The question of seigneurial tenure – the form of land ownership – was contentious since 1760. The French Canadians saw it as an aspect of their social identity, a means of protecting that identity against the threat of anglicization, while the British of the colony considered it archaic and feudal, an obstacle to the development of real estate, commerce, and industry. In 1830, petitions on seigneurial tenure circulating among French Canadians aimed not for its abolition, but rather for the correction of certain abuses. Committees of the House of Assembly investigated the issue, but without ever following up. An exchange of ideas in *La Minerve* from December 1836 to March 1837 between "Agricola," Dr Cyrille Côté, and "Jean-Paul," Amury Girod, about the seigneurial regime, shows the position of the more radical Patriotes and that of the Parti patriote. For Dr Côté, the seigneurial regime was aristocratic, anti-democratic, and unacceptable because it reserved for the seigneurs the riches of the present and the future (wood, minerals, mill sites on the water network). Girod recognized the reparable abuses of the system and favoured compensation in the event of its abolition, while also opposing the seigneurs' right of banality (their exclusive right to mill wheat). The debate came to an abrupt end with the news of the Russell Resolutions, which proposed, on the one hand, the abolition of seigneurial tenure in favour of a system of land tenure free of all constraints, and, on the other hand, the maintenance of the rights of the Crown over the land in the Eastern Townships and those of the speculators of the British American Land Company.[16] The problem of land ownership was thus doubly contentious.

The Patriotes of Sainte-Rose and Napierville felt that to "ensure sooner or later the triumph of the democratic principles that alone can form the basis of a free and stable government on this new continent," to "snatch from the government any hope of establishing in the country a core of aristocracy," that "this assembly regard as one of the most fitting ways to achieve this purpose the abolition of seigneurial rights while giving the owners just and reasonable compensation, and the institution of an entirely free tenure system, which our customs and our needs demand loudly and urgently." In Saint-François-du-Lac, the whole

Patriote assembly was on the seigneurial system, and it denounced the *lods et rentes* (fines of alienation) as an "immoral and unjust tax on the industry of the inhabitants of this country." The Patriotes of Vaudreuil felt that seigneurial rights were "incompatible with the liberty and feelings of the people."[17]

One thing is certain, the seigneurs knew where their interests lay; whether they were "weathercocks" or "turncoats" (Debartzch, Sabrevois de Bleury, Dumoulin, Dionne, Languedoc) or had always been pro-British (Hertel de Rouville, de Saint-Ours, de Tonnancour, Rolland, Masson, B. Joliette, not to mention Church seigneurs such as Saint-Sulpice and the Séminaire de Québec), all the francophone and anglophone seigneurs except Papineau sided with the established power. Some such as Debartzch in Saint-Charles-sur-Richelieu and Ellice in Beauharnois would even see their manors occupied by the Patriotes.[18]

PAPINEAU AND PARENT ON THE RUSSELL
RESOLUTIONS AND THE POPULAR ASSEMBLIES
(APRIL TO AUGUST 1837)

Papineau, who participated in the assemblies in Saint-Laurent, Sainte-Scholastique, and the counties of L'Islet, Bellechasse and L'Assomption, clearly expressed his disappointed expectations and the need to find another approach: in Saint-Laurent, he declared: "The new circumstance ... is that the British Parliament has taken a position against us." He said to the Patriotes assembled in Sainte-Scholastique: "We had hopes in the House of Commons; but that House tricked us; a wretched royal commission [Gosford] fooled the Lords, the ministers and the Commons in which we had misplaced our trust." Since the "persecutory government has dismissed each and every one of the reforms requested," it seemed clear, he acknowledged, that the time for petitions was over and "the time for a test has come," a test that would reveal the true Patriotes. The tone became more insistent, because the grievances were "becoming increasingly unbearable"; in L'Assomption, the Patriote leader stressed the gravity of the situation: "We must hope that we will not be pushed to the ultimate extremes." While he maintained that the "European colonial system must be remade and reshaped," that "all the colonies have the most urgent reasons to move forward the time of their separation" and that "we must be ready sooner or later to take what the iron fist of power would want to take from us," he noted that his approach was still constitutional resistance. Similarly, although a republican admirer of American institutions, he was not ready, for the time being, for a union with the large neighbouring republic: "That union is seductive, and ours at the present time is humiliating. Does it therefore follow that we must repudiate one to embrace the other? Caution!" But he did not miss the opportunity to say, in the same breath, for the benefit of the governor and the secretary of state for the colonies, that if "Lord Russell's determination is a firm plan," "the history of the old plantations will begin again with the same inevitable outcome."[19]

While, addressing the governor and the colonial Executive, Papineau continued to demand acceptance of the 92 Resolutions of 1834, it was clear that London's refusal through the Russell Resolutions forced him to maintain the strategy of boycotting imported goods, if not of encouraging contraband, so that the colony, with no tax revenue, would become a burden for the metropolis. With respect to the anglophones in the colony, Papineau reiterated his position: "Whoever comes to share our fate as an equal is a friend who will be welcome, regardless of the place of his birth." Silent on the political positions of Mgr Lartigue and the clergy and on the seigneurial question, Papineau made the following enigmatic comment to the Patriotes of Berthier-en-Bas in June 1837: "In the circumstances, the seigneur is no more than his *censitaire*."[20]

From the perspective of the history of the ideas of the francophone majority, the Rebellions of 1837 and 1838 form a chorus of three voices: that of the Patriotes and the Parti patriote, which was Papineau's; that of the more radical Patriotes – Dr Côté, Rodier, the Nelson brothers – who in 1837 were identified with certain counties and certain themes in the popular but radical assemblies that would emerge especially during the rebellion of 1838; and finally, that of Parent, which introduced discord. There was discord between Papineau and Parent, and between the Montreal region and the Quebec City region, where John Neilson, who had been Papineau's ally in both Quebec City and London, had distanced himself from the Parti patriote on the 92 Resolutions. The Patriotes would even have to found the short-lived *Le Libéral* in Quebec City to try to counter Parent's *Le Canadien.*

Even before the Russell Resolutions, Parent had shown his colours: "In the interest of [their] national existence, the *Canadiens* must remain united with the British Empire; in the interest of its domination on the American continent, England must protect the *Canadiens* in their national rights." After the Russell Resolutions, Parent opposed the idea that the time for petitions was over and opted for "submission accompanied by energetic and solemn protest"; he rejected constitutional opposition and proposed "decisive resistance carried out on the terrain where the ministers themselves have established themselves." He denounced the interference of the Imperial Parliament in the affairs of the House of Assembly – the "hand in the provincial coffers" that constituted an "act of aggression ... that breaks the social contract and that would make any resistance holy, even with physical force." But one metaphor best expressed this great journalist's position: the observation that "the vessel of our liberties has been thrown upon the reefs of British high-handedness and the debris is scattered on the beach"; he refused to attempt "the hazards of a new fate," proposing instead that the "pilot follow another course" and see "if we cannot repair the damage of the storm, enough to allow us to hope for tolerable navigation." This "tolerable" navigation was his position, which he also expressed more gravely, as follows: "A weak people can resign itself to an unhappy fate without dishonour; there is honourable submission, just as there is dishonourable domination."[21]

Parent suggested to the "moderates" that they organize their own popular assemblies, expressing his disagreement with the content of those of the Patriotes in the Montreal region. With respect to the resolutions of Saint-Ours-sur-Richelieu, which declared war on England and appealed to the United States, he remarked that they were counting a lot "on elsewhere," while the leaders did not have the credibility of those of the American colonies of 1774. He called the petition to the American Congress by the assembly of Saint-Laurent, and Papineau's idea of a rapprochement, if not an outright union, with the United States, "the work of a childish desire." A former ally of the Patriotes, he was wary of this "elsewhere" across the border because Americans "are born, live and die calculating," and he feared that the Canadian people would find themselves in the situation of "Poland, which counted a lot on the support of France in its last insurrection." It would thus be better not to rely too much on the Americans: "One dines poorly and late when one relies on one's neighbour." Well-informed on the international situation and conscious of the increase of Great Britain's imperial power, he replied to the Patriotes of Bellechasse county: "Strange conduct indeed that of a weak colony that, while admitting it is unable to repel the encroachment of a vital right, would nevertheless provoke an all-powerful metropolis to strip it of all its liberties."[22]

Parent's opposition to the Patriote approach even became more radical: "We have not repelled the oppression of a Dalhousie or an Aylmer to today accept shackles from the hands of the central committee, or from anyone else." He was the target of a concerted attack by *Le Libéral*, *La Minerve*, and *The Vindicator*, but he felt he represented the position of French Canadians: "Would they want to punish us for being right, for having hit the point where public opinion should rest?"[23]

Parent was prepared to give the colonial and metropolitan governments another chance on condition that they introduced the reforms that were necessary "and of a nature to satisfy free men and prevent them from seeking sympathies outside the empire." To him, the priority was the reform of the Legislative Council. While he was not very concerned about the seigneurial question, he intended "to defend our religious establishment" against the charges of "L.M.N.," a pseudonym of Thomas Storrow Brown in the *New York Daily Express*. And for the first time, in response to a certain Patriote radicalization against political interference by the clergy, Parent proposed "bringing together the standard of the cross with the standard of the defenders of our institutions, our language and our laws," marking the birth of a type of nationality that was destined for a long life.[24] Religion had implicitly been added to the motto of *Le Canadien*.

THE SESSION OF AUGUST 1837: PAPINEAU VS. PARENT

The session convened by Governor Gosford to officially inform the House of the content of the Russell Resolutions lasted only eight days (from the 18th to the 26th), but that week witnesssed the final effort of the moderates to modify the Patriotes' strategy. Papineau maintained that it was necessary "more than ever to stand tall" and not to waver in the demand for an elected Legislative Council. He denounced London's strategy of using the law of the strong to protect the British minority of the colony and "prolong the ruinous and fraudulent game that all the ministers and all the governments without a single exception from 1792 until today have played against the country in organizing the two Houses in a perpetual struggle that makes their lucrative amusement, which an elected Council would spoil and destroy straightaway." The Patriote leader envisaged the day when the connection with the Empire "will inevitably have to come to an end through the passage of time."

Taschereau, the member for Beauce, rose to suggest another response to the governor's speech. Some Patriote members also spoke, saying they could not vote in favour of a reply whose "father" they did not know, implying that they guessed that this "father" was Parent, the editor of *Le Canadien* and the spokesperson for the citizens of the Quebec City region. It was indeed the ideas of Parent that Taschereau was expressing: regret that the revenues had not been voted in the 1835–36 session, and in particular, criticism that so much – too much – emphasis had been placed on the demand for an elected Legislative Council. He was also critical of the popular assemblies, with their spirit of rebellion and the rash appeal to foreigners; he said he was still in favour of an elected Legislative Council, but he would nonetheless agree to legislate on the basis of a promise of reforms from the British authorities.

Augustin-Norbert Morin, the member for Drolet, spoke against this conciliatory approach: "If we do not make an elected Council a sine qua non condition, a question without which we want no conciliation, we will be taking a step back twenty years." He expressed indignation at Taschereau's words, which he called "worthy of the Legislative Council," and dismissed any impulse toward conciliation. A new stage had been entered, according to him, and the Executive was "no longer able, either in its leader or in its other members, to carry out the reforms absolutely required as the first step to any arrangement between the metropolis and the colony in a just, equitable, impartial way that [could] satisfy this House and the people."[25]

Several days later in *Le Canadien,* Parent defined nationality as he saw it, defended it and would continue to defend it: "the cause of freedom defended with prudence and moderation, and always in the interest of what we call nationality, the preservation of which constitutes us as a people, and of what makes *Canadiens* the happiest and most moral people that exists; in a word, it is the cause of true patriotism, as opposed to that of false patriotism, which, a new Esau, would be ready to sell our birthright for a mess of pottage, perhaps for something even less." Parent's major question was then whether Canada (and not only Lower Canada) would take its place among the nations, whether it would become part of the American union or whether a new union would be born.[26]

THE MANIFESTO OF THE FILS DE LA LIBERTÉ
(4 OCTOBER 1837)

Founded in September 1837 on the model of the Sons of Liberty of the American War of Independence, the Fils de la liberté presented themselves, at least at first, as a purely preventive and defensive association. In October 1837, they published a manifesto written by Thomas Storrow Brown and addressed to the "young people of the colonies of North America." The document recalled that 1776 and 1789 had shaken England, that "the authority of a motherland over a colony can only exist as long as that can please the colonials who live in it" and that, consequently, it was necessary to "shake off the yoke of monarchy." The republican and secessionist perspective of the manifesto was clear: "A separation has begun between parties whose union it will never be possible to cement again, but that will be pursued with increasing vigour, until one of those unexpected and unforeseen events as occur from time to time in the course of the present has provided us with a favourable opportunity to take our place among the independent sovereignties of America." The Fils de la liberté, who attributed "all our troubles to the deleterious

action of the colonial government," appealed to all youth, independently of beliefs, origins or ancestors, and in this scenario of the future, guaranteed "a strict equality before the law for all classes without distinction
of origin, language or religion."

Parent did not think much of the manifesto, the "insanity" of the "agitators" from Montreal or the Fils de la liberté, because of whom, he said,
"we find ourselves between grapeshot on one side and dishonour on the
other." As for Papineau and the Patriotes who had signed an address to
the London Working Men's Association, which had become aware of the
Canadian situation through British radicals, they shared this vision of a
continental future: "We have not mentioned independence from the
British Crown, but we have not forgotten that the destiny of the continental colonies is to separate from the metropolitan state when the unconstitutional action of a legislative power residing in a distant country is
no longer bearable."[27]

THE MAJOR ASSEMBLY OF THE CONFÉDÉRATION DES SIX COMTÉS (23–24 OCTOBER 1837)

The movement of popular assemblies that had started in May reached its
peak in Saint-Charles-sur-Richelieu on 23 and 24 October with the major assembly of the Confédération des Six Comtés. Thirteen members of
the House of Assembly took part, including Papineau, who appeared
dressed in locally produced homespun in accordance with his strategy
of boycotting imported products. Banners greeted the participants:
"Gosford persecutor of the *Canadiens*," "Honour to those who have sent
back their commissions and those who were dismissed," "INDEPENDENCE,"
"Legislative Council sine qua non!," "Long live Papineau and the elective
system." There was something military about the staging, with the firing
of cannons and muskets to welcome Papineau. The resolutions of the
assembly, written by Papineau and O'Callaghan, recapitulated the demands of the previous assemblies, but added an expression of concern
about the increase in the number of soldiers: "And the ultimate of our
misfortunes, this Governor-in-Chief has lately introduced great bodies of
armed troops into this province in a time of profound peace in order to
destroy by physical force any constitutional resistance, and to complete
by desolation and death, the work of tyranny already resolved and authorized overseas."

The address of the Confédération des Six Comtés, probably written by
Papineau, recalled both the constitutional approach taken until then
and the fact that French Canadians were bearing "the unbearable" – an
allusion to Parent – an irresponsible Executive, a non-elected Legislative

Council, judges dependent on the Executive, and the alienation of their lands. To these Patriotes, who believed that popular sovereignty conferred the right to change the system of government, London had shown a "guilty determination to sap and overthrow the very foundations of civil liberty," and they said they were no longer "attached to the British Empire": "Thus the experience of the past demonstrates the folly of waiting and hoping for justice from the European authorities." Once again, a reference to the experience of the United States was meant to warn the metropolis of a scenario other than that of the tie with the Empire: the address, written in the spirit of human rights as formulated in the American Declaration of Independence, recalled that "our history is but a recapitulation of the evils that the other colonies have endured before us. Our grievances are but a second edition of theirs." And the Patriotes were convinced that their republican neighbours "will not consent that the principles for which they fought with such success in the eighteenth century be in our persons trodden on in the nineteenth century." The text ended with an appeal to all, of whatever origin, language, or religion, and "having no more hope but in you," to organize vigilance committees, elect magistrates, increase the number of organizations of the Fils de la liberté "in order to be ready to act promptly and effectively when circumstances require it" and to place the militias under the officers of their choice.[28]

Parent said in *Le Canadien* that he was concerned about the impression given abroad that "the Canadian people is about to declare itself independent." He asked the Patriotes and their leaders if it was necessary "that the government know that to obtain *all* of our demands, we are *all* ready to risk *all*?" He called for the organization of a counter-federation of moderates who would draw their inspiration from Ireland rather than the United States: "We then show ourselves no longer in the position of the former colonies on the eve of their declaration of independence, but rather in that of O'Connell and Ireland, asking insistently for the suppression of abuses and wanting only to achieve that by peaceful means, believing with him that no political improvements are worth a drop of human blood; we are Reformers, we cease to be Revolutionaries." Because faced with "Revolutionaries ... Parliament will grant everything to the Ministers and the local oligarchy."[29]

THE ASSEMBLY OF THE MONTREAL CONSTITUTIONAL ASSOCIATION (24 OCTOBER 1837)

Simultaneously with the "Convention" in Saint-Charles, the Montreal Constitutional Association, which included British loyalists, St Patrick's

Society, St George's Society, St Andrew's Society, and the German Society, organized a big assembly in Montreal, the culmination of a dozen loyalist assemblies held in Rawdon, Napierville, Trois-Rivières, Quebec City, Aylmer, Yamaska, Milton, and Clarenceville. The banners waving above the crowd read "Reform Not Revolution," "United we Stand," "A Reformed Council not an Elective One," and "Registry and Abolition of Feudal Tenures." The assembly had been organized to maintain the order that was under attack by a revolutionary faction incapable of appreciating British institutions, and it passed resolutions that clearly stated the Loyalists' position: the right to protection by the government; support of the Crown, which was threatened by disloyal officers; organization of neighbourhood associations "in case of disturbance"; rejection of an elected Legislative Council; abolition of seigneurial tenure.

Peter McGill, an anglophone Protestant speaker at the assembly, did not spare the "vacillating policy" of the Colonial Office; he attacked the Patriote leaders, with their "disappointed ambitions," all of them "imbued with a mortal hatred of British supremacy" and "assailing alike the Altar, the Throne, and the Bench." McGill was respectful of order, and he stated that he was relying on the intervention of the Catholic clergy and the influence "of their venerable and respected pastors, and holy religion which inculcates loyalty to the Sovereign." The journalist Adam Thom, the very personification of opposition to French Canadians, stated that "our present evils do emanate from Downing Street" and, referring to the garrison on Île Sainte-Hélène, the bayonets of the troops on the Champ de Mars and the proud citadel of Quebec City, made the following provocative declaration: "Will Mr. Papineau be so valiantly infatuated as to hoist the tricolour of rebellion?"[30]

MGR LARTIGUE'S PASTORAL LETTER
(24 OCTOBER 1837)

Things were clearly reaching a point of no return. The Patriotes and the Loyalists held assemblies on 23 and 24 October 1837 and the bishop of Montreal, remembering the issue of the fabriques and the rise of the liberals, published a pastoral letter to the faithful of the diocese. Mgr Lartigue emphasized once again that the origin of civil power was divine power, and not the people – *Omnis potestas a Deo* – and recalled the duties of Catholics with respect to established, constituted power. Well aware of the rise of nationalities in Europe and the crisis of the liberal Catholics with regard to the insurrection in Poland, Mgr Lartigue attached to the pastoral letter Lamennais's declaration of submission to the papal condemnation of *L'Avenir* of Paris of 6 February 1831, Pope

Gregory XVI's encyclical of 15 August 1832 condemning the political ideas of the Polish Catholic liberals, and the papal bull to the bishops of Poland charging them to preach the submission of the Polish liberal Catholics to the constituted power of the Czar of all the Russias. Thus, anyone who "resists the Powers that be resists God's order," and the results of such insubordination could be horrible: "Did you ever seriously think about the horrors of a civil war? Did you ever represent to yourselves your streets and your countrysides deluged with blood, the innocent and the guilty wrapped up in the same series of woes?" A former Mennaisian who had submitted to Church authority, the bishop recognized in the rise of the Patriote movement the desire for popular sovereignty and the distinction of the religious and the political, if not the separation of church and state, that had inspired the liberal and nationalist Catholics in Poland.

A *Défense du mandement de Mgr. Lartigue* (Defence of Mgr Lartigue's pastoral letter), written by the bishop himself and dated 24 October, appeared in *La Minerve* of 17 November; it urged the Patriotes either to stop calling themselves Catholics or to renounce "the maxims of revolt against the civil government." For it was clear to the religious authority addressing Catholics that if "you reject their [the bishops'] teachings, you are not in the Church." Pointing out the contradictions of the Irish pro-Patriote *Vindicator* and at the same time subtly legitimizing the Church's intervention in temporal matters, Mgr Lartigue reminded the paper that it supported the union of the clergy and the people in Ireland while rejecting it in Lower Canada. But above all, the bishop established an equation that it would take a century to solve: political principles fall under the purview of religion, since the basis of politics is morality and the basis of morality is religion. This spiritual hierarchy of temporal goals – religion / morality / politics – had a bright future ahead of it.[31]

The bishop intervened in this way because his priests were reporting disturbing behaviour to him, in particular in the southwest district of Montreal. In Saint-Cyprien-de-Napierville, the habitants had passed a resolution in which they said, "we will continue to protest our most sacred attachment to our religion while nevertheless hoping that the people will be given the liberty to do and think whatever it wishes on the form of government, which should be described by the people and not by its religious leaders." The local priest wrote to his bishop that "spirits have become heated" since the pastoral letter, that resolutions had been passed when people were leaving services during which the pastoral letter had been read, that people were talking about "doing away with" tithes and seigneurial rights, and that if the collector of the *rentes* came to collect arrears, "he would receive more lashes of the whip than money." Some Patriotes gave him a charivari, singing a "Libera" in front of the presbytery. Recognizing privately that he used the confessional as an instrument of persuasion, the priest noted to his bishop: "At the tribunal of penitence, those that are questioned on fidelity to the king answer curtly, 'Father, I did not come here to talk politics. If you don't want to hear my confession, I'll leave.'" Annoyed, he added: "I don't know through what enchantment our good habitants have been persuaded that obedience to the authorities was a purely political question that does not concern religion." It was indeed worrying that people were seeking to distinguish between politics and morality, the sovereignty of the people and the sovereignty of God and the king, civil power and religious power. In rejecting these distinctions, the Church was taking a risk that the bishop of Quebec City recognized: "They shout loudly at the doors of the Churches that the clergy has sided with the enemies of the people in order to crush it." The alliance of the Church and political power, British or not, could be a costly principle.[32]

SKIRMISHES, CLASHES, AND COMBAT
(6 NOVEMBER TO 16 DECEMBER 1837)

All these resolutions and warnings indicate clearly that the situation had reached a point of no return; and with the clash in Montreal (6 November) between the Doric Club and the Fils de la liberté, and the defeat of the Patriotes in Sainte-Scholastique and Sainte-Thérèse (16 December), the phase of assemblies and speeches gave way to one of civil unrest in the Richelieu Valley region and northwest of Montreal. These events, described and analyzed briefly, are only of interest to the history of ideas for their symbolic importance and for the assessment they make possible of the scale of the initiatives taken.

The confrontation of 6 November marked the beginning of repression by the political and military authorities and by the Loyalists. From that time to the Battle of Saint-Denis, the Patriotes had no other choice but to organize themselves as best they could. The clash between the loyalist Doric Club, which had existed since 1834, and the Fils de la liberté, formed in September 1837, had a double significance. First, with respect to the Patriote movement in Montreal itself: the Doric Club, with the support of the majority of the anglophone population, the anglophone bourgeoisie and the army garrison on Île Sainte-Hélène, had an obvious advantage, which explains how it was able to best the Fils de la liberté. In addition to these demographic and economic factors, ten days after the confrontation, arrest warrants were issued for the Patriote leaders, including Papineau, and it became obvious that the Patriotes would have to avoid Montreal and move the resistance and fighting to the countryside. Second, the non-intervention or late intervention of the army during the sacking of the offices of *The Vindicator* would be perceived by French Canadians as an obvious case of collusion between the civil power and the military power and, in a sense, a repeat of the riot of 21 May 1832.[33]

It was around this time (on 10 November) that the Patriotes decided to form an armed guard for Patriote leaders such as Papineau and Nelson, who was in Saint-Denis. Three days later, the colonial political authority was carrying out its purge of the bench and the militia, dismissing magistrates, justices of the peace and officers of the militia who were pro-Patriote, in order to put in place a loyalist judicial and military structure. In September 1837, there were eighteen magistrates and thirty-three militia officers dismissed, while, in the Patriote community, the honourable course was felt to be resignation. A parallel judicial and military structure was established through the selection of magistrates and militia officers suggested by the Patriotes. The situation deteriorated to the point where there were two parallel legal structures that were prepared to judge possible offences according to criteria that were likely different, if not contradictory. The Patriote strategy was both more radical and more specifically Canadian than that of boycotting imported British goods, which had been borrowed from the Americans.[34]

At the same time as he was issuing arrest warrants against the Patriote leaders (16 November), Lord Gosford authorized the formation of a volunteer corps of 1,000 to 2,000 men in Montreal and 800 men in Quebec City. These motivated loyalist volunteers, who were often members of the Doric Club, supplemented a garrison that in August 1837 consisted of 1,000 soldiers in Montreal and 1,700 in Quebec City. The following day's successful ambush by the Patriotes near Longueuil to free their members who had been taken prisoner on the pretext of arrest warrants, and the establishment of a camp in Saint-Charles-sur-Richelieu on 18 November led to troop movements, with Colonel Wetherall leaving Montreal for Fort Chambly and Colonel Gore going (22 November) from Sorel to Saint-Denis-sur-Richelieu. In Saint-Denis (23 November), 800 Patriotes, of whom 200 were armed, routed 300 of Gore's soldiers. That would be the Patriotes' only victory. On the 25th, Wetherall, who had set out from Saint-Hilaire with 350 men, a cavalry troop, and two pieces of artillery, crushed 200 to 300 Patriotes, of whom

50 were armed, in Saint-Charles, in a battle that showed quite clearly the Patriotes' total lack of strategy. On 6 December, 80 Patriotes exiled in Vermont set out from Swanton, but they were defeated by the Missisquoi Volunteers; a week later, Governor Jenison of Vermont proclaimed the neutrality of the state, leading to some disillusionment for the Patriotes and their leaders, who had for a long time been counting on "elsewhere" – their republican neighbours.

On 14 and 15 December, in Saint-Eustache and Saint-Benoît, north of Montreal, General Colborne, with 1,200 soldiers, 230 volunteers, and 12 cannon, faced 200 to 250 Patriotes, of whom 70 to 100 were killed and a greater number taken prisoner. On the 16th, the Patriotes were also defeated in Sainte-Scholastique and Sainte-Thérèse.[35]

The clamour of arms silenced the voices of the Patriotes, the press in particular. *The Vindicator*, whose offices had been sacked by the Doric Club, stopped publishing. Facing exile, Duvernay published his last issue of *La Minerve* on 20 December, and the same day, *Le Libéral* of Quebec City stopped publishing. François Lemaître, who had been printing *Le Libéral*, launched *La Quotidienne* in Montreal on 30 November, but his arrest and the confiscation of his presses prevented the publication of the newspaper from January to June 1838. On the other hand, the voice of power made itself loudly heard through proclamations, arrests and jailings, the conservative press, and the directives of the bishops of Montreal and Quebec City. *Le Populaire* continued to appear until November 1838 and *L'Ami du peuple, de l'ordre et des lois*, which was the property of Sulpician loyalists and was founded by the head of the secret police during the Rebellions, Pierre-Édouard Leclère, would defend law and order until 1840.

The alliance of religious power with political and military power took many forms. On 4 December, the bishop of Quebec City asked the faithful to facilitate the movement of troops coming from New Brunswick, who "come only to protect the inhabitants and to maintain public tranquility"; he assured them that their "efforts toward this very laudable goal would certainly be duly appreciated by a government that has shown unequivocal proof of being well disposed toward the clergy." A week later, he suggested public prayers in reparation and denounced those "blinded men" who circulated "doctrines that favoured insubordination." The bishop of Montreal informed the priests that "the Church so loathes this crime that it refuses to bury in the cemeteries those who are guilty" of this rebellion against their sovereign. Mgr Lartigue even sent a petition from the clergy of Montreal to the young Queen Victoria, proclaiming his "extreme sorrow" and begging for an "act of clemency" in spite of "the crime of a few."[36]

MEANWHILE IN LONDON ...

One month after the battles of Saint-Denis and Saint-Charles, the affairs of Canada resurfaced in the House of Commons in London, where Lord Russell provided an imperial reading of the causes of the Rebellions: "The intention was not to obtain redress by means of representation from the Assembly, but to look for redress by arms, to obtain it by violence, and to oppose by force her Majesty's Government in that province." The responsibility was thus placed on the colonials and not the Colonial Office.

The Radical member of Parliament Leader rose to denounce the effects of the Russell Resolutions: "Canadians, before excited by long years of misgovernment, were driven to desperation." All that the Colonial Office's policy had done was to place Canadians before a dilemma: "this dilemma, either to submit to the resolutions and be slaves, or to resist them and run the risk of civil war. In this dilemma, they made that choice which would be made by every people who had since enjoyed any portion of freedom – they determined on resistance." And to avoid the worst, London had but one alternative: to respond to the grievances or to allow "an amicable separation of the two countries. The North American provinces are now strong enough to take care of themselves, and they know it." His colleagues Hume and George Grote shared this analysis of metropolitan responsibility for the events that had occurred in the Canadian colony. The member of Parliament Molesworth expressed indignation at Great Britain's refusal of reforms, "which would offer the world the disgracious and disgraceful spectacle of a free and mighty nation succeeding by force and arms in putting down and tyrannising over a free though feebler community struggling in defence of its just rights."[37]

Arthur Roebuck, the agent of the Lower Canada House of Assembly in London, wrote to Prime Minister Melbourne to make a suggestion: to establish a federation of the Canadian provinces.[38] The spectre of a new union appeared in the House of Commons.

8

1838

THE CONFRONTATIONS OF 1838 involving Patriotes who had gone into exile in the United States had two consequences for the Patriotes – a split during the assembly in Middlebury and Robert Nelson's "Declaration of Independence" – both of which the Catholic Church and the metropolitan government had already responded to before the failed battles of November and December 1838.

THE ASSEMBLY IN MIDDLEBURY AND ROBERT NELSON'S "DECLARATION OF INDEPENDENCE"

Leaders of the four to five hundred Patriotes in exile in the states of Vermont and New York met in Middlebury, Vermont on 2 January 1838 to take stock of the situation and develop a strategy after the defeats of November and December 1837 in the Richelieu Valley and northwest of Montreal. The decisions they made, in particular the decisions to carry out new attacks and to do away with the seigneurial system, would create divisions among the exiled Patriotes. And they would not have the backing of Papineau, who, disagreeing with their radicalism, left Albany for Philadelphia on 20 February 1838 before going into exile the next year in Paris, where he would undertake a mission to raise awareness of the situation of Lower Canada. Dr Robert Nelson described the differences between the radicals and Papineau this way: "Papineau has abandoned us for selfish and family motives regarding the seigneuries and his inveterate love for the old French laws. We can do better without him than with him."[1] He was not wrong about the reasons; to Papineau, the abolition of the seigneurial regime without compensation was illegal and unjust, and stealing from a seigneur was no more justified than stealing from anyone else. But from the perspective of the radical Patriotes, Papineau the seigneur had overtaken Papineau the democrat, and while there were different strategic visions behind this social disagreement – expectations of diplomatic and military support from the United States and perhaps from France – it also called into question Papineau's moderation with respect to England and his public silence on the political interventions of the Catholic clergy. In addition, Papineau's expectations with respect to United States had been dampened by the neutrality statement made by President Martin Van Buren on the previous 23 December, instructing officers and governors "to prevent any unlawful interference on the part of our citizens in the contest unfortunately commenced in the British Provinces" and warning that any persons "who shall compromit the neutrality of this Government ... will render themselves liable to arrest and punishment."[2]

The "Declaration of Independence" signed by Robert Nelson provides a good summary of the new radicalization displayed by the exiled Patriotes, although it arose under circumstances that made it somewhat ridiculous: the failed attack on Caldwell's Manor, near Lacolle, on 28 February 1838. It declared the end of the connection with England and the independence of the colony and proposed the establishment of a republican government. The sovereign republic would support the equality of all persons, including Indians, before the law; the abolition of seigneurial rights and customary law and the repossession of all public lands; the separation of church and state; the abolition of tithes and freedom of conscience; male suffrage starting at twenty-one years of age and the secret ballot; and finally, the use of French and English "in all public affairs."[3]

"REBELS AND BRIGANDS" ACCORDING TO MGR LARTIGUE

The convergence of the interests of the Catholic Church and British colonial power found a new opportunity for expression with the second pastoral letter from the bishop of Montreal on 8 January 1838. We can imagine parishioners hearing their priests lecturing those "brigands and rebels": "They have shown what kind of liberty they were promising you when they despoiled you of your barns and your houses, when they took away your animals, and reduced you to extreme poverty in order to gorge themselves on booty in their camps, where they corrupted our youth, keeping them in a constant state of drunkenness to numb their consciences." Faced with demoralized parishioners often with relatives in exile or jail, the Church castigated those false patriots "who sought only to advance themselves, to dominate in a new chimerical state, to take the place of those they could dispossess." The pastoral letter called the Patriote leaders "leaders of revolt" and "flatterers, who with the big words of liberty and independence are seeking to indoctrinate you only for their personal advantage." The bishop's directive to the clergy was clear: refusal of burial in Catholic cemeteries for people who died with arms in their hands.[4]

To reply to those who "assert[ed] that *all authority comes from the people*" and sought to confine the Church to spiritual tasks, the Church published a 129-page volume, *Doctrine de l'Église catholique d'Irlande et de celle du Canada sur la révolte*, that argued in favour of the Church's right of intervention in the affairs of civil government. It reproduced texts by bishops in Ireland and Lower Canada, including the bishop of Montreal's two pastoral letters and Gregory XVI's encyclical of 25 June 1834 against *Words of a Believer*, by Lamennais, which Duvernay of *La Minerve* had published in a pirate edition.[5]

Anticipating a new plan for union that would challenge the Catholic religion, the status of the Church, and tithes, the bishop of Quebec City took the initiative of writing to the Queen, reiterating "the inviolable attachment to the tie" with England, the loyalty of the clergy, and the loyalty it had inspired in the people. The superior of the Séminaire de Saint-Sulpice in Montreal, Joseph-Vincent Quiblier, considered it useful to write to the Sacred Congregation for the Propagation of the Faith in Rome to say that "the Seminary had contributed more [according to General Colborne] to putting down the rebellion than all his regiments."[6] The Church's offensive was such that some political prisoners took the trouble to write to Mgr Lartigue: "The prestige that surrounded you has collapsed ... The *Canadien* people, after all the sacrifices it has made for you, deserved a better bishop."[7]

NEW CONFRONTATIONS (NOVEMBER 1838)

In the summer of 1838, the exiled Patriotes recruited Frères chasseurs from among their ranks and their fellow citizens of Lower Canada; they gave them this name because the recruits had to operate in secret – as in the great wolf hunt – to foil spies and informers. The Frères chasseurs was a secret paramilitary society like the Italian Carbonari, and it planned attacks in the counties of southwestern Lower Canada, near the American border.[8]

The colonial power also took some measures: creation of a mounted police corps in August, reinforcement of the existing military force of five thousand men under the command of General Colborne and more than one thousand loyalist volunteers.

From 3 to 10 November 1838, there were confrontations in the counties of Laprairie, Beauharnois, and L'Acadie, which had been recognized for their greater radicalism in 1837. In Napierville, where the Patriote headquarters likely had four to five thousand men, Nelson repeated his "Declaration of Independence" and raised, not the flag with three horizontal stripes, but a white flag with two stars representing the two republics of Lower and Upper Canada – a possible reference to the American "Star-Spangled Banner." Another flag, another vision.

In Beauharnois, the anti-seigneurial Patriotes put their words into action and occupied the manor of Seigneur Ellice, the personification of the British colonial elite and a long-time lobbyist to the House of Commons and the House of Lords. The daughter-in-law of the seigneur, recently arrived from London and accustomed to evenings of conversation interspersed with songs and pieces for piano or guitar, was awakened on 4 November by the sounds of dogs and turkeys, and found herself "en *chemise de nuit* and robe de Chambre, in the midst of five or six of the most ruffian looking men I ever saw ... (except in my *dreams* of *Robespierre*)." She faced them "with a trembling heart and the most smiling face I could *put on*." Finally freed by British troops on 12 November, she was taken by canoe to Lachine while "the water was lighted up by the reflection of the villages burning in all directions."

But the insurgents were defeated in Lacolle and Odelltown and every other place, and not by Colborne's army, but by loyalist volunteers from the region, who were as motivated as they were well-armed.[9]

It was the end of something. And as if to turn the knife in the wound of the defeat, the bishop of Quebec City published a circular letter "for public prayers on the occasion of the insurrection in the district of Montreal," in which he urged that "we submit with humility to the chastisements divine providence sends us in punishment for our sins."[10] And on 21 November, President Van Buren published a second proclamation of neutrality of the United States. These occasions for guilt and disappointment completed the circle, and a week later trials of the political prisoners began.

FEAR AND REPRESSION

While the ambivalence and the long discussions in the night that so enraged the Patriote leader Girod were a sign of the not entirely voluntary nature of certain uprisings, rumour and counter-information, coupled with the slowness of communications, may explain some of the confusion that existed in the population. Or it was the ringing of alarms, or the sight of "bayonets gleaming in the sun at quite a distance" that sowed fear, or repression by the police, the army, the government, and the justice system together. Constables spied on people in Montreal while

mounted policemen criss-crossed the countryside on a manhunt, forcing Patriotes or people who had been denounced to hide in the woods
or in sugar shacks, cellars, or haylofts and avoid making fires or leaving
tracks in the snow; others fled toward the American border in the snow,
crossing "swamps and streams where the ice would break underfoot at
any moment" and living on half-frozen turnips left in the fields. The
looting by Patriotes themselves north of Montreal, which was denounced
both by Girod and by the priest Paquin, and that of the Ellice manor in
Beauharnois was minor compared to the looting by the military, which
included, for example, the theft of some eight hundred horses. The
military repression was intended to set an example: Gore returned to
Saint-Denis, although it was calm after the Patriotes' only victory, and set
about sacking part of the village. In Saint-Charles, eighteen houses and
barns were burned. In Saint-Eustache, sixty houses were destroyed.
Saint-Benoît, which had already surrendered, was reduced to ashes.
Beauharnois was razed, and eighty houses were burned in Napierville,
twenty in Châteauguay. It was said of the soldiers of Glengarry Regiment
that "they made war like Cossacks."[11]

The forced resignations of justices of the peace and the establishment
of a justice system parallel to the government system with its loyalist
judges in part explain the debatable and much debated decision by the
colonial authorities to set up a military court to judge civilians and their
refusal to let Patriote defendants choose French Canadian lawyers on
the pretext that rebels could not defend rebels. Of the 855 citizens arrested in the second rebellion, 108 were charged with high treason in
fourteen state trials held from 6 December 1838 to 1 May 1839. Of the
accused, nine were acquitted, and ninety-nine sentenced to death, exile,
or banishment; twelve were hanged in the new prison at Pied-du-Courant,
fifty-eight were deported to Australia, eight others having been exiled to
Bermuda in 1837, twenty-seven were freed on bail, and two were banished for life. These "wandering *Canadiens*" are described in the song
"Le Proscrit / Un Canadien errant," as "banished from their homes, and
travelling through foreign countries weeping."[12]

Before and after their death or exile, the Patriotes, whether prisoners
or not, were subjected to insults, humiliation, and other forms of abuse:
insults in the caustic prose of Adam Thom who, starting in 1835, had
made vicious attacks on French Canadians in the *Montreal Herald*, which
he later repeated in the Durham Report as advisor to the imperial inves-
tigator; insults from anglophones throwing coils of rope, mud, or stones
at Patriotes being transported to prison; the humiliation of Patriotes being called "brigands" by Mgr Lartigue and the priests, and the humiliation of their parents when church burial was refused to those who died;

the moral and physical suffering of those who were deported, crammed in the dark under the third deck of sailboats, bent over in a space four feet high without air, sickened by the smell of vomit, vermin and insects in the tropics, and then being forced to wear prison clothes marked "LB," for Long Bottom, the jail where they were taken; finally, the suffering of Chevalier de Lorimier, the bravest of them all, aware that he would "die thrown into the air" but thinking of the one he called "the Strong of the Strong."[13]

LONDON, WINTER 1838

John Arthur Roebuck, who had not been re-elected in the riding of Bath but remained the House of Assembly's agent in London, obtained permission to speak before the House of Lords on 19 January 1838. He had already – possibly with the agreement of the House of Assembly and Papineau – proposed a federation of the Canadian colonies, and he had only one concern: to "arrange all matters in Canada" so that the colonies would not throw themselves into the arms of the United States. This arrangement would mean that the Legislative Council would be abolished – rather than being made an elected body – and would be replaced by an advisory council appointed by the governor and made. up of people elected in the legislative assemblies of each of the colonies of British Canada, and that a superior court of the magistrature would be established to arbitrate any parliamentary conflicts.[14]

In the House of Commons, Lord Russell, who was determined not to abandon "the Province to the French party" and to ensure the commercial interests of the colony, had to follow up on his Resolutions: he proposed suspending the Constitution of 1791, establishing a governor in council as a form of temporary power, and sending Lord Durham on a mission – another one – to investigate the situation of the British provinces of North America. The strongest dissenting voices were those of the leader of the Radical Party, John Stuart Mill, and the member of Parliament Washburton, who was in favour of responsible government and an amicable separation. The Radical member of Parliament asked the House: "Was this country, that had favoured Greece, Poland, South America and Hanover in their struggles for freedom, prepared to deny that aid to Canada?" The philosopher Mill published an article in the *London and Westminster Review* in which he denounced the recent actions of the Colonial Office. First he criticized the Gosford Report itself, the real source of the Russell Resolutions and a reminder that "the local oligarchy, represented by the Council, have done their utmost to inflame those national differences which enable them to identify *their* cause with that of the English settlers and even of the mother country," and asked, "Is it to be wondered at that such animosities should exist?" Then he declared that the appropriation of £140,000 without the consent of the House of Assembly to pay the arrears owed by Lower Canada constituted a provocation, and he expressed surprise: "There is something very alarming to us in the nonchalance with which Englishmen treat so grave a matter as the infraction of a constitution." To Mill, the refusal to pass the revenues was the simple exercise of a right, because, he asked, was a constitution "a gift resumable at the discretion of the giver?" On the suspension of the Constitution of 1791, he declared that "an English Parliament has followed the example of Polignac and King Ernest, in treating a constitutional charter as waste paper." He understood Papineau for not necessarily having followed the path of O'Connell: "Ireland is at our doors, that Ireland has above a hundred representatives in the British Parliament," he said, "and ... it has required fifty years to procure even such imperfect justice ... can we wonder that Canada ... should not obtain justice?" Finally, he supported the plan that his former member of Parliament, Roebuck, had presented on 14 April 1837 and that had recently been taken up again in the House of Lords.[15]

The Constitution of 1791 was suspended on 27 March 1838 and a Special Council was set up until November 1840. Habeas corpus was also suspended in the district of Montreal from April to August 1838, opening the door to the possibility of summary justice. Lord Durham landed in Quebec City in May and stayed until November, and the amnesty measures he took with respect to prisoners and eight Patriotes exiled in Bermuda earned him a rebuke from London, which led to his resignation.[16]

PAPINEAU'S EXILE TO PARIS (FEBRUARY 1839)

Papineau sailed from New York City on 8 February 1839 on the *Sylvie-de-Grasse* to travel to Le Havre and then Paris. He no longer really had any reason to stay in the United States. Since 1830, he had been proposing the constitutional model of the United States. He had, among other things, sent a petition to Congress at the time of the popular assembly in Saint-Laurent on 15 May 1837. A refugee in the United States since 1 December 1837, he had written to the historian George Bancroft on the 18th: "We must carry out the purchase of ten thousand muskets, twenty pieces of artillery, ammunition and enough to pay the food of the volunteers who will make use of these during four months, so that our chances of success be almost infallible. If we do not obtain this help, you will have Poland and its horrors at your doors."[17] Nothing had been forthcoming, other than what the Patriotes in exile had been able to commandeer. Worse yet, the Middlebury assembly of 2 January 1838 had opened a serious breach in the unity of the Patriotes in exile. Living in Philadelphia from 20 February 1838, Papineau had waited a year before leaving, finally giving in to pressure by the Nancrède family, Hector Bossange, and especially radical Patriotes in exile who wanted the absence of this man who not only was no longer leading them but was creating a possible division in their ranks.[18] Papineau's disillusionment with the United States at this time was shared by other Patriotes, who bemoaned this "eminently dollariferous people" or sought consolation for the failure of the plan for "independence": "We would be delivered to the Americans who would, as in Texas, have invaded everywhere and would have flooded our unhappy homeland with moneybags and rogues. Our virtuous farmers would have been led by high prices to sell their lands and withdraw into the interior, leaving to their new masters the most beautiful properties, and voluntarily taking a lower rank in society. I say new masters! Yes, they would have been new masters and perhaps, believe me, less humane than the former ones."[19]

Although the diplomatic difficulties Papineau experienced when he arrived in Le Havre resulted primarily from his decision not to apply for a passport from the British consul in New York City, they were an indication of what France had to offer him. This is shown in the diplomatic correspondence of the French ambassador to Washington, Édouard de Pontois, who travelled in Lower Canada in the summer of 1837, attended the popular assembly in Saint-Constant, and met Papineau in Saratoga and New York City. The correspondence with the French Ministry of Foreign Affairs shows how Lower Canada and its geopolitics were perceived by France at the time. This diplomat from Canada's former mother country confessed that the "first impression felt by a Frenchman when entering Canada is a feeling of pain and regret." His perception was one of an admirer of the American republic: "The Canadian shore is sad, depopulated, without movement, without life, and presents, in a word, the faded features of a distant colony forgotten by the Metropolis," while on the American shore, "everything is alive with the fertile breath of Nationality." This man who had known 1789 said of the population of Lower Canada, "Time has not worked in its favour, the revolutions that have turned the world upside down have not changed either its ideas or its habits." He perceived submission to the feudal regime and "blind submission to the precepts of the ministers of Religion." This people, according to him, was "little prepared for political innovations, little made for revolutions," and "the feeling of Nationality ... that is awakening still [remains] vague and confused among the Canadians." This diplomat and ally of the United States was familiar with the history of relations between France and England, and he felt that the regime that prevailed in Lower Canada "has today ... nothing oppressive or wounding, and can hardly be reproached but for the disadvantages inseparable from the co-lonial regime." He considered that Papineau "has only received the im-perfect education of a very backward Country, that he has barely seen Europe" and that he was deluding himself about the support he could expect from the United States. As for the minister of foreign affairs, Count Molé, his words frankly expressed the place of francophone Lower Canada in France's policies: "The details on M. Papineau, this leader of the Canadian opposition, have for us all the interest of novelty"; as for "the sensation produced in Europe by events in Canada, it was all the more intense given that they had suddenly awakened awareness of a country that for a long time we were not in the habit of paying attention to, and that even for people who were not unaware of the problems of the colony with its metropolis, such events were still a subject of surprise, so little did they believe that things had reached that point." One year before Papineau's arrival in France, the ambassador could write to his minister that the Patriote leader "was sure of encountering among the people to whom he wanted to speak [that is, the ministers of the king] sympathy for the inhabitants of Canada and a desire to contribute to eas-ing their fate, *but nothing beyond that.*"[20] Such was the France that awaited Papineau, the France from which he was still expecting something.

The first months of his stay would reveal to Papineau that there had for more than half a century been an ocean between France and Lower Canada. Dr Gauvin, who was then in Paris, wrote to Duvernay, still in exile in Burlington, that he had just

learned from a reliable source that [the editors of French newspapers], while having much at heart the well-being and independence of Canada, could not agree with the opinions of Mr. Papineau, who saw no other means of making us free than becoming part of the United States. You may well believe that was enough ... to prevent those gentlemen, who wanted to preserve in Canada its customs and its language, from working, as they seemed to be disposed to do still today even, for the emancipation of our country. From what I can see, there may, I believe, be a way to renew the interest of these gentlemen in our cause, and we are proposing ourselves, Duchesnois, de Léry and myself, to see and consult the French on measures to take for the emancipation of Canada.[21]

The defection of the French was added to that of the Americans.

THE DURHAM REPORT (FEBRUARY TO MAY 1839)

After five months in the colony and a resignation that followed the condemnation of his way of dealing with political prisoners from 1837, Lord Durham returned to England in late November 1838 and started writing a report for the Colonial Office and the Imperial Parliament. His consultations with people such as Jonathan Sewell, Adam Thom and, in particular, Edward Ellice – who submitted a memorandum to him entitled "Suggestions for a scheme for the future government of the Canadas," dated 21 December 1838, from which the Durham Report would take most of its recommendations – clearly indicate that not only was the report based on an already old tradition of opposition to reform in Lower Canada, but above all, that it was the end of a long cycle of constitutional debates in which these advisors of his had been witnesses and actors. Just as the Rebellions of 1837 and 1838 should be considered the culmination of constitutional struggles that had been going on at least since 1810, the content of Lord Durham's report was the result both of previous investigations (the Committee of 1828, the Gosford Commission of 1835), political projects left unfinished (the plans for union of 1811 and 1822), and the outline of a settlement contained in the Russell Resolutions of March 1837, not to mention the suggestion of the House of Assembly's agent, John Arthur Roebuck, of a confederation of England's Canadian colonies. For Lord Durham, the way had already been paved – or "macadamized," as was said at the time in honour of the inventor of the process, John McAdam – and anyone who took it encountered figures known to the Colonial Office and Patriote circles. Drawing on the most recognized among the veterans of the battle against reform, the report Lord Durham submitted to the Commons on 11 February 1839 could not have been anything but colonialist, strongly marked by imperial certainties.[22]

This is shown in the perception Durham conveys of the *Canadiens* and of English superiority. To him, the *Canadiens* were "an utterly uneducated and singularly inert population, implicitly obeying leaders who ruled them by the influence of blind confidence and narrow national prejudices"; they had "the unreasoning tenacity of an uneducated and unprogressive people." The French of the ancien régime were "obviously inferior to the English settlers" in terms of political education; "the superior political and practical intelligence of the English cannot be, for a moment, disputed." In the interest of fairness, Durham remarked: "It is not any where a virtue of the English race to look with complacency on any manners, customs, or laws which appear strange to them; accustomed to form a high estimate of their own superiority, they take no

pains to conceal from others their contempt and intolerance of their usages. They found the French Canadians filled with an equal amount of
national pride."[23] He recognized that these were "different races engaged in a national contest."[24]

Sharing this consciousness of British superiority and the centuries-old
Anglo-French rivalry, Durham stated that the English settlers in Lower
Canada would "never … tolerate the authority of a House of Assembly, in
which the French shall possess or even approximate to a majority."[25] He
focused not on political struggle or possible class struggle, but on a "contest of races" as the main, fundamental cause of the colonial crisis: "I expected to find a contest between a government and a people: I found two
nations warring in the bosom of a single state: I found a struggle, not of
principles, but of races."[26] Later, he drew the consequences of this observation: "Until this is settled, no good government is practicable; for
whether the political institutions be reformed or left unchanged, whether the powers of the Government be entrusted to the majority or the minority, we may rest assured, that while the hostility of the races continues,
whichever of them is entrusted with power, will use it for partial purposes."[27] But in the same breath, he added that "the hostility of the races [is]
palpably insufficient to account for all the evils which have affected Lower
Canada, inasmuch as nearly the same results have been exhibited among
the homogeneous population of the other provinces," and "it may fairly
be said, that the natural state of government in all these colonies is that
of collision between the executive and the representative body."[28]

The report was hesitant with regard to other overall causes of the colonial crisis. Sometimes it minimized the fact that "the original and constant source of the evil was to be found in the defects of the political
institutions of the Provinces";[29] sometimes it asserted that "the origin of
the present extreme disorder may be found in the institutions by which
the character of the colony was determined" and that "those causes of
division" were in "the disorder produced by the working of an ill-contrived
constitutional system."[30] But all in all, the admitted deficiencies of the
political institutions constituted quite a complete list of the complaints of
Lower Canada: the exclusion of French Canadians from the public service, the army and the navy; favouritism in the government and the judiciary;[31] government negligence in public education;[32] the Executive and
administration beyond the control of the House of Assembly;[33] successive governors who were dependent on the same council members and
constantly referred back to a distant Colonial Office.[34]

While he paid attention to the "vices" of the colonial system, Durham
only briefly mentioned the Legislative Council and the repeated demand by reformers that it be elected. Being British, he preferred the

solution of responsible government to the emphasis on elections in the
American republican system, but he finally recommended the system of
an appointed, and not elected, Legislative Council.

In fact, the Legislative Council was practically hardly any thing but a veto in the
hands of public functionaries on all the acts of that popular branch of the legislature in which they were always in a minority. This veto they used without much
scruple. I am far from concurring in the censure which the Assembly and its advocates have attempted to cast on the acts of the Legislative Council. I have no
hesitation in saying that many of the Bills which it is most severely blamed for
rejecting, were Bills which it could not have passed without a dereliction of its
duty to the constitution, the connexion with Great Britain, and the whole English
population of the Colony.[35]

This was the fundamental blind spot of Durham's vision; he was culturally and politically an interested party in the questions he was investigating and reporting on. While he did see some flaws in the Constitution,
he was unable to see what the French Canadians and the Patriotes had
been complaining about since Bédard's brief of 1814, namely that the
Legislative Council had since 1774 and 1791 been a non-elected, essentially anglophone structure and that it was the real cause of the "national
distinctions" for which the *Canadiens* alone, the demographic and democratic majority, were being held responsible. The clamour of the
Executive and of anglophones in general against the project of a "nation
canadienne" or French Canadian nationality does not obscure the fact
of Lord Durham's silence on the Legislative Council as the vehicle, for
all parties, of a national project just as evident and determined as that of
the French Canadians. While such an analysis does not negate the cultural and ethnic component of the political crisis in the colony, it makes
it possible to balance the responsibility of the parties.

After Durham's diagnosis came his solution and his remedies: "I enter-
tain no doubts as to the *national* character which must be given to Lower
Canada; it must be that of the British Empire; that of the majority of the
population of British America; that of the great race which must, in the
lapse of no long period of time, be predominant over the whole North
American Continent" (our italics). The perspective was clear: "it must
henceforth be the first and steady purpose of the British Government to
establish an English population, with English laws and language, in this
Province, and to trust its government to none but a decidedly English
legislature."[36] Here was the real issue since 1791: who would control the
House? And preparations were being made to do what the Canadians
had been criticized for doing, insofar as they had been able, through the

representation by population granted by London in 1791, to achieve a parliamentary majority, which included anglophone members. The report stated, "The only power that can be effectual at once in coercing the present disaffection, and hereafter obliterating the nationality of the French Canadians, is that of a numerical majority of a loyal and English population," a system that, as in Louisiana, would be based on "the influence of perfectly equal and popular institutions in effacing distinctions of race without disorder or oppression."[37]

And while the people of Louisiana were in the process of assimilation, it was clear that the French Canadians "are and ever must be isolated in the midst of an Anglo-Saxon world," and that "whatever may happen, whatever government shall be established over them, British or American, they can see no hope for their nationality."[38] "It is but a question of time and mode" of assimilation: "it is but to determine whether the small number of French who now inhabit Lower Canada shall be made English, under a Government which can protect them, or whether the process shall be delayed until a much larger number shall have to undergo, at the rude hands of its uncontrolled rivals, the extinction of a nationality strengthened and embittered by continuance."[39]

The means chosen might appear radical, but it was not new; it had been in the air since 1811 and 1822, and had only been deferred: "I find in union the only means of remedying at once and completely the two prominent causes of their present unsatisfactory condition." And he specified: "I believe that tranquillity can only be restored by subjecting the Province to the vigorous rule of an English majority: and that the only efficacious government would be that formed by a legislative union," that is, one consisting of a single legislative assembly, and not a federal union of provincial legislative assemblies.[40] For this colony made up of Upper Canada, with 400,000 inhabitants, and Lower Canada, with 650,000 inhabitants, including 150,000 of British origin, Durham proposed a single legislative assembly elected according to "rep by pop," which would soon result in an English majority, a majority that would, in any case, increase through immigration: "I am averse to every plan that has been proposed for giving an equal number of members to the two Provinces, in order to attain the temporary end of out-numbering the French, because I think the same object will be obtained without any violation of the principles of representation, and without any such appearance of injustice in the scheme as would set public opinion, both in England and America, strongly against it."[41]

The Empire would thus finally use union to eliminate the French Canadian parliamentary majority in Lower Canada and put an end to the republican tendency that sought to give primacy to the elected

House. This would at the same time settle the thorny issue of the Legislative Council, which would not be elected; it would make it possible to eliminate "the necessity of relying, in Lower Canada, on the English character of the Legislative Council as a check on the national prejudices of a French Assembly" – the implication being that national prejudices could not be British and imperial, but only French Canadian and colonial. Like the Russell Resolutions, the Durham Report was responding five years later to the 92 Resolutions. With respect to the civil list: "All the revenues of the Crown, except those derived from [Public Lands and Emigration], should at once be given up to the United Legislature, on the concession of an adequate civil list," and "No money-votes should be allowed to originate without the previous consent of the Crown." As for public lands, they would come under imperial authority. The central problem of the financial situation of the two provinces would thus be solved:

The union of the two Provinces would secure to Upper Canada the present great objects of its desire. All disputes as to the division or amount of the revenue would cease. The surplus revenue of Lower Canada would supply the deficiency of that part of the upper Province; and the Province thus placed beyond the possibility of locally jobbing the surplus revenue, which it cannot reduce, would, I think, gain as much by the arrangement as the Province, which would thus find a means of paying the interest of its debt. Indeed it would be by no means unjust to place this burthen on Lower Canada, inasmuch as the great public works for which the debt was contracted, are as much the concern of one Province as of the other.[42]

In addition to these measures, there was a plan for British immigration and colonization,[43] and especially, the proposal that the metropolis grant responsible government in the administration of the colony. Durham deplored the "utter absence of all efficient control of the people over their rulers" and the imperial resistance to conceding this power of relative autonomy to the colony, and he therefore proposed that the actions of the government be subject to some responsibility and that the Executive, through a ministry made up of Assembly members of the majority, be responsible to the people.[44]

PAPINEAU AND PARENT ANALYZE LORD DURHAM'S REPORT

In Paris, Papineau, who received a copy of Lord Durham's Report through Roebuck or some member of Parliament of the Radical Party,

responded to it in an article in the *Revue du progrès* of May 1839, in which
he gave his account of the insurrection in Canada and undertook to refute Durham's conclusions and recommendations. Recalling "how heavy
was the yoke, and how humiliating the condition of our national thrall-
dom," Papineau imputed the responsibility for the Rebellions to the government, saying that the population had not wanted them and that they
had not been advised to take that path. To show the consistency of his
thinking, he recalled that he rejected union now as he had back in 1823
with Lord Bathurst, to whom he had instead proposed eventual independence "under the protection of Congress." He said he deplored the outcome of the resistance, but at the same time he had "great hope that it
will be resumed and will prevail" because the fate of Lower Canada was
as awful as that of Ireland, where an English aristocracy drove "the serfs
who live there" to "the small islands of all its external possessions every
time [they] want to stop being liable to forced labour, talliable and mort-
mainable at pleasure and at mercy."

He found the report "true when it accuses power, false when it accuses
the people," and the list of admissions of abuse and high-handedness
that Lord Durham provided led him to believe that the "English government was describing itself"; he also recognized the thinking of Adam
Thom, the gang leader of the Doric Club and Durham's table compan-
ion and advisor, and that of Edward Ellice, Durham's wife's uncle. It was
clear to Papineau that after the Durham Report, Canadians "no longer
have any hope of justice from England, and that for them, submission
would be a blot and a death sentence, and independence, on the contrary, a principle of resurrection and life." He stated his "conviction that
it is not English statutes that will settle the near future of Canada; but
that this future is written in the declarations of the rights of man and in
the political constitutions that have been established by our good, wise
and happy neighbours, the independent Americans."[45]

The refutation of Papineau's text by Clément-Charles Sabrevois de
Bleury, published in October 1839, was that of a "turncoat," as he was
called at the time, but it is also a reminder of the opposition to Papineau
in the Quebec City region since 1832. Sabrevois de Bleury was from an
aristocratic background, a soldier; a Patriote, he was elected to the
Assembly for Richelieu in 1832, was in favour of the 92 Resolutions of
1834, joined the more moderate elements of the Quebec City region in
1835, founded the most virulent anti-Papineau newspaper, *Le Populaire*,
in April 1837, and in August 1837, accepted an appointment to the
Legislative Council. His *Réfutation de l'Histoire de l'insurrection du Canada
de Papineau* was probably written by the editor of *Le Populaire*, Hyacinthe-
Poirier Leblanc de Marconnay, but was signed by Sabrevois de Bleury,

and it included some twenty texts that had already been published in their newspaper; it sought to show that Papineau alone was the cause of the ills of Lower Canada and that he had "prepared, desired and even planned the armed resistance." The 136-page text loses credibility because of its excesses, its references to Papineau's "perverse desire to overthrow Canadian institutions," his hope "to become Governor of one more State added to the American Union," his plans "to uproot the *Canadiens*' religious principles," and his "thirst for domination." But the text clearly expresses what may have been the day-to-day strategy of the Parti patriote and the Patriotes and shows the temptation to demonize an opponent of the regime.[46]

In *Le Canadien*, Parent had followed the popular assemblies closely and had criticized the address of the Confédération des Six Comtés and the manifesto of the Fils de la liberté. The events of November and December 1837 and January 1838 had, for him, compromised "the *Canadiens*' former reputation of loyalty to their sovereign, a reputation that, in the absence of the ties of a shared origin, constituted all our strength with respect to the metropolitan authorities." Against Papineau, he did his best to absolve the British government of responsibility, while sharing Papineau's opinion on the responsibility of the Executive: "It is against the local oligarchy, and not against the British Crown, that the insurrection really raised its hand" because that "dominant caste [had] become influential enough, powerful enough over time to laugh at all the efforts for Representation." He saw this oligarchy as the primary cause of those "national distinctions" wrongly attributed to French Canadians alone: "These are undue advantages that the British population has always received until now and that have made it hope for and demand still greater ones, that have given an apparently national character to our political divisions. Re-establish equality, destroy privilege, and you will see the national part of our problems extinguished for lack of fuel. Those who attribute our political ills to national distinctions are taking the cause for the effect and vice versa. It is the political differences that have ignited the national divisions."[47]

Parent, less antagonistic than Papineau toward London, sought, with the people of the Quebec City region and other ambivalent francophones, a middle way between Papineau and Mackenzie, on the one hand, and *La Gazette de Québec*, on the other hand: "Is there not between these two extremes the position of Mr. O'Connell, who has for so long been demanding the emancipation of his people?" He observed that the resistance had not prevailed and felt that it would not prevail because it was the action of a minority: "The idea of a separation from England has not put down deep roots anywhere, neither among the masses of the colonial populations nor in thoughtful minds." His middle way would be to prefer a "bearable trusteeship" to a "doubly ruinous emancipation."

But you think with us that, for peoples as for individuals, it is in a period of complete emancipation that it is most often dangerous for them to advance; for just as it is not good for the individual to be too early master of his actions, similarly it is not good for a people to take its place among the nations before its time, if it does not want to be exploited by them. You think with us that a bearable trusteeship is always better than a doubly ruinous emancipation; for while we could flatter ourselves with achieving the dream of immediate independence, this achievement would very certainly cost us more than the rather doubtful advantages that we could obtain in our geographic position, which, in leaving the domination of the Lion would cause us to fall under that of the Eagle.[48]

For Parent, political independence was thus equivalent to an acceptance of "Americanization," and, with some irony, he suggested that the Patriotes study the history of Louisiana more that than of Poland. This was then an opportunity for him to define his conception of nationality, a conservative conception that rejected the liberal principle of nationality, the right of peoples to self-determination.

We must rectify an error into which *La Gazette* has fallen ... by saying that we are here using the word nationality in the meaning in which it was used in Europe with respect to Poland and Belgium in their struggles, the former with Russia, the latter with Holland. For the Poles and the Belgians, it meant the establishment of a separate political existence, while here it is only a question of a purely social, provincial existence, to preserve customs and laws the abolition of which, in our opinion, would turn to the disadvantage of the *Canadien* people.[49]

To Parent, "Our institutions, our language and our laws" and "our" religion served to culturally identify this nationality without this nationality taking the step of seeking a unique political status.

Having, since the summer of 1837, recommended conciliation and compromise and accepted a "bearable trusteeship," Parent did not have a price put on his head as did Papineau and other Patriotes, but his sense of conciliation did not keep him from being arrested and imprisoned on 26 December 1838 for having written in *Le Canadien*, on Christmas eve.

In the century we are in, a century of publicity and opinion, when one wishes to crush a people, one does not proceed as summarily as one did in days gone by. One must today go through certain preliminaries, one must create a reason, a pretext, and the most ordinary and the easiest procedure is to exasperate a population, to push it to some excesses. We are ready, and the rigours are not long in coming; those rigours provoke new excesses, which are immediately followed by new and more terrible rigours. And governments are thus made to go from rigours to rigours, and peoples from excesses to excesses, until conciliation has become impossible. It is then that the true conspirators, the true authors of all the troubles, achieve their purpose, and that "a people is swept from the surface of the globe." This is what the Russians have done very recently in Poland, and we would like to prevent England from having the unenviable honour of seeing its name associated with that of the Autocrat of the North.

For these "seditious activities," the editor of *Le Canadien* would spend the next five months of his life in prison, where, through various stratagems, he continued to edit and write *Le Canadien*, in which he translated and published Lord Durham's Report. Behind bars, Parent understood that the report, far from favouring the nationality of French Canadians, would instead "work openly to eradicate it from the country." Endowed with a remarkable historical consciousness, he put in perspective the effect of the Durham Report on the fate of the French Canadians: "Let us take note, the work of Pitt [in 1791] isolated the French Canadian population of this continent and tied it to the metropolis through connections of interest, honour and recognition. The work of Lord Durham, on the contrary, will have the effect of breaking the ties that attached French Canadians to Great Britain and bringing them closer to the neighbouring heterogeneous populations, placing their hopes in them and identifying their social interests and their national affections with theirs."

But conciliation, compromise, and disappointments finally led Parent to resignation: "Situated as the French Canadians are, there is no alternative for them but to resign themselves with the best grace possible." Then resignation sank to anglicization: "Assimilation, in the new state of affairs, will take place gradually and smoothly, and will be all the more quick if we let it run its natural course and if French Canadians are led there by their own interest, without their pride being too wounded by it."[50] It was fated: "With knowledge of the dispositions of England, it would be for French Canadians the height of blindness and madness to persist in remaining a people apart in this part of the continent. Destiny has spoken."[51]

In keeping with the image of the prison in which he was confined, Parent convinced himself of the inevitability of things; the idea from September 1837 of a union "with the peoples of the river and the gulf" came to the fore again: "to make with all the scattered social elements on the banks of this great river one great and powerful nation." The metaphor of the storm, reefs, and shipwreck also came back. But this time, could the navigation be "bearable"? The man who had joined *Le Canadien* in 1822 to fight the plan for union of the time was opposed to the union recommended in the report, but he clung to the lifeline provided by Lord Durham: responsible government. To Parent, when the metropolis granted that to the colony, things would work out, "and soon we will hear no more of national animosities in Canada than we hear of them in Louisiana, Scotland and Wales."[52]

RESPONSIBLE GOVERNMENT IN THE THOUGHT AND STRATEGY OF PARENT AND OF PAPINEAU

Was Parent staking too much on responsible government? Was he taking too great a risk in putting all his hopes on it, given the place of this idea in French Canadian thought since 1830?

Parent and Papineau had not held the same views on this question since 1830. Parent declared himself in favour of an elected and responsible Legislative Council, and deplored the fact that the Executive was not accountable for its decisions, but he rejected the scenario of representation of Lower Canada in the Imperial Parliament. He asserted that Canadians could "conduct their affairs alone" and that the American colonies of Great Britain could govern themselves. He called for "a regular ministerial organization," a "provincial ministry," an "effective government responsible to the people": "Thus, instead of calling on influential members of one House or the other to make them simple political Advisors, one would now want them to be made heads of departments responsible jointly to the Houses ... but with the major difference that they would be tangible Advisors by whom all the acts of the government would have to be accounted for, and not invisible people without any responsibility, as is the case today."[53]

At a time when Mackenzie in Upper Canada was demanding responsible government increasingly directly and Part Three of the Report of the Gosford Commission had dealt with this question, Parent maintained that the *Canadiens* would be satisfied "when they will exercise over the acts of their local government the same influence that the English people exercises over its own local government." The lack of responsibility of the Executive made him see clearly the absurdity, if not the heinousness, of the situation in Lower Canada, in which "the minority, who in England can only act as the opposition, here plays the role of the majority, and that majority has been reduced to acting as the opposition." Already in September 1835, it was clear to Parent that the colonial political system based on representation must as soon as possible have the same attributes as the metropolitan system, or else "English liberties" would be a contradiction. Once again, he pointed out the consequences of the oligarchic system maintained by London in the colony: "The political struggle that exists in this country is not a struggle of people against people, origin against origin, but a struggle between liberals and tories, between reformers and anti-reformers, between the greater number who want a responsible government and the lesser number who want an irresponsible government."[54]

After the Russell Resolutions, but before the publication of the Durham Report, Parent demanded "as a means of peace and prosperity, that the colonies have full and entire administration of their local affairs under an extension of the constitutional system, without [it] affecting imperial unity with respect to the general interests of the empire." He called for "a form of representative government purged of any flawed principle, any seditious influence, a free and responsible government." And to those who considered the demand for responsible government excessive, he replied: "But it would be a quasi-independence, some say. Well, yes: it would be a quasi-independence."[55] This was thus the same man who, after the Durham Report, resigned himself to believing that everything would be resolved with responsible government and that no more would be heard of "national animosities in Canada."

Papineau did not accord the same importance to responsible government. Increasingly inspired by the American model and increasingly republican after 1830, he was, after 1833, in favour of a republican constitution for Lower Canada. Envisaging a regime of liberty similar to that of the United States, he considered the unelected Legislative Council incompatible with the customs and political culture of America.[56] He was perfectly conscious of the Executive's "venality" and the Legislative Council's "absolute irresponsibility," and he spoke of the desire for a "local, responsible and national Government" before February 1836, that is, before the House of Assembly, on the initiative of Dr O'Callaghan, passed resolutions in favour of a common front between Lower and Upper Canada to demand responsible government.[57] Papineau called for an elected Legislative Council and responsible government at the popular assembly in Sainte-Scholastique on 1 June 1837; in August, he observed that the Gosford Report contained nothing about responsible government, an approach that could have been of some value to the government if it had been chosen. In his last public speech before the Rebellions, he spoke of "the unbearable burden of an irresponsible Executive."[58]

But for the republican Papineau, political responsibility would not come primarily from the British approach of responsible government, but from respect for the people's sovereignty, delegated to the House of Assembly and to an elected Legislative Council. Then the governor would have to take into account representation in the two Houses, and as a result, all three branches would be responsible.[59] As spokesman for this old struggle for an elected Legislative Council, the Patriote leader could not, unlike Parent or Baldwin, opt for the solution of responsible government, for which there was then no model in the British colonies and no way to know whether or how it would work with an elected Legislative Council; and one could only speculate on what the metropolis would want to preserve of "imperial responsibility." Had not Lord Russell, in March 1837 and again in October 1839, considered responsible government incompatible with Canada's colonial status? And London had known since 1836 that granting responsible government would not have the same effect in Lower Canada and Upper Canada in terms of maintaining links with the empire; it is not inconceivable that in the absence of a French majority in Lower Canada, it could have been granted more quickly.[60]

THE POPULAR DIMENSION OF THE REBELLIONS

To evaluate to what extent the Rebellions of 1837 and 1838 were directed against the metropolis, the government, the seigneurial system, the Church, I will examine the social penetration of these ideas and the popular dimension of the Rebellions.

We need first to look at what I will call the political culture of French Canadian society of the time. It has correctly and elegantly been shown that politics and the political permeated every aspect of Quebec society during the half-century from the Constitution of 1774 to the Union of 1840.[61] Debates on the constitutions of 1774 and 1791, constitutional resistance since Governor Craig, petitions with tens of thousands of names in 1822 and 1828, tumultuous elections, signature campaigns such as the one in favour of an address accompanying the 92 Resolutions, popular assemblies from May to November 1837, reading out loud of *La Minerve* or *Le Canadien* on church steps or in inns for illiterate people – there was no lack of signs of the existence and vitality of a public sphere, a dynamic civic space.

It may be pointed out that the Rebellions did not reach Quebec City or Trois-Rivières, that they took place only in the Montreal region. But it should be remembered that the district or region of Montreal, the famous Six Comtés – Richelieu, Verchères, Saint-Hyacinthe, Rouville, Chambly, L'Acadie – plus those of La Prairie, Beauharnois, Missisquoi, Deux-Montagnes, Terrebonne, and Vaudreuil, contained between 55 per cent and 60 per cent of the total population of Lower Canada in 1831 and 1844. Of course, the participation varied according to place and occupation. The participation rate in the popular assemblies, calculated as the ratio of the number of Patriotes mentioned as being from a particular place to the population of the place, is evaluated at 6 per cent in the six counties that formed a confederation in November 1837, 8 per cent in La Prairie, L'Acadie, Chambly, and Beauharnois, 4 per cent in Richelieu, Verchères, and Saint-Hyacinthe, and 3 per cent in Deux-Montagnes, Terrebonne, and Vaudreuil. The same calculation applied to towns gives 20 per cent in Saint-Philippe-de-La Prairie, 18 per cent in Châteauguay, 14 per cent in Saint-Charles-sur-Richelieu, 13 per cent in L'Acadie, 12 per cent in Saint-Eustache and Saint-Denis, 11 per cent in Saint-Marc-sur-Richelieu, and 10 per cent in Saint-Jean-sur-Richelieu.[62]

Another list, consisting of 1,295 Patriotes involved in one way or another in the Rebellions, indicates that 56 per cent of them were country people, 30 per cent merchants, and 14 per cent in the liberal professions. Farmers and day labourers were under-represented compared to their presence in the population, unlike doctors and merchants, who were over-represented. There were fifty-five notaries, fifty-four doctors, and twenty-six lawyers among the leaders of the Parti patriote, which relied on their education and on their presence in the countryside. The forty-seven innkeepers or hotel keepers, who accounted for 10 per cent of the merchants, and the thirty blacksmiths involved in the Rebellions show the importance of their respective workplaces as sites of rural and village sociability.[63]

But the most obvious sign of the popular support for the Rebellions in the Montreal region is the fact that the Patriotes often used popular culture in forms of oral expression or actions that "spoke," that conveyed people's complaints and aspirations. Sometimes, they focused on the agricultural dimension of everyday life: they threatened to destroy harvests or open an Englishman's field of grain to a herd of cows, they cut the tail and mane of the horse belonging to Father Paquin of Saint-Eustache, or a peasant imitated the bleating of a sheep to make the dogs bark when a proclamation forbidding popular assemblies was being read. Sometimes, during planting in May, the ribbon-trimmed May tree planted in honour of a fellow citizen was cut down to show disapproval of an officer of the court or a militia officer who had refused to resign or who had been appointed and put in place by the British authorities. Or Papineau would arrive in Berthier-en-Bas among Patriotes wearing maple leaves on their lapels, or in Saint-Charles, he himself would wear homespun clothes and a *ceinture fléchée* in keeping with his policy of boycotting imported goods.

It was the politicization of charivaris that best shows the popular aspect of the events of 1837 and 1838. These were noisy nocturnal demonstrations where pots and pans were beaten like drums, carried out by people in disguise, wearing masks or hoods, in front of the houses of adulterers and bad payers. Now the targets of the charivari were seigneurs, notorious anti-Patriotes, and loyalist justices of the peace, and the purpose was to identify or intimidate opponents of the Patriotes.[64]

CONCLUSION ON 1837 AND 1838

Chapters 5 to 7 have put the Rebellions in perspective; their purpose was to understand these decisive events in political and intellectual history in the context of the cultural advancement of Lower Canada, the international situation, and discourses and practices. We now need to draw conclusions on the causes of the Rebellions and of their failure.

L'Ami du peuple had published in its edition of 17 July 1833 an article by a certain John Thomas, entitled "Ce qui est nécessaire pour l'indépendance d'un peuple" (What is required for the independence of a people). The author recalled that a country had to have a large enough population to be able to defend itself, or else it would have to call on outside assistance and risk a new domination. The "entire" population of the country had to be in favour of independence, form a common front, and avoid disagreements. Its financial resources, manufacturing, and commerce had to enable it to subsist during the struggle and the first days of independence, an independence that would also require the recognition of the major powers. Finally, this people had to be able to ensure better living conditions. Thomas's article laid out the issues four years before the first rebellion.

It should first be remembered that the Rebellions were the outcome of an escalating series of colonial crises that had clearly begun at the time of Governor Craig in 1810 and the first plan for union in 1811, which was followed by a second, more serious, plan in 1822, and then a Committee of the House of Commons on the Affairs of Canada in 1828. Delaying by the metropolis led to the 92 Resolutions, the Gosford Commission of 1835, and the Russell Resolutions of 1837. The Rebellions were the end result of a decades-long crisis.

First of all, let us look at the four factors already suggested, in addition to the economic and demographic pressures, to explain the Rebellions – London, the local oligarchy, the seigneurs, and the clergy – and their relative importance.

In the long term, there is no doubt that the primary cause of the Rebellions was the colonial crisis, the knot involving the "local oligarchy," its domination of the Legislative Council, its strategy of blocking constitutional change, its refusal to give the colony control of spending, and the overall fact that the governor and the Executive had become partisan. From this point of view, were Papineau, Parent, O'Callaghan, and Wolfred Nelson wrong in repeating that the "national distinctions" were made and maintained more by this system of colonial power than by the French Canadian majority, which welcomed anglophone defenders of English liberties, if not of republican freedoms, into the Parti canadien and then the Parti patriote? This point, which was made during the period, has had little impact on subsequent historical analysis. It should be added that at the very time of the Rebellions, the positions of the colonial oligarchy had decisive support: there was no longer only the *Montreal Herald* and Adam Thom heaping abuse on the majority, but also the Doric Club, the British Rifle Corps, the Montreal Constitutional Association, and the loyalist volunteers confronting the Patriotes in 1837, and especially 1838.

Opposition to the metropolis had developed after 1830, after the disappointing recommendations of the Committee of the House of Commons on the Affairs of Canada. The American model had then become an inspiration, as shown very officially in the 92 Resolutions of 1834, a response to which would be made three years after they were sent to London. The Russell Resolutions came like a "no" from a person who had seemed only to be deferring saying yes; they marked the end of any hope of a "disinterested arbiter," in Tocqueville's words. The desire and the power to maintain the colonial situation were then clearly revealed, and it became obvious that London had subtly masked its strategy of divide and rule and that it ultimately backed the colonial authority. The resolutions of the popular assemblies that followed the announcement of the Russell Resolutions said it: there was "no more justice to be expected" from a "government of force and oppression." Papineau's language also became stronger; at the assembly in Saint-Laurent on 15 May 1837, he observed that "the time for a test has come." With other signatories, he said in the petition to the London Working Men's Association in September 1837: "We have not mentioned independence from the British Crown, but we have not forgotten that the destiny of the continental colonies is to separate from the metropolitan state when the unconstitutional action of a legislative power residing in a distant country is no longer bearable." One month before the battle of Saint-Denis, the address of the Confédération des Six Comtés shows that they were aware that the British army was being deployed and that it was necessary to "be ready." It was indeed difficult, after the Russell Resolutions, to remain confined to "constitutionalism" when it could not include the satisfaction of demands that had been expressed for two decades. They could no longer be led to believe that their demands would be satisfied; they would not be satisfied, they would never be satisfied. In October and

November 1837, there had been many men more radical than Papineau; but the Patriotes were facing the same wall of refusal on the same question: could there be a solution other than anti-colonialism, although it was limited and slow in coming?

The anticlerical dimension of the Rebellions seems to have been expressed more than the anti-seigneurial dimension. It must be said that the latter was a practical issue, that it had been a grievance of the British colonials for some time and that there were a good number of French Canadians who were in favour either of the correction of the abuses or the abolition of the system with just and reasonable compensation. It should also be recalled that the question of the abolition of the seigneurial system, a key difference between Papineau and the proponents of an attack and a plan for independence at the assembly in Middlebury in January 1838, was also what distinguished the most radical of the Patriotes of 1837.

The resolutions of the popular assemblies said clearly that the Church and the priests should take care of spiritual matters and not make the pulpit and the confessional a political forum. Their aim was not the complete separation of church and state, but rather a strict distinction between the two spheres. The Catholic Church of Lower Canada threw all its weight into opposing the Parti patriote and the Rebellions, unlike the Orthodox Church in Greece or the Catholic clergy in Belgium and Poland. In a sense, the die was cast in 1835, when the Catholic Church in Lower Canada took a position with Rome against Lamennais and against all attempts to combine liberty and doctrine. All that was left was for Mgr Lartigue to repeat that power did not come from the people and that it was necessary to submit to "the Prince," and for his Quebec City colleague to ask the people to facilitate the movement of the British regiments coming from the east and to refuse church burial to those who died with arms in their hands.

How then can the failure of the Rebellions be explained? Five convergent reasons may be put forward: the dissension and obvious lack of unanimity within the Patriote movement, the many opponents of the Patriotes' position, their lack of organization and resources, their lack of outside support, and the imperial power of England.

While the dissensions between radical republican Patriotes and "reformist" Patriotes became pronounced at the assembly in Middlebury, they were perceptible in the Parti patriote as far back as 1831, when John Neilson distanced himself on the questions of an elected Legislative Council and the notables, and later with the 92 Resolutions. Bédard's reservations in 1836 concerning the action to take against Judge Bowen and concerning the publication of the directives to the Gosford

Commission by Governor Head of Upper Canada increased the solid
ongoing opposition of Étienne Parent, which had started with the popular assemblies in May 1837, fuelling the rivalry between Quebec City and
Montreal that went back to the winning of the leadership of the Parti
canadien by Papineau, a Montreal resident, around 1815.[65]

The lack of organization of the Patriotes was shown in many ways: first
in the lack of military strategy and leadership in Saint-Charles (Brown)
and Saint-Eustache (Girod), and then in the flagrant lack of guns and ammunition, which created the rather bizarre situation of a military undertaking in which not all the participants had weapons. Shipments of
weapons the Patriotes had counted on had never arrived. This lack of military organization and the fact that in November 1837, they were still taking the moderate approach of passing resolutions are the best indications
that the uprisings of 1837 were not premeditated, supporting the view
that, in a very volatile context of profound disappointments with regard to
London, accumulated tensions, escalating popular demands, arrest warrants issued and carried out by the colonial authorities, and military de-
ployments, some Patriotes took up arms to protect the Patriote leaders
who had a price on their heads.[66] The signs of resistance by the Patriotes
seem more numerous than the signs of premeditation and attack.

Opposition to the Parti patriote did not come solely from within its
ranks; it also existed in London among both Whigs and Tories, with the
exception of a few members of the Radical Party. It also came, it should
be recalled, from the British in the colony, well-armed loyalist volunteers
who, in the districts (Deux-Montagnes, Haut-Richelieu) where the two
"national" groups were more present, mobilized as much as the Patriotes
when they did not defeat them, as in Odelltown. Opposition also came
from the seigneurs who, except for Papineau, sided, as they had after
1760, with the British authorities. It was also expressed in the most dynamic cultural medium of the period – the press; Patriote newspapers
such as *La Minerve* and *Le Libéral* found serious opponents in *Le Canadien*,
La Gazette de Québec, and *L'Ami du peuple*, whose vigour they had underestimated. The entire population did not share the views of the Parti patriote. Opposition came, finally, from the Catholic Church, whose militant
loyalism won it legal recognition in 1839, a status it had lost in 1791 and
had worked hard to regain.

In addition, the support that was supposed to come or could have
come was not forthcoming. It was known, however, through international information that outside help could be needed, that foreign intervention was a double-edged sword and that the recognition of independence,
though slow, was necessary. The promises made to Poland by France
were known, as were the consequences of discord among the Poles.

France, absent since 1763, had forgotten the former New France. While its ambassador in Washington was somewhat moved, he still perceived the British colony of North America as a society of the ancien régime as measured against the standard of the admirable United States. Even in Paris, in 1839, they could not understand why Papineau would want independence under the wing of the United States at the risk of eventual loss of the French language and culture. Not only did Papineau lack the means to widen the circle of support for Lower Canada there, but the mission the Patriotes in exile in the United States had entrusted to him was hindered by the circumstances themselves: the consolidation of the power of Louis-Philippe, which was ruining "the republican influence that alone could be useful to the *Canadiens*," the consolidation of the relationship between France and England, and the special attention France was giving to its Algerian colony.[67]

From a distance, and given its own situation, what could Ireland do for Canada? While the Irish leader O'Connell had most often supported the demands of Lower Canada, his position after the first rebellion was clear. *Le Populaire* of 8 October 1838 reported his words spoken in Dublin on 15 August. He stated that while he had supported the Canadians and opposed Lord Russell's refusal to allow them to spend their own revenues as they saw fit, he refused to support them when they resorted to violence. He expressed the firm belief that moral power would prevail over the use of force and that when peoples turned to violence and rebellion, they invariably harmed their cause.

The United States was not going to burn its bridges with England for a colony that, in the opinion of some American journalists, could very well come to them as a windfall one day. Parent had understood this and had warned against counting too much on a country that, as republican as it was, had no interest in crossing swords with England for Upper and Lower Canada. The neutrality of Vermont and the United States was known very early, and neither weapons nor any kind of recognition came from the United States. In order to counteract any support that might come from the "colonies of the river and the gulf" or Upper Canada, London took care to undermine any common front, and the Patriotes of Lower Canada made little effort to ally themselves with the rebels of Upper Canada, another sign of their lack of organization.

French Canadians had not needed the recognition of a certain international press for the British constitutional and industrial model to express their own admiration for British constitutionalism. "English liberties" had been their inspiration until 1830, and they were aware of the maritime and military power of Great Britain that had humiliated Napoleon at Trafalgar and Waterloo. Some therefore had no illusions about the risks of a confrontation with this rising empire, already a counterforce to the Holy Alliance. Spoons melted into musket balls, old hunting muskets and scythes were no match for an experienced and well-equipped army; it was impossible not to know this. And this reality again gives weight to the view of the rebellion, the new resistance, as being without much hope except that of showing a certain cohesion, a certain dignity, a certain pride.

The symbolic foundations of the Rebellions were not much stronger than the logistical ones. While the French Canadians had carried out epic constitutional struggles since 1791 and had a keen consciousness of their "fathers" and of key moments in the past, this had not yet in 1837 found expression in history books and novels. In a patriotic society, there was poetry extolling homeland and patriotism. But the two great symbols of nationality, the motto of *Le Canadien* and the Patriote tricolour flag, still had a great deal of indeterminacy in relation to plans for greater respect for colonial prerogatives (control of public finances, elected Legislative Council), greater autonomy for the colony and, finally, for certain Patriotes, eventual independence.

The ultimate expression of nationality in 1837 combined three elements: the recognition that "no nation is willing to obey another, for the simple reason that no nation knows how to command another"; the clear recognition by Parent that the nationality of Lower Canada had nothing to do with that of Belgium or Poland, that it had everything to do with preservation and nothing to do with revolution; and the democratic affirmation, for both Papineau and Robert Nelson, that "national distinctions" were more the (obscured) effect of the oligarchic colonial system than of the Patriotes.

The bitter defeat of the first rebellion soon inspired poets, who wrote of "guilty brothers," "St Charles! St Eustache! oh, too ill-fated plains," the jailed Patriotes who missed their families and the peace of the fields, and the exiles. There was Joseph-Guillaume Barthe, who celebrated Papineau as a "sacred martyr for liberty," but there was also *Le Populaire*, which called him a "traitor" and imputed to him a desire "to be King," while P.-J.-O. Chauveau wrote in "L'insurrection": "But their shamed leaders, terror-stricken / Have disappeared – How? to fight they have nothing? / no arms, no more leaders? But Canadian blood." Already at the time of the 92 Resolutions, in 1834, people sang a song called "It's Papineau's fault"; its verses described both the actions of the Patriotes and the positions and reactions of their opponents, but the refrain unfailingly repeated that it was Papineau's fault.[68] From January 1838 until 1848, some would again say that everything was the fault of Papineau the fugitive; for lack of a valid explanation, a scapegoat was needed.

PART THREE

1840–1877

9

Union, Conservative Nationalism, and a New Liberal Failure (1840–1852)

THERE WAS DISMAY AND CONFUSION. 1837 and 1838 had been a long winter of discontent and frustration. In the Montreal region, some families had been left fatherless and some homeless. Family men had been imprisoned, hanged, or exiled to Australia, or had fled to the United States. The liberals' exhaustion was both physical and moral: a quarter-century of constitutional struggles had culminated in the Russell Resolutions, repression, and the Durham Report. What lay ahead? A new constitution, the Union Act, joining Upper and Lower Canada. What the métropolis had judged inadvisable or impossible in 1811 and 1822, it now saw as desirable, indeed, necessary.

LA FONTAINE AND THE FAILURE
OF OPPOSITION TO THE UNION

The two provinces now had a single Legislative Assembly. Notwithstanding Lord Durham's recommendations, Upper and Lower Canada received an equal number of representatives (forty-two each), rather than a number proportional to their respective populations in keeping with the great democratic principle of representation by population. Upper Canada had 400,000 inhabitants and Lower Canada had 650,000 at this time. In practice, this breach of democracy placed the francophone majority in Lower Canada at the mercy of the minority in Upper Canada, which could always make common cause with Lower Canada's anglophone minority, thus perpetuating the ethnic division in the colony. British strategy did not change; it merely became more radical, while flouting the democratic principle of representation by population. The least evident but most decisive effect of this strategy of depriving Lower Canada of its majority was to preclude any effort by Lower Canada to link liberalism and nationalism, the democratic impulse and the nationalist impulse. In addition, the act once again provided for a Legislative Council that was not elected, and whose members were appointed by the governor for life. The governor had the power to reserve decision on all legislation, as did the Queen of England, for a period of two years. The sole and official language of the Assembly of United Canada was English. The debt of Upper and Lower Canada was combined, although Upper Canada's debt was approximately $5 million, with annual interest of $224,000, while that of Lower Canada was $375,000. The debt was held in London by Barings Bank, one of whose main associates, the Right Honourable F.T. Baring, was a member of the Melbourne cabinet and chancellor of the exchequer. Finally, the new constitution did not grant responsible government; instead, there was a civil list of $300,000.

On 23 July 1840, the act was approved by 156 votes to 6 in the House of Commons and 107 to 10 in the House of Lords. O'Connell, shocked that the law had been adopted without consulting the people and Assembly of Lower Canada, voted against it. When Lord Gosford, the former governor of Lower Canada, was asked his opinion, he denounced the new constitution as a "mercantile intrigue." The failure to respect representation by population and the sharing of the unequal debt led him to ask: "Could any thing be more arbitrary and unfair?" The young poet and future Quebec premier (in 1867) Pierre-Joseph-Olivier Chauveau took up this theme of financial dealings in his own way, denouncing the Union as the "day of the bankers":

See: the table is set for a single meal,
   On a horrible blood-soaked cloth,
The ogres of trade have the two Canadas …
It is the day of the bankers, I tell you! It is their glory,
   That the royal posters proclaim on our walls;
The Union they announce is their song of victory,
   And nothing could resist such pure motives …
And yet, if Baring tells them: this is what I want …
   A single word from the banker determines life or death.[1]

In Canada East (still being called Lower Canada), opposition to the Union was unanimous among francophones, and it was based in Quebec City. The Comité des électeurs de Québec held its first anti-Union meeting on 24 January 1840, six months before the adoption of the act. Parent, Neilson, who once again joined the French Canadian majority, and Garneau participated. Parent was disillusioned and this was his last public comment. He was elected member for Saguenay on 8 May 1841 and appointed clerk of the Executive Council on 14 October 1842.

How can we hope for harmony, trust and cooperation on the part of people who have not uttered a word of sympathy for us, who have shown us only disdain, who have seen in our Union only a vile object of speculation and sectional interests, and who, not content to pillage us, to make us pay their debt, carry the injustice so far as to want to proscribe our language and banish it from the Councils of the State and the Tribunals? Such demands reveal too clearly the attitude of our future partner to allow any hope for a happy Union.

Parent, who had recently expressed a preference for a union of the provinces of the Gulf to one of Upper and Lower Canada, said he had "encountered the *Montreal Herald* and its ilk" in the attitude of the Upper Canadians. This was an understatement. He saw the union as an "unjust policy, comparable in this century only to Russia's policy in Poland." Although he had finally opted for assimilation in 1839, he summed up his position as follows: union "will tend to do nothing less than deprive us of what we hold dearest in the world, our language, customs and rights, in other words, our nationality."[2]

The Roman Catholic Church also joined the opposition to the Union; since the Durham Report, it had feared that the purpose of union was to "anglicize" and "de-Catholicize" French Canadians and eliminate the Catholic influence from education. The bishops of Quebec City and Montreal encouraged parish priests to sign the petitions against the union and to draw up their own petitions against it. The position of the Church was a source of some amazement to the Patriotes, one of whom observed that the clergy had abandoned its usual bowing and scraping and was no longer preaching servility.[3] For the Roman Catholic Church, heir to the legacy of Mgr Lartigue, was also developing a vision of the destiny of the French Canadians to counter the liberal and emancipating view of nationality of the Patriotes and their successors: "Here is how we see the *Canadien* nationality: religion, above all Catholicism, and then the homeland. But the latter derives its strength and its true character from its role in the support and protection of religion: Canada without Catholicism is a flag without colours ... Because it is not borders or even laws and political and civil administrations that make a nationality, it is a religion, a language and a national character." To the Church, it was "because we are Catholic that we are a nation in this corner of America."[4]

The petition campaigns throughout Lower Canada bore fruit: 39,928 Canadians signed them. But that did not change anything: the Union Act was adopted in July 1840.

Among the new actors on the political scene – in addition to the "old faithfuls" like the Catholic Church or absentees like Papineau, who was still in exile in France – Louis-Hippolyte La Fontaine is doubtless the most important. A young lawyer and the member for Terrebonne since 1830, La Fontaine had supported the 92 Resolutions in 1834 and the strategy of boycotting imported goods, and had been known for his anti-clerical views until 1837; he proved to be pragmatic and prepared to compromise a few days before the insurrections of November 1837. In London, Paris and, later, the United States from late December 1837 to June 1838, he argued for a constitutional solution and gradually became the interlocutor with British power in the metropolis and the colony. Briefly imprisoned in 1838, he remained outspoken: "Let local government in all its administrative and social dealings cease to make or to allow distinctions of race, let it advance openly towards a liberal but firm policy, let it abstain from favouritism towards the privileged classes." La Fontaine felt that if the Patriotes were granted an amnesty and the victims of 1837 and 1838 were compensated for their losses, they would accept the union. In a speech "To the electors of Terrebonne County," on 25 August 1840, thus after the adoption of the Union Act, he summed up his criticisms of the union, which he said was, "an act of injustice and of despotism, in that it is was imposed upon us without our consent; in that it deprives Lower Canada of a legitimate number of its representatives; in that it deprives us of the use of our language in the proceedings of the legislature, against the spirit of treaties and the word of the Governor General; in that it makes us pay, without our consent, a debt that we did not contract; in that it permits the executive to control illegally, under the name of the civil list, and without the votes of the representatives of the people, an enormous part of the revenues of the country."

He was opposed to the proposal put forward by some people for the repeal or abrogation of the union, and advocated the formation of parties identified with principles of reform rather than national identity. This was the basis on which La Fontaine intended to make common cause with the liberals of Upper Canada of whom Parent took such a dim view. To him, union was the price to be paid for responsible government, which had been promised only to the Canadians of Upper Canada.[5]

On the eve of the election, the Comité des électeurs de Québec, headed by John Neilson, published a letter from Quebec City electors opposed to the act to unite the two provinces, which recalled the main arguments against union. Although the union was already law, the hope was to make Governor Thomson understand that it faced unflinching opposition. The governor meddled in the electoral process just as in the glory days of Governor Craig, but the "anti-union" camp won twenty-three of the forty-two seats in Lower Canada – a small majority, but a majority only in Lower Canada. The union, adopted in London in July

1840, thus came into force on 10 February 1841, and although during the first session, which began on 15 June, the principle of ministerial responsibility seemed to be applied in practice, it was not recognized by London until 1848.[6]

After the Russell Resolutions, the failure of the Rebellions and the Durham Report, the opposition to union since 1839 was added to the list of failures. While La Fontaine had made inroads in Lower Canada, he would henceforth have to rely on the support of the Reformers in Upper Canada, who were equally dependent on the support of the anti-union members elected in Lower Canada. To what extent could La Fontaine count on the liberals of Upper Canada – of whom Parent had said he expected nothing? How could he count on men who had supported union, when it offered so little to the great majority of franco-phones of Lower Canada?

RELIGIOUS REVIVAL (1840–1848)

The Roman Catholic Church, which had lost its legal status in 1791, had long demonstrated its support for the alliance of throne and altar, and had given the ultimate proof of its loyalty during the Rebellions of 1837 and 1838. This loyalty was rewarded in 1839, when it regained legal status, that is, the right as a legal person to possess goods without risk of confiscation. It could henceforth invest with confidence in land and real estate. Mgr Lartigue, who died on 18 April 1840, was succeeded by Mgr Bourget. The former had awakened in some of his clergy a sympathy to the Catholic restoration under way in France, and after the censure of Lamennais in 1832 and 1834, the more cultivated of the Lower Canada clergy, such as Abbés Raimbault and Fournier in Nicolet, Raymond, Prince, Larocque, and Désaulniers in Saint-Hyacinthe, Painchaud in Sainte-Anne-de-la-Pocatière, and Viau in Montreal, had followed the ex-ample of the liberal Catholics who had distanced themselves from Lamennais, such as Abbé Gerbet, Father Lacordaire (who re-established the Dominican Order in France), and Count de Montalembert. Mgr Bourget provided some support for these views while at the same time he sought to exercise an increasingly conservative influence on them.

The religious revival occurred in the wake of the Rebellions, and it was based on human resources. Enrolments of future priests in the *grands séminaires* of Montreal, Quebec, and Saint-Hyacinthe increased: 156 new students enrolled in the Montreal seminary between 1840 and 1848, and twenty-five on average enrolled per year after 1853. The average number of ordinations of secular clergy from southwest Montreal dou-bled from 1844 to 1848. The number of women entering religious orders took off after 1840. A trip to Europe by the young bishop of Montreal on 23 June 1841 bore fruit: seventy-three religious arrived in Montreal between 1840 and 1848; forty-three of them in 1847–48 alone. The Jesuits, absent from the colony since 1800, returned in 1841 and founded Collège Sainte-Marie in 1848; the Oblate fathers of Mary Immaculate settled in Montreal in 1841 and Bytown (Ottawa) in 1844. Mgr Bourget recruited some sisters of the Dames du Sacré-Coeur in 1842, some Soeurs du Bon Pasteur in 1844, and some Soeurs de Sainte-Croix in 1847. The Clercs de Saint-Viateur and Clercs de Sainte-Croix arrived in 1847 and founded colleges in Joliette, Rigaud, and St Laurent. Many women's religious orders were also founded in Canada in this period: the Dames de la Charité de Saint-Hyacinthe were established in 1841, the Soeurs des Saints Noms de Jésus et de Marie and the Soeurs de la Providence in 1843, the Soeurs de la Miséricorde in 1846, the Soeurs de Sainte-Anne in 1848, and the Soeurs de la Charité de Québec in 1849. New supervisory structures were established, first in the dioceses of Quebec and Montreal, then, in 1847, in Bytown, which was included in the new (1844) ecclesiastic province of Quebec.[7]

Other measures that were part of the religious revival involved the founding of a newspaper and a parish library. After the bishop of Quebec City's refusal to fulfill Mgr Lartigue's request to found a Catholic "gazette" and the Sulpicians' founding of *L'Ami du peuple, des lois et de l'ordre*, a paper that was the unofficial voice of the diocese of Montreal, *Les Mélanges religieux*, appeared from January 1841 to 1852, with contributions from former followers of Lamennais such as Abbé Prince and Abbé Raymond, still eager to restore and defend the "genius of Christianity." Taking as their model the Oeuvre des Bons Livres de Bordeaux, the Sulpicians carried out the bishop of Quebec City's 1842 plan for a religious library; on 19 September 1844, the Oeuvre des Bons Livres de Montréal was inaugurated. This library, which had 2,500 volumes when it opened, loaned nearly 25,000 "good books" a year between 1844 and 1849. The new bishop approved and supported the initiative, reminding members of his diocese that thanks to it, they could "spend ... some very agreeable moments during the long winter evenings when, without it, you would, like many others, be tempted by profane pleasures."[8]

Pastoral strategies were developed and diversified, reinforcing each other. In France, the exiled bishop of Nancy, Mgr de Forbin-Janson, a royalist and a legitimist, founded a pastoral approach based on missionary work and intense preaching, which would be followed by the Oblate missionaries. In September and October 1840, this bishop, a supporter of the alliance of throne and altar, preached in about sixty places in Lower Canada. His new approach surprised the Patriote Louis Perrault, who wrote to Duvernay: "Since the Oblate fathers [four Frenchmen invited by the bishop of Montreal] have been in Canada, they have been travelling from one parish to another and holding retreats or missions of three weeks' duration." This blitz of fervour, already highly visible, was transformed into a spectacle when the bishop of Nancy concluded his pastoral marathon by blessing a huge cross on Mont Saint-Hilaire on 6 October 1841. His extravagant style of popular preaching, which also aimed to found a temperance movement, was perpetuated in Canada by Abbé Charles Chiniquy, who fired up parishioners and distributed his black cross of temperance for them to display in a prominent spot on the walls of their houses. Religious congregations were suddenly able to replenish their ranks.[9] If liberals were struck by the means used in this religious revival, Catholics were soon impressed by the effects: "It is a consolation to see religion flourishing again, indeed, triumphing in this province. It seems as though the political unrest that caused such anxiety and alarm among the people was merely a fog that gave rise to greater calm and greater fervour in the Church in Canada. Since 1840, a striking change of behaviour has been noticeable in all classes of our society." The practice of receiving communion at Easter and respect for the obligation for Catholics to take communion once a year, after reaching what was probably a low point in 1839 in the larger centres most affected by the recent rebellions, became more frequent. In Notre-Dame de Montréal parish, which made up 10 per cent of the faithful in the diocese, abstention from Easter communion fell from 61 per cent to 42 per cent between 1839 and 1842.[10] In this period of discouragement, when people were searching for their individual and collective destiny, religious practice revived, became more intense and reached ordinary people by means of spectacle, temperance campaigns, the Saint-Vincent-de-Paul or the Hôpital de la Miséricorde for "fallen girls." The Church, which had new resources, even began to bring religion into intellectual life, as shown by the reaction in ecclesiastical circles to the first volume of F.-X. Garneau's *Histoire du Canada* in 1845.[11]

ULTRAMONTANISM INTERVENES MORE
AND MORE ACTIVELY IN DAILY LIFE:
THE CASE OF PUBLIC EDUCATION

At the instigation of Mgr Bourget, ultramontanism became increasingly open about its geographical and ideological perspective. As they said in France, things were being done more and more as in Rome, *sic fit Roma*:

in 1842, the clergy abandoned the French-style clerical collar for the Roman collar and habit, and in 1853, the liturgy and ceremonial in effect in Rome were adopted. French Canadian clergy were increasingly familiar with these practices, for in 1852 they began what became a tradition of travelling to Roman universities, where they studied theology, canon law, and philosophy.

Ultramontanism involved far more than the alignment of studies and ecclesiastical practices with those of Rome. It was also a doctrine opposed to that of Gallicanism, which recognized the right of civil authorities to exercise a certain power in the religious domain. Not only did ultramontanism, the political philosophy of Rome, oppose the separation of church and state and promote the alliance of throne and altar, but it claimed that in "mixed" matters, those in which the spiritual was combined with the temporal, or the moral with the political, the Church had precedence over the state. In support of this principle, the Church put forward a hierarchy of ends – primacy of heaven over earth, the spiritual over the temporal, the soul over the body, and education over instruction – in order to lay claim to responsibility for health care (Hôtel-Dieu) and public education. Only after 1839, however, with the recognition of its legal status, was the Church finally able to carry out its plan to "seize control of education," which had been delayed by the laws establishing Royal schools (1801–24) and Assembly schools (1829–36).

Its vision of education had not really changed since the 1819 controversy over the Lancastrian schools. According to *Les Mélanges religieux* of 7 March 1845, "religious education must be essential, and intellectual instruction only accessory, and civil authority must thus make sure it does not seek to absorb religious authority, if there is to be cooperation between these two influences." In its 20 August 1841 issue, the voice of the diocese of Montreal formulated the same idea differently: "There is in the simple intelligence of the Catholic catechism a more complete and more profound education than is generally recognized." The Common School Act of 1841 gave churches the right to religious dissidence, the right to establish separate schools for religious (Catholic and Protestant) rather than linguistic (francophone and anglophone) minorities, and distinct structures for Catholic and Protestant school examiners. The act of 1846 extended this confessionalization of the education system: in Quebec and Montreal, teachers were to be chosen separately by Catholic and Protestant examiners, members of the clergy were to be exempted from the competency tests required of lay candidates, who also had to obtain a certificate of morality from a parish priest. The clergy won the right to supervise the choice of textbooks dealing with religious and moral topics, and in 1849 parish priests were allowed to hold positions as school commissioners. This amounted to the de facto recognition of a right to spiritual primacy for churches in "mixed" matters and in a crucial area, that of the formation and transmission of values.[12]

La Fontaine took advantage of this recognition of the primacy of the Church in educational matters in 1846 when he rose in the Assembly to demand the restitution to the Church of the Jesuits' assets and their use for education. Aware that they would be depending on anglophone Protestants for re-election, his liberal allies in Upper Canada voted against the bill. La Fontaine thus became at once the defender of the French language, the status and assets of the Church, and Catholic education. The alliance of the political and the religious could hardly have had a stronger footing.

A NEW LIBERAL IMPETUS

The liberal tradition had begun with the failure of constitutional struggles and of armed resistance, and the exile, voluntary or otherwise, of the most militant Patriotes. How could the liberal movement gain a new lease on life? In 1845, after La Fontaine succeeded in obtaining an amnesty, some Patriotes returned from exile. Papineau was among them, but the Patriote leader, back in Montreal, was not yet participating in public life.

Meanwhile, young Montrealers had not waited for Papineau's return to establish a place where they could socialize and hold discussions. The Institut canadien de Montréal opened on 17 December 1844, offering a number of activities for the long winter evenings. From 1844 to 1848, it presented some twenty public lectures, over twenty essays by members for their fellow-members, and a dozen debates of interest to law students. Wolfred Nelson was one of the lecturers, as were Amédée Papineau, Charles Mondelet, Charles Laberge, and Rodolphe Laflamme, but there were also more moderate speakers and lecturers, such as Étienne Parent, Augustin-Norbert Morin, and Antoine Gérin-Lajoie, which was a sign that the Institut did not yet have a clear ideological orientation. The Institut's library, which had about 1,300 volumes in 1848 and loaned an average of 725 a year, also made over twenty local and foreign newspapers available to members of the Institut and subscribers to the library.

The public lectures given by Parent at the Institut between 1846 and 1848 show that it had not yet radicalized its position, and that an alternative was still possible. Parent, the proponent of "honourable submission" in 1838 and an opponent of union in 1839 and 1840, presented a new vision of the preservation of nationality in what he called "the new order of things." Noting "the age of industry," and "the age of positivism," he stressed the importance of public education and the study of political economy in order to "honour" work and commerce and assign a new social task to capitalists, clerks, labourers, priests, and "the intellectual elite." The only hope of survival in this new union of Upper and Lower Canada was for French Canadians to participate in economic, commercial, and industrial life. Thus, between 1846 and 1848, within the Institut canadien de Montréal itself, a different form of liberalism was formulated, a moderate liberalism that was in favour of private enterprise, free trade, and a nationality based on cultural characteristics rather than political ones and opposed to anticlericalism if not supportive of clericalism. Parent, who had already, in the mid-1830s, seen responsible government as a solution to the colony's crisis, was to throw his support behind La Fontaine on this issue, even though he had also been one of the fiercest opponents of union.[13]

The young liberals also published a newspaper, whose very title was a program: *L'Avenir*. Its format and typography recalled those of the Parisian journal of the same name of 1830. The paper, which began publishing in July 1847, adopted a more liberal orientation in November, when Papineau returned to public life. *Les Mélanges religieux* saw in it Lamennais reborn from the ashes of his condemnations: "The doctrines of *L'Avenir* are indeed the same as those of its counterpart in Paris. These are the same doctrines as those in *Words of a Believer* and *Les Affaires de Rome*. And they are, finally, the doctrines of Mr. De Lamennais, that fallen angel whose loss the Church mourns." The contributors to Montreal's *L'Avenir* soon realized that times had changed: "Look now! In 1831 or 1832, Lamennais's *Words of a Believer* was published in full in the Quebec City paper *Le Canadien*. The people, moved by all the poetry, all the eloquence of that extraordinary genius, applauded it. Today, even the humblest, least ambitious text that expresses a little freedom is immediately decried as a threat to order and moral standards – a terrible, IMPIOUS thing! And all the pious souls and all the hypocrites and all the men with an interest in the perpetuation of the present regime close their eyes and cry 'God save us from our century's impiety!'"[14]

The publication of *L'Avenir* revived discussions about Lamennais, just as the return of Papineau recalled the period of valiant struggles. While Catholic circles had distanced themselves from Lamennais in 1832 and above all in 1834, liberals had followed the development of this former priest condemned by the Church. Papineau had come to know him well in Paris between 1839 and 1845, and his nephew, Louis-Antoine Dessaulles, on a visit to Paris in 1839, had discovered, either in the Bossange bookstore or in his dear uncle's library, *Les Affaires de Rome*, which Lamennais had published in 1836. The book contained a highly incriminating account of the collusion between the Polish Church and the czar to defeat the efforts of liberal Catholic Poles to free the country in 1830, which had led to the condemnation of *L'Avenir* of Paris in 1831. This explosive article revealed to the young Dessaulles "the honest and holy way in which things are done in Rome." Recalling the statements of the loyal Mgr Lartigue in 1837, he wrote to his cousin Denis-Emery Papineau: "It was only pure political considerations that led the Pope to take the position he did. It was Austria that condemned Mr. De La Mennais, it was Russia; it was not Gregory XVI." Papineau's nephew had seen his destiny traced out in Lamennais's work: to denounce all religious or spiritual interference by the Church in political or temporal affairs.

The moderate Denis-Benjamin Viger also engaged in polemics with *Les Mélanges religieux* on this issue in early 1842. To Viger, who seems to have read *Affaires de Rome*, it was clear that the pope's "brief to the bishops of Poland was paid for by the Russian government." This respectable and honourable public figure went further, identifying Lower Canada's situation with that of Poland: the pastoral letter issued by Mgr Lartigue on 24 October 1837 should, he argued, be interpreted exclusively in terms of politics, and not in terms of dogma. *Les Mélanges religieux* could hardly believe it: "To cite La Mennais [*sic*] as an indisputable authority against the Pope! To use La Mennais to slander the Pope; La Mennais, the most relentless foe the Church has at this time, who since his fall has devoted his entire life to opposing it by means of errors and lies ... La Mennais ... whom one of his erstwhile greatest admirers, who has since abandoned him for the voice of the Church, has so aptly called the Wandering Jew of politics."[15]

While there was also a new "liberal" spirit in Catholic circles after 1840, it was a particular, shifting sort of spirit that constantly imposed the obligation to establish what was liberal about this Catholicism and what was Catholic about this liberalism. Both the former followers of Lamennais and the editors of *Les Mélanges religieux* rejected Lamennais's kind of "Christian democracy" and referred only to the Lamennais refuted by Abbé Gerbet or Abbé Peltier, stressing that "all took their place to the right of the vicar of God." "All" meant essentially Lacordaire and Montalembert, Lamennais's former friends, who had made the pilgrimage to Rome in 1831 and had since submitted to God's vicar. But *Les Mélanges religieux* portrayed Lacordaire selectively: he had also refuted Lamennais's philosophical system and made a repentant pilgrimage to Rome, he was an orator, and he had recently re-established the Dominicans in France. This was the same Lacordaire admired by Abbé Raymond of Saint-Hyacinthe, who had submitted and distanced himself from Lamennais in a long confession on 24 November 1834.[16]

But Count de Montalembert above all fascinated certain Catholics throughout the nineteenth century, from Abbé Raymond to Abbé Lionel Groulx. Raymond had known Montalembert since the Parisian *L'Avenir* in 1830–31. The two had corresponded, with Montalembert confiding that he had stepped back from "the precipice from which de la Mennais, my former friend, fell, seeking to pull me down with him," and Raymond recognizing the existence of a "harmony" with the writings of his correspondent and also mentioning Lamennais, "our former friend." Raymond's trip to Europe in 1842–43, during which he visited Montalembert, Lacordaire, Gerbet, Chateaubriand, Dom Guéranger, Lamennais's opponent Father Rozaven, Father Perrone and Father Ventura in Rome, the Roman College, and the offices of *L'Univers*, played a decisive role in his resolution to spread the word about "the new Catholic school of thought" and to try to raise the intellectual level of the Canadian clergy. This is the essential meaning of the Catholic "liberalism" of Abbé Raymond or Abbé Bouchy of the Collège de Sainte-Anne-de-la-Pocatière.

The current of thought that became dominant, however, was that of *L'Univers*, the conservative Paris newspaper founded by Abbé Migne in 1833 and led after 1840 by Louis Veuillot, which was cited by the Quebec City paper *Le Canadien* beginning in late December 1839. Dioceses, presbyteries, and colleges subscribed to *L'Univers*, which Lacordaire described as "like Jansenism in disguise, subsuming the natural under the supernatural: 1° in politics, the state under the Church; 2° in philosophy, reason under authority; 3° in literature, the profane classics under the Christian classics." French Canadian liberals soon realized that "the party of *L'Univers* is among us. It follows the same approach and uses the same means to reach the same end."[17]

1848: A DECISIVE YEAR

Papineau, who had promised not to come home until all the Patriotes had been pardoned, returned to Montreal in September 1845 after eight years of exile in the United States and France. As he had been absent, he had not participated in the movement opposing union or witnessed the growing political influence of La Fontaine, who was increasingly seen as the new French Canadian leader. The situation had clearly changed: Papineau's cousin, Denis-Benjamin Viger, was now the joint premier, his brother, Denis-Benjamin Papineau was a minister, Ludger Duvernay had resumed publication of *La Minerve*, which supported La Fontaine, Abbé Chartier had returned to the priesthood, Thomas Storrow Brown had become an advocate of temperance, Wolfred Nelson had been re-elected in Richelieu, O'Callaghan was working as an archivist for the state of New York, Dr Robert Nelson had decided not to return to any place under the British monarch, and the former Patriote Dr Duchesnois had settled in Chile.

How would the great orator be received and how would he adjust his democratic, republican, and nationalist ideas to the new circumstances? Encouraged by the electors of Saint-Maurice, Papineau agreed to run in the December 1847 election. He was elected on 3 January 1848, and entered the Legislative Assembly of United Canada in Kingston on 14 March. In parliament and in his major speeches – to the electors of Saint-Maurice, to the Irish community, at Bonsecours Market, and to a Yamachiche meeting – the positions he took were those that would lead to a major parliamentary confrontation with La Fontaine on 22 and 23 January 1849, one year after his election.

In the speeches he made upon his return from exile, Papineau began by explaining his role in the events of 1837: until the last minute, armed resistance had been discouraged and had not been "planned or advised by anyone reasonable and influential." The instructions had been to surrender if served with a warrant, or flee to the United States. The real causes of the rebellion of 1837 lay in the armed anglophone volunteers who disturbed the peace and attacked houses, the arrests without warrant made by bands of soldiers, and above all, the proclamation of martial law: "If the weak Government of that period, guided by a weak consul, had not resorted to the extreme measure of unlawfully proclaiming martial law, there would have been no troubles." As Papineau saw it, "indignation and the taking up of arms were a spontaneous reaction to meet force with force."[18]

The politician had not changed; in his speech to the electors of Saint-Maurice, he declared, "All that I demanded in the Assembly in 1834 ... I demand once again in 1847": representation by population, resident electors, eligibility unrelated to property, putting an end to corruption, less costly administration.[19]

Papineau justified his opposition to union first and foremost in democratic terms: the fact that parliamentary representation was equal for Upper and Lower Canada, rather than proportional to population. This, he maintained, was "the first, the main defect of our present constitution," and thus the most urgent parliamentary reform: "Grant [this reform], the people is with you, and I am with the people; refuse it, the people is against you, and I remain with the people." As a democrat, he could not accept the principle of equal representation independent of population, which was to the advantage of Upper Canada; he pointed out that six "rotten boroughs" in Upper Canada of twelve thousand inhabitants had six representatives, whereas in Lower Canada, two counties of forty thousand inhabitants only had the right to elect two representatives. He proposed the principle of one representative per ten thousand inhabitants "throughout the Province"; to him, this was the only way to end a situation "of ongoing submission," and this was the reason for his rejection of Baldwin's strategy of increasing the number of representatives in Lower Canada – and in Upper Canada as well. In fact, there was a nationalist stake in this democratic argument: it was unthinkable to demand the repeal of the union without obtaining this reform, without a system of representation based on population that could give Lower Canada a parliamentary majority. Papineau was clear about this: "The men who cannot see this future are blind men, the men who do not want it are tyrants." To those who wondered why such a fuss about representation by population – which Upper Canada would soon demand when immigration made its population larger – Papineau answered, "There is no doubt that if the Union were to continue, Upper Canada would demand its full rights," and its demand would be justified, just as the present demand of Lower Canada was; "parliamentary reform based on population will lead to the judicious demand, useful to both sides and with their mutual consent, for a divorce to end their forced marriage."[20] Papineau was being a consistent democrat, but his reasoning was based on a condition: "if the Union were to continue." This was his wager.

He was no more attracted to responsible government than he had been at the time of the 92 Resolutions or in 1837. To him, it was "deceit," "an enigma interpreted differently by the one giving and the one receiving." Union had established only a falsely responsible government; a falsely liberal ministry made up of Upper Canada liberals who had helped impose the union and who were less liberal than Lord Durham, who had supported representation by population in his report. An alliance with the liberals of Upper Canada could only be a misalliance in democratic terms: "The liberals found it expedient to be, in a single day, more arbitrary and more oppressive than all the *Canadiens'* enemies had been in the previous eighty years; they have given us the measure of their morality."[21]

The measure of political morality was also evident, according to Papineau, in the corruption of the "rotten boroughs," which were sparsely populated and easy to intimidate or buy, that of a press well-paid for supplying *Canadien* "whisperers" to Lord Russell and Edward Ellice, that of the "so-called religious *Mélanges*," and that of finding "places" for those with a taste for power. At the Yamachiche assembly, he declared angrily, "An order based on commands and force has [been replaced by] one based on fraud and corruption. People are no longer whipped; they are bought."[22]

To Papineau, the only solution left was to demand the repeal of the union, the abrogation of a constitutional regime whose injustices had been decried since 1839. In the period immediately following his return to political life in December 1847, Papineau noted a sore spot: "How is it, then, that a law that hurt everyone – those who asked for it and those who opposed it – a law with which no one in Lower Canada is content, finds within the legislative chamber not a single voice that echoes the almost constant complaints heard outside it?" The union was "a deceitful system, a crude trap" that made Lower Canada a doubly colonized society: first by England and then by Upper Canada. Like Ireland, they must demand the repeal of the union, and must restore to Lower Canada "a separate government." The choice was "repeal of the Union or electoral reform," and to the former Patriote leader, the mere acceptance of the present situation showed "that we are already accustomed enough to abject servitude to submit to it without protest."[23]

Papineau was not the only one who wanted to revive the liberal spirit. The young people behind *L'Avenir*, and particularly his nephew Louis-Antoine Dessaulles, were engaged in the same struggle. Under the pseudonym "Anti-Union," Dessaules published two forceful articles in *L'Avenir*, on 31 December 1847 and 5 February 1848, decrying "the Tories of Lower Canada and the liberals of Upper Canada who brought about the Union." He spared no one.

It is thus universally recognized that the union is unjust, disastrous for us, bad in theory, impossible in practice; its effect is to give two distinct administrations to a single province that is too large for just one, and thus to complicate the administrative mechanisms by doubling them; it represents a monstrous amalgam of fundamentally opposed legislative systems; of different habits and customs, of essentially contradictory associations of ideas; in short, the only thing the constitution really pooled was the public coffers; but there too, practice has proven theory wrong, and Upper Canada has taken almost all of Lower Canada's contribution; furthermore, Union was imposed on Lower Canada without its consent and despite its opposition; the majority was delivered to the mercy of the minority; our taxes have been doubled and we are not the ones deriving the advantage from it.

The young Dessaulles, who had developed political consciousness in November 1837 when he helped his uncle flee Montreal, and was inspired by Lamennais's *Affaires de Rome*, proposed instead that they "follow a policy that is more durable and better suited to our needs and those of Lower Canada." He more clearly expressed the nationalist dimension in his strategy to repeal the union: "We are destined to form a separate people by ourselves, whether it be under the protection of the English flag or the American flag."[24]

The year 1848 was also extremely fraught in Europe. The revolution that broke out in France on 22 February made a strong impression on the press of Lower Canada, which gave it considerable space. The reformist newspaper *La Minerve* began publishing a regular feature of news from Europe, entitled "Revue européenne," and *L'Avenir*, which published "special pages" and reprinted material from the Paris paper *Le Siècle* and the New York-based *Courrier des États-Unis*, published "L'adresse à la jeunesse parisienne de la jeunesse canadienne," a letter from young Canadians to young people in Paris, on 17 May. The letter declared: "Members of the great French family fifteen hundred leagues from France, we are following in our hearts the path France has opened up to the world; and a thousand echoes rise up from our St Lawrence, repeating the cry of Liberty from the banks of the Seine."[25] How would the pro-government press interpret this enthusiasm for 1848?

Liberals had never before addressed the national question so explicitly. Papineau's speech at Bonsecours Market in Montreal on 14 April 1848 is an example. In it, he maintained that the words "*honour, homeland* and *nationality* embody the principle of the highest civic virtues, the most concise symbol of our foremost duties as citizens." Tracing the history "of our nationality" and swearing that, "until the final moment … the last beat of my heart will be for the French Canadian homeland and nationality," he recalled that "the principal cause of all nationalities is the defence of their mother tongue." But the choice in favour of nationality must not create "national distinctions" today, any more than it did in the past: "It is not in Lower Canada, which, to its credit, was the first of all the English colonies to pass a naturalization law applicable to all men, without distinction of religion or country of birth … and gives all members of the human family the right to come here and work the land, practise their various trades and enjoy the same civil, religious and political rights in free competition with the French constituents … who have consecrated this humanitarian principle of universal brotherhood."

The challenge was thus to combine liberalism and nationality because "the heart is too noble and reason too just and lofty to separate liberalism from nationality, to sacrifice the latter to the former," and "as long as true liberalism has not placed all national groups on a completely equal footing," Upper Canada would deceive itself and have people believe that it is liberal. Once again, Papineau mentioned Ireland, recalling that the English had given "Ireland, in order to destroy that nascent spirit of nationality, a Union on which our own is modelled." Whereas before 1837, he had avoided any reference to the movements of national awakening in Belgium, Poland, Italy, and Greece, he now allowed himself to say that Russia was to Poland what England was to Canada.[26]

As Papineau saw it, it was the liberals of Upper Canada who were lacking in liberalism. Once representation by population had been obtained, with the support of the real liberals of Upper Canada, then liberals in Lower Canada would face a challenge, as they would have to actually give "all members of the human family" the same rights.

AN APPEAL TO THE PRINCIPLE OF NATIONALITY?

On 14 April, a year after Papineau's return to political life and the launching of *L'Avenir*, three months after the revolution of February 1848 in France, and the day after Papineau's speech in Bonsecours Market, *L'Avenir* published the first of a series of articles on "the Union and the nation," which would preoccupy the pro-government press for the next few months.

L'Avenir, the paper of the Papineau camp, sought to revive patriotic feeling: "Long suppressed, stifled in the name of the public interest, the attachment to the nationality that characterizes us seemed destined to become one of those prejudices that may be dear to the heart but that reason had to proscribe as a weakness, an error of sentiment. No one dared make any demands in its name, to protect a position to which we had been led by a series of unfortunate events." Since 1838, it had been necessary "to cease considering ourselves French Canadians if we wanted to make something of ourselves in this system of social organization; and under the pretext of conquering it, we drowned [our nationality] in liberalism."

According to *L'Avenir*, union "demanded our national death in exchange for this constitutional political freedom that we had purchased so dearly"; it was an "act of both plunder and annihilation, a sort of political banditry that this century seems to want to repudiate and avenge everywhere today." This reference to the international situation is at the heart of the rehabilitation of nationalism: if the people "is unanimous, it will not be refused. These events that keep breaking out in Europe guarantee its success." The nationality involved was at once the "the life principle of peoples" and the idea that "we want only one thing, to *preserve* our institutions, our language, our laws and our customs" (our italics). Careful not to aggravate "national distinctions," *L'Avenir* concluded its first article as follows: "Cannot the history of our struggles be summed up in this motto of the Polish national movement, 'Liberty for us, liberty for you'? Indeed, would it be acceptable for six hundred thousand individuals to expect one hundred thousand to teach them their language and impose their institutions on them because among the one hundred thousand there are complainers who want to believe they are oppressed as soon as they are no longer the oppressors?"

The pro-government press, which supported La Fontaine, reacted promptly. The 18 April issue of the *Revue canadienne* claimed that the article in *L'Avenir* was "likely to have a terrible effect if public opinion is not immediately enlightened concerning [*L'Avenir*'s] leanings and if all good citizens do not work together to prevent its pernicious effects." The pro-government publication did not hesitate to ask supporters of Papineau and proponents of the repeal of the union where they were in 1840–41 when they needed to deal with the issue and in whose name they were today displaying "the sentimental politics" of the "flag of unrest, trouble and strife." *La Revue canadienne* stated that "the writers of *L'Avenir* wish to foment revolution in Canada," to stir up "winds and tempests amongst us," and "cast us on the high seas of politics." The paper was convinced that the people would consider a bird in the hand better than two in the bush, and that English-style constitutional monarchy remained more attractive than the republic of 1789 or 1793: "We are willing to wager that our compatriots, however much they may admire the French Revolution, prefer responsible government and the prospects it offers to the provisional government of Paris, with its bleak and menacing future. Our compatriots will not use the events occurring in Europe today to create an upheaval without knowing what would come next ... They know very well what you are getting at." According to the *Revue*, the union had not been carried out to defeat the French Canadians; rather, it had been their salvation.

The 22 April issue of *L'Avenir* spoke on behalf of those targeted by the *Revue canadienne*: "In the name of our institutions invaded by foreign institutions; in the name of our language eliminated from politics; in the name of our laws and customs, which we wish to preserve; in the name of our nationality, which we wish to awaken from its numbness and lethargy; in the name of our nationality, nullified and placed in a position of ever greater minority by the Union." Recalling that "since the Union, nationality has not been seen as a political or social relationship," the newspaper once again took the opportunity to define the sort of nationality it supported: "The government itself must grasp the close connection between our nationality and our tie with our country; this is the only binding tie we have with it, and the stronger our nationality is and the stronger its survival instinct, the more interest [our nationality] will have in maintaining this tie. But the day it loses this motivation, it [our nationality] will no longer have any interest in remaining united with it."

Les Mélanges religieux got involved in the controversy on 21 and 28 April with a typical question: "Is it possible that we are even disposed to risk. existing, guaranteed, protected freedoms for the pleasure of changing?" The paper of the diocese of Montreal suggested that the prospect of years of disorder "impels us to once again urge our colleagues of *L'Avenir*, in the name of religion, to abandon their enterprise and stop trying to drag their compatriots into a course of action with countless dangers and certain misfortune." For the doctrines put forward by *L'Avenir* would bring the people "a succession of woes, privations, oppression and total anarchy," all because repealing the union had become "the god of the day" for Papineau and the liberals of Lower Canada. *L'Avenir*, replying on the 26th, did not see why they should "give up in the name of religion," why "religion should order us not to prepare the people to demand the repeal of the Union when the time is ripe." It also made a point of observing that "*Les Mélanges* is trespassing onto the slippery slope of politics" and that the voice of the diocese was trying to make itself heard in the political arena. The intellectual and political conflict of the next few decades was now out in the open.

La Minerve, Duvernay's reformist paper, which had until then remained silent, merely pointed out, on 1 May, that "the better to create a sensation, one appeals to the strongest, most vibrant and indestructible sentiment of the people, that of nationality." Its intention was clear: the paper would not enter the debate "until the goal is somewhat better defined."

At the same time as Dessaulles, under the pseudonym of "Countryman," was repeating the arguments presented earlier by the editors of *L'Avenir*, while giving them his characteristic belligerent touch (3, 10, 13, 27, and 31 May), Joseph Cauchon's *Journal de Québec* joined the discussion. Cauchon, a brilliant and perseverant strategist, was a supporter of La Fontaine, and he rapidly perceived what his side was up against. "The major events occurring in Europe, the thrones that are toppling one after the other into the bottomless pit of democracy, must, we admit, be a powerful source of gigantic hopes to the men of *L'Avenir* and to agitators." This reference to O'Callaghan's "Agitate! Agitate!" also aimed to recall "the uncertainties of all possible systems and theories" and to make sure no one mistook "partial movements that are still incapable of defining themselves" for "the will of the country." The 4 May *Journal de Québec* decried this "nationalism," this "exclusive nationality": "You want to agitate for the repeal of the Union in the name of nationality; you reject liberalism, that is, justice for all." Clearly, the debate on the relationship between nationality and liberalism was heating up.

Two days later, *L'Avenir*, which maintained that the 24 June speeches "do not indicate that nationality has been recognized as a principle of public action," also stated that it was "seeking the repeal of the Union constitutionally and legally" and had no desire for "revolution in Canada." On 13 May, *Le Journal de Québec*, which considered "this national exclusivism" to be "a repudiation of liberalism," reopened the wound: "It is the substitution of a broad universal principle for human selfishness, for the shrunken *we* of the family and the exclusivism of nationality." Cauchon, like La Fontaine and the reformers, believed in responsible government and in the political generosity of the liberals of Upper Canada: "As a national group, they are more numerous than you, and as such (since you have made them remember their national identity) they will refuse you out of a sense of self-preservation what they would gladly have granted you in the name of justice and equal rights."

L'Avenir, which claimed on 17 May that it simply wanted the same rights as the inhabitants of Upper Canada had, on 20 May, questioned *Le Journal de Québec* on its definition of liberalism: "Unless you show that this liberalism is the reason that one third of Lower Canada is not represented, that the French Canadian population is pillaged and looted by the foreign population of Upper Canada, that the interests of Lower Canada are sacrificed and trodden on every time they come in contact with those of Upper Canada, which happens all too often. We ask you, Mr. Editor, *is that universal justice and equal rights for all?*" The parties were in a pitched battle: Papineau and *L'Avenir* championed a liberal nationalism that required the democratic principle of representation by population – which was rejected by Upper Canada and the French Canadian defenders of the union – and involved equal respect for the rights of everyone; the pro-government press called itself liberal without supporting the electoral reform of representation by population and suggested that the "sentimental politics" of nationality could only bring back the "national distinctions" and conflicts of 1837 and 1838, or even lead to those of 1848 in Europe. For the former, nationality was the political tie that united the French Canadians of Lower Canada, and their liberalism implied equal rights for the anglophone minority. For the latter, nationality – a forbidden word – served as a pretext to undermine the credibility of their fellow citizens' liberalism. For the former, it was a matter of principles; for the latter, a matter of principles and bogeymen.

Essentially, Cauchon the strategist did not share the hopes Papineau placed in the electoral reform of representation by population; on 27 May, his paper wrote: "You will have against you all the men of Lower Canada who do not speak French; but above all, Upper Canada will not want what you want. Thus you will not obtain a majority in the Assembly in favour of your proposition and your agitation." And "in five years, Upper Canada will have a larger population than Lower Canada and ... will in its turn complain bitterly about the inequality of representation."

As for the *Le Canadien*, which in the 22 September and 15 November issues identified itself "with the peoples' cause, with their suffering, with their hopes for emancipation" and found it "painful to see the obstacles created to delay the hour of justice and freedom for the people of the Canadas," it came too late to support *L'Avenir* but just in time to make it clear that "the word had been given" to make Papineau lose and to "cover it up."

"CONCERTED ACTION" AGAINST THE LIBERALS, AND A POINT OF NO RETURN FOR PAPINEAU (22–23 JANUARY 1849)

The resistance to Papineau after his return to political life and the opposition to the views expressed by *L'Avenir* on parliamentary reform and the repeal of the union, and by Dessaulles and the editors of the paper on nationality and liberalism, were planned down to the last detail by La Fontaine and the reformers. La Fontaine had won support from the press by granting exclusive rights to government announcements and printing work. The positions of *La Revue canadienne*, *La Minerve*, and *Le Journal de Québec* clearly show their loyalty, as does the decision by *Les Mélanges religieux* in March 1848 to publish a column entitled "Louis-Joseph Papineau."[27]

From May 1848 on, it was evident that the reformers and the clergy were carrying on "simultaneous action." Dr Wolfred Nelson launched an attack on Papineau, accusing him "of having fled" to the United States in November 1837. Nelson, who had not supported this view before 1848, began to spread it in his county, and he published his position in *La Minerve* on 25 May. Papineau replied in *L'Avenir* on 3 June, but withdrew from the discussion because Nelson refused to participate in a public debate.

In testimony, sworn or otherwise, in the form of affidavits, declarations or public oaths, the controversy raged on. There was a song going around, to the tune of "For he's a jolly good fellow":

Grandpa isn't going to war,
On his feet, on his hands, on his head,
Grandpa isn't going to war.
Who knows when he'll return,
Who knows when he'll return,

Who knows when he'll return? (Refrain)
He took to his heels
He fled to the States.
So where are you off to, my Grandpa
Where are you running so fast?
I'm looking for a hiding place
Until the fighting's over.
But it's not brave, Grandpa
To run away like that.
Don't say a thing, the Dessaulles boy
Will arrange everything.
After the battle of Saint-Denis,
Grandpa, he was still away.
But the Dessaulles boy
Will arrange everything.

In November 1848, convinced that there was a deliberate effort to "cast M. Papineau into disrepute," Dessaulles anonymously published a pamphlet, *Papineau and Nelson: White and Black*, with articles reprinted from *L'Avenir*. But things ended there. The damage was done: the reputation of the great man had been sullied and it was impossible to set the record straight.[28]

The fate of the liberal opposition and its policy of parliamentary reform and repeal of the union was decided on Monday and Tuesday, 22 and 23 January 1849. On Monday, Papineau rose in the Legislative Assembly of United Canada in Montreal and made a long speech. His political career had reached a point of no return. He began by welcoming the re-establishment of the French language in the Assembly "as an act of mere justice." This done, he went on the offensive. First he criticized the so-called liberal government of La Fontaine, whose policy seemed to him indistinguishable from that of the Tories. As he saw it, if this government had ever really been liberal, its Speech from the Throne would have included "some words of sympathy for the noble and courageous efforts that have been made in Europe against all tyrannies, and all forms of despotism. Surely our ministers, if they understand what they should by the word freedom ... should lend their support to the sublime struggles of the peoples against oppressors, to the efforts of generous men who dedicate themselves to the fight against despotism, in order to replace it with the democratic principle based on the ideas of human equality and fraternity?" This man who had followed politics for forty years refused to accept that individual wealth should be the criterion for eligibility to the Assembly when it was not for membership in the

Legislative Council. The responsible government London had finally granted the colony was still, he claimed, vested in Downing Street, and the ministers "can only do the will of the colonial office." He called once again for the repeal of the union, which "puts us, in relation to Upper Canada, in the same position as Ireland in relation to England," Ireland, "where more men die every year than anywhere else in Europe." He pointed a finger at the venality of the press, at certain newspapers that were "prompted" by the ministry. And since he was putting his cards on the table, he proposed an amendment that, if accepted, would change the electoral system and introduce proportional representation. But, tellingly, he had to beg for the support of at least one person in the Assembly in order to have his amendment debated.

The next day, La Fontaine rose to reply point by point to Papineau. He began by recalling that without him, Papineau "would still be in exile," and French would not have been re-established as a language of the parliament. A former Patriote, he denounced the "system of extreme opposition" of the former Patriote leader; he objected to the comparison between Lower Canada and Ireland and asked Papineau, sitting opposite him: "Do people starve to death in Canada as they do in Ireland? Has our population been decimated by famine, as the Irish population has? Is our population so dense and so large that there is no more uncultivated land in Canada?" Offended by the accusations concerning the venality of the pro-government press, La Fontaine challenged the member for Saint-Maurice: "to look each of my colleagues in the face; and to look me in the face; and then to place his hand on the spot where his conscience may be supposed to be and say whether he himself believes what he says." But La Fontaine reserved his most solemn declaration for Papineau's amendment. The leader of the government maintained that equal representation was precisely what "protects us today" and in the future; and this man who would die in 1864, before the implementation of the new political system that would have proven him wrong, stated: "Basing myself on the principle that the Union Act is only a confederation of two provinces, as Upper Canada itself declared in 1841, I state clearly that I will never accept that one section of the [united] province have a larger number of representatives in this assembly than the other, whatever the size of its population."[29]

Papineau's amendment was defeated. That was the end for electoral reform, for representation by population and for the strategy, now virtually impossible, of repealing the union. Twelve years after 1837 and two years after Papineau's return, the new liberal impetus had reached an impasse in both parliamentary and electoral terms. What was to be done?

At this time, the question of nationality arose again in Italy, where the liberals were trying to unify the country, which was fragmented by the domination of certain regions by neighbouring empires and by the "states" belonging to the Holy See, in particular, the pontifical territory in Rome. *Les Mélanges religieux*, taking its cue from Louis Veuillot's *L'Univers*, celebrated an idealized Rome – pagan Rome vanquished by that of the popes – magnified by the arrival of Pius IX on Peter's throne. The new pope, showing a certain liberalism at the outset of his papacy, supported the national positions of the liberals as long as they did not question his sovereignty over his territories. But when the time came to decide whether to declare war on Austria, which controlled a large part of the country, Pius IX first hesitated and then refused, maintaining that, "as an Italian and as a sovereign," he was favourable to Italian independence, but recalling that, "as a priest and as pope," he had a duty to seek peace.

The radicalization of the Italian liberals forced the pope to leave Rome on 24 November 1848, and this dramatic event raised two basic questions for Catholics: dispossessed of his territories by the nationalist liberals, at what cost could the pope be divested of his temporal power, his power as the political sovereign of his own territories, and was not the pope's temporal independence the heritage and responsibility of "all Catholic nations"?

Mgr Bourget's answer was presented in a circular letter to his clergy on 18 January 1849, four days before La Fontaine's dramatic speech in the legislature. The bishop, intervening for the first time in the affairs not of Rome but of Montreal, had understood that with responsible government, the alliance between throne and altar could no longer be maintained solely through the relationship between the bishop and the governor, and that it would be necessary to make himself heard on the actual terrain of popular sovereignty, that is, by the electorate. He suggested to his clergy: "The sufferings of Our Holy Father are, in our eyes, a precious mine that we must exploit for the advantage of the Faith of our good people, by inspiring it to a deep veneration of the Head of the Church, and a supreme horror of the revolutions of which he is the victim and which may one day affect us." In the pastoral letter that accompanied this circular, Mgr Bourget advised "his flock": "Be faithful to God, and respect all legitimately constituted authorities. Such is the will of the Lord. Do not listen to those who make seditious speeches to you, for they cannot be your friends. Do not read the books or papers inspired by the spirit of revolt, for they spread vile doctrines that, like a canker, have eroded and ruined the happiest and most flourishing States." Bishops of Montreal came and went, but their doctrine never changed. *L'Avenir* and the liberal supporters of Papineau, the propagandists of nationality, were clearly the targets of this document, in which the Church was not merely venturing into the political arena but was fully involved in it.³⁰

L'Avenir easily recognized itself in the bishop's warning, and on 14 March 1849, it published an anonymous article written by Dessaulles, entitled "The Temporal Power of the Pope." An admirer of Lamennais who had been following affairs in Rome for a decade, he described "the Pope's decline as king," and the proclamation of the republic in Rome. He expressed the wish that the pope would not use "foreign [Austrian] arms to regain a temporal power, in the name of him who said: My kingdom is not of this world." According to *L'Avenir*, Rome should act in keeping with "the doctrine that the people are the basis of power" because "the Pope's temporal power has no other basis than that of all the other political governments in the universe." In Rome as elsewhere, it was "a political issue and nothing else," and the political and religious spheres should be separate.

To the argument of *Les Mélanges religieux* that the pope should be able to play the role of arbiter between peoples and kings, Dessaulles replied: "Let us say that the last time the Pope arbitrated in the case of peoples versus kings he did not provide a convincing demonstration of the advantage for our time of such arbitration, which the Polish people did not ask the Pope for. The example of unhappy Poland cruelly delivered to the Emperor of Russia by the king of Rome [that is, the pope] was enough to make the peoples understand that their interests would be safer in their own hands than in those of an interested party, and that the much-vaunted independence of the Pope as king was in reality only a toy in the hands of Austria, Russia or any other great European power." Dessaulles concluded his article by reminding his readers that "this revolution in Italy has provided a pretext for endless attacks on democratic principles by sources who are all the more to be feared in that they are highly respectable. No doubt in good faith, they conflate everything: spiritual and temporal power, principles and men."³¹

The "concerted action" against the liberals and *L'Avenir* next took the form of a strategy that relied in equal measure on *Les Mélanges religieux*, a theologian, and a popular preacher. The diocese's newspaper tried to marginalize *L'Avenir*, to present it as "a foreign newspaper, a fanatical Protestant newspaper, or a socialist sheet" whose strategy was clear: "We should not be surprised; by praising the Roman usurpers and brigands, they seek to accustom the *Canadien* people to the idea that a few adventurers can seize sovereign authority and sit enthroned in our midst as sovereign masters." Then the canon of the cathedral of Montreal, Pierre-Adolphe Pinsoneault, plunged into the fray, armed with his theological studies with the French Sulpicians of Issy-les-Moulineaux. In three articles on the "New kind words of *L'Avenir*," the theologian zeroed in on "the limitless arrogance of these pygmies who keep wanting to take themselves for giants."

Finally, it was Abbé Chiniquy's turn, and the great preacher and temperance crusader used his popularity to serve this campaign against the liberals by advocating the marginalization of those who forgot "that religion and the homeland are two intimately related things in the heart of every good *Canadien*." To him, the *Canadiens* "will not want to separate from [their] Catholic brothers."

Under the pseudonym "Countryman," Dessaulles, the rising figure of radical liberalism, responded to this "desire for theocratic domination" by arguing that "temporal power has far more to fear than spiritual power" from the liberal ideas of sovereignty of the people and sovereignty of peoples. An unrepentant supporter of Lamennais, he asked those who denounced *L'Avenir*: "Do you believe you are strengthening Catholicism by showing that it is incompatible with liberalism?"[32]

AND WHY NOT ANNEXATION TO THE UNITED STATES?

Two circumstances would enable the liberals to answer their own question of what was to be done now that the strategy of demanding the repeal of the union and parliamentary reform had failed. First, the abolition in 1846 of the protectionist English laws on colonial grain placed Lower Canada in a competitive position with any other grain-exporting country. Then, in mid-March 1849, the Rebellion Losses Act provided for compensation for material losses during the Patriotes' uprising and the military intervention in 1837 and 1838. The threefold frustration of the failure to obtain the repeal of the union, the end of protectionism and the Rebellion Losses Act created a paradoxical common front made up, on the one hand, of anglophone Tory merchants disappointed by the repeal of the Corn Laws and London, by the law on compensation and the colonial authorities, by the re-establishment of French as a parliamentary language, and by the increasing role played by French Canadians in the government apparatus, and, on the other hand, francophone liberals conscious of the failure to repeal the union.

Expectations with regard to the United States were not new. Since 1830, Papineau had been citing – against England – the great republican experiment of the United States and stressing the value of the elected Senate. But the hopes placed in diplomatic and military assistance from the United States in December 1837 had been dashed despite the warm hospitality the Northeastern states had shown to some of the exiles. Now the republic that had disappointed French Canadian liberals again fascinated them. In 1848, Aubin wrote in *Le Fantasque*: "Each to his own taste: but for my part, I will never be an anglophile; because I prefer Brother Jonathan with his sharp eye, his free and easy manner and his egalitarian principles to that stupid John Bull with his fat stomach, sullen and aggressive expression and haughty, aristocratic air."[33] The liberal and annexationist press – *L'Avenir*, Napoléon Aubin's *Le Canadien indépendant*, and *Le Moniteur canadien* – proposed Louisiana as a model, inverting the observation Étienne Parent had once made. *L'Avenir* observed that there was, "however, a government beyond the 45th [parallel], which, without obliging its subjects to glorify it by calling it just, does not fear to grant them that which is just and reasonable," and continued: "Our brothers in Louisiana, French like us, have learned this. That government would grant us what we are asking and would require only that we submit to the general laws that govern the United States as a sovereign nation." It was clear to the people at *L'Avenir* that democracy and Catholicism were reconcilable: "Louisiana is there to tell us that it has not been put in the crucible of denationalization like Ireland in the claws of its dear ally the United Kingdom, because it remains French and Catholic because it is democratic." They had no doubt that the freedom of religion of the United States would ensure Catholicism's survival.[34]

The radical democrat Charles Laberge, under the pseudonym "34 stars," published a series of articles in *L'Avenir* between 2 June and 30 October 1849 that concluded with this pronouncement: "We have reached the point where *Canada* must become a republic, when our star must take its place in the American sky" (our italics). And in the hope of convincing his readers, he repeated Parent's old comment, changing it slightly: "After escaping from the claws of the British lion, which hold us down, our destiny is to be lifted in the talons of the American eagle." Meanwhile, from late August to late October 1849, *Le Moniteur canadien* published a delightful dialogue between Jean-Baptiste, son, an annexationist, and Jean-Baptiste, father, an anti-annexationist, which was aimed at the ordinary people to whom the newspapers were read out loud.

There was, however, a middle position between admiration for the United States model and annexationism, and this position was formulated by Denis-Benjamin Viger in the October and November 1849 issues of *Le Moniteur canadien*. Viger admired the American experiment, but he gave three reasons for not supporting annexation: England would not want to abandon its colony, despite the annexationists' claims; the United States was not interested in Canada at the time, especially not the South, which perceived the neighbour to the north as being against slavery; and the example of Louisiana, where the United States had imposed English, a different legal system and religious equality, could not safeguard French Canadian nationality. Viger, like Parent, believed the future lay in the British connection, and he thought England might one day grant Canada "greater independence under its protection, which would be consistent with good policy as it would be based on their reciprocal advantage."[35]

Not many French Canadians signed the two annexationist manifestos in October and December 1849, and those who did were generally members of the Institut canadien de Montréal or people around *L'Avenir*. Papineau, however, did publish a letter describing the advantages of annexation to the great republican neighbour.[36]

When Dessaulles began his six lectures on annexation at the Institut canadien de Montréal in April 1850, the subject was still topical, but it no longer really was by the time he gave his sixth lecture in May 1851. He dealt as much with the repeal of the union as with annexation, as if to say that the first was a precondition for the second. Annexation, he maintained, would solve many problems: there would be no more non-elected Legislative Council; they would be joining a successful republic without any reign of terror; they would enjoy the benefits of secular public education and freedom of conscience and religion; the value of land would increase, as in Texas, which had just become part of the United States (as a relatively impoverished seigneur, this mattered to him); and Congress would control public expenditures. Dessaulles also could not avoid the comparison with Louisiana; he dealt with it by observing that the inhabitants of Louisiana "are now a large minority," whereas the francophones of Lower Canada, once annexed, would constitute an "immense majority" in a state of their own.[37] Even turned upside down, the example of Louisiana was still a stumbling block for the liberal argument.

La Fontaine rapidly perceived the obvious contradiction between annexation and nationality, especially for the liberals who had been extolling nationality for two years. The pro-government press criticized them for their readiness "to sacrifice nationality on the altar of annexation." The whole idea of annexation was indeed shot through with contradictions: anglophone Tories together with francophone liberals (once again in the minority), democratic and republican leanings that could put the nationalist dimension at risk, and a paradoxical, if not uncertain, use of the example of Louisiana. It was the "logic of despair" after the failure of the strategy to repeal the union that led the liberals to prefer annexation to the United States to annexation to English Canada, that led them to ambivalence between the right to self-determination in relation to England and the right to self-determination as the 34th state of the American Union. Becoming the 34th star on the "Star-Spangled Banner" would mean becoming another state in the American federation, not a sovereign state in the concert of nations.

In 1849, French Canadian opinion did not rush to support annexation, while even the gold rush to California had a modest impact in comparison to the rush to cotton mills or brick factories in New England.

RADICALIZATION OF THE LIBERALS

The failure of both the strategy to repeal the union and annexation, and the further blow of Papineau's marginalization early in 1849, seriously damaged the liberals' hopes. The duo of liberalism and anticlericalism now succeeded that of liberalism and nationalism because the liberals were now able to express their anticlericalism after their frustration with regard to "concerted action" and corruption, and, above all, because they had lost their illusions regarding their political and electoral hopes.

The Institut canadien de Montréal, founded in December 1844, did not initially display any radical leanings. It was active, with over four hundred members in 1852, including Louis-Joseph Papineau; from 1844 to 1852, between thirty-nine and fifty meetings were held there a year, and between two and thirteen public lectures. The number of volumes in its library rose from four hundred to two thousand, while between 1,300 and 3,169 books were borrowed each year; in the periodicals room, the number of newspapers available varied between fifteen and sixty. Tensions emerged after the November 1847 election and in April 1848, when there was opposition to a vote of congratulations to Antoine-Norbert Morin on his election as speaker of the Legislative Assembly of United Canada. Tensions flared again in May 1848 when the "*L'Avenir* party" was elected to the board of directors of the Institut over the "*La Minerve* party." Rodolphe Laflamme was elected president over Antoine Gérin-Lajoie, while Jean-Baptiste-Éric Dorion, Louis Labrèche-Viger, Joseph Doutre, and Joseph Papin, who were to play a major role as radicals, were elected to the other positions. With fourteen representatives in the Assembly among its members in 1854, the Institut was already politicized internally. The way it celebrated the Saint-Jean-Baptiste holiday in June 1850 showed its democratic, republican, and nationalist militancy: it drank toasts to popular sovereignty, the republic of the United States, the European democrats, the Italian leader Mazzini, and the Hungarian Kossuth.[38]

But it was *L'Avenir* above all that became radicalized, as shown by its position on the revolution of February 1848 in France, and by the position of Dessaulles and some of the other editors in favour of the Italian liberals and against the temporal power of the pope. In the statement of its program published on 2 August 1848, the paper distanced itself not only from the positions of the Church and the supporters of La Fontaine, but even from those of Papineau himself, advocating annexation and the abolition of the Protestant clergy reserves, the tithe, and seigneurial tenure. In fact, the proposals to abolish the tithe and seigneurial tenure brought back the old radical demons of 1838. Papineau's deism never allowed him to lose sight of the political disadvantages of extreme anticlericalism; in this respect he differed from his nephew Dessaulles, whose anticlericalism was more confrontational. From the summer of 1849 to January 1850, *L'Avenir* waged an unrelenting campaign for the revision or abolition of the tithe. Dessaulles, Pierre Blanchet, known as "the Citizen," and Joseph-Guillaume Barthe undertook to debunk the myths about the generosity and disinterestedness of the clergy with regard to education, poverty, and sickness, recalling the revenue the clergy received from tithes, from its seigneuries, and from untaxed properties and the symbolic advantages it derived from its generosity. On the seigneurial question, uncle and nephew were agreed on the principle of abolition, but only with fair compensation. *L'Avenir* did not support the positions of these two leading liberals on the seigneurial question; it was in favour of abolition, and even organized an anti-seigneurial "convention." It was in 1850 that Papineau had to confront the issue of the seigneurial system; he made his position on it public, but was absent from the Legislative Assembly in 1853 when measures for abolishing the system were discussed, and absent when it was abolished in 1854, the year he retired from public life.[39]

Mgr Bourget, who in January 1849 had already criticized "this French newspaper [that] seeks to spread revolutionary principles" and had forbidden parish priests to absolve readers of *L'Avenir* in the confessional, said of the paper: "What a stinking bilge load of European corruption."[40] The positions of *L'Avenir* on sovereignty, universal suffrage, and the Italian republic, like the proposals in the Club démocratique's manifesto for a nationality established through "democratic renewal," led conservatives and clergy to present the liberals of 1848 as being the same as those of 1789 or, better still, 1793. Accusing them of "democratism" was not strong enough, "because yesterday's democrats are today's socialists." The attack on democracy, described as "the law of the fist, of the authority of numbers" – that is, of the people – was based on the identification of liberalism with socialism, English Chartism, and communism. Abbé Louis Proulx's pamphlet defending religion against the "socialist press" repeated the condemnation of the eighteenth-century philosophy that had given rise to the concept of democracy shared by the "thirteen apostles of Montreal," the thirteen editors of *L'Avenir*.[41]

PUTTING UP WITH THE SITUATION

Among the liberals, pessimistic assessments of the situation were widespread after 1850. *Le Moniteur canadien* of 24 May 1850 observed that the "clerical party [has become] a veritable political Inquisition of absolute rigorism," which seemed "to play a much more active role in temporal affairs than in those above." The 9 August issue of *L'Avenir*, assessing the progress or stagnation since 1837, observed "the humiliating sombre spectacle of seeing among political men today, with few exceptions, as many turncoats, as many servile men dedicated to maintaining a connection [with Britain] ... as we used to see independent thinkers and true patriots." Joseph Doutre, who had reached a point where he could no longer hide his exasperation in his religion column in *L'Avenir*, referred on 29 January 1851 to a people who had learned only "to eat and pray to God." Jean-Baptiste-Éric Dorion, known as the "enfant terrible," admitted in the 6 October 1852 issue of *L'Avenir*: "Only education can solve the problem and force the men of God to concentrate exclusively on religion or else to crawl out of their holes and participate openly in politics when they want to influence it and shape consciences and material interests. Until education has opened the eyes of the people in this regard, we must put up with the situation."

The Institut canadien was about to adopt an orientation that would mark the rest of its history. Not only had it succeeded in resisting the pressure by Abbé Chiniquy in 1850 to prevent access, in the Institut's periodicals room, to newspapers critical of the pope's temporal power, and his further efforts, in May 1851, to exclude *L'Avenir* from the same premises, but in October 1851, the Institut modified its constitution to admit anglophone Protestants as well as francophone Catholics as members. Its liberalism was open to pluralism and to those who were willing to make an effort to participate in the Institut's activities in the language of its founders.[42]

In this period, there were three signs of the democratic progress of the liberals. First, there was the interminable political program of J.-B.-É. Dorion in late 1851, at a time when the liberals no longer really had a leader. Then there were the eloquent results of the 1851 election: in the Montreal region, the Rouges (as they were beginning to be called ironically, after the red shirts worn by the liberal Italian supporters of Garibaldi) obtained 33 per cent of the vote, with a breakthrough of

56 per cent in Montreal East (where Papineau experienced his first defeat before getting elected in Deux-Montagnes), 39 per cent in the
"Patriote regions" of Chambly, Huntingdon, Rouville, Vaudreuil, Deux-
Montagnes, and Terrebonne, and 36 per cent in Joliette and Berthier,
although only 9 per cent in Richelieu, Verchères, and Saint-Hyacinthe;
in the enormous Quebec City region, the Rouge vote had been very low
in Kamouraska, where a letter from the bishop of Quebec City had
warned people not to vote Rouge. Finally, the disappearance of *L'Avenir*
in January 1852 provided a first measure of the relative success of the
liberal battles since union.[43]

CONCLUSION

Then as now, questions arise concerning the attitude of French Canadians
to the union. How can we explain the fact that they were consistently opposed to it in 1840 and that the majority were in favour in 1849, when in
the meantime, their patriotic sentiment and sense of nationality had
been reawakened by *L'Avenir*, the Institut canadien de Montréal, and
Papineau's speeches? The positions of Parent, Papineau, and La Fontaine
highlight the different reactions to the new constitutional system that
were possible at the time: Parent opposed rebellion in 1837 and opposed union but finally accepted it; Papineau waged a non-radical political battle in 1837, opposed the union (from Paris) in 1839 and called in
vain for its repeal in 1847; La Fontaine was already seeking compromise
in December 1837, opposed the union but decided to derive as much
benefit as possible from it for the French Canadians. The positions of
Papineau and La Fontaine define the real issue: what type of nationality
would prevail?

The liberals had led successful parliamentary campaigns from 1806 to
1837; they experienced their first defeat in 1837–38, and after that, one
defeat followed another. There was the failure – for all – of the opposition to union in 1839. Papineau made it clear after 1847 that by granting equal rather than proportional representation, London had put an
undemocratic end to the tradition of a French Canadian parliamentary
majority and that parliamentary reform would be needed to redress this
injustice – but could an empire have the same definition of justice as its
colonies? This reform, moreover, was the first step in another strategy,
that of repealing the union. It is here that we see that the Colonial Office
was right and Lord Durham wrong: if representation by population had
been implemented instead of equal representation, it is not inconceivable that before immigration had worked its favourable effects in Upper
Canada, Papineau might, without having to demand electoral reform,

have managed to have the union repealed with a possible parliamentary majority. A new series of failures ensued: the failure of parliamentary reform and of the repeal of the union, and Papineau's defeat in the Assembly in 1849. These were followed by the failure of the strategy of annexation to the United States, which was itself based on the failure of the repeal of the union.

These successive failures culminated in an overall failure, that of the appeal to the principle of nationality. While in Europe the appeal to the right of peoples to self-determination had reached its high point, in Lower Canada the appeal to the principle of nationality was minimal. *L'Avenir* indeed aimed to have nationality considered "as a political or social tie"; Papineau, in his famous speech of 22 January 1849, indeed proposed that the Legislative Assembly of United Canada support the struggle against despotism in Europe. But *L'Avenir* itself spoke in terms of the "preservation" of "our institutions, our language, our laws and our customs," and of "the close connection between our nationality and our tie with our mother land."

In fact, the liberals had not succeeded in combining nationality and liberalism in their own way. Although they had started, at the Institut canadien de Montréal, to formulate a model for reconciling the rights of a majority and those of a minority coexisting together, they were subsequently deprived of the place and the structure that would have allowed their endeavour to come to fruition in a larger public setting: a parliamentary assembly in which they had a majority. Papineau had been right: without parliamentary reform and representation by population, the repeal of the union and the strategy of appealing to the principle of nationality were impossible. Without a parliamentary foundation, nationalist demands could not be effective. The remaining option was radicalization, which is what happened to liberalism after 1852, at the Institut canadien de Montréal and in the newspaper *Le Pays*.

From 1840 to 1852, the liberals confronted a new form of alliance between the Church and conservatism, an alliance of religious and political power. In 1839, as a reward for the loyalty it had shown since 1763 and during the Rebellions of 1837 and 1838, the Catholic Church obtained legal recognition. Its positions on popular sovereignty, the liberal strategy to repeal the union, the dangers of annexation for religion, and the pope's temporal power served the vision and aims of La Fontaine's party, which, in exchange, allowed the ultramontanists to set up a confessional public education system under the responsibility and control of the Church. Henceforth, the values transmitted by the schools were those of religion and conservatism. From that time on, union no longer seemed threatening to the Roman Catholic Church. This new alliance also inspired a campaign against *L'Avenir* by *Les Mélanges religieux, La Revue canadienne,* and *Le Journal de Québec.* Ultramontanism became well-established in the 1840s: not only did the attacks on Rome by the liberals of Italy and Lower Canada become a major concern of Mgr Bourget, who was Romanizing the Church's practices at the time, not only was an alliance formed that offered reciprocal advantages to conservative religious and political power, but the Church succeeded in imposing the idea that in mixed matters such as education, it had priority over the civil power, over the state.

This alliance of principle and fact is the reason a certain type of nationality prevailed: the "preservation" or protection of nationality, later known as protective nationalism, which is a conservative nationalism in terms of values. This is the nationalism that Parent began to formulate around 1837, and its primary characteristic is that it is apolitical and is limited to cultural demands. It is apolitical because it refuses to combine nationalist demands with a description of the cultural characteristics of nationality or to appeal to the principle of nationality in order to give to a national community identified by its language, customs, religion, and legal system a territorial entity and sovereign state. La Fontaine could not accept the appeal to the principle of nationality because it challenged the tie with England. The Catholic Church had the same reasons for opposing it, and was motivated, as well, by indignation that this principle had been used to justify the Italian liberals' attacks on the pope, his states, and his temporal power.

Political conservatism would promote the "preservation" of the nation, language, laws, customs, and religion. Religious conservatism would promote the "preservation" of the same nationality, with the slight yet important difference that, in keeping with its spiritual and temporal interests, it would defend religion first, and then the language, laws, and customs. Thus, in the first case, one would speak of a Canadian who was French-speaking, Catholic, and rural, and lived under civil law; in the second case, one would speak of a Catholic who was French-speaking and rural and lived under civil law. This nuance was to have an impact on legislation regarding an education system that was religious or linguistic.

The union also modified the relative weight of its cultural "mother countries" – England, France, the United States, and Rome – as influences on the identity of the people of Lower Canada. The Russell Resolutions of 1837 and the establishment of the union had put an end to French Canadians' expectations of England. La Fontaine would rebuild these expectations by seeking amnesty for the Patriotes and compensation for citizens who had experienced material losses, and by obtaining responsible government, which was to lead to the famous double ministries in which a French Canadian leader could win power. Granted by London in 1848, responsible government gave the colony a certain autonomy, but not enough to satisfy Papineau or the liberals.

While the France of 1848 inspired the liberals of *L'Avenir*, they were a minority of French Canadians; the majority, according to *La Revue canadienne*, preferred responsible government to the still provisional government that had been set up in France. English-style reformism prevailed over the temptations of French-style revolution. Nationalism would be cultural and not political.

The United States still fascinated French Canadian liberals, even after the disappointments of 1837 and, above all, 1838. In despair after the failure to repeal the union, they embarked on the highly paradoxical strategy of annexation of Canada to the United States. But it is the "Louisiana syndrome" that is most revealing. Different groups rewrote the history of Louisiana to fit their interpretation. The liberals, who had the same information on Louisiana as the reformers, did not draw the same conclusions from its past and present. And paradoxically, the liberals had a concept of the states' "sovereignty" in the American federal system that seemed to satisfy their idea of a nationality "flying the American flag."

The period following union was one of religious, ideological, and political alignment of French Canadian Catholics with Rome, the capital of Catholicism. Rome came to experience the French Canadians' loyalty to the pope. But, significantly, it was less the Revolution of 1848 in France that served as the pretext for the Church to move forcefully against the local liberals than the questions of Rome and the pope's temporal power. Clerical denunciations of liberalism, such as those of Mgr Bourget, the Sulpician Pinsoneault and the popular preacher Chiniquy, turned on the question of the liberals' and the Red shirts' challenge to papal power. This reflected the importance of the religious factor in the liberals' successive failures.

Breaches in Radical Liberalism
(1852–1867)

PAPINEAU MET HIS PARLIAMENTARY Waterloo in 1849 and did not participate in the long debates on the abolition of the seigneurial system in 1853; he retired from politics in 1854, investing his time and money in his seigneury at Montebello. In 1854, under Antoine-Aimé Dorion, its first leader, the Liberal Party adopted a comprehensive political program that included popular education, an elected Legislative Council, which would be in effect from 1856 to 1867, abolition of the Protestant clergy reserves and those of the seigneurial system, which would affect Papineau and his nephew Dessaulles, and the choice of Montreal as the seat of the government of United Canada.

PROGRAM AND POLITICAL STRENGTH
OF THE LIBERAL PARTY (1852–1858)

In the election of 1854, the Liberals held on to their support. They obtained 34 per cent of the vote in the Montreal region, compared with 33 per cent in 1851, while in Montreal itself, they increased their share of the vote from 56 per cent to 62 per cent. The Patriotes' old area remained Liberal: the counties of Iberville, Châteauguay, Beauharnois, Saint-Jean, Napierville, Chambly, Vaudreuil, Deux-Montagnes, Joliette, and L'Assomption elected Liberals, while Liberals were defeated in Richelieu, Verchères, and Rouville. In Bagot, Louis-Antoine Dessaulles lost by twenty-five votes. The political strength of the Liberals remained considerable, since the Montreal region, where they obtained one third of the vote, with two thirds in Montreal itself, included 50 per cent of the total population of Lower Canada and 50 per cent of the francophone population.

In the following election, in 1857–58, however, the Liberals lost ground: they obtained 29 per cent of the vote in the Montreal region, and 41 per cent in Montreal itself, so that only 20 per cent of the members elected to the Legislative Assembly of United Canada were francophones from Lower Canada. Part of the challenge lay in electoral work, but the main problem was the split that was opening up between the party and doctrinal liberalism, whose proponents had to defend it tooth and nail.[1]

ELECTORAL LIBERALISM VERSUS DOCTRINAL LIBERALISM

Dorion gave the Liberal Party a new organ in 1852: the aptly named *Le Pays* (The country), which succeeded *L'Avenir* and was more moderate. With nearly 130 agents in as many towns, the new paper had a circulation of about 1,500 copies in its first year. Dessaulles, who was co-editor for four months with Labrèche-Viger, laid his cards on the table in the first issue on 15 January 1852. The "country" envisaged would be above all a democratic country: "Democracy knows no differences of origin." In this respect, the newspaper resembled the Institut canadien de Montréal, which, in its new constitution of 1850, had adopted the same principle for membership. Nationality was part of the spirit of democracy: "Democracy is the condition of man free to be himself in his dignity; it is the condition of the man who governs himself, subject to no law other than that of virtue and respect for others and himself; it is the conquest of equality in conditions and customs, and of popular sovereignty in government; it is the aim of human aspirations, the realization of the dreams of freedom that, although suppressed for centuries, live in the hearts of all men."

On 3 February, Joseph Cauchon's *Journal de Québec* made some distinctions: "It is true that we want to be with the country, but with the real country, not *Le Pays*, M. Dessaulles' paper, which will never be anything but the country of the Papineau family." Dessaulles, who could not leave Saint-Hyacinthe, where he lived, resigned from the management of the newspaper; it is also probable that he had not conveyed the moderate line Dorion's new team wanted.

From 1852 to 1858, the membership of the Institut canadien de Montréal rose from 336 to 741. In seven years, it hosted 250 meetings, presented 49 public lectures and 19 essays, and held 87 debates. The public lectures concerned popular education, the Patriotes (Édouard-Raymond Fabre, de Lorimier), Poland, Kossuth and Hungary, and national feeling. The Institut's foremost speaker, L.-A. Dessaulles, gave lectures on Lamartine, on progress and on Galileo, in the latter lecture drawing a parallel between the Peripatetic philosophers who had ostracized Galileo and the ultramontanists who denounced the liberals. In 1858, the Institut's library contained 4,270 volumes and a periodicals room with 117 different publications; subscribers could borrow over 3,100 books.[2]

The radicalization of the Institut in 1848 had left some bitterness and anxiety. Clouds began to gather over the association in June 1854 when a disciplinary rule of the Concile des évêques de Quebec stipulated: "When there are constantly in a literary institute books against the faith or customs; when lectures against religion are given there; when immoral or irreligious newspapers are read there, those who belong to it must not be given the sacraments, unless there is reason to hope that, given the strength of good principles, they [these principles] will be able to continue to reform them."[3]

A year later, the opposition no longer came from outside the Institut but from within it: on 28 February 1855, a proposal was made by Labrèche-Viger, the former co-editor of *Le Pays*, seconded by Hector Fabre, that the Institut subscribe to the Parisian ultramontanist newspaper *L'Univers*, edited by Louis Veuillot. It was narrowly defeated thanks to the deciding vote of the president of the Institut, who argued that the paper in question engaged in religious polemics, a veritable "plague" in Canada. This proposal was followed by a proposal that the Institut discontinue its subscriptions to *Witness*, *True Witness*, and *Le Semeur canadien*, a Canadian French-language Protestant paper. Joseph Doutre counterattacked, suggesting that there could be no censorship at the Institut because it accepted members of any origin and religious or political persuasion. Doutre's counter-proposal was defeated by 108 votes to 75. Wilfrid Dorion came to his assistance, suggesting that the proposal to discontinue the subscriptions be put off for twelve months, during which the Institut would continue to receive newspapers that were sent to it without cost, on condition that they contained no obscene or immoral material. Once again, the proposal passed (by 129 to 128) thanks to the tie-breaking vote of the president.[4] The war of procedure and internal opposition had begun, and the Institut was clearly the target: "By means of intrigue, by bringing in all their associates, [the radicals] succeeded in obtaining almost exclusive control, making the forum of this national institution ... a platform for discord, rebellion and irreligion. It is there that people like Doutre, Blanchet and Cyr go to spew their antisocial, antireligious and revolutionary doctrines at young *Canadiens* ... It is at the Institut that all the most extreme Rouge issues are discussed."[5] Rougism was strongly criticized and some former members of the *Avenir* team, hoping to relaunch the paper, which had ceased publication in 1852, were put off: "We will have the conviction that *L'Avenir* is unwelcome in this country, and that we would be preaching in the desert if we continued trying to expose abuse and defend freedom, justice and social well-being to a people whose majority sells itself in elections like a herd of slaves, and far from wanting to leave its slavery, wants more chains ... In our work, we have only the people's interest at heart, but the people, influenced and led by its enemies and a part of the clergy that has proscribed and denounced us in the name of religion, has not wanted to understand us."[6]

Four years after his first warning to literary institutes, it became clear to Mgr Bourget that there was no longer any hope of reforming the Institut; the external opposition to the Institut and its internal opposition thus joined forces. On 10 March 1858, the bishop of Montreal published a pastoral letter warning literary institutes against "books that are contrary to the faith and customs" and suggesting ways to "purge" libraries of "all the impious or obscene books." He advised the faithful: "Do not subscribe to any newspaper that is capable, by its antireligious doctrines, its passionate novels and its immoral serials, of harming the mind and the heart of your children."

On 13 April, the corresponding secretary of the Institut, Éraste d'Orsonnens, made a double proposal: that the Institut give up the principle of autonomous control of its library and that it form a committee, of which Hector Fabre would be a member, whose mandate would be to establish a list of books to remove from its library. The proposal was defeated by 110 votes to 88. Two days later, d'Orsonnens was relieved of his duties because of an article he had published in *La Minerve* on 6 April. On 22 April, 138 members out of 741, nearly 20 per cent, resigned from the Institut canadien de Montréal, including H. Fabre and L. Labrèche-Viger, who would cross the path of radical liberalism again later on. The resigning members went on to found the Institut canadien-français, which barely managed to survive for a few years.

On 30 April 1858, Mgr Bourget presented his views more explicitly in a document "on the Institut canadien and against bad books." He decried the Institut's claim to be "the only one competent to assess the morality of its library," which contained "far too many" books that were on the Index, as the printed catalogue of 1852 showed; he declared that only the Church was capable of leading "its flock into the green pastures of truth" and that it was "unquestionably invested with the right to govern the administration of all libraries in the world."

On 31 May 1858, a third document was published, this one concerning *Le Pays*, an "irreligious" newspaper that "combated the existence of God and his divine religion," a "heretical" newspaper that "attacked the Holy Catholic Church," an "impious" newspaper that pretended to respect religion, the better to destroy it, a "liberal" newspaper that "claimed to be free in its religious and political opinions [and] advocated the separation of church and state," an "immoral" newspaper that "offended modesty and good morals by its impure serial stories, love stories, suggestive songs, lewd poetry, shameless novels and plays." The bishop established a simple equation: disrespect for the clergy and the priest equals disrespect for Jesus Christ. Since the authority vested in him was that of Jesus Christ himself, any attempt to reduce the influence of the clergy constituted "an attack on that ultimate authority."

This condemnation of liberalism in both the library of the Institut canadien and *Le Pays* was once again based on the 1832 encyclical *Mirari vos*, which had condemned Lamennais's *L'Avenir*; it was also influenced by the new instructions from Rome on the "errors of our time," published in March 1858, which were the first formulation of the *Syllabus* of 1864, a sort of handbook of doctrinal errors of the eighteeenth and nineteenth centuries.[7] Henceforth, members of the Institut canadien would be refused the sacraments of the Catholic Church, including Extreme Unction and possibly the right to be buried in a Catholic cemetery.

DEMOCRACY AND NATIONALITY

The fact that liberalism was placed above nationality at the Institut canadien, as in the declaration by *Le Pays* on a democratic and liberal country with no distinction as to origins, worried conservatives and ultramontanists. This pro-democratic stance that tried to link nationality and democracy while giving priority to liberal values was a direct attack on conservative nationalism in two ways: first, in its emphasis on democracy, and second, in the effects it expected democracy to have on nationality. In 1857, the Sulpician Lenoir criticized "the rampant democracy that seeks to overthrow throne and altar" and recalled the history of Poland as proof of the evils sown by discord. In the ultramontanist *Courrier du Canada*, Cyrille Boucher, who was to become a personal enemy of Dessaulles and Rougism, began a series of articles entitled "On democracy," in which he attributed the origin of democracy to philosophism and Protestantism, two "evils" embodied in the Institut canadien, which promoted reason, individual reflection, and the admission of Protestants as well as Catholics as members. This democracy, which, according to Boucher, toppled thrones, erected gallows, and assassinated kings, was "the sickness of nations: when they return to health, they establish themselves in the shadow of thrones and live under the paternal government of kings." As for the sovereignty of the people, it was associated with equality, atheism, materialism, and revolutions. Boucher concluded by underlining the doctrinal orientation of liberalism, "the utterly philosophical direction that some newspapers have taken."[8]

The evolution of the patron saint's day of French Canadians, Saint-Jean-Baptiste Day, 24 June, and of the speeches on that day reflects these tensions. With the union, Saint-Jean-Baptiste Day had become a religious festival, whereas from 1834 on it had principally been a patriotic festival. Beginning in 1846, the celebratory speeches, in which the clergy participated, defined nationality above all in terms of religion and stressed universal "fraternity" while avoiding liberty and equality. Significantly, the Institut canadien was excluded from the Saint-Jean-Baptiste Day procession in 1858 for having launched a plan for a monument to the Patriotes of 1837 and 1838. The pro-government paper *La Minerve*, in announcing the event, also revealed its point of view: "It is to Catholicism alone that the *Canadien* people owes its nationality ... However, once a nation has contracted a debt so large to a religion; once a country owes its perpetuation in everyday life to its faith, its altars, it is hardly surprising that this people, this nation, this country should be religious in all its solemn proceedings ... Our people and our society are such that for us, in the most natural way in the world, Catholicism and Nationality are synonyms." In an earlier response to *Le Pays*, *La Minerve* did not beat around the bush regarding its agreement with ultramontanism: "Religion and politics come from God; they are sisters, they are great and sublime when united; but what anarchy ensues when ambition and jealousy separate them!"[9] The critique of democracy and popular sovereignty and the simultaneous glorification of monarchy show how conservative nationalism was constructed on the counter-revolutionary, anti-republican, and anti-democratic ideas whose genealogy went back, here and elsewhere, to 1789, perpetuated by 1793, 1830, and 1848.

THE ESTABLISHMENT OF A MODERATE DOCTRINAL LIBERALISM

Although the Liberals obtained more than half the vote in Montreal in 1854, and a third of the vote in the Montreal region, they lost ground there in the 1857–58 election. But above all, it is important to note that the political sentiment of the majority favoured La Fontaine and Cartier's reformers and that "the country of the Papineau family," in the words of the *Journal de Québec*, had yet to be built.

This electoral majority was beginning to rely on a moderate doctrinal liberalism that would reach its culmination in Laurier's speech of 1877, but that began in 1858 with the resignation of 138 members of the

Institut canadien de Montréal, including Hector Fabre, the instigator of
the split and the one who had proposed the abortive plan to establish a
censorship committee for the library of the Institut. The doctrinal dimension of this confrontation had been identified by C. Boucher in
1857 when he wrote, in *Le Courrier du Canada*, of "the utterly philosophical direction that some newspapers have taken." By situating the debate
at this level, the ultramontanists and conservatives who reaped the electoral benefits of this antagonism deepened the gap between radical doctrinal liberalism and electoral liberalism and made the Rouges a distinct
target for attacks and a major press war. One could now speak of philosophism, reason and rationalism and stigmatize liberalism as Rougism.
Other signs of the emergence of a moderate liberalism include the
launching, in November 1858, of the newspaper *L'Ordre*, which was to
spearhead this moderate liberalism as of June 1861, and the social marginalization of the Institut canadien de Montréal, which was excluded
from the symbolic 24 June parade in 1858.

A POLITICAL KNOT TO UNTIE:
THE CRISIS OF 1858

The union had created tensions not only among French Canadians but
also, and especially, among their fellow citizens in Upper Canada. The
political crisis that broke out in 1858 was like a Gordian knot, with its
main strands being the union, in the past, and a plan for confederation,
in the future (1864).

The crisis concerned four problems: possible constitutional changes
related to the question of parliamentary representation and that of the
double majority, the ephemeral nature of governments, and the choice
of a capital for United Canada, which could be Ottawa or Montreal.
Governments had been so fragile since the union that they fell one after
another; one of them had had the lifetime of a rose, surviving only forty-
eight hours. This instability was linked by contemporaries to the question of the double majority: was a Cabinet supported by one majority in
the House or by two, that is, by the majority of all the representatives
together or a majority of each group of representatives, from Lower and
Upper Canada? Was Macdonald supported only by Upper Canada, and
was Cartier supported only by Lower Canada, or should Macdonald-
Cartier have the majority of the votes of Upper Canada and the majority
of those of Lower Canada? The problem became acute in 1856, when
the Taché-Macdonald government was maintained in power exclusively
by its majority in Lower Canada. But the essential challenge of the political crisis concerned parliamentary representation: in a situation

where the population of Upper Canada was growing more rapidly than that of Lower Canada – 952,000 versus 891,000 in the 1851 census – it was tempting, even imperative, for the inhabitants of Upper Canada to object to equal representation between Lower and Upper Canada, which had previously served their interests, and to demand representation by population. The knot of this recurring question would be untied with Confederation. It is important to note, however, that 1858, like 1848, was a decisive year and that it too was a complex knot of politics and culture.

THE ITALIAN QUESTION (1859–1861)

The new twists and turns in the formation of the kingdom of Italy brought the Italian question to the centre of liberal debate, where it had been in 1848 during the anticlerical radicalization of liberalism. In return for the cession of Nice and Savoy to France, Napoleon III supported Piedmont, which defeated Austria at Magenta on 4 June 1859 and at Solferino on 24 June, resulting in Lombardy being attached to Piedmont, while Venetia remained under Austrian rule. In 1860, events accelerated: the Italian parliament met for the first time in April, following the liberation of Tuscany, Parma, Modena, and Romagna; in September, the Kingdom of the Two Sicilies and Naples was liberated by Garibaldi and his Thousand, and the Papal Zouaves, a small army raised by the pope to defend his states, were defeated at Castelfidardo. The unification of Italy became an international event, as it was the first concrete realization of the principle of nationality that had been invoked since 1830, and especially since 1848. And once again, the question of the political or temporal power of the pope sparked a crisis.

During the whole of 1860, Mgr Bourget, who played an increasingly dominant role in the Quebec episcopate, published document after document on the inviolability and integrity of the Papal States and the excommunication of the invaders of these states. According to the bishop of Montreal, in the Papal States, "the administration of justice is better," financial legislation and administration were exemplary, practices that had been criticized had been corrected. He maintained that the Church was "a perfectly organized society that, by virtue of its divine constitution, enjoys all the freedom necessary to it for the exercise of its sacred role; its independence from any other power is recognized in the person of its leader as a work of divine Providence, which succeeded in forming from the debris of the Roman Empire a temporal State for its Church, so that it would be on earth the kingdom of him whom the Scriptures call the King of Kings." For the bishop, the Italian question was also a Canadian question: "Make no mistake, the revolutionary spirit is making inroads here, as elsewhere, and there are some among us who condemn the pope and approve of Garibaldi." These French Canadian Garibaldians were to be found at *Le Pays*, whose "detestable writings" showed "such contempt for papal authority" that it preoccupied the bishop "day and night."[10]

One of the "Garibaldians" in question was without doubt Louis-Antoine Dessaulles, who now lived in Montreal and was editor of *Le Pays* from March 1861 to December 1863. A follower of Lamennais who had begun keeping up with "Roman affairs" in 1839 and had published articles on the temporal power of the pope ten years later in *L'Avenir*, once again argued, in the pages of *Le Pays*, for the integration of the Papal States into the national territory of Italy, and took the opportunity to once again ask the question of the preservation or abolition of the pope's temporal power. Replying to Mgr Bourget, whose texts had been read to the faithful by parish priests, Dessaulles, armed with information from the French periodical press, criticized every aspect of the temporal administration of the Papal States: the papacy was poorly advised by the Roman Curia, reforms had not been carried out since 1849, there was overspending, administrative controls were inadequate, Cardinal Antonelli and his family held too much power, the Roman tribunals were unjust, audiences were not public, and there were political detentions. And to justify his comments, he explained that "it is not anti-Catholic or anti-Christian to criticize a system under which the evangelical principle 'Do not unto others what you would not want done to you' is constantly violated in practice."[11]

No opportunity was missed to feed the crossfire of the controversy on the affairs of Rome and Italy. After a visit by the Institut canadien de Montréal to Prince Napoleon when he passed through Montreal on 13 September 1861, the conservative press heaped scorn on Dessaulles, *Le Pays*, the Institut, and liberalism. Prince Napoleon was the cousin of Napoleon III, Emperor of the French from 1852 to 1870. In 1849, Louis-Napoleon had helped restore the pope's political power when it was threatened by the Italian liberals. From 1858 on, however, the emperor followed a prudent policy of supporting Italian unity, which went as far as taking a non-interventionist line during the invasion of the papal territories by Victor-Emmanuel, who defeated the pope's weak army at Castelfidardo on 18 September 1860. But Prince Napoleon, who had married the daughter of King Victor-Emmanuel II of Italy in 1861, displayed an increasingly militant liberalism and anticlericalism and took a clear position in favour of Italian unity, and thus in favour of ending the temporal power of the pope. Although Cavour congratulated the prince – "The destruction of temporal power will go down in history as one of humanity's most glorious and most enduring feats, and the name of Y.H. [Your Highness] will forever be associated with it" – the Catholic clergy of Quebec City and Montreal condemned the prince for his position and constantly expressed their antagonism. The Institut canadien made a point of going to greet this international figure, if only to convey its thanks to Napoleon III for a generous donation he had made to the Institut in 1855 as a result of efforts by Joseph-Guillaume Barthe. The Institut's address to the prince was unequivocal: "The Institut-Canadien, which is a supporter of great causes, is pleased to communicate with its benefactors through a prince who, in his legislative work, has so eloquently developed the liberal views of the French government on the most important issues of European politics." The prince responded by recognizing the Institut as "the most enlightened institution in the country and independent from the clergy."[12]

THE FABRE-DESSAULLES CONTROVERSY
(JANUARY–MARCH 1862)

For four reasons, the controversy that began in 1862 was a turning point in the evolution of both radical and moderate liberalism. First, because of the participants: Dessaulles, who was becoming the scapegoat of the ultramontanists, conservatives, and moderates, and Hector Fabre, who had resigned from the Institut canadien in 1858 and was a cofounder of the Institut canadien-français and a champion of moderate liberalism. Second, because of the newspapers involved in the controversy: *Le Pays*, the main target of ultramontanism, and *L'Ordre*, which had been established as an ultramontanist paper in 1858 but had been evolving toward moderate liberalism since June 1861, under the leadership of none other than Fabre, who wrote on 1 July 1861: "We are Catholic and we belong to the nation," in that order. Third, because of the issues: Was a liberalism without anticlericalism conceivable, and why should nationalism be linked with Catholicism rather than with liberalism? And finally, because of the pretext: Montalembert, a repentant former supporter of Lamennais, was a symbol of the stubborn desire to find a Catholicism that could seem liberal without being the Catholic liberalism of Lamennais.

On 7 January 1862, *L'Ordre* published a letter from Count de Montalembert, who wrote to Fabre as follows: "I was terribly wounded by the address delivered to this prince [Napoleon] by some Institut-Canadien in Montreal or Quebec. I asked myself how there could have come to be, in this population of French origin that has been described to us as attached to religion and to its memories of old France, men so misguided as to pay a public homage of respect and sympathy to a man who did not shrink from insulting the Sovereign Pontiff along with all the opinions and traditions dear to respectable people." On 20 January, Fabre explained to his correspondent: "The behaviour of the Institut-Canadien toward Prince Napoleon was condemned by the whole population here with the exception of a small number of free-thinking democrats. The Institut itself was excommunicated four years ago by the bishop of Montreal, after an effort to reform it by my friends and myself."

In the 14 January issue of *Le Pays*, Dessaulles stressed the "little thoughtlessnesses" and contradictions displayed by the former friend of Lamennais: "M. de Montalembert has always managed to have a handy pretext for not putting into practice the fine and sonorous declarations he makes when he is making speeches. He is essentially the man of pretexts of the past twenty years of European history." To the editor of *Le Pays*, the visit to Prince Napoleon was clearly a pretext for attempting to crush the Institut: "The publication of M. de Montalembert's letter was certainly an attack on us, because it was followed by the incredible faux pas of admitting to us that they expected that we would 'bow' before this great name"; Dessaulles considered that *L'Ordre* had an "aggressive attitude toward the Institut-Canadien," which it sought to present as essentially unrepresentative of the Catholic and francophone French Canadian people.

In early January 1862, *L'Ordre* described the Institut canadien as an "evil and pernicious organization," to which Dessaulles replied that it had not been a sign of intolerance in 1858, when they had refused to establish an investigating committee on the library – in which Fabre would have participated – for the simple reason that the fact had been assumed before it had even been established. And to Dessaulles, they would not succeed today any more than they had four years earlier in proving that there were irreligious books in the library of the Institut.

This just set the stage. Next came the *pièces de résistance*: four articles by Fabre in *L'Ordre* on 3, 5, 7, and 12 February 1862 and four replies by Dessaulles in *Le Pays* on 22 February and 1, 11, and 13 March, entitled "To the detractors, great and small, of the Institut-Canadien," "great" referring to Montalembert and Mgr Bourget and "small" to Fabre. For the latter, "The hour of full and decisive explanations" had arrived. Determined not to allow himself "to be dragged into debates about minor details and quarrels about words, in which the winner [would be] the most patient and the most given to procedural nitpicking," Fabre intimated that the Institut canadien's cause was hopeless because its condemnation "was formulated by him who is responsible for our conscience." He then defined the guiding principles of the Institut canadien: "absolute freedom without taking into account any limits, duties or religious, moral or national principles" and a principle of universality that "admits of no distinction and makes no religious or national exceptions regarding members, books or speeches." To Fabre, this had social consequences: "In a Catholic society, if you create a forum in which the influence of religion may be combated directly or indirectly, you are striking a blow against that society." A "collective endeavour in our country" could not be neutral: it could only be Catholic and national. Fabre went on to formulate both his own very moderate liberalism and the credo of "real" nationalism, which could only be liberal: "Here more than anywhere else, the national interest is inseparable from the religious interest, and if liberalism disassociates itself from either one, it automatically becomes the enemy of the other." In his opinion, what the members of the Institut canadien wanted was "the fusion of the races; they have shaped the Institut in the image of the society of their dreams, without any religious or national distinctions." This anti-national goal would be the ruin of nationality: "They would lead the new generations off the Christian path, where they would encounter infallible geniuses who would expose them to all the adventures of the mind and all the dangers of study, delivering them to moral uncertainty and intellectual disorder."

Le Pays denounced Fabre's new crusade. Using the minutes of the Institut's meetings, the newspaper established a historical overview of the activities and ideological positions of the editor of *L'Ordre*, slyly pointing out the contradictions in his thinking and depicting him as "the man of good principles" whose positions today were the opposite of those he had held before.

Dessaulles also observed that the members of this "evil" Institut were nonetheless accepted within families, greeted fifty times a day on the street, asked to make offerings for the poor. The pressure was clearly rising: "Your influence is doubtless very great, and it takes courage to disagree with you even regarding a merely temporal subject. Nonetheless, you would not believe how much impact your harassment has on certain people who understand that once the Institut has been destroyed, if you succeed, others will be destroyed in turn. Many of these people are beginning to say that the pressure is too strong and that a reaction is becoming inevitable."

To those who "slandered [the Institut] because they could not burn it at the stake," Dessaulles explained that the Institut had only forty-four non–French Canadian members and between twenty-five and thirty Protestant members out of a total of 480. But did this enumeration resolve the question of principle? He challenged the accusation that the Institut's teachings were sometimes nationalist and sometimes anti-nationalist or that they sometimes promoted Catholicism and sometimes Protestantism, denying that it did any official "teaching." He stressed this point, and suggested that the institution could be neutral without its members being "indifferent to all religion, morality and nationality." The library of the Institut was not that of a college; it was the shared property of free and responsible men. Dessaulles confronted the conservatives with the implications of their system: "The more educated the people is, the less manageable it is ... Your system is rife with this idea. To the ignorant, you say that a little education is a dangerous thing; to the educated man, that nine-tenths of the books that contain the elements of human intelligence are dangerous. Who has the right to censor?" He ended his cry of anguish to the detractors by recalling the chronology of the events of 1858: on 13 April, a discussion at the Institut on the contents of the library; on the 22nd, the resignation of 138 members; on the 30th, publication of the first of Mgr Bourget's three letters condemning the Institut. This sequence of events "convinced the Institut that this whole movement was caused by an external influence that had become hostile to the Institut," that is, Mgr Bourget.

With a rare premonitory sense of the stakes involved, Dessaulles wrote: "If the Institut were to succumb before you, partisans of intolerance and general mindlessness, the political and social future of the country would suffer greatly, because that would demonstrate that the spirit of persecution can still smother individual free will."[13]

SEVEN LETTERS FROM MGR BOURGET TO *LE PAYS*
(FEBRUARY 1862)

On 24 February 1862, while Dessaulles was defending the Institut canadien against its detractors, Mgr Bourget concluded his seventh and final letter to *Le Pays*, and the secretary of the bishopric, Canon Paré, asked the editors to publish the letters. Dessaulles read the documents and noted that once again, the affairs of Rome were extremely relevant to the affairs of Canada.

After the censure of *L'Avenir* in 1849, and of *Le Pays* in 1858, the bishop of Montreal had attacked again in a pastoral letter issued on 31 May 1860, to which he had appended a "First supplement concerning the newspapers that have attacked the Bull issued by His Holiness Pius IX." This document contained the first formulation of the accusations he now brought against the newspaper edited by Dessaulles.

In this correspondence of about fifty pages, written between 12 and 24 February 1862, Mgr Bourget described *Le Pays* as anti-Christian because it had no religious principles, anti-Catholic because it showed little respect for the Church, antisocial because it was in favour of the overthrow of legitimate governments, immoral because it promoted the theatre and the novel, which presented marriage in a questionable light. The second letter observed that the liberal newspaper presented the Italian "revolution" and its heroes too favourably and suggested that a "similar revolution might be desirable in Canada." The bishop then aligned declarations by the pope that might convince *Le Pays* of the reforms carried out in the Papal States and asked the owners and the editor of the newspaper, "Are you not surprised now, Sirs, that *Le Pays* got on such a high horse to try to spit in the face of the Sovereign Pontiff, the Cardinals who surround him and, indirectly, 200,000,000 Christians?" As Chiniquy had in 1849, the bishop also suggested to the readers of *Le Pays* that they cease supporting the newspaper.

Mgr Bourget next tried to refute *Le Pays*'s statements concerning the financial and legal administration of the Papal States by saying that its sole information source was documents published by Piedmont. The bishop drew attention to *Le Pays*'s harsh treatment of the pope and Cardinal Antonelli and its praise for Prince Napoleon. To the bishop, who had censured the Institut canadien in 1858, its library remained "a stinking bilge that infects our city."

Dessaulles read and reread the letters; ever the polemicist, he thought they should be published. But the owners of *Le Pays*, "Dorion et Cie," decided otherwise and wrote to Mgr Bourget on 4 March: "It is to protect the boundary between things belonging to the spiritual order and those that God left open to disputes of the world that we wish to avoid a discussion with Your Highness on matters that are not, in reality, directly related to dogma and faith but to which Your Highness brings the dignity and authority of a Pontiff of the Church. We say we do not wish to discuss this for it cannot have occurred to Your Highness that *Le Pays* would publish, without intending to defend itself, seven long letters filled with accusations against it that are as serious as they are unjustified." The editors then claimed not to recognize the distinction the bishop had made between the managers and the editors of *Le Pays*, and concluded, with remarkable serenity: "Finally, we ask Your Highness to believe that, whatever may be the consequences of the position we have seen fit to take, we will find in our conscience, in the traditions left by the most distinguished men of our history and in the approval of our fellow citizens the strength necessary to protect freedom of discussion, the rights of the press and our own dignity."

Dessaulles considered the letters "as being addressed to me" and responded, on 7 March, to Mgr Bourget, accusing him, to start with, of a
"sovereign injustice." He listed the retractions the conservative European
press had had to make regarding the question of Rome and explained to
the bishop that his main source of information was not *Le Siècle* but rather the yearbook of the *Revue des deux mondes.* Concerning the revolutionary outlook of *Le Pays,* Dessaulles reminded him: "There is a very simple
reason why *Le Pays* does not want a revolution here; it is that we have
political institutions that, although still imperfect, allow for their own
modification without revolution ... In such a country, Monsignor, there
is no need for revolutions. It is only governments that seek to suppress
public opinion that are overthrown. Those that work with [the people]
never are, which shows that the people is the true sovereign."

Dessaulles noted the bishop's "instinctive hostility" to "anything that
resembles a popular right, to the participation of the people in the government." True to form, he admitted frankly to this man who had become an enemy: "Absolutism is indeed much more convenient for those
who do not want other nations to think and read, and who have always
placed human thought on the Index." His conclusion traced the path
that ideas would follow in the coming decades.

The most general conclusion that we can reach, Monsignor, is that Y.H. [Your
Highness], without stating it explicitly, maintains and wishes to apply in practice
the idea that there is no order of thought that cannot have some point of contact
with the religious idea, and in consequence, there is no order of ideas that
should not be judged in absolute terms of the idea of the supremacy of religion;
and thus, since there is no social or political principle that cannot affect religion,
directly or indirectly, for good or for ill, there is no social or political principle
whose application and practical operation should not be subordinated to Church
censure, and thus to supervision by the Clergy. Your Highness wishes to bring
into close interaction the spiritual and temporal domains in order to lead and
dominate the latter by the former, [whereas] we lay people (even those who flatter Y.H. today to satisfy political ambitions and their own egoism), want to avoid
confusion between these two orders of ideas and want the spiritual order to be
entirely distinct from the temporal order. In short, Monsignor, in the purely social and political order, we demand our complete independence from ecclesiastical power.

Dessaulles saw this as a fundamental issue, inasmuch as it eased or
heightened antagonism between the liberals and the ultramontanist
conservatives. This was the dividing line of ideas and rights. Distinction
or confusion, separation or alliance.[14]

A NEW OFFENSIVE AGAINST THE INSTITUT
CANADIEN DE MONTRÉAL (1862–1867)

By electing Louis-Antoine Dessaulles president of the association from May 1862 to November 1863, the Institut canadien de Montréal indicated in the clearest possible way its intention to pursue its work and its approach. The new president did not disappoint the five hundred-odd members of the Institut in his speech of 23 December 1862, on the occasion of the eighteenth anniversary of the Institut. Taking as his starting point the bishop's censure in 1858, he recalled the Institut's principles (tolerance, freedom of thought, and non-confessionality) and defended the contents of the library, while noting the irony that no bishop of Lower Canada had ever asked the members of the Legislative Assembly of United Canada to "purge" that library, which contained books considered unacceptable in the Institut's library. The president explained that the Institut had been condemned without proof and without the right to defend itself, and that the strategy of its opponents was based on "making people believe" their views. He attacked those who disparaged reason, suggesting "that it is not by denying our capacity to reason that they can give us a very high impression of theirs. Nor it is by challenging our right to judge that they can make us admit their right to judge us. Nor is it by advising us to abandon our own reason that they can persuade us of the superiority of theirs over ours ... Nor, finally, is it by carrying out persistent moral persecution against us – in fact, we almost have reason to believe that if they could practise legal persecution they would be overjoyed – that they can convince us of their spirit of conciliation and charity."[15]

This was obviously not the time of conciliation. In an announcement to all parish priests in the diocese on 18 January 1863, Mgr Bourget proposed: "Let us therefore pray that this terrible monster, rationalism, which has once again shown its hideous head in the Institut and which seeks to spread its venom in a pamphlet that repeats the blasphemies delivered from that stinking lectern, can harm no one." There was no doubt: it was Dessaulles's speech, published as a pamphlet, that was being targeted.

It was also in the spirit of opposition rather than that of conciliation that Abbé Louis-Herménégilde Huot decided to publish a series of articles on "Rougism in Canada" in *Le Courrier du Canada* in the summer of 1863; the articles were also published as a pamphlet in 1864. Under the pseudonym "An observer," Abbé Huot attacked Dessaulles directly on almost every page, calling him one of "the strongest supporters of Rougism." He had been studying Dessaulles's articles and speeches since

1848 in order to define what a Rouge was and to stigmatize the religious ideas, social principles, and anti-Canadian tendencies of Rougism. Concerning the popular sovereignty so dear to Dessaulles and the liberals, he wrote: "The axiom of the Rouges, *Vox Populi, Vox Dei*, which Mr. Dessaulles interprets as 'kings are subjects and subjects are kings!' weakens all respect for authority and seeks to destroy the balance of the social scale, which is the creation of God and not man."[16]

Not to be outdone, the tireless Cyrille Boucher dug up Dessaulles's 1858 speech on progress, eager to keep a topic with such inexhaustible potential for controversy from being forgotten. His aim was clear: as it had been with Papineau in 1848, it was to undermine the credibility of the president of the Institut canadien and editor of *Le Pays*.[17]

In October 1863, the Institut canadien, aware of the rising tensions and ready to try a conciliatory approach, created a committee made up of Dr Joseph Emery-Coderre, Joseph Doutre, Wilfrid Laurier, and Louis-Antoine Dessaulles to "enquire into ways to iron out the difficulties that have arisen between His Highness the Bishop of Montreal and the Institut." But a cordial meeting with the bishop on 27 October produced no results.

It was *L'Ordre*'s turn to strike, and it did so by borrowing an idea expressed by Cyrille Boucher in 1857 concerning the "the utterly philosophical direction that some newspapers have taken." Replacing Hector Fabre, who was now at *Le Canadien* in Quebec City, Louis Labrèche-Viger, who had been co-editor of *Le Pays* with Dessaulles at its start in 1852, wrote on the front page of the 27 November 1863 issue of *L'Ordre*:

We feel obliged, in the interest of the Ministerial Party, to express our sincere regret that the editors of *Le Pays* have embarked on philosophical dissertations that do little to advance the interests of the Liberal Party in Canada.

The small satisfaction that may result from success in an abstract discussion that has no political impact whatsoever should not outweigh, in the eyes of our colleague, the harm that it may do to the cause he serves ...

However strong his philosophical convictions may be, the editor of *Le Pays* is no doubt aware that his opinions are not shared by everyone; that maybe even the majority of the Ministerial Party does not share his views. Why then do you make a point of insulting the convictions, playing on the sensibilities, the prejudices, if you will, of your political allies, who know that these outdated discussions in our population have been the trap that has ensnared the Liberal Party?

L'Ordre thus repeated the reference to the philosophical direction of Dessaulles's "dissertations" in *Le Pays* and at the Institut canadien, but it went one step further than Boucher had in 1857: it blamed this radicalism for the damage to the Liberal Party. This was an idea with a future.

The next day, Dessaulles invoked his "right of defence" to explain that defending reason against religion in a moderate way and without hostility could not harm the Liberal Party: "Is allowing the Institut or any other association of a liberal nature to be crushed going to make the Liberal Party stronger?"

L'Ordre hid neither its intentions nor its interests: "The Liberal Party is in no way identified with the Institut-Canadien" and "neither supporting philosophical theses nor discussing the Inquisition are part of its mandate." The gap was widening and the radicals were being pushed to the margins.

In an article with an almost desperate title – "Do Our Articles Serve Any Purpose at All?" – Dessaulles put all his cards on the table: "There are nonetheless some who share our colleague's views, and see as a purely philosophical debate the great discussion on whether liberalism is the calamity for peoples that the reactionaries claim it is, and whether despotism is the greatest blessing they can receive. Nothing seems more mistaken to us."[18]

He had no illusions about this new "crusade" against liberalism and *Le Pays*, this "fire trained on the Institut by *La Minerve, Le Canadien, Le Courrier du Canada, Le Journal de Québec* and *Le Courrier de Saint-Hyacinthe.*" The situation at least allowed him to recall clearly the aims of the liberals: "We demand the independence of the human spirit in the legal domain, the political domain and the social domain! In the religious domain, we leave it to the conscience of each person: we want nothing to do with it!"[19]

In re-electing Dessaulles president from May 1865 to May 1867, the Institut canadien endorsed its leaders' new strategy; having failed to find a local solution with Mgr Bourget, they decided not to wait to deal with his eventual successor, but to submit an appeal to Rome, which had authority over the bishop. On 16 October, a petition was submitted to Pope Pius IX in the name of the Catholic members of the Institut by eighteen of their number, asking the pope to overturn the 1858 censure of the Institut. Among the signatories were three names that would go down in history: Wilfrid Laurier, a typographer named Joseph Guibord, and Dessaulles, who, in a brief accompanying the petition, drew the attention of Cardinal Barnabo, the prefect of the Sacred Congregation for the Propagation of the Faith, to the existence "here of a school, made up mainly of young people, recent graduates of the colleges, who seem to be expected to be much more Catholic than the Pope and his Councils."

Rome sought the opinion of Bishop Bourget, who replied in a brief on
21 September 1866 that it was not he but the Church that had censured the Institut in 1858. He added some details on Dessaulles's positions on the Italian question and the temporal power of the pope and,
characteristically, appended the articles Fabre had written against the
Institut in 1862,[20] so that their true importance and significance could
be understood.

On 17 December 1866, its twenty-second anniversary, the Institut canadien de Montréal inaugurated its new building on Notre-Dame Street.
The story was not over.

PHILOSOPHIA CONTRA RATIONALISMUM, DEMOCRATIAM ALIAQUE

Rationalism was frequently denounced in the mid-nineteenth century.
Mgr Bourget identified the Institut canadien with this intellectual attitude and *La Minerve* went further: "You are the representatives of the
philosophical spirit and rationalism; that is what you are. You fly the flag
of impiety; freedom of inquiry and of thought, that is your motto. That
is why we repudiate you. You believe that reason is all-powerful, you claim
that thought and philosophy promote regeneration and civilization,
whereas we claim that reason alone produces only error and leads societies to the abyss." The bishop of Saint-Hyacinthe, acting as a referee in
the controversy between Boucher and Dessaulles on progress, wrote to
Dessaulles: "But since human reason alone cannot enable humanity to
develop, because it cannot tell us enough about either our origin or our
destiny, it follows that progress that is based entirely on the principle of
human reason cannot, of course, be progress of humankind." Abbé
Huot had said the same thing: the "dogma" of Rougism was "independence of thought in the moral and religious realm."[21] Rationalism came
in for a lot of blame: it allegedly encompassed everything from Protestant
private judgment to "philosophism," from the "philosophical direction"
of debates to democracy.

Ever since the 1833 controversy on Cartesian reason and Lamennais's
common sense, the teaching of philosophy in the colleges had been
seeking its path. In 1864, the debate on the views of Gaume on the elimination of pagan authors in favour of Christian authors in the classical
colleges did not have any concrete results, but it gives a sense of a conservative milieu seeking to imbue every aspect of French Canadian culture
with religion.[22]

This desire to "Catholicize" everything included philosophy, which
was seen as inconceivable separately from religion and was taught in a

way that placed reason under faith. In search of a Catholic philosophy, textbooks, which were handwritten, copied from those of the teacher, and generally in philosophical Latin, taught students in the two final years of classical college that the "philosophy of St Thomas shows us that truth is entirely revealed, and there is need only to look for the relationships, reasons and causes of truths ... Thus, the philosopher must first believe, but after that he can seek to deepen his understanding of truths."

Moral education taught a hierarchy of human "ends" and "duties" and established the primacy of spiritual ends over temporal ends. This moral teaching was not merely abstract; the system of ends justified the Church's claim to responsibility in "mixed" questions, including that of schools: "civil society can build schools, it does not enter them." Thousands of students were taught that the state was in the Church, and not the Church in the state, that neither "absolute" liberalism (primacy of the state) nor "moderate" liberalism (danger of "indifference") nor "Catholic" liberalism (inconsistent) was acceptable, that *Omnis potestas a Deo* (All authority comes from God), that only monarchy was capable of maintaining the alliance of throne and altar, and that popular sovereignty was a "sophism."

The Church was moving toward a Catholic philosophy capable of serving as the foundation for ultramontanism, and toward the restoration of the philosophy of St Thomas Aquinas. In 1865, Abbé Isaac Désaulniers of the Séminaire de Saint-Hyacinthe acknowledged: "As for me, I know; I taught the likes of Descartes and Mallebranche [*sic*] for twenty years, and I can attest that this long study of false philosophy never satisfied the desires of my intelligence. But since I have been studying St Thomas, everything seems luminous, and I profoundly admire the marvellous harmony of all the principles in this philosophy, which is as broad as it is deep. Pius V was right to say that the philosophy of St Thomas is capable of refuting the errors of the past, present and future." This was also the period when the encyclical *Quanta cura* was issued, accompanied by the famous *Syllabus*, a sort of manual of errors of doctrine since the revolutionary period, to which religious authorities referred throughout the second half of the nineteenth century. Mgr Bourget noted: "You understand, as I do, that the arrival of the letters was opportune, because it is evident that many of the false principles criticized in them have already infiltrated even into our happy and peaceful countryside by means of the evil newspapers and speeches of our liberals."[23]

TOWARD CONFEDERATION (1864–1867)

During this period of increasing anticlerical tensions and efforts to marginalize radical liberalism, a new constitutional change began that was to have repercussions as far-reaching as those of 1791 and 1840. The crisis of 1858 had deepened, above all, because of demographic evolution and its political repercussions.[24] With Upper Canada's repeated demands for the replacement of equal representation with proportional representation, constitutional change became unavoidable and urgent because it took only a majority in the House – instead of the two thirds required by the constitution of 1840 – to make this change.

An alliance of Liberals from Upper and Lower Canada and then the Brown-Dorion government were unsuccessful in this, partly because of religious and conservative opposition to the school system that Brown wanted to establish and partly because of the difficulty the Liberals from Lower Canada had in formulating their positions regarding the crisis. The October 1859 report of the Liberal members from Lower Canada suggested elements of a solution: a federal union of the two Canadas (East and West), and not of the British provinces of North America; limited responsibilities for the central government, with the more important responsibilities going to the provincial governments; and guarantees for French Canadian institutions. While the crisis was institutional and constitutional, it was also a crisis of identity. How would one define a *Canadien* in 1860? *Le Pays* had an answer.

It must be understood that we have attained a state of society considerable enough to consider ourselves a distinct people, politically, socially, and even morally, in many cases, from England as from France.

Certainly our traditions, customs, religion, laws, language, etc., are influenced by both. We should not forget this; indeed, we cannot. But in order that an equitable social and patriotic balance be maintained, we must at least divide our affections between our two common mother countries and our true homeland, that is, the Canadian homeland. We must appear, and above all be, first and foremost Canadians.[25]

In the 1861 election, the Liberals maintained their popular support. Although they increased their share of the vote in the Montreal region relative to 1857 (38 per cent compared with 29 per cent), they obtained only 36 per cent of the vote in their stronghold of Montréal-Est, versus 64 per cent for the Conservatives, who were beginning to be called the "Bleus." Elsewhere in Lower Canada, the Conservatives obtained 59 per cent of the vote, the Liberals 6 per cent, and the Moderate Liberals 27 per cent, whereas the latter received only 17 per cent in the Montreal region. Behind the Conservatives, the Liberals and Moderate Liberals were neck and neck.[26]

The process of constitutional change really began in 1864 with the fall of another government – the tenth to fall in ten years – and the formation in June of a coalition government united around a plan for ending the crisis: a confederation.

The liberal press immediately signalled its opposition to the plan. *Le Pays*, without proposing any alternative, denounced George-Étienne Cartier for putting Lower Canada "on the path to a confederation based on the calamitous principle ... of representation based on population." In July, Charles Daoust, who had succeeded Dessaulles at the head of the newspaper, published a series of articles recalling the metropolis's previous plans for union and showing Britain's step-by-step plan: 1811, 1822, 1824, 1840, and the present plan for a federal union. *Le Journal de Saint-Hyacinthe* expected that confederation would confront French Canadians with not just two anglophone colonies but seven. One after another, Jean-Baptiste-Éric Dorion's *Le Défricheur* in Arthabaska, the young Félix-Gabriel Marchand's *Le Franco-Canadien* in Saint-Jean-sur-Richelieu, and Médéric Lanctôt's *Union nationale* came out against the plan for confederation, situating themselves above the parties. As for *L'Ordre*, the voice of the Moderate Liberals, for the moment, it was politically opposed to the project but its moderation would lead it to accept confederation for religious reasons.

In September 1864, the Charlottetown Conference gave the representatives of United Canada an opportunity to form an alliance with their colleagues from the "Gulf countries," who were meeting precisely to discuss a plan for the federation of the colonies. The conference was followed, from 10 to 22 October, by the Quebec Conference, in which all the political parties in the colony participated, except the Liberals of Lower Canada, who were excluded. This served as another reason for Antoine-Aimé Dorion, the leader of the Lower Canada Liberals, to publish a manifesto on 7 November criticizing the "secret sessions" and the negotiations among the ministers "within their cabinet." He noted that "the absence of any official communication of the proceedings of the conference, the complete silence of the ministers from Lower Canada concerning the details of this planned confederation, suggest that they want to rush this measure, without consulting the people." Dorion expressed concern about the number of representatives envisaged for Quebec (twenty-four of seventy-six Council members appointed for life; a fixed number of sixty-five elected members out of 194), the responsibilities of each level of government, the division of the debt, and above all, the fact that the plan was not for confederation but for legislative union.[27]

THE PRINCIPLE OF NATIONALITY IN 1864

Gonzalve Doutre's lecture on the principle of nationality at the Institut canadien de Montréal on 1 December 1864 revealed two important dimensions of the intellectual and political issues at this turning point: first, the liberals' emphasis on democracy, their insistence on placing their liberalism above nationality in confronting the clergy and the Conservative Party, who identified religion with nationality; and second, a novel element in the Americanity of Lower Canada, the phenomenon of international immigration. Doutre's words represented a shift in relation to the right of peoples to self-determination from the views of the 1830s and 1848, at the time of the Italian question.

While stating that he did not support the plan for confederation, Doutre observed "the phenomenon of universal immigration" and sought to demonstrate that Lower Canada was "not in a position to speak of nationality as France and England are; Canada, or rather, the New World, being open to the migration of all peoples, should not form distinct Nationalities for all the fractions of peoples within it, but rather one single Nationality based on the identical interests and needs of its inhabitants." He feared the consequences of these migratory movements: "What good will it do to have all these nationalities, which will lead only to internal divisions and not to the centralization of strength and power?" And he even foresaw the emergence in the New World of a quasi-universal nationality that "would unite all these distinct parts of nationalities to form a single nation." A law professor at McGill University, he refused to define nationality in terms of language, religion, blood, or skin colour. He rejected religious specificity and felt "that religious tolerance is everywhere" and "that there is only one God above us and all the differences of opinion ultimately concern the best way to adore him." To him, "the fundamental principle of nationality is that of best interest ... which links all the inhabitants of a country; it is the very simple way to facilitate moral and social relations; it is based on the highly logical calculation that everyone has an interest in maintaining domestic harmony and in cultivating the same feelings of conservation and shared well-being and prosperity." This concept of nationality resembles the much-criticized membership of the Institut canadien de Montréal, which welcomed members of all origins and all religious and political beliefs and which was a sort of microcosm of the "universal nationality" Doutre envisaged.

Doutre expanded on his ideas in a reply to Laurent-Olivier David, who had published an article in *Union nationale* entitled "Rationalism and Confederation": "I did not say that national distinctions should disappear, but only that one nationality should not have supremacy over others; that in Canada, all these distinct nationalities should combine into one general nationality." He added, "In saying that it was absurd to claim that language and religion constitute nationality, I was basing my assertion on facts that are undeniable because they are historical: the United States of America, the German Confederation, etc., etc., form nationalities that are not based on language and religion." Modifying his liberalism for a moment, he admitted having "condemned these fragments of nations that, refusing to accept the fate that Providence assigned them, to make a nation of Canada, seek to separate, to grow weaker, under the ridiculous pretext that they must remain just as they were in the place they left." And this self-image as a Canadian prompted him to situate himself with regard to France: "I love my country, Canada, first; before France, which no longer means much to us ... [which] is foreign to us."

In reality, this concept of nationality was not new among liberals; it had been circulating at the Institut canadien for the past ten years. In 1852, Charles Laberge had asked: "Is it not time to understand that whatever language an individual speaks, whatever religion he professes, he is a man first and a Canadian after that, and that he shares these characteristics with all the others; that these internal divisions cause suffering among people of all origins; that the country will not progress until people of every origin express an enlightened respect for others, allowing them complete freedom in their spheres and joining hands with each other on neutral terrain: the love of their common homeland." The following year, Charles Daoust, too, foresaw the possibility of "a citizen of the world:" "What is this nationality to which the people clings as if by instinct? Is it the French language? No! Religion? No! The old laws, disfigured and abridged by the statutes? No! Is it the blue wool cap, cowhide shoes and a coat made of the local cloth? Is it the old-fashioned sleigh, the pipe and the parish priest, as a newspaper from Upper Canada recently suggested? Certainly not! So what is it? ... It is neither the language nor the religion nor the laws nor the institutions considered individually; it is the essence, the abstraction, the ineffable form of all this, it is the cult of the homeland, the religion of the tombs."

In May 1854, Francis Cassidy, the Irish president of the Institut, for whom it had modified its constitution in 1850, also stated that "language and religion are not components of nationality." In December, Pierre-Richard Lafrenaye had anticipated Doutre, describing "this movement of populations that is occurring on our continent and that, in the nature of institutions, is leading toward the fusion of nationalities and the homogeneity of races."

But there was one exception to this radical liberal conception of nationality among the members of the Institut canadien, and that was

Arthur Buies, the only French Canadien to have worn the red shirt of the Garibaldians. In an 1862 lecture on "the future of the French race in Canada," Buies took a very different position: "We are in a century in which there are no battles left save that for nationality"; "furthermore," he continued, "a distinctive characteristic of our period is the fusion of the ideas and trends of different peoples, and while it may seem strange to the unobservant, it is in the context of such fusion that each people tends increasingly to reinforce and confirm its identity, its nationality, its own government and its autonomy. The reason for this is simple: the word fusion does not mean confusion: as they come closer together, peoples do not want to disappear, but to enjoy closer, more friendly relations, they need a strong and sure independence (there is no union between the strong and the weak)."[28]

THE GREAT DEBATE ON THE PLAN FOR CONFEDERATION (FEBRUARY 1865)

The questions of parliamentary representation, an elected Legislative Council, and the rights of religious minorities were among the causes of Confederation and were central to the discussions. But references to the dangers of annexationism and the need to build a railway that could create a country from east to west indicate that, in this period at the end of the Civil War, the United States and its power of attraction worried Canadians. The address of the terribly British Cartier to the Legislative Assembly of United Canada in February 1865 reflects this concern.

We, who had the benefit of being able to contemplate republicanism in action during a period of eighty years, saw its defects and felt convinced that purely democratic institutions could not be conducive to the peace and prosperity of nations ... Our attempt was for the purpose of forming a Federation with a view of perpetuating the monarchical element. The distinction, therefore, between ourselves and our neighbours was just this: In our Federation the monarchical principle would form the leading feature, while on the other side of the lines, judging by the past history and present condition of the country, the ruling power was the will of the mob, the rule of the populace. Every person who has conversed with the most intelligent American statesmen and writers must have learned that they all admitted that the government powers had become too extended, owing to the introduction of universal suffrage, and mob rule had consequently supplanted legitimate authority.

Like A.-A. Dorion, the Liberals countered Cartier's monarchism and conservatism with the democratic principle of the future elected Senate, the decentralization of powers toward the base, and assent to the plan by the people. Maurice Laframboise, Dessaulles's brother-in-law, underscored the anti-democratic behaviour of Upper Canada with regard to the system of proportional representation: "But I maintain that as they refused the application of it when the population of Lower Canada was in a majority, it is unjust of them to demand it now because they are in a majority, and I cannot see by what right they wish to obtain it now. I say that if the application of that principle was unjust twenty years ago, it is also unjust today, and that if it is just today, it was equally just twenty years ago."

Jean-Baptiste-Éric Dorion attacked the formula for constitutional change passed in 1854 in a clearly undemocratic move by the Imperial Parliament, which had reduced the two-thirds majority required by the constitutional law of 1840 to a simple majority in order to facilitate an eventual vote on parliamentary representation. He denied "that the House has power to change the political constitution of the country ... without appealing to the people" and referred to the American model of constitutional change recently applied to the question of slavery. Interest in annexation had not disappeared, as is shown by his reference to Louisiana. He felt that Louisiana had not become lost in the American Union and that its situation was not comparable to that of Lower Canada because its white population had initially consisted of both French and Spanish people and it was the Louisianans themselves who had abolished the use of French in their legislature "to mark their dissatisfaction at having been sold by France." Fearing the numerical marginalization of the French Canadians, Dorion recalled the scenario of a Lower Canada similar to Louisiana: it "would be as independent as any of the other states of the union" because it "would possess, like all the other states, full and entire sovereignty in all matters specially relating to [its] own interests ... With regard to local matters, [it] would be perfectly sovereign in [its] own country, and [it] could make all the laws [it] thought proper, provided such laws were not hostile to the other states." Dorion preferred Lower Canada to take the form of an American state rather than that of a Canadian province.[29]

On 10 March 1865 in the Legislative Assembly of United Canada, ninety-one members voted in favour of the plan for Confederation, and thirty-three against; the anglophones of Upper and Lower Canada and the Conservative and moderate francophones gave the plan its majority. Of the members from Lower Canada, thirty-seven voted for Confederation, twenty-five against. Among the forty-nine French Canadian members, twenty-seven voted for it, and among the forty-nine representatives of predominantly francophone counties, twenty-five voted for it, twenty-four against. On 13 March, *Le Pays* wrote: "On this memorable night, the most unjust act was committed, the most degrading act the parliamentary system has witnessed since the betrayal of the Irish members who sold their country to England for positions, honours and gold."[30] The Confederation plan received imperial and royal assent on 1 March 1867 and came into force on 1 July of the same year.

THE BISHOPS, CONFEDERATION, AND CATHOLIC, RATHER THAN FRENCH-LANGUAGE, EDUCATION

Since 1858, the Catholic Church of Lower Canada had fought Rougism and its stress on the separation of church and state, but it had not since 1864 expressed itself publicly regarding the plan for Confederation. Conservatives knew, even before the period of parliamentary debate on the question in February 1865, that the Catholic Church would be in favour of Confederation. It had not succeeded in blocking the law on divorce or preventing responsibility for it from being given to the federal government, but it had managed to make its view felt on the rights of religious minorities, especially with regard to schools.

The question of religion had been raised not by the Catholic Church but by the anglophone Protestants of Lower Canada. Since the Quebec Conference of 1864 had already proposed to give the provinces responsibility for education, the Protestants, as a minority in Lower Canada, feared for their educational institutions, and it was in this context that the question of the reciprocal rights of the Catholic minorities in Upper Canada, New Brunswick, and Nova Scotia was posed. At the time of the London Conference, in late 1866 and early 1867, where the draft of the Constitution was to be approved, Alexander Galt, the member for Sherbrooke, had a clause added stipulating that in places where schools of religious minorities existed by law at the time of the conference, it would be possible to appeal to the federal government if their rights were threatened or were not respected, and the federal government could pass remedial legislation. Meanwhile, Section 133 of the constitutional bill provided for the right of the provinces to decide on the language of instruction in public schools.

The Canadian education system was thus confessional rather than cultural or linguistic: schools were Catholic or Protestant and not francophone or anglophone. This suited Lower Canada for two reasons: the Protestants, who were the majority in Canada and North America, feared not for their language, but rather for their religion; and the loyalist Catholic Church – which had succeeded in making Lower Canada's schools confessional between 1841 and 1846, and whose ultramontanism had led it to promote an alliance of the religious and political spheres and the primacy of the Church in so-called mixed issues – defended its spiritual and temporal interests by making school children Catholics first, and francophones at the same time.[31]

It was in this context of both vigilance against doctrinal and electoral liberalism and a campaign for the rights of Catholic minorities that, shortly before the election of 1867, the Catholic hierarchy intervened publicly in the political debate. The election scheduled for September 1867 was not referendary, that is, it did not concern Confederation, which had come into effect on 1 July. But it was clear that if a Liberal government was elected, it could re-open the question. At the suggestion of the ultramontanist coadjutor bishop of Trois-Rivières, Mgr Louis-François Laflèche, the bishops of five Lower Canada dioceses intervened in the summer of 1867. Mgr Bourget did not join them because of his dispute with the archbishop of Quebec City concerning the dismembering of the Sulpician parish of Notre-Dame de Montréal and the Catholic university obtained by Quebec City with support from Rome. Mgr Bourget did, however, publish a circular letter to the clergy on 5 May, recommending that the Church submit in the present as it had in the past (1791, 1840), and that it make all voters understand the importance of their votes: "I know that I will one day answer for my vote to the tribunal of my Sovereign Judge." The old bishop of Trois-Rivières, Mgr Cooke, published a pastoral letter on 8 June, saying that Confederation was "decided and obligatory"; the only thing that mattered now was the right candidate and the right vote: "You will have occasion to fulfill this duty in the coming elections, making sure that the men you choose to represent you in the parliaments are moved by that spirit of conciliation and goodwill that is indispensible in order to derive from the new constitution all the good we must expect of it." Mgr Baillargeon of Quebec City made the same recommendation regarding Confederation on 12 June: "Make sure that you do not cast your votes for men who intend to combat it or create obstacles to its operation." The bishop of Rimouski, Mgr Jean Langevin, the former editor of *Les Mélanges religieux* and *Le Courrier du Canada* and the brother of Louis-Hector, Cartier's right-hand man, went further: "The new constitution ... is given to you as the expression of the supreme will of the legislator of the legitimate Authority, and thus of God himself." His 13 June pastoral letter added that the vote would be decisive for "the preservation of all that is dear to us as a nation, our Religion, our Language, our Institutions." Finally, in a sixteen-page document dated 18 June, Mgr Charles Larocque of Saint-Hyacinthe attacked any remaining annexationist aims: "Republican institutions would not suit us better than they did the great people from which we descend, the

French! And our fate, if ever God permitted that we enter the great American republic, would be exactly comparable to that of the various tributaries that flow into the deep, broad St Lawrence River, where they disappear without a trace."[32]

THE ELECTIONS OF SEPTEMBER 1867:
"HEAVEN IS BLUE AND HELL IS RED"

The Liberals fought one last battle of honour when the bishops took a public position.

Wilfrid Laurier, who had been vice-president of the Institut canadien de Montréal in 1865 and 1866, showed his propensity for conciliation in participating in the committee responsible for resolving the problems with Mgr Bourget and by signing the Petition to Rome in October 1865 with other Catholic members of the Institut. The young lawyer, who had been opposed to constitutional change without popular consultation since 1864 and was a partisan of "union without fusion," succeeded J.-B.-É. Dorion at *Le Défricheur* in the village of L'Avenir from November 1866 to late March 1867. On 27 December 1866, he wrote in *Le Défricheur* that Confederation would be "the tomb of the French race and the ruin of Lower Canada." On 7 March 1867, his tone was even more strident.

When the charter of 1841 was imposed on us ... we had only two possible options, and we had to choose one or the other. We could either follow Mr. Papineau's program ... or accept the new constitution, take advantage of the exemptions it allowed, and protect ourselves as best we could from the dangers it posed. The new leader [La Fontaine] chose the latter option, in the hope that with the help of the good aspects of the charter, the bad aspects would be paralyzed. Everyone followed him. In vain did Mr. Papineau later cry: "Responsible government is nothing but a trap." The opposite side cried, "Although the Union was made to destroy us, it has saved us." Now that the Union is due to end, where are those who will still dare to say, "Although the Union was made to destroy us, it has saved us." No, the Union made to destroy us has not failed in its aim.

Today [the French nationality] is larger and more numerous, but it bears the seeds of its own dissolution: it has no strength, it is divided, it is not yet anglicized, but it is well on the way there ... We are being handed over to the English majority ... We must return fully and directly to Mr. Papineau's policy. We must protest with all our strength against the new situation that has been imposed on us and use the influence we still have to demand and obtain a free and separate government.

In order to be married in the Catholic Church and satisfy the requirements of the diocese of Montreal, Laurier resigned from the Institut canadien on 13 May 1867. The path of moderation opened up ahead of him.[33]

At *Le Pays*, Alphonse Lusignan continued to oppose Confederation even after its promulgation, hoping that the election of the Liberals in September might reverse the situation. He even published an anonymous pamphlet describing Confederation as the "culmination of ten years of bad administration," to which Joseph-Alfred Mousseau replied in a pamphlet that spoke of Confederation as "the salvation of Lower Canada."[34]

But Confederation would survive: the results of the September 1867 elections in Canada and Quebec left no room for doubt. The Conservatives won 101 out of 181 seats in the new House of Commons of the new Canada, and in the Legislative Assembly of Quebec, they won 45 out of 65 seats, with more than half of the members – 23 members, 20 of them Conservatives – elected by acclamation. The cumulative Liberal vote in Ottawa and Quebec was 12 per cent. In the Montreal region, the Liberals received 18 per cent of the vote, compared with 33 per cent in 1863, and in Montreal itself, 8 per cent, compared with 42 per cent in 1863. They maintained their support with 41 per cent of the vote in Verchères, Richelieu, Saint-Hyacinthe, Rouville, Bagot, and Shefford; they lost half their votes (22 per cent) in Chambly, La Prairie, Châteauguay, Beauharnois, Napierville, Saint-Jean, and Iberville, and they obtained four times fewer votes (5 per cent) in Joliette, L'Assomption, Berthier, and Montcalm. Liberalism remained alive in Kamouraska, L'Avenir, and Drummond-Arthabaska, and it showed signs of life briefly in Trois-Rivières.[35]

Le Journal de Saint-Hyacinthe of 9 September 1867 was right "that the real struggle [had been] between the clergy and the Rouges." On 15 August, *Le Pays* predicted the strategies of the coming period: "The effort organized on such a large scale by the religious authority to influence the election is an abnormal phenomenon which must, in the interest of religion, disappear from future election contests." The Liberal press would have to wage these battles with reduced forces: of seven newspapers (*Le Pays* and *L'Union nationale* in Montreal, *Le Journal de Saint-Hyacinthe*, *Le Franco-Canadien* in Saint-Jean-sur-Richelieu, *L'Électeur* in Quebec City, *Le Journal de Lévis*, to which the liberal poet Louis Fréchette was a contributor, and *Le Défricheur* in L'Avenir), four disappeared after 1866, while the Conservative press (*La Minerve* in Montreal; *Le Canadien*, *Le Journal de Québec* and *Le Courrier du Canada* in Quebec City; and *Le Courrier de Saint-Hyacinthe*) was joined by four new papers after 1866: the highly ultramontanist *Nouveau Monde* in Montreal, *L'Événement*, founded in Quebec by Hector Fabre, the *Union des Cantons de l'Est* in Arthabaska, and *La Voix du golfe* in Rimouski.

Le Pays barely waited for the election results to be published to undertake a campaign denouncing the electoral alliance of the Conservatives and the clergy. Dessaulles – who had been "placed," according to *La Minerve*, in a job as court clerk and who had just finished a dispute of six months' duration on the alliance of throne, altar, and college with Abbé Joseph-Sabin Raymond, the superior of the Séminaire de Saint-Hyacinthe, who had declared that "every political question contains a theological question" – resumed duty at *Le Pays*, carrying out an anonymous investigation of the clergy's intervention in the election campaign from September 1867 to February 1868. The Liberal paper showed how, following the bishops' pastoral letters, parish priests had used the Sunday announcements on temporal aspects of parish life, the pulpit, the confessional and, in some places, even political patronage to discourage the Liberal vote against Confederation. In one place, the priest had made it an obligation of conscience to vote in favour of Confederation; elsewhere, women whose husbands were readers of the Rouge *Le Pays* or who refused to send the paper back were denied absolution in the confessional. At the Séminaire de Sainte-Thérèse, students were encouraged to write their parents asking them not to vote for the Liberals. Still elsewhere, a parish priest threatened to deny the Rouges the sacraments and Catholic burial, and preached from the pulpit that "Heaven is blue and Hell is red" or asked parishioners to vote for Lemieux [literally, "the best"] and not for the worst. There were beginning to be accusations of "undue" influence by the Church and clergy in politics. Ultramontanism was no longer a politico-religious theory; it was involved in the civil process itself. And the Catholic Church had the means to implement its policy: the number of priests in Quebec had risen from 225 in 1830 to 464 in 1840, to 620 in 1850, to 948 in 1860 and to 1,412 in 1870, and the number of the faithful per priest had gone down from 1,835 in 1830 to 1,185 in 1840, to 1,080 in 1850, to 893 in 1860, and to 658 in 1870.

In December 1867, four years before his death, Louis-Joseph Papineau briefly left his manor at Montebello to present a lecture at the Institut canadien de Montréal, a sort of political overview and testament, in which he denounced the new constitutional system "prepared in the dark," its religious and confessional choices regarding education, and the monarchism of the Senate, which was appointed, not elected. In July 1868, Étienne Parent, who had been busy with the tasks of a senior civil servant, also stepped back into the political arena, celebrating Confederation, one of "those providential events," in whose preparation he had, he said, played a role thirty years earlier, in 1838.[36]

CONCLUSION

Antoine-Aimé Dorion's efforts to keep liberalism alive after Papineau's defeat in 1849 were not as successful as he had hoped. Not only did political and ideological conservatism become stronger, but moderate liberalism did as well as radical liberalism in the election of 1861. The conservatives and ultramontanists sought to neutralize radical liberalism, or Rougism, by establishing an association between radical liberalism and the Liberal party, while the moderate liberals dissociated doctrinal liberalism and electoral liberalism.

This two-pronged process was in a sense facilitated by the constant radicalization of the liberals at *Le Pays* and the Institut canadien de Montréal during the period when the most radical of them, Louis-Antoine Dessaulles, was their leader. The liberals' affirmation of the priority of liberal values and democracy over nationality found its fullest expression at the Institut canadien, in both its constitution and its position on nationality and the principle of nationality. Indeed, its belief in democracy led to the Institut's censure by the bishop of Montreal in 1858. At *Le Pays*, it was the paper's position on the Italian question and the pope's temporal power that aroused the wrath of Mgr Bourget and *L'Ordre*.

After Cyrille Boucher's allusions in 1857 to the "the utterly philosophical direction" of some newspapers and after the split in the Institut canadien de Montréal and its exclusion from the Saint-Jean-Baptiste parade in 1858, the 1862 dispute between *L'Ordre* and *Le Pays* enabled the moderate liberals, who, after the conservatives, had as much electoral support as the Rouge liberals, to widen the gap between doctrinal liberalism and partisan electoral liberalism. Their criticism of *Le Pays*'s "philosophical dissertations" on the temporal power of the pope or on reason had only one purpose: to show the damage they did to the party. Five years later, Wilfrid Laurier resigned from the Institut canadien and undertook to develop what could be a viable moderate liberalism, that is, a liberalism that was not anticlerical. The breach that opened within radical liberalism in 1858 widened in 1862. Soon it would cripple it.

The political crisis over proportional representation in 1858 also challenged the liberals. The most insightful among them noted the emergence of a new factor: immigration, which was changing the face of North America, including Canada, altered the problem of nationalities and their relations. The liberals rejected the solution proposed to resolve the crisis – a Confederation of the provinces of British America – pleading repeatedly for democracy, and particularly for a new constitution that would be ratified by the people, but to no avail, as Confederation was decided in the back rooms.

Opposing Confederation thus meant opposing the conservatives, the moderates, and the clergy of Lower Canada and Upper Canada, to say the least. The Catholic Church, which denounced democracy and popular sovereignty and supported monarchy, was now more ultramontanist than ever. It defended Rome and the pope, argued for an alliance of religious power and political power, and, with the Protestant churches, gained control over the schools, which were defined more in confessional than linguistic terms. This demand, which was granted by conservative political power, was perfectly consistent with the Church's conception of the destiny of French Canada; Catholic first, and French after that. The Church, in return, made this concession to the state: it intervened in the non-referendary but crucial election of 1867, which placed it in a delicate position. What was beginning to be called "the undue influence" of the Church threatened to spill over into plans for a theocracy.

11

Tolerance:
An Issue for Liberals and Ultramontanists
(1867–1877)

THE 1865 APPEAL TO ROME by the Catholic members of the Institut canadien de Montréal had not been answered and clerical and conservative opposition to the liberals had been fanned by the long and virulent controversy between Dessaulles and Abbé Raymond of the Séminaire de Saint-Hyacinthe concerning the anachronistic instruction given by the clerical colleges with regard to political ideas; the antagonism had also been increased by the investigation undertaken by *Le Pays* and, again, Dessaulles, into clerical intervention in the 1867 election.

THE INSTITUT CANADIEN DE MONTRÉAL
AND TOLERANCE: THE SECOND CENSURE (1869)

On 12 December 1868, Dessaulles made a hard-hitting public speech on tolerance at the Institut canadien de Montréal, which he repeated at the Institut canadien de Saint-Hyacinthe. In it, he posed the crucial question regarding the dispute between the liberals of the Institut and religious authority: "To what do we owe our difficulties? To the fact that we have some Protestant members, that we receive some Protestant newspapers, and that we have some philosophical works that are on the Index." Invoking the idea that tolerance is Catholic because it is based on love for one's neighbour, he clarified the Institut's positions: "The fundamental principle of our association is tolerance, that is, respect for the opinions of others. We welcome all men of good will, whatever their nationality or religion. We are in favour of general fraternity rather than eternal hostility between races." But "all men of good will" did not think this way when they read the text of the speech in *Le Pays* or in the Institut canadien de Montréal's yearbook for 1868.

Abbé Raymond certainly did not. Replying in a public lecture at the Union catholique des jésuites de Montréal on 15 March 1869, he spoke of tolerance as "the war cry of all the enemies of the Church." To him, "any conviction is essentially intolerant" and "and any consideration is imprudence." After justifying the Index and the Inquisition, Abbé Raymond recognized, however, that "de facto tolerance" might be "acceptable at certain times and in certain places," as it was in Canada with regard to freedom of religion. But he foresaw the "reign of the cross over the nations" including that Canada of which Catholicism was the distinctive feature: "The glory of our homeland is the heroism of its colonists, the saints of its founding period, the religious and moral character of its inhabitants, its magnificent educational and charitable institutions, its devotion to noble causes, its Zouaves."[1]

Nor did Mgr Bourget have the same concept of tolerance as the members of the Institut canadien. He sent the Sacred Congregation of the Inquisition a thirty-six-page brief, dated 27 April 1869, which provided his answer to two basic questions: is the Institut canadien de Montréal evil and dangerous, and can it be reformed? Stressing the fact that Dessaulles's speech on tolerance had been published in the yearbook of the Institut and thus represented the Institut's thinking, he declared that the association was not reformable.

Indeed, to carry out a salutary reform in the Institut, we would above all have to make it renounce tolerance, which is the aim of its existence, and all the false, erroneous and impious principles it adheres to. The constitution and regulations, which contain the seed of that tolerance that unleashes every whim and every aberration of human reason, would obviously have to be modified. The library and the reading room would have to be purged of all books and newspapers contrary to faith and morality, either by eliminating them completely, or by putting them away in a place where only those authorized by the Holy See could read them. Topics that, according to the rules of the Church, cannot be subject to free inquiry by liberals, which today's free thinkers claim as a right, would have to be banished from discussions. All those inclined to present speeches like those included in the Yearbook would have to be excluded from the speaker's tribune.

Such a reform would necessitate a complete and radical reorientation of the Institut's founding principles and the content of its essential activities: the library and public lectures. The Institut's old opponent therefore demanded that it be censured and that its yearbook for 1868 be placed on the Index.

The Institut was censured by the Sacred Congregation of the Inquisition – the same one that had condemned Galileo, about whom Dessaulles had delivered a public lecture in 1856 – on 7 July 1869. The

"Most Eminent and Most Reverend General Inquisitors" informed Mgr Bourget that "the doctrines contained in a certain yearbook, in which are recorded the proceedings of said Institut, should be completely rejected, and ... the doctrines taught by the same institute should also be censured." They observed "that in addition, it was greatly to be feared that such evil doctrines posed a serious threat to the instruction and education of Christian youth" and they exhorted the bishop to do everything in his power "to keep Catholics, and especially young people, away from said Institut, as long as it is common knowledge that pernicious doctrines are taught there." The Tribunal placed the yearbook on the Index.

On the 16th, from Rome, Mgr Bourget sent a circular letter to the clergy of the diocese indicating that "it was clearly that evil book [the yearbook and the speech on tolerance] that led to the judgment and censure of that evil Institut" that wanted to "rob us of our people, and above all, our young people." Having attained his goal, the bishop had to take measures to ensure that the condemnation did not remain a dead letter.

(1) Parish priests are to publish the enclosed Announcement, observing what is ruled in it and taking care to see that their parishioners are not members of the Institut Canadien; (2) Confessors are to demand, with prudence and firmness, that their penitents respect the orders of the Holy Office ... (4) Superiors of Seminaries, colleges and other educational institutions are to protect their students from the pernicious doctrines of the Institut Canadien ... to enable them to resist invitations to join the Institut; (5) Journalists are urged to offer the support of the press against the dangerous doctrines of the Institut, which threatens to overthrow the throne as well as the altar; (6) The Institut canadien-français, the Cabinet de Lecture, the Union catholique, the Cercle Littéraire and other good institutions should contribute their zeal and devotion to the propagation of good principles ... (7) It is highly to be desired that pamphlets containing the antidote to the poison of the evil doctrines spread by the Institut Canadien be circulated in all classes of society; (8) Means must be taken, with prudence and discretion, to discourage the faithful, especially women, from attending lectures at the Institut Canadien and subscribing to its library or its newspapers.

Parish priests, confessors, superiors of seminaries, journalists, writers, and Catholic associations, the whole network of public and private communication, had a role to play.

Everything was planned. Sunday, 29 August 1869, in all the churches in the diocese of Montreal, it was announced that Rome had censured the Institut, and parishioners were reminded that "two things are especially and expressly forbidden here: 1° to belong to the Institut Canadien as long as it teaches pernicious doctrines, and 2° to publish, hold, keep or read the Yearbook of the Institut for 1868," at the risk of being deprived of the sacraments, including on the verge of death.[2]

The Institut canadien had to react. A special committee, of which Dessaulles was a member, sent the secretary of Bishop Bourget, who was still in Rome, two resolutions that it intended to submit to the members of the association: (1) that the Institut as an institution teach no doctrine and require that its members respect the doctrines of others; (2) that the Catholic members, upon learning of the censure of the 1868 yearbook by decree of the Roman authority, simply obey it. Not only was the proposal rejected by the chapter of the diocese, but it gave the very ultramontanist *Nouveau Monde*, edited by Canon Lamarche, a member of the chapter, a pretext to fan the flames and prevent any solution.

Once again, the Institut appealed to Rome; on 12 October 1869, it drew up a second petition, which Gonzalve Doutre delivered to the Sacred Congregation of the Inquisition, and which stated essentially that the Institut canadien de Montréal taught no doctrine. The animosity toward the bishop of Montreal was thinly veiled: "We have never found him to be either just or charitable as befits a pastor of the Church. Although he maintains an appearance of humility, those who have had occasion to deal with him know the rigidity and inflexibility with which he invariably reacts to all questions, great and small. He is a man who never changes his mind, whatever one may say to him. This is recognized by the Clergy as well as by lay people." The petition explained to Cardinal Barnabo the "mixed" situation of the country, the impossibility of requiring that the Protestant members of the Institut sign a statement of Catholic faith: "There was a very simple way to avoid these unfortunate consequences; and that was by not asking the association to make declarations that a good third of its members could not support, and to make do with the jurisdiction on individuals, a jurisdiction from which the Catholic members of the Institut never thought to exempt themselves," having, as Catholics, submitted to the decree of the Index. It was clear to the signatories of this second petition that their adversaries were not interested in reconciliation: they were aiming for the dissolution of the Institut. The petition sought one thing: that a clear distinction be made between "what the laws of the Church really require and what is inspired by partisanship."[3]

THE GUIBORD AFFAIR (1869–1875)

A new development: on 18 November 1869, five months after the second censure of the Institut canadien de Montréal, one of its members died. His name was Joseph Guibord.

The death of this typographer, who had been one of the eighteen signatories of the Institut's first petition to Rome in 1865, gave the Catholic hierarchy the opportunity to show that it meant what it said. Alleging that Guibord was under ecclesiastical censure – excommunication – Father Rousselot of the parish of Notre-Dame refused to let his widow, Henriette Brown-Guibord, bury her husband in consecrated ground; and when on the 21st, the funeral cortege arrived at Côte-des-Neiges cemetery, it was not admitted and had to take the body to the mass grave of the Protestant cemetery. Proceedings were instituted by the Institut canadien and Joseph Doutre, to whom Guibord's widow had turned for help.

Dessaulles made a speech at the Institut canadien on 29 December on what would come to be known as the Guibord affair. In it he maintained that because the 1865 appeal to Rome had not been judged and there had been no formal excommunication, Guibord could be buried in Catholic ground. In addition, the Sacred Congregation of the Inquisition was considering a new issue, that of the 1868 yearbook, and it had not yet heard the Institut's point of view. Although not a lawyer, Dessaulles took a keen interest in the law, and he claimed that the two conditions for refusing burial on consecrated ground had not been met: in ecclesiastical law, public and specific censure of the individual concerned, and in civil law, public abjuration of the faith. Dessaulles, whose published lecture on tolerance had been placed on the Index – the first document in Canada to suffer this fate – expressed surprise that a good citizen like Guibord was refused what non-believers, criminals, and suicides were granted.

There was also a broader issue: whether, because the Church was responsible for keeping the registers of civil status (baptisms, marriages, burials), it could grant itself power over cemeteries. More generally, there was the question of whether ecclesiastical or civil law took precedence. Dessaulles criticized the ultramontanist claim to precedence: "If the state must be the humble servant of ecclesiastical power and cannot curb its perpetual thirst for omnipotence, it would be better to know it immediately; but there is no evidence that this is so. On the contrary, I am convinced that it is impossible that the enlightened men in charge of the administration of justice in this country will not assert this fundamental principle of public law: that the church is in the state, and that the state is not in the church."[4]

The trial opened in Superior Court, and the arguments were presented from January to April 1870. Joseph Doutre and Rodolphe Laflamme represented the Institut canadien for Henriette Brown, and Francis Cassidy, a founder and two-time president of the Institut who had left in 1867 with L.-A. Jetté and F.-X.-A. Trudel, an ultramontanist whom the liberal press called "the Great Vicar," pleaded in favour of Father Rousselot and the fabrique of Notre-Dame parish. Doutre spoke of "the disregard for a temporal law under pretext of religion" and asked whether "the ecclesiastical power" was "subject to the jurisdiction of the tribunals," and added a few anticlerical barbs, and the opposing party subjected Dessaulles to a long cross-examination, reminding him that he had accused the pope of being a despot during his lectures on annexation in 1850.

On 2 May 1870, Judge Charles Mondelet pronounced judgment.

In consequence of which, this Court orders that a writ of peremptory mandamus be issued immediately, ordering the respondents and the parish priest to give the remains of the said late Joseph Guibord the aforesaid burial, according to the usages of the law, in the said cemetery, as they will be asked to do, and as burial is accorded to the remains of any parishioner who, like him, dies a Roman Catholic; and also to register according to the law in the registers of the said parish of Notre-Dame de Montréal, of which the respondents are the custodians, the death of the said late Joseph Guibord as prescribed by the law.

The judge required that a report be made of the execution of this judgment on 6 May and "condemn[ed] the respondents to pay the costs." The judgment was immediately appealed before the court of error, which reversed it on 10 December 1870. Then the petitioners filed an appeal before the Judicial Committee of the Privy Council in London, which, four years later, on 21 November 1874, reversed the decision of the court of error and, on 23 July 1875, issued a decree ordering that Guibord be buried in the Catholic cemetery of Côte-des-Neiges.[5]

This was a meagre success for Dessaulles, who fled to the United States five days after the decree, and to Europe in September, to escape his creditors. On 29 August, the faithful Doutre obtained a writ of execution of the judgment of the Judicial Committee. The first effort to move Guibord's remains from the Protestant cemetery to the Catholic cemetery was blocked by a crowd of Catholics at the entrance to the cemetery, and the hearse carrying Guibord's coffin had to turn back.

On 8 September, Mgr Bourget signed a pastoral letter to be read the following Sunday in the churches of the diocese, in which he said he understood the "peaceful demonstration" of the faithful who wanted to "keep the cemetery from being profaned" by a man who had died in disgrace. And using his power "to bind and unbind," the ever-combative bishop assured the faithful that "the place in the cemetery where the body of the late Joseph Guibord will be buried, if it is ever buried, will be de facto and will remain ipso facto off limits and separated from the rest of that cemetery." The threat was thus announced, and already the burial was being countered.

On 3 October, the bishop of Montreal published a new pastoral letter setting out the reasons for Guibord's excommunication: he had belonged to an Institut that taught evil doctrines and possessed books that were on the Index, he did not make his confession once a year, nor did he receive communion at Easter. The document also protested the decision of the "Noble Lords" of the Privy Council, which had saddened the bishops, "who had been steadfast in their loyalty."

Finally, on 16 November 1875, the mayor of Montreal mobilized the police force, along with 1,255 soldiers of the Canadian militia, and Guibord's burial in the "Catholic" cemetery took place. The funeral ceremony was minimal; Father Rousselot was present in his capacity as a civil official. In the plot, located in section N, lot 173, the coffin was even covered with cement to discourage vandalism.

The same day, Mgr Bourget signed a final pastoral letter on the Guibord affair; he even suggested a symbolic epitaph for Guibord.

"Here lies," he will exclaim in the recesses of his soul, "the body of the too famous Joseph Guibord, who died in rebellion against the common Father of the Church, under the anathema of the Church; who could not pass the gates of this sacred place save escorted by armed men, as if for battle against the enemies of the country; who, but for the good disposition of his fellow citizens, would have caused blood to flow; who was conducted to this sepulchre, not under the protection of the Cross, but under that of the bayonets of the military; who has been laid in this grave in two feet of earth, not to the impressive chant of the prayers which the Church is accustomed to make for her children, but amid the curses contained in the breasts of the attendants."[6]

The saga was over. The Guibord affair was to be the swan song, the culmination of the conflict between radical liberals and "ultra" ultramontanists.

THE END OF SOMETHING

At the time of Guibord's death, the end of another saga was drawing near, that of the Institut canadien de Montréal. Rome had still not answered the Institut's second petition. Influenced by the briefs of Mgr Bourget and Mgr Laflèche, who argued that an association could not be "indifferent" in religious terms, the Sacred Congregations of the Inquisition and of the Index placed the 1869 yearbook of the Institut canadien de Montréal – which contained two lectures by Dessaulles, one on Guibord and the other on the Index – on the Index. Although the Institut canadien remained active until 1880, the great saga that had begun in 1848 was over.[7] Its end coincided with the unification, in 1870, of Italy, which had also begun in 1848, and with the Vatican council that declared the pope infallible in matters of dogma.

Papineau's death on 25 September 1871 also recalls the trajectory of liberalism, which started around 1815, reached a high point in 1837, and began its decline around 1848. His death set in motion events that, although private, bore a certain similarity to the Guibord case.[8] It left a taste of ashes and the sense of an ending – the end of an era. Four months later, on 26 December, Le Pays ceased publication, after L'Union nationale (1867) and the ephemeral La Lanterne (1868–1869), published by Arthur Buies. Radical liberalism, which had had no significant electoral base since 1867, and which saw the Liberal Party of Quebec become the Parti national, was also without resources: Le Pays was dead, and although the Institut canadien continued to operate its library for a few more years, the voices of its speakers were stilled, with a final lecture by Buies on 22 April 1871.

THE "CATHOLIC PROGRAM": THE "HOLY WAR"
OF THE ULTRA ULTRAMONTANISTS (1871)

The infighting among the French Canadian Catholic clergy and the radicalization of some ultramontanists began in 1865 with the dismemberment of the Sulpician parish of Montreal, which had led the bishop of Quebec City, Mgr Taschereau, the Séminaire de Québec, and the bishop of Saint-Hyacinthe, Mgr Charles Larocque, to ally themselves with the Sulpicians against Mgr Bourget. This ecclesiastical rivalry was fuelled by the clergy's territorial ambitions: Montreal was the fief of the Sulpicians, Quebec City of the Séminaire de Québec, Ottawa of the Oblates, and Joliette of the Clercs de Saint-Viateur. The radicalization of individuals such as Abbé Alexis Pelletier, alias Luigi, and newspapers such as Le Nouveau Monde of Montreal led Abbé Raymond of Saint-Hyacinthe to observe in 1870: "The evil to be feared in this country at the moment is not Gallicanism or liberalism, but rather this Phariseeism that sees evil everywhere except in itself."[9]

It was Mgr Bourget's disciple in Trois-Rivières, Mgr Laflèche, who launched a plan for a Catholic theocracy that would have a popular aspect in the clergy's role in elections and a learned aspect in its definition of Catholic liberalism. On the eve of elections, the bishop of Trois-Rivières would invite his fellow Catholics to make sure "that the candidate to whom you give your vote is duly qualified in both respects [religious and temporal], and that he offers all the moral guarantees appropriate for the protection of such serious interests." He explained: "You must therefore distrust those false doctors ... who sometimes tell you that elections are not the concern of priests and that they should not speak of them in the pulpit."[10] The events during the election of 1867 came back to the forefront, as did what was beginning to be called "the undue influence" of the clergy.

The Guibord affair had alerted the most extreme ultramontanists, those most jealous of the supremacy of the Church over the state in mixed issues. The 1864 federal law on marriage – or divorce, depending on the point of view – the new Civil Code of 1866, the struggle for a confessional education system with Section 93 of the Constitution of 1867, and the bitter taste left by the British decision in favour of Guibord and the Institut canadien de Montréal led people such as F.-X.-A. Trudel, one of the lawyers for the fabrique of Notre-Dame, to create, if not a political party, at least a "Catholic program," which candidates would have to accept in order to be elected by "true" Catholics. On 20 April 1871, *Le Journal des Trois-Rivières* published this program, which stipulated: "Full and entire adherence to Roman Catholic doctrines in religion, politics and social economics must be the first and main qualification that Catholic electors must demand of Catholic candidates."

Mgr Bourget and Mgr Laflèche publicly supported the Catholic Program, while bishops Larocque, Langevin, and Taschereau opposed it; Taschereau disapproved of it because it was "formulated without any participation on the part of the bishops." The Catholic press also took sides in favour of (*Le Nouveau Monde*, *Le Courrier du Canada*, *Le Journal des Trois-Rivières*) or against (*L'Ordre*, *L'Union des Cantons de l'Est*, and *Le Pionnier* in Sherbrooke) the program. The situation was becoming embarrassing for Catholics, and *Le Constitutionnel* in Trois-Rivières expressed this in its 26 May 1871 issue: "Our population thus faces the deplorable choice of displeasing two bishops or disobeying three." The intervention of the Church in temporal and political affairs had a price, and Dessaulles had clearly indicated its consequences when he wrote, on 3 June 1871: "It should be evident to any reasonable man that the clergy cannot always remain unanimous once involved in the political arena, which is always turbulent." The celebration of the golden anniversary of the ordination of Mgr Bourget on 29 October 1872 deepened this internal conflict: the Jesuit Braun, whose order was about to ask for a university in Montreal, praised the ultramontanist option, which greatly displeased Mgr Larocque and Mgr Langevin, as well as Taschereau, who walked out.[11] The conservative *Journal de Québec* even wrote, on 2 November: "This golden anniversary has been nothing but a pretext, or to speak more frankly, an ambush to make bishops, priests and lay people fall into the chasm of the Program."

Catholics who were not "programists" or avowed ultramontanists were soon considered to be among the "Catholic liberals." It was mainly the clergy of the diocese of Quebec City around Mgr Taschereau, Université Laval, and the Séminaire de Québec who were targeted. Following the publication of a book on liberalism by Abbé Benjamin Pâquet in 1872, a scholarly quarrel broke out around orthodoxy. Abbé Pâquet, a theologian educated in Rome who served as the Quebec City clergy's agent to the Roman congregations, even had the second edition of his book praised by La Civilta cattolica: "Reading this book from Canada gave us the pleasure one feels in hearing a faithful echo from afar; the farther and the more faithful is the echo, the greater the pleasure." The theology professor summed liberalism up as "the spirit of evil": "free inquiry, free thought, independence of science and reason, rationalism, indifferentism, tolerance." Although he cited the Syllabus of Errors of 1864, which stated that the proposition that the pope should reconcile himself and come to terms with liberalism was false, he also claimed to favour "a free Church in a free State."

The ultramontanist Abbé Alexis Pelletier could not allow such laxity to go unchallenged. Under the pseudonym A. de F., he published a pamphlet attacking Abbé Pâquet's "doctrine of tolerance" and his "accommodations." For him, there could be no question of "tolerating" or "living in peace with error, as far as possible," since Jesus Christ had not done so.[12]

Abbé Raymond of Saint-Hyacinthe, the cultivated cleric who had been involved in a controversy with Dessaulles and had responded to his lecture on tolerance, came to the rescue of his colleague from Quebec City, declaring himself fundamentally in agreement with him. At the conclusion of a public lecture at the Union catholique de Saint-Hyacinthe on 8 December 1872 on "the action of Mary in society," he made the following remarks, which were unexpected but relevant to the circumstances: "There is no liberalism here in the sense condemned by the vicar of Christ; because this is clearly not political liberalism. No one among those professing Catholicism maintains that freedom of religion, speech and the press is an absolute principle; no one claims that the best political system is one in which the State is indifferent to all religion." Neither did he find Gallicanism, "the subjection of the Church to the State." The few provisions of the Civil Code that bore the mark of Gallicanism should be amended "when the time is right," without haste or conflict. The superior of the Séminaire de Saint-Hyacinthe was proud to be able to say that "orthodoxy prevails among us."

This was too much for Mgr Pinsoneault, alias Binan, and Abbé Pelletier, alias Luigi. In a pamphlet that first appeared as a series of articles in *Le Franc-Parleur* beginning on 11 January 1873, Mgr Pinsoneault identified Raymond as a "liberal Catholic" by virtue of his sympathies (Montalembert, Dupanloup, Falloux, even Lamennais) and antipathies (Veuillot, Mgr Pie, the ultramontanist school). He described Raymond's lecture on tolerance as "imitating Montalembert and Dupanloup" and claimed: "He can neither say nor write anything without burning the purest incense of his admiration on the altar of liberal Catholicism."

From January to March 1873, in the well-named *Franc-Parleur*, Abbé Pelletier, alias Luigi, published his response to the positions of Abbé Raymond, a long treatise in which he maintained that liberalism and Gallicanism were both present in Canada: "Moderate liberalism or Catholic liberalism teaches that peace, tranquillity and the conformity of thoughts and feelings are so precious that, to obtain them, one may sacrifice certain laws of truth; that to win over those who have erroneous beliefs, to lead them imperceptibly to renounce them, it is permissible to make some concessions, to bend certain principles a little to the viewpoints of adversaries when the inflexibility of these principles is too off-putting." According to Catholic liberalism as defined by "Luigi," truth must be softened and error treated with kid gloves, and compromise was acceptable in attenuating circumstances. And pressure was put on those who spoke "frankly and clearly," such as *Le Nouveau Monde* or Abbé Proulx exiled in the Beauce, a veritable "penal colony." To "Luigi," Canadian liberalism was no different from European liberalism in its nature, characteristics, and behaviour.

It was at this point that Dessaulles, still in Canada, published a pamphlet on "the great ecclesiastical war," whose title alone announced the author's intention: to criticize this fight among the clergy and point out that, sooner or later, clerics would be fighting in the political arena.[13]

The fact that liberals were capitalizing on their internal quarrels did not stop the clergy. Mgr Pinsoneault undertook to establish a connection between the Catholic electoral program and the quarrel on "Catholic" liberalism. In a book of "letters to a member of Parliament," first published as articles in the relentless *Franc-Parleur* from March to June 1874, the uncompromising cleric sought to provide a "course in Christian politics," identifying the "duties" of a member of Parliament battling "Compromisers."

A pamphlet published in 1875 by "Luigi," providing an "overview of European and Canadian liberalism," was the grand finale of this escalating battle around orthodoxy. In it, he demonstrated that the two liberalisms were utterly identical, summed up the ultramontanism expressed in the Catholic Program and reviewed the history of the French Canadian counter-revolutionary tradition. He compared "impious liberalism" in Europe (1789, the Rights of Man, the separation of church and state) and Canada (popular sovereignty, equality and freedom of religion as promoted by *L'Avenir* and the Institut canadien de Montréal) and blamed Catholic liberalism for having a policy of conciliation and a fear of "inflaming minds." *Le Courrier du Canada*, having on 21 July 1875 asked the question "What is liberalism?" must have expected an answer, sooner or later. And the answer came.[14]

In this context, two events occurred that were to be important in the long term: the arrival of the Dominicans in Canada in 1873 and the abolition of the Ministry of Public Instruction in Quebec in December 1875. The Dominicans, the Order of Preachers, had been re-established in France by Father Lacordaire, a former friend of Lamennais, and they inherited in Canada the reputation their superior had acquired in France. The order was perceived as liberal and "tolerant," and the first Dominicans who visited or settled in Saint-Hyacinthe were surprised to find that Canada reminded them of France of the ancien régime.[15]

It would seem that the ultramontanists, who, along with the Protestants, had obtained a confessional education system in 1867, had no reason to worry about the control of public education. Yet in some circles, the Ministry of Public Instruction created in 1867 seemed too much like a state institution. The circumstances in part explain its abolition. First there was the fact that Premier Chauveau's double mandate as premier and education minister was too demanding. Then there was the division of the ministry into two denominational sectors, one Catholic and one Protestant, as a concession to the Protestants, which created a precedent. But ultimately, the abolition was for ideological reasons. At the height of the ultramontanist radicalization and pressure, the Conservative premier Boucher de Boucherville decided to make "elementary education safe from any dangerous influences, in a refined and calm atmosphere in which neither the spirit of caste nor political agitation will be felt." Mgr Langevin was pleased "to see many of our politicians so well disposed to recognize and respect the rights of the Church in education."

This decision did not promote democracy: it replaced an elected minister who was responsible to the Legislative Assembly with a superintendent who had no public responsibility for his acts but, rather, executed the decisions of the Catholic and Protestant public education committees. These committees constituted a ministry without the name or responsibility, but with one crucial distinction: the Catholic committee was composed of the bishops of the province of Quebec ex officio and an equal number of lay people.

Given the infighting among the bishops and clergy, and the fact that a future superintendent of public education "with no political connections" would be Gédéon Ouimet, an embattled politician who had resigned as premier, Boucher de Boucherville's argument about calm is unconvincing.[16] The decision by the politicians to abolish the Ministry of Public Instruction was equivalent to simply abandoning education to the Catholic bishops and the Protestant authorities. The politicians had to give way so that the clergy could occupy a terrain it claimed as its own.

THE MANY WAYS OF BEING LIBERAL, AND "UNDUE INFLUENCE"

Catholics and ultramontanists had been trying since 1871 to answer the question, "What is liberalism?" and liberals had been preparing their own answer for some time. But since 1867, the answer had varied according to electoral and ideological ups and downs. Twice, in 1868 and 1876, Arthur Buies, who belonged to a new generation of liberals, provided the same answer: "Today there are many ways to be liberal; but it seems the most fashionable consists of being liberal while repudiating liberalism." Himself a radical who did not repudiate liberalism, he wrote: "Let us make a distinction between what is called, with cruel irony, the 'Liberal Party' and the many individuals, serious liberals, real liberals, who burn with desire to escape from this party that represents nothing, that signifies nothing, that is thus not a real principle expressed in a program, and whose constant motto, whether in power or in opposition, is: concession, hedging, equivocation, beating about the bush, playing for time, hypocrisy."[17]

The leadership of the Liberal Party had also changed: Wilfrid Laurier, who had left the Institut canadien de Montréal in 1865 and had opposed Confederation, was elected to the Legislative Assembly of Quebec in 1871 after experiencing first-hand what an election campaign was in the context of the Catholic Program, with intervention by the clergy and accusations of Rougism and radicalism. The day after the election, he wrote: "The liberals of 1871 cannot be the same in men or in principles as what they were in 1848, a period of liberal revival." The young member of the Assembly was beginning to foresee a future for this Liberal Party, even though he participated in 1872 in the founding of the Parti national, a moderate reformist party. Fabre, always present at turning points in the history of liberalism, had a different view of the situation from that of Buies: "The Liberal party is not dead … it still exists, although without *L'Avenir* and *Le Pays*. It has become a purely political party."[18]

On 29 January 1874, when Antoine-Aimé Dorion, the leader of the Quebec Liberal Party since 1854, was appointed a judge, Laurier was

elected to the House of Commons, where the Mackenzie government
took 206 out of 276 seats (34 out of 65 of them in Quebec). The hope
to which this gave rise justified the continued search for a political line,
even if some commentators, such as Oscar Dunn, felt that Quebec would
always be conservative.

This is not the triumph of liberal principles; not having suffered, the Liberals
have no glory now. It is very clear that the mass of the people has remained conservative: we mean the word not in the sense of being partisans of this candidate
or that, but in the broad sense of an innate or reasoned attachment to the country, its constitutions, its laws and Catholic doctrine. Our province is conservative
in this way, and anything that smacks of annexation to the United States or irreligion is met with an invincible antipathy. The majority is at the moment grouped
around the Liberal leaders, but it would be a serious mistake to suppose that that
means it approves of their past; rather, it has accepted them because it believes
they have gotten over their former exaggerations.

In his first speech in the House of Commons, Laurier provided some
elements of an answer concerning his party's definition of liberalism:
"The liberals among French Canadians are not like the liberals of France
and the other European countries ... who are ready to overthrow the
government at any moment. We are more like the liberals of England,
who have been working for so many years to introduce reforms by constitutional means."[19]

In 1875, the Quebec legislature passed a law on "undue influence"
based on the federal law of 1874. Section 258 of this law stipulated:
"Every person who, directly or indirectly, by himself or by any other person on his behalf, makes use of, or threatens to make use of any force,
violence or restraint, or inflicts or threatens the infliction by himself,
or by or through any other person, of any injury, damage, harm, or loss, or
in any manner practises intimidation upon or against any person, in
order to induce or compel such person to vote or refrain from voting,
or on account of such person having voted or refrained from voting at
any election" was liable to legal action. Henceforth, parish priests who
intervened in the electoral process, as had been the practice since at
least 1867, could be brought before the civil courts and obliged to defend themselves.

The bishop of Rimouski, Mgr Jean Langevin, took a dim view of this
law: he believed that "the partisans of these dangerous doctrines" wanted
to "reduce the just and salutary influence of the clergy over the masses
and destroy anything that can stand in the way of their plans against the
freedom and rights of the Church; they want to take exclusive hold of

the education of young people ... this is to make material interests predominate over spiritual and religious interests."[20]

Laurier was careful to distance himself from the "impious liberalism" of Europe so harshly criticized by "Luigi" and the "programists." At an election meeting in Sainte-Croix de Lotbinière, on 6 June 1875, he said:

When the Conservative Party dons the mantle of religion, it is merely putting on a mask. I recognize that there have been dangerous men in Europe who called themselves liberals, although the only thing liberal about them was the name. Theirs is not the liberalism of my party. We are liberals the way they are liberal in England, we are liberals like O'Connell, John Bright and Richard Cobden. O'Connell, who valiantly defended the [Catholic] religion in the British parliament, was one of our leaders; we draw our doctrines from there, and not from those so-called liberals who try to impose their ideas by violence and bloodshed ... I don't want anybody dredging up the old rags of the red party in France to throw in our face. No, the Liberal Party has nothing to do with socialists and communists.[21]

To accompany the Catholic Program and provide instructions for Catholic voters, the bishops of the ecclesiastical province of Quebec published a pastoral letter and a circular letter to the clergy on 22 September 1875. The pastoral letter, written by Mgr Langevin, gave rise to a lot of controversy. In it, he stated that "being a liberal Catholic cannot be permitted in all conscience," that seeking to restrict priests to the sacristy was equivalent to practising "moral independence" and that the intervention of priests was justified when spiritual ends were threatened: "There are indeed political questions that concern the spiritual interests of souls, either because they concern faith and morality, or because they may affect the freedom, the independence or the existence of the Church, even in temporal terms."

The document bore the imprint of the Catholic Program in the way it addressed the question of the masks of Catholic liberalism and that of "conciliation."

Do not trust this liberalism that wants to adorn itself with the fine name of Catholic the better to carry out its criminal work. You can recognize it easily by the description the Supreme Pontiff has often made: 1° Efforts to submit the Church to the state; 2° Constant attempts to break the ties that unite the children of the Church to each other and the clergy; 3° Monstrous mixture of truth and error, under the pretext of reconciling all things and avoiding conflicts; 4° Finally, illusion, and sometimes hypocrisy: beneath a religious exterior and fine protestations of submission to the Church hides measureless arrogance.[22]

Some non-intransigent Catholics – those the extreme ultramontanists called liberal Catholics – found it hard to live with this position. On 25 May 1876, Mgr Taschereau, the archbishop of Quebec, who had just learned that Rome had supported him on the establishment of a second Catholic university, in Montreal, published a pastoral letter qualifying the collective statement of 22 September 1875. In it, he said that the Liberal Party and the Conservative Party were on the same footing, which was a way of saying that the earlier pastoral letter was not aimed at the Liberal Party exclusively.

Beginning in the summer of 1876, two events helped settle the issue of the duty and right of the clergy to intervene in the civil and temporal process of elections. In Charlevoix county, the victory of the Conservative Langevin over Pierre-Alexis Tremblay in January was confirmed in the summer when the election was contested before Judge Routhier, a "pro-gramist" known for his militant ultramontanism. On 28 February 1877, the case was appealed on the grounds of undue influence, and Judge Taschereau, brother of the archbishop of Quebec, invalidated the election of Langevin, who was the brother of the bishop of Rimouski.

A similar scenario took place in Bonaventure county: Judge Casault annulled the election on the following grounds:

(1) That for a Catholic priest to threaten to refuse the sacraments to those voting for a certain candidate constitutes an act of undue influence according to clause 258 of the Quebec Electoral Act. (2) That when parish priests are actively involved in favour of one of the candidates in an election, who declares in a speech to the electors that he is the candidate of the clergy, that the clergy asked him to run, and that without the assurance of their support he would not have agreed to be a candidate, these priests will be considered the candidate's agents to the point of making him responsible for their actions. (3) That if, in the presence of a candidate, a priest acting as his agent threatens to refuse his parishioners the sacraments if they vote for an opposing candidate, the candidate present will be considered to have consented to this act of undue influence and to have approved of it, and will be disqualified if, in a speech delivered a few hours later, he presents himself as the candidate of the clergy and does not disavow the threats or otherwise withdraw his responsibility.

As Bonaventure county was in Mgr Langevin's diocese, which covered the lower St Lawrence region, he published a pastoral letter against Judge Casault's decision on 15 January 1877. Imitating the papal *Syllabus* of 1864, he declared "unworthy of the sacraments" those who supported the following five statements: "(1) Parliament is omnipotent and is competent to pass any law, even one opposed to the exercise of religion;

(2) Electors must have absolute freedom; (3) It is up to the civil courts to repress abuses that may occur in preaching and the refusal of sacraments; (4) The threat by Pastors of the Church to refuse the sacraments in connection with elections constitutes undue influence, a highly fraudulent manoeuvre of which the civil courts must be made aware; (5) An unjust oath must be observed."[23]

To Mgr Moreau, the new bishop of Saint-Hyacinthe, these judgments were "nothing but the public and solemn condemnation of our collective letter, the decrees issued by our recent councils, our instructions to parish priests, and finally, our instructions to the faithful concerning their duties during elections."

Although the period of conflict among bishops was not over, a period of conflict between bishops and the civil or temporal authority seemed to be starting. To avoid confrontation, in April 1877, Rome sent Mgr George Conroy, with the directive that the pope did not intend to condemn the Liberal Party, but only Catholics who professed a so-called liberal Catholicism.[24]

LAURIER'S SPEECH ON LIBERALISM (1877)

It was in this general context of debate on the meaning of liberalism and the trial regarding "undue influence," a context in which the Rouges were identified with Hell and the Bleus with Heaven, that Wilfrid Laurier – who had been a member of Parliament since 1874, after sitting in the Quebec legislature from 1871 to 1874, and was now the new leader of the Liberal Party – made a forceful speech at the Club canadien in Quebec City on 26 June 1877.

Aware that his party was in "a false position in public opinion," Laurier sought to define the principles of the Liberal Party and respond to the accusations against the party, which he summed up – the style of the *Syllabus* is present even in his speech – in "the following propositions: (1) Liberalism is a new form of evil, a heresy already virtually condemned by the head of the Church; (2) A Catholic cannot be a Liberal." Laurier's rhetoric of persuasion relied on four arguments. First of all, he claimed to be utterly unqualified to define Catholic liberalism, while maintaining at the same time that Catholic liberalism was not political Liberalism.

Then, he retold in his own fashion the history of the Liberal Party "since 1848," the history of *L'Avenir* and *Le Pays* and that of the Institut canadien de Montréal, excusing it and presenting it as commonplace: "The only excuse for these Liberals was their youth." And while recognizing their initiatives with regard to the abolition of seigneurial tenure, judicial decentralization, and colonization, he said: "As for the old programme, nothing whatever remains of its social part, while, of the political part, there only remain the principles of the English Liberal party."

He then minimized the threat of liberalism by presenting it as part of human nature, as a question of "diversities of temper ... drawn in opposite directions by the charm of habit and by the charm of novelty," by the attachment to "whatever is ancient" or the tendency to "give every change credit for being an improvement." He took advantage of the opportunity to make a little dig: "Indeed, more revolutions have been caused by Conservative obstinacy than by Liberal exaggeration."

He now came to the heart of his argument: to show that Canadian liberalism was of British and reformist inspiration, and not of French revolutionary inspiration. He began by explaining the origin of this confusion in the excessive respect for French history and the neglect of English history: "Our French education leads us naturally to study the history of modern liberty, not in the classic land of liberty, not in the history of old England, but among the peoples of the continent of Europe, of the same origin and faith as ourselves. And there, unfortunately, the history of liberty has been written in letters of blood ... In all classes of educated society may be seen loyal souls, who, frightened by these mournful pages, regard with terror the spirit of liberty, imagining that it must produce here the same disasters and the same crimes as in the countries I have just referred to."

The English, on the contrary, had been and were able to channel human aspirations; they had carried out "a series of reforms which has made the English people the freest people and the most prosperous and happy of Europe." And if the English people had not had this sense of reform, he asked, "Do you think that riot would not have raised its hideous head under the windows of Westminster and that the blood of civil war would not have reddened the streets of London, as it has so often reddened the streets of Paris?" His purpose here was to dissociate the Liberal Party of Canada from those European so-called liberals who were nothing more than revolutionaries, to put an end to accusations that judged "the political situation of the country, not according to what is happening in it, but according to what is happening in France" and to make people understand that in Canada, the principles of the Liberal Party were based on those of the great Liberal Party of England.

Finally, Laurier could not fail to speak of the question of undue influence. As a consistent liberal, he gave the priest "the right to take part in political affairs," "to instruct the people in what he believes to be their duty." But while recognizing this "indisputable right," he believed that the priest had "every thing to lose by meddling in the ordinary questions of politics" and that the right to participate ended "at the spot where it encroaches on the elector's independence" to vote according to his conscience, without intimidation.[25]

Hector Fabre, who had been paving the way for this reformism since 1858, stated in *L'Événement* that Laurier "opened up a path and showed us the way ... Now we know where we are going."

Mgr Conroy, who had most likely been sent the text of Laurier's speech, had already decided by August 1877 that the bishops' collective letter of 22 September 1875 hinted of censure of the Liberal Party. His dealings with the bishops led to the writing of a new pastoral letter on elections. Two days after Laurier joined the federal Liberal cabinet, the bishops wrote: "We are following the example of the Holy See, which, when it condemned the errors of Catholic liberalism, abstained from naming people or political parties. Indeed, there is no Pontifical condemnation of any political party; all the condemnations issued to date by this venerable source pertain only to the Liberal-Catholics and their principles." In a circular letter accompanying the pastoral letter, the bishops recommended to parish priests: "When you explain to your people the principles that should guide their choices, leave it up to each person's conscience to apply the principles to people and parties." They added: "The decree of the Fourth Council implicitly forbids teaching from the pulpit or elsewhere that it is a sin to vote for a specific candidate or political party, let alone telling people you will refuse them the sacraments for that reason."[26]

CONCLUSION

Against the backdrop of the disappearance of the Institut canadien de Montréal, *Le Pays*, *L'Union nationale*, and *La Lanterne* and the death of Louis-Joseph Papineau, the victory in the Guibord affair was bitter, a swan song heard in the cemetery. Guibord was buried in the Catholic cemetery of Côte-des-Neiges, which was later deconsecrated within the perimeter of his remains, but there was no real glory in this legal triumph.

The ultramontanist counterpart of this final liberal victory was the Catholic Program. Like the Guibord affair, this theocratic program was a final hurrah – in this case, of radical conservatism.

It is easier to understand, in the context of this escalating conflict, how tolerance became the real issue of the decade. It was to the principle of tolerance that Dessaulles appealed in his defence of the Institut canadien de Montréal; it was this principle Abbé Raymond rejected when he said that "all conviction is essentially intolerant." And it was a lack of tolerance that marked the behaviour of Mgr Bourget regarding the

Institut canadien de Montréal, which was censured by Rome and had two of its yearbooks placed on the Index.

Tolerance not only divided the liberals from the ultramontanists; it also distinguished ordinary ultramontanists from extreme ultramontanists. Those whom "Luigi," "Binan," and the aptly named *Le Franc-Parleur* described as Catholic liberals or liberal Catholics earned these epithets by their tolerance; unlike the radical ultramontanists, they were sometimes willing to compromise.

The liberals were divided by the same sort of questions about liberalism. Buies well understood how many varieties of liberalism there were at the beginning of the 1870s, a few years before Laurier's 1877 speech. Already in 1871, Laurier stated that the Liberal Party of 1871 was not the one of 1848. In 1874, in response to "Luigi"'s pamphlet likening European and Canadian liberalism, Laurier distinguished between Canadian liberalism and continental European liberalism, in particular, French and Italian liberalism. In 1877, he further distinguished between a liberalism that was "purely political" (as Fabre put it) and an ideological liberalism: a Catholic could thus vote Liberal, because the Liberal Party was not, was no longer, what it had been in 1848; it did not take the revolutionary liberalism of France or Italy as its model, but rather the reform-minded liberalism of England. This liberalism was reformist and not anticlerical.

This was what the delegate of Rome, Mgr Conroy, made the bishops recognize in their collective letter of 1877: the Church did not have to condemn one or several political parties; the age of undue influence was over, politics must be allowed to exist and individual voters must be allowed to vote according to their consciences. Can one imagine a sweeter victory than this triumph of the individual for an English-style liberal?

Reformist liberalism and moderate ultramontanism were the descending curves of two trajectories: that of a liberalism that became radicalized in 1848, changed in 1858 because of a split led by Hector Fabre, and culminated in Laurier's 1877 speech; and that of a battle led by the bishop of Montreal, who rebuilt the French Canadian Church in what had become the economic and cultural metropolis of the province of Quebec, and whose tenacity grew in proportion to the opposition he faced from the radical liberals. Mgr Bourget's fellow Catholics in Quebec City, who had not known the insurrections and the radical liberalism of the union period, found it easier to seek a middle ground and thus to seem liberal and tolerant.

A Manifest Destiny for French Canada in America (1854–1877)

LAURIER IN 1877 DEFINED the doctrine and electoral strategy of the Liberal Party by denying its French sources and emphasizing its English roots, as though one could at this time provide the electorate with an image of itself in which England featured more prominently than France. His 1877 speech was delivered in a context marked by the rejection of annexationism, the end of the Civil War in the United States, and the presence of Rome in Quebec, in the person of the papal delegate Mgr Conroy.

During the second half of the nineteenth century, with the development of Lower Canada, United Canada, and then Canada, French Canada's political and cultural "mother countries" played a larger role in its search for its identity. References to its cultural and political legacies from abroad became more frequent, making it necessary to weigh the relative contributions of France, England, the United States, and Rome to the identity under construction in French Canada.

ENGLAND IS ADMIRED ONCE AGAIN

The image of England in French Canada had changed since 1840. With the granting of responsible government in 1848, La Fontaine and Cartier had managed to convince their fellow citizens to forget the Russell Resolutions of 1837; at the same time, Papineau had fallen from the upper ranks of political popularity. Laurier took over from Sir Louis-Hippolyte La Fontaine and Sir George-Étienne Cartier, and became, in his turn, a "Sir." If the perfectly bilingual Laurier, with his Scottish mother and his English-style upbringing, could offer French Canadians this political Britishism, this liberal idealization of the metropolis, it was because the anti-colonialism of 1830 and 1837 had been forgotten and the great decade of constitutional struggles that had culminated in armed resistance had given way to admiration for Queen Victoria's empire. Under Laurier's influence, French Canada experienced anew the admiration for England it had felt before 1830.[1]

THE FRENCH CANADIANS REDISCOVER FRANCE

The publication of Isidore Lebrun's *Tableau statistique et politique des deux Canadas* (Statistical and political portrait of the two Canadas) in 1833 had failed to arouse much interest, while the France of the period following the coup d'état of 2 December 1851 was of interest mainly to Mgr Bourget, who recruited 225 religious of various congregations between 1837 and 1876.

French Canadians travelled in France before the middle of the century, taking advantage of the regular trans-Atlantic crossings between Le Havre and New York that began in 1864, but it was only in the mid-1850s that France resurfaced in Quebec current affairs. In spring 1855, in Paris, Joseph-Guillaume Barthe, a member of the Institut canadien de Montréal, published a book whose content was as odd as its title. In *Le Canada reconquis par la France* (Canada reconquered by France), Barthe proposed that the Institut canadien de Montréal affiliate with the Institut de France and wore himself out trying to persuade the administration and Paris literary circles to make this a reality. Barthe's goal, essentially a response to the ignorance of French Canada that he encountered in France, was more an alliance than an actual reconquest. He did, however, write: "France, this is what we are made of, look at what we have done to remain faithful to you. Now it is up to you to decide whether we should be punished for this loyalty by your complete abandonment."

The French press showed little interest in Barthe's efforts, while the French Canadian press used various arguments to criticize the whole idea of a reconquest of (French) Canada. The conservative newspapers were not interested in seeing the Rouges of the two continents join forces, especially since, as *La Minerve*, which had a way with words, put it, "today's Rouges in our country merely imitate those in France, who trampled on the crown of gold and the crown of thorns." *Le Canadien* of 17 September 1855 reprinted an article from Veuillot's *L'Univers* slamming Barthe's book: "The curious thing is that in Canada, M. Barthe is not a leader but a follower of the socialist and anti-religious party that exalts Protestantism and advocates annexation to the United States." *Le Journal de Québec* was even sceptical about whether democracy would continue if France were to reconquer Canada: "We do not see any moral or political interest for the Canadian populations in exchanging one imperial status for another, when their situation, which is more democratic

than otherwise, suits them well ... France would be morally and politically required to allow Canada to keep the full advantage of its liberal
and almost entirely democratic institutions, and that would not corre-
spond ... to the current state of French political life." But it was *La Patrie*
that subjected Barthe's efforts to the most irony, in a series of articles that
ran from July to October 1855. Alfred Rambaud, the editor, had a bit of
fun at Barthe's expense – "Reading M. Barthe two or three times is already enough torture to atone for all the capital sins committed by all
the staff of *La Patrie*" – before pointing out the extravagance of what was
not actually Barthe's plan: "Although we love France as one loves a distant relative, although we celebrate her triumphs and are pleased that
she is so highly esteemed throughout the world, although we are proud
to descend from the most civilized and most chivalrous people in the
world, the *Canadiens* are attached to their adopted land ... It would be
wrong to say that *Canadiens* want Canada to return to French domination, because they are aware that that would necessarily be accompanied
by bloody disorder and a murderous civil war, a horrible fate that they
would never embrace." Even *Le Pays* offered anti-colonial reasons for not
wanting a reconquest of Canada by France: "For self-respecting men,
colonial status, under whatever power, is so incompatible with the ideas
of national and individual dignity that it hardly matters whether the
mother country ... is on the continent or in the British Isles." A French
traveller who visited Canada in 1851 had the same impression: "Today,
there is not a soul that dreams of becoming French again."[2] Although
Barthe's efforts certainly led to no reconquest, they did have an advantage for the Institut canadien de Montréal and its little museum, which
received books and engravings from the government of Napoleon III.

"OUR PEOPLE" RETURN: *LA CAPRICIEUSE* SAILS UP
THE ST LAWRENCE (1855)

The arrival of the French frigate *La Capricieuse*, commanded by Paul-
Henri Belvèze, at the port of Quebec City on 13 July 1855, and its stay in
Quebec until 25 August, created great excitement in French Canada. It
was the first time since the British conquest and the cession of the colony
of Canada by France that a French ship had sailed up the St Lawrence.
The reasons are as follows. The abrogation of Britain's Navigation Acts in
1850 opened Canadian ports to non-British ships. Then, the old enemies Britain and France were brought together by the need to defend
Turkey against Russia in the Crimea. Their Entente Cordiale lasted from
April 1854 until September 1855. But most important, the ongoing development of capitalism in France led to a search for new markets, the

opening of new consulates to foster French trade, and the decision to host the second Universal Exhibition in 1855, four years after the London Exhibition, and rekindled France's colonial ambitions, whether regarding Algeria or Canada.

All the speeches, celebrations, receptions, and toasts reawakened old memories: on 26 June 1855 *Le Journal de Québec* described *La Capricieuse* as arriving "in the name and under the flag of the old country, our beautiful France, which is today England's closest ally; and Canada will greet her as one greets an old friend one has not seen for a long time, but whose memory has remained dear and is still present, and whom one finally sees again with all the heady joy of the beginning." At a banquet held for Captain Belvèze by the Institut canadien de Montréal, Robillard, its president, declared: "France left us French at the time of our last and painful goodbyes; she finds us still French after so many years of absence." The poet Octave Crémazie immortalized the nostalgia French Canadians felt for France in his poem "The Old Canadian Soldier":

Like that old soldier who sang your glory,
An unknown bard, I told his story,
On those same ramparts we will walk,
Surveying there that river flowing,
Waiting for you still, we will be saying:
Do they not appear?[3]

No, they did not appear, for the French Canadians had found in the Entente Cordiale the magic formula for their dual allegiance. A few days after Captain Belvèze unveiled a monument to the brave French and English soldiers who had died in the Battle of Sainte-Foy, Pierre-Joseph-Olivier Chauveau declared, in the name of the Association Saint-Jean-Baptiste of Quebec City, "that we have shown to the new flag the same loyalty our forefathers showed to the old one." The Entente Cordiale also resolved the conflict concerning two mother countries: "our old and new mother countries, despairing of being able to conquer each other, decided to dominate the rest of the world together."[4] How glorious it was to be the colony and ex-colony of the two greatest powers of the time!

The bubble of joyous unanimity was burst by *Le Moniteur*, the liberal Montreal counterpart of *Le Pays*, two days before the departure of *La Capricieuse*: "M. de Belvèze should put aside his dishonest mission … but not a single democrat was taken in by the sermons, answers and shouts of the servant of the coup d'état; not a single thinking man believed in the oral or written expression of this officer of Napoleon III; the Bible story of the master and the servant is too well-known." *Le Moniteur* recommended, "tearing off the veil that hides M. de Belvèze and his intentions." *La Patrie,* however, refused to see the visit of *La Capricieuse* in political terms: "France cannot conquer us, and neither would it want to try; the very idea is ridiculous; there would be no advantage in doing so, and it would be cruelly difficult."[5]

The symbolic value of the visit of *La Capricieuse* seems more important than the economic results: it did not come close to attaining its commercial objective, but a French consulate did open in Canada in 1858, and Canada participated in the Universal Exhibition in Paris in 1855, and, according to *Le Journal de Québec* of 16 February 1855, had to "maintain its reputation in France and show its mother country that she had abandoned a possession worthy of greater care." The paper viewed the exhibition as "an opportunity for a country to make itself known, especially when, like ours, it is essentially unknown; considered by a great many people as a few *arpents* of snow inhabited by tattooed cannibals, where a few colonists struggle to survive." Even Canada's representative to the Paris Exhibition, Joseph-Charles Taché, could not suppress a certain resentment in a "sketch of Canada" he prepared for the exhibition, in which he alluded to France's abandonment of Canada and the "million French people [who] who grew up forgotten there!" He regretted that "all too often in France, everything that is accomplished in North America is attributed to the Americans" and argued vigorously in favour of French emigration to Canada.[6]

France, which had just opened a consulate in Canada, had a very particular image of the North American continent – that is, the United States – as mercantile and materialistic, which reinforced the image held by French Canadians themselves. Returning to France after visiting the United States and Canada in 1851, Xavier Marmier wrote, in the spirit of Tocqueville twenty years earlier: "The republic of the United States, like the Israelites, worshipped the golden calf, kneeled before it ... There is only one true religion, the religion of material well-being. The bank is its temple, the double-entry accounts ledger its law, and the gold of California its sun." Captain Belvèze took up the idea, adding the notion of a more spiritual destiny for French Canadians in the New World: "The *Canadiens,* Gentlemen, alone in North America, have always claimed a distinct nationality; they have waged a glorious struggle for it and they have believed, correctly in my opinion, that the destiny of a people is not entirely a matter of improving material life, it is also revealed in the work of the spirit." Regarding French civilization in general, he recalled in his mission report "the antipathy between the heartless, mindless civilization of the United States and the gentle and affable, chivalrous and noble customs of our nation." His fellow citizen Manoël de Grandfort, the

only woman to lecture at the Institut canadien de Montréal, did not foresee an entente cordiale between France and the United States: "There is
an aristocracy in the United States: an aristocracy of suet and cod, haugh-
tier, more pitiless than the old aristocracy of Europe ever was." She saw
French Canadians, on the contrary, as open and frank: "What is surprising about that? Are not the *Canadiens* descended from the most sociable
and chivalrous nation in the world?" She, of course, hoped for an entente cordiale between France and Canada: "I hope that soon the
Canadiens will no longer be able to say: 'France has so long believed us
dead and buried that even if we told her we had come back to life, she
would not believe us.'" This perception was an enduring one, as is shown
in Claudio Jannet's book on the contemporary United States, published
in 1876: "The *Canadiens* undeniably have a richer intellectual culture
than the people of the United States, as well as a more chivalrous spirit
and a more religious nature. Their role is to preserve these superior elements of civilization in the New World."[7]

FRANCE REDISCOVERS FRENCH CANADA AND THE
VOCATION OF THE FRENCH RACE IN AMERICA

In this context of France's rediscovery of French Canada and the paired
representations of the United States as materialistic and France as spiri-
tually superior, the idea that French Canada had a special vocation in
America began to take shape. These elements, combined with existing
predispositions, were to give rise to an enduring self-image on the part of
French Canadians. The theme of a special vocation or mission was fuelled by the old idea that the British conquest of 1760 had been "providential" in that it had spared British Canada the horrors the French had
experienced in 1789 and, above all, in 1793. Revived by Mgr Plessis
at the turn of the nineteenth century, this idea had been formulated
by Judge Smith during the Terror. Then in 1847, Étienne Parent had
spoken of a special role French Canada was supposed to play on the
American continent. However, the annexation crisis of 1849 made conservatives fearful of American republicanism, so that although annexation was not much of a threat, it was countered by the formulation of a
different destiny for French Canada on the American continent. That
destiny finally found its logic in the rising ultramontanism, whose system
of ends and hierarchy of values placed religion above all else and gave
the spiritual order primacy over the temporal order. It then followed
that in America, French Canada embodied spiritualism, if not religion.
    The theme of the French Canadian destiny in America began to
be formulated in connection with Saint-Jean-Baptiste day in 1854. On

28 June 1854, *La Minerve* referred to the "best-preserved nation in all of America." In 1856, Chauveau spoke of the "Gesta Dei per Francos," the deeds of God carried out by the French and by France, the eldest daughter of the Church (despite 1789 and 1793). In 1857, during the period when the French Sulpician Étienne Faillon was working on his history of Ville-Marie (Montreal), his colleague and fellow citizen Hyacinthe Rouxel gave two public lectures at the Cabinet de lecture paroissial de Montréal, one on "the first colonists of Montreal," which described them as "a colony of apostles" representing "the purest ideal of a colony," and the other on "the vocation of the colony of Montreal," in which he maintained that "societies, like individuals, have their vocation through the Divine Wisdom," and that already in the seventeenth century, Ville-Marie had been "the boulevard and centre of Catholicism in the New World."[8]

But it was two other Frenchmen who rediscovered Canada who, in 1859, proposed an idea that many French Canadians found convincing: the idea that they had a specific destiny in America. The first one, Henry-Émile Chevalier, was one of those republicans who, like Eugène Sue or Alexandre Dumas, had had to go into exile after the coup d'état of 2 December 1851. Some of them, such as Chevalier, ended up with French-language newspapers in the United States, such as *L'Abeille* in New Orleans or the *Courrier des États-Unis* in New York. Chevalier later lived in Montreal, from 1853 to 1859, and gravitated to *Le Pays* and the Institut canadien, while also editing *La Ruche littéraire*. He imagined a French America that would unite the French of the United States, the French Canadians of Quebec, and the French Canadians of New England; he envisaged an American press and a "Franco-American literary phalanx" in which a French Canadian national literature would stand out, fuelled by the saga of 1760 and the exoticism of nature, Indians and pioneers, and written in language specific to French Canada. However, it was not this graft that took, but rather that of the second Frenchman, Edmé Rameau de Saint-Père, who had first heard about French Canadians from some Oblate missionaries in Algeria, of all places.

Rameau de Saint-Père was a disciple of Le Play, as was the first French consul in Quebec City, Charles-Henri-Philippe Gauldrée-Boilleau, who wrote "Le paysan de Saint-Irénée," published in 1875 in *Ouvriers des deux mondes*, a publication of the followers of Le Play. Rameau de Saint-Père saw in French Canada the confirmation of his master's theories on the social importance of moral and religious factors; at the same time, these theories provided ideological legitimacy for the conservatives and the clergy.[9] In 1859, the centenary of the British conquest of Canada, Rameau de Saint-Père, curious about the real or possible colonial evolution of France in Algeria and Canada, published a book on "France in the colonies," one chapter of which, on "the moral and intellectual future of the *Canadiens* in America," was to become the matrix of what would later be called the ideology of messianism on the vocation of the French race in America.

Rameau de Saint-Père shared his fellow citizens' perception of America as materialistic and thus proposed that "the national repulsion, better than a customs barrier, blockade anything that smells of Americanism at the border of the *Canadien* country, that each person mistrust and reject with disdain the contagion of that unhealthy civilization." This "Americanism" was industry and trade, "shopkeepers' calculations and the keen desires of cupidity," "the cult of money," comfort and material well-being. The future of Catholic French Canada was to be different: "While in the United States spirits are absorbed in an exhausting preoccupation with trade, industry and the adoration of the golden calf, it is up to Canada to claim, disinterestedly and with a noble pride, the intellectual, scientific and artistic side of the American movement, devoting itself in preference to the cult of feeling, thought and beauty." Striking a prophetic note, Rameau made a pronouncement that was to have a bright future: "It does not seem to us that it is Canada's destiny to be an industrial or commercial nation."[10]

His impassioned vision of the future of the French Canadians even led him to predict "the progressive retreat of the Anglo-Saxon population before them." He pointed out that among this "chosen people" as among the Jewish people, "the association of nationality with religion was a source of support," and proposed a destiny characterized by the "dual development of simplicity of customs and cultivation of the spirit." This future would have the grace of an unchanging village: "The Canadian countryside has all the rusticity of our peasants, without the brutality of [American] materialism; the simple lives, the sweet fraternity of families, the happy harmony that unites the whole parish under the paternal and loved guidance of the parish priest sometimes recall those dreams of a golden age that seem from here to belong only to the fantasies of the imagination." To other Frenchmen, this "golden age" evoked the ancien régime; the Dominican Chocarne admitted: "What good people these *Canadiens* are! Good heart, unpretentiousness, generosity, and they still love France despite all its betrayals, as a dog licks the hand that beats it. It is like France of two centuries ago, with its customs, song and traditions. The Conquest, far from changing the character of the *Canadiens*, fixed it more in national sympathies: this is a country of the ancien régime in every respect." In 1877, Albert Lefaivre, the French consul in Canada, described French Canada as the "debris of old France on the other side of the Atlantic Ocean" and as a backward-looking utopia:

"Fourrier, Considerant and Cabet never suspected that their theories were being peacefully applied in Canada by priests."[11]

As the title of Rameau's book suggests, this vision of the future of the former New France also included a vision of the future of colonial France: he saw French Canada as the "fulcrum of the preservation and proper development of the French name and genius in North America"; it would be the place from which French civilization, and thus French greatness, were disseminated: "It thus depends on you, the descendents of Catholic, Greco-Latin and French civilization, to imbue the American spirit with this loftiness, this fullness of heart and mind, on which the renown and the essential character of every great civilization have been based." Étienne Parent, who in 1837 had moderated the continental visions of the Patriotes by citing the example of Louisiana, wrote to Rameau: "I have been working for nearly forty years for the survival of our beloved nationality, to make an American France, and I have not yet lost hope of success ... I do not fear Anglo-Saxonism per se; if we perish, it will be for political reasons, in other words, by our own hands." It was of an "American France," a reproduction of metropolitan France, that Parent still dreamed: "Lower Canada is still France, France in America. May our nationality spread and consolidate, it is a reliable ally for France ... Yes, like me, you must deplore the fact that thousands of Frenchmen are being drowned among peoples of foreign races whereas by coming here they would be helping us create on the shores of the St Lawrence a France as beautiful, maybe as glorious, as the France of the Seine and the Rhône."[12]

After Rameau's travels in Canada and the United States in the summer of 1860, the theme of the vocation of the French race was taken up in Montreal and Quebec City in connection with 24 June. The French Sulpician Sentenne stated that every people has a mission to fulfill and that French Canada's mission was to propagate religion and civilization. Abbé Hercule Beaudry outlined "true civilization": "Descendents of the great French race, we are the heirs of its religious traditions and the sublime role France has played in the upper sphere of European influence. That influence must be exercised in the moral and intellectual order. The material progress of our neighbours – the astonishing development of their manufacturing, trade and industry – matters very little; that is not the basis of true civilization."[13]

But the greatest promoter of the providential vocation of the French race in America was Abbé Henri-Raymond Casgrain, who was also the impresario of a national literature with this spiritual – and ultimately religious – vocation. Inspired by Rameau de Saint-Père, Abbé Casgrain asked: "What action has Providence reserved for us in America? What role does it call on us to play?" His answer was that "as representatives of the Latin race facing an Anglo-Saxon population whose excessive expansion and abnormal influence must be balanced, as in Europe, for the progress of civilization, our mission and that of societies with the same origin, whose number is limited on this continent, is to create a counterweight by uniting our forces, to fight the materialistic instincts and crude egoism of Anglo-American positivism with the higher tendencies that are the heritage of the Latin races and an unmatched superiority in the moral order and in the realm of thought."

Convinced of France's civilizing "superiority," a message that had been repeated by Belvèze, Rameau, and others, Casgrain confidently predicted the "moral superiority" of French Canada in America: "Failing one of those uncontrollable reactions that occur without notice, of which we see no indication, this huge market of men called the American people, brought together without any other principle of cohesion than greed, will be crushed by its own weight. Who says that the only people in North America (which is still nascent today) that possesses the sap of life, the unchanging principles of order and morality will not rise like a radiant column amid the ruins all around it?"[14]

The providential and messianic theme was present from June to the fall of 1866. The Oblate Thibault took it up on 24 June: "It is this little corner of America as big as Europe bequeathed us by our forefathers that we must consider sacred and inviolable; it is this national diploma given us by God and France that we must not let our neighbours tear up, and even more important, that we must not tear up with our own hands." Mgr Laflèche put more stress on the providential mission: "Since we are a nation, we have a homeland; it is the land our fathers left us, the beautiful and rich St Lawrence Valley. It was Providence itself that gave it to our ancestors as a reward for the zeal with which they worked to convert the poor heathens who were its first occupants." From Philippe Masson in 1875, who posed the question, "What purpose did Providence have for preserving us on this American soil?" and answered it, "Providence wants us to provide in America the example, rare in the world today, of a race, a nation over which Christ reigns socially," to Mgr Louis-Adolphe Pâquet in 1902, this theme became the inevitable leitmotif of patriotic speeches, particularly by the clergy, and of the representation of French Canada's manifest destiny in America.[15] It was accompanied by a myth of a northern population destined to settle the Ottawa Basin and create a belt through northern Ontario linking the francophone populations of eastern and western Canada. There was even an effort in France to provide resources to help put this policy into practice. The geographer Onésime Reclus became a promoter of immigration to Canada; and in 1872, the

Compagnie de colonisation franco-canadienne was founded in Paris. Hector Bossange, the great Parisian friend of the French Canadians, was appointed recruitment agent, responsible for finding emigrants, while Auguste Bodard undertook a propaganda tour and Paul de Cazes tried to recruit immigrants from Alsace and Lorraine. After 1880, Father Labelle would perpetuate this vision and this policy.[16]

The Franco-Prussian War of 1870 gave rise to various reactions in French Canada. To *Le Canadien*, it was clear that, despite the expressions of sympathy and collections for France in its hour of need, "our political and national interests no longer concern European politics. America is ours. Let us let old Europe tear itself to pieces." Quebec City's *L'Événement* of 29 July 1870 felt more involved: "French blood courses through our veins once again, as though nothing had ever chilled it; and we salute the flag of our old mother country as though it had never ceased to fly over our heads." To this paper, "France is still France to us. It is our sole national love, the very source of our patriotism. We esteem England, we are grateful to it for having given us freedom, the greatest treasure of all, we admire the United States, whose prosperity dazzles us, but it is only France that we love with passion."

The founding of the Third Republic on 4 September 1870 revived the strife between liberals and conservatives. One of the latter, Faucher de Saint-Maurice, even used providentialism to explain contemporary events: "God spoke to the Emperor Napoleon III and France from the mouth of Prussian machine guns." The poet Octave Crémazie, who had written the poem "The Old Canadian Soldier" in 1855 and was in forced exile in France, kept a diary of the siege of Paris in 1870, a record of "the return of the bad times of 1848." Seeing how politically divided France was, Crémazie, who knew what he was talking about, noted: "France's great misfortune is that its children are partisans rather than patriots." As a good Catholic, he deplored the situation in Italy, where the liberals were taking advantage of the fall of Napoleon III to invade Rome in order to put a final end to the pope's temporal power. The Commune of 1871, which led Crémazie to flee to Orléans, seemed to him to be the work of "Communard thugs," of "mob rule" and "Belleville riffraff."[17]

The liberals had a completely different understanding of the evolution of France. These men, who had visited Prince Napoleon when he passed through Montreal in 1861, criticized the ultramontanists for "their strange attachment to the France of Louis XV." Gonzalve Doutre, recalling France's despicable abandonment of Canada, confessed that France "means almost nothing to us now" and thought it advisable to "calm this enthusiasm for France, legitimate, but often misplaced, which today provides an example of a nation where thought is not free."

At the time of the Commune, the ultramontanists had other reasons to denounce France. Adolphe-Basile Routhier, a Canadian Veuillot, declared that "Paris has become Satan's capital in this world."[18] And to Laurier in his 1877 speech, this was not the France that French Canadians held dear.

THE REAL AMERICA

About 1860, the myth of the vocation of the French race in America, which had been created by Frenchmen influenced by the renewal of French colonialism, came together with the failure of the annexation movement to give rise to an alternative. Although the idea of annexation was not popular at the time, it nonetheless reflected the appeal the United States had for some French Canadians, just as the emigration of French Canadians by the thousands to the manufacturing towns of New England was a response to both an economic need and a symbolic attraction. By the time of Laurier's speech, annexation had lost some of its glamour because for people like Arthur Buies, it had taken another, more concrete form: "Annexation is not only a commercial and political fact, it is above all a geographic and physical fact. We are already annexed through our rivers, our laws and our railways ... We are already American by virtue of our customs, which have been overtaken by a gradual yet rapid democracy; and the same can be said of our new interests, our aspirations, and the inevitable tendencies of modern societies ... We must be primarily American if we want to live on this continent, and we will only be truly American if we become part of the great republic."[19]

Given the political-religious division in French Canadians' perceptions of the Civil War in the United States, from 1860 to 1865, not everyone agreed with Buies. The conservatives favoured the Southern states: "Do not the Southern states have as much right to autonomy as Hungary, Poland and Italy, whose cause received so much support from our neighbours? This model government that was supposed to give Europe republics is now following in the footsteps of the most oppressive governments in Europe." Rameau de Saint-Père, who pointed out the presence of "French blood" in the South in a lecture on the American crisis, claimed that slavery did not justify breaking up the Union – contrary to the position of the liberals, and of Dessaulles in his lectures on the Civil War – and considered that the North's principal concern was to save its profits: "It would have been astonishing if a Yankee question did not turn out to be, ultimately, about the bottom line." Quebec's conservative Catholic press, which had to resolve the contradiction of slavery, declared itself in favour of secession but anti-slavery.

The vision of a national literature that was taking form at the time was also a useful indicator of the way French Canadians saw the United States. Serial novels filled the press, and novels with exotic themes were at the height of their popularity in France, where Gustave Aimard's *Les trappeurs de l'Arkansas* (The Arkansas trappers) (1858), *L'eau qui court* (The flowing water) (1861), and *Les chasseurs d'abeilles* (The bee hunters) (1863) were published. The Frenchman Henry-Émile Chevalier mined the same vein from 1853 to 1859 in the Montreal-based *Ruche littéraire*. In 1866, like Abbé Casgrain, the moderate liberal Hector Fabre gave a lecture on the present and future of French Canadian literature and described its unique features as follows: "The role of our literature is to identify and describe what is special about us, what distinguishes both the race from which we come and the race in the midst of which we live, which makes us resemble an old people exiled in a new country and growing gradually younger. In this broad portrait of America, which is merely a crude image of Europe, we have a place apart, a whole corner of the horizon ... Our society is neither French nor English, nor American, it is Canadian."

Fabre echoed Garneau's vision of a literature based on the exoticism of the nature and climate and imagined a *Canadien* Fenimore Cooper: "Our great and beautiful nature, in its infinite variety, is also made to attract brilliant imaginations. And yet it is the feeling for nature that our writers most lack. There are some broad descriptions in the work of Charles Guérin, but where is the passion for every green nook and cranny? Our winters have not yet found their bard. Let us celebrate our countryside, our great forests and our chains of mountains, but please, say as little as possible about the Iroquois; let sleeping Hurons lie. Those proud and naïve heroes were eloquent reflections of their age and style, but when they express themselves in modern language and gesticulate in Alexandrines, I find them quite mediocre and they spoil the best parts for me."

Unlike Abbé Casgrain, Fabre did not insist that rural scenes, forests, and winters be Catholic; and he also distinguished himself from Chevalier, a French immigrant, in rejecting the exoticism of the "noble Savage."

But by the following year, the poet Crémazie had already lost faith in the idea of a *Canadien* Cooper: "Canada could have conquered its place among the literatures of the old world if, before Fenimore Cooper, there had been among the *Canadiens* a writer capable of introducing Europe to the vast nature of our forests and the legendary exploits of our trappers and *voyageurs*. Even if a talent as powerful as that of the author of *The Last of the Mohicans* were to appear amongst us today, his works would not create a sensation in Europe, because they would have the irreparable flaw of arriving second, which is to say, too late."[20]

"*ITE AD ROMAM*": GO TO ROME

Rome, which was also a conduit of cultural and political influence on French Canada, took on a new importance in this period. Since 1848, Rome and the papacy had been central in the question of Italian unity and in the dispute between the Catholic Church and the French Canadian liberals; the quarrels with *L'Avenir* and Dessaulles as editor of *Le Pays* attest to this. The sending of Canadian Zouaves to defend the Papal States during the 1860s clearly indicates the connection between French Canada and Rome created by the Italian question.

However, during the 1850s, with the renewal of the material and human resources of the Catholic Church in French Canada and especially Montreal, Rome figured increasingly as a model of orthodoxy. Mgr Bourget wanted to make Montreal "a little Rome," and its cathedral was a miniature of St Peter's in Rome. The bishop also imposed the Roman liturgy and collar during these years, and the clergy began to make pilgrimages to Rome and spend time studying there. It was also during this decade that the bishops of Quebec delegated priest diplomats such as Abbé Baillargeon and Abbé Benjamin Pâquet to Rome, where they pleaded the many cases that were brought before the Roman congregations. Mgr Bourget, Mgr Laflèche, and Mgr Taschereau travelled with increasing frequency between Rome and Quebec to defend their points of view on the dismemberment of Notre-Dame parish in Montreal, answer the petition of the Institut canadien de Montréal, defend or censure the "liberalism" of the diocesan clergy of Quebec City, and argue for or against the establishment of a Catholic university in Montreal. Rome was truly harassed by the infighting of Quebec's clergy. What Dessaulles had called the Great Ecclesiastical War degenerated to the point where, in 1877, Rome had to appoint a delegate, Mgr Conroy, to ensure that the dissension did not destroy the credibility of the local Church. This set a precedent that would give the Congregation of Propaganda – and Laurier – the idea of having an apostolic delegation in Canada that could act as arbiter in the conflicts that had so often been taken to Rome.

CONCLUSION

It was after 1850 that the rich, complex identity of French Canada took form, under the influence of what may be called its four cultural and political metropolises: Paris, London, Washington, and Rome.

The backlash after the insurrections, the new Constitution of 1840 and the granting of responsible government enabled La Fontaine to triumph over Papineau in 1848, and allowed Cartier, with London's support, to establish the new constitutional regime of 1867. Indeed, by around 1867, French Canada had regained the admiration it had felt for England before 1830, and had thus put its anti-colonialism on ice. The reforming spirit that prevailed under the leadership of La Fontaine, Cartier, and Laurier is reminiscent of French Canadians' attitude in response to 1774 and 1793.

French Canada's rediscovery of France is paradoxical in several respects. The reference to a reconquest by France in the title of Joseph-Guillaume Barthe's book did not fool anyone: it was unthinkable that after abandoning the French Canadians and forgetting them for a century, France would risk a civil war to reconquer Canada. Especially since some French Canadians were opposed, either because they feared it would bring together the Rouges of the two continents or because they thought they had finished with colonial situations of any sort. And the arrival of *La Capricieuse*, a supremely symbolic event, linked the reunion of France and Quebec to the Entente Cordiale; in the celebrations in honour of that alliance between France and Great Britain, care was taken to include the unveiling of a monument to the French and British soldiers who had died in the Battle of Sainte-Foy. Chauveau, the superintendent of public education and future premier, even found a certain glory in Canada's being the ex-colony and colony of the two greatest colonial powers of the period. This did not, however, prevent the French Canadian press from expressing some resentment because it wanted Canada to be a more active participant in the Paris Universal Exhibition of 1855.

One might say that when *La Capricieuse* sailed up the St Lawrence, it bore a new plan for the former French colony in America, one that was based on a representation of the United States as materialistic and France as chivalrous, and that cast French Canada in a spiritual role, with the destiny of spreading the "superior elements of civilization." This conception became associated with a French Canadian belief in providentialism that had existed since the eighteenth century and shared a similar view of the United States, opposing annexation and linking French Canada's spiritual and religious destiny to an ultramontanist vision in which heaven took primacy over earth, and religion over civil values.

The new vocation was welcome and culturally viable. Conservatives and members of the clergy took up the idea of a spiritual destiny, and it became the principal theme of their speeches on 24 June, the French Canadians' patron saint's day. It was not Henry-Émile Chevalier's vision of a "French America" that would prevail, but rather the more colonial idea of an "American France" mentioned by Parent, formulated by Rameau de Saint-Père and adopted by Abbé Casgrain. This American France would not be a combination of French and American republican ideas; on the contrary, the pairing of religion with nationalism and the primacy accorded to rural and spiritual values suggested a New France of the ancien régime, as was noted by the French Dominicans, who were thinking of establishing themselves in French Canada. It is easy to understand how and why, in this context, clerics such as Abbé Casgrain and later Mgr Pâquet clericalized an idea about values of civilization and turned it into a Catholic religious destiny, especially since the Third Republic of 1870 and the Paris Commune of 1871 brought back the image of two Frances created by 1793 and maintained by 1830 and 1848.

The ideological antagonism in French Canada was so great at this time that it influenced all perception, including that of the Civil War in the United States between 1860 and 1865, reproducing the division between pro-South conservatives and pro-North liberals. Still, the "vocation of the French race in America" did not completely extinguish the idea of annexation. Buies, for example, spoke of the geographic and commercial annexation of Canada to the United States, and then of political annexation. In doing so, he was acknowledging an unavoidable – and lasting – reality.

But the vision of a Catholic and spiritual vocation for the French race in America triumphed in one symbolically decisive domain: literature. The symbolic expression of French Canada would not be the expression of America in French for France – not after Cooper and Gustave Aimard – but that of a particular "exoticism" that was Catholic and rural. This conception, Catholic and French – in that order – was fed by ultramontanism, which in the years after 1850 found its first definition of geographic reality: one went to Rome, and soon Rome would come to Canada, in the form of an apostolic delegation, an idea that had been in the air since 1878. Papal Rome was no longer merely the opposite of the liberal Rome of the Italian revolutionaries; it became the model for what the ultramontanists wanted to do on a miniature scale in Montreal. To the motto *Ite ad Romam*, which was popular in Quebec ecclesiastical circles, a new motto soon had to be added: in Rome, *Ite ad Quebecum*, because the dissension within the Quebec clergy made it necessary to send a first delegate. Mgr Conroy's presence could only strengthen Laurier.

It was at the intersection of these "four roads" that the identity of French Canada was forged.

The Spread of Ideas and Cultural Takeoff (1840–1877)

LOWER CANADA'S BILATERAL RELATIONS with France, Great Britain, the United States, and Rome intensified under the union, while society was undergoing major changes demographically, economically, and technologically and providing the means for its development.

During the period from the political crisis of the union to Laurier's moderate and moderating speech in 1877, the two main schools of thought became radicalized at different points and for different reasons: after driving liberalism from the electoral scene to the rooms of the Institut canadien de Montréal in 1848, moderate liberalism and conservatism became more prevalent, until conservatism itself became radicalized in 1871, with the Catholic Program, a sort of extreme ultramontanism. The liberal-ultramontanist antagonism took form during the religious revival, fuelled by polemics about education, democracy, and tolerance.

During nearly four decades of this intellectual and ideological ferment, resources and media such as the press and associations were put to use, and debate often revolved around them – the orientations of the associations and the content of their libraries or periodical reading rooms – with the information made public in newspapers, magazines, lectures, and novels. After the union, these exchanges of ideas, the participants and content of which are familiar to us, used new channels of communication. And it was precisely when political debate and ideological conflict reached their apogee at the beginning of the 1860s that Lower Canada underwent a definitive cultural takeoff accompanied by the emergence of a new type of sociability.

THE CIRCULATION OF PEOPLE AND GOODS

The population of Lower Canada, which doubled between 1844 and 1881, remained predominantly rural, with the traditional oral and material culture of rural life. In 1851, one person in six lived in a town or city, compared with one in three in 1891. This urbanization had a definite impact on culture and the cultural infrastructure such as schools, the press, and libraries. Montreal, whose population surpassed that of Quebec City during the 1830s, had 140,000 inhabitants in 1881 compared with Quebec City's 62,000. Throughout the period, Montreal and Quebec City were still the only cities with more than ten thousand inhabitants. From 1861 to 1881, the number of towns with at least six thousand inhabitants rose from three to five – Trois-Rivières, Lévis, Sherbrooke, Saint-Hyacinthe, and Hull – while the number of towns with five thousand inhabitants or more increased from four to nine.

This demographic growth was due first to the natural increase of the population, but also to immigration. From 1839 to 1843, there were 24,772 immigrants who arrived in the ports of Quebec City and Montreal; from 1844 to 1848, there were 39,270; from 1849 to 1853, there were 187,737. Notwithstanding the essentially British, and mainly Irish, nature of this immigration, Montreal regained its status as a majority francophone city around 1865,[1] due to the migration of francophones from the country to the city, despite the large wave of emigration of rural francophones to the New England states. The British immigration enabled the anglophone community to consolidate cultural institutions that in many cases had been established before 1840.

The use of steam power in transportation facilitated international population movement and communications. After 1840, more than two hundred ocean-going steamships per year put in to the port of Montreal, including those of the Allan Company, which provided regular transportation between Quebec City and Liverpool after 1856. The ocean-going paddle steamer, which took fifteen days to cross the Atlantic in 1840, improved its performance by five days in 1870, thanks to the screw propeller. "Pyroscaphes," as they were called in 1840, also navigated the St Lawrence and went into the interior of United Canada and the United States using the system of canals developed around the Ottawa Valley and the Great Lakes.

Steam also powered locomotives. Three railway lines transported people and goods between Lower Canada and the United States: the La Prairie–Saint-Jean–Rouses Point–New York–Boston line starting in 1851, the St Lawrence and Atlantic line, which linked Longueuil and Portland, Maine, in 1853 via Saint-Hyacinthe (1845) and Sherbrooke, and the Montreal–Saint-Jean–Vermont line from 1864. The passengers were as likely to be French Canadian emigrants on their way to Manchester or Lowell as French Canadian "tourists," such as P. Verchères de

Boucherville, who travelled to California in 1849, Arthur Buies, who did so in 1874, and Pierre de Sales Laterrière, who went to Boston in 1873. These French Canadian travellers met American tourists, with their "Strangers' Guides" that provided names of hotels and train schedules. They might even cross paths with Henry David Thoreau, who toured Lower Canada in 1850 and wrote *A Yankee in Canada*, published in 1856.

Thoreau, the "philosopher of the woods," who crossed the "invisible border" between the United States and Canada, had the impression that he was travelling in time as much as in space, and described Canadians as "a rather poor-looking race," with their "rusty" institutions. The free-thinker, pacifist, and antimilitarist considered the population of Lower Canada "to be suffering between two fires: the soldiery and the priest-hood." Seeing the ramparts of Quebec City as symbolizing his impres-sions, he wrote that they "do not consist with the development of the intellect" and "rather oppress than liberate the mind."[2]

The railway freight service made it possible to import books, news-papers, engravings, lithographs, geographic maps, and musical instru-ments from the United States, and after the Reciprocity Treaty of 1854, to send massive quantities of goods to the belligerents in the Civil War (1860–65). Montreal was finally linked to the United States by way of the Victoria Bridge, which was completed in December 1859 and inaugurated in the summer of 1860. The royal and imperial event was lavish: when the Prince of Wales arrived in Montreal, his carriage passed under six arches of triumph on its way to his residence. The son of the Queen for whom the new tubular bridge was named opened the local Crystal Palace, a sort of industrial cathedral modelled on the one built in London for the first International Exhibition in 1851. His Highness graced the opening of the Art Association of Montreal with his presence, attended a game of lacrosse, the local sport par excel-lence, took railway rides, and opened a grand ball in his honour. The railway was king.[3]

Europeans also took advantage of the increased speed and comfort of steam-powered transportation. British, French, Italian, and other people intensified their relationship with Lower Canada. Charles Dickens, visit-ing Lower Canada in 1842, observed first-hand the arrival of huge num-bers of Irish immigrants in the colony when he took a steamboat from Quebec City to Montreal. Dickens admired Quebec City, "this Gibraltar of America," and its monument dedicated to both Wolfe and Montcalm, "worthy of two great nations," and noted, in May, the sudden arrival of spring, "which is here so rapid, that it is but a day's leap from barren winter, to the blooming youth of summer."

After the visit of *La Capricieuse* (1855), France established a consulate (1858) in Quebec City and then one in Montreal, and its consuls participated actively in local cultural life, writing in the spirit of Le Play about the peasants of Saint-Irénée (Gauldrée-Boilleau) or about French literature (Lefaivre). The philanthropist Alexandre Vattemare, Mgr Forbin-Janson, the writer Joseph Marmier, Ampère, Rameau de Saint-Père, and Prince Napoleon all visited Lower Canada, and books from publishers such as Bossange and Gaume brought Canadian bookstores up to date with literary trends. Delegates from Rome, such as Mgr Conroy, also made the transatlantic crossing from east to west.

In the opposite direction, Paris and elsewhere in France, such as Lourdes, became more popular than Rome as destinations. Mgr Bourget recruited religious orders in France in 1841 and 1846–47. Joseph-Guillaume Barthe made efforts in 1855 to associate the Institut de France with the Institut canadien de Montréal, and a bit later the poet Octave Crémazie and the radical liberal Louis-Antoine Dessaulles lived in exile in Paris. And Canada, including Lower Canada, participated in the Universal Exhibitions held in Paris in 1855, 1867, and 1878.

Clergy and laymen made increasingly frequent trips to Italy, especially to Rome. Their primary destination was Christian Rome, but they took in pagan Rome while they were there. Abbés Taschereau, Louis-Honoré and Louis-Adolphe Pâquet, and Chandonnet studied in Rome after 1852 or, with Bishop Bourget, Laflèche, or Taschereau, discussed Canadian ecclesiastical matters before various Roman congregations. Among the lay visitors, some were Zouaves sent to defend the pope and the Papal States against the liberal Italian "usurpers" who in 1848 had raised the "Roman question." Some Zouaves, such as G. Drolet, L.-E. Moreau, C.-G. Rouleau, and F. Lachance, repeated the pilgrimage to Rome between 1868 and 1870.[4]

The use of steam power for maritime and rail transportation also facilitated communication within Lower Canada. A trip from Montreal to Quebec City was no longer a lengthy adventure, and by the end of the period, travelling to resort areas (Cacouna, Murray Bay) had become commonplace, as shown in Arthur Buies's *Chroniques*. Hotels, which gradually replaced inns, were built near docks, stagecoach stations, and railway stations, whether modest country structures or city stations with daring architecture.[5] Railway lines, such as the Montreal–Lachine (1847), Montreal–Toronto (1856), Montreal–Rivière-du-Loup (1860), Montreal–Saint-Jérôme, and Lévis–Beauce lines, now covered much of Lower Canada, and an intercolonial line linked Montreal with Halifax (1876) before Halifax was linked to Vancouver in 1885.[6]

THE CIRCULATION OF IDEAS

As we have seen, the period of the union was one of political and religious reconstruction. After the failure of the Rebellions, the population of Lower Canada sought ways to shake off the lethargy resulting from the failure of the French Canadian consensus against union. Civic reconstruction in general, and political reconstruction in particular, with the debates and conflicts they gave rise to, were accompanied by an equally remarkable cultural reconstruction. The intellectual and institutional takeoff that had been in the works since the end of Napoleon's blockade in 1815, but had been interrupted by the Rebellions, finally took place.

While journalists such as Étienne Parent of *Le Canadien* and Ludger Duvernay of *La Minerve* had published crusading newspapers of high editorial quality, the francophone press before 1840 was essentially limited to Quebec City and Montreal. Participation in associations, a widespread form of sociability among anglophones who had the means and the model of their mother country, was, among francophones, limited to membership in patriotic societies before 1837. The 1836 decision of the Legislative Council not to renew the Assembly Schools Act of 1829, which was also opposed by the Catholic Church, added to the interruption caused by the Rebellions and weakened an education system that had begun to show results. In the period from 1815 to 1840, libraries were still an Anglo-British phenomenon, with the exception of some colleges and well-off francophones. Édouard-Raymond Fabre remained a maverick among booksellers, the majority of whom were Montreal anglophones, and he had to join forces with the printer Duvernay to play the role of "publisher" to meet the needs of schools and the highly active political life of the period.

STRENGTH IN UNITY: THE RISE OF ASSOCIATIONS

It was the rise of associations and the new desire to join forces and help each other that led to the intellectual and institutional takeoff. In cultural terms, "strength in unity" was the watchword of the 1840s. Associations brought together people who shared an interest – be it science, history, literature, or art – on a voluntary basis. In the previous decades, the British population of the colony had taken the initiative, founding the Literary and Historical Society of Quebec (1824), the Natural History Society of Montreal (1827), and the Mechanics' Institute of Montreal (1828) and that of Quebec City (1831). They were inspired by an international movement that took the form of the Society for

Useful Knowledge or the Mechanics' Institute in Great Britain, the Lyceum or the Atheneum in the United States, and Le Cercle in France.

From November 1840 to March 1841, Alexandre Vattemare, a French ventriloquist who was also a philanthropist and proponent of the international exchange of books, launched a project to create institutes that would bring together the Literary and Historical Society, the Mechanics' Institute, and the Quebec Library in Quebec City, and the Natural History Society, the Mechanics' Institute, and the Montreal Library in Montreal. The project was unsuccessful because of the hesitation of the associations concerned, the intensity of the political struggles and the fact that all the associations were essentially anglophone.[7]

The union was not only a political and constitutional regime; it was also a cultural regime within which the idea of association was promoted early on. Young French Canadians of 1840 saw the anglophones of the colony as a cultural inspiration: "[The anglophones] who are fighting with us form associations for everything. Most of them were born in a place where political and religious institutions link the idea of association to all ideas, they all tend to join an association to develop themselves, derive strength and pursue their goal, so much so that today, association is, so to speak, part of their way of life." This generation was becoming aware of the new demographic and economic competition of an anglophone business community that was founding banks, and insurance, gas, and telegraph companies, and whose entrepreneurship found expression in sociability, whether in the Board of Trade or the Mechanics' Institutes, clearly reflecting the new demand for skilled labour created by industrialization.

For the twenty-year-olds of 1840, faced with commercial and industrial development, ignorance was unacceptable. Parent, who after 1846 gave lecture upon lecture to promote the study of political economy, approved. These young people, who understood that the "old simplicity" was finished and the old institutions were crumbling around them, also made a connection between knowing and having: "Like money in business, the accumulation of knowledge creates a fund whose dividends give the shareholders wealth with almost no labour." Political union, cultural union, economic union: the vocabulary of exchange referred as much to dividends and wealth as to knowledge.

The cultural takeoff of the union period was based on these young people's sense of belonging to the same generation: "The generation of Canadian youth preceding that of the founders of the Institut canadien [1844] was indistinguishable from all the generations before it. Then as now, no doubt, it was composed of young people with various intellectual endowments, but they were all lost in an amorphous mass, feeling isolated, not knowing their neighbours, and were powerless to further their individual interests and or those of society." This rising generation expressed the need for a "public spirit" and for places in which to discuss "common concerns"; it intended to counter the new competition with new mutual aid, and the "mutual discouragement" following 1837–38, with "mutual encouragement." But above all, it sought to free French Canadians from their isolation and create a "theatre" of sociability for them: "Every house, every family has its near and dear; but no house and no family has enough people over, and especially enough different kinds of people, of different occupations and even different levels, who can, all together, express our spirit, our customs, our ways and our air. In all countries, a foreigner who wants to get to know a society can meet it somewhere, in theatres, in concerts, in learned societies, in circles, in meetings, and in the homes of people whose wealth and standing permit them to receive company ... In our society, there is no theatre, there are no concerts, there are no learned societies and there are no circles. So the foreigner would not meet people anywhere, except in church." Indeed, neither Quebec City nor Montreal at the time had a permanent francophone theatre, a concert hall with a French name, or francophone associations for science, literature, history, or painting. There was minimal public space, and sociability was primarily domestic and familial.[8]

Along with the anglophone initiatives, Vattemare's project, and the new interest in college academies – one was founded in Nicolet in 1842 – there was a proliferation of associations: several Instituts canadiens, discussion societies, artisans' institutes, and Catholic circles or unions. Over 130 cultural associations were established between 1840 and 1880, with the peak, identifiable by requests for government subsidies, in 1858.[9] In Quebec City, Montreal, and Saint-Hyacinthe, from the Mauricie to Plessisville and from New Carlisle and Baie-Saint-Paul through Aylmer, Matane, Rimouski, L'Islet, Rigaud, and Bagotville, towns of every size created meeting places where common concerns could be discussed.

Although it was not the first "literary society," the Institut canadien de Montréal (founded 17 December 1844) set the tone and became the benchmark. In Quebec City, which remained the cultural hub of Lower Canada during the first decade of the union, there was an effort to implement the Vattemare project in 1843 with the Société des jeunes gens, which was followed by the Société canadienne d'études littéraires et scientifiques, half of whose young founding members were lawyers or notaries. Its thirty-odd members belonged to La Fontaine's Reformers. The Société de discussion de Saint-Roch (1843–49, with an interruption from 1845 to 1847) had about 145 members, a fifth of them in the legal professions. La Fontaine's Reformers, who were close to the *Journal de Québec,* sometimes joined in groups. The Quebec Library Association, founded in January 1844, was mainly anglophone, although it organized some activities with and for francophones.

The Institut canadien de Montréal gave rise to a number of other Instituts canadiens, in Quebec City (1848), Saint-Hyacinthe (1854), and elsewhere. Few of them, however, shared the ideological orientation of those of Montreal and Saint-Hyacinthe. The Institut canadien de Montréal became radicalized after 1848 because of the failure of the liberals' strategy of calling for the repeal of the union; that led to a polarization, which in turn led to a split (1858) and to the Institut's first censure by the Church. Catholic associations, such as the Cabinet de lecture paroissial des Sulpiciens (1857), the Union catholique des Jésuites de Montréal (1859), the Cercle catholique (1858), and the Union catholique de Saint-Hyacinthe (1865), were soon established to counter the liberal influence of the Institut canadien de Montréal and that of Saint-Hyacinthe. As we have seen, the associations and the press were instrumental in developing and maintaining the liberal-ultramontanist antagonism that marked 1848 to 1870.[10]

The social and occupational composition of the associations depended on their location. In Longueuil, which at the time was a railway town, the members of the Institut canadien were shopkeepers and carpenters. In Quebec City, the first associations were formed by young people in the legal field – lawyers, notaries, or students. At the Institut canadien de Montréal, 15 per cent of the 926 members who joined between 1855 and 1880 were lawyers (130), law students, (71), or notaries (14). Whereas shopkeepers represented 16 per cent of the membership and leadership of the Institut, legal people, who made up only 15 per cent of the membership, held 39 per cent of the officers' positions. This set the tone for the activities of these associations, which created a culture of lawyers, in the image of political and parliamentary life.[11]

ACTIVITIES OF THE CULTURAL ASSOCIATIONS: A CULTURE OF ELOQUENCE

Associations were the matrix of the cultural takeoff that occurred during the union because they made possible and also drew on the three key forms of nineteenth-century culture: the press, the forum, and the library. In varying proportions, associations offered their members public lectures, "essays" (lectures on a more modest scale, intended only for the members of the association), debates, libraries, newspaper reading rooms, and, in the case of the Institut canadien de Montréal, a small museum. In doing so, the associations fulfilled their principal role, that of providing concentrated activities to fill the long winter evenings from October to May, when economic activity began again with the thaw and the ice run and the movement of sailing vessels and steamers up-river.

Public lectures, essays, and debates were part of a culture of eloquence that, in a rural society with an oral tradition, predominated even among the elites, who were trained to speak in their rhetoric course and in the college academies. This elite was preparing to preach in the pulpit, to argue in court, or to make speeches on the hustings. One young man admitted in 1859: "For us, most of whom are going into law, it is above all a sort of prelude to the battles we will have to fight later on, serious and difficult battles, for which we cannot be too well prepared."

Not including the Institut canadien de Québec and the Union catholique de Montréal, over 650 public lectures were delivered in fourteen associations in Lower Canada between 1845 and 1880: 128 public lectures at the Institut canadien de Montréal from 1845 to 1871, with an annual maximum of thirteen lectures in 1858; 149 at the Sulpicians' Cabinet de lecture paroissial from 1857 to 1867; 93 at the Union catholique de Saint-Hyacinthe from 1865 to 1871. The lectures, held in halls designed for the purpose – in the case of the Sulpicians' Cabinet de lecture paroissial, the Institut canadien de Montréal and the Institut canadien de Québec – were something of a social event: women were welcome, although, with the exception of Manoël de Grandfort, a French speaker invited to the Institut canadien de Montréal, they did not give lectures. The phenomenon of the *lecture public* – a literal translation of "public lecture" – allowed a few important figures such as Étienne Parent, Louis-Antoine Dessaulles, Arthur Buies, Abbé Joseph Raymond, and the Sulpicians Antoine Giband and Dominique Granet, to rise to prominence in an activity that was also at the height of its popularity in the United States at the time. The lectures addressed the subjects of freedom, progress, tolerance, the defence of the Institut canadien de Montréal, and political economy from different, if not opposing, viewpoints depending on the speaker.[12]

Essays, which were presented only to the members of an association, served as a trial run for young people who, like Antoine Gérin-Lajoie, wondered: "And what have we that could help the young man who feels he has some talent for speaking? Where can he receive lessons in eloquence? Theatres cannot survive among us; and where are our podiums and public forums?" Essays represented a sort of eloquence typical of the beginning of a certain sociability and public self-expression, and they were especially popular at the Société des Amis, which hosted sixty-four of them from 1845 to 1847, and the Institut canadien de Montréal, which hosted sixty-eight from 1845 to 1871.[13] Indeed, the fact that the essay so rapidly reached its peak at the latter, which presented eleven essays in 1847, shows that the forms associated with the beginning of public sociability were soon abandoned. The fact that thirty of the sixty-eight essays given at the Institut were delivered by law students or young lawyers confirms that this culture of eloquence was especially suited to people in the field of law.

Debates, which involved arguing for or against a position on a question, to some extent continued on from the college academies, and prepared participants to plead in court and make speeches in parliament if not sermons from the pulpit. They were less frequent than public lectures, but more so than essays.[14] Fourteen associations offered their members about 575 debates between 1845 and 1880, of which 240 were held at the Institut canadien de Montréal, which presented twenty-five debates in 1858. Lawyers and journalists were most likely to debate topical questions in Canadian and international politics.

The public lectures, essays, and debates are a clear indication of the central role the middle class of the liberal professions played in the cultural takeoff that occurred during the union. Not only did legal practitioners find in the associations a place to exercise leadership, but they developed a culture of rhetoric there that prepared them for professional life. Law could lead anywhere, including to literature: the writers of this period were usually lawyers, and their flights of oratory in the associations sometimes concerned literature.[15]

THE ASSOCIATIONS' LIBRARIES AND READING ROOMS

At the heart of the culture of eloquence, associations also promoted reading, with libraries of books and newspaper reading rooms. In 1851, when the government adopted the Act for the Incorporation and Better Management of Library Associations and Mechanics' Institutes, it recognized that the recent trend toward opening libraries was related to the associations. More generally, the associations' libraries were a decisive step in the long process leading to public libraries. Although they claimed to be public, the Quebec Library (1778–) and the Montreal Library (1796–) were based on individual subscription, and not public libraries open to all without distinction as to language, religion or occupation and financed by local public funds. Unlike the libraries of specific "communities" – subscribers, occupational groups, or colleges – the associations' libraries were open to a broader public than that made up of lawyers, doctors, artisans ("mechanics"), clerks or clerical students, and to people who could not afford to subscribe to an elite library. These libraries were a new and decisive step in the process that would make libraries truly public at the end of the nineteenth century.

Associations thus launched a trend of reading as a more public activity. From 1840 to 1880, there were 105 libraries founded by specific groups in Montreal, of which sixty-four were francophone. Of the latter, twenty-nine – almost half – were established between 1850 and 1860. They included associations' libraries, of course, but also those of lawyers, artisans, schools, parishes, and companies (Sun Life, Grand Trunk Railway, Bank of Montreal) and quasi-public anglophone libraries such as the Fraser Library (1885) and the Westmount Public Library (1899). Another sign of the importance of the associations' libraries: at a time before card catalogues, they published the most catalogues, enabling members to diversify their book borrowing.

The law of 1851 put an end to the practice of libraries incorporating under private law; it provided a legal framework for associations' libraries and granted them subsidies, which had hitherto been limited to a few institutions. Five years later, on the initiative of the new superintendent of public education, Pierre-Joseph-Olivier Chauveau, the law was extended to parish and township libraries, which were to be administered by local school commissioners, and in 1876 the law was amended to include cities, towns, and villages. The results were rapid; the number of these libraries, which Chauveau called public in his annual reports, reached a peak in 1863–64, with 284 of them in Lower Canada, and the size of their combined collections was also at its maximum, with 196,204 volumes.[16]

In addition to being subject, in the case of the Institut canadien de Montréal, to debate and censure by the Church for having books on the Index and Protestant newspapers, libraries were part of the everyday activities of the most dynamic associations, which provided their members or subscribers with proper libraries and periodicals rooms.

The collection of the library of the Institut canadien de Montréal reached a first peak in 1855, with over 4,000 volumes, despite a devastating fire in February 1850. By 1879, it had 10,657 books.[17] Thanks to the printed catalogues (1852, 1870, 1876), we know that 80 per cent of the books were in French and that in 1852, for example, one third of the collection consisted of works by novelists such as Alexandre Dumas *père*, Balzac, and Eugène Sue and writers such as Chateaubriand, and that one quarter consisted of history books. The library's American collection contained, for example, the writings of Alexis de Tocqueville, while the Canadian collection was rich in parliamentary documents and offered histories of Canada by Michel Bibaud, François-Xavier Garneau, and Robert Christie, novels by Joseph Doutre and François-Réal Angers, the poetry collection of the same Bibaud and James Huston's *Répertoire national.* From 1870 to 1876, literature (46 per cent) and history (21 per cent) accounted for two thirds of the books in the collection, and included the French serial novelists (Dumas, Sue, Féval, Aimard).

Supply is one thing, demand another. The former can be assessed by means of the library's printed catalogues, the latter by the handwritten loan registers, when, by a miracle, they survive, as they have in the case of the Institut canadien de Montréal. From 1845 to 1880, the Institut's library loaned 78,850 books, with a first peak of 4,175 in 1854. These records bring to light a little-known aspect of public reading: the difference between the content of the collection – the supply – and what the members and subscribers borrowed – the demand. Thus, while literature represented 33 per cent of the collection, it accounted for 77 per cent of the circulation, or demand. Loans of French novels rose from 66 per cent of overall book circulation in 1865 to 85 per cent in 1875. On 13 August 1861, the secretary of the Institut recorded in the minutes of the meeting: "A lot of books have been borrowed, especially in the light literature category; let us hope that interest will also be shown in the other categories; they are much more deserving of it." One book out of five was by Dumas *père*, although, like Eugène Sue, he was on the Index. In 1870, a total of 13 per cent of the books in the Institut canadien de Montréal library were on the Index; in 1868, there were 50 per cent of the books in circulation, essentially novels, on the Index.

It is clear, then, that the censure of the Institut canadien de Montréal for the presence of books on the Index in its library concerned less Voltaire, Volney, or the Encyclopedists, but rather the French authors of serial novels, where the freedom to read had a different significance.

The press gave associations publicity, and associations gave the press exposure in their newspaper reading rooms. When Antoine Gérin-Lajoie complained that the Sulpicians' Oeuvre des bons livres "has no newsroom attached to its library" although that was "something businessmen absolutely cannot do without," he was recognizing three things: that in 1847, a library could not afford not to have a section of newspapers, that the term *chambre de nouvelles*, as it was called, was a literal translation of the word *newsroom* used by the colony's anglophones, and that this newsroom was of enormous interest to businessmen. This tradition of the newsroom in Quebec City and Montreal recalls the fact that newspaper reading rooms were first attached to commodity markets, reflecting an aspect of exchange characteristic of the economic liberalism of the period, especially after the abolition of British protectionism in 1846. In this rapidly growing market economy, circulation concerned information as much as products on the markets; exchange was both material and intellectual, and knowing also meant having.

The library of the Institut canadien de Montréal had a very dynamic newsroom, which at its most active point, in 1857, received 126 different newspapers and magazines from Lower Canada, Upper Canada, the "Gulf provinces," the United States (*Le Courrier des États-Unis,* from New York, and the *North American*), France (*L'Écho des feuilletons, La Semaine de Paris, Le National, Le Magasin pittoresque*), and Great Britain (*Blackwood's Magazine, The Dublin Magazine, The Enquirer*).[18]

The "Catholic" libraries had other objectives: "The parish library is the antidote to those unwholesome novels that infest our cities and are already invading our countryside, violating the sanctuary of the family and bringing with them perversion of the spirit and corruption of the heart." Although the Oeuvre des bons livres (1844–57), which was run by the Sulpicians of Montreal and modelled on the organization of the same name in Bordeaux, France, had a "disparate, insipid" religious collection, that was no longer true for its Cabinet de lecture paroissial (1857–67), which had been founded to combat the "poison" of the Institut canadien and had 2,225 works in 1862, of which 32 per cent were religious writing and 48 per cent letters and philosophy.[19]

THE PRESS AND THE TELEGRAPH

Parent had said that the press was the library of the people, and Chauveau, the superintendent of public education, felt that it "had replaced the forum, the public square that in ancient times was the only way to speak to the people." Chauveau, who could not imagine schools without public libraries, or public libraries without newspaper reading rooms, wrote in 1857: "The newspaper is a step forward; it is more than a book. The book is the serious, discreet doctor who awaits you in his office. The newspaper is the ardent, tireless missionary who runs after you and allows you no rest. The newspaper is also ... the book that got bored on the shelves of its library and tore out all its pages and flung them to the four winds ... One can always not pick up a book; one cannot escape from the newspaper."

Associations benefited from the rise of the press and also contributed to it: newspapers announced and reported on the activities of associations and published the texts of public lectures or essays, while newsrooms made newspapers accessible to everyone. In Lower Canada, from 1840 to 1879, there were 222 new newspapers launched, of which 127 were French (57 per cent) and 90 English (40 per cent). The number of papers available doubled from 1840 to 1869, and tripled from 1840 to 1879, not counting those from the United States.[20] The regions outside Montreal and Quebec City finally had regular papers: 45 per cent of the papers were published in these regions, and 59 per cent of the French-language papers. In Trois-Rivières, there were *Le Journal des Trois-Rivières*, *L'Ère nouvelle*, and *Le Constitutionnel*; in Mascouche, *Le Courrier de Saint-Hyacinthe*, *Le Journal de Saint-Hyacinthe*, and *L'Union*; in Arthabaska, *L'Union des Cantons de l'Est*; in Sorel, *La Gazette de Sorel*; in Joliette, which also had a seminary, *La Gazette de Joliette*; in Sainte-Anne-de-la-Pocatière, *La Gazette des campagnes*; in Rimouski, *La Voix du Golfe*; in L'Avenir, *Le Défricheur*; and in Saint-Jean-sur-Richelieu, *Le Canada français*. In Montreal, thirty-five of the sixty-eight papers published were French, compared with thirty-three of fifty-four in Quebec City.

The expansion of the press clearly shows the relationship between the cultural takeoff and urbanization; the demographic threshold required to support the publication of a daily paper in Lower Canada and Quebec was forty-two thousand inhabitants in 1851; it was thirty-four thousand in 1871; for a weekly, the threshold was respectively three thousand and two thousand inhabitants in those years. The same exercise may be carried out for schools, associations, or inns in order to establish the population required for the different types of cultural activities and institutions.[21]

In addition to spreading into the regions, the press became confessionalized and specialized. The Catholic hierarchy, which before 1840 had not seen any need "to establish a public paper," launched *Les Mélanges religieux* in Montreal in 1840. The religious newspapers were not necessarily the voice of the bishops, but the ultramontanist line was unmistakable in *Le Courrier du Canada* and *La Vérité*, published by Tardivel in Quebec City, as well as in *Le Journal des Trois-Rivières*, *Le Nouveau Monde*, *L'Étendard*, and *Le Franc-Parleur*, published in Montreal. This shows that the press was a press of opinion, in which opinions were strongly marked by the government or the opposition and by the ideological war of words that occurred in the union and post-Confederation periods. Papers such as *L'Opinion publique* popularized illustrations; they also specialized after 1860, with publications for doctors, legal professionals, science buffs, or music lovers.[22]

This rise of the press was connected, as we shall see, to the growth of literacy, the importance of newspapers in the associations, and the ideological polarization of the papers. Other contributing factors were economic prosperity, the ability to send information more rapidly, and the development of the railway system, which prolonged the economic and commercial year, previously limited in winter by navigation conditions. Year-round economic activity made information, advertising, and daily newspapers necessary. Although the majority of dailies were English until 1883, *La Patrie* (1857), *La Presse* (1863–64), published by Médéric Lanctôt, *La Minerve* and *Le Journal de Québec* (1864), *Le Pays* (1868), *L'Ordre* (1870), and *Le Canadien* (1874) published on working days. However, in 1881 as in 1851, the Quebec press was predominantly weekly.

Information travelled faster because of the mail system, increased access to the international press, which arrived on transatlantic steamships, the introduction of national and international telegraph service, the installation of the transatlantic cable, and the organization of press agencies. Post offices proliferated to process the increasing volumes of mail and newspapers. Lower Canada had 260 post offices in 1851, or 2.9 per 10,000 inhabitants. The mail processed rose from nine million letters in 1871 to eleven million ten years later. In 1851, a total of 32 per cent of the population had postal service six times a week; by 1881, the figure was 71 per cent. Of course, postal service varied by region: in 1881, fully 37 per cent of the population of Saguenay–Lac-Saint-Jean had no postal service. In 1851, only 11 per cent of the population had access to railway mail service, whereas three decades later, 41 per cent had it, particularly subscribers to newspapers sent by railway mail – 45 per cent of newspapers in 1871, and 54 per cent in 1881.

The press of Lower Canada obtained articles from foreign newspapers through exchange or subscription. In 1848, three quarters of the international news came from Europe and one fifth from the American press. *La Minerve*, *L'Avenir*, and *Le Canadien* often reprinted French correspondents published in *Le Courrier des États-Unis* of New York. *Le Journal de Québec*, *Le Canadien*, and *Les Mélanges religieux* had correspondents in France for varying periods.

The introduction of telegraph service in Montreal in May 1846 made it much easier to obtain information. In August 1847, Montreal and Toronto were linked by telegraph; in October of the same year, Montreal and Quebec City; in 1851, Montreal and Halifax, a crucial step, which made it possible to transmit Atlantic news to the interior of the country, even in winter, before the railway connected Montreal and Halifax in 1876. From 1849 to 1856, European news was distributed by European press agencies – Wolff in Germany, Havas in France, Reuter in Britain – and beginning in 1856, by the Associated Press of New York. Not even technology was safe from the ideological antagonism of the period. On 29 September 1866, *Le Pays* waxed ironic about *Le Courrier du Canada*, which had attacked the Associated Press: "Organize, form a society, find an agent and you will receive news that suits your taste. Let a religious agency be the counterpart to the freethinkers' agency."

In winter, the news arrived by boat in Halifax, which sent it by telegraph to Boston and New York. When the St Lawrence was open to navigation, the Montreal Telegraph Company had a station in Pointe-au-Père and the British North American Company had a transmitter in

Rivière-du-Loup to receive printed news by ship and telegraph it west-
ward even before the ship berthed in Quebec City or Montreal. Once the
transatlantic cable was installed in August 1866, European news was sent
from London to New York, and transmitted to Montreal by the Associated
Press via the Montreal Telegraph Company. News was received two days
after it happened, and the "telegraphic style" became the norm in the
press, alongside the poems and novels of a "national" literature in the
making.[23]

ASSOCIATIONS, MUSEUMS, AND SOCIABILITY

In the early days of the union, the idea of associations was promoted in
terms of the need for a public life. Literary associations, by various
means, created a sociability based on public lectures and the reading of
newspapers. The press reported on each public lecture as a cultural and
social event, describing the details and playing up its urbane character.

Museums developed after 1840 as part of the trend to form associations, growing out of the interest in science, the arts, "curiosities," agriculture, and industry. This interest in museums remained an essentially
anglophone phenomenon and was mainly associated with the museum
of the Natural History Society of Montreal (1827) and to a lesser extent
those of the new Geological Society of Canada (1844) and the Montreal
Society of Artists (1847–48).

Francophones took some initiatives in this area, but for the most part,
they were short-lived. In Quebec City, in the wake of the Vattemare project for a big umbrella institute made up of existing organizations, the
painter Joseph Légaré tried to maintain as a "National Museum" an "Art
Gallery" (1833–53) consisting of his own collection of paintings. In
Montreal, Guilbault's Botanic and Zoological Garden (1852–69) combined demonstrations of "curiosities," a menagerie, concerts, a circus,
and hot-air balloons. The Institut canadien de Montréal, with its support
from prominent citizens and literary figures, in 1854 developed a plan
for a museum; following Joseph-Guillaume Barthe's trip to France in
1855, it created the museum between 1866 and 1869, when the Institut's
new building was inaugurated. The museum offered the Institut's members a few natural "curiosities," some works of art – prints, oil paintings,
and sculptures – historical memorabilia, and coins. Its collection was later turned over to the Art Association of Montreal (AAM), founded in
1860 on the occasion of the Prince of Wales's visit to Montreal to inaugu-
rate Victoria Bridge – the symbol of Montreal as an industrial city, named
for his mother, the Queen. The Art Association had no artists among its
members; it was created by anglophones (twelve of the 205 founding

members were francophones) and for anglophones, as shown by the choice of the Anglican bishop of Montreal as president. In 1879, the AAM built itself a permanent museum, which exhibited works from private collections and paintings by members of the Royal Academy of Canada, which was founded the following year.

Referring implicitly to the ideological dissension in the francophone community of Montreal at the time, and recognizing once again the anglophones' "spirit of association," the young painter Napoléon Bourassa commented in 1864:

The spirit of association is very strong among our fellow citizens of English origin; their social education has developed this quality in them so well that it has become part of their character. An Englishman brings it with him wherever in the world he settles; and it is doubtless his most precious piece of baggage, because this quality is the most vital factor in his success, giving him wealth and indisputable political superiority everywhere, without great effort, and without internal warring. We people of French origin spend a lot of time fighting at the beginning of any undertaking, we fight during it, and we almost always fight at the end.

This anglophone colonial merchant bourgeoisie, which cared about the prestige of its city when a representative of the mother country's monarchy visited and was eager to exhibit its wealth and knowledge, already had experience with industrial exhibitions because of its economic power. As early as 1843, the Mechanics' Institute of Montreal organized an exhibition of new industrial products made in the colony, and awarded prizes to products selected by a committee. The first provincial exhibition was organized in 1850 to select the furnishings for the Canadian pavilion at the first Universal Exhibition, which was held in London in 1851; subsequent exhibitions took place in Montreal's Crystal Palace, also inaugurated in 1860 by the Prince of Wales.[24]

NOT MUCH SOCIABILITY IN THEATRE AND MUSIC

Those who promoted the idea of associations had been right to bemoan the lack of a theatre in which a French Canadian and Montreal sociability could have developed and found expression. They lacked theatre, concerts, learned societies or circles, they said in 1845, and this was still true for theatre and music in 1877.

Before 1880, as in the case of museums, the sociability of shows in Montreal was anglophone, centred on the Royal Theatre and the Dominion Theatre. While travelling theatre companies from Paris via

New York or New Orleans presented plays in Montreal between 1840 and 1880, the city was still unable to support a permanent francophone troupe. It should be noted that the theatre was frowned on by the Catholic Church. At the same time Mgr Bourget began his offensive against the Institut canadien de Montréal, he also condemned shows and theatre, deploring the fact that "these unconfessed foreigners who come and expose us to the wrath of heaven ... take from us considerable amounts that we sacrifice to pleasure while we refuse them to charity." "Foreign actors" were like a "new visitation of cholera or typhus"; they showed "a revolting immorality," knew how to "affect all the senses with sensual and carnal impressions" and used gestures to excite "the most shameful passions with a truly infernal malice." The theatre was thus utterly "foreign" and the danger it posed, like the serial novels one could borrow at the Institut canadien de Montréal, was more of a moral than an intellectual nature. By the beginning of the 1860s, the bishop had understood that Dumas, Eugène Sue, gestural language, and the speech and costumes of shows were likely to reach more people than Voltaire or Volney. Although the Sulpicians were unbending on these matters, the French Canadian bishops allowed "innocent recreation" that respected Christian prudence. The Church supported college theatre, whose repertoire was carefully selected and in which the inevitable female roles were played by young men. It also permitted amateur theatre presented for "worthy causes." Since they could not combat this popular activity, they adopted it and tried to adapt it. The wolf was in the fold.[25]

Montreal concert halls were also anglophone until 1890, as the names show: Royal Theatre (1825), City Concert Hall (1852), Mechanics' Hall (1854), Bonaventure Hall (1857), St Patrick's Hall (1868), Nordheimer Hall (1859), after a brand of piano; Dominion (1872), Queen's Theatre and Academy of Music (1875). From 1852 to 1875, two thirds of the lyric theatre productions in Montreal were presented at the Royal, and later, the Academy of Music took over. From 1840 to 1912, the repertoire was American (218 titles out of 560) and French (171 titles). The great successes of the day were *Il Trovatore*, *The Bohemian Girl*, *Faust*, *La mascotte*, *Carmen*, *Les cloches de Corneville*, *Lucia di Lammermoor*, and *La fille du régiment*. There was only one French Canadian work presented in this period: in 1868, *La conversion d'un pêcheur de la Nouvelle-Écosse* (The conversion of a Nova Scotia fisherman) by Jean-Baptiste Labelle, which had a highly political libretto. Labelle was part of the small group of French Canadians (which also included Edmond Hardy and Charles Lavallée) who were beginning to make names for themselves as leaders of bands or orchestras or in music publishing (A.-J. Boucher), and who were joined in 1865 by the Belgian musicians Jules Hone and Frantz Jehin-Prume.

Secular music and lyric theatre were no more popular with the Church than dramatic theatre. In 1843, *Les Mélanges religieux* stated that musicians and singers were part of the "nomadic race," to which *La Minerve* replied: "Canadians will not forbid a kind of entertainment that the most enlightened governments in Europe subsidize and that the monarchs, princes and princesses best known for their religious sentiments attend and encourage in France, Russia, Germany and Britain." The clerical opposition continued; on 28 August 1868, *Le Nouveau Monde*, the coloratura soprano of ultramontanism, wrote of some planned performances of Offenbach's *La duchesse de Gérolstein* and *La belle Hélène.* "Paris enjoyed these performances for six months; but the Paris that could thus applaud the spectacle of honest husbands being ridiculed, prostitutes idolized, and filial respect presented as idiotic was not the Paris of decent people in the true sense of the word." Morality was threatened, all the more so in that the evil serpent once again took a seductive form.[26]

THE SPREAD OF PUBLIC EDUCATION AND LITERACY

The public education system had to be reconstructed after the Rebellions, and especially after the Legislative Council's failure to extend the Assembly Schools Act in 1836. In 1843, responsibility for education was returned to the Catholic Church, which had demonstrated its unfailing loyalty during the Rebellions.

Early in the union period, the old question debated in 1819 was still relevant: should religious instruction be the mainstay of primary education? *Les Mélanges religieux*, recently founded by Mgr Bourget, maintained that "there is a more complete and profound education in the simple intelligence of the little Catholic catechism than is generally thought." To this organ of the bishopric, "the way to improve the situation of the people does not precisely consist in instructing it, but in making its masters compassionate, charitable and human," and "the religious education is the only one that can enable them to bear the hardship of their labours with patience and even joy." The danger of education was that it created "semi-scholars, semi-doctors who disturb the tranquility of families and who resist both civil and ecclesiastical authority."

Others had a different view of education. At the Institut canadien de Montréal, lecturers and debaters discussed the question of "popular education" quite often. P.-R. Lafrenaye held that "national education is simply a corollary of the sovereignty of the people" and that "without instruction in the duties of public and social life, the elective principle becomes a bitter joke." Taking his reasoning even further, he maintained that education enabled "society to free itself from the errors and

prejudices that have been used so long to exploit it."[27] Clearly, "authority" was to be resisted, and just as clearly, school was still a social issue.

This tone was to mark public debate on education from the confessionalization of the system in 1843 to the establishment of a Ministry of
Public Instruction in 1867 and its abolition in 1875. But it did not prevent a remarkable takeoff of education, which was made necessary by
economic development and made possible by two superintendents of
public instruction, Dr Jean-Baptiste Meilleur (1842–55) and Pierre-
Joseph-Olivier Chauveau, who later became the minister responsible
(1855–67). The legislative action of these two men (laws of 1841, 1845,
1846, 1849, 1851, and 1856) re-established the system, although it met
with some resistance. Large landowners and seigneurs described the
Education Act of 1846 as a machine for taxing a peasant population
that already had obligations to the seigneur and tithes and the cost of a
pew in church to pay. The resulting "guerre des éteignoirs" (candle
snuffers' war) took the form of a refusal to elect school commissioners,
withdrawal of students from school, legal challenges, and even the destruction and burning of schools; it touched a nerve in a peasantry that
had large families and relied on their children's labour, and was now
being asked to pay a monthly fee per child, whether or not all the children attended school.[28]

The superintendents' legislative action was accompanied by government investment in education: in ten years, its spending tripled, growing
from £9,764 in 1849 to £29,037 in 1859,[29] the dollar having become
the currency after 1858. The increase in the number of schools was
remarkable: 804 in 1842; 1,298 in 1843; 1,832 in 1844; 2,005 in 1850;
3,199 in 1859; 4,028 in 1870.[30] A pool of teachers was formed through
a government initiative to establish normal schools (École normale
Jacques-Cartier in Montreal and École normale Laval in Quebec City,
both founded in 1857), which produced, on average, 144 graduates a
year from 1857 to 1875. At the primary and secondary school levels, the
teachers continued to be primarily lay, but after 1877, there was a rise in
the proportion of clergy. The proportion of female teachers also increased, and the great majority of them were laypersons.[31] In the early
years of the union, the issue of the teaching certificate had been raised
in connection with teacher training, but only for laypersons, not for religious. This issue arose again with the new normal schools, most of
which granted teachers a professional diploma.[32]

With the exception of the three years (1846–48) of the "guerre des
éteignoirs," the number of students rose constantly, from 4,935 in 1842
to 39,397 in 1843, to 61,031 in 1844, to 74,857 in 1850, to 108,284 in
1853, and to 202,648 in 1865.[33] The fact that the growth of the student

population between 1850 and 1855 was greater than that of the overall population is another indication of the cultural takeoff that was under way.[34] So is the literacy rate, which had remained in the 20 to 30 per cent range from the 1830s through the 1850s, but rose to 41 per cent between 1860 and 1869 and passed the 50 per cent mark between 1870 and 1879 (52 per cent), except for French Canadian farmers (47.8 per cent) and day labourers (19.6 per cent).[35]

This was the general trend. It should be remembered that the test of literacy was the ability of spouses to sign their marriage certificates. The chronology varied depending on a number of factors. The literacy rate was higher in the St Lawrence Valley than in newly settled villages, although colonization of some regions was much more recent than of others; the Mauricie region was colonized long before the Saguenay–Lac-Saint-Jean region, for example. Literacy was also generally higher in urban than rural areas, although it took the population of Trois-Rivières a decade longer to reach the 50 per cent literacy mark than it took Lower Canada as a whole.[36] This gap is explained by the rate of economic development in the Mauricie region, where the construction lumber sector took off after 1850 and pulp and paper followed shortly after 1875. It could also happen that an urban area had a low literacy rate because of the presence of large numbers of unskilled or semi-skilled workers. Wives were more often able to sign their names than their husbands as of 1850 in Lower Canada, and as of 1830 in Trois-Rivières. One thing is certain: schools were bringing literacy to a population in the urban, commercial, and industrial areas that increasingly needed it, and for whom it affected the practices of voting and reading newspapers or novels, and attitudes to religion.[37] Although schools were the instrumental cause of increased literacy, the interaction of economic and cultural incentives and the wealth of resources provided to develop and maintain the ability to read and the pleasure of reading – newspapers, libraries, bookstores – should be stressed.

COLLEGES, UNIVERSITIES, AND THE LIBERAL PROFESSIONS

This effort to establish schools was spearheaded by people in the liberal professions, who made up the great majority of francophone members of the legislature, and the Catholic clergy, which replenished its ranks by recruiting religious congregations, generally from France, and founding ten new college seminaries. These college seminaries, which provided a classical secondary education in the Greco-Roman humanities, produced priests and lawyers, notaries and doctors, who went on to debate, in the associations and the press, the value of the classical education provided by the clergy; and at times the clergy itself revealed its internal division on the issue of the pagan and non-Christian authors studied in the humanities courses.

Ten new colleges were added to the eight that already existed. Some of these new institutions were initiatives of recently arrived religious orders: the Clercs de Saint-Viateur opened a college in Joliette (1846) and one in Rigaud (1850); the Pères de Sainte-Croix founded Collège de Saint-Laurent (1847); the Jesuits, who had returned to the country, founded Collège Sainte-Marie (1848). In other cases, the new colleges were founded by the secular clergy of recently established dioceses: this was the case in Lévis (1853), Trois-Rivières (1860), Rimouski (1870), Chicoutimi (1873), and Sherbrooke (1875). The clergy in charge of these colleges sought to ensure the uniformity of the education they provided. They began by creating a bachelor's degree in 1854, and then, in 1865, requested the affiliation of the colleges to the arts faculty of Université Laval. Using the same textbooks – which they had refused to do for the primary level when it was proposed by the state – and providing a uniform examination for the bachelor's degree, the clergy educated youth systematically in versification, rhetoric, scholastic philosophy and, later, Thomist philosophy. The college seminaries trained both clergy and professionals in a sort of de facto ultramontanism, an alliance of the religious and the civil that continued until 1937, when for the first time, graduates "going into the world" were more numerous than those "going into orders." The 2,500 to 3,000 students who attended these eighteen colleges each year reproduced the patterns of social relations in the nineteenth century: they were the sons of parents of all social conditions; in the early union period, a small number of the parents belonged to the liberal professions, but later, the liberal professions consolidated and they eventually came to be overrepresented in the colleges.[38]

The liberal professions, fed by the college seminaries, first organized outside the university, establishing the School of Medicine and Surgery of Montreal (1843), the Chambre des Notaires (1847), and the Barreau du Bas-Canada (1849). The anglophone community of Lower Canada had founded McGill College in 1821, but it was not until 1852 that the French Canadian community established Université Laval in Quebec City, and it was only in 1876, after endless plans and internal disputes, that the Catholic Church, under pressure from Rome, agreed to open a branch of Université Laval in Montreal. The university faculties offered theology, law, medicine and, secondarily, arts. In the field of law, Université Laval in Quebec City faced strong competition: not only did some francophone students attend McGill University (for example,

Gonzalve Doutre, Antoine-Aimé Dorion, Wilfrid Laurier) but others studied at Maximilien Bibaud's law school (1851–67) at the Jesuit Collège Sainte-Marie or one established by the Institut canadien de Montréal in association with Coburg College in Ontario (1866–71). It was this competition that filled the cultural associations with law students and fostered a culture of lawyers. As for the teaching of the sciences, it was developed mainly at Université Laval in Quebec City, where it appears that Darwinism and evolution gave rise to little debate, until the École polytechnique de Montréal opened in 1874.[39]

FRENCH CANADIAN BOOKSELLING AND PUBLISHING

Although the cultural takeoff of francophone Quebec had little effect on the institutions and sociability of museums, theatre, and music, it was nonetheless clearly evident in the development of associations and the rise of literacy, for example, and it was consolidated in the area of bookselling and publishing.

Édouard-Raymond Fabre was no longer the only francophone bookseller in Montreal. Beauchemin and Rolland had both opened bookstores in 1842, followed by Chapeleau in 1849 and by Cadieux and Derome in 1878. The number of catalogues published by booksellers to help their individual and institutional customers choose titles was another sign of life in this cultural area. Twelve such catalogues were published between 1840 and 1880, eight of them from 1870 to 1880.[40] Quebec bookstores continued to obtain their stock from France, competing with the clergy and religious institutions, which imported directly from Catholic bookstores such as Mame in Tours or Poussielgue and Jouby in Paris. It is probable that the six million dollars' worth of books imported between 1850 and 1867 went principally to the English-language bookstores of Lower Canada.[41] Indeed, 45 per cent of them came from Great Britain and 49 per cent from the United States; this situation led the colonial authorities in 1843 to set up a committee to evaluate the extent of book importing from the United States. Legislation was passed in 1850 to protect British authors from much cheaper reprints arriving from the United States via the Richelieu River and Saint-Jean-sur-Richelieu. An 1841 law on literary property in the colony encouraged local authors to demand their rights. From 1842 to 1858, applications for copyright came mainly from Lower Canada and Montreal. One indication of the situation in publishing in this period is the fact that copyright holders tended to be printer-"publishers" of schoolbooks rather than authors of fiction.[42] And although 1,067 literary works were "registered" in Ottawa between 1842 and 1867, the real takeoff for authors occurred after 1880.[43]

While the situation was improving, authors still published novels or other works by subscription; examples include Joseph Doutre (*Les fiancés de 1812*, 1844), James Huston (*Répertoire national*, 1848), and Mgr Laflèche (*Quelques considérations sur les rapports de la société civile avec la religion et la famille*, 1866). Even in 1873, Arthur Buies could write, with his characteristic irony: "Today, I am relatively rich; subscription is an admirable lever when one knows how to use it artfully; for me, as God is my witness, it has enabled me to uncover treasures."

But there were also examples such as that of the printer Ludger Duvernay, who joined forces with the bookseller Fabre to publish textbooks, prayer books, and political pamphlets, "printed" by Duvernay and "available at the bookstore" of Fabre. Efforts to actually publish, to take charge of the whole process of publishing, became more common. G.H. Cherrier, who was presenting himself as a publisher in 1853, wrote in the preface to P.-J.-O. Chauveau's *Charles Guérin*: "We thus believe that we have shown courage and a good example in being the first to buy a literary work, in giving one of our writers a reliable income ... in sparing him the troubles and risks of publishing." The lawsuit of the Brousseau brothers printers against the editors of *Les Soirées canadiennes* (1860–65) reveals the fragility of the discourse and the situation of the printer-publisher. Initially, the Brousseaus stated that they appreciated "the *Soirées canadiennes* a little for the profits and much for the honour" it brought them; but in the course of the legal case, they answered one of the editors as follows: "Mr. Lajoie's writing probably amuses and interests our workers; but he would be wrong to think that they can live on that alone. We cannot, for that very reason, print out of pure patriotism."

Musical publishing contributed to the takeoff of publishing. After 1850, mainly because of Adélard-Joseph Boucher, music seller, composer, "publisher" of music periodicals, sheet music, and collections, it became possible to publish works by Lower Canada composers. Among the published works were "marches" of the union, Confederation or Saint-Jean-Baptiste Day, the "galop" of the telegraph, the waltz "Souvenirs de Cacouna," and the "St Lawrence Tubular Bridge Mazurka" celebrating the inauguration of Victoria Bridge. Although the bookseller Beauchemin's publishing production really expanded after 1880, he published some fifty titles between 1870 and 1879, half of which were textbooks and practical publications such as almanacs.[44]

The clearest indication of the takeoff of the publishing sector is the change from the publication of novels in serial form to their publication in the form of volumes. From 1840 to 1850, four novels were published serially at the bottom of the front page of newspapers, while only one, *Les fiancés de 1812* by Joseph Doutre (1844), was published in book form. Not only did the Catholic Church disapprove of novels; so did a class of professionals polarized by politics and economic reconstruction at the beginning of the union period. In 1846, for example, Étienne Parent felt that "a population like ours" had "forests to clear, fields to improve and all sorts of factories to establish," and that "the time for light literature has not yet come and will not come any time soon in Canada." James Huston tried to counter the ephemeral nature of literary and intellectual creations in the colony by publishing his *Répertoire national* beginning in 1848. In the preface, he admitted: "For we are convinced that what sickens the heart of Canadian writers is to see the fruit of their studies and labours pass with the periodical newspapers into eternal oblivion."

Four novels appeared in book form from 1850 to 1860, including three by Henry-Émile Chevalier and Chauveau's *Charles Guérin*, which was published by Cherrier. During the publication of *Les Soirées canadiennes* (1860), *Le Foyer canadien* (1863), *La Revue canadienne* (1864), and a follow-up to Huston's *Répertoire national* entitled *La littérature canadienne de 1850 à 1860*, there were six novels published in book form between 1860 and 1870, and fifteen between 1870 and 1880, including thirteen published in Montreal by printer-publishers or bookseller-publishers. It was a sign of the times that "Canadian" literature figured in the catalogues of Quebec booksellers: a few pages of the 1873 catalogue of the Rolland bookstore devoted to "Canadian publications" described 116 works by Canadian authors, including some twenty novels. In 1877, the same bookseller published a catalogue of Canadian works, with some sixty titles. Beauchemin included in its 1879 catalogue six pages of "Canadian publications or works on Canada." Starting in 1857, bookstores benefited from the purchase of books to be awarded as prizes in schools, an indication of the development of the schools; over two hundred thousand volumes were awarded as prizes between 1857 and 1880, a quarter of which were by Canadian authors.[45] After 1876, Abbé Casgrain helped ensure that French Canadian authors figured more prominently among those whose works were awarded to students.[46]

The ability of these authors and writers to live on their writing was limited; practically all of them had a principal occupation that provided for their basic needs: from 1840 to 1900, they were first journalists, next civil servants, and then lawyers. While French Canadian writers had gained visibility through their texts and in institutions related to writing, their status remained precarious and subject to the effects of partisan politics, which Buies described as follows in 1877: "We have in our country so many reasons to become rapidly disgusted by the muses, to renounce all intellectual culture, and politics is so joyless that I wonder how one can be involved in it for thirty years and still remember that there are books and people who write them!" Indeed, people had being doing so for over thirty years, as Edmond Lareau observed in the first history of Canadian literature (*Histoire de la littérature canadienne*), published in 1874 after various intellectual assessments, defences, and illustrations of a "national literature" produced by Joseph-Guillaume Barthe in 1855, Maximilien Bibaud in 1858, Laurent-Olivier David in 1861, Hector Fabre and Henri-Raymond Casgrain in 1866, Emmanuel Blain de Saint-Aubin in 1871, and Louis-Michel Darveau in 1873.[47]

CONCLUSION

The development of associations and the adoption of education laws during the first decade of the union made possible the cultural takeoff of the late 1850s and early 1860s. The associations were the matrix for the creation of libraries and were key places for reading and discussion of the press, and they were themselves at their height in the late 1850s, as is shown by applications for government subsidies and by Mgr Bourget's first censure of the Institut canadien de Montréal. The first law on libraries, in 1851, and the record number of libraries founded by groups in Montreal between 1850 and 1860 attest to the dynamism of the associations. It was also at the end of the 1850s that there were the largest number of public lectures and debates, and the rhetorical culture of the legal professions became established. The number of newspapers and magazines received by the periodicals reading room of the Institut canadien de Montréal was highest in 1857; in the same year, the press began to become regionalized, and the first French-language daily paper, the aptly named *La Patrie*, was founded in Montreal.

The impact of the education laws passed in the 1840s was already perceptible by the following decade. Government investment in education continued, student enrolments doubled from 1844 to 1854 and from 1850 to 1858, and at the point in the 1850s when the student population was growing faster than the total population, the practice of awarding books as prizes in school contributed to the growth of bookstores. With the founding of Université Laval in 1852 and the establishment of normal schools in 1857, higher education began to spread. But it was not until the 1870s that the education laws of the 1840s and 1850s and the increase in the number of schools and accredited teachers led to a rise in the rate of literacy, to 41 per cent between 1860 and 1870, and to 52 per cent between 1870 and 1880.

Maximilien Bibaud, who published a book on Canada's "material and intellectual progress" (*Tableau historique des progrès matériels et intellectuels du Canada*) in 1858, took note of the cultural and literary takeoff. There was also a proliferation of national literary magazines and there were assessments by Fabre, Casgrain, and David between 1860 and 1870. All this activity was in a sense reflected in Lareau's 1874 *Histoire de la littera-ture canadienne*. But why was there this cultural takeoff during the union period?

A cultural takeoff would have been attainable after the end of the economic blockade in 1815 if it had been possible to build on the advances that had been made. This was impossible for three reasons: the interruption caused by the Rebellions; the conflict between the Assembly and the Legislative Council, which led, for example, to the non-renewal of the Assembly Schools Act in 1836; and the positions of the Church with regard to schools, libraries, theatre, and new ideas in general.

After 1837 and 1838, political, cultural, and religious reconstruction took place under the banner of economic reconstruction, which was a precondition for the existence of institutions and even symbols. The economic recovery was stimulated by the end of British protectionism and the beginning of free trade, particularly with the United States, with which reciprocal trade relationships increased. The economic reconstruction was helped by the investment of British capital in the development of canal and railway systems and by new technologies such as steam power and telegraphy. The inauguration of Victoria Bridge in 1859 perfectly symbolized the alliance of the imperial metropolis and the anglophone colonial bourgeoisie: the Queen gave her name to a railway bridge inaugurated by her son the Prince of Wales, who also presided over the opening of the Crystal Palace – an imitation of the one in London – and the first exhibition of the Art Association of Montreal.

The anglophone bourgeoisie of Montreal had the means to provide for its sociability and institutions; the anglophones of Lower Canada, who lived in the cities, had rates of school attendance, literacy, and newspaper ownership that were higher than their percentage of the total population. It was this bourgeoisie in Montreal and Quebec City that set up associations, libraries, and bookstores, and between 1840 and 1877, created museums, theatres, and concert halls without equal in the French Canadian community; it exhibited both its industrial products and the paintings of its masters, major or minor.

This colonial reality weighed heavily on French Canadian culture of the period. French Canadians, as they readily admitted, modelled certain of their institutions on those of the anglophone community and adopted its cultural forms, adapting them to their needs and customs. The very terms used for the public lecture and newsroom are borrowed directly from the English terms, confirming the borrowing of these forms. The French Canadians adapted these cultural forms to their aspirations, creating a new sociability, whose absence and necessity they had recognized at the beginning of the union. Their cultural institutions also benefited from the fact that more and more of them were living in towns or cities. Their adaptation of cultural forms meant that the culture they created reflected the social structure: it was a culture of the liberal professions, in particular, lawyers. Law students and young lawyers were in their element delivering lectures, presenting essays, or debating in associations. If their prominence was out of proportion to their number, it was because the membership was composed mainly of merchants and clerks and artisans, recalling the predominance of the economy in the general reconstruction following the union. As Étienne Parent, who had been politically demoralized by the Rebellions and the union, liked to say shortly after, industry and political economy would be the lifelines for the French Canadians' sorely tested nationality.

The cultural takeoff of the early 1860s may be explained and summed up in two words: *union* and *exchange*. The union of Upper and Lower Canada was a constitutional regime; there was also an economic union, that of the Board of Trade; there would soon be unions of workers; and union was also cultural – the unity of the French Canadians that made them strong. This spirit of union reached a sort of apotheosis in the commercial union of a market economy involving the exchange not only of goods, but also of information and ideas.

PART FOUR

1877–1896

Battles of Honour at the Close of the Century
(1877–1896)

THE ANTAGONISM BETWEEN LIBERALS and ultramontanists began in the late nineteenth century to look like a battle only for honour. After the neutralization of the extremes, there was a final flare-up, as if the last great friction between these visions of society made them luminous one last time.

ULTRAMONTANISTS VS. LIBERALS,
ULTRAMONTANISTS VS. ULTRAMONTANISTS

The old fight the Liberals and Laurier had fought against undue influence was still showing signs of vitality. The bishops published a new pastoral letter on the freedom of pastoral ministry and respect for the confessional, still maintaining that priests could not be summoned before civil courts where they would have to reveal the reasons for refusing absolution. Cardinal Simeoni, prefect of the Sacred Congregation for the Propagation of the Faith, who urged priests not to mention any names in the pulpit at the risk of civil trials, wrote to Mgr Taschereau: "Your Lord will have to notify each of the suffragans, on behalf of His Holiness, that each of the prelates, individually, must abstain from brandishing or allowing to be brandished, either in parliament or in the press, the question of the modification of the law concerning undue influence."

The election in the county of Berthier-en-Haut in 1878 continued to fuel the debate. In 1881, Mgr Laflèche of Trois-Rivières, a disciple of Mgr Bourget (who would die in 1885), published a volume on undue spiritual influence in relation to religious and civil liberty, in which he stated that the law forbidding electoral interference by the clergy infringed on their freedom. He based his argument in favour of a right to clerical immunity on other forms of immunity: parliamentary, senatorial, judicial, and military immunity.

In this period of increased urbanization and land development, the debate around clerical immunity took the form of the exemption of fabriques, educational and charitable institutions, and religious communities from property tax. For the episcopate, there had to be no change in this situation, "other than its recognition," because "it is an established fact in our history that it is the Church that formed our country," and without the Church, the government and the municipalities "would be required to provide for all necessities." This was indeed what would happen in 1884 and 1885 in the case of insane asylums; the government resisted the ultramontanist slogan "the state out of the asylums," but finally continued, for economic reasons, to call on the religious communities.[1]

A bishop's circular letter from 1885 on the prohibition of clerical involvement in politics and the use of the pulpit as a political soapbox for fear of creating a "spectacle of disunity" corroborates Cardinal Simeoni's observation of the "disastrous division that is ruining us."[2] For there were divisions between liberals and ultramontanists, among liberals and among ultramontanists. Pamphlets, books, and series of articles in newspapers fuelled intellectual and ideological fireworks. They had the tone of judgments, suggesting that this was also a battle of honour.

At the end of 1881, a volume by the tireless Abbé Alexis Pelletier on the "source of the ills of the time" described from the first pages the contemporary habit of leaving decisions to Rome: "Because of this, it has occurred that the Roman congregations to which many of our most important affairs were submitted were constantly as if enveloped in such a network of combined intrigues and ruses." Pelletier therefore intended to enlighten the Roman congregations and explain the source of the liberal evil.

The same year, Abbé Alphonse Villeneuve, a protégé of Mgr Bourget, wrote a book published in Paris entitled *Étude sur le mal révolutionnaire en Canada,* in which he argued against Mgr Conroy, who had stated in 1877 that "the perverse principles that are disrupting Europe have not yet crossed the ocean." For Abbé Villeneuve, the revolutionary evil, that "social poisoning that is circulating in the veins of old Europe" and is the "negation of the rights of God and of His Church in civil societies," did indeed exist in Canada. In 333 pages, he provided a good overview of the liberal symptoms of this evil and the internecine struggles of the clergy, from the debate on undue influence to the university question.

In turn, Mgr Laflèche knocked on the door of the Roman congregations to submit a brief on "the religious difficulties in Canada," which included an appendix. In more than two hundred pages, he gave his version of religious problems related to political and university issues and undue influence. He went on the offensive again with a letter to "Cardinal NN" explaining "the necessity of an inquiry into the religious affairs of Canada," an excellent example and proof, if any was required, of the internecine war being fought within the clergy. Mgr Laflèche complained that his brief had been transmitted to his adversaries before being studied by Rome, and wondered if "that is the justice of the Holy See." To him, Abbé Benjamin Pâquet and Mgr Zitelli, those who governed the Church of the province of Quebec, were the source of the intrigue. The bishop had himself experienced what the liberals had gone through: "In Rome, it is even more difficult than at home to make oneself heard." Without doubt, this was because there were many there pleading their cases. One of them was Mgr Taschereau, who made 103 comments on Mgr Laflèche's brief, examining in his own way liberalism, the Catholic Program, undue influence, the university question, and the new Civil Code.

In *Le libéralisme dans la province de Québec*, a little book of ninety-five pages published in 1897, an anonymous author gave an overview of French Canadian liberalism from the Guibord affair to Laurier, a kind of reply to Laurent-Olivier David's pamphlet on the mission and work of the Canadian clergy published the year before. It is not known if this very critical assessment of liberalism reached Rome, where Mgr Laflèche suffered another defeat, with regard to the division of his diocese and the creation of a new diocese in Nicolet.[3]

LIBERALS AGAINST LIBERALS

In 1877, Laurier had hoped and believed that his speech would ease the conflicts and create an electorally advantageous and politically governable centre. In the main, he was proven right in the immediate present, and liberals such as Edmond Lareau continued to distinguish between conservatism and liberalism and between political liberalism and Catholic liberalism. The spirit of Laurier endured and became dominant, although it did not prevail with everyone. While the leading figures of radical liberalism were dying (Dessaulles, Laflamme, Joseph, and Gonzalve Doutre) and the library and archives of the Institut canadien de Montréal were being moved to the "Protestant," anglophone Fraser Institute, one of the first "public" libraries in Montreal and Quebec, new liberal figures were emerging and making their mark, in particular Arthur Buies, Louis Fréchette, Honoré Beaugrand, Aristide Filiatreault, Marc Sauvalle, and Godfroy Langlois. Beaugrand, confined by his image as a Freemason, made no attempt to hide his anticlerical liberalism: "Our cause would not be worth our efforts to make it triumph if the best way to make it triumph was to hide its nature. The Liberal Party has been in opposition for twenty-five years, and it can stay there for another twenty-five years if the people have not yet accepted its ideas, but may it march head high, banners unfurled, before the country." Beaugrand also suggested that his liberalism came from France and not from England; he wrote to Laurier in 1895: "You repudiate the French Revolution and I admire it; not in its excesses nor in its exaggerations, but in its effects, in its legislation and its traditions. I prefer Thiers, Henri Martin and Michelet to the Englishman Macaulay or to Hume. I prefer the French Republic of today to the aristocratic and notoriously anti-democratic English government."[4]

Beaugrand's *La Patrie*, founded in 1879, showed a good deal of staying power, and around 1890, *L'Avenir* and *Le Pays* established a certain intellectual and ideological lineage. Aristide Filiatreault published *Le Canada artistique* (January 1890–January 1891), which became *Canada-Revue* (January 1891–August 1894) and then *Le Réveil* (September 1894–November 1901). Godfroy Langlois, who began his career as a journalist with *Le Clairon* of Montreal in December 1889, took up *L'Avenir*'s battle against tithes, adapting it to the question of immunity from taxation:

Our clergy has always been sovereign on our shores and it does not like any more today than in the past seeing some of the faithful evading its control … ; it has shaped the people to make it simple-minded and submissive and the French Canadian priest has never been accustomed to boldness or to movements that do not originate with his influence. In addition, it has accustomed the inhabitants of this province to consider all its material interests as immunities, and when we ask the religious corporations to help us with the payment of taxes, certain of the devout, holier than thou, impiously veil their scandalized faces and even cry impiety.[5]

Going on to *L'Écho des Deux-Montagnes* (1890–91) of Sainte-Scholastique, which was replaced by *La Liberté* (1891–95), Langlois continued his denunciation of political interference by the clergy and the teaching in the classical colleges. The ideological pressure of liberalism was also maintained by *L'Union* (1873) of Saint-Hyacinthe, *Le Progrès de Valleyfield* (1878), *L'Électeur* (1880–96), and then *La Paix* (1884) of Quebec City and *Le Clairon* (1884) of Trois-Rivières.

These were the papers that denounced scandals among members of the clergy, Dessaulles having only threatened to do so twenty years earlier. In the summer of 1892, a score of cases of indecency involving the clergy were discussed in *Canada-Revue*, *La Patrie*, and *L'Écho des Deux-Montagnes*, and the liberal poet Louis Fréchette intervened in the affair of the Sulpician Guihot, who was accused of sending licentious writings to the wife of an important Montreal lawyer. A collective pastoral letter from the bishops against these accusations did not, however, put an end to the liberal initiatives. In 1894, Fréchette offended again, denouncing a French parish priest by the name of Bruneau who had murdered another priest and a florist. Fréchette used the Bruneau affair to promote accountability of the clergy before the civil courts and call into question clerical immunity.[6]

The rivalry between the liberal press and the ultramontanist newspapers such as Tardivel's *La Vérité* (1881) and *La Croix* (1893) of Montreal led to legal proceedings such as those of Marc Sauvalle against Tardivel, who had accused Sauvalle of being a "Methodist," and Aristide Filiatreault against Abbé David Gosselin of *La Semaine religieuse* of Quebec City, the official organ of the archdiocese. But the most spectacular case of censure was that of *Canada-Revue* by Mgr Fabre, who did not appreciate its serialization of *The Three Musketeers*, which was on the Index. On 11 November 1892, the bishop condemned *Canada-Revue* "to protect the flock," and ordered the refusal of sacraments for those who printed, sold, and read the newspaper. On 12 May 1893, the editors of *Canada-Revue* took Mgr Fabre to court to determine whether canon law could be allowed to harm the material interests of an author, a newspaper owner, or a printer. "Duroc," (Marc Sauvalle), wrote on 25 April: "all we want to establish is that the clergy is always on the side of the oppressor, and has at all times worked to ensure its own domination by subjugating us to the yoke of a powerful conqueror. The history of the clergy since the Conquest is one of the triumph of selfishness."

The lawyers for *Canada-Revue* were aware that they were taking up the battle of the Institut canadien de Montréal, and in the case of Rodolphe Laflamme, that of the Guibord affair, and the publication of the trial documents under the title *La Grande Cause ecclésiastique* [The great clerical case] was a thinly veiled reference to *La Grande Guerre ecclésiastique* [The great clerical war] by Dessaulles. But it was in vain; the judges decided in favour of Mgr Fabre in the lower court and on appeal. The editor of *Canada-Revue*, A. Filiatreault, then published an incendiary book, *Ruines cléricales*, in the most radical tradition of Dessaulles. The tone was unmistakable: it was a battle of honour in which the opponents did not hold back, as demonstrated in three anonymous pamphlets on clericalism that were published in 1896.[7]

In addition to the fireworks of the *Canada-Revue* case, there were other, less spectacular cases of censure: Mgr Laflèche banned *La Sentinelle* in

1886, Mgr Fabre condemned *L'Écho des Deux-Montagnes* at the same time as the *Canada-Revue,* Mgr Bégin and Mgr Fabre condemned *L'Électeur* of Quebec City, which had published L.-O. David's book, *Le clergé canadien, sa mission et son oeuvre.* After being condemned on 27 December 1896, *L'Électeur* came out the following day under the title *Le Soleil.*[8]

THE STATE IN OR OUT OF THE SCHOOLS?

Laurier's speech of 1877 did not keep the schools question from once again becoming a bone of ideological and political contention between liberals, on one hand, and conservatives and ultramontanists, on the other. The debate and the strategies took place on many fronts. The 1875 law abolishing the Ministry of Public Instruction and making bishops ex officio members of the Catholic Committee was already being challenged in 1879. An experienced educator, Urgel-Eugène Archambault, stated: "This law ... may have been a skilful political operation, but I am not afraid to say that I am one of those who doubt the effectiveness of this measure from a pedagogical point of view."

Archambault, the superintendent of the Montreal Catholic School Commission (MCSC), who had recently founded the École Polytechnique, took his opposition to the Montreal level and proposed standardizing the MCSC curriculum while giving the Brothers of the Christian Schools the right to use their methods and textbooks. Archambault was supported by his colleague Jean-Baptiste Cloutier, the future editor of *L'Enseignement primaire* (Primary education), who in September 1880 gave a lecture on the standardization of education. But a royal commission of inquiry on the administration of the MCSC and the issue of religious education in 1882–83 did not lead to any concrete results.[9]

The debate that fuelled the opposition revolved around the bill of 24 July 1880 on the creation of a "book depository," a selection of textbooks, a single one for each school subject, that would be reviewed every four years. Since at least 1855, the very great diversity of school books had been considered an obstacle; the superintendent of public education, P.-J.-O. Chauveau, had written in his 1855 report: "The inspectors, in their reports, are constantly complaining about the huge variety of them that are in use. The choice of textbooks, in practice, is left to the teachers; and, since each has his habits and particular predilections, it follows that a change of books usually takes place with each change of teacher, which occurs too frequently, as we know. Nothing does more to delay the children's progress and to discourage the parents with the useless expenses that are thus imposed on them." The 1880 bill stipulated that schools that did not comply with the law by September 1882 would lose their grants. This measure, which challenged the quasi-monopoly of the religious communities in educational publishing and tried to provide relief for families who were forced, from year to year or from school to school, to purchase more schoolbooks for their children, created an outcry. Father Rousselot of the parish of Notre-Dame in Montreal – the priest in the Guibord affair – saw it as a tactic to get rid of the methods and textbooks of the Brothers of the Christian Schools, which, he noted, the republican and anticlerical Jules Ferry had not done in France. The new Canadian superior of the Brothers of the Christian Schools, Brother Réticius, who had just arrived from France of the Third Republic and of Jules Ferry, argued first with Abbé Verreau, principal of École normale Jacques-Cartier (teachers' college), over the standardization of education and the value of religious versus secular education. He then debated with U.-E. Archambault, who had just published a brief on the question, and he formulated the slogan "the state out of the school." In 1881–82, Premier Chapleau's "small bills à la Ferry" on the book depository and the organization of an inspection system were blocked.[10]

In 1881, Honoré Mercier, the member of Parliament for Saint-Hyacinthe, who was soon to be leader of the provincial Liberals, opened up a new front, that of compulsory schooling, with the argument that ignorance and illiteracy led to "political incapacity in young people," who reached the age of majority without knowing how to read and write. He would have the support of the nascent trade unions, the Knights of Labour and the Trades and Labour Congress of Canada, as well as the radical liberal press and the moderate liberal press. *Le Moniteur du commerce* of Montreal wrote on 19 August 1892:

In the area of education, until twenty years ago, the clergy proved its worth, it is true; but in the last twenty years or so, all the time it has not devoted to its State duties, it has used sometimes to start internecine squabbles and weaken the discipline so necessary to ministry, sometimes to stir up fights among various regular communities in order to maintain or increase, for this one or that one according to the favourable mood of the moment, its sum of influence or wealth. For twenty years, the clergy has done nothing to spread and appreciably increase education among the people.

And the business and labour communities pointed out the imperative need for public education in a context of industrialization, which increasingly demanded knowledge. It was therefore not surprising that, in the absence of the will or the ability to pass a compulsory education law, the function was fulfilled by free evening classes, which were set up from 1889 to 1892 and were denounced by the ultramontanists but welcomed by Cardinal Taschereau because of the social morality that they could inculcate.[11]

The central issue remained that of "the state out of the school." While the archbishop of Quebec City was more favourable to lay teachers, his colleague in Trois-Rivières, Mgr Laflèche, published a pastoral letter against state education, supported by the tireless Mgr Pinsoneault and by Abbé L.-P. Paquin, who gave lectures to the Cercle catholique de Québec against compulsory education. This battle reached a turning point in 1886 when Cardinal Taschereau, writing to Premier Ross, acknowledged that the state had a role to play in schools, thus marginalizing the extremists of "the state out of the school" movement.[12]

While church control of education loosened a little, it was maintained, as is shown by the political attempt – which failed – to require clergy to have a teaching certificate equivalent to that of lay teachers. From 1892 to 1895, efforts to require equal diplomas from religious and lay teachers were opposed by the Catholic Committee of the Council of Public Instruction and by the Legislative Council, where Thomas Chapais made every effort to recall Ferry and the republican clouds that were supposedly hanging over Quebec education: "The teaching congregations object to this measure out of mistrust because it is the first step down a path that leads naturally to State interference, to State tyranny, to the State trampling on their rights, to the State reducing their mission and their educational activities, to the violation by the State of their freedom and their autonomy."[13]

The awareness of industrialization that had led Mercier, the business world, and the trade unions to promote compulsory schooling, standardization of textbooks, and technical education also led moderate and radical liberals to challenge the value of the education provided by the clergy in the classical colleges. Laurier wrote to the premier of Ontario, Edward Blake: "When students graduate from the classical colleges, they are ignorant as well as being fanatical conservatives." *Le Moniteur du commerce*, the voice of the Montreal business community, considered the education of the classical colleges a capital "without market value." The radical liberal poet Louis Fréchette, arguing against Abbé Baillargé, stated: "If the current system is extended, our colleges will soon be nothing more than factories of obsolete graduates too educated to plough and too ignorant to run a store or wield a pen." Referring to Dessaulles's comment that under the prevailing mentality, "we make monks, never men. We organize a convent, never a nation," Fréchette wrote, "It is not the clergy that is made for the country, but the country that is made for the clergy." This was shown in particular in the teaching of philosophy, which had been based on Thomism since the encyclical *Æterni Patris* of 1879.[14]

After the primary school and the classical college, the normal school was the last context of the battle on education and the disagreement within the Church. In 1881, Abbé Verreau, the director of the École Normale Jacques-Cartier and an opponent of Brother Réticius's initiatives, also crossed swords with Mgr Laflèche on the funding of normal schools and the value of religious versus lay teachers in them. Verreau argued in favour of the superiority of lay teachers, who had to obtain a teaching certificate.[15]

A TENACIOUS BATTLER: JULES-PAUL TARDIVEL

Tardivel was an exemplary figure of the swan song of ultramontanism in the late nineteenth century. He equated free, compulsory, neutral, and state schooling and saw Mercier as a man "who is following in the footsteps, he too, of the Jules Ferrys." Raised in the shadow of the presbytery and of Louis Veuillot, Tardivel began his public life at *Le Canadien* in 1873, in the enthusiasm following the Catholic Program of 1871. In 1881, he founded a weekly newspaper with the revealing title *La Vérité*, a Catholic paper first and foremost, non-partisan and dedicated to promoting agriculture and colonization. A sworn enemy of republican France, Tardivel in *La Vérité* denounced liberalism, to him a synonym for "the suppression of the rights of God in the civil and political order" and the "secularization of politics." Laurier's distinctions did not impress Tardivel, who wrote that there "are not two liberalisms, one English, the other French, one religious, the other political. There are only various nuances of the same political-religious error." In 1882, he rejected democracy, and, faithful to the philosophy textbook he used, stated that political power came from God and that the sovereignty of the people, according to which the majority makes the law, was a false doctrine.[16]

Tardivel was the first French Canadian to use Freemasonry as a scapegoat for the "sins" of the Revolution, the Republic, and liberalism. Borrowing from the French press, *La Croix* of Paris, the anti-Masonic league of the French Jesuits, and Claudio Jannet's book on secret societies and society, from which *La Vérité* reprinted long excerpts in 1883–84, Tardivel challenged the archbishop of Quebec City on this in 1884, when the Jesuit Édouard Hamon, under the pseudonym Jean d'Erbrée, published a book on Freemasonry in Quebec and Leo XIII promulgated the encyclical *Humanum genus* on Freemasonry.

The episcopate – from Mgr Taschereau to Mgr Laflèche – wasted no time in dissociating themselves from Tardivel's excessive language and some of his positions, and after 1885, Tardivel was isolated by the Catholic hierarchy.[17]

In spite of his isolation, this uncompromising Catholic conceived a nationalism that was in keeping with his intransigence, completely original and a harbinger of things to come. It was a nationalism different from that of Parent, La Fontaine, and Cartier, which was limited to the affirmation of the characteristics of French Canadians (Catholicism, French language, rural life, civil law) and from that of the radical liberals, which was associated with liberalism and occasionally with the principle of nationality. Tardivel's nationalism was triggered by a series of events that caused him to become disillusioned with the Confederation of 1867. Following the hanging of Riel in 1885, he wrote in *La Vérité* of 21 November: "The Canadian government has thus shed the blood of a madman to quench the ignoble thirst of the Orangemen. How sad! What a shame for our country. This vile stain will never be erased ... The gallows of Regina will grow, will keep growing; its sinister shadow will be cast more and more menacingly over the country ... Always will the image of Louis Riel's corpse be there, swinging between heaven and earth, before the eyes of our population." Already keenly aware of the fact that, four years after Confederation, the francophone Catholics of New Brunswick had lost their right to Catholic schools, Tardivel stated in his newspaper on 2 November 1889:

Since Confederation does not protect the rights of minorities whenever those minorities are French and Catholic, what then is its raison d'être from the point of view of our interests, we French Canadians and Catholics? It may suit the purposes of sectarians who want the anglicization and religious and national apostasy of the French Canadians; but it cannot suit our purposes ... Our enemies will only stop when they have trampled underfoot the last right of the French race in America ... Already there is talk of abolishing the French language as an official language in Ottawa and even in Quebec City ... What will they dare to do when we are no more than one fifth or one sixth [of the population]?

After the loss of school rights by the Franco-Manitobans in 1890, it became clear to Tardivel that "it is necessary to do one of two things: demand respect for our rights in confederation or leave confederation."

This nationalism founded on disillusionment with regard to respect for the Catholic religion and the French language was also fuelled by providentialism, the idea of an interventionist, active Providence. Tardivel wrote in *La Vérité* of 18 March 1893:

When and how will the French Canadian people take the place that is ardently destined for it among the autonomous nations of the earth? That is God's secret. But that hour will surely sound, sooner or later, if we remain faithful to the providential mission that has been entrusted to us ... That providential hour will sound, be assured of that; for it is impossible that God did not want to make a true nation of this French Canadian people whose birth and youth he has so obviously protected ... Let events run their course. The dissolution ... of the interprovincial link will come at the hour and in the manner set by divine Providence.

Tardivel subscribed to the idea of a nationality identified first with its religion and then with its language, and moreover, linking those two distinctive features: "for our nationals, language is closely linked to faith. If they lose the former, they risk losing the latter." Already, he was denouncing the absence of French in federal departments and in the railway and telegraph companies. But the originality of his vision of nationality lay in his choice of a separation of Quebec from Canada, without appealing to the liberal principle of nationality. In this sense, he was the first one to explicitly combine what we call cultural nationalism and political nationalism, to use the distinctive characteristics of a people to propose that it should be provided with a state.

From 1885 to 1895, Tardivel formulated and defined the nature of this ultramontanist Catholic and French Canadian state, this nation "enjoying the benefits of religious unity." This state would cover the northeast of the American continent; it would guarantee the rights of Protestants until they disappeared and it would oppose emigration to the West by French Canadians and immigration into its territory. This state would be, paradoxically, a Catholic republic, republic here meaning the rejection of monarchy and the creation of a presidency, as in the Ecuador of Garcia Moreno. The constitutional regime of this Catholic state would exclude ministerial responsibility and would be based on two houses, one elected and the other made up of the "main groups of the nation." Suffrage would be by family. The union of Church and state would be sealed and the state would be dedicated to the Sacred Heart.

Tardivel presented this vision of French Canadian nationality in a remarkable novel, *Pour la patrie* (For the homeland), published in 1895. This futuristic (the action takes place in 1945) suspense novel of love surpassed by national feeling involved the theft of archives from the Freemasons and had three themes: opposition to republican France in favour of loyalty to the "old France," denunciation of Freemasonry, and advocacy of the separation of the provinces rather than the status quo or a legislative union. It drew from Tardivel's journalism, using Freemasonry as a dramatic plot element, and featuring a "League of Progress," a federal prime minister who is a Freemason and who presents a law favouring a single Canadian nationality or a sect whose archives, obtained by "nationals," provide "irrefutable proof that this constitution [of the country] is the direct work of the lodges; that we are facing a truly diabolical conspiracy to prevent New France, the eldest daughter of the Church in America, from taking her place among the nations of the earth." An acceptable novel, whose characters pray, practise, and witness miracles and the resurrection of a protagonist, *Pour la patrie* already presents a world of leagues, magazines (*La Nouvelle-France*, *La Libre pensée*), and manifestos typical of the turn of the century.

A remarkable novel for its unprecedented vision of nationality, *Pour la patrie* was also the work of a radical Catholic who transformed his religious radicalism into political radicalism and became a supporter of independence out of disillusionment and a desire to protect religion and language. This marginal work is in the image of its author, a tenacious battler, isolated in his "ultra" ultramontanism – his own description – whose newspaper was finally not that of the elites nor that of the common people, rural or urban.[18]

ANOTHER VISION OF "INDEPENDENCE":
THE FUTURE OF CANADA ACCORDING TO MERCIER
(1893)

In 1893, after being ousted from power, Honoré Mercier gave a ringing speech on the future of Canada in Sohmer Park. At a time when preparations were under way to celebrate the sixtieth anniversary of Queen Victoria's reign in 1897, the call for Canada to take its place "under the sun of nations" was one of the first signs of a French Canadian anti-imperialism that would become important at the turn of the century.

Considering himself a francophone who was not an anglophobe, although he confessed that England left him "quite indifferent, almost cold," Mercier felt that England had done more harm than good to the French Canadians, that they "owed it nothing," and that they "could, if necessary, separate from it." Canadians owed their "loyalty to Canada first, and not to foreign countries," and to Mercier it was not disloyal to talk about breaking the colonial tie.

The former premier of Quebec examined three possible solutions: the status quo, political union with the United States, and the independence of Canada. The status quo was unacceptable: the colonial state was transitory, and there were moral reasons (the divorce bill passed by the federal government) and religious reasons (the loss of school rights in New Brunswick and Manitoba) that justified a change of allegiance.

Political union of Canada with the United States seemed tempting to Mercier: American capital already made it possible to exploit mines in

Quebec and Americans would help exploit the forests. A union would make emigration unnecessary, labour would be better remunerated, French Canadians would be spared prejudices of race and religion that were absent in the United States. Each province in the union would be a "virtually independent" state, and unlike the Louisianans, French Canadians would set their own conditions and impose French in all their institutions, except in the House of Representatives.

But Mercier preferred independence for Canada, and "the idea of independence seems to have put down deep roots in Young Canada." Using the Monroe Doctrine, he stated that America belonged to all Americans and that Canada had to free itself from all ties and create a "Canadian Republic."[19]

A TURNING POINT: THE MANITOBA SCHOOLS QUESTION (1890–1896)

The political and cultural debate brought about by the Manitoba schools question marked the end of something, and the beginning of an intellectual and political trajectory that would continue through the twentieth century. The 1896 crisis challenged Confederation itself and again focused scrutiny on the problem of political and electoral intervention by the clergy – which Laurier's speech of 1877 should have laid to rest – at a time when Laurier, the first French Canadian leader of the Liberal Party of Canada, was about to become the first French Canadian prime minister of Canada. The crisis revealed disillusionment with Confederation, an unprecedented political attitude, a "party spirit" that would give rise to a renewal of nationalism and a new split in the French Canadian and Irish Catholic hierarchy.

The tensions of 1896 went back to the summer of 1888, when the Anglo-Protestant press of the Eastern Townships denounced Honoré Mercier's solution to the question of the Jesuit properties. The opposition movement spread to Montreal in the autumn of 1889, and then took the form of opposition in the House of Commons, which refused to pass a motion disallowing the law of July 1888 on the question of the division of the Jesuit properties. The foundation of the Equal Rights Association in Ontario and its activities led in 1890 to the abolition of French as a parliamentary language in Manitoba and the abolition of separate, or Catholic, schools. This was not the first crisis concerning schools. Four years after Confederation, which recognized confessional schools where they existed legally before 1867 and which gave the federal government the power to disallow and remedy any violation of this right by a province, New Brunswick had in 1871 taken away the right of Acadians, the Catholic minority, to separate schools.

By creating a confessional school system rather than a linguistic one, the Constitution of 1867 had entrusted the clergy of the different denominations with the defence of the language and culture associated with them. The pastoral letter of March 1891 from the Catholic bishops on the Manitoba schools question was therefore to be expected. The bishops expressed surprise that "our social and political institutions guaranteed us the protection of all rights and now these same rights are being violated by those who were supposed to safeguard them." To the Catholic hierarchy, this was a flagrant case of persecution, but it was a "shrewd" move "because the legislature, while abolishing the Catholic schools, passed laws that not only maintain the Protestant schools in all their integrity, but even ensure for them, although they are sectarian, the entire share of public money to which the Catholics would have been entitled." It was clear to the bishops "that the Protestant idea dominates this legislature."

The Catholic hierarchy also seized the opportunity of a judgment by the Privy Council in London on 29 January 1895, according to which the Manitoba law of 1890 violated the rights of the Catholic minority; it published two new pastoral letters, the first one calling for respect for these rights in light of the judgment of the Privy Council, the second asking the press and the Catholic clergy to leave the task of carrying out the struggle to the bishops alone.[20]

In the middle of the 1896 election campaign, a cardinal, seven archbishops, and twenty bishops confronted the ruling Conservative Party, which promised a remedial order, and Laurier's Liberal Party, which gave a vague commitment to restore the rights of the Catholics to the satisfaction both of the Protestant majority and the Catholic minority.

In his first public statement as the voice of the episcopate, the young theologian Louis-Adolphe Pâquet listed the guiding principles of the position of the Catholic authorities: "it is not for us a matter of party interest, but an issue of doctrine and ecclesiastical public law of the greatest religious and national significance." Recalling the fundamental ultramontanist principle that "the Church is, because of its purpose, a society essentially superior to the state" and basing himself once again on the judgment of the Privy Council, Abbé Pâquet called on the political parties to take a clear stance: "Would it not be infinitely better for the central power, since it has the right and the opportunity to do so, to raise now against all present and future persecutors a rampart of justice and religious protection?"

A few weeks before the election, the bishops made another appeal, recalling that the highest court in the Empire had recognized "the merits of the Catholics' demands, the legitimacy of their grievances and the right of intervention of the federal authorities so that justice can be done for the oppressed." Their pastoral letter of 6 May 1896 declared that the last session had "betrayed our hopes" and prescribed that "all Catholics should give their votes only to candidates who commit formally and solemnly to vote in Parliament in favour of legislation that restores for the Catholic minority in Manitoba the school rights that were recognized by the Honourable Privy Council of England."

Despite the warning in the pastoral letter that it was up to the bishops "to designate or approve the appropriate means to fulfill the spiritual purpose they propose to pursue," the uncompromising Mgr Laflèche gave a sermon interpreting the bishops' message as a condemnation of Laurier and the Liberal Party. The bishops did not disavow him, and some went so far as to suggest voting for the Conservatives. In a circular letter, the episcopal authority recalled that the priests "will be the first to set an example of prudence and submission in such solemn circumstances."[21]

On 23 June 1896, out of the sixty-five members from Quebec in the House of Commons, Laurier was able to win forty-nine seats, compared to sixteen seats for the Conservatives. The electorate followed Laurier rather than the bishops, and did not re-elect the Conservatives, who had done nothing to protect the rights of Catholics in Manitoba from 1890 to 1896. Louis Fréchette, the radical liberal poet, wrote with obvious satisfaction: "So here is the much-vaunted power of the clergy that made and unmade ministries and ministers; that imposed on the weak its power and on the strong its fear; here it is lying at our feet, and we can measure it at our leisure. Come close, good people, don't be afraid anymore!"[22]

AN EDITORIAL BATTLE OF HONOUR:
CLERGÉ CANADIEN, SA MISSION ET SON ŒUVRE
PLACED ON THE INDEX

In July 1896, Laurent-Olivier David published a book entitled *Le clergé canadien, sa mission et son œuvre*, a moderate look at Church intervention in politics from the troubles of 1837 to the Manitoba schools affair. As respectful as it was, the conclusion of the book was firm: the ministers of religion were portrayed as "men subject to human passions and errors"; one should therefore not "confuse the priest and the religion." As for the Church leaders, David took the view that "the truth came to them laboriously through the cloud of incense that envelopes them." The message was clear: "But what we refuse to the clergy is the right to expel from the Church men who wish to freely exercise their rights as citizens ...

following their judgment and conscience"; what was being demanded was that when the bishops intervened, "the teaching be the same everywhere." The book was used as a pamphlet by the former Zouave Gustave Drolet, who had been sent as an emissary to Rome by Laurier to protest the interference by the clergy in the 1896 election. The prime minister did not want to lose the effects of his 1877 speech.[23]

David's book was put on the Index on 18 December 1896 and it drew the ire of the Dominican Dominique-Ceslas Gonthier, alias Pierre Bernard, the author of *Un manifeste libéral: M.L.-O. David et le clergé canadien,* who suspected that David's book was "written under the inspiration of the Liberal leader." The Vatican saga continued: after the ex-Zouave Drolet, it was Abbé Jean-Baptiste Proulx's turn to go to Rome at Laurier's request. His arguments, which were printed in Rome with a number of documents on the Manitoba schools question, including Laurier's 1877 speech, his speeches on the issue of the Jesuits' properties and the Greenway agreement in Manitoba, the bishops' pastoral letter of 6 May 1896, and Mgr Laflèche's sermon. Abbé Proulx even made public his efforts in Rome in a "travel journal" published in 1897.[24]

The tangible result of this Liberal lobbying of the Vatican was that Rome sent a delegate, Mgr Merry del Val, to Canada from March to May 1897, just after the condemnation by the bishops of Quebec City and Montreal of *L'Électeur* of Quebec City, which had published David's book in full. The apostolic delegate managed to impose a certain silence on the bishops and the Catholics of Canada, and in spite of Father Gonthier being sent to Rome to counter Mgr Merry del Val's arguments, Leo XIII on 8 December 1897 published the encyclical *Affari vos,* which recognized that the Manitoba law of 1890 was a "noxious law," that the remedial order was "defective, imperfect, insufficient" and that it was the bishops' duty to "publicly protest against injustice." But the encyclical also noted the division generated by the election campaign and found it "deplorable" that "Catholic Canadians themselves were unable to act in concert in the defence of interests which so closely touch the common good." The circular letter that accompanied the promulgation of the encyclical recalled the "solemn pact which could not in honour and in justice be broken, and in which [the Catholics] placed absolute trust," while in Quebec, the rights of the Protestants, who were economically powerful, were fully respected.[25]

In 1897, after the Quebec Liberals had spent thirty years in the political wilderness, the Liberal Félix-Gabriel Marchand was elected premier, and Laurier continued his representations in Rome with a view to obtaining an apostolic delegation from Vatican diplomacy; the delegation would be established in Ottawa in 1899. For Laurier, this meant appointing an observer from the Canadian Catholic episcopate. The Manitoba schools question had revealed a new breach in the usual unanimity of the bishops with respect to confessional education: they were now divided between francophone bishops and Irish anglophone bishops, who had different views of the reciprocal protection of the Catholic religion and the French language.

"PARTY SPIRIT"

The Manitoba schools question did not only create divisions among Catholics and the Catholic clergy. Very early on, questions were raised about Laurier's endorsement of the Greenway agreement and what appeared to be a vague and unfulfilled electoral promise because he had placed the interests of the Liberal Party above those of the country and his French Canadian and Catholic compatriots, although they had trusted him despite the bishops' warnings. Indeed, how could he have promised so much – to satisfy the Anglo-Protestant majority and the Franco-Catholic minority in Manitoba and in the country in general?

The question of "party spirit" did not first arise in 1896; it dated back to the foundation of the Parti national in 1879 and the desire to temper radical liberalism by placing "the national interest above that of the party." The paper *La Concorde* of Trois-Rivières adopted as its motto the same year "The interests of the country before those of parties." In 1885 at the time of the Riel affair, F.-X.-A. Trudel in *L'Étendard* had accused Premier Chapleau of putting the interests of his party before those of the country. In 1886, Father Labelle wrote to Rameau de Saint-Père: "To me, the major enemies to be feared are not the English, but the French Canadians ... You would not believe how politics is spoiling our population and accustoming it to respect nothing when it comes to political questions. Politicians blithely lie as long as the party benefits."

Tardivel countered the party spirit with "Catholic spirit" and told his editor Amédée Denault that the country needed Catholic polemicists who were independent of the political parties. The clergy quickly identified what Mercier would in 1889 call "fratricidal conflicts." In a public statement on February 1896, the theologian L.-A. Pâquet stated: "I will add that, given the party spirit that so deeply divides our public figures, it is not from any one specific political group that we can expect the strength of unity needed to rally all Catholics in a single way of thinking and under a single flag." The bishops' letter on the Manitoba issue had itself spoken of "this party spirit that distorts judgment and produces in the mind a kind of obstinate willed blindness." In 1898, the bishop of Quebec City, Mgr Bégin, would write to his colleague Langevin in

Saint-Boniface that politicians are "puppets ... capable of betraying the most holy causes in order to stay in power."[26]

The discourse of "the vocation of the French race in America" was perpetuated by conservatives and ultramontanists such as Adolphe-Basile Routhier and J.-P. Tardivel and priests such as Abbé Henri-Raymond Casgrain. But it should be recognized that this discourse of the elites was contradicted by reality: 120,000 French Canadians emigrated to the United States from 1870 to 1880; 150,000 from 1880 to 1890; 140,000 from 1890 to 1900, primarily for economic reasons but also because of the attraction of success. As Mercier said in 1893, US capital was already at work in Quebec, but the world of labour was also beginning to be organized by "international unions," the American Knights of Labor, who established themselves in Quebec around 1880 and who extracted acceptance from Mgr Taschereau under pressure from the American bishops. Signs of American influence were also evident in a culture of leisure, from lyric theatre to amusement parks such as Sohmer Park (1889–1919). It was in this park, which was open on Sunday (they even sold beer there on the "Lord's day"), and on "the Main," St Lawrence Boulevard, that the first signs of a *holy day* being transformed into a *holiday* could be seen.[27]

During the two decades 1877 to 1897, there was significant development in relations between French Canada and Great Britain. Beginning with the famous speech by Laurier and the idea of a Canadian liberalism of the English, rather than the French, kind, and then the appeals (in the Guibord affair and the Manitoba schools question) to the Privy Council as the highest court, the period ended with the grand finale of Queen Victoria's Diamond Jubilee in 1897. That event, which marked the high point of the Empire, enjoyed a certain unanimity, starting with Mercier's speech of 1893 on the future of an independent Canada – an idea that the young Henri Bourassa would take up in 1899 during the Boer War in South Africa.

In 1890, French Canadian ultramontanism was more than fifty years old and was engaged in a battle of honour, facing opposition after the Catholic Program of 1871 and through the marginal figure of Tardivel. The papacy still remained central in Quebec Catholicism. The encyclicals

(*Aeterni Patris,* on Thomist philosophy, *Rerum novarum,* on labour issues, *Affari vos,* on the Manitoba schools question) – with the possible exception of *Inter sollicitudines,* which advised French Catholics to accept the Republic – were still received as words of truth and principles for action. Rome was still turned to, in particular for arbitration on the interminable local quarrels (Mgr Laflèche vs. Mgr Taschereau, the tireless Abbé Alexis Pelletier, the Zouave G. Drolet, Abbé J.-B. Proulx). On education and other "mixed" questions, the ultramontanist principle of the supremacy of heaven over earth, religion over politics, the Church over the state continued to be upheld. The clergy still journeyed to Rome, in an Italy that had finally achieved unity, and about which Abbé Léon Provancher wrote in 1881: "We then went to Piazza del Quirinale, where ... the usurper Humbert lives. The papal arms in relief on the marble above the main entrance are still there to attest to all eyes to the sacrilegious usurpation of the impious king." And in 1882, a visit to Quebec by the French general de Charette revived the fervour of the Canadian Zouaves whom he had commanded in Italy in 1869–70.

The most decisive change in the relationship between Rome and French Canada came about in the context of the emergence of the demographic and economic power of the United States and the evolution of English-speaking Canada. This North American context would transform French Canadians' view of Rome and Vatican diplomacy and change relationships within Canadian Catholicism. The reorientation of Vatican policy began in 1888 when Leo XIII recommended to the Irish bishops of the United States that they ensure that Italian immigrants have priests who spoke their language. During a period of intense immigration to the United States, the Vatican sensitivity to the languages and cultures of "national" clergies was inevitable. The Liberal leader F.-G. Marchand was conscious of this with respect to the possibility of the subdivision of dioceses in the Ottawa Valley and the Northwest; he wrote to Rameau de Saint-Père: "The only danger that threatens us ... is coming to us by way of Rome, if information is lacking there." Once again, all roads led to Rome.

In 1891, the crisis became obvious: in Ogdensburg, in a New England with many Catholic parishes of French Canadians, Franco-Americans were asking for a French-speaking coadjutor bishop. Rome turned them down; Cardinal Mazella wrote: "The English language must in the end be the only language in North America." Worried, Mgr Bégin, then bishop of Chicoutimi, expressed the hope that, in this issue and in that of the possible subdivision of Canadian dioceses, Rome would not sacrifice the French Canadians of Quebec and the United States to the Irish and the proponents of "Americanization." The situation became so worrying that in 1892, Mgr Racine, the bishop of Sherbrooke, took to Rome a brief from the Quebec episcopate on the attitude of Irish priests toward Franco-Americans.

Seen from Rome, the situation of Quebec and the French Canadians was more than ever that of a minority. The association of faith and language did not necessarily hold for the Roman congregations, which included Catholics in North America and saw them as majority English-speaking. Mgr Satolli wrote to his colleague Mgr Rampolla: "It is ridiculous ... to affirm that if they do not maintain their native language exclusively in the home and at church they risk losing their faith, as if the latter were tied to one or another language for every nation. Indeed, the inevitable course of events for every immigrant nationality shows that change and uniformity of language and customs [occur] within one generation at the latest." Was what was "inevitable" for Franco-American Catholics also inevitable in the medium term for the French-speaking Catholics of Quebec and Canada? In the aim of converting Anglo-Saxon America to Catholicism, should the responsibility and initiative belong to the Anglo-Irish bishops and clergy, even though 70 per cent of Canadian Catholics in 1890 were francophone? Was the Vatican going to side with the most numerous, with the North American majority against the Catholic majority of Canada, which at the same time was a francophone minority in Canada as well as in North America? Mgr Lynch, the bishop of the diocese of Toronto, wanted it to, even seeing a linguistic and religious providentialism in the example of Ireland: "Ireland was subdued ... in order the more effectively to amalgamate with the English nation ... They resisted but were compelled by force to learn the language. God has his designs in this. Little did Irish children suspect when they were whipped in school for not knowing the English lesson that God destined the English language in their mouths to spread the true faith of his Divine Son throughout the greater part of the world."[28]

FRANCE OF THE THIRD REPUBLIC

In the last quarter of the nineteenth century, relations between Quebec and France became institutionalized. The visit of *La Capricieuse* had permitted the re-establishment of official relations in 1855 and led to the opening of a French consulate in Canada in 1858. This rediscovery of French Canada by France in the context of the reformulation of its colonial policy had taken the form of Rameau de Saint-Père's statement on the vocation of the French race in America.

Canada took part in the Paris World's Fair of 1878; the provinces, including Quebec, were especially present in the international school exhibition. Economic exchanges between Quebec and France were formalized with the foundation in 1880 of the Crédit Foncier Franco-Canadien, the success of which was rather limited in spite of the opening, in 1886, of a French chamber of commerce in Montreal. Except for two loans to Quebec by France in 1890 and 1893, economic relations remained below expectations.[29]

Diplomatic relations between Canada and France took a new direction in 1882 with the appointment of Hector Fabre as Quebec's representative and Canada's commissioner and commercial agent in France. The commission established a bimonthly journal, *Paris-Canada*, which was published from 1884 to 1914. Along with the commission, the "La Boucane" group was formed and became a meeting place for Canadians living in Paris. The awarding of the Montyon Prize of the Académie française to poet Louis Fréchette in 1881 provided individual recognition for literary work, but the creation four years later of a French group, Les Amis du Canada (Friends of Canada), which included Rameau de Saint-Père and the geographer Onésime Reclus, was the real result of a desire to provide a basis for the vocation of the French race in America. In order to achieve this, Les Amis du Canada, in an ongoing relationship with Father Labelle, the "apostle of colonization" in northern Quebec, wanted to link Quebec and Manitoba through northern Ontario and set up the Société de colonisation du Témiscamingue. In the summer of 1888, Rameau de Saint-Père visited Canada and travelled through the north with the deputy minister of colonization, Father Labelle, who spent eight months in France and Belgium in 1890 to encourage emigration and recruit colonists. But Father Labelle's premature death struck a fatal blow to this network of men who, as Reclus said, loved Canada and "proved it through deeds, not through words, phrases, invocations of Cartier, of Champlain, remarks about Montcalm and Saint-Jean-Baptiste Day festivities."[30]

Rameau de Saint-Père, a member of the Le Play school since 1853, was the mainstay of a new interest by some French Canadians in this empirical and Catholic method of studying society. Rameau gave a lecture on French Canada to the Société d'économie sociale in 1873, two years before that organization published the results of a study by the first French consul in Canada, Count Gauldrée-Boileau, on the inhabitants of Saint-Irénée in Charlevoix. The Canadian commissioner in France, Hector Fabre, published in *La Réforme sociale*, a journal of the Le Play school, and Premier Honoré Mercier lectured at the Société d'économie sociale in 1891.

In 1888, a Quebec branch of the Le Play school was created, the Société d'économie sociale de Montréal, which existed until 1911, recruiting about fifteen members and organizing some seventy meetings over a period of twenty years. Léon Gérin, who had been interested in Le Play and his disciple Demolins since 1888, joined the society in 1892. But aside from one person who would become Quebec's first sociologist, the members, with the possible exception of Abbé Stanislas-Alfred Lortie – whose *Compositeur typographe* was published in 1905 – were more interested in the social doctrine formulated in *Rerum novarum* in 1891 than in any actual surveys carried out using the Le Play method.[31]

These exchanges took place in the context of the Third Republic, which conservatives and ultramontanists had warned against in the debates on the state within or outside the school. Jules Ferry was probably, after Louis Veuillot, the Frenchman most quoted in those years of looking for enemies. The Republic was under constant attack from the ultramontanists. In *Le Canadien* of 14 January 1879, Tardivel declared: "We love the France of yore, the powerful, great and glorious France, the eldest daughter of the Church; we also love the Catholic France of today. But modern France, as the Revolution has made it, the France fallen from its ancient splendour, impious France, in a word, republican France, inspires in us only a feeling that is a mixture of horror and pity." His compatriot A.-B. Routhier, who presented himself as "an American Vendean" in La-Roche-sur-Yon and declared that "we have remained French because we have remained Catholic," tried to reconcile his two homelands by repudiating the France of 1789: "Owing to circumstances that we may well call providential, England would save us from France, while our love for France saved us from England."

With the rhetorical skill of radicals of all stripes, Tardivel summarized the two Frances of conservative and ultraconservative French Canadians by contrasting Sacré-Coeur Basilica on Montmartre with the iron tower designed by Gustave Eiffel for the Paris World's Fair of 1889: "Two monuments dominate Paris ... both are modern, both represent an *idea*, a *principle*": the basilica on Montmartre symbolized expiation and "just punishment" following the Commune of 1870–71; the Eiffel Tower, which recalled the Tower of Babel, "pretends to greatness" but "achieves only the grotesque." Tardivel brought to its climax a debate that had gone on for six months, starting in January 1888, in Beaugrand's *La Patrie*, on one side, and in his own *La Vérité* and the ultramontanist F.-X.-A. Trudel's *L'Étendard*, on the other side, concerning Canada's participation in the World's Fair of 1889, which celebrated the centenary of 1789. The government of Canada was absent, wanting at all costs to avoid the trap of participating in an international event identified with the Third Republic, as well as 1789 and 1793.[32]

The French Canadian Catholic hierarchy and press do not seem to have ascribed much importance to the "toast of Algiers" after the 1889 election in France, when Cardinal Lavigerie asked Catholics to rally to the Republic – nor did they subscribe to Leo XIII's encyclical *Inter sollicitudines* (16 February 1892) on that question. This is not very surprising in view of the fact that they suspected even the Alliance française, including its Montreal branch, of Freemasonry. Fréchette, who had just denounced the scandal involving Father Guihot and argued with Abbé Baillargé about the classical colleges, explained this suspicion as follows: "The whole secret of the matter lies in this: there are in Montreal members of the Alliance française who refuse to bow down devoutly to certified Baillargism and guaranteed Guihotism; they must be crushed at any price. And since slander is the only thing that can be used against these citizens who are above reproach, then slander must be employed." It was therefore not surprising that a certain anticlerical community in France explained the reservations of some French Canadians with regard to their country as follows: "Its inhabitants are not at all French, on the contrary, they are Canadians and nothing else. How could they love a France that has silenced the demands of the clergy, when they grovel more and more before them? How could they respect a country that, in their eyes, has corrupted the whole world?"³³

The tensions in France were reflected in Quebec. In 1881, before General Boulanger's actions had given rise to Boulangism (1887), a veritable "union of the discontented," the general, a symbol of France's policy of revenge on Germany, visited Quebec, where he was well received in spite of the political divisions. Appointed minister of war in July 1886, he pleased French Canadians by maintaining the name of the barracks on Rue du Faubourg Poissonnière, the Caserne de la Nouvelle-France. While *Paris-Canada*, the newspaper of the Canadian commission, was written by Boulangists, members of Déroulède's Ligue des Patriotes in Quebec City, Tardivel called Boulanger a "vulgar adventurer" in 1889, when the general had to flee to Brussels, where he committed suicide.³⁴

A visit by General Marquis de Charette to Quebec City and Montreal in June and July 1882 provided another opportunity to reignite the dissension among French Canadians regarding their French heritage. A relative of Count de Chambord, the heir of the Bourbons, de Charette was a Legitimist who had commanded the French Canadian Zouaves in Rome in 1869–70. Invited by the Union Allet des zouaves, de Charette was described as a "counter-revolutionary standard-bearer" by the ultramontanist *Courrier du Canada* of 3 July 1882, which used his visit as a pretext to denounce the Third Republic and republicanism in general. Fréchette, who was a liberal sentinel in those years, wrote a long series of articles in Beaugrand's *La Patrie*, entitled "Petite histoire des rois de France" (anecdotal history of the kings of France), enumerating the injustices and excesses of the French monarchy.[35]

In October 1890, the Count of Paris passed through Montreal. Invited to the Jesuit college, he was introduced by George Drummond as "the distinguished descendant of Kings" and the symbol of a stable society. At the Société des antiquaires (antiquarians' society), he was welcomed as "the glorious personification of the Christian and chivalrous spirit." His journey took him among the bishops and the Ursulines of Trois-Rivières and Quebec City. In Quebec City, he was shown the old flag of Carillon. But this monarchist voyage in the Canadian – and liberal – land gave rise to demonstrations. The young Raoul Dandurand considered it "unacceptable that a Canadian of French origin could be a partisan of an heir of Louis XV, who so odiously abandoned us."[36]

The publication of *La Croix* (1893–95) of Montreal, which was modelled on *La Croix* of Paris, published in a few cities in France and Belgium, is a good example of a certain cultural mimicry that went so far as to import debates that had little to do with the local situation. *La Croix*, a biweekly paper edited by A. Denault, who had come from Tardivel's *La Vérité*, led a crusade of young people in favour of faith in the workplace, drawing on the encyclical *Rerum novarum* of 1891. The newspaper believed in a link between God and homeland, between Catholicism and nationality, between faith and language. Virulently anti-Freemasonry, the paper imported anti-Semitism into a society where the Jewish community was still numerically insignificant. Starting in November 1894, *La Croix* published excerpts from *La Libre parole*, the paper of the anti-Semite Drumont, and articles in the same vein by a certain Raoul Renault of Quebec City.[37]

Finally, the Canadian representation of France in the official discourse, that of commissioner Fabre, Premier Mercier, and Prime Minister Laurier, is surprising. Speaking at the Société des études maritimes et coloniales (society for maritime and colonial studies), Hector Fabre waxed lyrical: "Countries that have loved France at certain times, when they needed her, when they needed her blood and her gold, are not rare in the world; but do you know many countries that have always loved her as mine has? That have loved her for having received from her the benefit of existence, that have loved her after the pain of separation, across the shadows of forgetting, that have loved her for herself, without expecting anything, without judging her, without criticizing her, simply loving her, do you know many?" This steadfast loyalty did not cause this friend of Laurier to forget another loyalty: "If we owe to you the first possession, that of existence, it is to England that we owe the second, liberty." Writing on "French society in Canada" in Le Play's *La Réforme sociale*, Fabre presented French Canada as "a little people that has remained French and become free," that had been able to "renew itself without upsets" while "keeping the old ways." The commissioner emphasized the cordial understanding that prevailed in Canada, where the two influences, French and English, "balance each other." For this man who since 1858 had traced a path of moderate liberalism, 1867 had made Quebec "a kind of French state." As for Canada's independence in relation to England, "it can be defined in a few words: it is independence except in name; the thing without the label."

Mercier also spoke for a Canada where there was an ethnic and religious cordial understanding: "in Canada, we live in peace with all the nationalities; English, Scottish and Irish gladly join hands with the French." During a visit to the Marist Brothers, he said that while the Jesuits in France were being dispossessed of their property, in Canada it was being restored to them. A month earlier, at the Alliance française in Paris, he had reiterated the idea that the French Canadians had survived thanks to the Catholic clergy.

In 1897, Laurier took up his friend Fabre's ideas. At the British Chamber of Commerce in Paris, he said, "In Canada, we are proud of this dual loyalty to distinct ideas and aspirations. We are loyal to the great nation that gave us life, we are loyal to the great nation that gave us liberty." As a good liberal who had since 1877 stressed the British heritage of Canadian liberalism over its French heritage, Laurier put it this way: "Liberty, Equality, Fraternity. Well, everything there is in that motto of valour, greatness and generosity, we have today in Canada." He took part as prime minister of Canada in the imperial celebration of the Jubilee in London, and he observed at the banquet of Les Amis du Canada in Paris: "Today Canada is a nation. Yes, I repeat it with pride, Canada is a nation, although it is still just a colony," expressing the same paradox as Fabre and Routhier: a nation that had the appearance of a state, but that was still a colony.[38]

CONCLUSION

The period 1867–77 had been the high point of outspoken expression of opinions, marked by the Guibord affair and the Catholic Program. The uncompromising Louis-Antoine Dessaulles had raised the question of tolerance, as intolerable as it was in certain quarters. In his famous speech of 1877, Laurier had contributed to clarifying the liberalism of

1837 and 1848. And thanks to the intervention of the apostolic delegate, Mgr Conroy, the undue influence of a certain segment of the clergy had been moderated.

The two decades from Laurier's speech to his election as prime minister (1877–96) marked the end of a certain ideological fervour. The end of the episcopal trinity of Mgr Bourget, who died in 1885, and Cardinal Taschereau and Mgr Laflèche, both of whom died in 1898, was a first sign of the passing of a certain style of political presence of bishops. Then, extremists of all stripes faded from sight: Tardivel, with his *La Vérité*, was quickly isolated; radical liberals such as Aristide Filiatreault, the author of *Ruines cléricales*, did not have the kind of radical liberalism that would survive Laurier's speech of 1877; and a certain type of clerical censure abated after the condemnation of L.-O. David's book.

The very style of radical liberalism was changing: while there were still trials around magazines and newspapers, and denunciations of the behaviour of members of the clergy, articles were no longer on tithes, but on the clergy's immunity from property tax, one sign among others that urbanization was influencing the ideological debates. But the liberal struggle focused on the issue of schools and, particularly in Montreal, on the Catholic School Commission and its administration, the standardization of instruction and the textbooks used. The issue of education was clearly brought to the fore by urbanization and industrialization, as is shown by the questions of compulsory schooling and evening schools, as well as the involvement of the unions in the debate; education was no longer enough, training was required. The antagonism over the question of the state's role in the schools was lessened in 1886 by Cardinal Taschereau, who was beginning to make distinctions, as did his colleague Abbé Verreau, principal of École normale Jacques-Cartier, who, unlike Mgr Laflèche, recognized the value of lay teachers with their mandatory teaching certificates.

Along with this sense that the "knots" of old antagonisms were being untied, there was a formation of new knots – which the twentieth century would have to undo. While the strands of these knots had begun to come together with the loss of the Catholic Acadians' school rights in New Brunswick in 1871 and the hanging of Louis Riel in 1885, it was the Manitoba schools question that pulled them together to form a knot that would become increasingly entangled in the first quarter of the twentieth century. Laurier was elected, and with him the Liberal Party, emerging from a long purgatory. He reaped the rewards of his 1877 speech and consolidated them with the arrival of a delegate from Rome, Mgr Merry del Val and, especially, the establishment of an apostolic delegation close to Parliament. But that victory left a doubly bitter taste: the abolition of French in the Manitoba legislature and the loss of school rights by the French-speaking Catholics of that province opened the eyes of French Canadians with regard to the possible meaning of Confederation, leading to a certain disillusionment. At the same time, the view emerged that Laurier had promised too much, and in failing to keep his word on the Manitoba schools question, had ended up placing the interests of the Liberal Party above those of his French Canadian compatriots. He was now identified with the "party spirit." As for England, which had given Laurier a knighthood, its imperial sun was clouded by little plans for Canadian independence formulated by Honoré Mercier and soon taken up by the young Henri Bourassa, and by Tardivel's vague idea of a French Canadian "homeland," another idea that would be carried into the twentieth century.

The Manitoba schools question contributed to tying another knot, a religious one. The French Canadian bishops and clergy, used to thinking of Rome as the tribunal for the settlement of its many internal disputes, was beginning to raise questions about Vatican diplomacy, which seemed to accept that French-speaking Catholics would be in the minority in Canada and that the equation of faith with language might not be necessary or even useful.

A new knot was forming in Franco-Canadian and Franco-Quebec relations, made up of new official representations and messages sent to the French by French Canadians. Indeed, how could the French not be perplexed by the denunciations of the Third Republic, Quebec's reception of the Count of Paris, General de Charette and General Boulanger, and the refusal of Canadian participation in the 1889 World's Fair? How did they understand the message of Fabre, Laurier, and Mercier emphasizing the dual loyalty of French Canadians and stating that this little people of the ancien régime was free, that the Confederation of 1867 had created a "kind of French state," and that Canada was independent of England in everything but name?

15

Culture at the Close of the Century
(1877–1896)

THE DECLINE OF ASSOCIATIONS:
CAUSES AND SIGNIFICANCE

The phenomenon of cultural associations reached its peak in Montreal and Lower Canada in general at the end of the 1850s, while its decline began in Quebec City in the middle of the decade. A minor dispute in 1853 between *Le Journal de Québec* and *Le Pays* was symptomatic of the general causes of this decline. In *Le Journal de Québec* of 14 May 1853, a correspondent hiding behind the pseudonym "Un Canadien," looked at the question of why the Institut canadien de Montréal and the one in Quebec City were so different with respect to the debates that took place in them. The response of *Le Pays* was rather provocative: "Because for two years now, the Institut canadien de Québec has always been run by men who do not at all desire the advancement of youth." *Le Pays*'s old enemy, *Le Journal de Québec*, replied on 28 May by alluding to the political divisions of 1848: "But the great division of the Liberal Party came ... The hatreds accumulated in political struggles did not stop even in the refuge of letters, and the fight, though it changed terrain, was still animated enough for us to fear the ruin of the Institut"; then, "the discussions were adjourned until better times." *Le Pays* concluded that "the administration of the Institut [in Quebec City] did not want to let youth advance except curbed and wrapped in swaddling."[1] Starting in the middle of the decade, the Institut canadien de Québec emphasized its library function, until it became Quebec City's municipal library. It was in that respect exemplary of a tendency formalized in a law of 1890, which revised those of 1851 and 1856, giving cities, towns, and villages assistance to maintain free public libraries. Created in part to favour the foundation of libraries in the francophone community, associations saw one of their initial objectives being fulfilled by the province and the cities. Once they had become autonomous and legal and were funded, the libraries no longer needed the associations. It was in this context that public libraries came into being, first in the anglophone community, with the Fraser Institute founded in 1885 and the Westmount Public Library in 1899.[2]

Likewise, the periodicals rooms of the associations no longer really had their raison d'être. The press became consolidated in terms of frequency of publication and geography: more or less short-lived weeklies, triweeklies, and dailies were published in Montreal and Quebec City, and were also starting to be published in other regions.

Public lectures stopped being given at the Institut canadien de Montréal in 1871; Arthur Buies, who gave the last one in April of that year, described in 1885, in *Une évocation*, how the Institut had become more and more deserted. The railway had put an end to the kind of urban sociability established to "occupy the long winter evenings": now economic activity was spread out over the whole year, and commercial activity would soon invade even the area of culture and recreation, day and evening. The public lecture would survive at the Union catholique and the Cercle Ville-Marie in Montreal, for example, but it would no longer have the significance that it had during the union.

Not only were the old objectives of associations reached through the increased cultural autonomy of libraries and the press, but there was a decline of public lectures and competition from new ways of spending time. The little dispute of 1853 is a concrete example of the malaise that was eroding associations: ideological and political contamination of the institution itself and its activities. The radicalization of the Institut canadien de Montréal in 1848, its censure by Mgr Bourget in 1858 and by Rome in 1869, the split of 1858 that gave birth to the Institut canadien-français, and the failure of a plan to merge the Catholic associations of Montreal in 1869 provide ample evidence that associations in the sphere of culture were plagued with debates, disputes, and excommunications, official or not. The very foundation of many political clubs – the Club Canadien, the Club Saint-Denis, the Club Cartier, founded by the friends of Chapleau in 1874, the Club National (1875), led by M. Laframboise, E. Lareau, and R. Préfontaine, the Club conservateur de Montréal (1889), the Club Letellier (1890) – indicated that political partisanship was flourishing after the Confederation of 1867 and a "party spirit" was being established. The ideology-based associations were succeeded by partisan political clubs. This politicization may have been what put an end to government subsidies to associations around 1865, and the economic crisis of 1875 would have further weakened the most active associations.[3]

There is another reason that explains the decline of associations before 1877, which Gonzalve Doutre of the Institut canadien de Montréal pointed out in 1870: "The other rival institutions have no methods of education other than billiards, convinced that they will never be accused of having pernicious doctrines for getting balls in pockets or accumulating caroms." Obviously, people were occupying themselves differently in associations in times when competing cultural forms were proliferating. And billiards was one of the new activities. French Canadians did well at it; the Dion brothers, for example, organized tournaments and won championship after championship in North America. Halls were transformed into billiards palaces for the duration of a tournament or permanently, as was the case for St Lawrence Hall, Nordheimer Hall, and the Mechanics' Hall. Billiards was played in taverns and inns; at the Club Saint-Denis and the Club Canadien the players smoked cigars. By 1888, Montreal had some fifty billiards halls.

Billiards was perhaps the indoor sport that was developing the most around 1870. It was closely linked to associations, as were other organized or professional sports activities that were becoming established. Voluntary associations moved from bringing people together through lectures, discussions, debates, and libraries to the shared pleasure of physical, sporting, and recreational activities.[4]

It was the anglophones of the colony – the middle class and the military – who shaped a sporting tradition in Lower Canada. Taking advantage of the climate, adopting traditional Amerindian activities such as snowshoeing and lacrosse, or simply importing metropolitan sports such as curling (1807), cricket or horse racing, anglophones increased their sporting activities at the time of the union. These activities were all forms of sociability practised in rather closed clubs. The approach changed around 1850, when competitions were organized between clubs, in particular for cricket. This competition was possible because national associations were formed – lacrosse (1860), rugby football (1868), baseball (1870), swimming (1876) – that regulated play and organized matches. The change was not only organizational. It was primarily social: carrying on from the bourgeoisie and the military, the middle class of merchants and clerks, who were familiar with organization and business, occupied the space of sport. It was precisely these social groups who had traditionally accounted for most of the membership of the Institut canadien de Montréal.

Like the cultural associations, the sports associations were incorporated. There were 651 sports club incorporations in Quebec from 1867 to 1900; 78 per cent of the clubs were English-speaking, 68 per cent had their headquarters in Montreal or Quebec City, 32 per cent were incorporated by merchants, clerks, manufacturers, and lawyers. Francophones joined the movement after 1870, and devoted themselves in particular to baseball before 1877, with fourteen teams organized in Montreal.[5]

With billiards competing with cultural associations in terms of indoor activities, and sports offering an alternative for relaxation and camaraderie, there were now places for sociability – the lack of which had been used in 1840 as an argument to promote associations. People could come together at the theatre, at concerts, in scholarly societies or in parks. At the turn of the 1880s, francophone theatre finally became permanently established when the "divine" Sarah Bernhardt made her first visit to Montreal. Now the stage was winning out over the political arena. There were also concerts, with the Academy of Music in Montreal offering the musical repertoire of the period starting in 1875. While a "Latin Quarter" had grown up in Quebec City around Université Laval beginning in 1852, a student and scholarly community became possible in Montreal with the opening in 1876 of a branch of Université Laval in Montreal. This scholarly community gave rise to the founding in 1882 of the Royal Society of Canada, which included a French-language section. And people developed the habit of going to parks: the one on Île Sainte-Hélène, which opened in 1874, to which a ferry carried strollers for free on Sundays; the one on Mount Royal, designed by the well-known Frederick Law Olmsted, which opened in 1876 and was initially frequented by the anglophone middle class.[6]

CULTURAL CHANGE AFTER 1877: THE PENNY PRESS

The large-circulation newspapers provide the most revealing indication of cultural change at the turn of the 1880s. The editorial of the first issue of the daily *La Presse*, on 17 November 1884, took up the idea of a newspaper for the common people: "The rich, the well-to-do classes are served by their books, magazines and special newspapers. The worker, the artisan – the people, in a word – possesses nothing of that; he lacks the leisure and the means to read books; what he needs is a library of his own, a pocket library he can carry everywhere, to the workshop, to the fields or in the home; this is the penny newspaper!" But it emphasized the break with the past: "Our newspapers are no longer abstract tracts as in the past; it is now only by the force of tradition that we find in them the vestiges of the old interminable disputes that made the glory and fortune of our predecessors twenty-five years ago. The public today wants information, facts and news. It is quite capable of forming opinions, drawing conclusions and making inferences by itself." What that editorial did not mention was the new mode of production of the newspaper itself: how and why was it able to be "a penny newspaper"? Three factors made the penny daily possible: urbanization, technology, and advertising. Montreal, with some 217,000 inhabitants in 1891, provided the press with a pool of literate readers; the new technology of typesetting, printing, and folding made it possible to quickly print and reproduce the newspaper in thousands of copies; the advertising in the newspaper, which was sold according to the circulation, justified lowering the sale price to a penny precisely in order to increase circulation and seek profit from the advertising sold. The linotype made it possible to go from typesetting the newspaper by hand to mechanical typesetting, doing the work of three typographers. First installed at the *New York Tribune* in 1886, the linotype was adopted by the *Montreal Witness* in 1892, the *Montreal Herald* in 1893, and *La Presse* in 1894. The big stores and the popularity of mail-order remedies brought the dailies steady lucrative advertising – 50 per cent of the contents of *La Presse* was advertising in 1884, and 70 per cent in 1914 – and agencies such as McKim (1889) kept track of newspaper circulation, which was now crucial for selling that advertising. It was in this context that the first French Canadian book specifically on the "science of advertising," by W.A. Grenier, was published in 1896.[7]

There was a proliferation of daily newspapers in Quebec: in Lévis in 1879, Hull in 1884, Saint-Jérôme in 1885, Sorel in 1887, and Saint-Hyacinthe in 1888. The press continued to specialize, and for the first time, gave a voice to women, with *Le Coin du feu* (1893), created and written by Joséphine Marchand-Dandurand.

THEATRE AND SHOWS

Another aspect of urban sociability in Montreal after 1880 was the growing numbers of theatres, which were also advertised in the press. When Sarah Bernhardt gave her first triumphal performance in 1880, the city had three theatres, but there were ten permanent theatres for professional troupes between 1890 and 1899. The Empire Theatre housed the first permanent francophone troupe from 1893 until it moved to the Théâtre de l'Opéra français in 1898.

During the last decade of the century, eight permanent troupes, five of them francophone, performed more than 1,800 plays. The French playwrights who were presented most were Alexandre Dumas, father and son, and Victorin Sardou. Plays by seventeen Canadian playwrights were performed. This was a new phenomenon, with thirty-two plays by French Canadians presented from 1800 to 1880 and twenty-one from 1880 to 1890. A similar blossoming of the theatre took place in the colleges:

while fewer than one hundred productions were put on from 1800 to 1890, more than 160 were presented in the 1890s. The Church tolerated this, while remaining vigilant. But the uncompromising Tardivel had little appreciation for the theatre; he decreed in *Le Canadien* of 27 December 1880: "The actors and actresses are not merely public entertainers. In social life, they occupy the same position as the keeper of the performing bear, the clown, the circus rider, the menagerie organizer, the puppeteer."

The construction on St Lawrence Boulevard of the Monument National theatre, the flagship of French Canadian sociability in Montreal and the counterpart of the anglophones' Her Majesty's Theatre, was revealing of the period. It was an initiative of the Association Saint-Jean-Baptiste; the first stone of "the temple, the arsenal, the sanctuary" of the homeland was laid in 1884, and the building was officially opened nine years later, on 25 June 1893, after a period of economic depression. Located on "the Main" in the heart of the newly cosmopolitan area of Montreal, the Monument National, "the unassailable boulevard of our language, our institutions, our laws, and to a some extent, our religion itself" (said Abbé Lévesque), held the fort against American vaudeville, which brought in its famous "chorus lines" starting in 1880, and against the many "museums" that offered "variety shows" to audiences and that were denounced by bishops Fabre of Montreal and Taschereau of Quebec City. The very term "dime museum" is an indication of a commercial culture that was developing; the penny press, the nickelodeon, and the dime museum ushered in the era of "5 / 10 / 15 cents."[8]

French Canadians also attended concerts. On 24 June 1880, they heard Calixa Lavallée's "Ô Canada" for the first time, with words written by the ultramontanist Adolphe-Basile Routhier. Some conducted orchestras or bands: Guillaume Couture was the conductor of the Montreal Symphony Orchestra, born of the Sohmer Park orchestra (1890); Edmond Hardy conducted a few bands and the Association des corps de musique (1887). Music was the most active area of the specialized press: *L'Album musical* (1882), *L'Écho musical* (1888), *Le Canada artistique* (1890), *L'Orchestre* (1893), *Piano-Canada* (1893), *Le Passe-temps* (1895), and *L'Art musical* (1896) announced concerts and published scores. Edmond Archambault's music store, which opened its doors in 1896, also sold sheet music.[9]

FRENCH CANADIANS MAKE SPORTS THEIR OWN

A symbol of the north-south economic and cultural axis, baseball was remarkably popular starting in 1876, as shown by articles in the press. The founding of the English-speaking Montreal Bicycle Club in 1878 involved an activity French Canadians also participated in on summer Sundays.

But it was hockey, played in covered rinks, that was at the forefront after the first game played at the Victoria Skating Rink (1862) on 3 March 1875. The first team, made up of McGill University students, established the rules of the game, indicating that this new sport belonged to the anglophone elite. This was true until 1890. But with the presence of the anglophone working class and francophones in general, hockey became an organized sport for the masses. Hockey was discussed in the new sports columns in the press, including "Sports and Pastimes" in the *Montreal Gazette*, starting in 1884. Leagues and associations began to form in 1886, and in 1893, an emblematic trophy, the Stanley Cup, named after the then governor general of Canada, was created.

The colleges were sometimes the door to a sport for French Canadians; this was the case for hockey at Collège Sainte-Marie in Montreal, starting in 1886, and its team played a match with Mont-Saint-Louis in 1893. But francophones really devoted themselves to hockey after 1895. There were then some thirty-five players with French names, and the first French Canadian team, Le National (1895), organized by the snowshoe club of the same name, included ten francophone players and fifteen anglophones. The number of French Canadian players increased to 123 in 1900, to 256 in 1905, and to 314 in 1910; the number of French Canadian teams went from four in 1900 to eight in 1905, to twenty-one in 1910, the year following the creation of the Club de hockey Canadien (the Montreal Canadiens) (1909). The name *Canadien* had been a success since the founding of the newspaper *Le Canadien* in 1806; the first French Canadian snowshoe club (1878) was also called Le Canadien. The variant Le National was used for a lacrosse team (1894), a baseball team (1895), and a sports association, the Association athlétique d'amateurs Le National, which was intended to counterbalance the Montreal Amateur Athletic Association (MAAA, 1881) and which would later become the Palestre nationale.[10]

CULTURE AND RECREATION BECOME MUNICIPAL

The investment of capital in culture and recreation had made possible the growth of theatre, music, and sport, and had essentially taken the place of voluntary associations and bourgeois patronage. A new actor became involved in the area of culture toward the end of the century: the city or municipality. Starting in 1875, the City of Montreal became aware of the cultural change toward the commercialization of recreation and decided to tax amusements – theatre, concerts, shows, the circus, or sport. The revenues from this tertiary sector were used in part to open the public parks of Île Sainte-Hélène, Mont Royal, and La Fontaine (1875), to establish a policy on public baths – Wellington in 1883, Île Sainte-Hélène in 1884, Hochelaga in 1890 – and to take part, starting in 1895, in serious discussion around the creation of a public library. The cultural change was such that the concept of public services, which had until then been applied to water mains, sewers, and transportation, was extended to recreation to include parks, baths, and soon libraries. This "municipalization" of culture did not, however, replace traditional forms of culture and behaviour, in particular those within the parish structure, which declined to some extend under the pressure of urban organization but also adopted and adapted the new forms of recreation.[11]

All the social and economic actors – municipality, business community, railway companies, and sports clubs – joined forces in 1883 to organize a winter carnival in Montreal and gain real and symbolic profit from the winter snow and ice. Francophones became involved in 1885 and took part in sleigh rides, snowshoe races, masquerades on ice, tobogganing, curling matches, and simulated attacks on the ice palace. These festivities ended in 1889, less as a result of Mgr Fabre's pastoral letters and circular letters complaining about the skating rinks and toboggan runs, those "places of immorality for young girls," than because of financial problems.[12]

NEW THINGS IN ENTERTAINMENT, STORES,
AND TECHNOLOGY

Capital succeeded in 1889 in organizing summer entertainment in a lasting way. When Ernest Lavigne, a former cornet player with the papal Zouaves, and Louis-Joseph Lajoie, an accountant, opened Sohmer Park on 1 June 1889, they combined the café-concert as depicted by Renoir, Vienna's Prater park as popularized by Strauss, and Coney Island in New York City, which had opened the same year. The associates realized that, given the popularity of the public park on Île Sainte-Hélène since 1874, a private park for relaxation and entertainment had every chance of success. They were also counting on the population density in Montreal to enable them to attract families to music and variety performances on weekdays and Sundays alike. Sohmer Park – named for a brand of piano sold by Lavigne in his music store – always strived to maintain a reputation for respectability. It became a place for workers' celebrations: plasterers, typographers, and train conductors assembled there once a year. Honoré Mercier, who had understood the new dynamics of the press and of spectacle, gave a resounding speech there. But above all, groups of Montrealers went to Sohmer Park on the tramways to hear the park orchestra play Meyerbeer and Strauss and see the latest of the variety acts Lavigne had discovered in New York City through the big new touring agencies.[13]

This interest in new things, which had been developing through the tradition of industrial and agricultural exhibitions since the early 1850s, was further fuelled by new consumption habits, such as shopping in department stores, and the appeal of technology, which was changing everyday life and leisure activities. The people drawn to the new kinds of shows in Sohmer Park were often the same ones who went shopping in the big department stores of Montreal: Morgan's, which had opened in 1854 and started displaying merchandise in show windows in 1872, became a department store in 1874, and moved to St Catherine Street in 1891; and Dupuis Frères opened its doors in 1868. As well, there was Eaton's mail-order service inaugurated in Toronto in 1888, imitating that of Montgomery Ward (1872) in the United States, and soon adopting the catalogue system introduced by Sears and Roebuck in 1887.[14]

In 1889, when Sohmer Park first welcomed its evening visitors under electric lighting, electricity had only been around for a short time. After a first public demonstration of the arc lamp on 16 May 1879 and the use of electric lighting for a lacrosse game and for night work by stevedores in the port of Montreal in 1880, the irreversible breakthrough of the new technology came with the inauguration of electric lighting in the streets in Montreal on 17 July 1886. Electricity had been the subject of a major exhibition at the Paris World's Fair in 1881, in which French Canadian inventor Charles Dion and exiled liberal Louis-Antoine Dessaulles took part. The Royal Electric Company, established in 1884, was one the first electricity generating companies, providing its customers with nearly twenty-five thousand incandescent lamps in 1892, thirty-nine thousand in 1893, and seventy-nine thousand in 1899.

In addition to all the new things in the theatres, parks, dime museums, and department stores, there were new technologies. At the same time, Thomas Edison obtained a Canadian patent for his phonograph (1878), Emile Berliner introduced his gramophone (1877), and Alexander Graham Bell brought the telephone to Montreal (1877). Telephone subscribers were mostly business people and merchants, and in 1882, francophones made up 18 per cent of them. From 1880 to 1896, Montreal accounted for 20 per cent of the telephone lines in Canada, and there were also lines to Granby (1880), Sorel (1881), Lévis (1882), Stanstead, Saint-Jérôme, Buckingham (1891), and Terrebonne (1893).

And electricity enabled the representatives of the Cinématographe Lumière of Lyon to present the first motion picture show in Canada at the Palace Theatre on 27 June 1896.[15]

THE DESACRALIZATION OF TIME: THE SUNDAY QUESTION

The relationship to time and to the weekly calendar of life was also new. And it would be at Sohmer Park from 1891 to 1893 that a decisive struggle would take place over the Sunday question, although it had already been discussed for a quarter of a century. This was, first, because the workers and unions had not been able to preserve the gains they had made regarding the Saturday half-holiday, and Sunday was thus the only day of rest in the week for the working majority of the population. In addition, the new forms of culture and recreation practised in free time had eaten into Sunday: bicycle riding and bicycle races starting in 1869, Sunday relaxation in the park on Île Sainte-Hélène starting in 1874, Sunday horse races in Côte-Saint-Paul and elsewhere starting in 1880. Cities and municipalities had also taken initiatives to deal with this change. Outremont and Westmount went further than Saint-Henri and Maisonneuve with regard to respecting Sunday: they banned the sale of ice cream, candy, and cold drinks in the streets and public squares. On 19 September 1876, Montreal passed Regulation 103 prohibiting the operation on Sunday of theatres, circuses, menageries, or places of amusement where athletic, gymnastic, musical, or bicycle performances were presented or noisy games took place.

The church authorities, directly concerned by the question of respect for the "Lord's day," reacted quickly, and their prohibitions provide a good indication of the activities that took place on Sunday. In 1871, Mgr Laflèche of Trois-Rivières railed against the violation of Sunday by public transportation. In 1881, his Montreal colleague criticized Sunday picnics and excursions by train or steamboat as opportunities for sin. In *La Vérité*, Tardivel, who was up against popular publications such as *Le Journal du dimanche* (1883) and *Le Nouveau Samedi* (1889), attacked Sunday work, the primary cause of non-observance of the "Lord's day." Mgr Fabre warned his flocks against Sunday political assemblies, which were "of a nature to distract" from the religious spirit of the day; on 20 May 1890, he denounced "the unfortunate tendency shown among us to change Sundays and feast days, into days of entertainment and days of disorder," recalling that "until recent years, the regular observation of the Lord's day was a distinctive characteristic of our country." In

another circular letter, he observed the effects of these changes on morals: "These picnics, these pleasure excursions that, in addition to the
fact that they are in themselves a source of debauchery and intemper-
ance, would carry the scandal into our countrysides that are so good
and so religious."[16]

On 20 April 1891, a pastoral letter from the bishop of Montreal took
aim at Sohmer Park: "We deplore in particular this kind of amusements,
introduced recently to this city, and in which, through the announcement of harmless concerts and walks, invite the people at great expense
to crowd into public places to be witness there to dances, perilous feats
and games contrary to morality, in a word, what is seen in the least repu-
table circuses; and these shows are not only presented without any scru-
ples on Sundays and feast days, but even during services, so as to lead
people away from the churches."

It was the beginning of a concerted attack on Sohmer Park that was
taken up by the Protestant Ministerial Association of Montreal, which
informed the municipal authorities of its opposition to Sunday shows.
Resistance came from the liberal councillor Raymond Préfontaine, who
presented to the City Council a request from police magistrates and a
petition of two thousand signatures in favour of opening Sohmer Park
on Sunday. The saga continued regarding the sale of beer in the park.
Although Montreal's charter had been amended in 1889 by the Quebec
legislature to allow the sale of candy, fruit, and refreshments on Sunday
in Montreal and on Île Sainte-Hélène, and although provincial law had
since February 1892 permitted the Sunday sale of beer containing less
than 4 per cent alcohol, Sohmer Park was charged in Recorder's Court
in June 1892 with selling alcohol on Sunday and fined one hundred
dollars on 2 October, three weeks before the City Council permitted
the sale of "lager" on Sunday. *La Presse* of 1 April 1893 found the lobby
of the common front of English-speaking ministers and priests against
the opening of Sohmer Park on Sunday and the sale of beer there excessive: "Our customs are French and we do not have on this question
the same way of seeing things as our citizens of the Anglo-Saxon race.
We live in an English country, under the shadow of English laws and the
English flag, and we ask that no one try to make us Englishmen more
English than the English themselves, who drink lager on Sunday." A
historic moment occurred on 2 June 1893, when in an almost absolute
ethnic split between francophones and anglophones, the city councillors voted by seventeen votes against sixteen in favour of opening
Sohmer Park on Sunday and allowing the sale there of beer containing
less than 4 per cent alcohol.[17]

"LE LAGER," "LE CURLING," "LE BASEBALL,"
"LE HOCKEY," "LE FOOTBALL," "LA MAIN"

New things and cultural change did not affect only customs and activities; they also had an impact on "our institutions, our language," in the words of the motto of *Le Canadien* of 1831. After 1880, there were increasing numbers of appeals for linguistic vigilance. Tardivel came out with the slogan, modelled on the French republican Gambetta's "Le cléricalisme, voilà l'ennemi" (clericalism, that is the enemy), "L'anglicisme, voilà l'ennemi!" (anglicism, that is the enemy). The press and many pamphlets were full of examples of the contamination of the French language with the English vocabulary of business, technology and tools, trades, sport, and new consumer products. *Les Fautes à corriger: Une chaque jour, Corrigeons-nous,* and *Dictionnaire de nos fautes contre la langue française* came out one after the other, identifying the large numbers of anglicisms that had come with changes in systems of production, distribution, and consumption. But Tardivel, Buies, and their colleagues were soon also denouncing the syntactic contamination of the spoken and written French of politicians, lawyers, and journalists. Anglicisms were the enemy but a new element was that canadianisms were presented and justified by Napoléon Legendre as the expression of "our right to contribute to the enrichment of the French language." This attitude was new in that, for the first time, a culture that was differentiated from the culture of France was being thought about and presented in a positive way. This was the beginning of discussion of the specificity of the French language in Canada and, in part, of the pertinence of a Canadian French-language literature different from the French literature of France.[18]

EXPLAINING CULTURAL CHANGE

How did the shift take place from voluntary associations to the diversity of forms of culture and recreation that became predominant at the start of the 1880s? How did traditional culture become commercialized recreation? The explanation lies in the transformation of the economic system in general and the systems of production, distribution, and consumption in particular. The conditions of production (urbanization, industrialization, technology), distribution (organization, commercialization, tertiarization), and consumption of goods now applied to the world of culture and non-work activities. These causes of change obviously acted simultaneously, and their presence in Montreal does not imply that they affected Quebec as a whole at the same time and the same rate.

In a Quebec that was still mainly rural, urbanization was limited. But it was this urbanization that gave rise to population densities capable of expanding the consumer market for manufactured goods and creating a readership for daily newspapers, an audience for theatre, and visitors to amusement parks, and that made possible the formation of social groups such as the middle class, the source of the new sports enthusiasts. In this cultural change, the space itself was modified, not only under the influence of land speculation, but also in response to a need for the definition and regulation of space for lacrosse, baseball, football, hockey, and amusement parks.

This pool of urban consumers could only be satisfied through industrialization supported by technology. The factories producing rolling stock provided culture and recreation with the locomotives, railway cars, and tramways that permitted the creation of local and inter-city lacrosse and hockey leagues, the stocking of department stores, the distribution of mail-order catalogues and products, and the transportation of Montrealers to Sohmer Park. How would hockey and piano and band concerts have been possible without the industrial capacity to mass-produce skates, pianos and horns? Without the telegraph, the transformation of the partisan political press into the information press would have been practically impossible. Not only did the telegraph enable the dissemination of sports scores, for example, but it also created a style of writing, the telegraphic style. The industrially produced linotype completed the sequence of technological innovations that made possible large-circulation newspapers. Electricity replaced hydraulics in factories and brought light to the night in the port of Montreal, the streets of the city, Sohmer Park, and the Opéra français. The spirit of competition that fuelled capitalism and economic liberalism was transposed to sport, which went from being a form of sociability to an arena of amateur and professional competition. Finally, it was industrialization that made the ability to read and write necessary, stimulating efforts to increase literacy in the Quebec population; the literacy rate rose from 62 per cent in the period 1880–89 to 74 per cent in 1890–99.[19]

These new conditions of production imposed a new mode of distribution: it was necessary to sell the mass-produced goods, the shoes that had been manufactured on assembly lines rather than being produced a pair at a time in shops of artisan shoemakers. The development of the tertiary sector, services, followed that of the secondary sector, production. The retail trade and a few department stores would serve as intermediaries between production and what was becoming consumption. Morgan's and Dupuis Frères became showcases for the new products, which were displayed in sidewalk windows and advertised with great fanfare in newspapers. It was necessary to familiarize people with the products, to make them look attractive and publicize them in the streets and on the walls of buildings, in the press and in catalogues, which in many houses were the only printed matter other than the missal and the prayer book. Those who organized and managed the distribution of goods and services also applied their skills to culture and recreation. The cornet player and music merchant Ernest Lavigne opened Sohmer Park. Merchants and clerks organized sports clubs, lacrosse leagues, and professional and amateur hockey associations; employees in the insurance industry even had their own hockey league in Montreal. It was an era of organization of recreational activities, including winter carnivals.

The organization of culture and recreation was no longer carried out only by volunteers. Certain people and certain businesses became involved in the organization of theatre, music, and sport, while the former members of voluntary associations were gradually turned into clients and consumers of the recreation activities organized by capital. The citizens of the city who sold their labour for wages spent that money not only to purchase essentials that they did not produce themselves, but also to pay for entertainment and relaxation, recreation that they did not produce themselves. Commercialized culture and recreation thus transformed producers of their own culture into consumers of culture produced by others. In a sense, just as industrial workers lost their means of production to capital, citizens delegated the responsibility for providing their cultural services to capital or to the city. Thus was born the cultural consumer – the reader of daily newspapers, the theatregoer, the vaudeville spectator, the hockey fan, the viewer of "moving pictures," and the listener to the music of Strauss and Berlioz. The bishop of Montreal, Mgr Fabre, saw very well how the city was being exported to the country, how the railway was carrying magazines, newspapers, catalogues, and mail-order merchandise, and people were going to pick them up at the little red railway stations that dotted the Quebec countryside.[20]

This material – to some people, materialistic – culture often came from the United States; examples include catalogue sales, baseball, vaudeville, burlesque, the variety shows in Sohmer Park, and even operetta and opera. The new urban culture challenged "the spiritual, religious, Catholic vocation of the French race in America" that had been constructed since the 1850s on the rejection of American materialism and mercantilism. In spite of the discourse of the elites, French Canadians were emigrating to the New England states by the thousands, capital was increasingly coming from the United States, as were as the so-called international unions, and the shows for "the Main" and Sohmer Park were being imported from New York. But in 1882, the major promoter of the idea of the spiritual and Catholic vocation of the French race in America since 1866, Abbé H.-R. Casgrain, wrote from Florida, where he was staying for health reasons: "What a vulgar mob this American people is! Can you imagine a poet dressed as a Yankee? And the creations of their mercantilism, their cities lined up in straight lines, their blocks of houses with their grotesque, pretentious architecture that they have created in their image, and the gouache spread everywhere on that classic land of whitewash and glitter; can you conceive of anything more prosaic, more philistine, more opposed to art and poetry?"[21]

CONCLUSION

The decline and replacement of associations clearly shows their importance, in terms of both causes and effects, as a cultural form since the union. Undermined by politicization and the formation of partisan political clubs, recognized for contributing to the development of libraries and the press, which became more autonomous at the beginning of the 1880s, witness to the establishment of forms of sociability such as theatre and concerts, whose absence in French Canada they had bemoaned around 1840, and subjected to competition from the organized sport that was coming into being, associations were also the crucible of national feeling, despite ongoing antagonisms. If not, how could we explain the meaning of *national* in the names of a lacrosse club and a baseball club, an amateur sports association, and the Monument National (theatre) and the Palestre nationale (sports centre)? At the beginning of the 1880s, cultural life in French Canada experienced a second period of expansion, after the one in the 1860s: French Canadians established *La Presse*, a permanent professional theatre troupe, the Monument National, and musical institutions; they became interested in sports, drawing once again on the initiatives of Anglo-Montrealers.

It was culture transformed into recreation that gradually replaced voluntary associations. This transformation can be explained by the implementation of systems of mass production, distribution, and consumption involving the tertiary sector. Now non-work activities were among the services offered for payment by capitalist enterprises or provided by the city for free or in return for taxation. As a result, the cultural actors had changed: while the culture of the associations had been that of the legal profession (lawyers, notaries, judges, law students), commercialized culture was that of business people and merchants. The participants in cultural activities changed too: volunteer members of associations or sports clubs became the public, clients of the capital invested in culture and recreation and citizens of a city that redefined the public and the civic in parks, baths, and libraries.

The years 1877 to 1896 saw the development of a sense of novelty, the novelty of the shows in Sohmer Park, the consumer goods in the department stores or mail-order catalogues, and the "moving pictures," all of these new things having developed, in one way or another, as a result of electricity. In another register, this phenomenon was noted by Pope Leo XIII when he called his encyclical on social issues *Rerum novarum*, "On New Things."

Cultural change involved customs, space, time, religion, and language. A new relationship to urban and industrial space led to a new relationship to time: the traditional activities of the Lord's day were disrupted by the work done that day in the mechanized factories that never shut down, the imperatives of public services (gas, electricity, transportation), the public culture of parks, and the private culture of commercial recreation. The Catholic Church had to make concessions though it pretended not to, but it adopted and adapted to these new things: steamboat excursions could take people to pilgrimage sites; the theatre could be edifying and even morally acceptable in colleges or in troupes. And what was to be done about all the English words that were coming with sports, catalogues, and industrial trades in a North American economy controlled in Quebec by anglophones? Anglicisms were the enemy. Materialism was another enemy, a new Trojan Horse that had come from the United States and entered the city!

Conclusion

HOW DO THE CLEARINGS DISCOVERED or created in this exploration of ideas enable us to see more clearly the major chronological and thematic strands in Quebec of the eighteenth and nineteenth centuries?

Key moments are the primary indicators of situations and developments that have marked this history of over a century. In these terms, it seems clear that we cannot speak of the conquest of Canada by England without speaking at the same time of the cession of the colony by France. This obliges us not only to take into account the two empires that colonized Canada and Quebec, but also to consider the ways in which Quebecers shaped their identity on the basis of these two mother countries.

In 1774, another component of the political and intellectual identity of Quebec was added when the Americans asked the "Canadians" to support the cause of their independence and invaded the British colony. In about fifteen years, the Canadians were thus exposed to the three main forms of government of the period: the French monarchy of divine right, the British constitutional monarchy, which granted a representative regime in 1791, and the republican aspirations of the British colonies to the south.

The perception of the French Revolution and its culmination in the Terror of 1793 was filtered through Great Britain and British colonial power. Hence, for the metropolitan and colonial authority – to which the Roman Catholic Church would add its loyal authority – France had become regicidal and "impious," and it would be seen as such for a long time. Here began Quebec's dominant trajectory of conservatism vs. reformism and the subsequent antagonism of liberalism vs. ultramontanism.

The end of the Napoleonic Wars and the Treaty of Vienna of 1815 meant, first, the lifting of the economic blockade and a certain resumption of the movement of people, goods, and ideas to and from France, and, second, an increase in the power of Great Britain, along with that of the empires of the Holy Alliance. The colony of Lower Canada developed in the shadow of this rising power that had put an end to the ambitions of Napoleon and of France, which was still trying to find its way politically and constitutionally.

In Lower Canada, the Parti canadien, which became the Parti patriote in 1826, had to recognize that the reforms it had been demanding since 1815 were not forthcoming from London, as shown by the lack of follow-up to the report of the Committee of the House of Commons on the Affairs of Canada in 1828. After 1830, Papineau and the liberals found inspiration in the great neighbouring republic, and models with which they could compare and contrast British institutions.

The escalation of events and demands (the riot of 1832, the 92 Resolutions of 1834, popular assemblies) led to the ten Russell Resolutions, the end of the hopes placed in the metropolis – the colonial administration having given no reason for hope – and then the Rebellions and their failure. French Canadians went from nearly total opposition to the union of 1840 to acceptance by the majority in 1848–49. After the first great surge of liberalism of 1815 to 1837, there was a second surge, which died out in 1849 with the triple failure of the Rebellions, the resistance to union, and the brief flirtation with the idea of annexation, and with the beginning of Papineau's marginalization. The way was paved for political reformism, moderate liberalism, the alliance of political and religious powers, and conservative, mainly cultural nationalism.

The new demographic superiority of Upper Canada beginning in 1851 added to the recurring political crises the issue of a return to proportional rather than equal parliamentary representation, which would prove decisive. Circumstances had profoundly modified the democratic principles of anglophone Canada and would lead to Confederation, which was welcomed by the Catholic Church but condemned, in vain, by the liberals.

Ten years after Confederation, during a relative decline in radical liberalism, Wilfrid Laurier gave a landmark speech on political liberalism, putting his double stamp of moderation and British influence on the liberalism that was then becoming predominant. The old antagonisms were practically neutralized and cultural forms were put in place that replaced those shaped under the union.

In an overview of 150 years of history, Quebec identity appears extremely multi-faceted, marked by the successive mother countries of France and Great Britain, strongly attracted by its powerful continental neighbour, and influenced by Rome, the source of politico-spiritual directives. There is no escaping the fact that the French Canadians of the eighteenth and nineteenth centuries were culturally and politically Franco-British Catholics living in America.

We must also chart the major trends of this intellectual history. This involves examining the many facets of Quebecers' identity, looking more closely at their support for monarchism or republicanism, measuring the influence of the Catholic Church, tracing the development of the democratic ideas of the francophones and anglophones of the colony and defining the liberalism expressed and practised in it. We also need to measure the intensity of the demands of Lower Canada and Quebec, to understand the type of nationality that finally became dominant and to assess cultural and intellectual development over 150 years.

What about this multiple nature of Quebecers' identity? While France was perceived through the mist of a certain nostalgia, a certain feeling of abandonment and a certain loyalty, it was primarily seen through the prism of the new British colonial situation. Canadians of French origin, and then French Canadians, had many reasons for distancing themselves from France: France's having forgotten Canada, its revolutionary Terror, its chronic political instability, and its militant anticlericalism. They also had reasons for gradually moving closer to England: the granting of an assembly, which, though somewhat forced, also permitted the establishment of the press and printing; the political stability of an imperial system that seemed capable of reforms, however slow. After the 92 Resolutions, England, in which the Parti patriote had placed all its hopes, disappointed it bitterly with the Russell Resolutions; London in 1837 no longer showed the willingness to listen that had sustained hope in the colony since 1815. Then, with the undemocratic imposition of the union of Lower and Upper Canada with equal, and not proportional, representation, England, which was at the peak of imperial power, granted responsible government to its colony and agreed to compensation for the Patriotes. So in 1855, the great reunion with *La Capricieuse* and with France was celebrated under the banner of the Entente Cordiale between France and England. This approach would continue until the end of the nineteenth century in the discourse of the Canadian commissioner in Paris, Hector Fabre, and that of Laurier: France had given French Canadians their "first possession, existence"; England had given them "the second, liberty." And when Laurier in 1877 gave a speech identifying Canadian liberalism with the reformist liberalism of England and not the revolutionary liberalism of France, that speech was very well received. Above and beyond the resulting electoral successes (so fervently desired by the Liberals), the speech had to relate to French Canadians' political experience, and it did: from Bédard to Laurier, through Papineau, father and son, Parent, La Fontaine and Cartier, as well as the Roman Catholic Church, Quebec's political and intellectual history in the eighteenth and nineteenth centuries was seen through the prism of a constant, though sometimes qualified, admiration for the English Constitution.

The majority of "Canadians" having finally said no to the American colonies of 1774 and the "Yankees" of 1812, they were in 1837 given the same medicine they had given the Americans: "benevolent neutrality" for "benevolent neutrality." After 1830, Papineau's admiration for the great republic was undermined by Parent's Louisiana argument, an argument that was equally valid for any plan for rapprochement or annexation: what future would there be for the French language, the Catholic religion, and French civil law in the American union? What remained then as a destiny for French Canada in America? A spiritual vocation that had become religious and then Catholic.

In the identity of Quebec and its religious dimension, Rome had been the beacon of orthodoxy, the ultramontanist reference point, the arbiter of conflicts among the ultramontanists of Quebec, certain of whom also considered themselves as Catholic as the Pope, if not more so. Drawn into the politico-religious conflicts of French Canada and Canada (the Manitoba schools question), the Vatican awakened to the risks of the association of faith with language, and concluded that, all things considered, Catholic America, that of both Canada and the United States, was English-speaking. In this situation, the vocation of a French-speaking Catholicism in America lost its strategic interest.

In a Canada that was a constitutional monarchy, the majority of people in Quebec of the eighteenth and nineteenth centuries preferred monarchy to a republic. Having lived under the French absolute monarchy until 1763, the colony discovered constitutional monarchy under the English regime and again during the 1830s, when restored thrones and empires in Europe were being shaken by movements of national emancipation. The newspapers in Lower Canada usually favoured constitutional monarchy as the most desirable form of government for countries that had gained their independence. During the discussions on Confederation, Cartier would see the system proposed as the best way to ensure that the British monarchy endured against the American republic. The fact that the majority was in favour of monarchy did not preclude the existence of a republican current, which began in 1774 and was consolidated around 1830, when the Parti patriote denounced any attempt by the metropolis to create an aristocracy in the forests of America and took the elected American Senate as the concrete model for its demand for an elected Legislative Council.

There were undoubtedly French Canadian republicans in the French style in 1830 and 1848, but after 1840, and especially after 1867, reformers, conservatives, and ultramontanists all generally took a critical view of the French Third Republic, so much so that in 1889, Canada chose not to participate in the celebrations around the centenary of 1789. As for the republic as conceived by Tardivel in his novel *Pour la Patrie* in 1895, it was only republican in that it had a president, as was the case for Ecuador under Garcia Moreno.

The choice of monarchy was very British in inspiration, but it was also religious, giving an indication of the influence of the Catholic Church. In the teaching of philosophy in the colleges where generations of future priests and future citizens studied, the clergy constantly presented the monarchy of divine right as in principle the best form of government, while tolerating the reality of the constitutional monarchy under which Lower Canada lived. One thing is certain: the Church took a dim view of the sovereignty of the people and democracy: *omnis potestas a Deo*. This belief was based on its political philosophy and its perception of its interests after the loss of its legal status in 1791, which also explain its loyalty to British metropolitan and colonial power, and provide the basis for its ultramontanism: it was in favour not only of the alliance of throne and altar, but of the primacy of the Church over the state in "mixed" questions such as education and social welfare.

The Church made repeated declarations of loyalty, in 1775, 1793, 1812, 1837, 1838, 1867: political sovereignty did not belong to the people and it was forbidden to overthrow legitimate authority. The Catholic Church of Quebec was particularly involved in temporal affairs. Not only did it construct a political theology and philosophy on the hierarchy of ends and the superiority of its mission in order to justify its intrusion into the temporal sphere (any political issue is moral, and therefore religious), but it became deeply involved in it. It took control of the school, the college, the university, the asylum, and the hospital. Denouncing the Patriotes, the liberals, the repeal of the union, and annexation, it supported local British power, which restored its legal recognition in 1839 and paved the way for La Fontaine and the Reformers, who accepted the confessionalization of the school system in 1845. The confrontation of liberals and the Church in 1848 around Italian unity, the Roman question and the temporal power of the pope was in a way the religious counterpart of the political marginalization of Louis-Joseph Papineau in the House and by the electorate. In this sense, 1848 was a decisive year; it was also important in the definition of a cultural and apolitical nationality that did not appeal to the principle of nationality. The Church had sought social, political, and temporal power; it had obtained that power, and conservative and reform politics had to allow it to exercise it. The alliance involved both parties.

The imprint of the Catholic Church was still perceptible in culture itself. Its simplistic conception of primary education, along with its desire for control of the school system, its reservations and prejudices against associations, which it still suspected of being "secret societies," its claiming the right to control the reading of the members of the Institut canadien de Montréal and to supervise a civil association, its condemnation of theatre, shows, and sports, the censorship it exercised on books, novels, newspapers, and shows, its use of the confessional and the pulpit to dissuade parishioners from holding certain political ideas – all these positions delayed and influenced the cultural and intellectual development of Quebec.

It was said in the 1950s that, historically, French Canadians did not want democracy for themselves and that anglophones did nothing to give them a taste for it. What about the democratic strand in Quebec history in the eighteenth and nineteenth centuries? Thanks to the work of Pierre Tousignant, who re-established the official documents, we now know that French Canadians participated in the demand for a house of assembly starting in 1784. They wanted it and subsequently defended it, aware as they were that majority representation was their lifeline and their hope for development. With John Neilson, Daniel Tracey, Dr Edmund O'Callaghan, and some dozen English-speaking members, the *Canadien* majority of the Parti canadien and the Parti patriote defended democracy, opposing the civil list and demanding control by the House over public revenues and expenditures; fighting for the separation of political and judicial powers; promoting the idea that the House of Assembly should take precedence over the Legislative Council in various conflicts; proposing, in the name of the sovereignty of the people, an elected Legislative Council and elected administrators of fabriques; and pointing out that the existence of similar demands coming from Upper Canada refuted any accusations of "national prejudices" in their struggle.

Moreover, what had the British done to promote the democracy they boasted of having established in 1688, long before 1776 and 1789? After the Conquest, some anglophones of the colony conceived of a house of assembly in which only Protestants would vote; others expressed support for the presence of judges in the House of Assembly; they minimized the principle of "no taxation without representation" in the colony by giving the governor and the executive a civil list that shielded them from the people's representatives; they sought and accepted almost all the positions on the Legislative Council, knowing that in doing so they were obstructing political life in the colony and participating in the Machiavellian metropolitan policy of "divide and rule." They set up a military rather than a civil court to judge the Patriotes arrested and charged with treason; they refused to permit them to have French Canadian lawyers on the pretext that rebels could not defend rebels. And at the time of the union, they decreed a division of the new shared debt that was unfair and disadvantageous for Lower Canada; they abolished in the House the language of those with whom they were uniting. They created a "little lottery" to buy support; they imposed a regime of equal representation, not representation proportional to population, without the consent of the colony, violating the principle of "rep by pop." Then, with the increase in their demographic weight after 1850, they returned to the "rep by pop" they had refused to Lower Canada when it had the majority of the population – a double standard, a democracy based on the power of the stronger, the colonizer.

The "English liberties" were won in 1688 and applied in Great Britain, and then in the colonies with certain adjustments and limitations. Quebec's liberal tradition was founded on these "English liberties," and people in Lower Canada wanted them to be as complete in the colony as in the metropolis; that was the destiny of the colonies. The liberalism of the tradition was English in origin, but it was influenced by the republican liberalism of the neighbours to the south. Quebec liberalism was of English inspiration until 1830; Laurier knew this and took it into account.

This liberalism became more radical after 1830, and then went from failure to failure: the failure of the Rebellions of 1837 and 1838; the failure of the opposition to the union and then of the movement for its repeal, at a time when nationalist liberalism, having lost its parliamentary majority, no longer had much chance of success; the failure of the strategy of annexation of Canada to the United States; and the failure of the opposition to Confederation.

The most obvious failure of radical liberalism under the union was due to the reaffirmation of moderate liberalism, the liberalism of La Fontaine and Cartier as well as Hector Fabre, which, as much as Mgr Bourget and the Catholic Church or Étienne Parent, undermined radical liberalism and paved the way for Laurier. Laurier's strategy in 1877 consisted of ridding liberalism of its radical anticlericalism and clearly identifying the Canadian liberal tradition with English reform liberalism rather than French revolutionary liberalism. Laurier's speech must be understood not only as the electoralist response of a moderate liberal to the "philosophical dissertations" of the radicals but, more fundamentally, as the outcome of a political and intellectual tradition that went back to the eighteenth century in Quebec. It is thus understandable that the liberalism of the last quarter of the nineteenth century in Quebec was dominated, not by the pyrotechnics of the Guibord affair or the Catholic Program or the battles of a Tardivel, but by a search by people on both sides for tolerance, moderation, and compromise.

The predominance, finally, of this moderate liberalism attests to some extent to the moderate nature of colonial demands in Lower Canada before and at the time of union. The first period of colonial demands was from 1791 to 1828, at the time of the purely administrative recommendations and good will of the Committee of the House of Commons on the Affairs of Canada. London's delaying then became more flagrant, and the decision of the House of Assembly of Lower Canada to bypass the approval of the Legislative Council in 1831 and appoint an agent to London was indicative of the urgent need for a lobby to express the views of the colonials, and no longer only those of the local oligarchy. Similarly, the increasingly frequent references to the republicanism of the United States conveyed a new vision of the potential destiny of the colony. A new level of impatience was reached with the 92 Resolutions of February 1834, a list of grievances of the Parti patriote, which had the electoral support of three quarters of the population. Dissatisfaction continued to mount, and in spite of a formal prohibition, the parliamentary majority held extra-parliamentary popular assemblies in the spring and summer of 1837. Finally, the Russell Resolutions were the last straw. In 1837 and especially in 1838, a few radicals had called for independence, but now Papineau saw it not only as natural and necessary in the Americas, but also as possible. The most advanced principle for a project of national emancipation in Lower Canada in 1837 was also the most "constitutionalist" formulation of what would become a right, the principle of nationality: "No nation is willing to obey another, for the simple reason that no nation knows how to command another." But Étienne Parent, who had been discussing nationality in *Le Canadien* since 1831, confined himself to the idea of the "preservation" and not "revolution" of French Canadian nationality. In this respect, Papineau and Parent represented two sides of the coin of the intellectual and political history of Lower Canada and Quebec, and personified the conceptions of nationality promoted in the nineteenth century.

Parent would finally agree to the union in exchange for responsible government, which he had been demanding for some time, and La Fontaine, for other reasons, would apply Parent's view of nationality. It was this conservative version of nationality that predominated after 1848, for three reasons. The principle of nationality put forward by the

liberal Rouges was identified with that of the Italian liberals against the
pope, the Papal States, and the temporal power of Rome. It was denounced both by the Church and by La Fontaine's Reformers; after the
union, the radical liberals were not sufficient in numbers to defend this
principle in the legislature of United Canada, in which representation
was equal and not proportional to population. Finally, the conception of
nationality that was acceptable and promoted was cultural – the "preservation" of national characteristics such as language, religion, French law
– and not political, without the objective of self-determination. The destiny of French Canada would thus be to preserve its culture and, soon, to
make it the essential component of its vocation in America.

London did not have to impose the federation of 1867 as it had the
union of 1840; French Canada found its place – or at least a place – in it
with the assurance of a majority in the government of the province of
Quebec. And when Laurier gave his speech on English and French liberalism in 1877, French Canadian anti-colonialism was put aside. Tardivel
brought it back, but it was Honoré Mercier who showed a new way toward French Canadian autonomy, a way that would be followed and
broadened by Henri Bourassa in the twentieth century.

As much as its political development, the intellectual development of
Quebec shows the transfer of the cultural forms of the metropolis to the
colony, and even their imitation, and attests to the essential colonial dimension of the Quebec of the eighteenth and nineteenth centuries.
With this first observation comes the recognition that French Canadians
themselves adopted and adapted the cultural institutions of the anglophones, such as the press, associations, libraries, reading rooms, museums, and sports. This explains the politicization of the culture: printed
matter, the press, associations, and the school system were marked by
politics, the necessary and primary form of struggle, survival, and development. If cultural forms and content were so marked by ideology, it was
because they were promoted by a middle class in the liberal professions
that not only gave them a civic and political content, but also stamped
them with the culture of the law, which was the dominant liberal profession: the culture of printed matter, eloquence, and argument.

Stimulated by the establishment of printing, the press, and parliamentarism, debates on ideas were driven by the cultural dynamics of the
media, exchanges, and institutions, which had a rhythm of their own:
they became established at the beginning of the nineteenth century, began to develop with the lifting of the economic blockade in 1815, and
exierenced an abortive takeoff at the end of the 1830s. Economic and
political reconstruction under the union was combined with a cultural

reconstruction that made possible an irreversible cultural takeoff at the beginning of the 1860s. The cultural forms that marked this takeoff – the press and associations – were precisely those in which significant cultural changes would occur at the end of the century.

Intellectual Quebec would enter the twentieth century with the recurring issue of its fragile destiny in the face of the British Empire, American expansionism, school crises, the "party spirit," and urbanization. Its challenge would be to formulate a doctrine capable of providing a basis for action.

Notes

IN A WORK OF SYNTHESIS such as this one, references are necessarily numerous, especially when a study is drawing on primary sources. Many notes in this book contain references to more than one source. In principle, these notes have a simple and logical connection to the text: multiple sources are listed in the order in which they pertain to citations or references in the text. This choice was made so that the overall number of notes and length of the book would remain reasonable and the reading experience of the text would not be overburdened with references while still allowing sources and scholarship to be visible.

ABBREVIATIONS

AAQ	Archives de l'archevêché de Québec
ACAM	Archives de la chancellerie de l'archevêché de Montréal
ACSAP	Archives du Collège de Sainte-Anne de la Pocatière
ASN	Archives du Séminaire de Nicolet
ASQ	Archives du Séminaire de Québec
ASSM	Archives Saint-Sulpice de Montréal
ASSP	Archives Saint-Sulpice de Paris
BANQ	Bibliothèque et Archives nationales du Québec
BRH	*Bulletin des recherches historiques*
CD	*Cahiers des Dix*
CHSTH	Centre d'Histoire de Saint-Hyacinthe (ex Archives du Séminaire de Saint-Hyacinthe)
CIHM	Canadian Institute for Historical Microreproductions
DC	*Documents Relating to the Constitutional History of Canada*
DCB	*Dictionary of Canadian Biography* (www.biographi.ca)
GM	*Gazette de Montréal*
GQ	*Gazette de Québec*
JHALC	*Journal of the House of Assembly of Lower-Canada*

LAC   Library and Archives Canada
LJP   Louis-Joseph Papineau
MEM   *Mandements des évêques de Montréal*
MEQ   *Mandements des évêques de Québec*
METR   *Mandements des évêques de Trois-Rivières*
PPBC   Parlement provincial du Bas-Canada
PUL   Presses de l'Université Laval
PUM   Presses de l'Université de Montréal
RAPQ   *Rapport de l'archiviste de la province de Québec*
RHAF   *Revue d'histoire de l'Amérique française*
RL   Registre des lettres

INTRODUCTION

1 Ouellet, "L'histoire socio-culturelle: colloque exploratoire"; Mamdrou, "L'histoire socio-culturelle: retrospective européenne."

2 I have dealt with some of these aspects in the following articles: "Canadian Print and the Emergence of a Public Culture in Eighteenth and Nineteenth Centuries"; "La culture urbaine au Canada"; "Cultural Crossroads" (with Patricia Lockhart Fleming); "Public Libraries and the Emergence of a Public Culture" (with Peter F. McNally and Andrea Rotundo); "L'histoire du livre et de l'imprimé au Canada."

3 Lamonde, "Le médium est le message."

4 Curtis, "Comment étudier l'État?"

5 Curtis, *Politics of Population*; Curtis, "Y-a-t-il une histoire de la statistique de l'éducation au Bas-Canada?" 5–11 and 43–51.

6 Curtis, "Le redécoupage du Bas-Canada dans les années 1830"; Curtis, "Tocqueville and Lower Canadian Educational Networks."

7 Nelles, *The Art of Nation-Building*; Rudin, *Founding Fathers*.

8 Radforth, *Royal Spectacle*.

9 Curtis, "The 'Most Splendid Pageant Ever Seen.'"

10 Radforth, "Political Demonstrations and Spectacles."

11 Constant and Ducharme, *Liberalism and Hegemony*, which reproduces McKay's text; Ducharme, *Le concept de liberté au Canada*.

12 Bannister, "Canada as Counter-Revolution."

13 Harvey, *Le printemps de l'Amérique française*.

14 See the end of Chapter 11; Laurier's speech is reproduced in *Wilfrid Laurier on the Platform*, 51–80.

15 Lamonde and Livernois, *Papineau: Erreur sur la personne*.

16 Bédard, *Les Réformistes*.

17 Lamonde, "La confiance en soi du pauvre."

18 Julie Papineau, *Une femme patriote*; L-J Papineau, *Lettres à Julie*; Rosalie Papineau-Dessaulles, *Correspondance.*

19 Béique, *Quatre-vingt ans de souvenirs*; Lamonde and Simard, *Inventaire chronologique et analytique d'une correspondance de Louis-Antoine Dessaulles.*

20 H. Dessaulles, *Journal*; the bibliography provides a list of Fadette's letters.

21 Dessaulles Family Fonds, McCord Museum.

22 Marchand, *Journal intime*; Montreuil, "(Se) lire et (se) dire."

23 Lévesque, *Éva Circé-Côté*; Circé-Côté, *Chroniques d'Éva Circé-Côté.*

CHAPTER ONE

1 Quoted in Deschênes, *L'année des Anglais*, passim; quotation from Wolfe in Wright, *The Life of Major-General James Wolfe*, 517.

2 "Mandement pour des prières publiques. Dispersion des Acadiens," 15 February 1756, *Mandements des Évêques de Québec [MEQ]*, II:106–7; circular letter, winter 1761, ibid., 150.

3 Letters of 1 and 4 February 1762, *MEQ*, II:157 and 160.

4 Mgr Briand to M. Perrault, 22 February 1762, *RAPQ* (1929–1930), 51; Briand to M. Montgolfier, [1762], *RAPQ* (1929–1930), 50; Briand to James Abercrombie, [1762], *RAPQ* (1929–1930), 50.

5 Letter of 4 June 1763, *MEQ*, II:169–70.

6 Father Théodore, Récollet, to Mgr Briand, quoted in Brunet, *La présence anglaise*, 46.

7 Cardinal Castelli, Rome, to Abbé de l'Isle-Dieu, 17 December 1766, quoted in Lanctôt, *Canada and the American Revolution*, 8.

8 "Adresse des principaux habitants de Québec," 7 June 1762, quoted in Brunet, *Les Canadiens après la Conquête*, 41.

9 "Adresse des bourgeois de Québec à l'occasion du traité de paix," 4 June 1763, quoted in Brunet, *La présence anglaise*, 46–7; see also the petition of the citizens of Montreal, 12 February 1763, ibid., 42.

10 Quoted in Galarneau, *La France*, 89.

11 Ibid.

12 Mother d'Youville to M. Villars, 5 August 1763, quoted in Brunet, *Les Canadiens après la Conquête*, 78–9; Mother d'Youville to Abbé La Rue, 18 September 1765, quoted in Galarneau, *La France*, 91–2; on the perceptions of France and the French, see Frégault, *Canada: The War of the Conquest*, 268–74, 321–6, 334–5.

13 *DC*, I:84–90, 119–23, 123–4, 132–49.

14 Carleton to Count Shelburne, 20 January 1768, *DC*, I:207; Tousignant, "The Integration of the Province of Quebec."

15 "Letter of the committee to Maseres," 8 November 1773, *DC*, I:343.

16 H.T. Cramahé to Lord Dartmouth, 13 December 1773, *DC*, I:344.

17 Petition to the King, 31 December 1773, *DC*, I:347–9; Memorial from Quebec to Lord Dartmouth, 31 December 1773, *DC*, I:349–51; Memorial from Montreal to Lord Dartmouth, 15 January 1774, *DC*, I:351–2.

18 Maseres to Dartmouth, 4 January 1774, *DC*, I:340.

19 Dartmouth to H.T. Cramahé, 4 May 1774, *DC*, I:352.

20 Harris, *Historical Atlas of Canada*, vol. I, plate 51.

21 Quebec Act, *DC*, I:401–5.

22 Lawson, *The Imperial Challenge*, 142.

23 Lawson, "'Sapped by Corruption,'" 302–24.

24 *To the people of Great-Britain*, 21 October 1774, reproduced in Lanctôt, *Canada and the American Revolution*, 244.

25 *To the Inhabitants of the Province of Quebec*, 26 October 1774, in Lanctôt, *Canada and the American Revolution*, 247–5; or *CIHM*, no. 36657.

26 Trudel, *La Révolution américaine*, 73, 81–3, 90–1.

27 "Mandement au sujet de l'invasion américaine," 22 May 1775, *MEQ*, II:264–5; plans for sermons by M. Montgolfier in Lanctôt, *Canada and the American Revolution*, 52.

28 "Circulaire au sujet du rétablissement des milices," 13 June 1775, *MEQ*, II:265–6.

29 "To the Inhabitants of the Province of Canada," 24 January 1776, *Journals of the Continental Congress, 1774–1789*, vol. 4, 85; Lanctôt, *Canada and the American Revolution*, chap. 6–10; Trudel, *La Révolution américaine*, chap. 2.

30 M. Montgolfier to Mgr Briand, 9 October 1775, quoted in Lanctôt, *Canada and the American Revolution*, 88.

31 *MEQ*, II:266.

32 Mgr Briand to Curate Maisonbasse, 25 October 1775, quoted in Hare, "Le comportement de la paysannerie," 146.

33 Mgr Plessis to Grand Vicar Bourret in London, 15 May 1807, *AAQ, RL*, VI:20–37.

34 Lanctôt, *Canada and the American Revolution*, 120–3; *Journal de MM. Baby, Taschereau et Williams*, 40.

35 Ouellet and Therrien, *L'invasion du Canada*, 71–2.

36 Carleton to General Burgoyne, 29 May 1777, *DC*, I:462n1.

37 "Mémoire de l'évêque de Québec à Lord Dorchester," 20 May 1790, in Dionne, *Les ecclésiastiques*, 326–31.

38 "Petitions for the Repeal of the Quebec Act," 12 November 1774, *DC*, I:414–16; "Petition of Merchants for Repeal of Quebec Act," 2 April 1778, *DC*, I:473–4.

39 Haldimand to Germain, 25 October 1780, *DC*, I:48290; Haldimand to North, 24 October 1783, *DC*, I:4978; Haldimand to North, 6 November 1783, *DC*, I:499.

40 Text from 1784, quoted in Ouellet, *Lower Canada, 1791–1840,* 18.
41 "Petition for House of Assembly to the King's Most Excellent Majesty,"
24 November 1784, *DC,* I:502–9; on this question and on the correction of
the *DC* of Shortt and Doughty, which omitted the 1,436 signatures of the
Canadiens, see Tousignant, "La genèse," Appendix A, 447–59; the petition
was also published in London in 1791 in *Petitions from the Old and New Subjects,*
and *Le Canadien* of 9 August 1809 republished the list of signatories; the
committees in favour of a house of assembly summed up their position in a
pamphlet, *Aux Citoyens et Habitants des Villes et Campagnes de la Province de
Québec;* Tousignant, "Problématique"; Tousignant, "Les Canadiens et la réforme constitutionnelle," 13f.; Tousignant, "Les aspirations libérales des
réformistes canadiens-français."
42 "Objections to the Petition of November 1784," 30 November 1784, *DC,*
I:514–16.
43 "The very humble address of the Roman Catholic citizens and inhabitants
of different conditions in the province of Quebec in Canada," [November
1784], *DC,* I:518–20.
44 Tousignant, "Pierre du Calvet," *DCB;* Tousignant, "*Appel à la justice*"; Jean
Delisle to J.-B. Adhémar, 15 January 1785, *LAC,* Verreau collection, G.5,
7:49; "Letter from Merchants of Montreal," 2 November 1784, *DC,* I:544–5;
"Letter from Merchants of Quebec," 9 November, *DC,* I:545–6; on the position of *La Gazette de Montréal,* see de Lagrave, *Fleury Mesplet,* 257–90.
45 Finlay to Nepean, 9 February 1789, *DC,* I:656–8.
46 Grenville to Dorchester (Private and Secret), 20 October 1789, *DC,*
I:662–3.
47 Grenville to Dorchester, 20 October 1789, *DC,* I:663–6.
48 Already in 1772, Wedderburn had realized, "To exclude the Canadian subject would be impossible, for an Assembly chosen only by the British
Inhabitants could no more be called a representative body of that colony"
(quoted in Tousignant, "Problématique," 186).
49 *GM,* 16 April and 11 June 1789, quoted in Guimond, *La Gazette de Montréal,*
14–19; *GQ,* 6 August 1789; Galarneau, *La France,* 105–39.
50 *GM,* 8 October 1789, 21 October 1790, 20 January 1791; L'homme libre,
"À l'imprimeur," *GM,* 27 November 1790; see also 19 August, 2 September,
9 December 1790, 24 February 1791, 9 February 1792.
51 Tousignant, "La *Gazette de Montréal,*" 221; see also Un Canadien du manoir
de Berthier, "Aux Canadiens," *GM,* 4 March 1790, quoted in Guimond, *La
Gazette de Montréal,* 255, 265–8; de Lagrave, *Fleury Mesplet,* 371–86.
52 Brassier to Mgr Hubert, November 1789, *AAQ,* portfolio of vicars general, 12.
53 J.-O. Duchêne à Mgr Briand, 1 January 1792, quoted in Galarneau, *La
France,* 80; see also 76.
54 *GQ,* 6 December 1792, quoted in Galarneau, *La France,* 128.

55 Text of the law in *DC*, I:694–708; the English version was published in *GM*, 26 and 27 May 1791, the French version 2 and 9 June and the official version 8, 15, 22, 29 December 1791.

56 Abbé Gravé to Abbé Hody, Paris, 25 October 1791, quoted in Galarneau, *La France*, 133.

57 Hare, *Aux origines du parlementarisme québécois*, 38, 44 and texts, 131–48; Tousignant, "La première campagne électorale," 128.

58 *DC*, I: 698–700, sections XVIII-XXIV; Garner, *Franchise and Politics*, 73–82.

59 Texts of the pamphlets in Hare, *Aux origines*, 150–91, quotations 165 and 191; or *CIHM*, in order, nos. 57292, 55039, 47236, 52824, 52827, 55152, 57291; Vlach and Buono, *Catalogue collectif*, 160 (in indexes).

60 Ouellet, *Lower Canada*, 44.

61 Hare, *Aux origines*, 207–21, 228.

62 Ibid., 93, 230–92; on the text of the law, 239, 102–3.

63 Letter from the House of Assembly, *JHALC*, 27 April 1793, 604; quotation from Smith in Galarneau, *La France*, 227–8.

64 Galarneau, *La France*, 291–8, 308.

65 Document published by Brunet in "La Révolution française," 159; "Un Mémoire de Henry Mézière"; Galarneau, *La France*, 233–4; Greenwood, *Legacies of Fear*, 76–9; de Lagrave, *Fleury Mesplet*, 406–18.

66 Galarneau, *La France*, 231.

67 Ibid., 230, 244–50; Greenwood, *Legacies of Fear*, 99–101.

68 On the "seditious" activities: Galarneau, *La France*, 234–42; Greenwood, *Legacies of Fear*, 80–2, 87–91, 96–9, 101–3; Robichaud, "Le pouvoir, les paysans et la voirie au Bas-Canada"; Knafla, "The Influence of the French Revolution"; Lalancette, "La Malbaie"; on McLane, Galarneau, *La France*, 252–9; Greenwood, *Legacies of Fear*, 139–70; the transcripts of the testimony in the trial were published in *Les Soirées canadiennes*, II:353–400.

69 *Lettre de Mgr. de Léon aux ecclésiastiques français réfugiés en Angleterre*, 18.

70 "Circulaire aux curés," 9 November 1793, *MEQ*, II:471–3; Mgr Hubert to Abbé Jones, 29 March 1794, *RAPQ* (1930–1931): 298–9; see also "Circulaire recommandant la fidélité au gouvernement," 5 November 1796, *MEQ*, II:50–2.

71 Mgr Denaut, "Mandement prescrivant des actions de grâces après la victoire de l'amiral Nelson," 22 December 1798, *MEQ*, II:515–17; Mgr Plessis, *Discours à l'occasion de la victoire remportée par les forces navales de Sa Majesté britannique*, 10 January 1799, quotations, 239 and 251; Roy, "Napoléon au Canada"; see also Greenwood, *Legacies of Fear*, 193–202.

72 Poems published in *GQ* and quoted in Galarneau, *La France*, 266, and Lortie, *La poésie nationaliste*, 12–2, 129.

73 *Quebec Mercury*, 27 October 1806; still on the strategy of assimilation, the same paper, 6 April 1805, October–December 1806, 26 January, 9 and

16 March 1807, 31 October and 7 November 1808, 3 April 1809, 15
January and 16 April 1810, according to Hare and Wallot, *Les imprimés,* 309.

74 Smith, "*Le Canadien,*" 97–100.

75 *Le Canadien,* 31 January 1807, 25 June, 2, 9, 16, 23 July 1808, 25 March, 3,
24 June, 1, 29 July, 23 September 1809.

76 Craig to Castelreagh, 5 August 1808, quoted in Smith, "*Le Canadien,*" 104–5.

77 *Le Canadien,* 31 January 1807, quoted in Hare and Wallot, *Les imprimés,*
324–5; see also 24 January 1807, 24 April, 27 May and 9 December 1809.

78 [Denis-Benjamin Viger], *Considérations sur les effets,* 7, 21–2, 38–40, 43–4,
15, 30, 32–3; CIHM, no. 20923; *Le Canadien,* 29 November 1806, 17 and
31 October, 5 and 26 December 1807, 23 September and 11 November
1809.

79 Pierre-René de Saint-Ours à Herman Witsius Ryland, 20 June 1808, quoted
in Wallot, *Un Québec qui bougeait,* 291–2; Mgr Plessis to M. Roux, 4 December 1809, *RAPQ* (1927–1928): 270; *Le Vrai-Canadien,* 4 April 1810.

80 "Chanson du Canadien patriote," *GQ,* 1 August 1807; *Courier de Québec,*
28 January 1807; Craig to Lord Castelreagh, 13 May, 15 July, 4 August
1808, quoted in Roy, "Napoléon au Canada," 107–8; Craig to Liverpool,
5 March 1810, and Craig to H.W. Ryland, 10 June 1810, quoted in Wallot,
Un Québec qui bougeait, 290–2.

81 Chapais, *Cours,* 3:190; on the rejection of the laws by the Legislative
Council, *JHALC, 1804,* 226–9, 288–9, 308–13, 328–33, 374–81, 392–9.

82 Hare and Wallot, *Les imprimés,* 229–31; *DC,* II:367.

83 Craig's proclamation, 21 March 1810, *MEQ,* III:45–50.

84 Circular letter accompanying the proclamation, 21 March 1810, *MEQ,*
III:43–5; on the loyalty of the clergy, 22 March 1810, ibid.:50–1; Mgr Plessis
to M. Roux, to M. Noiseux and to M. Conefroy, 22 March 1810, AAQ, RL 7,
81, 131–3; Mgr Plessis to the coadjutor and the bishop of Saldes, 23 March
1810, ibid., 136–7 and *RAPQ* (1928–1929), 273; Abbé Jean Raimbault's sermon on "loyalty to the Prince," 1810, ASN, Polygraph IV, no. 9.

85 Craig to Liverpool, Quebec, 30 March 1810, *DC* II:372–8.

86 Speech of Sir James Craig on Proroguing Parliament, 1810, *DC,* II:371–2;
*Sermon prêché par l'Évêque catholique de Québec dans sa cathédrale le IVe dimanche
du Carême, 1er April 1810,* 7–9; CIHM, no. 53687; Abbé de Calonne,
[c. 15 April 1810], quoted in *Histoire du monastère,* I:100–1.

87 Craig to Liverpool, 1 May 1810, *DC,* II:387–400; Liverpool to Craig,
12 September 1810, ibid.:407–8; Craig to Ryland, 9 November 1810,
ibid.:411–12.

88 Chapais, *Cours,* 2:206–16, 405–10; Sewell, *A Plan for the Federal Union;* CIHM,
no. 21154; Greenwood and Lambert, "Sewell, Jinathan," *DCB.*

89 Henry, *An Enquiry into the Evils;* see also, in the same vein, Cuthbert, *An
Apology;* CIHM, no. 20924; Gray, *Letters from Canada;* CIHM, no. 35926;

Fleming, *Some Considerations*; Lambert, *Travels Through Lower Canada*; Hare and Wallot, *Les imprimés*, nos. 194, 201E, 243, 248, 250E.

90　Mgr Plessis to M. Burke in Halifax, 16 August 1810, AAQ, RL 7, 190–1; see also Plessis to M. de Bouveres in London, 21 November 1810, ibid., 224–5; on conversations in November 1811 between Plessis and Craig, *MEQ*, III:59–82; Plessis's brief to the new governor Prevost on the future of the Catholic episcopate, 15 May 1812, ibid.:79–82.

91　Mgr Plessis to Abbé Jean Raimbault, 18 September 1806, ASN, E, 3–4.

92　Lamonde and Beauchamp, *Données statistiques*, Table 14. All tables referred to in this book may be found in this source.

93　Lamonde and Beauchamp, *Données statistiques*, Table 13.

94　Mgr Plessis to Abbé Bourret, ecclesiastical agent in London, 10 May 1807, AAQ, RL, 6:20–37; see also Mgr Plessis to Vicar General Roux, 3 June 1805, AAQ, bishops' portfolio, III:139–41; Abbé Boucher to Mgr Plessis, 28 March 1810, AAQ, RL, 6:52.

95　Ouellet, *Lower Canada*, 145–72.

96　Mgr Plessis's circular letter on the war, 29 June 1812, *MEQ*, III:86–88; Beaudin, "Sermon de M. Lartigue," 5 July 1812, *RHAF*, XXII, 2:303–5; Wallot, "Une émeute à Lachine" [1964–65], *Un Québec qui bougeait*, 107–41; see also *MEQ*, III:88–91, 95, 108. Mgr Plessis would receive an annual pension of $1,000 beginning in 1813 and would be appointed to the Executive Council in 1818.

97　Guitard, *The Militia of the Battle of the Châteauguay*.

98　The brief is published in Christie, *A History*, VI:313–23; Bédard to Neilson, 15 January 1815, LAC, Neilson papers, II:438; Ouellet, "Bédard, Pierre-Stanislas", *DCB*; Finlay, "The State of a Reputation"; Ajzenstat, "Canada's First Constitution"; on the question of judges, *DC*, II:443–85.

99　Abbé Denis Chaumont to Abbé Robert, 19 May 1814, ASQ, letters T:84.

100　*Le Canadien*. On Spain: 8 and 15 October, 12 December 1808; 29 July, 22 December 1809; 3 and 10 February 1810. On Portugal: 22 October, 12 and 19 November 1808; 7 January, 22 April, 25 November 1809. Latin America: 2 and 16 February 1809. On the relations between colonies and empires: 30 December 1809, 6 and 20 January 1810.

CHAPTER TWO

1　Lamonde and Beauchamp, *Données statistiques*, Table 46.

2　On the Académie de Montréal, de Lagrave, *Fleury Mesplet*, 127–60; on the Société des Patriotes: ibid., 399–402; Galarneau, *La France*, 130–1; Greenwood, *Legacies of Fear*, 59–60; on the Société littéraire de Québec and *Séance de la Société*, Hare and Wallot, *Les imprimés*, 197–200; on the Montreal Society United for Free Debate, Tousignant, "La *Gazette de*

Montréal", 210–20; on some public lectures in English in 1795–96, ibid., 201–4; on Masonic lodges, Le Moine, "Francs-maçons."

3 Lamonde and Beauchamp, *Données statistiques*, Tables 47–52.

4 The concept of "public" recurs in the prospectuses of newspapers; for example, *GQ*, 21 January 1764 and 9 July 1795, *GM*, 28 August 1785 and 23 February 1786, *Courier de Québec*, 29 October 1806.

5 Lamonde and Beauchamp, *Données statistiques*, Table 1.

6 Ibid., Table 62.

7 On the ordinances, Gallichan, *Livre et politique*, 106–7; on the reading aloud of newspapers for people who were illiterate, *GQ*, 16 May 1793; Montgolfier to Mgr Briand, 2 and 6 January 1779, Haldimand to Montgolfier, 15 February 1779, quoted in Buono, "Imprimerie," 24–7.

8 Mesplet to Governor Carleton, May 1778, quoted in Buono, ibid., 24; *GM*, 21 October 1778, 28 April and 2 June 1779, and de Lagrave, *Fleury Mesplet*, 161–97.

9 D.P., "Idées sur la Liberté de la Presse et sur les avantages qu'on en peut espérer," *Le Canadien*, 25 July 1807; see also extracts from Delolme on freedom of the press in *Le Canadien*, 2, 9, 16, 23 July, 5 September and in December 1808.

10 Lamonde and Beauchamp, *Données statistiques*, Tables 1 and 3.

11 Goudreau, "Mail Conveyance"; Lee, *The Canadian Postal System*, 93, 106–7.

12 Lamonde and Beauchamp, *Données statistiques*, Table 61.

13 Ibid., Table 82.

14 Vlach and Buono, *Catalogue collectif*, passim.

15 *GM*, 3 June, 4 November 1778, 13 January, 17 and 24 February 1779, quoted in de Lagrave, *Fleury Mespet*, 98, 116, 131.

16 Haldimand to General Buade, 1 March 1779, quoted in Wade, *The French Canadians*, I:79.

17 M. Montgolfier to Mgr Briand, 1779, quoted in Drolet, *Les bibliothèques*, 91; see also Mgr Hubert to the prefect of the Sacred Congregation for the Propagation of the Faith, 26 October 1792, quoted in Galarneau, *La France*, 133; Mgr Hubert, "Mémoire sur l'état du diocèse de Québec en 1794," *MEQ*, II:487; pastoral letter of Mgr Plessis, 22 August 1814, *MEQ*, II:121.

18 Gallichan, "Bibliothèques," Chap. 3; Buono, *Imprimerie*, 130.

19 *Catalogue of English and French Books in the Quebec Library; Catalogue of English and French Books in the Montreal Library / Catalogue des livres françois et anglais dans la Bibliothèque de Montréal; Catalogue of English and French Books in the Quebec Library; Catalogue of the English and French Books in the Quebec Library.* We have not been able to trace the catalogues of the Bibliothèque de Québec published in 1780, 1781, 1783, 1784, 1787, 1789, 1796, 1798, 1799, or 1800.

20 Lamonde and Beauchamp, *Données statistiques*, Table 59.

21 Laurent, "Le catalogue de la bibliothèque du Séminaire de Québec," 13.
22 Lamonde and Beauchamp, *Données statistiques*, Tables 79 and 85.
23 Ibid., Tables 71–74.
24 Ibid., Tables 75–78.
25 Ibid., Tables 54–58.
26 Gallichan, "Bibliothèques," 50–7, 63–9.
27 Lamonde and Beauchamp, *Données statistiques*, Tables 64–70.
28 Ibid., Table 80.
29 Ibid., Tables 83 and 84.
30 Buono, "Imprimerie," 127–9, 202–16.
31 Lamonde, *La librairie*, 26.
32 *Le Canadien*, 20 January 1810, quoted in Lebel, "François-Xavier Garneau"; Audet and Gauthier, *Le système scolaire*, 8.
33 Gentilcore, ed., *Historical Atlas of Canada*, II, plate 51.
34 "Report of the committee of Council on commerce and police," 5 January 1786, *DC*, I:618; brief and correspondence of Mgr Hubert and brief of Mgr Bailly de Messein, *MEQ*, II:415–21, 385–409, 421–23; Galarneau, *La France*, 46–9, 134–5; de Lagrave, *Fleury Mesplet*, 327–34.
35 Jacob Mountain to Robert Shore Milnes, 19 October 1799, quoted in Christie, *A History of the Late Province of Lower Canada*, 5, 40.
36 Ryland, "Observations relative to the political state of Lower Canada," May 1808, *DC*, II:249.
37 Audet, *Le système scolaire*, III:68–90, 112, 140–2; Boulianne, "The French Canadians."
38 Lamonde, *La philosophie*, 80, 87–95.

CHAPTER THREE

1 Lamonde and Beauchamp, *Données statistiques*, Table 13.
2 Ibid., Table 22.
3 Ouellet, *Lower Canada*, 270, 225, 280, 298, 331; Bourassa, "Regards sur la ressemblance," 36–49, passim; Rosenfeld, "Miniatures and Silhouettes"; Burger, *L'activité théâtrale*, 356–64.
4 Quoted in Gagnon and Lebel-Gagnon, "Le milieu d'origine," 393; see also Mgr Lartigue to Mgr Plessis, 6 October 1824, *AAQ*, *DM*, II:113.
5 Rousseau, *La prédication*, 99; Lemieux, *Histoire du catholicisme*, vol. 1, *1760–1839*, 103–4; Lenoir, "Montréal et ses principaux monuments," 295; Rousseau, "À propos du 'réveil religieux,'" 239, and "La conduite pascale."
6 Ouellet, *Lower Canada*, 218.
7 Lamonde and Beauchamp, *Données statistiques*, Tables 1 and 11.
8 Chapais, *Cours*, III, 17–40; *LJP*: "PPBC. Continuation des débats sur le message de Son Altesse Royale ... concernant les accusations contre

l'Honorable juge Foucher, [c. 7 March]," *L'Aurore*, 20 March 1819; on the uncertainty regarding the leadership of the Parti canadien after 1810, Ouellet, *Lower Canada*, 300–6.

9 *DC*, II:369–70, 484–6; *DC*, III (1818–1829):96–7, 224, 329–31, 484–6, 501.

10 Chapais, *Cours*, 3:81–100; *DC* (1819–1828):55, 69, 88, 214, 222, 269; *JHALC*, 1822, appendix K.

11 LJP, "PPBC. [Civil list]," 19 March 1818, *L'Aurore*, 18 April 1818.

12 Chapais, *Cours*, 3:101–7, 114–44; "Bill for uniting the Legilatures of the Provinces of Lower and Upper Canada," *DC* (1819–1828):123–31.

13 Stuart, *Observations on the Proposed Union*, [6 June 1823], 11–12, 14, 31, 37–8; quotations, 26 and 94; petitions in favour of union, *DC*, II (1819–1828):131–9; Kolish, "Stuart, Sir James" *DCB*.

14 Petitions against union, *DC*, II:139–40; LJP: "Discours prononcé par l'Hon. L.J. Papineau ... au dîner patriotique du mois d'October," [7 October 1822], *Le Spectateur canadien*, 19 and 26 October 1822, reprinted in LJP, *Un demi-siècle*, 46–53; *At a Meeting of the General Committee Appointed for the District of Montreal, for the Purpose of Preparing Petitions*; LJP to Wilmot, 16 December 1822, *DC*, II:144–6; "Observations de MM. L.-J. Papineau et John Neilson sur le projet de réunir les législatures du Haut et du Bas-Canada," in Chapais, *Cours*, 3: 263–82, published in English in London in 1824; Lamonde, "Conscience coloniale."

15 *GQ*, 13 June and 12 December 1822, for example; Neilson–Papineau correspondence, June–December 1822, LAC, MG24, Neilson papers.

16 Parent's articles in *Le Canadien* are not signed; the quotations are taken from the following articles: [Editorial], 30 October 1822; "Le lecteur," 4 December 1822; "Nous avons déjà dit," 22 October 1823; "Nous publions dans un extraordinaire," 1 January 1823, reprinted in Parent, *Étienne Parent*, 48; Parent, *Discours*.

17 *DC* (1819–1828):146.

18 Ibid., 240–3; J. Stuart did not share the views of Sewell and Robinson; he wanted a union of Upper and Lower Canada first, as a prelude to a broader union, ibid., 243.

19 Mgr Plessis to Mgr Lartigue, 25 November 1822, AAQ, RL, XI:67; Mgr Lartigue to Mgr Panet, 1 December 1827, quoted in Lemieux, *Histoire du catholicisme*, 376.

20 Bathurst to Sherbrooke, July 1816, quoted in Lambert, "Plessis, Joseph-Octave," *DCB*.

21 Bathurst to Mgr Plessis, 5 June 1817, quoted in Lemieux, *Histoire du catholicisme*, 48–9; Bathurst to Sherbrooke, 6 July 1817, *DC*, II:556; Mgr Plessis to Bathurst, 16 September 1819, AAQ, bishops of Quebec diocese, 3, 163; "Sermon prêché à la cathédrale de Québec par Mgr Plessis."

22 LeSaulnier to Garnier, 22 September 1829, quoted in Rousseau, *La prédication*, 86n50; Chaussé, *Jean-Jacques Lartigue*, 187.

23 Mgr Plessis to M. Jacques Panet, parish priest in L'Islet, 30 December 1815, *RAPQ* (1927–1928):313; "Sermon prêché à la cathédrale," 165; Mgr Plessis to Abbé Louis Lamothe, 6 November 1823, AAQ, RL, XI:346.

24 "Lettre d'un curé du Canada."

25 Mgr Plessis to Abbé Roby, 28 January 1811, AAQ, RL, VII:251; Abbé Jean Raimbault to Mgr Plessis, 17 December 1820, ASN, Raimbault collections, correspondence; M. Bernier, Paris, to M. Robert, 28 March 1803, ASQ, Letters, T:72.

26 Lamonde, "Classes sociales," 43–7.

27 [François Blanchet], *Appel au Parlement impérial et aux habitans des colonies angloises dans l'Amérique du Nord sur les prétentions exorbitantes du Gouvernement Exécutif et du Conseil législatif de la Province du Bas-Canada*, 37, 11–12, 16, 35; Bernier, "Blanchet, François," *DCB*.

28 Governor's speech of prorogation, 7 March 1827, in *Speech of Louis J. Papineau on the Hustings*, 41–3; Papineau and other signatories, "To Our Constituents," 2 April 1827, *DC* (1819–1828):412–15.

29 "Discours prononcé par Louis-Joseph Papineau, Écuier, Avocat, à l'ouverture de l'élection pour le Quartier Ouest de la Ville de Montréal," 11 August 1827, *La Minerve*, 13, 17, 20, 24, 27 September, 1 October 1827, text in LJP, *Un demi-siècle*, 93 and 112; LJP, "Aux Électeurs du Quartier Ouest de Montréal," 20 August 1827, *La Minerve*, 23 August 1827, text in LJP, *Un demi-siècle*, 126–30.

30 On the speaker's refusal, *DC* (1819-1828), 416-419.

31 Petitions of the citizens of Quebec City and Montreal in *Report from the Select Committee on the Civil Government of Canada*, Appendix, in Chapais, *Cours*, 3:188–204.

32 "Précis du Discours prononcé par le Docteur Labrie," 26–27 December 1827, *La Minerve*, 7 January 1828; B. Chassé, "Labrie, Jacques," *DCB*.

33 Jean-Marie Mondelet to D.-B. Viger, 23 April 1828, quoted in Ouellet, *Lower Canada*, 327.

34 Burroughs, *The Canadian Crisis*, 28–42; for the speeches in Parliament in London: *Hansard* [Parliamentary Debates], Second Series, XIX, 2 May 1828, 300–40: Huskisson, 299–315; Labouchère, 316–18; Mackintosh, 318–31; Wilmot, 331; Hume, 339–42; extracts in Burroughs, *British Attitudes*, 42–8.

35 Testimony before the committee in *Report from the Select Committee on the Civil Government of Canada*, 11–328; list of witnesses, vi.

36 Recommendations in *Report from the Select Committee on the Civil Government of Canada*, 1-10, and in Chapais, *Cours*, 3:283–301, and in *DC* (1819–1828), 466–7, and in *JHALC*, 1828–1829, 38, appendix HH.

37 *DC* (1819–1828), 502–5; see the instructions of the secretary of state for the colonies, Murray, to Governor Kempt and Kempt's response, 29 September and 22 November 1828, *DC* (1819–1828), 487–98.

38 Ouellet, *Lower Canada*, 329–30.

39 LJP, "Sur les diverses références relatives à la composition du Conseil législatif," 10 January 1833, *Le Canadien*, 16, 18 and 23 January 1833; LJP, "Que Dominique Mondelet," 24 November 1832, *La Minerve*, 3 December 1832; Garon, "La fonction politique et sociale des chambres hautes canadiennes, 1791–1841," and "Le Conseil législatif du Canada-Uni."

40 LJP, "État du pays," 11 March 1831, *La Minerve*, 21, 24 and 28 March 1831, text in LJP, *Un demi-siècle*, 158–9; also on the historical perspective: LJP, "Sur les diverses références," 10 January 1833, *Le Canadien*, 16, 18 and 23 January 1833.

41 LJP, "Indépendance des juges," 11 January 1832, *Le Canadien*, 28 January and 1 February 1832.

42 LJP, "État du pays," 11 March 1831, *La Minerve*, 21, 24 and 28 March 1833, text in LJP, *Un demi-siècle*, 161; LJP, "Composition du Conseil," 16 January 1832, *La Minerve*, 2, 9 and 13 January 1832, text in LJP, *Un demi-siècle*, 204.

43 LJP, "Électivité des institutions gouvernementales," 10 January 1833, *La Minerve*, 21 and 24 January 1833, text in LJP, *Un demi-siècle*, 235.

44 LJP, "Rejet des Résolutions Goderich," 16 January 1832, *La Minerve*, 2, 9 and 13 February 1832, text in LJP, *Un demi-siècle*, 200; LJP, "État du pays, douzième résolution," 10 March 1831, *La Minerve*, 21 March 1831, text in LJP, *Un demi-siècle*, 151; LJP, "Conseil législatif, 16 March 1833, *Le Canadien*, 12 April 1833; Abbé Jacques Paquin to Mgr Lartigue, 31 January 1832, quoted in Chabot, *Le curé de campagne*, 97.

45 LJP, "Rejet des Résolutions Goderich," 16 January 1832, *La Minerve*, 2, 9 and 13 January 1832, text in LJP, *Un demi-siècle*, 208; LJP, "Électivité des institutions gouvernementales," 10 January 1833, *La Minerve* 21 and 24 January 1833, text in LJP, *Un demi-siècle*, 226; LJP, "État du pays," 11 March 1831, *La Minerve*, 21, 24 and 28 March 1831, text in LJP, *Un demi-siècle*, 171; LJP, "Constitution du Conseil législatif," 10 January 1833, *Le Canadien*, 28 and 30 January 1833.

46 [É. Parent], *Le Canadien*, 15 August and 7 November 1832, 29 April and 19 June 1833.

47 Chapais, *Cours*, 3: 237–44; on the previous disagreement between Neilson and Papineau on the question of revenues, *JHALC*, 1824, 316–17, and *GQ*, 26 February 1824.

48 On the petitions, the questionnaire sent by the House and the vote: *JHALC*, 40 (1831): 30–31, 74, 90, 138, 202; 41:203 and appendix QQ; Lemieux, *Histoire du catholicisme*, 155–8, and Chaussé, *Jean-Jacques Lartigue*, 179–84, refer to the bishops's writings and the quotation is from *La Minerve* of

31 March 1831; the text of the bill and the clergy's *Mémoire* against the "bill des notables" are in *La Minerve*, 11 April 1831 and 15 and 19 December 1831; LJP, "Notables, [26 March]," *La Minerve*, 11 and 14 April 1831; LJP, "Les Fabriques," *La Minerve*, 2 December 1831; LJP, "Bill des Fabriques," *La Minerve*, 5 and 9 January 1832, texts in LJP, *Un demi-siècle*, 178–87 and 195–8; Abbé Jacques Paquin to Mgr Lartigue, 31 January 1832, quoted in Chabot, *Le curé de campagne*, 97.

49 Chapais, *Cours*, 3:237–44; LJP, "Subsides," 19 March 1831, *La Minerve*, 24 March 1831, text in LJP, *Un demi-siècle*, 175; LJP, "Subsides," 21 March 1831, *La Minerve*, 28 March; also LJP, "Liste civile," 21 January 1832, *Le Canadien*, 22 February 1832; LJP, "Bill des subsides et la liste civile," [16 March], *Le Canadien*, 8 April 1833.

50 Galarneau, "L'élection dans le quartier-ouest de Montréal"; candidates' platforms, *La Minerve*, 23 April 1832; on the vote, Galarneau, "L'élection partielle du quartier-ouest"; judicial and parliamentary enquiries, *JHALC*, 42 (1832–1833), appendix M and unnumbered app.; 43 (1834), unnumbered app., after Nn; verdict of 1 September 1832, *La Minerve*, 7 January 1833; LJP, lettre to the governor, 22 May 1832, *La Minerve*, 11 March 1833; LJP, "Affaire du 21 mai," 11 December 1832, *La Minerve*, 11 March 1833; LJP, "Lieutenant colonel Eden," 28 February 1833, *La Minerve*, 13 March 1833; "La Marseillaise canadienne" [1832], reproduced in Carrier and Vachon, *Chansons politiques*, I:30–2.

51 [Parent], "Les écrivains," *Le Canadien*, 20 December 1833; see also de Sales Laterrière, "Correspondances," *Le Canadien*, 5 October 1831; the *Quebec Mercury*, 18 August 1806, had already discussed the possible example of Louisiana.

52 [Parent], "Adresse au public canadien," *Le Canadien*, 7 May 1831, reproduced in Parent, *Étienne Parent*, 69–73; *La Minerve*, 26 April 1827, quoted in Lebel, "François-Xavier Garneau," 233.

53 Ibid.

54 Roussellier, *L'Europe des libéraux*, 19, 27, 39, 47, 53, 56, 64.

CHAPTER FOUR

1 *La Minerve* of 15 and 22 February 1834 and *Le Canadien* of 17 February published the 92 Resolutions; *Les Quatre-Vingt-Douze Résolutions*; reprinted in Dionne, *Les trois comédies du "Statu Quo" 1834*, 127–235. On the contemporary debates and documents on the 92 Resolutions, *Affaires du pays depuis 1828*, and *Précis des débats de la Chambre d'Assemblée, état de la Province*. On the bills rejected by the Legislative Council, An Old Countryman [Edmund O'Callaghan], *The Late Session of the Provincial Parliament of Lower Canada*.

2 LJP, "État de la Province, 1re Résolution, [18 February]," *La Minerve*, 27 February and 3 March 1834, text in LJP, *Un demi-siècle*, 255, 260–1, 269.

3 Abbé Jacques Paquin to Mgr Lartigue, 31 January 1832; Jean-Baptiste Saint-Germain to Mgr Lartigue, 22 April and 11 November 1834, quoted in Chabot, *Le curé de campagne*, 97, 99, 189–91.

4 LJP, *To the honorable the knights, citizens and burgesses, the Commons of the United Kingdom of Great Britain and Ireland in Parliament assembled.*

5 *Hansard*, Third Series, vol. 22, 14 April 1834, 767–817, quotations, 767, 775, 781, 784, 790, 811.

6 LJP, *Observations sur la réponse de Mathew Lord Aylmer à la députation du Tattersall et sur le discours du Très Honorable E.G. Stanley ... sur les affaires du Canada le 15 April 1834*, 12, 16, 20, 39. Like Jean-Paul Bernard, I attribute this text to Papineau.

7 LJP, *Address of the Hon. L.J. Papineau to the Electors of the West Ward of Montreal*," 3 December 1834; French version, *La Minerve*, 4 and 8 December 1834 and LJP, *Un demi-siècle*, 325–56.

8 Chapman, *What is the Result of the Canadian Election? Fully Answered*, [from *The Daily Advertiser*]; *Canada*, from the *Monthly Repository* (September 1835); Laporte, "Le radical britannique Chapman et le Bas-Canada."

9 Charpentier-Dufour, "La question des agents du Bas-Canada en Grande-Bretagne"; Burroughs, "Roebuck, John Arthur", DCB; *Hansard*, Third Series, vol. 26, 9 March 1835, 660–715; Roebuck, *The Canadas and their Grievances*; Papineau-Roebuck correspondence, LAC, FM24, A19; Hamburger, *Intellectuals in Politics*.

10 "Continuation des débats du 22 février. État de la province et subsides," *Le Canadien*, 9, 11, 14, 16 March 1836, text in LJP, *Un demi-siècle*, 382–416; quotation from La Fontaine, Chapais, *Cours*, 4:81.

11 LJP to Roebuck, 13 March 1836, LAC, FM24, A19, I, 5, 82.

12 LJP, "Continuation des débats du 22 février. État de la province et subsides," *Le Canadien*, 9, 11, 14, 16 March 1836, quotation from *Le Canadien*, 14 March 1836, text in Lamonde and Larin, *Louis-Joseph Papineau*, 382–416; Chapman, *Recent Occurences*; Roebuck's speech, *Hansard*, Third Series, 35, 16 May 1836, 925–53, quotations, 926, 927, 941.

13 *Fourth Report of The Standing Committee of Grievances made to the Assembly of Lower Canada Respecting the Conduct of Lord Aylmer*, 419–29.

14 Roebuck, *Existing Difficulties in the Government of the Canadas*; Chapman, *Progress of Events in Canada*.

15 Gosford Report, 15 November 1836: *The Reports of the Royal Commissioners Appointed to Enquire into the State of Canada*; British Parliamentary Papers, Shannon, Irish University Press, 1968, Colonies, Canada 4, Session 1837, 1–173, quotations, 5, 6, 7, 9.

16 The fourteen anglophone members who voted in favour of the 92 Resolutions were James Leslie (Montréal-Est), Ed Toomey (Drummond), Robert Nelson (Montréal-Ouest), John Pickel (William-Henry), Edmund B. O'Callaghan (Yamaska), Meritt Hotchkiss (L'Acadie), Jacob de Witt and James Perrigo (Beauharnois), W. Henry Scott (Deux-Montagnes), James Blackburn (Outaouais), C.W. Tolford (Sherbrooke), Robert Layfield (Mégantic), and Marcus Child and John Grannis (Stanstead), according to Bolduc, "Les élections générales de 1834," 80n37.

CHAPTER FIVE

1 Lamonde and Beauchamp, *Données statistiques,* Table 1.

2 Ouellet, *Le Bas-Canada,* 218.

3 Lamonde and Beauchamp, *Données statistiques,* Table 1.

4 Ibid., Table 4.

5 Goudreau, "Mail Conveyance," 20–3; Lee, "The Canadian Postal System," 93.

6 Gagnon, "L'infrastructure touristique."

7 Galarneau, "Les Français au Canada," 215–20; Galarneau, "Leblanc de Marconnay, Hyacinthe-Poirier" and Sylvain, "Rambau, Alfred-Xavier," *DCB*; Yon, *Le Canada français,* 11–13.

8 Pavie, *Souvenirs atlantiques,* I:183; Vallée, *Tocqueville au Bas-Canada,* 84–106; quotations, 91, 101, 90, 100, 101.

9 Galarneau, "Les Canadiens en France," 135–81; Mgr Plessis, *Journal d'un voyage en Europe,* 88, 395, 410–11, 357–8, 409, 416; Mgr Lartigue, "Journal de voyage," quoted in Galarneau, ibid., 60–161.

10 Roy, *Édouard-Raymond Fabre,* Galarneau, "Reiffenstein, John Christopher" and "Langlois, *dit* Germain, Augustin-René," *DCB*.

11 Garneau, *Voyage en Angleterre et en France,* 123 and 191; Galarneau, "Holmes, John," *DCB,* and Gallichan, "Berthelot, Amable," *DCB*.

12 La Fontaine, "Journal de voyage," manuscript, quoted in Galarneau, *Voyage en Angleterre et en France,* 169–71; White, *Louis-Joseph Papineau et Lamennais.*

13 Lamonde, "La librairie Bossange."

14 Barker, "Essai historique et politique sur le Canada," quotations, 384 and 386; Lebrun, *Tableau statistique et politique des deux Canadas;* Vindex [Thomas Maguire], *Le clergé canadien vengé par ses ennemis.*

15 de Vigny, "Les Français du Canada."

16 Granger-Remington, "Étude du journal politique et littéraire *Le Courrier des États-Unis*"; Masson-Juneau, *"Le Courrier des États-Unis."* Articles from *Le Courrier des États-Unis* were reprinted or debated; see, for example *L'Ami du peuple, de l'ordre et des lois,* 25 July 1832, *L'Écho du pays,* 3 July 1834, *Le Canadien,* 21 October 1836.

17 Lamonde and Beauchamp, *Données statistiques,* Table 62 and 62A.

18 P. Bédard to J. Neilson, 18 February 1815, quoted in Ouellet, *Lower Canada*, 305; J. Neilson to LJP, 12 November 1822, LAC, Neilson collection, MG24 B1, XV:25; *Le Canadien*, 22 January 1823; P. Bédard to J. Neilson, 26 March 1824, quoted in Ouellet, *Lower Canada*, 323; *Le Canadien*, 19 January 1825.

19 Cambron, "Pauvreté et utopie"; M. Bibaud, "Mes pensées," *Bibliothèque canadienne*, November 1828; Lamonde, "Les revues"; É. Parent, "Adresse au Public canadien," *Le Canadien*, 7 May 1831, in Parent, *Étienne Parent*, 69–73; "Au Public," *Courrier du Bas-Canada*, 9 October 1819; "Prospectus," *L'Écho du pays*, 1 January 1833.

20 Teyssier, "La distribution postale," 45; Boucher-Belleville, *Journal d'un Patriote*, 22; statement of J. Normandin, quoted in Ouellet, "Les insurrections de 1837–1838," 364n32; statement of Paul Martin, quoted in Ouellet, *Lower Canada*, 444; statement of Paul Brazeau, 8 January 1838, "Documents relatifs à 1837–1838", RAPQ (1925–1926); on reading out loud, see also 12, 13, 19, 356.

21 É. Parent, "Prodesse civibus," *Le Canadien*, 18 February 1824; other positions taken by Parent in *Le Canadien*, 25 December 1822, 22 January and 19 February 1823, 22 February 1832, 23 August 1833, 26 December 1834, 16 June 1837; *Mémoires relatifs à l'emprisonnement de l'honorable D.-B. Viger*, 8–9, 26–34; list of Patriotes in Bernard, *Les rébellions*, 290–315, and Beaulieu and Hamelin, *La presse québécoise*, vol. I.

22 Mgr Plessis to Mgr Lartigue, 5 January 1824, AAQ, RL, XI:406; Abbé Brassard to L. Duvernay, 21 August 1832, quoted in Ouellet, *Lower Canada*, 353; Vicar General Viau to L. Duvernay, August 1832, RAPQ (1926–1927): 160.

23 Mgr Lartigue to Mgr Panet, 11 September 1830, ACAM, RLL, 5:305–6; Abbés Paquin and Lefebvre to Mgr Lartigue, 3 October 1831, ACAM 901.021,931–9; Mgr Lartigue to Mgr Panet, 16 December 1831, ACAM, RLL, 6:174, 190, 194, 204, 209, 218; Mgr Lartigue to Mgr Panet, 18 February 1832, ibid.: 228; Mgr Lartigue to Mgr Panet, 20 February 1832, ibid.: 232; Mgr Lartigue to Mgr Panet, 20 March 1832, 257; Désilets, "Sicotte, Victor," DCB. Some priests even met at the presbytery of Sainte-Geneviève to start a newspaper, 29 December 1831 and 3 January 1832, ASQ, polygraph 8, nos. 44 and 45. A plan for a newspaper called *L'Ecclésiastique* had been formulated from 1823 to 1826, RAPQ (1933–1932): 273, 295; (1941–1942): 430, 436–7, 452, 475, 481, 490; Mgr Lartigue to Mgr Plessis, 23 October 1824, ACAM, RLL, 3:118; prospectus in *La Bibliothèque canadienne* (December 1826). See Thomas-Marie Charland, "Un projet de journal ecclésiastique."

24 J.-L. Roy, "Leclère, Pierre-Édouard," DCB.

25 Metcalfe, "Le sport au Canada français au xixe siècle"; *Canada Learns to Play*, passim.

26 Bernatchez, "La Société littéraire et historique de Québec"; Lamonde, *Les bibliothèques de collectivités*, 41–3; Chartrand, Duchesne and Gingras, *Histoire*

des sciences au Québec, 87–92; Gagnon, "Le projet avorté de musée d'histoire naturelle de la Montreal Library."

27 Lamonde, *Les bibliothèques de collectivités,* 43–5; Robins, "1828–1870: the Montreal Mechanics' Institute."

28 "Société littéraire de Montréal," *L'Aurore,* 11 August 1817; Campagnard, *L'Aurore,* 18 August 1817; *La Bibliothèque canadienne,* June and October 1827, March 1828.

29 Garneau, *Voyage,* 155–6, 295, 212, 256; P. de Sales Laterrière to D.-B. Viger, 1833, quoted in Manon Brunet, "Documents pour une histoire de l'édition au Québec avant 1900," 347; Papineau frequented the news room in Albany in November 1838, Julie Papineau, *Une femme patriote,* 156; see also *La Minerve,* 18 July 1831, 11 December 1834, and *Le Populaire,* 30 August 1837.

30 Muzzo, *Les mouvements,* 72–6, 30–4, 47–50, 77–8, 82–4, 79–82.

31 Boucher de la Bruère, "La Société Aide-toi et le ciel t'aidera," 107–11; see also Le Franc-Parleur, "Des associations et des banques," *La Minerve,* 11 December 1834; Muzzo, *Les mouvements,* 29.

32 Curé Mignault, Chambly, to Mgr Lartigue, 12 February 1834, ADSJQ, 1A/109; Dr C.-H.-O. Côté à ses constituants, 4 September 1835, ibid., 16A/58.

33 Un Trifluvien, *L'Ami du peuple,* 27 March 1837; Un jeune Canadien, "Observations sur un article lu à la société Aide-toi et le ciel t'aidera," *La Minerve,* 10 and 24 April, 15 May 1837; manuscript, 31 March 1837, ASSH, Raymond correspondence, folder 43; Anonymous, "Article [sur l'éducation] lu devant la société Aide-toi et le ciel t'aidera," *La Minerve,* 20 March 1837; *Le Fantasque,* 5 November 1838; Amédée Papineau "Littérature canadienne," 119–21.

34 Audet, *Histoire de l'enseignement,* I:344; idem, *Le système scolaire,* III: 137, 140–42, 159; V: passim.

35 "Lettre d'un curé du Canada," 7–15.

36 Lamonde, "Classes sociales, classes scolaires," 49, 50, 53, 55; see also "Un autre ami de l'éducation," *Le Canadien,* 5 November 1823.

37 Le Franc-Parleur, *Le Canadien,* 26 January 1825; Mgr Lartigue to Mgr Plessis, 27 January 1825, ACAM, RLL, 3: 159; *JHALC,* 1825, vol. 34: 17 and 32; Mgr Plessis to Mgr Lartigue, 2 February 1825, AAQ, RL, 12: 179-180; the Borgia who is referred to was a member of the legislature.

38 Lamonde and Beauchamp, *Données statistiques,* Tables 30–39.

39 Dufour, "Diversité institutionnelle."

40 Abbé Painchaud to Mgr Signay, 2 February 1829, quoted in Dionne, *Vie de C.-F. Painchaud,* 157–8.

41 Lamonde and Beauchamp, *Données statistiques,* Tables 29 and 40; Dufour, *Tous à l'école,* 44–52; Audet, *Histoire de l'enseignement,* I:381–7.

42 Lamonde and Beauchamp, *Données statistiques*, Table 46.

43 Ibid., Table 47.

44 Ibid., Table 50.

45 Verrette, "L'alphabétisation au Québec," 148, 202, 250, 263; "L'alphabétisation de la ville de Québec," 51–76.

46 Mgr Lartigue to Abbé Turgeon, 28 March 1836, ACAM, RLL, 8:147; Mgr Lartigue to Mgr Signay, 1 May 1836, ACAM, RLL, 8:183; see also *MEQ*, III:341–2.

47 Audet, *Le système scolaire*, VI:75–179; *JHALC*, 1836, appendix Oo; Mgr Lartigue to Mgr Signay, 1836, quoted in Ouellet, *Le Bas-Canada*, 267.

48 *Le Canadien*, 29 January 1823; see also Victor, "De l'éducation," *L'Écho du pays*, 13 August 1834.

49 Maurault and Dansereau, *Le Collège de Montréal*, 235, 500, 122–5; Maurault, "Une révolution collégiale"; Mgr Lartigue to Abbés Viau and Maguire, 12 November 1830, quoted in Maurault, "Une révolution au Collège de Montréal," 40; *Montreal Gazette*, 11 November 1830.

50 *Journal d'un voyage en Europe par Mgr J.-O. Plessis*, 357-358, 409–11, 416; Lartigue, "Journal d'un voyage," 11 September 1819, ACAM, RCD 134:24; Lartigue to Thavenet, 8 March 1821, ACAM, RLL I:33; Lartigue on Lamennais: "Journal d'un voyage," 18 January 1820, ACAM, RCD 134:77. Mgr Lartigue would be a subscriber to *Mémorial catholique* from 1825 to 1830, when *L'Avenir* by Lamennais came out; Lartigue to Thavenet, 25 January 1825, ACAM, RLL, 3:156.

51 Abbé Viau to Mgr Lartigue, 19 October 1829, ACAM 295.101, 829-47; Mgr Lartigue to Abbé Viau, 27 October 1829, ACAM 901.013, 829-1.

52 M. Garnier to M. Roque, 15 July 1829, ASSM, Garnier correspondence.

53 Lemire, ed., *La vie littéraire au Québec*, II:440–52; Abbé Painchaud to Chateaubriand, 19 January 1826, and Chateaubriand to Abbé Painchaud, 29 April 1827, in Lebon, *Histoire du Collège de Sainte-Anne-de-la-Pocatière*, I:359–62; Galarneau, "L'abbé Joseph-Sabin Raymond," 85.

54 Mgr Lartigue to Vicar General Pierre Viau, 9 October 1830, ACAM 901.013, 830-2; Abbé Larocque to Abbé J.-S. Raymond, 16 November 1830, CHSTH, old classification, A,G11; "Des doctrines du *Mémorial* dans leurs rapports avec les circonstances actuelles," *La Minerve*, 21 October 1830.

55 Mgr Lartigue to the Rev. Dr Wiseman, President of the English College at Rome, 20 January 1832, ACAM, RLL, 6:208; Abbé Prince to Mgr Lartigue, quoted in Choquette, *Histoire du Séminaire de Saint-Hyacinthe*, I:135–6; see also "Procès de M. l'abbé de La Mennais, rédacteur du journal *L'Avenir*," *La Minerve*, 14 April 1831; Abbé Viau to Abbé Ignace Bourget, 3 September 1831, ACAM, 295.101, 831-7; Mgr Lartigue to Abbé Viau, 9 February 1832, ACAM, 901.013, 832-2; Mgr Lartigue to Abbé Viau, 12 May 1832, ACAM, 901.013, 832-4.

56 "Examen critique des ouvrages de M. de La Mennais par G. Rozaven," *Le Canadien*, 16 May 1832; Mgr Lartigue to Abbé Prince, 4 June 1832, ACAM, RLL, 6:330.

57 Mgr Lartigue to Abbé Viau, 17 November 1832, ACAM, RLL, 6:492–3; Mgr Signay to Mgr Provancher, 11 April 1832, AAQ, RL, 15:367; see also Mgr Lartigue to Abbé Viau, 27 February 1833, ACAM, 901.013, 833-2; Mgr Signay to Mgr Lartigue, 1833, *RAPQ* (1936–1937):216; Mgr Signay to Mgr Lartigue, 11 October 1834, AAQ, RL, 16:326 and 341; English text of *Mirari vos*, available at http://www.papalencyclicals.net/Greg16/g16mirar.htm.

58 [Abbé Prince], "Doctrine," *L'Écho du pays*, 13 March and 8 May 1834; Lamonde, *La philosophie*, 96–109.

59 Abbé J.-S. Raymond to Félicité de Lamennais, [late 1833–early 1834], quoted in Plourde, *Dominicains au Canada*, I:16–19; Lamennais, *Words of a Believer*, 95, 114, 132, 177.

60 Extracts from *Paroles d'un croyant: L'Écho du pays*, July 1834, *Le Canadien*, 16 July 1834; about the book: *La Minerve*, 21 August 1834, *Le Canadien*, 29 August and 26 December 1834; English text of *Singulari nos*, available at http://www.papalencyclicals.net/Greg16/g16singu.htm; Le Guillou, *La condamnation*, 729–36.

61 Mgr Lartigue to Abbé Prince, 30 August 1834, ACAM, RLL, 7:525–6, see also Mgr Lartigue to Abbé Viau, 8 February 1835, ibid., 669–70; submission of Abbé Prince, *La Minerve*, 11 September 1834, or *Le Canadien*, 15 September 1834; Un Croyant catholique [J.-S. Raymond], "Mr. de la Mennais," 24 November 1834, CHSTH, fonds du Séminaire, CH001/S2/SS10, folder 42, 78–105, copy of the original; Mgr Lartigue to Abbé Prince, 8 November 1834, ACAM, RLL, 7:593; Mgr Lartigue to Abbé Prince, 29 November 1834, ibid.: 613, 772; Mgr Lartigue to Abbé Raymond, 29 November 1834, ibid., 613–14; Mgr Lartigue to Abbé Prince, 1834, quoted in Choquette, *Histoire du Séminaire de Saint-Hyacinthe*, I:169.

62 Abbé Jean Holmes to Abbé Prince, 24 November 1834, CHSTH, old classification, box 43, no 2:25, now in fonds du Séminaire (CH001); Lamonde, *La philosophie*, 109–14.

63 Mgr Signay to Mgr Lartigue, 28 February 1838, AAQ, RL, 18:236; "Mémoire pour justifier l'enseignement et la conduite des Prêtres du Collège de St-Hyacinthe lors de l'insurrection de 1837," February 1838, CHSTH, RL d'affaires, fonds du Séminaire, CH001/S2/SS8, 123–36; Mgr Lartigue to Mgr Signay, 5 March 1838, ACAM, RLL, 9:26.

64 Lamonde, *Les bibliothèques de collectivités*, 37–9, for the printed catalogues of the Montreal Public Library for 1824, 1833, and 1842; the Quebec Public Library published catalogues of its collection in 1821, 1832, 1834, and 1844; *L'Écho du pays*, 22 May 1836.

65 Lamonde and Beauchamp, *Données statistiques*, Table 85.

66 Gallichan, *Livre et politique*, passim; for the library of the House of Assembly, there are catalogues for 1818, 1825, 1831, and 1832; for that of the Legislative Council, there are catalogues for 1822, 1830, 1831, and 1832; Lamonde and Morel, "Faribault, Georges-Bathélemy," *DCB*.

67 Lamonde, *Les bibliothèques de collectivités*, 39–41, 47.

68 Lamonde, *Les bibliothèques de collectivités*, 39, 47; Buono, "Imprimerie," 130–1; *Catalogue of Cary's Circulating Library, Quebec*.

69 Lamonde, *Les bibliothèques*, 40, 48; Buono, "Imprimerie"; E.D., "Le 4 juillet, le Canada et les États-Unis," *L'Écho du pays*, 13 August 1835; Amédée Papineau, *Journal d'un Fils de la Liberté*, 87, entry of 2 March 1838.

70 Lamonde and Beauchamp, *Données statistiques*, Table 54.

71 Ibid., Table 56B.

72 Ibid., Table 55B.

73 Ibid., Tables 57B and 58; Labonté, "Les bibliothèques privées."

74 Buono, "Imprimerie", 202–16; Lamonde and Olivier, *Les bibliothèques personnelles*, 37, 75–6, 83–4, 91–2.

75 Lamonde, "La librairie Hector Bossange," 66–7; *Catalogue général de la librairie canadienne d'Édouard R. Fabre*, 120.

76 Lamonde, *La librairie et l'édition à Montréal (1776–1920)*, 171–87.

77 Lamonde and Beauchamp, *Données statistiques*, Tables 64–66.

78 Lamonde, "La librairie Hector Bossange," 66.

79 Lamonde and Beauchamp, *Données statistiques*, Table 68.

80 Ibid., Table 70; Lamonde, *La librairie et l'édition*, 146–8, for bookstore catalogues published between 1815 and 1840.

81 *Catalogue général de la librairie canadienne*; for the inventory of the Hector Bossange bookstore in 1816 and in 1819, Lamonde, "La librairie Hector Bossange," 66–79.

82 Françoise Parent, "Les envois de livres de Paris au Bas-Canada de 1824 à 1827"; Quiblier-Carrière correspondence, Archives Saint-Sulpice de Paris, dossier 99, and Lajeunesse, "Le livre dans les échanges sulpiciens Paris-Montréal"; ASQ, polygraph 44 and Séminaire 75, no. 85; ACSAP, Painchaud 5, XLIII.

83 Lebel, "Ludger Duvernay et *La Minerve*."

84 Mgr Lartigue to Mgr Signay, 26 January 1836, ACAM, RLL, 8: 07; Mgr Lartigue to Mgr Signay, 10 March 1836, ibid.: 144; Gallichan, *Livre et politique*, 88–91; Joseph Lettoré to L. Duvernay, 6 September 1838, *RAPQ* (1926–1927): 195; see also on the matter of the *Words of a Believer*: C.-O. Perreault to E.-R. Fabre, 22 February 1836, BANQ, Quebec's Centre, Fabre papers; Mgr Lartigue to Mgr Signay, 1 May 1836, ACAM, RLL, 8: 185; Mgr Lartigue to Mgr Signay, 11 May 1836, ibid.: 191–2; "Circulaire aux curés,"

10 August 1837, MEM, I:13–14; [Abbé Thomas Maguire], *Doctrine de l'Église d'Irlande et de celle du Canada sur la révolte,* 121; Matheson, "Un pamphlet politique au Bas-Canada."

85 Deutsch, *Nationalism and Social Communication,* xii; Gellner, *Nations and Nationalism.*

86 Hayne, "Lamartine au Québec "; Lemire, *La vie littéraire,* II:337–49, 363–82, 440–52; Hare, *Contes,* I:1778–859, 49–66, 102–26; *Magasin du Bas-Canada,* 1 January 1832; "Littérature américaine," *La Minerve,* 20 August 1832; Chasles, "De la littérature dans l'Amérique du Nord," *Le Glaneur,* February 1837.

87 Prospectus for *Le Glaneur* in *L'Ami du peuple,* 14 September 1836; on Angers and de Gaspé, parliamentary reporters: *La Gazette de Québec,* 4 February 1834, *Le Canadien,* 5 February 1834, *La Minerve,* 10 February 1834 and Hare, *Contes,* 69; on the morals of de Gaspé's novel, *Le Populaire,* 11 October, 15 and 17 November 1837.

88 Dostaler, *Les infortunes du roman,* 46; Lacourcière, "Aubert de Gaspé *fils*"; in 1825, Louis Plamondon was not able to obtain enough subscriptions for a five-volume work on Canadian civil law; Abbé Holmes had subscription forms signed for a philosophy textbook by Abbé Demers, Holmes to Abbé J.-C. Prince, 24 November 1834, ASSH, box 43, no. 2:25.

89 *Provincial Statutes of Lower-Canada* (1831–1834), Guill. IV:52–3, 25 February 1832.

90 *Bibliothèque canadienne,* 1825–1830; B. Chassé, "Labrie, Jacques," DCB; "Monsieur l'éditeur," *Le Canadien,* 13 July 1831; Perrault, *Abrégé de l'Histoire du Canada;* "Histoire du Canada," *L'Écho du pays,* 14 March 1833 to 16 January 1834.

91 Grisé and Lortie, *Textes poétiques,* III, nos. 205, 146, 220, 230, 15, 143, 224, 101, 16.

92 "Airs nationaux de différens pays," *La Minerve,* 3 April 1834; "Chant patriotique," *L'Ami du peuple,* 12 April 1834; "Hymne de Riego," *Le Populaire,* 12 April 1837; "Navarin. Chant national," *Le Populaire,* 8 May 1837; "Chant patriotique du Canada," *Le Libéral,* 17 June 1837.

93 "Détails sur l'assemblée anti-coercitive des Comtés de l'Islet et de Bellechasse," *Le Libéral,* 1 July 1837; "Assemblée de Sainte-Scholastique," *La Minerve,* 12 June 1837; "L'agitation," *La Gazette de Québec,* 8 June 1837; Aubin, "Chronique des patriotes de 1837–1838."

CHAPTER SIX

1 *L'Ami du peuple, de l'ordre et des lois:* 21 July 1832 to July 1840; *L'Aurore:* 10 March 1817 to September 1819; *La Bibliothèque canadienne:* June 1825 to June 1830; *Le Canadien:* 22 November 1806 to 17 March 1810; 14 June

1817 to 12 March 1825; 7 May 1831 to 1 January 1839; *L'Écho du pays*: 28 February 1833 to July 1836; *Le Fantasque*: 1 August 1838 to 31 December 1840; *The Quebec Gazette / La Gazette de Québec*, 1 January 1808 to 31 December 1838; *Le Magasin du Bas-Canada*: January to December 1832; *La Minerve*: 9 November 1826 to 20 November 1837; *L'Observateur*: 10 July 1830 to 2 July 1831; *Le Populaire*: 10 April 1837 to 3 November 1838; *Le Libéral*: 17 June to 20 November 1837; *La Quotidienne*: 30 November 1837 to 3 November 1838; *Le Spectateur canadien*: 1 January 1813 to 1 October 1822; *Le Télégraphe*: 22 March to 3 June 1837; *The Vindicator*: 12 December 1828 to October 1837. These newspapers were analyzed as part of the cultural section of the Institut interuniversitaire de recherches sur les populations (IREP), whose director then was Gérard Bouchard.

2 "Statistiques des États d'Europe," *La Minerve*, 18 August 1828; "Statistique de la Turquie," *La Minerve*, 10 July and 4 August 1828; "Statistique de l'Irlande," *La Minerve*, 10 April 1828; "Chronology," *The Vindicator*, 19 January 1829.

3 "Les nouvelles d'Europe," *Le Spectateur canadien*, 3 November 1821; "Du Journal des Débats," *La Minerve*, 10 September 1829; "Politique étrangère," *La Minerve*, 28 September 1829; D. de Saint-Quentin to Abbé de Calonne, 18 March 1816, ACSAP, Calonne 36, XXVII; "Entre les dates," *Le Spectateur canadien*, 19 May 1821.

4 Mgr Plessis to M. Roux, 15 May 1815, AAQ, RL 8:339; de Sales Laterrière, *Fortunes et infortunes d'un dandy canadien*, 39; Abbé Raimbault to Mgr Plessis, 23 May 1815, AEN, sheet 22; Mgr Plessis to Abbé Raimbault, 23 May 1815, ASN, letters from Plessis to Raimbault, II: 232–3; "Nous sommes encore sans nouvelles," *Le Spectateur canadien*, 7 August 1815; J.C. de Saint-Morys to Abbé de Calonne, [after March 1815], archives des Ursulines de Trois-Rivières, RL, 71–2; M. Duvier to Abbé Raimbault, 11 May 1818, ASN, Séminaire II:57; "Les dernières nouvelles de France," *Le Canadien*, 20 March 1822.

5 "Révolution de Naples," *Le Spectateur canadien*, 9 and 16 September 1820; *La Gazette de Québec*, 11 September 1820; *Le Canadien*, 13 September 1820; "Extrait d'une lettre datée," *Le Spectateur canadien*, 21 October 1820; "Dernières nouvelles d'Europe," *Le Spectateur canadien*, 12 May 1821.

6 "S'il faut en croire," *Le Spectateur canadien*, 27 May 1820; "La Révolution," *Le Spectateur canadien*, 16 September 1820; "Les derniers journaux," *Le Spectateur canadien*, 28 April 1821; "Les nouvelles d'Europe," *Le Spectateur canadien*, 11 August 1821; "Révolution à Naples," *Le Canadien*, 20 September 1820.

7 "Les derniers journaux," *Le Spectateur canadien*, 23 June 1821; "De la Révolution Piémontaise," *Le Spectateur canadien*, 16 March 1822; "Quelques politiques," *Le Spectateur canadien*, 11 May 1822; "S'il faut en croire," *Le Spectateur canadien*, 28 October 1820; "L'Europe," *Le Spectateur canadien*, 27 January 1821.

8 "Vienne, le 30 mars," *La Gazette de Québec*, 13 June 1816; "Insurrection des Grecs," *Le Spectateur canadien*, 2 June 1821; "Voici le serment," *Le Spectateur canadien*, 21 July 1821; "Dernières nouvelles d'Europe," *Le Spectateur canadien*, 6 July 1822; "Les différents," *Le Spectateur canadien*, 20 July 1822; "Les nouvelles du théâtre," *Le Canadien*, 5 January 1825; "Ibrahim Pacha," *La Gazette de Québec*, 22 May 1826; "Journaux de France," *La Gazette de Québec*, 26 July 1827; "*L'Observateur de Trieste*," *La Gazette de Québec*, 30 August 1827; "Nouvelles étrangères," *La Gazette de Québec*, 24 December 1827; "By the Packet-Ship," *The Irish Vindicator*, 20 February 1829; "Les conditions de paix," *La Gazette de Québec*, 5 November 1829.

9 "Les dernières nouvelles," *Le Spectateur canadien*, 4 August 1821; "Les nouvelles d'Orient," *Le Canadien*, 27 March 1822; "Les Thermopyles ont été de nouveau," *La Gazette de Québec*, 14 October 1822; "Québec lundi," *La Gazette de Québec*, 23 July 1821; "Nous avons rempli," *Le Canadien*, 11 June 1823.

10 "Les dernières nouvelles," *Le Spectateur canadien*, 4 August 1821; "La question," *Le Spectateur canadien*, 24 August 1822; "Nous avons informé nos lecteurs," *La Gazette de Québec*, 22 July 1824; "*Gazette de Québec*," *La Gazette de Québec*, 8 November 1827.

11 "Extraordinaire. Révolution en France," *La Minerve*, 8 September 1830; "France," *The Irish Vindicator*, 4 June 1830; "Dissolution officielle," *La Minerve*, 21 June 1830; "France," *The Irish Vindicator*, 9 July 1830; "France," *La Gazette de Québec*, 12 July 1830; "The *Paris Moniteur*," *La Gazette de Québec*, 9 August 1830; "Révolution en France," *La Gazette de Québec*, 9 September 1830; "Discours," *La Minerve*, 20 September 1830; "Chambre des Députés," *La Minerve*, 28 October 1830, and issues until 17 February 1831.

12 Amédée Papineau, *Souvenirs de jeunesse*, 83, 87.

13 "If we are," *The Irish Vindicator*, 15 January 1830; "Politique européenne," *La Minerve*, 24 June 1830; "Lorsque nous faisions part," *La Minerve*, 9 September 1830; "La voie de Québec," *La Minerve*, 23 September 1830.

14 "Les partis," *L'Observateur*, 7 August 1830; "The French Revolution," *The Irish Vindicator*, 10 September 1830; "Nous avons reçu nos papiers," *La Gazette de Québec*, 30 September 1830; "L'extrait suivant," *La Gazette de Québec*, 23 September 1830; "Les événements se succèdent en Europe," *La Minerve*, 18 November 1830.

15 "The Struggle Prevailing," *The Irish Vindicator*, 6 August 1830; "Les nouvelles de France," *La Gazette de Québec*, 7 October 1830.

16 "Aux dernières nouvelles," *L'Observateur*, 30 October 1830; "L'éditeur de," *La Minerve*, 4 November 1830; Un Québéquois, "Correspondance," *La Minerve*, 15 November 1830.

17 "Ambition démocratique," *L'Ami du peuple*, 18 August 1832; "Les dernières nouvelles," *L'Ami du peuple*, 15 February 1834; "De la position des agitateurs," *Le Populaire*, 14 June 1837.

18 "Mouvements révolutionnaires dans les Pays-Bas," *La Gazette de Québec,*
14 October 1830; "Latest News," *The Irish Vindicator,* 22 October 1830; "We
have on our Columns," *The Irish Vindicator,* 9 November 1830; "Pays-Bas,"
La Gazette de Québec, 15 November 1830; "Nouvelles récentes d'Europe," *La
Gazette de Québec,* 2 December 1830; "Pays-Bas," *La Minerve,* 30 December
1830; "Belgique. Ouverture du Congrès national," *La Minerve,* 10 January
1831; "Québec. Jeudi," *La Gazette de Québec,* 17 February 1831; "Québec.
Lundi," *La Gazette de Québec,* 28 February 1831; "France," *L'Observateur,*
5 March 1831; "La France et la Belgique," *L'Observateur,* 19 March 1831;
"Belgique," *La Minerve,* 18 April 1831.

19 "Les événements," *La Minerve,* 18 November 1830; "Québec. Jeudi," *La
Gazette de Québec,* 11 November 1830; D.-B. Viger, "Réflexions sur la Belgique,"
La Minerve, 12, 16, 19, 23, and 26 May 1831, also published as a pamphlet
under the title *Considérations relatives à la dernière révolution de la Belgique.*

20 "Manifesto of the Nation," *The Irish Vindicator,* 11 March 1831; "Address to
the People of Poland," *The Irish Vindicator,* 26 April 1831; "Adresse du gouvernement polonais aux habitans de la Lithuanie," *Le Canadien,* 6 August
1831; "Extraits des journaux," *La Gazette de Québec,* 4 November 1831; the
text of Warsaw's capitulation was reprinted in *Le Canadien* on 5 November
1831 and in *La Minerve* on 10 November; "Détails sur la prise de Varsovie,"
La Minerve, 2 January 1832.

21 "Révolution en Pologne," *La Minerve,* 14 February 1831; "Russia and Poland,"
The Irish Vindicator, 22 March 1831; "Manifeste," *La Minerve,* 30 May 1831;
"Pologne," *L'Observateur,* 26 March 1831.

22 "Nouvelles étrangères. Pologne," *La Minerve,* 15 February 1831; "Québec.
Lundi," *La Gazette de Québec,* 26 September 1831; "De la nationalité politique," *La Minerve,* 12 March 1832; "Address to the Poles by their Countrymen in England and France," *The Times,* 8 November 1831 in *Le Canadien,*
4 January 1832.

23 "Le reste de l'Europe," *L'Ami du peuple,* 31 December 1833; "Dîner public
au Dr Nelson," *Le Populaire,* 22 June 1838; MEM, I:14–21.

24 "Détails sur les causes," *Le Canadien,* 14 January 1832; "De la nationalité
politique," *La Minerve,* 12 March 1832; "De la manière dont se forment,"
La Minerve, 11 September 1834.

25 "Correspondance," *La Gazette de Québec,* 9 February 1815; "Extraits de
quelques-uns," *La Gazette de Québec,* 8, 17, 18, 19, and 24 August 1822;
"Irlande," *La Gazette de Québec,* 21 February 1825; "Dublin," *La Gazette de
Québec,* 21 August 1828; "Irlande. Motion de M. Hume," *Le Canadien,* 14,
21, 28 July, and 4 August 1824; "Votre écrit," *Le Canadien,* 30 May 1831;
"The Following is a Sketch," *The Irish Vindicator,* 30 June 1829; the question
of the repeal of the union drew the attention of *The Irish Vindicator* from
September 1830, and it was frequently discussed until 1834; "Insurrections

et outrages en Irlande," *Le Spectateur canadien,* 26 January 1822; "L'Irlande paraît," *Le Spectateur canadien,* 13 April 1822; "Nous voyons," *Le Canadien,* 18 December 1822.

26 "[Ireland]," *The Canadian Spectator,* 25 June 1834; Un Canadien [D.-B. Viger], "Analyse d'un entretien," quotation from 230; "Dialogue entre deux amis," *La Minerve,* 4 June 1827; "Irlande," *La Minerve,* 6 March 1828.

27 "Société des amis de l'Irlande en Canada," *La Minerve,* 2 October 1828; see also *The Irish Vindicator,* 20 November and 16, 23, 26, 30 December 1828, 23 January, 13 and 27 February 1829 and *La Gazette de Québec,* 29 January 1829; "Assemblée générale," *The Irish Vindicator,* 3 and 20 March 1829; "Adresse aux habitants des provinces britanniques de l'Amérique du Nord," *La Minerve,* 7 and 14 April 1831; V.P. [Vallières de Saint-Réal], "Si l'honnête homme," *La Gazette de Québec,* 27 October 1828; "J'ai fait savoir," *La Gazette de Québec,* 3 November 1828, reprinted in *The Irish Vindicator,* 19 December 1828.

28 On the debates on Catholic emancipation in the House of Commons and the House of Lords, *La Minerve, La Gazette de Québec* and *The Irish Vindicator* between 23 April and 28 May 1829; on O'Connell's first speech in the House, "The Following," *The Irish Vindicator,* 30 June 1829; on the repeal of the Union: "Dernières nouvelles d'Europe," *La Gazette de Québec,* 29 November 1830; "Extrait d'une lettre de M. O'Connell," *La Gazette de Québec,* 25 October 1832 and *Le Canadien,* 13 February 1833; *The Irish Vindicator,* 7 and 11 January, 27 May, 26 June 1832, 25 January, 5 and 8 February, 27 March and 8 October 1833.

29 The election of 1832 is discussed in Chapter 3.

30 "Irish Vindicator," *The Irish Vindicator,* 10 March, 21 and 24 April 1829; "Ireland," *The Irish Vindicator,* 8 September 1829; André Lacroix to L. Duvernay, 6 September 1833, quoted in Ouellet, *Le Bas-Canada,* 335; O'Callaghan in *The Vindicator* of 24 May 1835, quoted in Finnegan, "Irish-French Relations in Lower Canada," 45; A. Roebuck, July 1835, in *The Canadas,* 7.

31 "Fête de St Patrice," *La Minerve,* 20 March 1834; "Banquet de St Jean-Baptiste," *La Minerve,* 26 June 1834, 29 June 1835, 30 June 1836; "La saint Jean-Baptiste," *La Minerve,* 27 June 1836, 29 June 1837; see also *The Vindicator,* 29 June 1835.

32 "Nous avons par les derniers arrivages," *L'Ami du peuple,* 27 March 1833; "Discours de Sa Majesté," *L'Ami du peuple,* 22 March 1834; "Irlande," *La Gazette de Québec,* 29 March 1834; "Coercion Bill for Canada," *The Vindicator,* 11 April 1837; "Hurrah for Agitation," *The Vindicator,* 21 April 1837; "Le sort du Canada," *Le Populaire,* 12 April 1837; "On lit dans *La Minerve,*" *L'Ami du peuple,* 17 June 1837.

33 "L'Irlande dément," *Le Populaire*, 21 June 1837; "Loyauté des Irlandais," *L'Ami du peuple*, 14 August 1837; "Nos amis irlandais," *L'Ami du peuple*, 21 October 1837; "O'Connell et Papineau," *Le Populaire*, 4 September 1837; "Correspondance. Conversation," *Le Populaire*, 27 October 1837.

34 Quoted in Finnegan, "Irish-French Relations in Lower Canada," 45; Daley, *Edmund Bailey O'Callaghan*, 247; Abbé Thomas Maguire, "Doctrine de l'Église d'Irlande et de celle du Canada sur la révolte," *La Gazette de Québec*, 1 February to 3 March 1838, and published as a pamphlet under the same title.

35 See *La Minerve*, 29 March 1830, 12 and 16 December 1833, 1 May 1834; *Le Canadien*, 24 and 27 August 1831, 14, 17, 20, and 24 December 1832, 18 March 1833, 24 July and 15 December 1835, 16, 19, 21, and 22 December 1836, 31 January 1837; *The Vindicator*, 12 March and 13 December 1833, 12, 16, and 19 December 1834, 11, 17 and 21 March, 15 and 19 September 1837.

36 See *La Minerve*, 10 July 1834; *The Vindicator*, 4 July 1837; exerpts from the history of the American Revolution: *The Vindicator*, 18, 21, and 28 July 1837, 10, 13, 17, 20, 24, and 27 October 1837.

37 "De l'abolition de l'esclavage dans les colonies britanniques," *Le Canadien*, 11 October 1833; "Abolition de l'esclavage," *Le Canadien*, 29 April 1836; "Correspondance. Conversation," *Le Populaire*, 27 October 1837; see also *The Vindicator*, 18 July 1834.

38 "De la démocratie en Amérique," *Le Canadien*, 18 and 30 September, 2, 5, 7, and 16 October 1835, 20 May and 4 July 1836; "Lettres sur l'Amérique," *La Minerve*, 15, 26, and 29 December 1836 and 23 February 1837.

39 "Depuis longtemps," *L'Ami du peuple*, 4 February 1837; "*La Minerve* commence," *L'Ami du peuple*, 19 April 1837; "De la position des agitateurs," *Le Populaire*, 14 June 1837; "De l'espoir d'une coopération," *Le Populaire*, 4 October 1837.

40 "Il y a environ," *Le Spectateur canadien*, 6 July 1822; "Le Général San Martin," *Le Canadien*, 22 August 1818, reprinted from *La Gazette de Québec* of 20 August 1818; "L'histoire de la révolution," *Le Spectateur canadien*, 5 January 1822; "Bolivar," *Le Canadien*, 5 May 1824; "Extraits de la nouvelle Constitution," *La Minerve*, 8 July 1830; "Baltimore, le," *La Gazette de Québec*, 24 October 1816.

41 "Québec, jeudi," *La Gazette de Québec*, 7 December 1815; "Ce qui précède," *Le Canadien*, 9 April 1823; "Ce qui suit," *Le Canadien*, 23 April 1823; exchanges between Parent and "the man of the woods" on the intervention of France in Spain, *Le Canadien*, 17 September to 10 December 1823.

42 "L'Espagne enfin," *Le Spectateur canadien*, 15 May 1819; "Amérique méridionale," *La Gazette de Québec*, 29 April 1819; "Si les dernières nouvelles," *L'Aurore*, 19 May 1817; "Proclamation du Général Mina," *L'Aurore*, 4 August 1817

and *La Gazette de Québec*, 7 August 1817; "Des six numéros," *Le Spectateur canadien*, 16 June 1821.

43 "Le lecteur doit avoir lu," *Le Canadien*, 7 May 1823; "Desseins de la Russie," *L'Aurore*, 15 and 22 November 1817; "La décision du Congrès d'Aix-la-Chapelle," *L'Aurore*, 19 December 1818; "Si l'écrit publié," *Le Spectateur canadien*, 17 March 1821.

44 "Nouvelles étrangères," *Le Spectateur canadien*, 11 December 1819; "Du National," *La Gazette de Québec*, 25 March 1822; "Le message," *Le Spectateur canadien*, 30 March 1822; "La nouvelle," *Le Canadien*, 22 May 1822; "Le Courrier," *Le Spectateur canadien*, 1 June 1822; "Coup d'œil…," *La Gazette de Québec*, 3 February 1823; "Indépendance de l'Amérique Espagnole," *La Gazette de Québec*, 21 February 1825; "Le gouvernement français," *La Minerve*, 28 June 1827.

45 "Québec, jeudi," *La Gazette de Québec*, 29 October 1818; "Extrait d'une lettre," *Le Canadien*, 18 July 1821.

46 "Nos derniers journaux," *Le Spectateur canadien*, 3 February 1821; "Selon les derniers avis du Paraguay," *L'Aurore*, 23 June 1817; "Mexique," *Le Spectateur canadien*, 14 September 1822; "Quoique devienne," *Le Spectateur canadien*, 24 November 1821; "Ce qu'on dit," *Le Spectateur canadien*, 9 March 1822; "Il paraît," *Le Spectateur canadien*, 17 August 1822; "L'Espagne enfin," *Le Spectateur canadien*, 15 May 1819.

47 M. Langlade, Bordeaux, to L. Duvernay, 10 February 1836, Duvernay Papers, *RAPQ* (1926–1927), 173; Resolutions of the assembly of Sainte-Scholastique, in Bernard, *Assemblées publiques*, 47–56; "Adresse des Fils de la Liberté," 4 October 1837, ibid., 214–22; "Adresse de la Confédération des Six comtés," 24 October 1837, ibid., 277–85.

48 É. Parent, "Le mouvement politique," *Le Canadien*, 28 May 1834; the study of the positions of Papineau, Parent, and Garneau was summarized and published in Lamonde, "Papineau, Parent, Garneau," 41–9, from which I have borrowed and developed certain parts here; for a more detailed analysis, see Lamonde, "Conscience coloniale et conscience internationale"; Lamonde, "'L'ombre du passé'"; Parent, *Discours*, Introduction.

49 Garneau, "À Lord Durham," 8 January 1838, in Grisé and Lortie, *Les textes poétiques*, IV:80–3; É. Parent, "Ainsi M. Howe," *Le Canadien*, 8 January 1838.

50 É. Parent, "Le *Vindicator* revient," *Le Canadien*, 7 April 1837; "Il y a quelque temps," *Le Canadien*, 13 September 1837.

51 LJP, Papineau, "Élection du Quartier Ouest," *Le Canadien*, 19 July 1820; É. Parent, "Nous publions," *Le Canadien*, 1 January 1823; LJP to Wilmot, 16 December 1822, *DC* (1819–1828), 144–6; LJP, [Appointment of an agent by resolution], *La Minerve*, 23 November 1835.

52 Garneau, *Voyage*, 123, 191–3; É. Parent, "Nous sommes en possession," *Le Canadien*, 15 May 1837.

53 LJP, "Composition des Conseils," *La Minerve*, 2, 9, 13 February 1832; LJP, "État de la province. 1ère résolution," *La Minerve*, 27 February and 3 March 1834.

54 É. Parent, "Grand doit être l'embarras," *Le Canadien*, 18 September 1835; É. Parent, "La sympathie de nos voisins," *Le Canadien*, 17 July 1837; É. Parent, "La Louisiane et le Bas-Canada," *Le Canadien*, 24 October 1838; LJP, "Discours de l'honorable ... à l'assemblée du comté de Montréal tenue à St Laurent," 15 May 1837, text in LJP, *Un demi-siècle*, 428, 429; É. Parent, "Les écrivains," *Le Canadien*, 20 December 1833; É. Parent, "Si nous avions," *Le Canadien*, 26 December 1836; É. Parent, "Nous sommes en possession," *Le Canadien*, 15 May 1837.

55 É. Parent, "50. Résolu," *Le Canadien*, 26 February 1834; LJP, "Rapport du comité sur les contingents," *La Minerve*, 6 and 10 February 1834; LJP, "État de la province. 1ère résolution," *La Minerve*, 24 February 1834; LJP, "À Messieurs les Électeurs du Quartier Ouest de Montréal," *La Minerve*, 20 and 30 October 1834; LJP, "Discours de l'honorable ... à l'assemblée du comté de Montréal tenue à St Laurent," text in LJP, *Un demi-siècle*, 431.

56 F.-X. Garneau, *Voyage*, 261; É. Parent, "Le *Mercury*," *Le Canadien*, 21 March 1834; É. Parent, "Nous sommes en possession," *Le Canadien*, 15 May 1837; there are very few references to South America in Papineau, other than statements that England had prepared the United States for independence better than Spain and Portugal had their colonies.

57 F.-X. Garneau, *Voyage*, 59; É. Parent, "Qu'allons-nous faire?," *Le Canadien*, 19 April 1837; É. Parent, "La sympathie de nos voisins," *Le Canadien*, 17 July 1837.

58 "De l'Amérique du Sud," *Le Canadien*, 19 September 1818; "Extrait d'une lettre," *L'Aurore*, 24 July 1819; "Pérou," *La Gazette de Québec*, 2 December 1824; "Amérique du Sud," *Le Spectateur canadien*, 17 November 1821; "Pensées sur l'État social," *Le Spectateur canadien*, 29 January and 2 February 1816; "L'idée d'un patriote," *L'Ami du peuple*, 8 August 1832.

59 Weill, *L'éveil des nationalités*, 5; "De la manière dont se forment," *La Minerve*, 8, 11, 13, 18 September 1834.

60 Papineau: "À nos constituans," *La Minerve*, 26 March 1827; "Discours prononcé," *La Minerve*, 1 October 1827; "État de la province. 1ère résolution," *La Minerve*, 27 February and 3 March 1834; LJP, *Address of the Hon. L.J. Papineau to the Electors of the West Ward of Montreal*," 3 December 1834; French version, *La Minerve*, 4 and 8 December 1834; "Bill des subsides et liste civile," *Le Canadien*, 8 April 1833; "Continuation des débats," *Le Canadien*, 16 March 1836.

61 Papineau on national distinctions: "Finances," *La Minerve*, 18 March 1830; "Réélection des employés," *La Minerve*, 14 February 1831; "Nomination d'un agent," *La Minerve*, 14 March 1831; "Discours prononcé," *La Minerve*,

30 October 1834; "Musée Chasseur," *La Gazette de Québec*, 12 March 1836; "Continuation des débats," *Le Canadien*, 16 March 1836; *To the Honorable*, 1 March 1834; "Ouverture de la session parlementaire" *La Minerve*, 11 September 1837, text in LJP, *Un demi-siècle*, 484.

CHAPTER SEVEN

1 *Hansard*, 3rd Series, XXXVI, 6 March 1837: 1287–1306; Leader: 1306, 1308, 1310; Roebuck: 1336; O'Connell: 1324–1327; see also *Hansard*, 3rd Series, XXXVII, 14 April 1837: 1209–93.
2 McInnis, "A Letter from Alexis de Tocqueville on the Rebellion of 1837."
3 Allan Greer and Léon Robichaud note that the petitions to the House of Assembly for help in the famine of 1831 to 1836 came from districts other than Montreal, "La rébellion de 1837–1838 au Bas-Canada," 366.
4 Ouellet, *Lower Canada*, 117–26, 136–57, 158–65, 177–82.
5 Muzzo, *Les mouvements réformistes et constitutionnels à Montréal*, 30–4, 40–53, 72–6; the idea of the committees of correspondence is found in Resolutions 89 and 91 of the 92 Resolutions.
6 Ibid., 95–106; Bernard, *Les rébellions*, 25–6.
7 Maps of the geographic distribution of the assemblies may be found in Bernard, *Assemblées publiques*, 21, and Greer and Robichaud, "La rébellion," 349; Gosford's proclamation against public assemblies, RAPQ (1923), 305–6.
8 Bernard, *Assemblées*, 23, 25, 48; see also 69, 101–2, 113, 138, 144.
9 Ibid., 97, 108, 176; see also 50, 52, 117–18.
10 Ibid., 31–2, 39, 118; see also 50, 60.
11 Ibid., 49, 52, 68, 79, 87, 138, 165, 183, 228.
12 Ibid., 40, 52–3; see also 58.
13 Greer, *The Patriots*, 183.
14 Bernard, *Assemblées*, 187; see also 201; speech by Mgr Lartigue reported in *L'Ami du peuple* of 26 July 1837 and *Le Canadien* of 28 July 1837; see also the circular letter requesting a "Te Deum" for Queen Victoria's coronation, MEM, I:13–14.
15 "Mardi dernier," *La Minerve*, 27 July 1837; *Le Libéral*, July 1837, quoted in Ouellet, *Lower Canada*, 298–9; "Nous avons exprimé," *La Minerve*, 7 August 1837; on the position of the Montreal permanent central committee, Muzzo, *Les mouvements*, 137.
16 Greer, *The Patriots*, 277–81; Gendron, *Tenure seigneuriale et mouvement patriote*.
17 Bernard, *Assemblées*, 81, 141, 180–2, 186, 197–8; on the circumstances of the assembly in Saint-François-du-Lac, Greer, *The Patriots*, 285.
18 Greer, *The Patriots*, 287.

19 LJP, *Procédés de l'assemblée des Électeurs du Comté de Montréal, tenue à Saint-Laurent*, 15 May, *La Minerve*, 25 and 29 May 1837, text in LJP, *Un demi-siècle*, 418; [Assemblée de Sainte-Scholastique, Comté des Deux-Montagnes], 1 June 1837, *La Minerve*, 12 June 1837, text in LJP, *Un demi-siècle*, 452; Lamonde, "Conscience coloniale," passim.

20 LJP, *Procédés de l'assemblée des Électeurs du Comté de Montréal, tenue à Saint-Laurent*, 15 May, *La Minerve*, 25 and 29 May 1837, text in LJP, *Un demi-siècle*, 430; [Assemblée de Sainte-Scholastique], ibid., 4505; "La voix du Peuple [Assemblée de Berthier]," 18 June 1837, *La Minerve*, 22 June 1837.

21 Étienne Parent, "Le *Vindicator* revient," *Le Canadien*, 7 April 1837; "Nous étions tellement engagés," *Le Canadien*, 17 April 1837; "Qu'allons-nous faire?," *Le Canadien*, 19 April 1837; Parent, *Discours*.

22 É. Parent, "Nous sommes en possession," *Le Canadien*, 15 May 1837; "Nous publions," *Le Canadien*, 22 May 1837; "La sympathie de nos voisins," *Le Canadien*, 17 July 1837; "Santés," *Le Canadien*, 3 July 1837.

23 É. Parent, "La presse accueille," *Le Canadien*, 16 June 1837; "Les brouillons," *Le Canadien*, 26 June 1837.

24 É. Parent, "Nous n'aimons," *Le Canadien*, 19 June 1837; "Nous publions," *Le Canadien*, 22 May 1837; "Clôture de l'élection," *Le Canadien*, 7 July 1837; "Convocation de la législature," *Le Canadien*, 10 July 1837; "Le bateau à vapeur," *Le Canadien*, 19 July 1837; "Le clergé et le parti révolutionnaire," *Le Canadien*, 6 October 1837; "Nous reproduisons," *Le Canadien*, 31 July 1837.

25 Gallichan, "La session de 1837"; Papineau: 151, 159–60, 154; Taschereau and opponents: quoted in Gallichan, 181–5, 186, 202.

26 É. Parent, "Nous terminons aujourd'hui," *Le Canadien*, 30 August 1837; "Nos affaires politiques," *Le Canadien*, 1 September 1837.

27 L'Adresse des Fils de la liberté in Bernard, *Assemblées*, 215–21; É. Parent, "Il y a quelque temps," *Le Canadien*, 13 September 1837; [Response of the permanent central committee of the county of Montreal to the Address of the London Workingmen's Association], in French in *La Minerve*, 7 September 1837, reprinted in de Lorimier, *Lettres d'un Patriote*, 30–39.

28 Bernard, *Assemblées*, 259–60, 266, 273, 277, 285.

29 É. Parent, "Nous publions," *Le Canadien*, 13 November 1837, reprinted in Parent, *Discours*, 82, 84–5.

30 Bernard, *Assemblées*, 231–51.

31 MEM, I:14–21; attribution of the *Défense du mandement de Mgr Lartigue* to Mgr Lartigue, Chaussé, *Jean-Jacques Lartigue*, 169, note 13; *Défense du mandement de Mgr Lartigue*.

32 Resolutions in *La Minerve*, 30 October 1837; Abbé Amiot to Mgr Lartigue, 7 November 1837, quoted in Chabot, *Le curé de campagne*, 213–14; Greer,

The Patriots, 235–6; bishop of Quebec diocese to M. Mailloux, 15 November 1837, ACSAP, 100.2, 228–9.

33 Senior, *Redcoats and Patriots*, 43–50; Amédée Papineau, *Journal d'un Fils de la Liberté*, 57–67; Lanthier, "La violence selon la presse patriote et loyale", 85–9, 100–3.

34 Greer, *The Patriots*, 151, and Chap. 8.

35 On the military operations, Senior, *Redcoats and Patriots.*, Chap. 5–7; Bernier, "Étude analytique et critique"; Bernard, *Les rébellions*, 7–14; Greer, *The Patriots*, Chap. 10; proclamation by the governor of Vermont in Christie, *A History of the Late Province of Lower Canada*, V:16–19.

36 Circular letter, 4 December 1837, and pastoral letter, 11 December 1837, *MEQ*, III:369–73; Mgr Lartigue to M. Marcoux, priest at Saint-Barthélémy, 7 December 1837, ACSAP, Painchaud 4, L; "Requête du clergé catholique du diocèse de Montréal à la Reine," 26 December 1837, *MEM*, I:23–4.

37 *Hansard*, 3rd Series, XXXIX, 22 December 1837: 1428–1507; quotations: 1429, 1433, 1444, 1467.

38 Roebuck to Melbourne, 29 December 1837, quoted in Dufour-Charpentier, "La question des agents," 193; Roebuck's suggestion would be transmitted to Lord Durham, who was about to be appointed governor general of Lower Canada.

CHAPTER EIGHT

1 R. Nelson to J.-B. Ryan, 25 February 1838, quoted in Ouellet, *Lower Canada*, 312; on the split with Papineau: various correspondents with Duvernay, also in exile, *RAPQ* (1926–1927), 186, 190, 193–4, 199–203, 210, 214, 216, and articles probably by Dr Côté in the *North American* of Swanton, Vermont, 11 September, 16 October 1839, 25 March 1840, and 31 March 1841, quoted in Kenny, "Strangers' Sojourn," 195; Abbé Étienne Chartier even went to meet Papineau in Paris to tell him of the Patriotes' "discontent" and suggest that he "clear his name" with them, Montarville Boucher de la Bruère, "Louis-Joseph Papineau, de Saint-Denis à Paris," 79–106.

2 Declaration of President Van Buren, 5 January 1838, in Corey, *The Crisis of 1830–1842*, 44–57.

3 "Déclaration d'Indépendance" and "Proclamation" by Robert Nelson on 28 February 1838 in Bernard, *Assemblées*, 301–4; Bernard, *Les rébellions de 1837–1838*, 118–19.

4 "Second mandement à l'occasion des troubles de 1837," *MEM*, I:24–9; see Mgr Lartigue, "Des doctrines du philosophisme moderne sur les gouvernements," [1838], ACAM, 901.037, 838-2, and comments by the Patriote priest Étienne Chartier, who wrote to the bishop from Philadelphia on 21 July 1838, text in Chabot, *Le curé de campagne*, 311–14.

5 Mgr Turgeon to Mgr Bourget, 22 August 1838, quoted in Lemieux, *Histoire du catholicisme*, 391; [Abbé Thomas Maguire], *Doctrine de l'Église d'Irlande et de celle du Canada sur la révolte.*

6 "Circulaire," 7 February 1838, MEQ, III:377–8; Vincent Quiblier to the Sacred Congregation, September 1838, quoted in Lemieux, *Histoire du catholicisme*, 390.

7 Political prisoners to Mgr Lartigue, 6 June 1838, ACAM, 901.106, 838-4; the author of the letter was Jean-Philippe Boucher-Belleville, see his *Journal d'un Patriote (1837–1838)*, 158. Other anticlerical reactions: Abbés Perrault and Amiot to Mgr Lartigue, 7 and 26 September 1838, Archives du diocèse de Saint-Jérôme, 16A/59 and 13A/99.

8 Bernard, "Vermonters and the Lower Canadian Rebellions"; Caron, "Une société secrète dans le Bas-Canada"; Kenny, "The Canadian Rebellions and the Limits of Historical Perspective"; Johnson, "The New York State Press and the Canadian Rebellions."

9 Bernard, *Les rébellions*, 126–30; Greer, *The Patriots*, 345; de Lorimier, *Lettres d'un Patriote condamné à mort*, 63, which also refers to the flag with two stars; Ellice, *The Diary of Jane Ellice*, 128–52, quotations: 133 and 137.

10 Circular letter of 19 November 1838, MEQ, III:392–3.

11 Girod, "Journal tenu par feu Amury Girod," 408–19; Boucher-Belleville, *Journal*, 61, 50; Paquin, *Journal historique des événemens arrivés à Saint-Eustache*, 59; Prieur, *Notes d'un condamné politique de 1838*, 105; Greer, *The Patriots*, 351.

12 Fecteau, "Mesures d'exception et règle de droit," 465–95; Greenwood, "The Chartrand Murder Trial," 129–59, and Greenwood, "The General Court Martial of 1838-1839 in Lower Canada," 249–90; Bernard, *Les rébellions de 1837–1838*, 131–4; Greer, *The Patriots*, 352–3; Senior, *Redcoats*, 200–2; *Report of the State Trials*; [André-Romuald Cherrier], *Procès de Joseph N. Cardinal*; *Procès politique: la reine vs Jalbert*; Laforte on the song "Le Proscrit / Le Canadien errant," written in 1842 by Antoine Gérin-Lajoie, DOLQ, I:714–16, text in Grisé and Lortie, *Les textes poétiques du Canada français (1606–1867)*, IV:504–6.

13 On the *Herald* and the anglophone press, there are many quotations in Lefebvre, *La "Montreal Gazette" et le nationalisme canadien*; on the deportees in Australia, memoirs by Ducharme, Lepailleur, and Prieur; de Lorimier, *Lettres*, 67 and 72.

14 *Hansard*, 3rd Series, XL, 19 January 1838: 263–310; 5 February 1838: 735 and 770.

15 *Hansard*, 3rd Series, XL, 16 and 17 January 1838: 5–95 and 96–162; 25 January 1838: 430 and 470; Mill, "Radical Party and Canada," 406–35; [Chapman], *An Impartial and Authentic Account of the Civil War in the Canadas.*

16 Bernard, *Les rébellions de 1837–1838*, 119–22; Mill, "Lord Durham and his Assailants," August 1838, and Mill, "Lord Durham's Return," December 1838.

17 LJP, Albany, to George Bancroft, 18 December 1837, reproduced in Howell, "The Political Testament of Papineau in Exile," 295–9.

18 White, *Louis-Joseph Papineau et Lamennais,* 17–30.

19 E.N. Duchesnois to L. Duvernay, 9 July 1839, quoted in *RAPQ* (1926–1927): 208–9; C. Drolet to L. Duvernay, 8 November 1839, ibid.: 215–16.

20 Correspondence of M. de Pontois to Count Molé: 9 August, 23 July, 29 September 1837, 13 January and 30 November 1838 in Roquebrune, "M. de Pontois et la rébellion des Canadiens français," *Nova Francia,* III, 4 (1927–1928): 246, 245, 248; 5: 278; IV, 1 (1929): 7; 2: 90.

21 Dr Gauvin, Paris, to L. Duvernay, 27 November 1839, *RAPQ* (1926–1927): 217.

22 On Ellice, Thom, and Sewell in the *DCB,* see in the bibliography Colthart, Bindon, and Greenwood; Buckner, *The Transition to Responsible Government,* 252–3; on plans to subdivide Lower Canada, from Gosford, through Stephen and Charles Grey, to Ellice, according to the "principle of divide and impera," ibid., 208, 211, 218, 219, 253.

23 Lambton, *Lord Durham's Report,* 88–9.

24 From Durham's dispatch to the Colonial Office of 9 August 1838, in which he provided his detailed impressions of Lower Canada.

25 Lambton, *Lord Durham's Report,* 105, 71, 113.

26 Ibid., 67–8, 79.

27 Ibid., 123.

28 Ibid., 123–4.

29 Ibid., 66.

30 Ibid., 115, 279.

31 Ibid., 84–5, 87.

32 Ibid., 81, 175.

33 Ibid., 126–8.

34 Ibid., 127–8, 147.

35 Ibid., 131–2.

36 Ibid., 303–4, 312, 318.

37 Ibid., 315.

38 Ibid., 307.

39 Ibid., 308–9.

40 Ibid., 319, 321, 323.

41 Ibid., 321, 334.

42 Ibid., 336–7.

43 Ibid.

44 Ibid., 124, 128, 281, 298–301.

45 LJP, *Histoire de l'insurrection du Canada en réfutation du rapport de Lord Durham,* 5, 10, 8, 13, 20, 25–8, 34–5; text in LJP, *Un demi-siècle,* 506–27. Papineau would repeat that he had only acted in "constitutional opposition"; see, for

example, his letter to Dr Nancrède of 14 May 1838, quoted in Ouellet, "Papineau dans l'insurrection de 1837–1838," 26.

46 Sabrevois de Bleury, *Réfutation de l'écrit de Louis[-]Joseph Papineau*; en collaboration, "Sabrevois de Bleury, Clément-Charles," DCB.

47 É. Parent, "Nouveaux développements," *Le Canadien*, 15 December 1837; "La *Gazette de Québec* de samedi," *Le Canadien*, 12 February 1838; "Proclamation de Lord Durham," *Le Canadien*, 15 October 1838; see also "*Le Courrier de Montréal*," *Le Canadien*, 7 October 1839.

48 É. Parent, "Puisque La *Gazette de Québec*," *Le Canadien*, 21 February 1838; "Ainsi M. Howe," *Le Canadien*, 8 January 1838; "Nouveaux développements," *Le Canadien*, 15 December 1837.

49 É. Parent, "Les préparatifs de guerre," *Le Canadien*, 14 February 1838; "La Louisiane et le Bas-Canada," *Le Canadien*, 24 October 1838; "La *Gazette de Québec*," *Le Canadien*, 23 February 1838.

50 É. Parent, "La *Gazette de Québec* interprète," *Le Canadien*, 13 May 1839.

51 É. Parent, "Le *Canadian Colonist*," *Le Canadien*, 23 October 1839.

52 É. Parent, "Nos affaires politiques," *Le Canadien*, 1 September 1837; "Le *Canadian Colonist*," *Le Canadien*, 23 October 1839.

53 É. Parent, *Le Canadien*, 15 August 1832, quoted in Gosselin, *Étienne Parent*, 25–6; *Le Canadien*, 7 November 1832, ibid., 30–1; "Remarques," *Le Canadien*, 8 October 1831; "Nous publions l'extrait," *Le Canadien*, 25 April 1834; quotation from "Dans la dernière partie," *Le Canadien*, 19 June 1833, reproduced in Parent, *Étienne Parent*, 75–9; see also "Il est dans notre histoire," *Le Canadien*, 23 November 1834.

54 É. Parent, "La malle d'hier," *Le Canadien*, 19 June 1835; "Nous publions en détail," *Le Canadien*, 29 July 1835; "Nous revenons," *Le Canadien*, 11 September 1835. In Upper Canada, the most explicit demand for responsible government by Robert Baldwin was in his letter to the Secretary of State for the Colonies Baron Glenelg on 13 July 1836; document in Kennedy, ed., *Statutes, Treatises and Documents of the Canadian Constitution (1713–1929)*, 335–42.

55 É. Parent, "Puisque La *Gazette de Québec*," *Le Canadien*, 21 February 1838; "Proclamation de Lord Durham," *Le Canadien*, 15 October 1838; "Les préparatifs de guerre," *Le Canadien*, 14 February 1838.

56 LJP, "PPBC: Sur les diverses références relatives à la composition du Conseil législatif," 10 January 1833, *Le Canadien*, 16, 18, 23 January 1833 ; LJP to A. Roebuck, 16 January 1835, LAC, MG24, A19, I-5, 12; *Address to the Nonorable*, 1 March 1834; Greenwood, "Les Patriotes et le gouvernement responsable."

57 LJP, *Address of the Hon. L.J. Papineau to the Electors of the West Ward of Montreal*, 3 December 1834; French version, *La Minerve*, 4 and 8 December 1834 and LJP, *Un demi-siècle*, 333 and 349; LJP, "Constitution du Conseil législatif," 10 January 1833, text in LJP, *Un demi-siècle*, 211–38.

58 LJP, [Assembly of Sainte-Scholastique], 1 June 1837, ibid., 450–5; "PPBC: État de la province," 19 August 1837, ibid., 456–70; "Adresse de la Confédération des Six Comtés," 23–24 October 1837, ibid., 497.

59 LJP, "PPBC: Composition des Conseils," 16 January 1832, ibid., 199–210; "PPBC: Lieutenant colonel Eden," 28 February 1833, ibid., 239–47.

60 Buckner, *The Transition*, 235, 357.

61 Dumont, *Genèse de la société québécoise*, 145–8.

62 Greer and Robichaud, "La rébellion de 1837–1838 au Bas-Canada," 356–7; Blanchette-Lessard and Daigneault-Saint-Denis, "La participation des groupes sociaux aux rébellions dans les comtés de Laprairie et de Deux-Montagnes," in Bernard, *Les Rébellions de 1837–1838*, 320–5. The participation rate was calculated on a list of 2,083 Patriotes, for 1,812 of whom the place of residence is mentioned.

63 Ouellet, "Les insurrections de 1837–38."

64 Greer, *The Patriots*, 170, 154, 150, 241–2, 230–3, 243ff.; Hardy, "Le charivari," 47–69.

65 Ouellet, "Papineau et la rivalité Québec Montréal."

66 Boucher-Belleville, *Journal*, 41–2, 48–9, 54–5, 57; Nelson, *Écrits d'un Patriote*, 66, 78, 81–2.

67 Boucher de la Bruère, "Louis-Joseph Papineau."

68 Grisé and Lortie, *Les textes poétiques*, IV:3–5, 66, 50–1, 103–5, 109–10, 136–7, 22, 57; Carrier and Vachon, "De 'C'est la faute à Papineau' aux Quatre-vingt-douze Résolutions."

CHAPTER NINE

1 Union Act, Statutes of Lower Canada, *Provincial Statutes of Canada, 1840–1841*, reprinted in Kennedy, *Documents of the Canadian Constitution, 1759–1915*, 536–50; O'Connell quoted in Chapais, IV:301–2; *Hansard* [British Parliamentary Debates] 3rd Series, 55, 23 March 1840: 246–7 and Garneau, "Une conclusion d'histoire," 422–4; Chauveau, "L'Union des Canadas," 5 April 1841, in Lortie and Grisé, *Textes poétiques du Canada français*, IV:373–8; Bernard, in Gougeon, *Histoire du nationalisme québécois*, 42–3.

2 É. Parent, "Procédés contre l'Union," *Le Canadien*, 27 January 1840; "Il faut que le *Herald*," *Le Canadien*, 3 February 1840; "Indemnités," *Le Canadien*, 31 August 1840; "Nous sommes donc maintenant," *Le Canadien*, 22 March 1841.

3 Mgr Lartigue to Mgr Griffiths, apostolic vicar of London, 17 June 1839, quoted in Pouliot, "Les évêques du Bas-Canada," 162, 169; Abbé Jean Raimbault to the bishop of Quebec diocese, 11 May 1840, AAQ, SN, a-107; E.-L. Pacaud to L. Duvernay, 11 February 1840, quoted in *RAPQ* (1926–1927): 223–4.

4 *Les Mélanges religieux,* 26 November 1842; ibid., 1843, quoted in Dumont, *Genèse de la société québécoise,* 227.

5 Quioted in Monet, "La Fontaine, Louis-Hippolyte," *DCB*; "Adresse aux Électeurs de Terrebonne," 25 August 1840, *L'Aurore des Canadas* or *Le Canadien,* 31 August 1840; English translation, "The Terrebonne Manifesto: the Collaborator," in Elizabeth Nish, ed., *Racism or Responsible Government,* 35–7.

6 "Lettre des électeurs de Québec," *La Gazette de Québec* and *The Quebec Gazette,* 23 December 1840; the anti-union newspapers of Lower Canada (*Le Canadien, The Canadian Colonist, L'Aurore des Canadas, The Times and Commercial Messenger, The Sherbrooke Gazette*) and those of Upper Canada in Toronto, Brockville, Bytown, St Catharines, London, and Kingston published the letter in French or English; Bolduc, "Les élections générales de 1834," 50–5, 109.

7 *Grand Séminaire de Montréal. Album du centenaire;* Rousseau and Feuvrier, "Morphologie des carrières pastorales," 195–6; Rousseau, "Les rapports entre le 'réveil' et la réorganisation ecclésiale."

8 Lajeunesse, *Les Sulpiciens et la vie culturelle à Montréal,* 19–55, quotation from 35.

9 Sylvain, "Forbin-Janson, Charles-Auguste-Marie-Joseph de," *DCB*; Galarneau, "Mgr de Forbin-Janson au Québec"; L. Perrault to L. Duvernay, 4 February 1842, quoted in *RAPQ* (1926–1927): 247; Rousseau, "Boire ou ne pas boire."

10 Nun at the Hôpital général de Québec to a nun in France, 1842, quoted in Hardy, "L'activité sociale du curé de Notre-Dame de Québec," 6; Rousseau, "La conduite pascale dans la région montréalaise"; Hardy, "À propos du réveil religieux dans le Québec du xixe siècle"; Rousseau, "À propos du 'réveil religieux' dans le Québec du xixe siècle."

11 Saint-Martin, "L'Histoire du Canada de F.-X. Garneau"; Abbé Jean-Baptiste Pelletier, Sainte-Anne-de-la-Pocatière, to Abbé Désaulniers, Nicolet, 1 December 1845, ASN, Séminaire 5, no. 5.

12 Audet, *Histoire de l'enseignement,* II:30–66; Heap, "Les relations Église-État dans le domaine de l'enseignement primaire public"; Carignan, "La place faite à la religion dans les écoles publiques."

13 Parent, *Discours,* Introduction.

14 Lamonde, *Les bibliothèques de collectivités à Montréal,* 53–4; Lamonde, *Gens de parole,* 17–24; "Les principes de L'Avenir," *Les Mélanges religieux,* 27 March 1849; *L'Avenir,* 9 August 1850.

15 White, *Louis-Joseph Papineau et Lamennais,* passim; Lamonde, *Louis-Antoine Dessaulles,* 36–8; Dessaulles, *Écrits,* 67–77; *L'Aurore des Canadas,* 18 and 25 January, 1 and 8 February 1842; *Les Mélanges religieux,* January and February 1842, quotation from January 1842, 43; Ouellet, "Le mandement de Mgr Lartigue de 1837," 101–3.

16 "Mr. de Lamennais," *Les Mélanges religieux,* 12 February 1841, 46–9; Abbé B., "Biographie. Abbé Lacordaire," ibid., (6 September 1842), 315–20; "Bibliographie," ibid. (4 June 1841), 330.

17 Abbé Raymond to Count de Montalembert, 16 July 1839, CHSTH, fonds
    Raymond, CH004/S3/SS2, folder 187 (copy); Montalembert to Raymond,
    17 June 1841, ibid.; Raymond, correspondence while travelling in Europe,
    1842–1843, ibid., box 35 bis, 21 or folder 190; Raymond to Montalembert,
    [1844], ibid. (copy); Raymond to Montalembert, 29 May 1844, reproduced
    in Sylvain, "Le premier disciple canadien de Montalembert"; Abbé Pierre
    Bouchy to Abbé de la Treiche, 30 October 1843 and 12 October 1844,
    ACSAP, Collège 51, LXIII and LXIV. On Louis Veuillot, see Sylvain,
    "Quelques aspects de l'antagonisme libéral-ultramontain," 130; Sylvain,
    "Libéralisme et ultramontanisme au Canada français," 113, 123, 133–4;
    Sylvain,, "Lamartine et les catholiques de France et du Canada," 387.
18 Filteau, Les Patriotes, 475–6; LJP, "Discours parlementaire" [c. 16 March
    1848], L'Avenir, 24 March 1848; [Compensation for losses during the rebel-
    lions], 19 February 1849, L'Avenir, 28 February, 3 and 10 March 1849; see
    also "Débats sur les documents de 1837 et 38," 28 February 1849, L'Avenir,
    17 March 1849; on the bands of Loyalists feared by Papineau's wife, Julie
    Papineau, Une femme patriote, 101, 107–12, 120–1.
19 LJP, [Extracts from the manifesto to the electors of Huntingdon and Saint-
    Maurice counties], 24 December 1847, L'Avenir, 22 January 1848 or CIHM,
    no. 62928; "Rien ne serait plus compromettant," 15 May 1848, L'Avenir,
    18 May 1849 or CIHM, no. 59475.
20 LJP, "Discours parlementaire" [c. 16 March 1848]; "Correspondances. Le
    docteur Wolfred Nelson," 31 May 1848, L'Avenir, 3 June 1848; "Assemblée
    d'Yamachiche," 6 June 1848, L'Avenir, 14, 17, 21, 28 June 1848, reprinted
    in LJP, Un demi-siècle, 530, 532, 555.
21 LJP, [Extracts from the manifesto to the electors of Huntingdon and Saint-
    Maurice counties], 24 December 1847, 22 January 1848 or CIHM,
    no 62928; "Assemblée d'Yamachiche," 6 June 1848, L'Avenir, 14, 17, 21,
    28 June 1848, reprinted in LJP, Un demi-siècle, 528–62; "Discours parlemen-
    taire," [c. 16 March 1848]; [Compensation for losses during the rebel-
    lions], 19 February 1849.
22 LJP, [Extracts from the manifesto to the electors of Huntingdon and Saint-
    Maurice counties], 24 December 1847, 22 January 1848 or CIHM, no 62928;
    "Correspondances. Je ne vois qu'aujourd'hui," 19 May 1848, L'Avenir,
    24 May 1848; "Assemblée d'Yamachiche," 6 June 1848, L'Avenir, 14, 17, 21,
    28 June 1848, reprinted in LJP, Un demi-siècle, 528–62.
23 LJP, [Extracts from the manifesto to the electors of Huntingdon and Saint-
    Maurice counties], 24 December 1847, L'Avenir, 22 January 1848 or CIHM,
    no. 62928; "Rien ne serait plus compromettant," 15 May 1848, L'Avenir,
    18 May 1849 or CIHM, no. 59475; "Assemblée d'Yamachiche," 6 June 1848,
    L'Avenir, 14, 17, 21, 28 June 1848, reprinted in LJP, Un demi-siècle, 528–62.

24 Anti-Union [Louis-Antoine Dessaulles], "M. le Directeur," *L'Avenir*, 31 December 1847; "L'Union," *L'Avenir*, 5 February 1848; texts reproduced in *L.-A. Dessaulles, Écrits*, 82–7, 88–94.

25 The letter was also reproduced in *Le Canadien*, 8 May 1848; on *L'Avenir*'s response to 1848, see, for example, the 24 April, 4 and 22 November 1848 issues; see also Samuel, "L'image de la révolution française de 1848."

26 LJP, "Assemblée du Marché Bonsecours," [c. 14 April], *L'Avenir*, 15 and 19 April 1848; "Correspondances. Je ne vois qu'aujourd'hui," 19 May 1848, *L'Avenir*, 24 May 1848; "Assemblée d'Yamachiche," 6 June 1848, *L'Avenir*, 14, 17, 21, 28 June 1848, reprinted in LJP, *Un demi-siècle*, 528–62.

27 Monet, *The Last Cannon Shot*, 316.

28 Text reproduced in Dessaulles, *Écrits*, 63–4.

29 Speeches by Papineau and La Fontaine in Chapais, *Cours*, VI:248–86, 286–307; quotations, 254, 283, 303, 307, 294. Arthur G. Doughty. ed., *The Elgin-Grey Papers, 1846–1852*, 1:152–5 for Papineau's speech and 155–60 for that of La Fontaine.

30 Sylvain, "Libéralisme et ultramontanisme," 111–22; Eid, "*Les Mélanges religieux* et la révolution romaine de 1848"; Brunn, "Les Canadiens français et les nouvelles de l'Europe," 469–80, 515–34, 590–612; Abbé André Pelletier, Paris, to Abbé Henri Dionne, 10 May 1858, ACSAP, Pelletier, 57, 1; see Savard, "L'Italie dans la culture canadienne-française"; Savard, "La Rome de Pie IX vue par un prêtre québécois," 5–13; MEM, II:20, 31.

31 Text reproduced in Dessaulles, *Écrits*, 94–102.

32 The editors, "Pouvoir temporel du Pape," *Les Mélanges religieux*, 20 and 23 March 1849; "Les principes de *L'Avenir*," ibid., 23 March and 10 April 1849; Adolphe Pinsoneault, "Nouvelles gentillesses de *L'Avenir*," ibid., 9, 19, 23 April 1849, or *La Minerve*, 9, 19, 20 April 1849; Abbé Charles Chiniquy, "M. le Directeur," *L'Avenir*, 18 April 1849, and "Lettre de M. Chiniquy," *Les Mélanges religieux*, 20 April, 18, 28 May and 19 June 1849; Campagnard, "Tribune du peuple," *L'Avenir*, 23 June 1849, reproduced in Dessaulles, *Écrits*, 103–14.

33 Bernard, *Les Rouges*, 61–73, quotation from 61; Monet, *The Last Cannon Shot*, 334–5, 344–53.

34 Bas-Canada, "La nationalité," *L'Avenir*, 24 February 1849; "Les États-Unis," ibid., 28 July 1849; Un Québecquois, "L'annexation," ibid., 4 September 1849; see also *L'Avenir*, 20 May 1848 and 29 February 1849.

35 *Le Moniteur canadien*, 30 October 1849; Ouellet, "Denis-Benjamin Viger et le problème de l'annexation," 195–205.

36 Manifesto in *La Minerve*, 11 and 15 October 1849, and *L'Avenir*, 13 October 1849; the second annexationist manifesto is reproduced in Chapais, *Cours*, VI:307–45; 176 of the 1,016 signatories (17 per cent) had French

surnames; LJP, "À Messieurs les membres du comité annexionniste," 25 October 1849, *L'Avenir*, 3 November 1849, reprinted in LJP, *Un demi-siècle*, 563–8.

37 Dessaulles, *Six lectures sur l'annexion du Canada aux États-Unis*, 85–6, 100, 174–5.

38 Lamonde, *Les bibliothèques de collectivités*, 53–4; *L'Avenir*, 6 November 1847, 4 March and 24 May 1848; Lafontaine, ed., *L'Institut canadien en 1855*; Dorion, *L'Institut canadien en 1852*; Bernard, *Les Rouges*, 60.

39 On the tithe, Bernard, *Les Rouges*, 77–84; Dumesnil, *De l'abolition des droits féodaux au Canada*; on Papineau and seigneurial tenure, "Assemblée législative du Canada-Uni: Tenure seigneuriale [14 June 1850]," *L'Avenir*, 28 June 1859, text in LJP, *Un demi-siècle*, 569–73; Campagnard [L.-A. Dessaulles], "Tribune du people," *L'Avenir*, 13, 20, 27 April 1850, and Lamonde, *Louis-Antoine Dessaulles*, 90–3; on the difference of opinion between Joseph Doutre and Pierre Blanchet, *L'Avenir*, 4 May 1850, and on disagreement at the newspaper itself, *L'Avenir*, 27 and 29 October and 22 November 1849; on the anti-seigneurial convention, *L'Avenir*, 11 and 25 October, 12 and 22 November 1849.

40 *MEM*, "Circulaire au clergé" and "Lettre pastorale," 18 January 1849, II: 20–31; Mgr Bourget to Abbé L.-A. Maréchal, curate at Saint-Jacques-de-l'Achigan, 2 October 1849, ACAM, RLB, V: 306–8; Mgr Bourget to Abbé J. Marcoux, missionnary in Sault Saint-Louis, 18 November 1850, ACAM, RLB, VI:226–7.

41 *Manifeste du Club national démocratique*, XXX, "Démocratie et socialisme," *L'Ami de la Religion et de la Patrie*, 11 April 1849; "Le socialisme" and "Le communisme," *Les Mélanges religieux*, 3 and 8 August 1849; [Abbé François Pilote], "Socialisme en Canada," [after 1849], ACSAP, Pilote 14, XCII; [Louis Proulx], *Défense de la Religion et du Sacerdoce*; identification of Proulx, Lebon, *Histoire du Collège de Sainte-Anne-de-La Pocatière* I: 431–4; Mgr Bourget to Mgr Turgeon, 9 April 1850, ACAM, RLB, VI:51–2; "Le socialisme devant le bon sens populaire," *Les Mélanges religieux*, 13 April 1852; Le villageois du comté de D., "Le libéralisme et *L'Avenir*," *L'Ordre social*, 13 April 1850.

42 Bernard, *Les Rouges*, 59–60.

43 Program of J.-B.-E. Dorion in Bernard, *Les Rouges*, 341–74; election results, ibid., 97–9; Abbé C.-J. Cazeau to Abbé Bégin, 2 February 1851, ACSAP, Gauvreau 10, LIX; on liberalism in Kamouraska, see the Gauvreau collection, 10, LXXII, LXXVII, LXXIX, LXXXIV-LXXXIX.

CHAPTER TEN

1 Julie Papineau, *Une femme patriote*, 426, 432, on Papineau's attachment to Montebello; Bernard, *Les Rouges*, 114–20, 150.

2 Prospectus of *Le Pays* reproduced in Dessaulles, *Écrits*, 128–33; Dessaulles, "Galilée, ses travaux scientifiques et sa condamnation," public lecture at the Institut canadien de Montréal on 11 March 1856, ibid., 134–84; Lamonde, *Gens de parole*, passim, and *Les bibliothèques de collectivités*, passim.

3 *MEM*, June 1854, II:466.

4 *Le Pays*, 27 February, 6, 20, 24 March and 10 April 1855; the minutes (PV) of the Institut canadien de Montréal from 1855 on are at the BANQ, Montreal centre.

5 Alfred Rambaud in *La Patrie*, 10 July 1855, quoted in Sylvain, "Libéralisme et ultramontanisme au Canada français," 131.

6 *L'Avenir*, 22 December 1857, quoted in Bernard, *Les Rouges*, 144–5.

7 Letters of Mgr Bourget: 10 March 1858, *MEM*, III:367–71; 30 April: *MEM*, VI:24–38; 31 May, *MEM*, III:380–411; resignations from the Institut canadien, Minutes of the Institut canadien de Montréal, II, 25 March, 12 and 22 April 1858, BANQ or *Le Pays*, 22 April 1858; Mgr Bourget, "Lettre pastorale ... contre les erreurs du temps," *MEM*, III:356–76; Simard and Vaugeois, "Fabre, Hector," *DCB*.

8 [Speech of the Sulpician Lenoir], *Le Pays*, 25 June 1857; see also 9 July for the beginning of a debate that continued until August; C. Boucher, "De la démocratie," *Courrier du Canada*, 4, 7, 9, 11 September 1857 and "Où allons-nous?" *Courrier du Canada*, 6 16 August 1858; see also on democracy, *Le Courrier de Saint-Hyacinthe*, October 1857 and *La Minerve*, 18 January 1858; E. de Bellefeuille, "Essai sur le rougisme," *L'Ordre*, 13–27 May 1859.

9 Guay, "La fête de la Saint-Jean-Baptiste à Montréal"; *La Minerve*, 23 June 1858; *Le Pays*, 24 June 1857; *La Minerve*, 27 June 1857; see also Achille Belle, "La nationalité canadienne-française," *Écho du cabinet de lecture paroissial*, 3 August 1861: 243–5.

10 "Lettre pastorale ... sur l'inviolabilité du pouvoir temporel du St Siège," *MEM*, IV:24–42; "Instructions pastorales de Mgr l'Évêque de Montréal sur l'indépendance et l'inviolabilité des États Pontificaux," 31 May 1860: ibid., 42–152; "Premier supplément au mandement du 31 May 1860," [n.d.], ibid., VIII:208–14; between 1860 and 1870, the bishops of Quebec and Montreal published forty documents on the Roman question alone.

11 Dessaulles, "La France, Rome et l'Italie," *Le Pays*, 16 and 21 March 1861; "Encore les marchands de religion," *Le Pays*, 12 November 1861; "De l'administration des états romains," *Le Pays*, 14 November 1861; "Un nouveau libelle," *Le Pays*, 16 November 1861; "De l'administration des états romains. Justice et tribunaux," *Le Pays*, 19 November 1861; "Nos adversaires sur la question du pouvoir temporel," *Le Pays*, 26 November, 3, 7, 10, 14 December 1861; the editors, "*Le Pays* nous accuse," *La Minerve*, 14 November 1861; see also Dessaulles's debate with Maximilien Bibaud: "M. Bibaud et le droit romain," *Le Pays*, 23 November 1861; "Le bataillon

sacré," *Le Pays*, 5 December 1861; "Une séance à l'école de droit du Professeur Bibaud" and "M. Bibaud," *Le Pays*, 17 December 1861; Bibaud, *L'Honorable L.A. Dessaulles*; Dessaulles, "M. Bibaud," *Le Pays*, 8 February 1862.

12 *Le Pays*, 14 September 1861; Sylvain, "La visite du prince Napoléon au Canada (1861)."

13 Dessaulles, "*L'Ordre*," *Le Pays*, 18 and 25 January 1862; "L'Institut-Canadien," *Le Pays*, 28 January 1862; "Une dernière croisade," *Le Pays*, 6 February 1862; "Plus sensible pour lui-même que pour autrui," *Le Pays*, 8 February 1862; A friend of *Le Pays*, "L'Institut-Canadien. Les détracteurs," *Le Pays*, 15 February 1861; H. Fabre, "Institut-Canadien," *Le Pays*, 20 February 1862; Dessaulles, "Un mot à certains calomniateurs," *Le Pays*, 1 March 1862; the editors, "Lettre de Montalembert," *L'Ordre*, 7 and 15 January 1862; the editors, "Nous répondrons," *L'Ordre*, 20 January 1862; see also *L'Ordre*, 22 and 24 January 1862.

14 Lamonde and Nolin, "Des documents cruciaux du débat libéral-ultramontain."

15 Text of the 18 January 1863 announcement by Mgr Bourget in Dessaulles, "L'Index," 55; Dessaulles, *Discours sur l'Institut-Canadien*, reproduced in Dessaulles, *Écrits*, 218.

16 [Louis-Herménégilde Huot], *Le Rougisme en Canada*.

17 Dessaulles, *Écrits*, 145–52.

18 Dessaulles, "Un dernier mot," *Le Pays*, 28 November 1863; the editors, "Dans son article de samedi," *L'Ordre*, 30 November 1863; Dessaulles, "Nos articles n'ont-ils aucune actualité?" *Le Pays*, 1 December 1863, reproduced in Dessaulles, *Écrits*, 236–42.

19 Dessaulles, "Encore une croisade," *Le Pays*, 21 November 1863; "Une dernière croisade," *Le Pays*, 24 November 1863; "L'Institut-Canadien-français et les mauvaises tendances du siècle," *Le Pays*, 26 November 1863; "Encore une croisade," *Le Pays*, 28 November 1863; see the letter from Dessaulles to Mgr Bourget, 16 November 1864, which made the break between them definitive, in Dessaulles, *Écrits*, 251–63.

20 Petition to Pius IX, 16 October 1865, Bibliothèque de la Ville de Montréal (now at BANQ), Institut canadien de Montréal Collection, document no. 1; brief from Dessaulles to Cardinal Barnabo, ibid., no. 2, and reproduced in Pouliot, *Mgr Bourget et son temps*, IV:116–39; Dessaulles to Cardinal Barnabo, 30 October 1865, Institut canadien collection, unnumbered document, 96–116, and no. 24; LAD, *Dernière correspondance entre S.E. le Cardinal Barnabo et l'Hon. M. Dessaulles*, 7–8; brief by Mgr Bourget on the Institut canadien, 21 September 1866, ACAM, RLB, 16:39–54.

21 Laurent-Olivier David, in *La Minerve*, quoted in Bernard, *Les Rouges*, 241–2; Mgr Larocque to L.-A. Dessaulles, 28 December 1863, ACAM, 901.135, 863-4; [L.-H. Huot], *Le Rougisme en Canada*, 32.

22 Charland, "Un gaumiste canadien: l'abbé Alexis Pelletier": 195–236, 463–8;
    Voisine, "Pelletier, Alexis," *DCB*; Lamonde, " Chandonnet, Thomas-Aimé," *DCB*.

23 Lamonde, *La philosophie et son enseignement*, 130–5, 157–75, quotations, 158
    and 163; on the encyclical *Quanta cura* and the *Syllabus* and Mgr Bourget's
    pastoral letter of 1 January 1865 introducing the papal publications, *MEM*,
    V:42–77; Catholic newspapers of the time reproduced the papal encyclicals.

24 Taché, *Des provinces de l'Amérique du nord et d'une union fédérale*, 73–5.

25 On the report on this convention, *Le Pays*, 29 October 1859; *Le Pays*,
    6 October 1860; Bernard, *Les Rouges*, 165–85.

26 Bernard, *Les Rouges*, 188–91.

27 A.-A. Dorion's manifesto, published in *Le Pays* and *L'Ordre*, is reproduced in
    Chapais, *Cours*, 8: 224–36, and in Bonenfant, *La naissance de la
    Confédération*, 82–90.

28 G. Doutre, "Le principe des nationalités," *Le Pays*, 15, 17, 20 December
    1864, reprinted as a pamphlet, quotations, 60, 51–2, 45, 62–3, 50, 57, 73;
    Doutre, "Le Rationalisme et la Confédération," *Le Pays*, 17 December 1864;
    Lamonde, *Gens de parole*, 59–66; Rioux, "Doutre, Gonzalve," *DCB*; Buies,
    "L'avenir de la race française en Canada," *Le Pays*, 27, 29, 31 January 1863.

29 *Parliamentary Debates on the Subject of the Confederation of the British North
    American Provinces*: Cartier: 53–62, quotation from 59; A.-A. Dorion: 248–
    78; Laframboise: 843–58, quotation from 854; J.-B.-E. Dorion: 858–73, quo-
    tations 864, 870; *In memoriam. Sir A.A. Dorion*. On Cartier's monarchism,
    Bonenfant, "Les idées politiques de George-Étienne Cartier." Other plans
    for federation had already been formulated: from 7 July to 23 October
    1857, Joseph-Charles Taché published thirty-three articles in Le *Courrier du
    Canada*, which were reprinted as a pamphlet, *Des provinces de l'Amérique du
    Nord et d'une union fédérale*; in 1858, Joseph Cauchon published *Étude sur
    l'union projetée des provinces britanniques de l'Amérique du Nord;* he took the op-
    posite position in 1865 in *L'union des provinces de l'Amérique britannique du
    Nord*, which was first published in *Le Journal de Québec* from 30 January 1865
    on, and then reprinted as a pamphlet.

30 Bernard, *Les Rouges*, 265.

31 Audet, *Histoire de l'enseignement*, II:69–80, 81–98; Carignan, "La raison d'être
    de l'article 93 de la loi constitutionnelle de 1867"; Carignan, "L'incubation
    de la crise politique soulevée en août 1866: I: Les remous au Bas-Canada."

32 *MEM*, 5 May 1867, V:212–14; *Mandements des évêques de Trois-Rivières*, 8 June
    1867, or *La Minerve*, 12 June 1867; *MEQ*, 12 June 1867, IV:579–82;
    Mandements des évêques de Rimouski, 13 June 1867, 137–41, or *Le Courrier du
    Canada*, 26 June 1867; *Mandements des évêques de Saint-Hyacinthe*, 18 June
    1867, II:421–437. On 29 July 1867, Mgr Bourget published a pastoral letter
    contradicting the Liberals, who had pointed out divisions among the bishops:
    MEM, V:236–44. The bishops' letters and pastoral letters are reproduced in

Nouvelle Constitution du Canada; Bellavance, *Le Québec et la Confédération: Un choix libre?*, 72–5.

33 Bélanger, *Wilfrid Laurier. Quand la politique devient passion*, 43–65; BANQ, Montreal's Centre, PV, Institut canadien de Montréal, II:331.

34 [A. Lusignan], *La Confédération, couronnement de dix années de mauvaise administration*; [Joseph-Alfred Mousseau], *Contre-poison. La Confédération c'est le salut du Bas-Canada*; see also: [Boucher de la Bruère], *Réponses aux censeurs de la Confédération*, and Berenard, "Boucher de la Bruère, Pierre," DCB.

35 Bernard, *Les Rouges*, 298–310, 324; on Kamouraska, Rumilly, *Histoire de la province de Québec*, II:105–10, and ACSAP, Gauvreau collection; on L'Avenir, archives of the diocese of Nicolet, parish of Saint-Pierre de Durham; de L'Isle, "Arthabaska et son élite"; Verrette, "Le libéralisme en région."

36 On the Dessaulles-Raymond polemic and the post-election inquiry, Lamonde, *Louis-Antoine Dessaulles, un seigneur libéral et anticlérical*, 182–90 and 191–4; Bellavance, *Le Québec et la Confédération*, 89–90, 123, 127, 129–32; Louis-Edmond Hamelin and Colette Hamelin, "Évolution numérique séculaire du clergé catholique dans le Québec," 189–241; LJP, *Un demi-siècle*, 603–6; "Discours de M. Étienne Parent," *La Voix du golfe*, 14 July 1868, in Étienne Parent, *Discours*.

CHAPTER ELEVEN

1 Dessaulles, [On tolerance], *Annuaire de l'Institut-Canadien pour 1868*, 4, 5, 12, 18; Lamonde, *Louis-Antoine Dessaulles*, 201; Raymond, *Discours sur la tolérance*, 3–4, 6, 17, 23; Abbé Raymond's lecture was based on one given by the Sulpician Antoine Giband at the Cabinet de lecture paroissial on 18 March 1858, "Essai sur la tolérance."

2 Brief by Mgr Bourget on the Institut canadien, 27 April 1869, ACAM, 901.135, 869-4; MEM, VI:46–7, 38–45, 46–9.

3 BANQ, Montreal's Centre, Institut canadien de Montréal Collection, Minutes, September and October 1869; Dessaulles-Truteau correspondance, September 1869, ACAM, 901.135, 869-9, 869-11, 869-12, 869-13 and RLB, 19:349; the editors, "C'est ce soir," *Le Nouveau Monde*, 9 September 1869; the editors, "Bulletin du jour," *Le Nouveau Monde*, 10 September 1869; the editors, "Nous recevons de l'hon. M. Dessaulles," *Le Nouveau Monde*, 14 September 1869; the editors, "La séance que va tenir," *Le Nouveau Monde*, 23 September 1869; the editors, "Nos lecteurs," *Le Nouveau Monde*, 24 September 1869; Dessaulles to Cannon G. Lamarche, September–October 1869, BANQ, Quebec's Centeer, Dessaulles collection, Penn Letter Book, 44–45, 47–52, 52–5, 62–72, 129–129A; Dessaulles, "Nous avons reçu de M. Dessaulles," *L'Ordre*, 16 September 1869; Dessaulles, "Depuis que l'Institut s'est réuni," *Le Pays*, 18 September 1869; L.-A. Dessaulles, "M. Dessaulles nous fait parvenir, " *Le Courrier de*

Saint-Hyacinthe, 28 September 1869; the editors, "À la demande de M. Dessaulles," *Le Courrier de Saint-Hyacinthe,* 2 October 1869. Dessaulles and others to His Eminence Cardinal Barnabo, 12 October 1869, ACAM, 901.135, 869-15.

4 Dessaulles, "Affaire Guibord," *Annuaire de l'Institut-Canadien pour 1869,* 8, 12, 16–21, 31, 34–5, 39, 32, 36–7, and quotation from 50; CIHM, no. 404; Mgr Bourget to Abbé Truteau, 8 January 1870, ACAM, 901.060, 870-2.

5 Argument presented by Joseph Doutre in Hébert, *Le procès Guibord,* 41, 73, 29, 36, 49, 52, 59; Dessaulles, "Affaire Guibord. Témoignage de L.-A. Dessaulles," *Le Pays,* 26, 29, 31 January, 1, 2, 3 February 1870; judgment: Superior Court, Montréal; *Plaidoirie des avocats in RE Henriette Brown vs la Fabrique de Montréal,* 17; CIHM, no.10538; judgment of the Court of Error in *Le Nouveau Monde,* 8 September 1871; judgment of the Judicial Committee of the Privy Council in Dougall, *History of the Guibord Case,* 29–55, 56–61; excerpts in Clark, *The Guibord Affair,* 56–68; judgment also published in *Le Bien public,* 22 November 1874 and *La Minerve,* 23 November 1874.

6 *MEM,* VII:196–200, 234–47, 267–74; English version of Bourget's pastoral letter: "Pastoral After the Burial," quotation from 123.

7 Response of the bishop of Montreal to the appeal by four members of the Institut canadien, 27 May 1870, ACAM, 901.135, 870-4; Opinion of the bishop of Trois-Rivières on the Institut canadien de Montréal, 16 June 1870, ibid., 870-6; decision of Rome: Cardinal Barnabo to Mgr Baillargeon, 13 August 1870, published in *Dernière correspondance entre S.E. le Cardinal Barnabo et l'Hon. M. Dessaulles,* 14; Lamonde, "Histoire et inventaire des archives de l'Institut canadien de Montréal."

8 Lamonde, *Louis-Antoine Dessaulles,* 219–20.

9 Abbé Joseph-Sabin Raymond to the superior of the Séminaire de Québec, 7 February 1870, ASQ, Université 108 no. 13.

10 *METR,* Mgr Laflèche, I:219–28, quotation from 226; Voisine, *Louis-François Laflèche,* I:152–77, 197–8; Eid, "Les ultramontains et le Programme catholique."

11 Mgr Taschereau, "Circulaire au clergé," 24 April 1871, *MEQ,* Cardinal Taschereau, I:37; Voisine, "Taschereau, Alexandre-Elzéar", *DCB;* Mgr Bourget, "Circulaire au clergé concernant les élections," 6 May 1871, *MEM,* VI:170–7; Mgr Laflèche, "Circulaire au clergé," 15 May 1871, *METR,* Laflèche, I:259–68; L.-A. Dessaulles to Cardinal Barnabo, 3 June 1871, BANQ, Quebec's Centre, Dessaulles collection, "Penn Letter Book," 199–202; *Noces d'or de Mgr l'évêque de Montréal,* 4–11; CIHM, no. 23799.

12 Pâquet, *Le libéralisme,* 24–6, 61; CIHM, no. 64193; S. Chassé, "Pâquet, Benjamin," *DCB;* on the approval of the *Civiltà cattolica, Annuaire de* Université Laval, 56; A. de F. [Abbé Alexis Pelletier], *Le libéralisme ou quelques observations critiques,* 12-14; CIHM, no. 11481.

13 Abbé J.-S. Raymond to Abbé B. Pâquet, 2 May 1872, ASQ, Université 107, no. 6; Raymond, *Discours sur l'action de Marie,* 140–3; Binan [Mgr

Pierre-Adolphe Pinsoneault], *Le Grand-Vicaire Raymond et le libéralisme catholique*, 1–7, 7–13, 2; Choquette, "Pinsoneault, Pierre-Adolphe," *DCB*; Luigi [Abbé Alexis Pelletier], *Il y a du libéralisme et du gallicanisme en Canada*, 3, 36, 30–1; Luigi [Abbé Alexis Pelletier], *Du modérantisme;* Dessaulles, *La grande guerre ecclésiastique;* reply by "Luigi" [Abbé A. Pelletier], *Le Don Quichotte montréalais;* Voisine, "Pelletier, Alexis," *DCB*.

14 Mgr Pinsoneault, *Lettres à un député;* CIHM, no. 23978; Luigi [Abbé A. Pelletier], *Coup d'œil sur le libéralisme*, 11–12, 34–9.

15 Plourde, *Dominicains au Canada*, I:179, 245–6, 251–2, 269, 511.

16 Audet, *Histoire de l'enseignement*, II:115–22; Audet, *Histoire du Conseil de l'instruction publique.*

17 Buies, *La Lanterne*, 1 September 1868, and *Le Réveil*, 7 October 1876.

18 Quoted in Bélanger, *Wilfrid Laurier*, 82–3.

19 Oscar Dunn quoted in Bernard, *Les Rouges*, 319; Laurier quoted in Bélanger, *Wilfrid Laurier*, 94.

20 Quebec Election Act, *Statutes of the Province of Quebec passed in the thirty-eighth year of the reign of Her Majesty Queen Victoria;* MER, Mgr Langevin, 216; N. Bélanger, "Langevin, Jean," *DCB*.

21 Quoted in Marcel Hamelin, *Les premières années du parlementarisme québécois*, 215.

22 "Lettre pastorale et circulaire au clergé des évêques de la province ecclésiastique de Québec," 22 September 1875, *MEM*, VII:203–24, quotations 207, 209, 211, 218; on Protestant reactions, Galt, *Civil Liberty in Lower Canada;* Kesteman, "Galt, Alexander Tilloch," *DCB*; Mgr Bourget, "Lettre pastorale sur le libéralisme catholique," 1 January 1876, *MEM*, VII:299–310, quotations 299, 301. Mgr Bourget resigned in July 1876.

23 Mgr Taschereau, "Mandement sur les devoirs des électeurs pendant les élections," 25 May 1876, *MEQ*, V:403–9; on Charlevoix and Bonaventure, Voisine, *Louis-François Laflèche*, I:210–25, 251–60; *Reports of the Supreme Court of Canada*, I (1877):145–234; *Rapports judiciaires de Québec*, III (1877):75–92; Bélanger, "Une introduction au problème de l'influence indue; Chassé, "L'Affaire Casault-Langevin; "Mandement ... portant condamnation de certaines propositions contraires aux droits de l'Église," 15 January 1877, *MER*, Mgr Langevin, 455–64.

24 Mgr Moreau, quoted in Voisine, *Louis-François Laflèche*, I:258; "Déclaration des évêques au sujet de la loi électorale," 26 March 1877, *MEQ*, VI:10–13; Voisine, "Conroy, George," *DCB*; Voisine, *Louis-François Laflèche*, I:260–72, and Voisine, "Laflècje, Louis-François," *DCB*.

25 Laurier, "Political Liberalism: Lecture at Quebec 26th June, 1877," *Wilfrid Laurier on the Platform*, 51–80; Louis-Georges Desjardins, *M. Laurier devant l'histoire;* CIHM, no. 24213.

26 H. Fabre, quoted in Bélanger, *Wilfrid Laurier*, 109; instructions to Mgr Conroy, Sylvain and Voisine, *Histoire du catholicisme québécois*, 469n25; "Lettre pastorale des évêques sur les élections" and "Lettre circulaire au clergé," 11 October 1877, *MEM*, IX:132–4, 126–31; Perin, "Troppo Ardenti Sacerdoti."

CHAPTER TWELVE

1 Lamonde, "Le lion, le coq et la fleur de lys," 168–73.
2 Barthe, *Le Canada reconquis par la France*, article signed by "Michel," *La Minerve*, 3 May 1855; "Le Canada vengé des platitudes d'un fanfaron ou M. Barthe et son livre," *La Patrie*, July–October 1855, quotations 13 and 20 July 1855; Sylvain, "Rambaud, Alfred-Alexis," *DCB*; *Le Journal de Québec*, 18 August 1855; *Le Pays*, 5 July 1855, articles quoted in Vaucamps, "La France dans la presse, 105–8; Ampère, *Promenade en Amérique*, I:109; on the French perception of Canada, Simard, *Mythe et reflet*.
3 Kinsman, "The Visit to Canada of 'La Capricieuse'"; Portes, "La reprise des relations"; Bossé, *"La Capricieuse" à Québec*, remarks by President Robillard, *La Minerve*, 18 August 1855; Crémazie, "Le vieux soldat canadien," 18 August 1855, in Grisé and Lortie, *Textes poétiques*, V: 634–9; for the eight songs composed by A. Marsais, Kinsman, "The Visit to Canada," A60–A75.
4 "Discours de M. Chauveau," *La Minerve*, 24 July 1855.
5 *Le Moniteur*, 23 August 1855 and *La Patrie*, 28 August 1855; on the subject of the controversy, Kinsman, "The Visit to Canada,"A2–A29; on the objectives of Belvèze's mission, Portes, "'La Capricieuse' au Canada."
6 *Le Journal de Québec*, 24 March 1855, quoted in Vaucamps, "La France dans la presse," 89–90; Taché, *Esquisse sur le Canada*; Savard, *Le consulat général*; Benjamin Sulte compiled a collection of strange perceptions of Canada, *Le Canada en Europe*.
7 Marmier, *Lettres sur l'Amérique*, I:270; Belvèze's statements reported in *Le Journal de Québec*, 31 July 1855 and his *Rapport de mission*, 1 November 1885, quoted in Portes, "'La Capricieuse' au Canada," 362; Grandfort, *L'Autre Monde*, 249, 253, 272, and Lamonde, *Gens de parole*, 152; Jannet, *Les États-Unis contemporains*, quoted in Beaudoin, *Naissance d'une littérature*, 32; Savard, "Du Lac Saint-Jean au Texas."
8 Gosselin, *Étienne Parent*, 168, 133; "Discours de M. É. Parent," *La Voix du golfe*, 14 July 1868; Guay, "La fête de la Saint-Jean-Baptiste," passim, from which I have taken the choice of texts of the 24 June speeches; Chauveau, *La Minerve* 27 June 1856; Rouxel, *Annales du cabinet de lecture paroissial*, nos. 1 and 2, 1857.
9 Chevalier, "La langue française et la nationalité canadienne," and "La presse franco-américaine"; Beauchamp, "Henry-Émile Chevalier et le feuilleton

canadien-français (1853–1860)"; Gauldrée-Boilleau, "Le paysan de Saint-Irénée"; Dussault, "Un réseau utopique franco-québécois."

10 Rameau de Saint-Père, *La France aux colonies*, 250–69, and *Les Français en Amérique*, 262–9; see also "La race française en Amérique," speech on 23 October 1860, *Écho du cabinet de lecture paroissial*, 1 and 15 November 1860: 325–30, 339–46, and "La race française au Canada," speech presented to the Société d'économie sociale de Paris on 26 January 1873, in Sulte, *Le Canada en Europe*, 46–62; on the comparison between the colonization of Canada and that of Algeria, see the text of the lecture by Rameau de Saint-Père in *Le Courrier de Saint-Hyacinthe* from 4 to 18 June 1861.

11 Rameau de Saint-Père, *La France aux colonies*, 12, 14; Father Bernard Chocarne to his brother, 4 August 1868, quoted in Plourde, *Les Dominicains au Canada*, I:47–8; Guénard [Albert Lefaivre], *La France canadienne*, and *Conférence sur la littérature canadienne*, 48.

12 Rameau de Saint-Père, *La France aux colonies*, 346; É. Parent to Rameau, 9 August and 25 October 1861, quoted in Jean Bruchési, "Les correspondants canadiens de Rameau de Saint-Père," 108, 105–6.

13 Sentenne, *La Minerve*, 19 June 1860; Abbé Hercule Beaudry, *La Minerve*, 25 June 1862; Trudel, "Les destinées du peuple canadien," *Écho du cabinet de lecture paroissial* (1861): 141–4, 148–9, 155–60.

14 Casgrain, "Le mouvement littéraire au Canada," I: 370, 373; Beaudoin, *Naissance d'une littérature*, passim.

15 Speech by Father Thibault, *La Minerve*, 26 June 1866; Laflèche, *Quelques considérations sur les rapports de la société civile avec la religion et la famille*, 60; Masson, *Le Canada français et la Providence*, 6, 49; see also Thibault, "Mission providentielle des Canadiens," *Écho du cabinet de lecture paroissial* (1867): 949–58.

16 Rameau de Saint-Père, "La race française en Amérique," *Écho du cabinet de lecture paroissial*, 1 November 1860: 325–30; 15 November 1860: 339–46; "Lecture de M. Rameau sur le patriotisme," *Écho du cabinet de lecture paroissial* (1860): 372–77; (1861): 4–5, 12–15, 28–30, 37–9; "La race française au Canada," lecture to the Société d'économie sociale de Paris, 26 January 1873, in Sulte, *Le Canada en Europe*, 46–62.

17 *Le Canadien*, quoted in Rambaud, "Québec et la guerre franco-allemande," 315; Vaucamps, "La France dans la presse," 259–72; Faucher de Saint-Maurice, *Le Courrier du Canada*, 7 September 1870; Crémazie, "Journal du siège," quotations 138, 151, 146, 255, 252, 248; see also Abbé J.-S. Raymond, "Les enseignements des événements contemporains," lecture on 8 December 1870, *Revue canadienne* (June 1871): 27–56.

18 On Prince Napoleon, Lamonde, *Louis-Antoine Dessaulles*, 121–3; Doutre, *Le principe des nationalités*, 39–40, 28, 56; A.-B. Routhier, *Le Courrier du Canada*,

23 and 30 September, 10 October, 2 and 9 November 1871, quotation from 9 November 1871.

19 Buies, "De la réciprocité avec les États-Unis" (1874), *Chroniques*, II:89–95.

20 Quoted in Savard, "1861. La presse québécoise et la guerre de Sécession," 113; Rameau de Saint-Père, "Conférence sur la crise américaine," *Le Courrier du Canada*, 10, 13, 15, 17 May 1861; Dessaulles, *La guerre américaine*; Fabre, [*Canadien* literature]: 90, 93; O. Crémazie to Abbé H.-R. Casgrain, 29 November 1867, in *Oeuvres complètes*, 40–1.

CHAPTER THIRTEEN

1 Lamonde and Beauchamp, *Données statistiques*, Tables 1, 6, 5, 10, 7–9, 17, 11.

2 Hare, *Les Canadiens français aux quatre coins du monde*, 90–137; Rajotte, Carle, and Couture, *Le récit de voyage*, 248–64; Thoreau, *A Yankee in Canada*, 19, 21, 103, 107, 99.

3 *Journal of the Legislative Assembly of United-Canada*, "General Statements of Exports," 1850–; on the railway and Victoria Bridge: *Montreal in 1856*; Triggs et al., *Le pont Victoria / Victoria Bridge*, 74–95; Chauveau, *The Visit of His Royal Highness the Prince of Wales to America*; Lenoir, "Montréal et ses principaux monuments."

4 Dickens, *American Notes for General Circulation*, 249–54; Hare, *Les Canadiens français*; Rajotte, *Le récit de voyage*; Jaumain, "Paris devant l'opinion canadienne-française"; Crémazie, "Journal du siège de Paris, août 1870-mai 1871"; Lamonde, *Louis-Antoine Dessaulles*, chap. 16–17; Dessaulles, *Écrits*, 274–309; Kroëller, *Canadian Travellers in Europe*.

5 Courville, Robert, and Séguin, *Atlas historique du Québec*, 103–4, 107, 115.

6 Gerald Tulchinsky, *The River Barons*, 69–70, 106.

7 Bibliographic information on associations from an international point of view in Lamonde, *Gens de parole*, 124, 136; on Vattemare: Galarneau, "Le philanthrope Vattemare"; Revai, *Alexandre Vattemare*.

8 Tulchinsky, *The River Barons*, 24–5; source of quotations: Lamonde, "Les associations au Bas-Canada"; on the need for a public space: *Le Fantasque*, 28 September 1840; Charles Mondelet, "Les jeunes gens du Canada," lecture at the Institut canadien de Montréal, 3 February 1848, *L'Avenir*, 12 February 1848; Joseph Doutre, "Sixième anniversaire de la fondation de l'Institut canadien," lecture, 17 December 1850, *L'Avenir*, 29 January 1851; Lamonde, "La sociabilité et l'histoire socio-culturelle."

9 Lamonde and Beauchamp, *Données statistiques*, Tables 11, 114.

10 On associations in Québec: Lamonde, "Liste alphabétique de noms de lieux" and *Territoires de la culture québécoise*, 177n7; Lebel, "François-Xavier Garneau et la Société de discussion de Québec."

11 On the membership of the Institut canadien de Montréal, Lamonde, *Gens de parole*, 134.

12 On public lectures, Lamonde, *Territoires de la culture québécoise*, 152–4, and *Gens de parole*, 37–81; Lajeunesse, *Les Sulpiciens*, 89–121; Rajotte, "Pratique de la conférence publique" and *Les mots du pouvoir*; quotation from Senécal, "Discours de clôture," *Cercle littéraire*, 1 May 1859, quoted in Lajeunesse, *Les Sulpiciens*, 126. On the public lecture given by Herman Melville in Montreal on 11 December 1857, Kennedy, "Herman Melville's Lecture in Montreal"; on the lecture by Orestes Brownson on 4 April 1850, Sylvain and Voisine, *Histoire du catholicisme québécois*, 78–9.

13 Lamonde and Beauchamp, *Données statistiques*, Table 112.

14 Ibid.

15 On essays and debates, Lamonde, *Territoires de la culture québécoise*, 175, and *Gens de parole*, 83–109, 137, 163–9; quotation from Gérin-Lajoie, "Éloge de l'Honorable Rémi Vallières de Saint-Réal," 360; on literature, Lamonde, *Territoires de la culture québécoise*, 152–4, 174; on the law and literature, Lemire, ed., *La vie littéraire au Québec*, III:105.

16 Lamonde, *Les bibliothèques de collectivités*, 21, 115–29, and "Une contribution à l'histoire de la bibliothèque publique," 21–6; Lamonde and Beauchamp, *Données statistiques*, Tables 99–102.

17 Lamonde and Beauchamp, *Données statistiques*, Tables 95, 97, 106–108.

18 Ibid., Table 94.

19 Lamonde, *Territoires de la culture québécoise*, 117–47, 86–7 and studies by Mark V. Olsen and Louis-Georges Harvey cited 146n2; Institut canadien de Montréal, minutes, 13 August 1861, BANQ, Montreal's Centre; Angenot, "Le roman français dans la bibliothèque de l'Institut canadien de Montréal"; A. Gérin-Lajoie, "Bibliothèques publiques. Leur importance," essay at the Institut canadien de Montréal, *La Minerve*, 14 May 1847, reproduced in Dionne, *Antoine Gérin-Lajoie*, 367–77; Cambron, "Les bibliothèques d'Antoine Gérin-Lajoie"; Lajeunesse, *Les Sulpiciens*, 19–55, 165–76, 197; quotation from *L'Écho du Cabinet de lecture paroissial* (1868), 624; the development of private libraries took place alongside that of libraries formed by groups, see Lamonde and Olivier, *Les bibliothèques personnelles*.

20 Lamonde and Beauchamp, *Données statistiques*, Table 105.

21 Parent, "La presse," lecture, 1844, in Parent, *Discours*; P.-J.-O. Chauveau, "Inauguration de la salle de lecture," *La Minerve*, 25 February 1857; Beaulieu and Hamelin, *La presse québécoise*, vols. I and II, and "Aperçu sur le journalisme québécois"; Galarneau, "La presse périodique au Québec," 147; de Bonville, *La presse québécoise*, 78; on the question of the cultural threshold, Bernard, "La fonction intellectuelle de Saint-Hyacinthe."

22 On the religious press: Mgr Bourget to Mgr Signay, 31 August 1840, ACAM, corr. Bourget, II:204; Abbé Prince to anonymous, 5 November 1840, in

Choquette, *Histoire du Séminaire de Saint-Hyacinthe*, 235; Circular letter on the founding of a Church newspaper, 14 April 1842, ACSAP, Pilote 14, LXXXV; M. Hudon to Abbé Pilote, 4 July 1842, ibid., XC; correspondence regarding the founding of *Le Courrier du Canada*, 20 November 1856–20 January 1857, ibid., Gauvreau 11, LXIX–LXXIII.

23 de Bonville, *La presse*, 359, 366, 371; Teyssier, "La distribution postale de la presse périodique québécoise," appendix H, 50, 93, 99, 102, 91, 117; Lapointe, "La nouvelle européenne"; Brunn, "Les Canadiens français et les nouvelles de l'Europe"; on the telegraph: the McKay and Lovell Directories; Murray, *A Story of the Telegraph*; on its inauguration, *La Minerve*, 22 May 1846; on the transatlantic cable, *Le Courrier du Canada*, 31 July 1866; *Le Pays*, 31 July, 16 August and 1 September 1866; *L'Ordre*, 1 August and 3 September 1866; *Le Canadien*, 22 August 1866; on writers and the press, Lemire, ed., *La vie littéraire au Québec*, III: 112–17; quotation from *Le Pays*, 29 September 1866.

24 Porter, "Un projet de musée national"; Gagnon, "Les musées accessibles au public"; Trudel, "The Montreal Society of Artists" and "Aux origines du Musée des Beaux-Arts de Montréal," quotation from 54–5; on the industrial exhibitions: Dray, *Address Delivered at the Provincial Industrial Exhibition*; Dufresne, "Attractions, curiosités," and Montpetit, "Fêtes et société"; Drouin, "Les meubliers du Québec"; Kröller, "Canadians at World Exhibitions," in *Canadian Travellers*; on sociability and public markets: Murray, "Les marchés de Trois-Rivières."

25 See Montpetit and Dufresne in Montpetit, ed., *Rapport du Groupe de recherche en art populaire*, 48–128, 187–257; Laflamme and Tourangeau, *L'Église et le théâtre au Québec*, 130, 149, 139–43; Larrue, *Le théâtre à Montréal*, 20–1; Camerlain, "Trois interventions du clergé"; articles repeating the bishop's statements in *L'Écho du Cabinet de lecture paroissial*, 21 June 1860 to 28 June 1861.

26 Barrière, "La société canadienne-française et le théâtre lyrique", 51–61, 79–117, 311, 314, 317, 456, 345–53, quotation from *La Minerve*, 347; Kallman, Potvin and Winters, eds., *Encyclopedia of Music in Canada*, "Royal Theatre," "City Concert Hall," "Mechanics' Hall," "Nordheimer Hall," "Academy of Music," "Labelle, Jean-Baptiste," "Hardy, Edmond," "Lavallée, Charles," "Boucher, Adélard Joseph," "Hone, Jules," "Jehin-Prume, Frantz," and "Concert halls and opera houses."

27 *Mélanges religieux*, 20 August 1841, 19 January 1844, 14 May 1847; Pierre-Richard Lafrenaye, lecture at the Institut canadien de Montréal, 17 December 1854, *Le Pays*, 28 December 1854; Lamonde, *Gens de parole*, 54.

28 Audet, *Histoire de l'enseignement*, II:56–62, 69–72; Dufour, *Tous à l'école*, 110–20; Nelson,"The 'Guerre des Éteignoirs'"; É. Parent, "Considérations sur notre système d'éducation," lecture at the Institut canadien de Montréal, 19 February 1848, in Parent, *Discours*.

29 Lamonde and Beauchamp, *Données statistiques*, Tables 41 and 42.

30 Ibid., Table 29.

31 Ibid., Tables 43 and 44.

32 Ibid., Table 45.

33 Ibid., Table 29.

34 Dufour, *Tous à l'école*, 48; the increase in the number of schools and students was similar everywhere, with some chronological variation from place to place: Hamelin, "L'alphabétisation de la Côte du Sud", passim, Table 114, and J. Ouellet, "Le développement du système scolaire au Saguenay–Lac-Saint-Jean," 14, 18–19.

35 Lamonde and Beauchamp, *Données statistiques*, Table 46.

36 Ibid., Tables 47–51.

37 Verrette, "L'alphabétisation au Québec," 202, 212, 201; "L'alphabétisation de la population de la ville de Québec"; Lessard, "L'alphabétisation à Trois-Rivières"; Hamelin, "L'alphabétisation de la Côte du Sud"; Bouchard, "Nouvelle mesure de l'alphabétisation"; Bouchard, "Évolution de l'alphabétisation au Saguenay"; Saint-Hilaire, "Mobilité et alphabétisation au Saguenay."

38 Lamonde, *La philosophie et son enseignement*, 252–3; the Collège de Monnoir, founded in 1853, lasted only a few years.

39 Hamelin, *Histoire de l'Université Laval*; Lavallée, *Québec contre Montréal*; Pouliot, *Mgr Bourget et son temps*, V:178–90; Chartrand, Duchesne, and Gingras, *Histoire des sciences au Québec*, 216–20, 167–82, 227–33; Gagnon, *Histoire de l'École polytechnique*.

40 Lamonde and Beauchamp, *Données statistiques*, Table 88.

41 Ibid., 95 and 96.

42 Ibid., 93.

43 Lamonde, *La librairie et l'édition à Montréal*, 57–62; Mativat, *Le métier d'écrivain au Québec*, 65.

44 Lamonde, *La librairie et l'édition*, 62–71, quotations: 64 and 61; Mativat, *Le métier d'écrivain au Québec*, 258–61; Landry, *Beauchemin et l'édition au Québec*, 218–26.

45 Lamonde and Beauchamp, *Données statistiques*, Table 103.

46 Quotation from Mativat, *Le métier d'écrivain*, 257; Parent, "Importance de l'étude de l'économie politique," public lecture at the Institut canadien de Montréal, 19 November 1846, in Parent, *Discours*; Lamonde, *La librairie et l'édition*, 63–77; Landry, *Beauchemin*, 324–5, 226–33.

47 Mativat, *Le métier d'écrivain*, 57; Buies, *Chroniques II*, 331–2; Barthe, *Le Canada reconquis*, 261–276; Bibaud, *Tableau historique*; Laurent-Olivier David, "Essai sur la littérature nationale," *Écho du Cabinet de lecture paroissial* (12 October 1861): 315–18; Fabre, "On Canadian Literature," *Transactions of the Quebec Literary and Historical Society* (1865–1866): 85–102; Casgrain,

"Le mouvement littéraire au Canada," I, 353–75; Blain de Saint-Aubin, *Quelques notes*; Darveau, *Nos hommes de lettres*.

CHAPTER FOURTEEN

1 "Lettre pastorale des évêques sur la liberté du ministère paroissial," 1 January 1880, MEM, IX:298–303; Cardinal Simeoni to Mgr Taschereau, 13 September 1881, quoted in Voisine and Sylvain, *Histoire du catholicisme québécois*, II:390; Mgr Laflèche, *L'influence spirituelle indue devant la liberté religieuse et civile*, 12–32; CIHM, no. 8579; "Lettre pastorale des évêques. Taxes sur les biens ecclésiastiques," 8 December 1887, MEM, IX:360; Mgr Laflèche, *Des biens temporels de l'Église et de l'immunité de ces biens devant les pouvoirs civils*; see also Mgr Laflèche, *Lettre pastorale … concernant les dangers auxquels la foi des catholiques est exposée en ce pays*; on the election in Berthier, see Tarte, *Le clergé, ses droits, nos devoirs*; on the question of the insane asylums, Laperrière, *Les congrégations religieuses*, I:183–5; Rodrigue, "L'exemption fiscale des communautés religieuses."

2 Mgr Fabre, "Circulaire. Défense au clergé de se mêler de politique," 17 December 1885, MEM, XI:346–60; letter from Cardinal Simeoni on undue influence, 31 December 1881, MEM, IX:397–401.

3 Un catholique [Abbé Alexis Pelletier], *La source du mal de l'époque au Canada*; Villeneuve, *Étude sur le mal révolutionnaire en Canada*; *Mémoire de l'évêque des Trois-Rivières sur les difficultés religieuses en Canada*; *Appendice au Mémoire de l'évêque des Trois-Rivières sur les difficultés religieuses en Canada*; Mgr Taschereau, *Remarques sur le mémoire de l'évêque de Trois-Rivières sur les difficultés religieuses en Canada*; *Lettre de Mgr Laflèche à son Éminence le cardinal NN établissant la nécessité d'une enquête sur les difficultés religieuses en Canada*; [Anonymous], *Le libéralisme dans la province de Québec*.

4 Beaugrand, *La Patrie*, 4 February 1890, quoted in Laurin, "Le nationalisme et le rationalisme du journal *La Patrie*," 210; Ricard, "Beaugrand, Honoré," DCB.

5 G. Langlois, *Le Clairon*, 8 February 1890, quoted in Dutil, "The Politics of Muzzling "Lucifer's Representative," 114; Dutil, *L'avocat du diable*.

6 Fréchette, *Satires et polémiques*, I:563–75; II:733–7; circular letter on the accusations made against members of the clergy, 29 September 1892, MEM, XI:89–106.

7 Sauvalle-Tardivel trial, *Canada-Revue*, August 1894: 292-293; "Circulaire de Mgr Fabre à propos de *Canada-Revue* et de *L'Écho des Deux-Montagnes*," 11 November 1892, MEM, XI:107–8; [J.-N. Marcil], *La Grande cause ecclésiastique*, 186–7; Circular letter of Mgr Fabre on bad newspapers, 28 February 1895, MEM, XI:45–6 and "Lettre pastorale des Pères du Premier Concile provincial sur la presse, 9 October 1895, ibid., XII:1–36; Filiatreault, *Ruines*

cléricales.; Brassard and Hamelin, "Filiatreault, Aristide," *DCB*; de Bonville, "La liberté de presse à la fin du xixe siècle"; [Anonyme], *Le cléricalisme au Canada*; [Anonyme], *Le cléricalisme au Canada. II: Saintes comédies*; [Anonyme], *Propagande anti-cléricale. Première série.*

8 Condamnation de *L'Électeur* par les évêques de Montréal et de Québec, 22 et 27 décembre 1896, *MEQ*, IV:335–48.

9 Heap, "L'Église, l'État et l'éducation au Québec," 156, 174; Cloutier, *Pédagogie: conférence sur l'uniformité de l'enseignement*; the report of the Commission sur l'administration de la CECM, 30 June 1883, was not made public at the time, but it was later published in Savaète, *Voix canadiennes*, vol. VIII, 148–65.

10 *Rapport* du Surintendant de l'instruction publique (1855), 16; on the disagreement between Verreau and Réticius: Labarrère-Paulé, *Les instituteurs laïques au Canada français*, 335–53; Heap, "L'Église, l'État et l'enseignement public catholique au Québec," 111–285, and Voisine, *Les Frères des Écoles chrétiennes au Canada*, vol. 2, 63–116; five letters by Abbé Verreau were published, first in *Le Courrier de Montréal* between 29 November and 6 December 1880; Brother Réticius responded with his *Réponse aux cinq lettres du R.M. Verreau*; Voisine, "Réticius, Brother," *DCB*. On the disagreement between Archambault and Réticius: Audet, "Épisode scolaire," *CD*, 39 (1974), 9–43, in which Archambault's brief and Mgr Taschereau's response are reproduced.

11 Pelland, *Biographie, discours, conférences de Mercier*, 603–4, 210; Heap, "Un chapitre dans l'histoire de l'éducation des adultes au Québec"; Gagnon, "Les discours sur l'enseignement pratique au Canada français"; Hamel, "L'obligation scolaire au Québec"; Cardinal Taschereau's letter to Premier Ross, 14 September 1886, in Heap, "L'Église, l'État et l'éducation," 252–3; *La Liberté*, 9 and 23 March 1893, 31 January and 27 September 1895.

12 Heap, "L'Église, l'État et l'éducation," 169; Paquin, *Conférences sur l'instruction obligatoire*; Pinsoneault, *Observations sur le Mémoire des instituteurs laïques*; pastoral letter of the bishops of the ecclesiastical province of Quebec on education, 19 March 1894, *MEM*, XI:646–93.

13 On Masson's proposal regarding the teaching certificate: Fréchette, *Satires et polémiques*, I:344n20; Chapais, *Les congrégations enseignantes*, 25.

14 Laurier to Blake, 10 July 1882, quoted in Fréchette, *Satires et polémiques*, I:30–1; Heap, *L'Église, l'État et l'éducation*, 142–5, 381; the disagreement between Fréchette and Baillargé, Fréchette, *Satires et polémiques*, I:426 and 472; Dessaulles, *La grande guerre ecclésiastique*, 54; Lamonde, *La philosophie et son enseignement*, Chap. III and IV.

15 On the dispute between Verreau and Fréchette: Labarrère-Paulé, *Les instituteurs laïques*, 341–8; Hamel, "Verreau, Hospice," *DCB*, for the texts published in the dispute.

16 Savard, *Jules-Paul Tardivel, la France et les États-Unis*, 7, 14, 177–86, 82–100, quotation from 184; "Programme de *La Vérité*," *La Vérité*, 14 July 1881; opposition to liberalism: "Les partis politiques. Qu'est-ce qu'un libéral?," *La Vérité*, 22 April 1882, reprinted in Tardivel, *Mélanges*, I: 310–12; *La Vérité*, 6 October 1889; Savard, *Jules-Paul Tardivel, la France*, 74–6; "L'avenir," *La Vérité*, 27 May 1882; on L. Veuillot: Savard, "Jules-Paul Tardivel et Louis Veuillot," and Savard, *Jules-Paul Tardivel, la France*, 82–97.

17 On Freemasonry, Savard, *Jules-Paul Tardivel, la France*, 170–6; isolation of Tardivel, ibid., 137, 139, 154, and Tardivel, *Mélanges*, III:XXXV–XXXVIII.

18 Bélanger, "Le nationalisme ultramontain," quotations 285–6, 291, 276, 287; Tardivel, *Pour la patrie*, 50–1, 58, 60, 85–6, 104, quotation from 176.

19 Mercier, *L'avenir du Canada*, 4–5, 8–9, 14, 26, 28–30, 33–8, 41, 47–8, 50, 57, 59, 65, 86; Joseph Royal took up the same subject the following year in *La crise actuelle*.

20 Miller, *Equal Rights: The Jesuits' Estates Act Controversy*; Groulx, *L'enseignement français au Canada*; bishops' pastoral letter on the question of the Manitoba schools, March 1891, *MEM*, XI:482–90; Cardinal Ledochowski, secretary of the Congregation for the Propagation of the Faith, to Cardinal Taschereau, 14 March 1895, in *MEM*, XII:94–7, or Bernard [the Dominican D.-C. Gonthier], *Un manifeste libéral*, II:1–4; bishops' pastoral letter on the Manitoba schools question, 25 March 1895, *MEM*, XII:53–4, 58; Crunican, *Priests and Politicians*; Brassard and Hamelin, "Gonthier, D.-C.," *DCB*.

21 Pâquet, *L'électeur*, 18 February 1896, reprinted in Lamonde, *Louis-Adolphe Pâquet*, 49–52; bishops' pastoral letter on the Manitoba schools question, 6 May 1896, in Bernard, *Un manifeste libéral*, 33–43, and circular letter, 45–8; Mgr Laflèche's sermon, in Proulx, *Documents pour servir à l'intelligence*, 44–55.

22 Fréchette, 4 July 1896, *Satires et polémiques*, 114–15.

23 David, *Le clergé canadien, sa mission et son œuvre*; Hébert, "Laurent-Olivier David," in Lamonde, ed., *Combats libéraux*.

24 Bernard, *Un manifeste libéral*, passim; Proulx, *Documents pour servir*; Proulx, *Dans la ville éternelle*.

25 Censure of L.-O. David, *MEM*, XII, sheet; Charland, *Le Père Gonthier*; text of *Affari vos*, 8 December 1897, and circular letter of the same date, *MEQ*, IX:17–24, 5–16; English text of *Affari vos* available at www.papalencyclicals.net/Leo13/l13affar.htm.

26 Trudel's accusation against Chapleau, see Dufour and Hamelin, "Mercier, Honoré," *DCB*; Curé Labelle to Rameau de Saint-Père, 28 October 1886, quoted in Bruchési, "Les correspondants," 109; Tardivel, *La Vérité*, 20 February 1886, reprinted in Savard, *Jules-Paul Tardivel, la France*, 28–32; Tardivel to A. Denault, 31 March 1891, quoted in Senese, "*La Croix de Montréal*," 85; Pâquet, *L'électeur*, 18 February 1896, quoted in Lamonde, *Louis-Adolphe*

Pâquet, 53; Mgr Bégin to Mgr Langevin, 4 December 1897, quoted in Hamelin and Gagnon, *Histoire du catholicisme québécois*, 91.

27 Lamonde, *Ni avec eux ni sans eux*, 43–7; Barrière, "Montréal, microcosme du théâtre lyrique nord-américain."

28 Abbé Léon Provancher, *De Québec à Jérusalem*, quoted in Savard, "L'Italie dans la culture," 263; Bruchési, "Les correspondants," 97–9; quotations from Mgr Satolli and Mgr Lynch in Perin, *Rome in Canada*, 19, 226.

29 Audet, "Le Québec à l'Exposition internationale"; Quinn, "Les capitaux français et le Québec."

30 Pénisson, "Le Commissariat canadien"; Pénisson, "Les commissaires du Canada en France"; Chartier, "Hector Fabre"; Dussault, "Un réseau utopique franco-québécois"; Dussault, "Labelle, Antoine," *DCB*; Clapin, *La France transatlantique*, 231, 235.

31 Trépanier, "Les influences leplaysiennes"; Trépanier, "La Société canadienne d'économie sociale de Montréal, 1888–1911: sa fondation, ses buts et ses activités"; Trépanier, "La Société canadienne d'économie sociale de Montréal (1888–1911): ses membres, ses critiques et sa survie."

32 Tardivel quoted in Savard, *Jules-Paul Tardivel, la France*, 27; Tardivel, *Notes de voyages*; Routhier in Bellerive, *Conférences et discours*; on the Exposition universelle of 1889: Savard, "Autour d'un centenaire"; Lamonde, *Louis-Antoine Dessaulles*, 278–9; Fréchette, *Satires et polémiques*, 1065.

33 Fréchette, *Satires et polémiques*, 1035; on the Alliance française, ibid., 577–600, and *Alliance française*; Jousselin, *Yankees fin de siècle*, 222.

34 Doty, "The Appeal of Boulanger."

35 Fréchette, *Satires et polémiques*, 20–31, 1035–50.

36 *Voyage de Mgr le Comte de Paris*, 25, 28, 41–2; Gagnon, *Le Comte de Paris à Québec*; Dandurand, *Les mémoires du sénateur*, 27–8.

37 Senese, "*La Croix de Montréal.*"

38 Fabre's speech in Bellerive, *Conférences*, 135–63, and "La société française au Canada," *La Réforme sociale*, 15 August 1886: 183–96; Mercier's speech in Bellerive, 33–51; Laurier's speech in Bellerive, 5, 1, 14, 24; Prévost, "Les relations franco-canadiennes."

CHAPTER FIFTEEN

1 Lebel, "Francois-Xavier Garneau et la Société de discussion de Québec," 118–19.

2 Lamonde, *Les bibliothèques de collectivités*, 25.

3 Trudel, *Mémoire sur la question de la fusion*; *Constitution du Club Jacques-Cartier de Montréal*; Decelles, *Constitution et règlements du Club Cartier*; Dumont, *Constitution du Club Letellier*.

4 G. Doutre, "Sur les affaires de l'Institut canadien à Rome," lecture at the Institut canadien de Montréal, 14 April 1870, *Le Pays*, 14, 15, 17, 18 June 1870; Guay, *Introduction à l'histoire des sports au Québec*, 39–58.

5 Metcalfe, *Canada Learns to Play*; Metcalfe, "Le sport au Canada français"; Guay, *Introduction*, 17–38; Guay and Couture, "Inventaire des incorporations."

6 Hathorn, *Lady of the Snows*, 54; Berger, *Honour and Search for Influence*; Schmidt, "Domesticating Parks."

7 de Bonville, *La presse québécoise*, 231; Dansereau, *L'avènement de la linotype*, 20, 86, 95; Ouellet, "La clé du succès," 135.

8 Larrue, *Le théâtre à Montréal*, 12–13, 21, 25, 46–7, 91, 118; Larrue, *Le monument inattendu*, 39; Hébert, *Le burlesque au Québec*; Hathorn, *Lady of the Snows*, 263; MEM, X:131–3, 376–7.

9 Kallman, Potvin, and Winters, eds., *Encyclopedia of Music in Canada*, "Calixa Lavallée," "'O Canada,'" "Guillaume Couture," "Montreal Symphony Orchestra," "Edmond Hardy," "Fédération des harmonies du Québec," "Adélard Joseph Boucher," "Archambault Musique."

10 Vigneault, "The Cultural Diffusion of Hockey in Montreal," 1–2, 12, 18–26, 30, 85, 100, and Appendix A; Guay, *Introduction*, 15–35, 101–15; Janson, *Emparons-nous du sport*, 128.

11 Collin, "La Cité sur mesure," 28; Metcalfe, "The Evolution," 156; Ferretti, *Entre voisins*, 139–66.

12 Dufresne, "Le carnaval d'hiver à Montréal"; Dufresne, "Fête et société," 173; MEM, 26 December 1885, X:226; *La Patrie*, 28 janvier 1889.

13 Lamonde and Montpetit, *Le parc Sohmer*.

14 Comeau, "Les grands magasins"; Lessard, "De l'utilité des catalogues commerciaux"; Rousseau, "La santé par correspondance"; Lefebvre, "Dupuis, Nazaire," DCB.

15 Hogue, Bolduc, and Larouche, *Québec, un siècle d'électricité*, 11, 22, 24, 42; *La Minerve*, 17 May 1879; Moogk, *Roll Back the Years*, 4–5, 11–12, 14–15; Babe, "Sise, Charles Fleetford," DCB; Bell Canada archives, Montreal and Quebec City telephone directories, 1880; "The World and Bell Exchange," Catalogue 24085; see also Catalogues 18908, 18912.

16 Metcalfe, "The Evolution," 148, 163–4; de Bonville, *La presse québécoise*, 50; *La Presse*, 27 June, 1 and 22 August 1885, 4 June 1887; *The Montreal Star*, 15 August 1869, 25 May and 15 October 1870; Collin, "La Cité sur mesure," 26–8; METR, 8 May 1871, I:255; MEM, 29 May 1881, IX:376–8, see also 26 October 1882 and 13 December 1883, IX:468 and 527; Tardivel, "Le travail du dimanche"; MEM, 18 August 1886, X:301, and 1 February 1887, X:314–15; MEM, 20 May 1890, X:697–8 and 24 June 1892, XI:46.

17 MEM, 20 April 1891, X:742; Lamonde and Montpetit, *Le parc Sohmer*, 197–202; *Statutes of the Province of Quebec*, 52 Victoria chap. 9, 8–11 (1892).

18 Dulong, *Bibliographie linguistique,* 23–48; Tardivel, *L'anglicisme, voilà l'ennemi!;* Lusignan, *Fautes à corriger;* "Corrigeons-nous," articles by Louis Fréchette in *La Patrie,* 18 July 1893 to 6 July 1895; Rinfret, *Dictionnaire de nos fautes;* Buies, *Anglicismes et canadianismes;* Legendre, *La langue française au Canada.*

19 Lamonde and Beauchamp, *Données statistiques,* Table 46.

20 Lamonde, Ferretti, and Leblanc, *La culture ouvrière à Montréal,* 149–52; Lamonde, "Pour une histoire de la culture de masse et des médias."

21 Lamonde, *Ni avec eux ni sans eux,* 45.

Sources and Studies

ARCHIVES

Archives de l'archevêché de Montréal

Diocèse de Québec: 295.101, 828–47, 831–37
Lartigue, "Journal d'un voyage en Europe," RCD 134
Mgr Lartigue. Questions diverses: 901.021, 931-9
Mgr Lartigue. Travaux: 901.037, 838-2
 901.135, 863-4, 869-4, 869-9, 869-11, 869-12, 869-13, 869-15, 870-4, 870-6
 901.160, 870-2
Notice sur Mgr Plessis: 901.013, 829-1, 830-2, 832-2, 832-4, 833-2
Pinsoneault, Pierre-Adolphe. *Observations sur le Mémoire des instituteurs laïques de la Province de Québec*, n.d.: 871-000.
Registre des lettres de Mgr Bourget: II, V, VI, XVI, XIX
Registre des lettres de Mgr Lartigue: I, III, V, VI, VII, VIII, IX

Archives de l'archevêché de Québec

Cartables des évêques: III
DM (Diocèse de Montréal): II
Évêques de Québec: III
Registre des lettres: VI, VII, XI, XII, XV, XVI, XVIII
SN (Séminaire de Nicolet): a-107

Archives de l'évêché de Nicolet

Correspondance Raimbault-Plessis
Paroisse de Saint-Pierre de Durham

Sources and Studies

Archives des Ursulines de Trois-Rivières

Registre des lettres

Archives du Collège de Sainte-Anne-de-la-Pocatière

Calonne 36, XXVII
Collège 51, LXIII, LXIV
Gauvreau, 10, LXIX–LXXIII, LXXVII, LXXXIV–LXXXIX, LIX
Mailloux, 100.2
Painchaud 4, L; 5, XLIII
Pelletier 57, 1
Pilote 14, LXXXV, XC, XCII

Archives du diocèse de Saint-Jean (Quebec)

1A/59; 1A/101

Archives du diocèse de Saint-Jérôme

Mgr Lartigue to Abbés Perrault and Amiot: 13A/99 and 16A/59

Archives du Séminaire de Nicolet

Fonds Raimbault: correspondance
Polygraphie: IV
Séminaire: III, V

Archives du Séminaire de Québec

Lettres: T
Lettres de Mgr Plessis à l'abbé Raimbault: II
Polygraphie: 8, nos. 44, 45
Séminaire: 75, no 85
Université: 107, no 6; 109, no 13

Archives Saint-Sulpice de Montréal

Correspondance Garnier

Archives Saint-Sulpice de Paris

Correspondance Quiblier-Carrière, dossier 99

Bell Canada Archives

Catalogues 18908, 18912, 24085
Phone Books (Montreal and Quebec), 1880–1896
"The World and Bell Exchange"

Bibliothèque et Archives nationales du Québec

CENTRE DE QUÉBEC
Fonds Dessaulles, "Penn Letter Book"
Papiers Fabre

CENTRE DE MONTRÉAL
Fonds de l'institut canadien de Montréal (autrefois à la Bibliothèque de
la Ville de Montréal)
Institut canadien de Montréal, procès-verbaux, 1855–1885

*Centre d'Histoire de Saint-Hyacinthe (formerly
Archives du Séminaire de Saint-Hyacinthe)*

Fonds du Séminaire de Saint-Hyacinthe, CH001/S2/SS8 et CH001/S2/
SS10
Fonds Joseph-Sabin Raymond, CH004/S3/SS2, folders 3, 42, 187, 190
The old call number A, G11 has not been retrieved due to reclassification;
probably in fonds du Séminaire (CH001)

Library and Archives Canada

John Neilson Papers, MG 24 B1: II, XV
Papineau Papers, MG 24 B-2 and MG 25 G172
Verreau Collection, MG 23 GV7 and MG 29 D6

McCord Museum, Montreal

Dessaulles Family Papers

PRINTED SOURCES

Periodicals

Note: dates refer to period covered by present research
Canada-Revue (1890–1894)
La Bibliothèque canadienne (1825–1830)

La Gazette du commerce et littéraire de Montréal pour la ville et le district de Montréal (1798–1815)

La Gazette de Québec / The Quebec Gazette (1764–1840), passim

La Lanterne (1868–1869)

La Minerve (1826–1849)

L'Ami du peuple, de l'ordre et des lois (1832–1840)

La Patrie (1879–1897), passim

La Quotidienne (1837–1838)

L'aurore des Canadas (1839–1849), passim

L'Avenir (1847–1851)

La Vérité (1881–1890), passim

Le Canadien (1806–1810, 1817–1825, 1831–1839)

Le Courier de Québec (1806)

Le Courrier de Saint-Hyacinthe (1853–1861)

Le Courrier des États-Unis (New York, 1828–1840)

Le Courrier du Canada (1857–1867), passim

L'écho du cabinet de lecture paroissial (1859–1875)

L'écho du pays (1833–1836)

Le Fantasque (1838–1840)

Le Franc parleur (1870–1878), passim

Le Libéral (June–November 1837)

Le Magasin du Bas-Canada (January–December 1832)

Les Mélanges religieux (1840–1842)

Le Nouveau monde (1867–1871), passim

L'observateur (1830–1831)

L'ordre (1858–1871), passim

L'ordre social (1850)

Le Pays (1852–1871)

Le Populaire (1837–1838)

Le Spectateur canadien (1813–1822)

Le Télégraphe (March–June 1837)

The Vindicator (1828–1837)

Parliamentary Documents

British Parliamentary Papers, vols. 1 to 18. Shannon: Irish Univerity Press.

Great Britain. Parliament. House of Commons. *Report from the Select Committee on the Civil Government of Canada*. Quebec: Reprinted by order of the House of Assembly of Lower Canada, 1829.

Hansard (British Parliamentary Debates)

Second Series, 19, 2 May 1828, columns 299–340

Third Series, vol. 22, 26, 35, 36, 37, 39, 40

Third Series, 55 (March 23 1840)

Journal of the House of Assembly of Lower-Canada

1793
1804
1822 Appendix K
1824
1825 Appendix K
1828–1829, Appendix HH
1831 Appendix QQ
1832–1833 Appendix M
1834 Unnumbered appendix, after Nn
1836 Appendix Oo

Journal of the House of Assembly of United-Canada (1850)

Parliamentary Debates on the Subject of the Confederation of the British North American Provinces, 3d session, 8th provincial Parliament of Canada. Compiled by M.A. Lapin; edited and rev. by J.S. Patrick. Ottawa: King's Printer, 1951.

Provincial Statutes of Canada, 1840–1841. Kingston: Stewart Derbishire and George Desbarats, Law Printer to the Queen's Most Excellent Majesty, 1841.

Provincial Statutes of Lower Canada (1831–1834), Guill. IV, 52–53, 25 February 1832.

Statutes of the Province of Quebec passed in the thirty-eighth year of the reign of Her Majesty Queen Victoria. Quebec: printed by Charles-François Langlois, Printer to Her Most Excellent Majesty the Queen, 1875.

Various Printed Sources

Abrégé de l'Histoire du Canada en quatre parties. Quebec: Imprimé par P. et W. Ruthven, 1831; n°s 39948-39953.

Adam Shortt, and Arthur G. Doughty, eds. *Documents Relating to the Constitutional History of Canada.* Vol. I, *1759–1791.* Ottawa: J. de L. Taché (King's Printer). http://www.canadiana.org/cgi-bin/ECO/mtq?doc=9_03424.

Ade F. [abbé Alexis Pelletier]. *Le libéralisme ou quelques observations critiques sur l'opuscule de l'abbé Benjamin Pâquet intitulée "Le libéralisme".* Montreal: les presses du Nouveau Monde, 1872; CIHM, n° 11481.

Affaires du pays depuis 1828, Québec, [Extrait de *La Gazette de Québec*], 1834; CIHM, n° 50640.

Alliance française [...] Délégation de Montréal. Montreal: La Patrie, n.d.; CIHM, n° 17949.

Ampère, Jean-Jacques. *Promenade en Amérique: États-Unis, Cuba, Mexique.* Vol. 1. Paris: Michel Lévy frères, 1855.

An Old Countryman [Edmund Bailey O'Callaghan]. *The Late Session of the Provincial Parliament of Lower Canada.* Montreal: [from *The Vindicator*], April 1836; CIHM, n° 49085.

Andrès, Bernard, and Pierre Lespérance, eds. *Fortunes et infortunes d'un dandy canadien. Pierre-Jean de Sales Laterrière. Journal de voyage (1815)*. Montreal: UQAM, Cahiers de l'ALAQ, n° 3, 1994.

Annuaire de l'Institut-Canadien pour 1868. Montreal: Le Pays, 1868; CIHM, n° 404.

Annuaire de l'Université Laval (1873–1874).

Appendice au Mémoire de l'évêque des Trois-Rivières sur les difficultés religieuses en Canada. Rome: imprimerie Éditrice, 1882; CIHM, n° 11782.

At a Meeting of the General Committee Appointed for the District of Montreal, for the Purpose of Preparing Petitions [...]. N.p., (18 November 1822), 2 p.; CIHM, n° 41323.

Aux Citoyens et Habitants des Villes et Campagnes de la Province de Québec. Quebec: Brown, February 1785; CIHM, n° 20675.

Barthe, Joseph-Guillaume. *Le Canada reconquis par la France*. Paris: Ledoyen, 1855.

Beaudin, François. "Sermon de M. Lartigue, July 5, 1812." *Revue d'histoire de l'Amérique française* 22, no. 2 (1968): 303–5.

Béique, Caroline. *Quatre-vingt ans de souvenirs*. Montreal: Éditions Bernard Valiquette and Éditions de l'Action canadienne-Française, 1949.

Bellerive, Georges. *Conférences et discours de nos hommes politiques à l'étranger*. Quebec: Léger Brousseau, 1902.

Bernard, Pierre [dominicain Dominique-Ceslas Gonthier]. *Un manifeste libéral. M. L.-O. David et le clergé canadien*. Vol. II. Quebec: L. Brousseau, 1896.

Bibaud, Maximilien. *L'honorable L.A. Dessaulles*. Montreal: P. Cérat, 1862; CIHM, n° 32740.

– *Tableau historique des progrès matériels et spirituels du Canada*. Montreal: Cérat et Bourguignon, 1858.

Binan [Mgr Pierre-Adolphe Pinsoneault]. *Le Grand-Vicaire Raymond et le libéralisme catholique*. Montreal: le Franc-Parleur, 1873; CIHM, n° 25374.

Blain de Saint-Aubin, Emmanuel. *Quelques notes sur la littérature canadienne-française*. Montreal: E. Senécal, 1871.

[Blanchet, François]. *Appel au Parlement impérial et aux habitans des colonies angloises dans l'Amérique du Nord sur les prétentions exorbitantes du Gouvernement Exécutif et du Conseil législatif de la Province du Bas-Canada*. Quebec: imprimé par Flavien Vallerand, 1824.

Boucher-Belleville, Jean-Philippe. *Journal d'un Patriote (1837–1838)*. Montreal: Guérin, 1992.

[Boucher de la Bruère, Montarville]. *Réponses aux censeurs de la Confédération*. Saint-Hyacinthe, QC: imprimerie du Courrier de Saint-Hyacinthe, 1867; CIHM, n° 23412.

Bourget, Ignace, Mgr. "Pastoral After the Burial." In *History of the Guibord Case: Ultramontism Versus Law and Human Rights*, 120–7. Montreal: Witness Printing House, 1875.

Buies, Arthur. *Anglicismes et canadianismes.* Quebec: Darveau, 1888; CIHM, n° 336.

– *Chroniques II.* Critical Edition by Francis Parmentier. Montreal: Presses de l'Université de Montréal, 1993.

Casgrain, Henri-Raymond. "Le mouvement littéraire au Canada (1866)." In *Œuvres complètes.* Vol. I, 353–75. Montreal: C.-O. Beauchemin et fils, 1896.

Catalogue général de la librairie canadienne d'Édouard R. Fabre. Montreal: n.p., 1837.

Catalogue of Cary's Circulating Library, Quebec. Additions will be constantly made. Quebec: printed by T. Cary & Co., 1830.

Catalogue of English and French Books in the Montreal Library/Catalogue des livres françois et anglais dans la Bibliothèque de Montréal. Montreal: chez E. Edwards, [1797].

Catalogue of English and French Books in the Quebec Library [...]. Quebec, Printing at the New Printing Office, 1801.

Catalogue of English and French Books in the Quebec Library [...]. Quebec: printed by Samuel Neilson, [1792].

Catalogue of the English and French Books in the Quebec Library [...]. Quebec: Printing at the New Printing Office, 1808 [with addenda up to 1813].

Cauchon, Joseph. *Étude sur l'union projetée des provinces britanniques de l'Amérique du Nord.* Quebec: A. Côté, 1858; CIHM, n° 22672.

– *The Union of the Provinces of British North America.* Translated by George Henry Macaulay. Quebec: Hunter and Rose, 1865; CIHM, n° 32356.

Chapais, Thomas. *Les congrégations enseignantes et le brevet de capacité.* Quebec: Léger Brousseau, 1893.

[Chapman, Henry S.]. *An Impartial and Authentic Account of the Civil War in the Canadas.* London: n.p., 1838; CIHM, n°s 8240-8241.

Chapman, Henry S. *Canada.* n.p., (September 1835), [from the *Monthly Repository*]; CIHM, no 37322.

– *Progress of Events in Canada.* N.p., January 1837; CIHM, n° 28197.

– *Recent Occurences.* [London: T.C. Hansard], 1836.

– *What is the Result of the Canadian Election? Fully Answered.* Montreal, [from *The Daily Advertiser*], December 1834; CIHM, n° 21427 or n° 43720.

Chauveau, Pierre-Joseph-Olivier. *The Visit of His Royal Highness the Prince of Wales to America, reprinted from the Lower Canada Journal of Education.* Montreal: Eusèbe Sénécal, 1860.

[Cherrier, André-Romuald]. *Procès de Joseph N. Cardinal, par un étudiant en droit.* Montreal: J. Lovell, 1839.

Chevalier, Henry-Émile. "La langue française et la nationalité canadienne." *La Ruche littéraire* (mars 1859): 2–10.

– "La presse franco-américaine." *La Ruche littéraire* (mars 1859): 41–8.

Choquette, Charles-Philippe. *Histoire du Séminaire de Saint-Hyacinthe depuis sa fondation jusqu'à nos jours,* Montreal: Imprimerie des sourds-muets, 1911–12.

494 Sources and Studies

Christie, Robert. *A History of the Late Province of Quebec.* Vol. V and VI. Montreal: Richard Worthington, 1866.

Circé-Côté, Éva. *Chroniques d'Éva Circé-Côté: lumière sur la société québécoise, 1900– 1942,* edited by Andrée Lévesque. Montreal: Éditions du Remue-Ménage, 2011.

Clapin, Sylva. *La France transatlantique: Le Canada.* Paris: Plon, 1885; CIHM, n° 655.

Le cléricalisme au Canada I. Curés et bedeaux. Montreal: n.p., 1896.

Le cléricalisme au Canada II. Saintes comédies. Montreal: n.p., 1896.

Cloutier, Jean-Baptiste. *Pédagogie: conférence sur l'uniformité de l'enseignement, 9 octobre 1880.* Quebec: n.p., 1880; CIHM, n° 4145.

Constitution du Club Jacques-Cartier de Montréal. Montreal: Perrault, 1864.

Cour Supérieure. Montréal. Plaidoirie des avocats in RE Henriette Brown vs la Fabrique de Montréal. Montreal: Typographie de Louis Perrault, 1870; CIHM, n° 10538.

Crémazie, Octave. "Journal du siège de Paris." *Œuvres. II Prose.* Critical Edition by Odette Condemine, 117–269. Montreal: Editions du fleuve, 1989.

– *Œuvres complètes.* Montreal: Beauchemin et Valois, 1882.

– *Œuvres II.* Edited by Odette Condemine. Montreal: Éditions du fleuve, 1985, 1989.

Cuthbert, Ross. *An Apology of Great Britain in Allusion to a Pamphlet intitled Considérations etc par Un Canadien.* Quebec: J. Neilson, 1809; CIHM, n° 20924.

Dandurand, Raoul. *Les mémoires du sénateur Raoul Dandurand (1861–1942).* Edited by Marcel Hamelin. Quebec: Presses de l'Université Laval, 1967.

Darveau, Louis-Michel. *Nos hommes de lettres.* Montreal: A.A. Stevenson, 1873.

David, Laurent-Olivier. "Essai sur la littérature nationale." *Écho du Cabinet de lecture paroissial* (12 October 1861): 315–18.

– *Le clergé canadien, sa mission et son œuvre.* Montreal: n.p., 1896; CIHM, n° 2510.

de Lorimier, Chevalier. *Lettres d'un Patriote condamné à mort.* Préface de Pierre Falardeau. Montreal: Comeau et Nadeau, 1996.

Débats parlementaires sur la question de la Confédération des provinces de l'Amérique britannique du nord. Quebec: Hunter, Rose et Lemieux, 1865.

Decelles, Alfred-Duclos. Constitution et règlements du Club Cartier. Montreal: n.p., 1874; CIHM, n° 23970.

Défense du mandement de Mgr Lartigue. 1837, n.p.; CIHM, n° 39816.

Desjardins, Louis-Georges. *M. Laurier devant l'histoire. Les erreurs de son discours et les véritables principes du Parti conservateur.* Quebec: imprimerie du Canadien, 1877; CIHM, n° 24213.

Dessaulles, Henriette [Fadette]. *Journal.* Critical édition by Jean-Louis Major. Montreal: Presses de l'Université de Montréal, 1989.

Dessaulles, Louis-Antoine. "Affaire Guibord." In *Annuaire de l'Institut-Canadien pour 1869,* 7–50. Montreal: Perreault, 1869; CIHM, n° 404.

– *Dernière correspondance entre S.E. le Cardinal Barnabo et l'Hon. M. Dessaulles.* Montreal: imprimerie d'Alphonse Doutre et Cie, 1871; CIHM, n° 2972.

- *Écrits.* Edited by Yvan Lamonde. Montreal: Presses de l'Université de Montréal, 1994.
- *La grande guerre ecclésiastique. La Comédie infernale et les Noces d'or. La suprématie ecclésiastique sur l'ordre temporal.* Montreal: Alphonse Doutre, 1873; CIHM, n° 23883.
- *La guerre américaine, ses origines et ses causes.* Montreal: Le Pays, 1865; CIHM, n° 34768.
- "L'Index." In *Annuaire de l'Institut-Canadien pour 1869,* 51–136. Montreal: Perreault, 1869; CIHM, n° 404.
- *Six lectures sur l'annexion du Canada aux États-Unis.* Montreal: Pierre Gendron, 1851; CIHM, n° 35066.
- "[Sur la tolérance]." In *Annuaire de l'Institut-Canadien pour 1868,* 4–21. Montréal: Le Pays; CIHM, n° 404.
Dickens, Charles. *American Notes for General Circulation.* Edited and with introduction by John S. Whitley and Arnold Goldman. London: Penguin Books, 1972.
Dionne, Narcisse-Eutrope. *Les trois comédies du Statu Quo.* [1834]. Quebec: Typographie Laflamme et Proulx, 1909.
- *Vie de C.-F. Painchaud, fondateur du Collège de Sainte-Anne-de-la-Pocatière.* Quebec: L. Brousseau, 1894; CIHM, n° 2718.
Dorion, Jean-Baptiste-Éric. *L'Institut canadien en 1852,* Montreal: Rowen, 1852; CIHM, n° 37510.
Dougall, John. *History of the Guibord Case: Ultramontanism versus Law and Human Rights.* Montreal: Witness Printing House, 1875; CIHM, n° 5643.
Doughty, Arthur G., ed. *The Elgin-Grey Papers, 1846–1852.* 4 vols. Ottawa: J.O. Patenaude, I.S.O., Printer to the King, 1937.
Doughty, Arthur G., and Duncan A. McArthur, eds. *Documents Relating to the Constitutional History of Canada.* Vol. II, *1791–1818.* Ottawa: Printed by C.H. Parmelee, 1914.
Doutre, Gonzalve. *Le principe des nationalités.* Montreal: Le Pays, 1864; CIHM, n° 34769.
Dray, Charles Dewey. *Address Delivered at the Provincial Industrial Exhibition.* Montreal: Rollo Campbell, 1850.
Dumesnil, Clément. *De l'abolition des droits féodaux au Canada.* Montreal: Starke, 1849; CIHM, n° 34625.
Dumont, Georges A. Constitution du Club Letellier adoptée le 15 janvier 1890. Montreal: G.A. et W. Dumont, 1890; CIHM, n° 688.
Ellice, Jane. *The Diary of Jane Ellice.* Edited by Patricia Godsell. Ottawa: Oberon Press, 1975.
Fabre, Hector. "On Canadian Literature." *Transactions of the Quebec Literary and Historical Society* (1865–1866): 85–102.
- "La société française au Canada." *La Réforme sociale* (August 15 1886): 183–96.

Filiatreault, Aristide. *Ruines cléricales.* Préface de Joseph Doutre. Montreal: A. Filiatreault, 1893; reprinted Montreal: Leméac, 1978; CIHM, n° 12782.

Fleming, John. *Some Considerations on this Question; wether the British Government Acted Wisely in Granting to Canada her Present Constitution.* Montreal: J. Brown, 1810; CIHM, n° 29286.

Fourth Report of The Standing Committee of Grievances made to the Assembly of Lower Canada Respecting the Conduct of Lord Aylmer, British Parliamentary Papers, 419–29. Shannon: Irish University Press, 1969, Colonies, Canada 7, Sessions 1833–1836.

Fréchette, Louis. *Satires et polémiques.* Vol. 1 and 2. Critical Edition by Jacques Blais, Guy Champagne, and Luc Bouvier. Montreal: Presses de l'Université de Montréal, 1993.

Gagnon, Ernest. *Le Comte de Paris à Québec.* Quebec: C. Darveau, 1891; CIHM, n° 3277.

Galt, Alexander Tilloch. *Civil Liberty in Lower Canada.* Montreal: Bentley, 1876; CIHM, n° 24095.

Garneau, François-Xavier. "Une conclusion d'histoire." *Revue canadienne* (1864): 422–4.

Gauldrée-Boilleau, Charles-Henri-Philippe. "Le paysan de Saint-Irénée." In *Paysans et ouvriers québécois d'autrefois,* edited by Pierre Savard, 19–76. Quebec: Presses de l'Université Laval, 1968.

Gérin-Lajoie, Antoine. "Bibliothèques publiques. Leur importance." In *Antoine Gérin-Lajoie. Homme de lettres,* edited by René Dionne, 367–77. Sherbrooke, QC: Naaman, 1978.

– "Éloge de l'Honorable Rémi Vallières de Saint-Réal." In *Antoine Gérin-Lajoie, homme de lettres,* edited by René Dionne, 356–67. Sherbrooke, QC: Naaman, 1978.

Girod, Armury. "Journal tenu par feu Amury Girod." *Report of the Public Archives of Canada for 1923,* 408–19. Ottawa: F.-A. Acland, King's Printer, 1926.

Gosselin, Paul-Eugène. *Étienne Parent.* Montreal: Fides, 1964.

Grand Séminaire de Montréal. Album du centenaire. Montreal: Association des Anciens, 1940.

Grandfort, Manoël de. *L'Autre Monde.* Paris: La Librairie nouvelle, 1855.

Gray, Hugh. *Letters from Canada.* London: Printed for Longman, Hurst, Lees, and Orme, 1809; CIHM, n° 35926.

Grisé, Yolande, and Jeanne d'Arc Lortie. *Textes poétiques du Canada français, 1606–1867.* Montreal: Fides, 1990.

– *Textes poétiques du Canada français.* Vol. III, *1827–1837.* Montreal: Fides, 1990.

– *Textes poétiques du Canada français.* Vol. IV, *1838–1849.* Montreal: Fides, 1991.

– *Textes poétiques du Canada français.* Vol. V, *1850–1855.* Montreal: Fides, 1992.

Guénard, A. [Albert Lefaivre]. *Conférence sur la littérature canadienne.* Versailles: Bernard, 1877; Saint-Jacques, QC: Éditions du pot de fer, 1992; CIHM, n° 24209.

– *La France canadienne. La question religieuse, les races française et anglo-saxonne.* Paris: Douniol, 1877; CIHM, n° 8665.

Henry, John [Camillus]. *An Enquiry into the Evils of General Suffrage and Frequent Elections in Lower Canada.* Montreal: Nahum Mower, 1810; CIHM, n° 57284.

Howell, Ronald F. "The Political Testament of Papineau in Exile, 1837." *Canadian Historical Review* 38, no. 4 (1957): 295–9.

[Huot, Louis-Herménégilde]. *Le Rougisme en Canada* (1864), reprinted in *les Écrits du Canada français* 34 (1972):181–252; CIHM, n° 39131.

In memoriam. Sir A.A. Dorion. Hommage du journal La Patrie. Montreal: La Patrie, 1891; CIHM, n° 4480.

Journal de MM. Baby, Taschereau et Williams. Quebec: Aegidius Fauteux, 1929.

Journals of the Continental Congress, 1774–1789. Edited from the original records in the Library of Congress by Worthington Chauncey Ford, Chief, Division of Manuscripts, 1906.

Jousselin, Stéphane. *Yankees fin de siècle.* Paris: J. Ollendorf, 1892.

Kennedy, William Paul McClure, ed. *Documents of the Canadian Constitution.* Toronto: Oxford University Press, 1918.

– *Documents of the Canadian Constitution, 1759–1915.* Toronto: Oxford University Press, 1943.

– *Statutes, Treatises and Documents of the Canadian Constitution (1713–1929).* 2nd ed. Toronto: Oxford University Press, 1930.

Laflèche, Louis-François Mgr. *Des biens temporels de l'Église et de l'immunité de ces biens devant les pouvoirs civils.* Trois-Rivières, QC: n.p., 1889; CIHM, n° 8283.

– *L'influence spirituelle indue devant la liberté religieuse et civile.* Trois-Rivières, QC: Typographie du Journal des Trois-Rivières, 1881; CIHM, n° 8579.

– *Lettre pastorale de [...] concernant les dangers auxquels la foi des catholiques est exposée en ce pays.* Trois-Rivières, QC: P.V. Ayotte, 1895; CIHM, n° 54694.

– *Quelques considérations sur les rapports de la société civile avec la religion et la famille.* Montreal: Eusèbe Senécal, 1866.

Lafontaine, J.-L. *L'Institut canadien en 1855.* Montreal: Senécal et Daniel, 1855; CIHM, n° 45468.

Lambton, John George (Earl of Durham). *Lord Durham's Report: An Abridgement of* Report on the Affairs of British North America. Edited by G.M. Craig. Introductions by G.M. Craig and Janet Ajzenstat. Afterword by Guy Laforest. Montreal and Kingston: McGill-Queen's University Press, 2007.

Lambert, John. *Travels Through Lower Canada...* London: Printed for C. Cradock and W. Joy, 1813; CIHM, n° 36170.

Lamennais, Félicité Robert de. *Words of a Believer.* New York: Charles de Behr, 1834.

Lamonde, Yvan, and Pierre Nolin. "Des documents cruciaux du débat libéral-ultramontain: les lettres (1862) de Mgr Bourget au journal *Le Pays.*" *Littératures* 3 (1989): 115–204.

Lamonde, Yvan, and Sylvain Simard. *Inventaire chronologique et analytique d'une correspondance de Louis-Antoine Dessaulles (1817–1895)*. Montreal: Bibliothèque nationale du Québec, 1978.

Laurier, Wilfrid. *Wilfrid Laurier on the platform; collection of the principal speeches made in parliament or before the people by the Honorable Wilfrid Laurier, member for Quebec-East in the Commons, since his entry into active politics in 1871*, compiled by Ulric Barthe, 51–80. Quebec: Turcotte & Menard's Steam Printing Office, 1890.

Lebrun, Isidore. *Tableau statistique et politique des deux Canadas*. Paris: Treuttel et Würtz, 1833.

Legendre, Napoléon. *La langue française au Canada*. Quebec: Darveau, 1890; CIHM, n° 4769.

Lenoir, Joseph. *Œuvres*. Critical Edition by John Hare and Jeanne d'Arc Lortie. Montreal: Presses de l'Université de Montréal, 1988.

Lettre addressee aux Habitants de la Province de Québec, ci-devant le Canada de la part du Congrès general de l'Amérique septentrionale tenu à Philadelphie, imprimé et publié par Ordre du Congrès, à Philadelphie, de l'imprimerie de Fleury Mesplet. MDCCLXXIV; CIHM, n° 36657.

Lettre de Mgr de Léon aux ecclésiastiques français réfugiés en Angleterre. Quebec: John Neilson, 1793; reprinted in *Les Écrits du Canada français* 30 (1970): 207–22.

Lettre de Mgr Laflèche à son Éminence le cardinal NN établissant la nécessité d'une enquête sur les difficultés religieuses en Canada: Trois-Rivières, QC: n.p., 1882; CIHM, n° 4525.

"Lettre d'un curé du Canada [Fournier]." *Bulletin des recherches historiques* 17, no. 1 (1911): 3–15.

Lettres pastorales, mandements et circulaires des évêques de Trois-Rivières, Trois-Rivières, QC: Ayotte, 1867–1898.

Le libéralisme dans la province de Québec. n.p., 1897; CIHM, n° 11819.

Luigi [abbé Alexis Pelletier]. *Coup d'œil sur le libéralisme européen et sur le libéralisme canadien. Démonstration de leur parfaite identité*. Montreal: le Franc-Parleur, 1876; CIHM, n° 4851.

– *Le Don Quichotte montréalais sur sa rossinante ou M. Dessaulles et La grande guerre ecclésiastique*. Montreal: publié par la Société des écrivains catholiques, 1873; CIHM, n° 23881.

– *Du modérantisme ou de la fausse moderation*. Montreal: le Franc-Parleur, 1873; CIHM, n° 23882.

– *Il y a du libéralisme et du gallicanisme en Canada*. Montreal: le Franc-Parleur, 1873; CIHM, n° 23875.

[Lusignan, Alphonse]. *La Confédération, couronnement de dix années de mauvaise administration*. Reprinted in *les Écrits du Canada français* 31 (1971): 173–247; CIHM, n° 23425.

Lusignan, Alphonse. Fautes à corriger. Une chaque jour. Quebec: Darveau, 1890; CIHM, n° 7727.

[Maguire, Thomas]. *Doctrine de l'Église d'Irlande et de celle du Canada sur la révolte.* Quebec: W. Neilson, 1838; CIHM, n° 38864.

Mandements, lettres pastorales, circulaires de Mgr Jean Langevin et statuts synodaux du diocèse de Rimouski, Rimouski: A.G. Dion, 1867-1889.

Mandements, lettres pastorales et circulaires des évêques de Chicoutimi, Chicoutimi : n.p., 1892.

Mandements, lettres pastorales et circulaires des évêques de Québec, Quebec: H. Tétu et C.-O. Gagnon, 1888; Taschereau, nouvelle série, Quebec: A. Côté, 1893.

Mandements, lettres pastorales et circulaires des évêques de Saint-Hyacinthe, Montreal: C. Beauchemin, 1888-1940.

Mandements, lettres pastorales, circulaires et autres documents publiés dans le diocèse de Montréal depuis son érection, Montreal: Chapleau et fils, 1869-1952.

Manifeste du Club national démocratique. Montreal: des presses de L'Avenir, 1849; CIHM, n° 22164.

Marchand, Joséphine. *Journal intime, 1879-1900.* Montreal: éditions de la pleine lune, 2000.

[Marcil, J.-N.]. *La Grande cause ecclésiastique. Le Canada-Revue vs Mgr E.-C. Fabre. Procédure, pièces du dossier, plaidoyers des avocats.* Montreal: John Lovell, 1894.

Marmier, Xavier. *Lettres sur l'Amérique.* Vol. I. Paris: A. Bertrand, 1851.

Masson, Philippe. *Le Canada français et la Providence.* Quebec: Léger Brousseau, 1875; CIHM, n° 24053.

McInnis, Edgar. "A Letter from Alexis de Tocqueville on the Rebellion of 1837." *Canadian Historical Review* 19 (1938): 394-7.

Mémoire de l'évêque des Trois-Rivières sur les difficultés religieuses en Canada. Trois-Rivières, QC: G. Désilets, 1882; CIHM, n° 11617.

Mercier, Honoré. *L'avenir du Canada.* Montreal: imprimerie Gebhardt-Berthiaume, 1893; CIHM, n° 9875.

Mill, John Stuart. "Radical Party and Canada: Lord Durham and the Canadians" (January 1838). In *Collected Works of John Stuart Mill.* Vol. VI, edited by John Robson. Toronto: University of Toronto Press; London: Routlegde and Kegan Paul, 1982.

Mirari vos: On Liberalism and Religious Indifferentism. Encyclical of Pope Gregory XVI. 15 August 1832. http://www.papalencyclicals.net/Greg16/g16mirar.htm.

Montreal in 1856, a Sketch for the Celebration of the Opening of the Grand Trunk Railway of Canada... Montreal: Lovell, 1856.

[Mousseau, Joseph-Alfred]. *Contre-poison. La Confédération c'est le salut du Bas-Canada.* Reprinted in *les Écrits du Canada français* 32 (1971): 171-253; CIHM, n° 23423.

Sources and Studies

Nelson, Wolfred. *Écrits d'un Patriote*. Edited by Georges Aubin. Montreal: Comeau et Nadeau, 1998.
Noces d'or de Mgr l'évêque de Montréal. Compte rendu des fêtes du 29 octobre [...]. Montreal: Le Nouveau Monde, 1872; CIHM, n° 23799.
Nouvelle Constitution du Canada. Ottawa: Le Canada, 1867; CIHM, n° 23496.
Ouellet, Richard, and Jean-Pierre Therrien. *L'invasion du Canada par les Bastonnois. "Journal de M. Sanguinet."* Quebec: Éditeur officiel du Québec, 1975; CIHM n° 51826.
Papineau, Amédée. *Journal d'un Fils de la Liberté...* Montreal: Réédition-Québec, 1972.
– *Souvenirs de jeunesse (1827–1837)*. Edited, introduction, and notes by Georges Aubin. Quebec: Septentrion, 1998.
Papineau, Julie. *Une femme patriote. Correspondance, 1823–1862*. Edited, Introduction, and Notes by Renée Blanchet. Sillery, QC: Septentrion, 1997.
Papineau, Louis-Joseph. *Address of the Honorable L.J. Papineau to the Electors of the West Ward of Montreal*. 3 December 1834. Montreal: Fabre et Perrault, CIHM, n°. 21431.
– *Un demi-siècle de combats. Interventions publiques*. Texts selection and presentation by Yvan Lamonde and Claude Larin. Montreal: Fides, 1998.
– *Histoire de l'insurrection du Canada en réfutation du rapport de Lord Durham* (1839). In Louis-Joseph Papineau, *Un demi-siècle*, 506–27.
– *Lettres à Julie (1820–1862)*. Text and Notes by Georges Aubin and Renée Blanchet. Introduction by Yvan Lamonde. Sillery, QC: Septentrion and Archives nationales du Québec, 2000.
– "Observations de MM. L.-J. Papineau et John Neilson sur le projet de réunir les législatures du Haut et du Bas-Canada." In *Cours d'histoire du Canada* by Thomas Chapais. Vol. III: 263–82 and in Louis-Joseph Papineau, *Un demi-siècle de combats. Interventions publiques*. Text Selection and Presentation by Yvan Lamonde and Claude Larin, Montreal: Fides, 1998, 54–71; CIHM, n° 38546.
– *Observations sur la réponse de Mathew Lord Aylmer à la députation du Tattersall et sur le discours du Très Honorable E.G. Stanley [...] sur les affaires du Canada le 15 avril 1834*. Montreal: n.p., juillet 1834; CIHM, n° 39135.
– *Procédés de l'assemblée des Électeurs du Comté de Montréal, tenue à Saint-Laurent, 15 mai*; CIHM, n° 21619.
– *Speech of Louis J. Papineau on the Hustings, at the Opening of the Election for the West Ward of the City of Montreal...* Montreal: printed by Ludger Duvernay, 1827; CIHM, n° 39126.
– *To the Honorable the Knights, Citizens, and Burgesses, the Commons of United Kingdom of Great Britain and Ireland, in Parliament assembled*, 1 March 1834, n.p.; CIHM, n° 62050.

Papineau, Louis-Joseph, and John Neilson. *Letter from L. J. Papineau and J. Neilson, Esqs., Addressed to His Majesty's Under Secretary of State on the Subject of the Proposed Union of the Provinces of Upper and Lower Canada.* 10 May 1823. *JHALC,* 1825, Appendix K.

Papineau-Dessaulles, Rosalie. *Correspondance 1805–1854.* Edited, presented, and annotated by Georges Aubin and Renée Blanchet. Montreal: Les Éditions Varia, 2001.

Pâquet, Benjamin. *Le libéralisme.* Quebec: de l'imprimerie du Canadien, 1872; CIHM, n° 64193.

Paquin, Jacques. "Journal historique des événemens arrivés à Saint-Eustache pendant la rébellion du comté du Lac des Deux-Montagnes." Rprt in *La rébellion de 1837 à Saint-Eustache* by Maximilien Globensky. Presentation by Hubert Aquin. Montreal: Éditions du Jour, 1974.

Paquin, Louis-Philibert. *Conférences sur l'instruction obligatoire faites au Cercle catholique de Québec.* Quebec: imprimerie du Canadien, 1881; CIHM, n° 11625.

Parent, Étienne. *Discours.* Edited by Claude Couture and Yvan Lamonde. Montreal: Presses de l'Université de Montréal, 2000.

– *Étienne Parent (1802–1874).* Texts selection by Jean-Charles Falardeau. Montreal: Éditions La Presse, 1975.

Pavie, Théodore. *Souvenirs atlantiques. Voyage aux États-Unis et au Canada.* Vol. I. Paris: Bossange, 1832.

Pelland, Joseph-Octave. *Biographie, discours, conférences de Mercier.* Montreal: n.p., 1890.

"Pétitions des citoyens de Québec et de Montréal." In *Rapport du Comité Choisi pour s'enquérir sur le gouvernement civil du Canada.* Quebec: réimprimé par ordre de la Chambre d'Assemblée, Neilson et Cowan, 1828, appendix; original english text in *British Parliamentary Papers:* Colonies, Canada 1, Sessions 1828–1837, Shannon: Irish University Press, 1966.

Petitions from the Old and New Subjects, Inhabitants of the Province of Quebec to the Honorable the House of Commons. London: n.p., 1790; CIHM, n° 49532.

Pinsoneault, Pierre-Adolphe, Mgr. *Lettres à un député.* Montreal: le Franc-Parleur, 1874; CIHM, n° 23978.

Plessis, Joseph-Octave, Mgr. *Discours à l'occasion de la victoire remportée par les forces navales de Sa Majesté britannique…* 10 janvier 1799, CIHM n° 20857 or *Les Écrits du Canada français* 30 (1970): 191–254.

– *Journal d'un voyage en Europe.* Edited by Mgr Henri Têtu. Quebec: Pineau et Kérouac, libraires-éditeurs, 1903.

Précis des débats de la Chambre d'Assemblée, état de la Province. Quebec: n.p., 1834; CIHM, n° 46690.

Prieur, François-Xavier. *Notes d'un condamné politique de 1838,* reprinted with *Journal d'un exilé politique aux terres australes de Léandre Ducharme.* Montreal: Éditions du Jour, 1974.

Procès politique : la reine vs Jalbert. Montreal: F. Cinq-Mars, 1839; CIHM, n° 12810.

Propagande anti-cléricale. Première série. Les hommes noirs. Montreal: n.p., 1896.

Proulx, Jean-Baptiste. *Dans la ville éternelle...: journal de voyage.* Montreal: Granger Frères, 1897; CIHM, n° 12238.

– *Documents pour servir à l'intelligence de la question des écoles du Manitoba.* Rome: imprimerie Befani, 1896; CIHM, n° 30463.

[Proulx, Louis]. *Défense de la Religion et du Sacerdoce, ou Réponse à la Presse Socialiste.* Quebec: n.p., 1850; CIHM, n° 37809.

Rameau de Saint-Père, François-Edmé. *La France aux colonies.* Paris: Jouby, 1859.

– *Les Français en Amérique. Acadiens et Canadiens.* Paris: Jouby, 1859.

Rapport de l'archiviste de la province de Québec: 1925–1926: Inventaire des documents relatifs aux événements de 1837–1838; 1926–1927: Papiers Duvernay; 1927–1928 and 1928–1929: correspondance de Mgr Plessis; 1929–1930: Journal de la tournée faite par MM Baby, Taschereau et Williams, 1776–1777; 1932–1933: lettres reçues de Mgr Plessis, 1792–1831; 1942–1943: inventaire de la correspondance de Mgr Lartigue, 1827–1833.

Rapport du Surintendant de l'instruction publique, 1855.

Rapports judiciaires de Québec. Vol. III, 1877.

Raymond, Joseph-Sabin. *Discours sur l'action de Marie dans la société, prononcé à l'Union catholique de Saint-Hyacinthe, 8 décembre 1872.* Quebec: Ovide Fréchette, 1873; CIHM, n° 9982.

– *Discours sur la tolérance.* Montreal: typographie Le Nouveau Monde, 1869.

Relation du voyage de son Altesse royale le Prince de Galles en Amérique... Translation by Joseph Lenoir. Montreal: Eusèbe Senécal, 1860.

Report of the State Trials. 2 vols. Montreal: Armour and Ramsay, 1839.

The Reports of the Royal Commissioners Appointed to Enquire into the State of Canada, [Gosford Report]. Quebec: Thomas Cary, 1837; CIHM, n° 61771.

Reports of the Supreme Court of Canada. Vol. I, 1877.

Réticius, Brother. *Réponse aux cinq lettres du R.M. Verreau.* Montreal: n.p., 1881; CIHM, n° 12425.

Rinfret, Raoul. *Dictionnaire de nos fautes contre la langue française.* Montreal: Cadieux et Derome, 1896; CIHM, n° 12486.

Roebuck, Arthur H. *Existing Difficulties in the Government of the Canadas.* London: printed by C. and W. Reynell, 1836; CIHM, n° 21521.

– *The Canadas and Their Grievances,* n.p., 1835, [from the *London Review,* July 1835]; CIHM, n° 21566.

Royal. Joseph. *La crise actuelle. Le Canada république ou colonie.* Montreal: Senécal, 1894; CIHM, n° 12732.

Sabrevois de Bleury, Charles-Clément. *Réfutation de l'écrit de Louis[-]Joseph Papineau [...] intitulé Histoire de l'insurrection du Canada [...].* Montreal: Imprimerie de John Lovell, October 1839; CIHM, n° 21719.

Savaète, Arthur. *Voix canadiennes: vers l'abîme.* Vol. VIII. Paris: n.p., 1913.

"Sermon prêché à la cathédrale de Québec par Mgr Plessis." 6 April 1815. *Bulletin des recherches historiques* 35 (1929): 161–9.

Sermon prêché par l'Évêque catholique de Québec dans sa cathédrale le IVᵉ dimanche du Carême, 1ᵉʳ avril 1810, À la suite de la Proclamation de Son Excellence le Gouverneur en Chef, du 21ᵉ mars même année. Quebec: imprimé à la Nouvelle-Imprimerie, 1810; CIHM, n° 53687.

Sewell, Jonathan. *A Plan for the Federal Union of the British Provinces in North America.* London: Printed by W. Clowes, [1814?]; ICMH, n° 21154.

Shortt, Adam, and Arthur G. Doughty, eds. *Documents Relating to the Constitutional History of Canada.* Vol. I, *1759–1791.* Ottawa: Printed by S.E. Dawson, 1907.

Singulari nos: On the Errors of Lamennais. Encyclical of Pope Gregory XVI. 25 June 1834. http://www.papalencyclicals.net/Greg16/g16singu.htm.

Stuart, James. *Observations on the Proposed Union of the Provinces of Upper and Lower Canada [...],* [6 June 1823]. London: printed by William Clowes, 1824.

Sulte, Benjamin. *Le Canada en Europe.* Montreal: Senécal, 1873; CIHM n° 23868.

Taché, Joseph-Charles. *Esquisse sur le Canada considéré sous le point de vue économiste.* Paris: Hector Bossange, 1855.

– *Des provinces de l'Amérique du nord et d'une union fédérale.* Quebec: Des presses à vapeur de J.-T. Brousseau, 1858; CIHM, n° 22742.

– *Sketch of Canada, Its Industrial Conditions and Resources.* Paris: Hector Bossange, 1855.

– *The Union of the Provinces of British North America.* Translated by George Henry Macaulay. Quebec: Hunter, Rose and Co., 1865; CIHM, n° 32355.

Tardivel, Jules-Paul. *L'anglicisme, voilà l'ennemi!* Quebec: Le Canadien, 1880; CIHM, n° 24458.

– *Mélanges.* Vol. I and III. Quebec: imprimerie de La Vérité, 1887, 1903.

– *Notes de voyages.* Montreal: Senécal et fils, 1890.

– *Pour la patrie.* Presentation by John Hare. Montreal: Hurtubise HMH, 1975.

– "Le travail du dimanche." *Mélanges.* Vol. I, 95–108. Quebec: imprimerie de La Vérité. 1887.

Tarte, Joseph-Israël. *Le clergé, ses droits, nos devoirs.* Quebec: de l'imprimerie de L.J. Demers, 1880; CIHM, n° 24642.

Taschereau, Alexandre-Elzéar Mgr. *Remarques sur le mémoire de l'évêque de Trois-Rivières sur les difficultés religieuses en Canada.* Quebec: n.p., 1882; CIHM, n° 24469.

Thoreau, Henry David. *A Yankee in Canada.* Montreal: Harvest House, 1961.

Trudel, François-Xavier-Anselme. Mémoire sur la question de la fusion des sociétés littéraires et scientifiques de Montréal. Montreal: E. Senécal, 1869; CIHM, n° 14789.

Un Canadien [D.-B. Viger]. "Analyse d'un entretien ..." (1809). *Les Écrits du Canada français* 40 (1976): 215–34.

Un catholique [abbé Alexis Pelletier]. *La source du mal de l'époque au Canada.* n.p., 1881; CIHM, n° 9832.

"Un Mémoire de Henry Mézière." *Bulletin des recherches historiques* 37, no. 4 (1931): 193–201.

Vallée, Jacques. *Tocqueville au Bas-Canada*. Montreal: Éditions du Jour, 1973.

Viger, Denis-Benjamin. *Considérations relatives à la dernière révolution de la Belgique*. Montreal: Printed by F. Cinq-Mars, 1831; CIHM, n° 32389.

[Viger Denis-Benjamin]. *Considérations sur les effets qu'ont produits en Canada, la conservation des établissemens du pays, les mœurs, l'éducation, etc de ses habitans, et les conséquences qu'entraineroient leur décadence par rapport aux intérêts de la Grande-Bretagne*. Quebec: James Brown, 1809; CIHM, n° 20923.

Viger, Denis-Benjamin. *Mémoires relatifs à l'emprisonnement de l'honorable D.-B. Viger*. Montreal: F. Cinq-Mars, 1840.

Vigny, Alfred de. "Les Français du Canada." In *Xavier Marmier et le Canada*, edited by Jean Ménard, 179–88. Quebec: Presses de l'Université Laval, 1967.

Villeneuve, Arthur. *Étude sur le mal révolutionnaire en Canada. Humble recours au Saint-Siège*. Paris: Plon; CIHM, n° 2078.

Vindex [Thomas Maguire]. *Le clergé canadien vengé par ses ennemis…* Québec: Neilson et Cowan, 1833.

Voyage de Mgr le Comte de Paris et de Mgr le Duc d'Orléans aux États-Unis et au Canada. Paris: Librairie nationale, 1891; CIHM, n° 33485.

Wright, Robert. *The Life of Major-General James Wolfe*. London: Chapman and Hall, 1864.

SECONDARY SOURCES

Ajzenstat, Janet. "Canada's First Constitution: Pierre Bédard on Tolerance and Dissent." *Canadian Journal of Political Science / Revue canadienne de Science politique* 23, no. 1 (March 1990): 40–57.

Angenot, Marc. "Le roman français dans la bibliothèque de l'Institut canadien de Montréal (1845–1876)." *Littératures* 1 (1988): 77–90.

Aubin, Georges. "Chronique des patriotes de 1837–1838." *Bulletin d'histoire politique* 5, no. 3 (Summer 1997): 109–13.

Audet, Louis-Philippe. "Épisode scolaire de la lutte ultramontaine à Montréal." *Cahiers des Dix* 39 (1974): 9–43.

– *Histoire de l'enseignement au Québec*. 2 vols. Montreal: Holt, Rinehart et Winston, 1971.

– *Histoire du Conseil de l'instruction publique de la province de Québec (1856–1964)*. Montreal: Leméac, 1964.

– "Le Québec à l'Exposition internationale de Paris en 1878." *Cahiers des Dix* 32 (1967): 125–55.

– *Le système scolaire de la Province de Québec*. Vol. III. Quebec: Les Presses universitaires Laval, 1952.

Audet, Louis-Philippe, and Armand Gauthier. *Le système scolaire du Québec.* Montreal: Beauchemin, 1969.

Babe, Robert E. "Sise, Charles Fleetford." www.biographi.ca.

Bannister, Jerry. "Canada as Counter-Revolution: The Loyalist Order Framework in Canadian History." In *Liberalism and Hegemony*, edited by Jean-François Constant and Michel Ducharme, 98–146. Toronto: University of Toronto Press, 2009.

Barrière, Mireille. "Montréal, microcosme du théâtre lyrique nord-américain (1893–1913)." In *Québécois et Américains*, edited by Gérard Bouchard and Yvan Lamonde, 369–85. Montreal: Fides, 1995.

– "La société canadienne-française et le théâtre lyrique à Montréal entre 1840 et 1913." PhD thesis, Université Laval, QC, 1990.

Beauchamp, Claude. "Henry-Émile Chevalier et le feuilleton canadien-français (1853–1860)." MA thesis, McGill University, Montreal, 1992.

Beaudoin, Réjean. *Naissance d'une littérature. Essai sur le messianisme et les débuts de la littérature canadienne-française (1850–1890).* Montreal: Boréal, 1989.

Beaulieu, André, and Jean Hamelin. "Aperçu sur le journalisme québécois d'expression française." *Recherches sociographiques* 7, no. 3 (1966): 305–48.

– *La presse québécoise des origines à nos jours.* Vol. I, *1764–1959.* Quebec: Presses de l'Université Laval, 1973.

Bédard, Éric. *Les Réformistes. Une génération canadienne-française au milieu du XIXᵉ siècle.* Montreal: Boréal, 2009.

Bélanger, Noël. "Une introduction au problème de l'influence indue, illustrée par la contestation de l'élection de 1876 dans le comté de Charlevoix." MA thesis, Université Laval, Québec, 1960.

– "Langevin, Jean." www.biographi.ca.

Bélanger, Réal. "Le nationalisme ultramontain: le cas de Jules-Paul Tardivel." In *Les ultramontains. Études d'histoire religieuse présentées en hommage au professeur Philippe Sylvain*, edited by Nive Voisine and Jean Hamelin, 267–303. Montreal: Boréal.

– *Wilfrid Laurier. Quand la politique devient passion.* Montreal: Entreprises Radio-Canada; Quebec: Presses de l'Université Laval, 1986.

Bellavance, Marcel. *Le Québec et la Confédération: Un choix libre?* Sillery, QC: Éditions du Septentrion, 1992.

Berger, Carl. *Honour and Search for Influence: A History of the Royal Society of Canada.* Toronto: University of Toronto Press, 1996.

Bernard, Jean-Paul. *Assemblées publiques, résolutions et déclarations de 1837–1838.* Montreal: vlb éditeur, 1988.

– "Boucher de la Bruère, Pierre." www.biographi.ca.

– "La fonction intellectuelle de Saint-Hyacinthe à la veille de la Confédération." *Sessions d'études.* Société canadienne d'histoire de l'Église catholique, 47 (1980): 5–17.

– *Les rébellions de 1837–1838.* Montreal: Boréal Express, 1983.
– *The Rebellions of 1837 and 1838 in Lower Canada.* Ottawa: Canadian Historical Association, 1996.
– *Les Rouges : Libéralisme, nationalisme et anticléricalisme au milieu du xixe siècle.* Montreal: Presses de l'Université du Québec, 1971.
– "Vermonters and the Lower Canadian Rebellions of 1837–1838." *Vermont History* 58, no. 4 (1990): 250–63.
Bernatchez, Ginette. "La Société littéraire et historique de Québec (The Quebec Literary and Historical Society), 1824–1900." *Revue d'histoire de l'Amérique française* 35, no. 2 (September 1981): 179–92.
Bernier, François. "Étude analytique et critique de la controverse sur la question de la 'fuite' de Papineau de Saint-Denis le 23 novembre 1837." MA thesis, Université de Montréal, 1986.
Bernier, Jacques. "Blanchet, François." www.biographi.ca.
Bindon, Kathryn M. "Thom, Adam." www.biographi.ca.
Bolduc, Marc. "Les élections générales de 1834 (Bas-Canada) et les élections générales de 1841 (ancien Bas-Canada): continuités et ruptures." MA thesis, Université du Québec à Montréal, 1997.
Bonenfant, Jean-Charles. "Les idées politiques de George-Étienne Cartier." In *Les idées politiques des premiers ministres du Canada / The Political Ideas of the Prime Ministers of Canada*, edited by Marcel Hamelin, 31–50. Ottawa: Éditions de l'Université d'Ottawa, 1969.
– *La naissance de la Confédération.* Montreal: les Éditions Leméac, 1969.
Bossé, Éveline. *"La Capricieuse" à Québec en 1855.* Montreal: La Presse, 1984.
Bouchard, Gérard. "Évolution de l'alphabétisation au Saguenay: les variables géographiques (1842–1971)." *Historical Papers / Communications historiques* (1989): 13–35.
– "Nouvelle mesure de l'alphabétisation à l'aide de la reconstitution automatique des familles." *Histoire sociale / Social History* 22, no. 43 (May 1989): 91–119.
Boucher de la Bruère, Montarville. "Louis-Joseph Papineau, de Saint-Denis à Paris." *Cahiers des Dix* 5 (1940): 79–106.
– "La Société Aide-toi et le ciel t'aidera." *Bulletin des recherches historiques* 34, no. 2 (February 1928): 107–11.
Boulianne, Réal G. "The French Canadians and the Schools of the Royal Institution for the Advancement of Learning (1820–1829)." *Histoire sociale / Social History* 5, no. 10 (1972): 144–63.
Bourassa, Paul. "Regards sur la ressemblance: le portrait au Bas-Canada." In *La peinture au Québec (1820–1850)*, edited by Mario Béland, 36–49. Quebec: Musée du Québec / Les Publications du Québec, 1991.
Brassard, Michèle, and Jean Hamelin. "Filiatreault, Aristide." www.biographi.ca.
– "Gonthier, Dominique-Ceslas." www.biographi.ca.

Bruchési, Jean. "Les correspondants canadiens de Rameau de Saint-Père." *Cahiers des Dix* 14 (1949): 87–114.

Brunet, Manon. "Documents pour une histoire de l'édition au Québec avant 1900." MA thesis, Université de Montréal, 1979.

Brunet, Michel. *Les Canadiens après la Conquête, 1759 à 1775: de la révolution canadienne à la révolution américaine.* Montreal: Fides, 1969.

– *La présence anglaise et les Canadiens. Études sur l'histoire et la pensée des deux Canadas.* Montreal: Beauchemin, 1964.

– "La Révolution française sur les rives du Saint-Laurent." *Revue d'histoire de l'Amérique française* 11, no. 2 (September 1957): 158–62.

Brunn, Denis. "Les Canadiens français et les nouvelles de l'Europe: le cas des révolutions de 1848-1849." PhD thesis, Université de Paris I, 1978.

Buckner, Phillip. *The Transition to Responsible Government. British Policy in British North America (1815–1850).* Westport, CT: Greenwood Press, 1985.

Buono, Yolande. "Imprimerie et diffusion de l'imprimé à Montréal (1776–1820)." MA thesis, Université de Montréal, 1980.

Burger, Baudoin. *L'activité théâtrale au Québec (1765–1825).* Montreal: Parti pris, 1974.

Burroughs, Peter. *British Attitudes Towards Canada (1822–1849).* Scarborough, ON: Prentice-Hall, 1971.

– *The Canadian Crisis and British Colonial Policy (1828–1841).* Toronto: Macmillan, 1972.

– "Roebuck, John Arthur." www.biographi.ca.

Cambron, Micheline. "Les bibliothèques d'Antoine Gérin-Lajoie." *Études françaises* 28, no. 4 (1993): 135–50.

– "Pauvreté et utopie: l'accommodement poétique selon le petit gazetier du journal *Le Canadien*." In *Écrire la pauvreté*, edited by Michel Biron and Pierre Popovic, 301–17. Toronto: Éditions du Gref, 1996.

Camerlain, Lorraine. "Trois interventions du clergé dans l'histoire du théâtre à Montréal (1789–1790, 1859, 1872–1874)." MA thesis, Université de Montréal, 1979.

Carignan, Pierre. "L'incubation de la crise politique soulevée en août 1866 par la question de l'éducation: I: Les remous au Bas-Canada." *Revue juridique Thémis* 30, no. 3 (1996): 323–446.

– "La place faite à la religion dans les écoles publiques par la loi scolaire de 1841." *Revue juridique Thémis* 17 (1982–1983): 9–78.

– "La raison d'être de l'article 93 de la loi constitutionnelle de 1867 à la lumière de la législation préexistante en matière d'éducation." *Revue juridique Thémis* 20, no. 3 (1986): 375–455.

Caron, Ivanhoé. "Une société secrète dans le Bas-Canada: l'Association des Frères-Chasseurs." *Proceedings of the Royal Society of Canada.* 20, 3rd series (1926): 17–34.

Carrier, Maurice, and Monique Vachon. *Chansons politiques du Québec*. Vol. I, *1765-1833*. Montreal: Leméac, 1977.

– "De 'C'est la faute à Papineau' aux Quatre-vingt-douze Résolutions avec Jacques Viger." *Revue d'ethnologie du Québec* 5 (1977): 108–12.

Chabot, Richard. *Le curé de campagne et la contestation locale au Québec de 1791 aux troubles de 1837-1838*. Montreal: Hurtubise HMH, 1975.

Chapais, Thomas. *Cours d'histoire du Canada*. 8 vols. Quebec: Librairie Garneau, 1921–1934.

Charland, Thomas. "Un gaumiste canadien: l'abbé Alexis Pelletier." *Revue d'histoire de l'Amérique française* 1, no. 2 (September 1947): 195–236; 3 (December 1947): 463–8.

– *Le Père Gonthier et les écoles du Manitoba, Sa mission secrète en 1897-1898*. Montreal: Fides, 1979.

Charland, Thomas-Marie. "Un projet de journal ecclésiastique." *Report of the Canadian Catholic Historical Society* (1956–57): 39–54.

Charpentier-Dufour, Jacqueline. "La question des agents du Bas-Canada en Grande-Bretagne et l'appui d'éléments britanniques au Parti canadien et patriote (1791–1838)." MA thesis, Université d'Ottawa, Ottawa, ON, 1983.

Chartier, Daniel. "Hector Fabre et le Paris-Canada au cœur de la rencontre culturelle France-Québec de la fin du xixᵉ siècle." *Études françaises* 32, no. 3 (1996): 51–60.

Chartrand, Luc, Raymond Duchesne, and Yves Gingras. *Histoire des sciences au Québec*. Montreal: Boréal, 1987.

Chassé, Béatrice. "Labrie, Jacques." www.biographi.ca.

– "L'Affaire Casault-Langevin." MA thesis. Université Laval, QC, 1965.

Chassé, Sonia. "Pâquet, Benjamin." www.biographi.ca

Chaussé, Gilles. *Jean-Jacques Lartigue, premier évêque de Montréal*. Montreal: Fides, 1980.

Choquette, J.E. Robert. "Pinsoneault, Pierre-Adolphe." www.biographi.ca.

Christie, Robert. *A History of the Late Province of Lower Canada, Parliamentary and Political, From the Commencement to the Close of its Existence as a Separate Province*. Vol. V. Quebec City: T. Cary, 1855.

Clark, Lovell C. *The Guibord Affair*. Toronto and Montreal: Holt, Rinehart and Winston, 1971.

Collin, Jean-Pierre. "La Cité sur mesure: spécialisation sociale de l'espace et autonomie municipale dans la banlieue montréalaise (1875–1920)." *Urban History Review/Revue d'histoire urbaine* 13, no. 1 (June 1984): 19–34.

Colthart, James M. "Ellice, Edward." www.biographi.ca.

Comeau, Michelle. "Les grands magasins de la rue Sainte-Catherine à Montréal: des lieux de modernisation, d'homogénéisation et de différenciation des modes de consommation." *Material History Review/Revue d'histoire de la culture matérielle* 41 (Spring 1995): 58–68.

Constant, Jean-François, and Michel Ducharme. *Liberalism and Hegemony: Debating the Canadian Liberal Revolution.* Toronto: University of Toronto Press, 2009.

Corey, Alfred. *The Crisis of 1830–1842 in Canadian–American Relations.* New York: Russell and Russell, 1941.

Courville, Serge, Jean-Claude Robert, and Normand Séguin. *Atlas historique du Québec. Le paysage laurentien au XIXe siècle.* Quebec City, QC: Presses de l'Université Laval, 1995.

Crunican, Paul. *Priests and Politicians: Manitoba Schools and the Election of 1896.* Toronto: University of Toronto Press, 1974.

Curtis, Bruce. "Comment étudier l'État?" *Bulletin d'histoire politique* 15, no. 3 (2007): 103–7.

– "The 'Most Splendid Pageant Ever Seen': Grandeur, the Domestic, and Condescension in Lord Durham's Political Theatre." *Canadian Historical Review* 89, no. 1 (2008): 55–88.

– *Politics of Population. State Formation, Statistics, ans the Census of Canada, 1840–1875.* Toronto: University of Toronto Press, 2001.

–. "Le redécoupage du Bas-Canada dans les années 1830: un essai sur la 'gouvernementalité' coloniale." *Revue d'histoire de l'Amérique française* 58, no. 1 (2004): 27–66.

– "Tocqueville and Lower Canadian Educational Networks." *Encounters in Education* 7 (Fall 2006): 113–29.

– "Y-a-t-il une histoire de la statistique de l'éducation au bas-Canada?" In *L'école en chiffres? Réflexions sur les statistiques scolaires au Québec, XIXe-XXe siècles,* edited by Brigitte Caulier and Thérèse Hamel, 5–11, 43–51. Quebec: Presses de l'Université Laval, 2006.

Daley, Robert. "Edmund Bailey O'Callaghan: Irish Patriot." PhD diss., Concordia University, Montreal, 1986.

Dansereau, Bernard. *L'avènement de la linotype: le cas de Montréal à la fin du xixe siècle.* Montreal: vlb éditeur, 1992.

de Bonville, Jean. "La liberté de presse à la fin du xixe siècle: le cas de *Canada-Revue.*" *Revue d'histoire de l'Amérique française* 31, no. 4 (1978): 501–23.

– *La presse québécoise de 1884 à 1914. Genèse d'un média de masse.* Quebec: Presses de l'Université Laval, 1988.

de Lagrave, Jean-Paul. *Fleury Mesplet (1734–1794).* Montreal: Patenaude éditeur, 1985.

de L'Isle, Gilles. "Arthabaska et son élite." MA thesis, Université Laval, QC, 1991.

Deschênes, Gaston. *L'année des Anglais. La Côte-du-Sud à l'heure de la conquête.* Quebec: Septentrion, 1988.

Désilets, Andrée. "Sicotte, Louis-Victor." www.biographi.ca.

Deutsch, Karl. *Nationalism and Social Communication. An Inquiry into the Foundation of Nationality.* Cambridge, MA: MIT Press, 1966.

Dionne, Narcisse-Eutrope. *Les ecclésiastiques et les royalistes français réfugiés au Canada à l'époque de la Révolution (1791–1802)*. Quebec: Laflamme, 1905.

Dostaler, Yves. *Les infortunes du roman dans le Québec du XIXᵉ siècle*. Montreal: Hurtubise HMH, 1977.

Doty, Stewart. "The Appeal of Boulanger and Boulangism to North Americans (1881–1889)." *Quebec Studies* 3 (1985): 113–25.

Drolet, Antonio. *Les bibliothèques canadiennes (1604–1960)*. Montreal: Cercle du livre de France, 1965.

Drouin, Daniel. "Les meubliers du Québec aux expositions provinciales, internationales et universelles (1850–1900)." MA thesis, Université Laval, QC, 1993.

Ducharme, Michel. *Le concept de liberté au Canada à l'époque des révolutions atlantiques, 1776–1838*. Montreal and Kingston: McGill-Queen's University Press, 2010.

Dufour, Andrée. "Diversité institutionnelle et fréquentation scolaire dans l'île de Montréal en 1825 et en 1835." *Revue d'histoire de l'Amérique française* 41, no. 4 (1988): 507–35.

– *Tous à l'école. État, communautés rurales et scolarisation au Québec de 1826 à 1859*. Montreal: Hurtubise HMH, 1996.

Dufour, Pierre, and Jean Hamelin. "Mercier, Honoré." www.biographi.ca.

Dufresne, Sylvie. "Attractions, curiosités, carnaval d'hiver, expositions agricoles et industrielles: le loisir public à Montréal au XIXᵉ siècle." In *Rapport du Groupe de recherche en art populaire: travaux et conférences 1975–1979*, edited by Raymond Montpetit, 233–57. Montreal: Université du Québec à Montréal, Département d'histoire de l'art, 1979.

– "Le carnaval d'hiver à Montréal (1883–1889)." *Urban History Review / Revue d'histoire urbaine* 11, no. 3 (1983): 25–45.

– "Fête et société: le carnaval d'hiver à Montréal (1883–1889)." In *Montréal: activités, habitants, quartiers*. 138–88. Montreal: Fides / Société historique de Montréal, 1984.

Dulong, Gaston. *Bibliographie linguistique du Canada français*. Quebec: Presses de l'Université Laval; Paris: Klinksieck, 1966.

Dumont, Fernand. *Genèse de la société québécoise*. Montreal: Boréal, 1993.

Dussault, Gabiel. "Labelle, Antoine." www.biographi.ca.

– "Un réseau utopique franco-québécois et son projet de reconquête du Canada (1860–1891)." In *Relations France-Canada au xixᵉ siècle*. Vol. III, 59–68. Paris: Cahiers du Centre culturel canadien, 1974.

Dutil, Patrice. *L'avocat du diable. Godfroy Langlois et la politique du libéralisme progressiste à l'époque de Laurier*. Montreal: Robert Davies, 1995.

– "The Politics of Muzzling 'Lucifer's Representative': Godfroy Langlois's Test of Wilfrid Laurier's Liberalism (1892–1910)." *Journal of Canadian Studies / Revue d'études canadiennes* 28, no. 2 (1993): 113–29.

Eid, Nadia F. "Les *Mélanges religieux* et la révolution romaine de 1848."
   Recherches sociographiques 10, no. 2–3 (1969): 237–60.
– "Les ultramontains et le Programme catholique." In *Les ultramontains
   canadiens-français. Études d'histoire religieuse présentées en homage au professeur
   Philippe Sylvain,* edited by Nive Voisine and Jean Hamelin, 161–81. Montreal:
   Boréal, 1985.
En collaboration. "Sabrevois de Bleury, Clément-Charles." www.biographi.ca.
English, John, and Réal Bélanger, eds. *Dictionary of Canadian Biography
   Online/Dictionnaire biographique du Canada (DCB/DBC). 2011. www.biographi.ca.*
Fecteau, Jean-Marie. "Mesures d'exception et règle de droit: les conditions
   d'application de la loi martiale au Québec lors des rébellions de 1837–
   1838." *McGill Law Journal/Revue de droit de McGill* 32, no. 3 (1987): 465–95.
Ferretti, Lucia. Entre voisins. La société paroissiale en milieu urbain, Saint-
   Pierre-Apôtre de Montréal (1848–1930). Montreal: Boréal, 1992.
Filteau, Gérard. *Histoire des Patriotes.* Montreal: L'Aurore, 1975.
Finlay, John R. "The State of a Reputation: Bédard as Constitutionalist." *Journal
   of Canadian Studies/Revue d'études canadiennes* 20, no. 4 (1985–86): 60–76.
Finnegan, Mary. "Irish-French Relations in Lower Canada." *Canadian Catholic
   Historical Association, Historical Strudies* (1985): 35–49.
Frégault, Guy. *Canada: The War of the Conquest.* Translated by Margaret M.
   Cameron. Toronto: Oxford University Press, 1969.
Gagnon, France. "L'infrastructure touristique appréhendée à travers les guides
   touristiques et les annuaires : rapport de recherche." In *Le pays laurentien au
   xixe siècle,* edited by Serge Courville, Jean-Claude Robert, and Normand
   Séguin, 153–81. Quebec: Université Laval, 1992.
Gagnon, Hervé. "Les musées accessibles au public à Montréal au xixe siècle.
   Capitalisme culturel et idéal national." *Historical Reflections/Réflexions histo-
   riques* 22, no. 2 (1996): 351–87.
– "Le projet avorté de musée d'histoire naturelle de la Montreal Library
   (1822–1827). Notes de recherche sur l'histoire des premiers musées au
   Québec." *Cahiers d'histoire* 12, no. 2 (Summer 1992): 75–88.
Gagnon, Robert. "Les discours sur l'enseignement pratique au Canada français
   (1850–1900)." In *Sciences et médecine au Québec,* edited by Marcel Fournier,
   Yves Gingras, and Othmar Keel. Quebec: Institut québécois de recherche sur
   la culture, 1987.
– *Histoire de l'École polytechnique (1873–1990).* Montreal: Boréal, 1991.
Gagnon, Serge, and Louise Lebel-Gagnon. "Le milieu d'origine du clergé
   québécois (1774–1840): mythes et réalités." *Revue d'histoire de l'Amérique fran-
   çaise* 37, no. 3 (1983): 373–97.
Galarneau, Claude. "L'abbé Joseph-Sabin Raymond et les grands romantiques
   français (1834–1857)." *Report of the Canadian Historical Society* (1963): 81–8.
– "Les Canadiens en France (1815–1855)." *Cahiers des Dix* 44 (1989): 135–81.

- "Les Français au Canada (1815–1860)." *Études canadiennes / Canadian Studies* 17 (December 1984): 215–20.
- *La France devant l'opinion canadienne (1760–1815)*. Quebec-Paris: Presses de l'Université Laval-Armand Colin, 1970.
- "Holmes, John." www.biographi.ca.
- "Langlois, *dit* Germain, Augustin-René." www.biographi.ca.
- "Leblanc de Marconnay, Hyacinthe-Poirier." www.biographi.ca.
- "Mgr de Forbin-Janson au Québec en 1840–1841." In *Les ultramontains canadiens-français. Études d'histoire religieuse présentées en hommage au professeur Philippe Sylvain*, edited by Nive Voisine and Jean Hamelin, 121–42. Montreal: Boréal Express, 1985.
- "Le philanthrope Vattemare, le rapprochement des 'races' et des classes au Canada (1840–1855)." In *The Shield of Achilles / Le bouclier d'Achille*. W. L. Morton, 94–110. Toronto: McLelland and Stewart, 1968.
- "La presse périodique au Québec de 1764 à 1859." *Proceedings of the Royal Society of Canada*, 4th series, 22 (1984): 143–60.
- "Reiffenstein, John Christopher." www.biographi.ca.
Galarneau, France. "L'élection dans le quartier-ouest de Montréal en 1832: analyse politico-sociale." MA thesis, Université de Montréal, QC, 1978.
- "L'élection partielle du quartier-ouest de Montréal en 1832: analyse politico-sociale." *Revue d'histoire de l'Amérique française* 32, no. 4 (1979): 565–84.
Gallichan, Gilles. "Berthelot, Amable." www.biographi.ca.
- "Bibliothèques et culture au Canada après la Conquête (1760–1800)." MA thesis, Université Laval, QC, 1975.
- *Livre et politique au Bas-Canada (1791–1849)*. Sillery, QC: Septentrion, 1992.
- "La session de 1837." *Cahiers des Dix* 50 (1995): 117–208.
Garneau, François-Xavier. *Voyage en Angleterre et en France dans les années 1831, 1832 et 1833*. Edited by Paul Wyczynski. Ottawa: Éditions de l'Université d'Ottawa, 1968.
Garner, John. *The Franchise and Politics in British North America (1775–1867)*. Toronto: University of Toronto Press, 1969.
Garon, André. "Le Conseil legislatif du Canada-Uni." *Histoire sociale / Social History* 4, no. 8 (1971): 61–83.
- "La fonction politique et sociale des chambers hautes canadiennes, 1791–1841." *Histoire sociale / Social History* 3, no. 5 (1970): 166–87.
Gellner, Ernest. *Nations and Nationalism*. Ithaca, NY: Cornell University Press, 1987.
Gendron, Mario. "Tenure seigneuriale et mouvement patriote. Le cas du comté de l'Acadie." MA thesis, Université du Québec à Montréal, QC, 1986.
Gentilcore, R. Louis, ed. *Historical Atlas of Canada*. Vol. II, *The Land Transformed, 1800–1891*. Toronto: University of Toronto Press, 1987.

Goudreau, Serge. "Mail Conveyance between Montreal and Quebec City at the Beginning of the 19th Century." *The Postal History Society of Canada Journal* 28 (1995): 15–30.

Gougeon, Gilles. *Histoire du nationalisme québécois*. Montreal: vlb éditeur, 1993.

Granger-Remington, Françoise. "Étude du journal politique et littéraire *Le Courrier des États-Unis* de 1828 à 1870." Doctorat de 3ᵉ cycle, Paris-Sorbonne, 1980.

Greenwood, F. Murray. "The Chartrand Murder Trial: Rebellion and Repression in Lower Canada, 1837–1839." *Criminal Justice History* 5 (1984): 129–59.

– "The General Court Martial of 1838–1839 in Lower Canada: An Abuse of Justice." In *Canadian Perspectives on Law and Society, Issues in Legal History*, edited by Wesley Pue and Barry Wright, 249–90. Ottawa: Carleton University Press, 1988.

– *Legacies of Fear: Law and Politics in Quebec in the Era of the French Revolution.* Toronto: The Osgoode Society / University of Toronto Press, 1993.

– "Les Patriotes et le gouvernement responsable dans les années 1837–1838." *Revue d'histoire de l'Amérique française* 33, no. 1 (1979): 25–37.

Greenwood, F. Murray, and James H. Lambert. "Sewell, Jonathan." www.biographi.ca.

Greer, Allan. *The Patriots and the People: The Rebellion of 1837 in Rural Lower Canada.* Toronto: University of Toronto Press, 1993.

Greer, Allan, and Léon Robichaud. "La rébellion de 1837–1838 au Bas-Canada: une approche géographique." *Cahiers de géographie du Québec* 33, no. 90 (1989): 345–77.

Groulx, Lionel. *L'enseignement français au Canada.* Vol. II, *Les écoles du Manitoba.* Montreal: Granger, 1933.

Guay, Donald. *Introduction à l'histoire des sports au Québec.* Montreal: vlb éditeur, 1987.

Guay, Donald, and Ginette Couture. "Inventaire des incorporations des clubs sportifs et récréatifs publiées dans la Gazette officielle du Québec (1867–1900)." Pro manuscripto, 1973, 116 folios.

Guay, Michèle. "La fête de la Saint-Jean-Baptiste à Montréal (1834–1909)." MA thesis, Université d'Ottawa, Ottawa, ON, 1973.

Guimond, Lionel. "*La Gazette de Montréal* de 1785 à 1790." MA thesis, Université de Montréal, QC, 1958.

Guitard, Michelle. *The Militia of the Battle of the Châteauguay: A Social History.* Ottawa: Parks Canada, 1983.

Hamburger, Joseph. *Intellectuals in Politics: John Stuart Mill and the Philosophic Radicals.* New Haven: Yale University Press, 1965.

Hamel, Thérèse. "L'obligation scolaire au Québec: enjeu pour le mouvement syndical et agricole." *Labour/Le Travail* 17 (Spring 1986): 83–102.

– "Verreau, Hospice." www.biographi.ca.

Hamelin, Jean. *Histoire de l'Université Laval: les péripéties d'une idée.* Quebec City, QC: Presses de l'Université Laval, 1995.

Hamelin, Jean, and Nicole Gagnon. *Histoire du catholicisme québécois. Le xxᵉ siècle.* Vol. I. Montreal: Boréal Express, 1984.

Hamelin, Louis-Edmond, and Colette Hamelin. "Évolution numérique séculaire du clergé catholique dans le Québec." *Recherches sociographiques* 2, no. 2 (1961): 189–241.

Hamelin, Marcel. *Les premières années du parlementarisme québécois (1867–1878).* Quebec: Presses de l'Université Laval, 1974.

Hamelin, Pierre. "L'alphabétisation de la Côte du Sud." MA thesis, Université Laval, QC, 1982.

Hardy, René. "À propos du réveil religieux dans le Québec du xixᵉ siècle: le recours aux tribunaux dans les rapports entre le clergé et les fidèles (district de Trois-Rivières)." *Revue d'histoire de l'Amérique française* 48, no. 2 (1994): 187–212.

– "L'activité sociale du curé de Notre-Dame de Québec: aperçu de l'influence du clergé au milieu du xixᵉ siècle." *Histoire sociale / Social History* 3, no. 6 (1970): 5–32.

– "Le charivari: divulguer et sanctionner la vie privée?" In *Discours et pratiques de l'intime,* edited by Manon Brunet and Serge Gagnon, 47–69. Quebec: Institut québécois de recherche sur la culture (IQRC), 1993.

Hare, John. *Aux origines du parlementarisme québécois (1791–1793).* Quebec: Septentrion, 1993.

– *Les Canadiens français aux quatre coins du monde: une bibliographie commentée des récits de voyage, 1670–1914.* Quebec: Société historique de Québec, 1964.

– "Le comportement de la paysannerie rurale et urbaine dans la région de Québec pendant l'occupation américaine, 1775–1776." *Revue de l'Université d'Ottawa* 47, no. 1–2 (1977): 145–50.

– *Contes et nouvelles du Canada français. I: 1778-1859.* Ottawa: Éditions de l'Université d'Ottawa, 1971.

Hare, John, and Jean-Pierre Wallot. *Les imprimés dans le Bas-Canada (1801–1810).* Montreal: Presses de l'Université de Montréal, 1967.

Harris, R. Cole, ed. *Historical Atlas of Canada,* Vol. I, *From the Beginning to 1800.* Toronto: University of Toronto Press, 1987.

Harvey, Louis-Georges. *Le printemps de l'Amérique française. Américanité, anticolonialisme et républicanisme dans le discours politique québécois, 1805–1837.* Montreal: Boréal, 2005.

Hathorn, Ramon. *Lady of the Snows: Sarah Bernhardt in Canada.* New York: Peter Lang, 1996.

Hayne, David. "Lamartine au Québec (1820–1900)." In *Questions d'histoire littéraire: mélanges offerts à Maurice Lemire,* 31–43. Quebec: Nuit blanche éditeur, 1996.

Heap, Ruby. "Un chapitre dans l'histoire de l'éducation des adultes au Québec: les écoles du soir (1889–1892)." *Revue d'histoire de l'Amérique française* 34, no. 4 (March 1981): 597–625.

– "L'Église, l'État et l'éducation au Québec (1875–1898)." MA thesis, McGill University, Montreal, QC, 1978.

– "L'Église, l'État et l'enseignement public catholique au Québec (1897–1920)." PhD diss., Université de Montréal, QC, 1987.

– "Les relations Église-État dans le domaine de l'enseignement primaire public au Québec (1867–1899)." *Sessions d'études*. Société canadienne d'histoire de l'Église catholique, 50 (1983): 183–200.

Hébert, Chantal. *Le burlesque au Québec. Un divertissement populaire*. Montreal: Hurtubise HMH, 1981.

Hébert, Pierre. "Laurent-Olivier David: le libéral malgré lui ou Réflexions sur l'année 1896." In *Combats libéraux au tournant du siècle*, edited by Yvan Lamonde, 145–58. Montreal: Fides, 1995.

Hébert, Robert. *Le procès Guibord ou l'interprétation des restes*. Montreal: Triptyque, 1992.

Histoire du monastère des Ursulines des Trois-Rivières. Vol. II. Trois-Rivières, QC: P.-V. Ayotte, 1892.

Hogue, Clarence, André Bolduc, and Daniel Larouche. Québec, un siècle d'électricité. Montreal: Libre Expression, 1979.

Janson, Gilles. *Emparons-nous du sport. Les Canadiens français et le sport au XIXe siècle*. Montreal: Guérin, 1995.

Jaumain, Serge. "Paris devant l'opinion canadienne-française: les récits de voyage entre 1820 et 1914." *Revue d'histoire de l'Amérique française* 38, no. 4 (Spring 1985): 549–68.

Johnson, Arthur L. "The New York State Press and the Canadian Rebellions (1837–1838)." *American Review of Canadian Studies* 14, no. 3 (1984): 279–90.

Kallman, Hellmutt, Gilles Potvin, and Kenneth Winters, eds. *Encyclopedia of Music in Canada*. Toronto: University of Toronto Press, 1981.

Kennedy, F.J. "Herman Melville's Lecture in Montreal." *New England Quarterly* 50, no. 1 (1977): 125–37.

Kenny, Stephen. "The Canadian Rebellions and the Limits of Historical Perspective." *Vermont History* 58, no. 3 (1990): 179–98.

– "'Strangers' Sojourn: Canadian Journalists in exile (1831–1841)." *American Review of Canadian Studies* 17, no. 2 (1987): 181–205.

Kesteman, Jean-Pierre. "Galt, Alexander-Tilloch." www.biographi.ca.

Kinsman, Ronald Desmond. "The Visit to Canada of 'La Capricieuse' and M. le Commandant de Belvèze in the Summer of 1855 as seen throught the French-Language Press of Lower Canada." MA thesis, McGill University, Montreal, 1959.

Knafla, Louis L. "The Influence of the French Revolution on Legal Attitudes and Ideology in Lower Canada, 1789–1798." In *Le Canada et la Révolution française,* edited by Pierre H. Boulle and Richard A. Lebrun, 83–102. Montreal: Centre interuniversitaire d'études européennes, 1989.

Kolish, Evelyn. "Stuart, Sir James." www.biographi.ca.

Kroëller, Eva-Marie. *Canadian Travellers in Europe.* Vancouver, BC: University of British Columbia Press, 1987.

Labarrère-Paulé, André. *Les institueurs laïques au Canada français, 1836–1900.* Quebec: Presses de l'Université Laval, 1965.

Labonté, Gilles. "Les bibliothèques privées à Québec (1820–1829)." MA thesis, Université Laval, QC, 1986.

Lacourcière, Luc. "Aubert de Gaspé *fils* (1814–1841)." *Cahiers des Dix* 40 (1975): 275–302.

Laflamme, Jean, and Rémi Tourangeau. *L'Église et le théâtre au Québec.* Montreal: Fides, 1979.

Laforte, Conrad. "Un Canadian errant, chanson d'Antoine Gérin-Lajoie." *Dictionnaire des oeuvres littéraires du Québec.* Vol. 1, *Des origins à nos jours,* 714–16. Montreal: Fides, 1978.

Lajeunesse, Marcel. "Le livre dans les échanges sulpiciens Paris-Montréal au cours de la première moitié du xixe siècle." In *Livre et lecture au Québec (1800–1850),* edited by Claude Galarneau and Maurice Lemire, 93–112. Quebec: Institut québécois de recherche sur la culture, 1988.

– *Les Sulpiciens et la vie culturelle à Montréal au xixe siècle.* Montreal: Fides, 1982.

Lalancette, Mario. "La Malbaie et la Révolution française." In *Le Canada et la Révolution française,* edited by Pierre H. Boulle and Richard A. Lebrun, 45–67. Montreal: Centre interuniversitaire d'études européennes, 1989.

Lambert, James. "Plessis, Joseph-Octave." www.biographi.ca.

Lamonde, Yvan. "Les associations au Bas-Canada: de nouveaux marchés aux idées (1840–1867)." In *Territoires de la culture québécoise,* 105–16. Quebec: Presses de l'Université Laval, 1991.

– *Les bibliothèques de collectivités à Montréal (17e–19e siècle).* Montreal: BNQ, 1979.

– "Canadian Print and the Emergence of a Public Culture in Eighteenth and Nineteeth Centuries." In *Les idées en mouvement: perspectives en histoire intellectuelle et culturelle du Canada,* edited by Damien-Claude Bélanger, Sophie Coupal, end Michel Ducharme, 175–90. Quebec City, QC: Presses de l'Université Laval, 2004.

– "Chandonnet, Thomas-Aimé." www.biographi.ca.

– "Classes sociales, classes scolaires: une polémique sur l'éducation en 1819." *Rapport de la Société canadienne d'histoire de l'Église catholique* (1974): 43–7.

– "La confiance en soi du pauvre: pour une histoire du sujet québécois." *Cahiers des Dix* 58 (2004): 21–36; reprinted in *Historien et citoyen: Navigations au long cours,* with the collaboration of Claude Corbo, 129–49. Montreal: Fides, 2008.

- "Conscience coloniale et conscience internationale dans les écrits publics de Louis-Joseph Papineau (1815–1839)." *Revue d'histoire de l'Amérique française* 51, no. 1 (Summer 1997): 3–37.
- "Une contribution à l'histoire de la bibliothèque publique au xixᵉ siècle." In *Les bibliothèques québécoises d'hier à aujourd'hui*, edited by Gilles Gallichan, 21–6. Montreal: Éditions ASTED, 1998.
- "La culture urbaine au Canada et les formes de la culture de l'imprimé aux XVIIIᵉ et XIXᵉ siècles." *Urban History Review / Revue d'histoire urbaine* 33, no. 1 (2004): 46–50.
- *Gens de parole: Conférences publiques, essais et débats à l'Institut canadien de Montréal (1845–1871)*. Montreal: Boréal, 1990.
- "L'histoire du livre et de l'imprimé au Canada et les percées en histoire culturelle et intellectuelle." *Cahiers de la Société bibliographique du Canada / Papers of the Bibliographical Society of Canada* 46, no. 1 (2008): 43–54.
- "Histoire et inventaire des archives de l'Institut canadien de Montréal (1855–1900)." *Revue d'histoire de l'Amérique française* 28, no. 1 (1974): 77–93.
- "A History of Mass Culture and the Media." *Cultures* (UNESCO) 8 (1981): 9–17.
- "La librairie Bossange de Montréal (1816–1819) et le commerce international du livre." In *Territoires de la culture québécoise*, edited by Y. Lamonde, 181–218. Quebec: Presses de l'Université Laval, 1991.
- *La librairie et l'édition à Montréal (1776–1920)*. Montreal: Bibliothèque nationale du Québec, 1991.
- "Liste alphabétique de noms de lieux où existèrent des associations littéraires au Québec (1840–1900)." *Recherches sociographiques* 16, no. 2 (1975): 277–80.
- *Louis-Adolphe Pâquet*. Montreal: Fides, 1972.
- *Louis-Antoine Dessaulles. Un seigneur libéral et anticlerical*. Montreal: Fides, 1994.
- "Le médium est le message: un message impératif pour l'historien?" In *Interkulturelle Kommunikation in der Frankophonen Welt. Literatur, Medien, Kultutransfert. Fetschrift zum 60. Geburstag von Hans-Jürgen Lüsebrink*, edited by Robert Dion, Ute Fendler, Albert Gouaffo und Christoph Vatter, 349–60. St. Ingbert: Röhrig Universitätsverlag, 2012.
- *Ni avec eux ni sans eux. Le Québec et les États-Unis*. Quebec: Nuit blanche éditeur, 1996.
- "'L'ombre du passé': François-Xavier Garneau et l'éveil des nationalités." In *François-Xavier Garneau, une figure nationale*, edited by Gilles Gallichan, Kenneth Landry, and Denis Saint-Jacques, 51–83. Quebec: Éditions Nota Bene, 1998.
- "Papineau, Parent, Garneau et l'émancipation nationalitaire (1815–1852)." *Bulletin d'histoire politique* 7, no. 1 (1998): 41–9.
- *La philosophie et son enseignement au Québec (1665–1920)*. Montreal: Hurtubise HMH, 1980.

– "Les revues dans la trajectoire intellectuelle du Québec." *Écrits du Canada français* 67 (1989): 25–38.

– "La sociabilité et l'histoire socio-culturelle: le cas de Montréal (1760–1880)." In *Territoires de la culture québécoise*, 71–104. Quebec: Presses de l'Université Laval, 1991.

Lamonde, Yvan, and André Morel. "Faribault, Georges-Barthélemi." www.biographi.ca.

Lamonde, Yvan, and Claude Beauchamp. *Données statistiques sur l'histoire culturelle du Québec (1760–1900)*. Chicoutimi, QC. http://classiques.uqac.ca/contemporains/lamonde_yvan/donnes_stats_hist_culture/donnes_stats_hist_culture.html.

Lamonde, Yvan, and Daniel Olivier. *Les bibliothèques personnelles au Québec*. Montreal: Bibliothèque nationale du Québec, 1983.

Lamonde, Yvan, and Jonathan Livernois. *Papineau. Erreur sur la personne*. Montreal: Boréal, 2012.

Lamonde, Yvan, and Raymond Montpetit. *Le parc Sohmer de Montréal (1889–1919). Un lieu populaire de culture urbaine*. Quebec: Institut québécois de recherche sur la culture, 1986.

Lamonde, Yvan, Lucia Ferretti, and Daniel Leblanc. *La culture ouvrière à Montréal (1880–1920): Bilan historiographique*. Quebec: Institut québécois de recherche sur la culture, 1982.

Lamonde, Yvan, Peter F. McNally, and Andrea Rotundo. "Public Libraries and the Emergence of a Public Culture." In *History of the Book in Canada*. Vol. II, *1840–1918*. Edited by Y. Lamonde, Patricia Lockhart Fleming, and Fiona A. Black, 250–71. Toronto: University of Toronto Press, 2005.

Lanctôt, Gustave. *Canada and the American Revolution, 1774–1783*. Toronto: Clarke, Irwin, 1967.

Landry, François. *Beauchemin et l'édition au Québec. Une culture modèle (1840–1940)*. Montreal: Fides, 1997.

Lanthier, Martin. "La violence selon la presse patriote et loyale, à la veille de la rébellion de 1837." MA thesis, Université du Québec à Montréal, QC, 1997.

Laperrière, Guy. *Les congrégations religieuses. De la France au Québec (1880–1914)*. Quebec City, QC: Presses de l'université Laval, 1996.

Lapointe, Pierre-Louis. "La nouvelle européenne et la presse québécoise d'expression française." *Revue d'histoire de l'Amérique française* 28, no. 4 (1975): 517–37.

Laporte, Gilles. "Le radical britannique Chapman et le Bas-Canada (1832–1839)." MA thesis, Université du Québec à Montréal, 1988.

Larrue, Jean-Marc. Le monument inattendu. Le Monument national (1893–1993). Montreal: Hurtubise HMH, 1993.

– *Le théâtre à Montréal à la fin du xixᵉ siècle*. Montreal: Fides, 1981.

Laurent, Monique. "Le catalogue de la bibliothèque du Séminaire de Québec [1782]." DES thesis, Université Laval, Québec, 1973.

Laurin, Luc. "Le nationalisme et le rationalisme du journal *La Patrie* (1879–1897)." MA thesis, McGill University, Montreal, QC, 1973.

Lawson, Philip. *The Imperial Challenge: Quebec and Britain in the Age of American Revolution.* Montreal and Kingston: McGill-Queen's University Press, 1990.

– "'Sapped by Corruption': British Governance of Quebec and the Breakdown of Anglo-American Relations on the Eve of Revolution." *Canadian Review of American Studies* 22, no. 3 (1991): 302–24.

Le Guillou, Louis. *La condamnation de Lamennais.* Paris: Beauchesne, 1982.

Le Moine, Roger. "Francs-maçons francophones du temps de la 'Province of Quebec' (1763–1791)." *Cahiers des Dix* 48 (1993): 93–115.

Lebel, Jean-Marie. "Ludger Duvernay et *La Minerve:* étude d'une entreprise de presse montréalaise de la première moitié du xixᵉ siècle." MA thesis, Université Laval, QC, 1983.

Lebel, Marc. "François-Xavier Garneau et la Société de discussion de Québec." In *François-Xavier Garneau, figure nationale,* edited by Gilles Gallichan, Kenneth Landry, and Denis Saint-Jacques, 85–166. Quebec: Éditions Nota bene, 1998.

– "François-Xavier Garneau et le caractère national des Canadiens français." In *François-Xavier Garneau, figure nationale,* edited by Gilles Gallichan, Kenneth Landry, and Denis Saint-Jacques, 223–41. Quebec: Éditions Nota bene, 1998.

Lebon, Wilfrid. *Histoire du Collège de Sainte-Anne-de-la-Pocatière.* Vol. I. Quebec: Charrier et Dugal, 1948.

Lee, Ian R. "The Canadian Postal System: Origins, Growth and Decay of the State Postal Function (1765–1981)." PhD diss., Carleton University, Ottawa, ON, 1989.

Lefebvre, André. *La "Montreal Gazette" et le nationalisme canadien (1835–1842).* Montreal: Guérin éditeur, 1970.

Lefebvre, Jean-Jacques. "Dupuis, Nazaire." www.biographi.ca.

Lemieux, Lucien. *Histoire du catholicisme québécois. Les xviiiᵉ et xixᵉ siècles.* Vol. I, 1760–1839. Montreal: Boréal, 1989.

Lemire, Maurice, ed. *La vie littéraire au Québec.* Vol. II, 1806–1839. Quebec City, QC: Presses de l'université Laval, 1992.

Lemire, Maurice, and Denis Saint-Jacques, eds. *La vie littéraire au Québec.* Vol. III, *Un peuple sans histoire ni literature.* Québec: Presses de l'Université Laval, 1996.

Lenoir, Joseph. "Montréal et ses principaux monuments (1860)." In *Œuvres* by Joseph Lenoir. Édition critique by John Hare. Montreal: Presses de l'Université de Montréal, 1988.

Lessard, Claude. "L'alphabétisation à Trois-Rivières de 1634 à 1939." *Cahiers nicolétains* 13, no. 3 (1990): 83–117.

Lessard, Michel. "De l'utilité des catalogues commerciaux en ethnohistoire du Québec." *Cahiers des Dix* 49 (1994): 213–46.

Lévesque, Andrée. *Éva Circé-Côté. Libre-penseuse, 1871–1949.* Montreal: Éditions du Remue-Ménage, 2010.

Lockhart Fleming, Patricia, and Yvan Lamonde. "Cultural Crossroads: Print and Reading in Eighteenth-and Nineteenth-Century Montreal." *Proceedings of the American Antiquarian Society* 112, no. 2 (2002): 231–67.

Lortie, Jean d'Arc. *La poésie nationaliste au Canada français (1606–1867)*. Quebec: Les Presses de l'Université Laval, 1975.

Mandrou, Robert. "L'histoire socio-culturelle: rétrospective européenne." *Histoire sociale / Social History* 17 (May 1976): 10–17.

Masson-Juneau, Jacques. "*Le Courrier des États-Unis* (1828, 1869, 1898)." MA thesis, Université de Montréal, 1975.

Matheson, Thomas. "Un pamphlet politique au Bas-Canada. Les *Paroles d'un croyant* de Lamennais." MA thesis, Université Laval, QC, 1958.

Mativat, Daniel. *Le métier d'écrivain au Québec (1840–1900)*. Montreal: Triptyque, 1996.

Maurault, Olivier. "Une révolution collégiale à Montréal il y a cent ans." *Cahiers des Dix* 2 (1937): 35–44.

Maurault, Olivier, and Antonio Dansereau. *Le Collège de Montréal (1767–1967)*. Montreal: n.p., 1967.

Metcalfe, Alan. *Canada Learns to Play: The Emergence of Organized Sport (1807–1914)*. Toronto: McLelland and Stewart, 1987.

– "The Evolution of Organized Physical Recreation in Montreal (1840–1895)." *Histoire sociale / Social History* 11, no. 21 (May 1978): 144–66.

– "Le sport au Canada français au xixᵉ siècle: le cas de Montréal (1880–1914)." *Loisirs et société / Society and Leisure* 6, no. 1 (1983): 105–19.

Miller, J.R. *Equal Rights: The Jesuits' Estates Act Controversy*. Montreal and Kingston: McGill-Queen's University Press, 1979.

Monet, Jacques. "La Fontaine, Louis-Hippolyte." www.biographi.ca.

Monet, Jacques, S.J. *The Last Cannon Shot: A Study of French-Canadian Nationalism 1837–1850*. Toronto: University of Toronto Press, 1976.

Montpetit, Raymond. "Fêtes et société au Québec: la visite du prince de Galles et la construction du Crystal Palace en 1860." In *Rapport du Groupe de recherche en art populaire: travaux et conférences 1975–1979*, edited by Raymond Montpetit, 258–85. Montreal: Université du Québec à Montréal, Département d'histoire de l'art, 1979.

Montreuil, Sophie. "(Se) lire et (se) lire: Joséphine Marchand-Dandurand et la lecture (1879–1886)." In *Lire au Québec au XIXᵉ siècle*, edited by Yvan Lamonde and Sophie Montreuil, 123–50. Montreal: Fides, 2003.

Moogk, Edward B. *Roll Back the Years: History of Canadian Recorded Sound and Its Legacy: Genesis to 1930*. Ottawa: National Library of Canada, 1975.

Murray, Jocelyne. "Les marchés de Trois-Rivières: étude de sociabilité urbaine (1850–1900)." MA thesis, Université du Québec à Trois-Rivières, QC, 1987.

Murray, John. *A Story of the Telegraph*. Montreal: Lovell, 1905.

Muzzo, Johanne. "Les mouvements réformistes et constitutionnels à Montréal (1832–1837)." MA thesis, Université du Québec à Montréal, 1990.

Nelles, Henry Vivian. *The Art of Nation-Building: Pageantry and Spectacle at Quebec's Tercentenary.* Toronto: University of Toronto Press, 1999.

Nelson, Wendie. "The 'Guerre des Éteignoirs': School Reform and Popular Resistance in Lower Canada (1841–1850)." MA thesis, Simon Fraser University, Vancouver, BC, 1989.

Nish, Elizabeth, ed. *Racism or Responsible Government: The French Canadian Dilemna of the 1840s.* Toronto: Copp Clark, 1967.

Ouellet, Fernand. "Bédard, Pierre-Stanislas." www.biographi.ca.

– "Denis-Benjamin Viger et le problème de l'annexion." *Bulletin des recherches historiques* 57, no. 4 (1951): 195–205.

– "L'histoire socio-culturelle: colloque exploratoire." *Histoire sociale / Social History* 17 (May 1976): 5–10.

– "Les insurrections de 1837–1838: un phénomène social." In *Éléments d'histoire sociale du Bas-Canada.* Montreal: Hurtubise HMH, 1972.

– *Lower Canada, 1791–1840: Social Change and Nationalism.* Translated by Patricia Claxton. Toronto: McClelland and Stewart, 1980.

– "Le mandement de Mgr Lartigue de 1837 et la réaction libérale." *Bulletin des recherches historiques* 58, no. 2 (1952): 97–104.

– "Papineau dans l'insurrection de 1837–1838." *Canadian Historical Association Report* (1958): 13–34.

– "Papineau et la rivalité Québec Montréal (1820–1840)." *Revue d'histoire de l'Amérique française* 13, no. 3 (1959): 311–27.

Ouellet, Jacques. "Le développement du système scolaire au Saguenay–Lac-Saint-Jean depuis 150 ans." *Saguenayensia* 30, no. 1 (1988): 12–20.

Ouellet, Marc. "La clé du succès: le discours publicitaire au Québec du tournant du siècle à la Crise." MA thesis, Université Laval, QC, 1993.

Pénisson, Bernard. "Les commissaires du Canada en France (1882–1928)." *Études canadiennes / Canadian Studies* 9 (1980): 3–22.

– "Le Commissariat canadien à Paris (1882–1928)." *Revue d'histoire de l'Amérique française* 34, no. 3 (1988): 357–76.

Perin, Roberto. *Rome in Canada: The Vatican and Canadian Affairs in Late Victorian Age.* Toronto: University of Toronto Press, 1990.

– "Troppo Ardenti Sacerdoti: The Conroy Mission Revisited." *Canadian Historical Review* 61 (September 1980): 283–304.

Plourde, J. Antonin. *Dominicains au Canada.* Vol. I. Montreal: Éditions du Lévrier, 1973.

Porter, John R. "Un projet de musée national à Québec à l'époque du peintre Joseph Légaré (1833–1853)." *Revue d'histoire de l'Amérique française* 31, no. 1 (1977): 75–82.

Portes, Jacques. "'La Capricieuse' au Canada." *Revue d'histoire de l'Amérique française* 31, no. 3 (1977): 351–70.

– "La reprise des relations entre la France et le Canada après 1850." *Revue française d'histoire d'outre-mer* 228 (1975): 447–61.

Pouliot, Léon. "Les évêques du Bas-Canada et le projet d'Union (1840)." *Revue d'histoire de l'Amérique française* 8, no. 2 (1954): 157–70.

– *Mgr Bourget et son temps*. Vol. IV and V. Montreal: Éditions Bellarmin, 1975, 1976.

Prévost, Philippe. "Les relations franco-canadiennes de 1896 à 1911." MA thesis, Paris IV, 1984.

Quinn, Magella. "Les capitaux français et le Québec (1855–1900)." *Revue d'histoire de l'Amérique française* 24, no. 4 (March 1971): 527–66.

Radforth, Ian. "Political Demonstrations and Spectacles during the Rebellion Losses Controversy in Upper Canada." *Canadian Historical Review* 92, no. 1 (March 2011): 1–41.

– *Royal Spectacle: The 1860 Visit of the Prince of Wales to Canada and the United States*. Toronto: University of Toronto Press, 2004.

Rajotte, Pierre. *Les mots du pouvoir et le pouvoir des mots: essai d'analyse des pratiques discursives ultramontaines au xixe siècle*. Montreal: L'Hexagone, 1991.

– "Pratique de la conférence publique à Montréal (1840–1870)." PhD diss., Université Laval, QC, 1991.

Rajotte, Pierre, Anne-Marie Carle, and François Couture. *Le récit de voyage. Aux frontières du littéraire*. Montreal: Triptyque, 1997.

Rambaud, Alfred. "Québec et la guerre franco-allemande de 1870." *Revue d'histoire de l'Amérique française* 6, no. 3 (1952): 313–30.

Revai, Elisabeth. *Alexandre Vattemare. Trait d'union entre deux mondes*. Montreal: Bellarmin, 1975.

Ricard, François. "Beaugrand, Honoré." www.biographi.ca.

Rioux, Jean-Roch. "Doutre, Gonzalve." www.biographi.ca.

Robichaud, Léon. "La Malbaie et la Révolution française." In *Le Canada et la Révolution française*, edited by Pierre H. Boulle and Richard A. Lebrun, 83–102. Montréal, Centre interuniversitaire d'études européennes, 1989.

– "Le pouvoir, les paysans et la voirie au Bas-Canada à la fin du XVIIIe siècle." MA thesis, Department of History, McGill University, Montreal, QC, 1989.

Robins, Nora. "1828–1870: The Montreal Mechanics' Institute." *Canadian Library Journal* 38 (December 1981): 373–9.

Rodrigue, Lise. "L'exemption fiscale des communautés religieuses." *Cahiers de droit* 37, no. 4 (1996): 1109–40.

Roquebrune, Robert de. "M. de Pontois et la rébellion des Canadiens français en 1837–1838", *Nova Francia*, vol. III (1927–1928), 4:238-249; 5:273-278; 6:362-371; IV (1928–1929), 1:3–32; 2:79–100; 3:293–310.

Rosenfeld, Rosalyn M. "Miniatures and Silhouettes in Montreal (1760–1860)." MA thesis, Concordia University, Montreal, 1981.

Rousseau, Guildo. "La santé par correspondence : un mode de mise en marché des médicaments brevetés au début du siècle." *Histoire sociale / Social History* 28, no. 55 (1995): 1–25.

Rousseau, Louis. "À propos du 'réveil religieux' dans le Québec du xixᵉ siècle: où se loge le vrai débat?" *Revue d'histoire de l'Amérique française* 49, no. 2 (1995): 223–45.

– "Boire ou ne pas boire, se sauver ou se perdre ensemble. Le mouvement de tempérance dans le Québec du xixᵉ siècle." *Études canadiennes / Canadian Studies* 35 (1993): 107–22.

– "La conduite pascale dans la région de Montréal, 1831–1865: un indice des mouvements de la ferveur religieuse." In *L'Église de Montréal, aperçus d'hier et d'aujourd'hui (1836-1986)*, 270–84. Montreal: Fides, 1986.

– *La prédication à Montréal de 1800 à 1830. Approche religiologique.* Montreal: Fides, 1976.

– "Les rapports entre le 'réveil' et la réorganisation ecclésiale dans le Québec du 19ᵉ siècle." In *Le diocèse au Québec et en France aux xixᵉ et xxᵉ siècles*, edited by Pierre Guillaume, 126–39. Bordeaux: Maison des sciences de l'homme de l'Aquitaine, 1990.

Rousseau, Louis, and Pierre Feuvrier. "Morphologie des carrières pastorales dans le sud-ouest québécois." In. *Le bas clergé catholique au dix-neuvième siècle*, edited by L. Rousseau, 195–6. Quebec: Université Laval, Groupe de recherche en sciences de la religion, 1995.

Roussellier, Nicolas. *L'Europe des libéraux.* Paris: Éditions Complexe, 1991.

Roy, Jean-Louis. *Édouard-Raymond Fabre, libraire et patriote canadien (1799–1854) contre l'isolement et la sujétion.* Montreal: Hurtubise HMH, 1974.

Roy, Joseph-Edmond. "Napoléon au Canada." *Proceedings of the Royal Society of Canada*, 3rd series (1911): 69–117.

Rudin, Ronald. *Founding Fathers: The Celebration of Champlain and Laval in the Streets of Quebec, 1878–1908.* Toronto : University of Toronto Press, 2003.

Rumilly, Robert. *Histoire de la province de Québec.* Vol. II. Montreal: Valiquette, 1948.

Saint-Hilaire, Marc. "Mobilité et alphabétisation au Saguenay (1840–1940)." In *Espace et culture / Space and Culture*, edited by Serge Courville and Normand Séguin, 227–36. Quebec City, QC: Presses de l'Université Laval, 1995.

Saint-Martin, Louis-Philippe. "L'Histoire du Canada de F.-X. Garneau et la critique." *Revue d'histoire de l'Amérique française* 8, no. 1 (1954): 380–94.

Samuel, Rodrigue. "L'image de la révolution française de 1848 dans la presse du Canada français." MA thesis, Université Laval, QC, 1978.

Savard, Pierre. "1861. La presse québécoise et la guerre de Sécession." *Mosaïque québécoise. Cahiers d'histoire de la Société historique de Québec* 13 (1961): 111–28.

– "Autour d'un centenaire qui n'eut pas lieu." In *L'image de la Révolution française au Québec (1789–1989)*, edited by Michel Grenon, 105–21. Montreal: Hurtubise HMH, 1989.

– *Le consulat général de France à Québec et à Montréal de 1859 à 1914*. Quebec: Presses de l'Université Laval, 1970.

– "Du Lac Saint-Jean au Texas. Claudio Jannet à la recherche de l'Amérique idéale." *Revue française d'histoire d'outre-mer*, 288 (1990): 1–16.

– "L'Italie dans la culture canadienne-française au xixᵉ siècle." In *Les ultramontains canadiens-français: Études d'histoire religieuse présentées en hommage au professeur Philippe Sylvain*, edited by Nive Voisine and Jean Hamelin, 255–66. Montreal: Boréal, 1985.

– "Jules-Paul Tardivel et Louis Veuillot." *L'enseignement secondaire* 45, no. 2 (1966): 85–99.

– *Jules-Paul Tardivel, la France et les États-Unis (1851–1905)*. Quebec: Presses de l'Université Laval, 1967.

– "La Rome de Pie IX vue par un prêtre québécois (1850–1851)." *Annali academici canadesi* 1 (1990): 5–13.

Schmidt, Sarah. "Domesticating Parks and Mastering Playgrounds: Sexuality, Power and Place in Montreal (1870–1930)." MA thesis, McGill University, Montreal, 1986.

Senese, Phyllis. "*La Croix de Montréal* (1893–1895): A Link to the French Radical Right." *Canadian Catholic Historical Association Historical Studies* 53 (1986): 81–95.

Senior, Elinor Kyte. *Redcoats and Patriots: The Rebellions in Lower Canada (1837–1838)*. Ottawa: Canada's Wings and Canadian War Museum, 1985.

Simard, Sylvain. *Mythe et reflet de la France. L'image du Canada en France (1850–1914)*. Ottawa: les Presses de l'Université d'Ottawa, 1987.

Simard, Sylvain, and Denis Vaugeois. "Fabre, Hector." www.biographi.ca.

Smith, Lawrence A.H. "*Le Canadien* and the British Constitution (1806–1810)." *Canadian Historical Review* 38, no. 2 (1957): 97–100.

Sylvain, Philippe. "Forbin-Janson, Charles-Auguste-Marie-Joseph de." www.biographi.ca

– "Lamartine et les catholiques de France et du Canada." *Revue d'histoire de l'Amérique française* 4, no. 1 (June 1950): 29–60; 4, no. 2 (September 1950): 233–48; 4, no. 3 (December 1950): 375–97.

– "Libéralisme et ultramontanisme au Canada français: affrontement doctrinal et idéologique (1840–1865)." In *The Shield of Achilles / Le bouclier d'Achille*, edited by W.L. Morton, 111–38 and 220–56. Toronto: McLelland and Stewart, 1968.

– "Le premier disciple canadien de Montalembert: l'abbé Joseph-Sabin Raymond." *Revue d'histoire de l'Amérique française* 17, no. 1 (June 1963): 93–103.

- "Quelques aspects de l'antagonisme libéral-ultramontain au Canada français (1967)." In *Les idéologies québécoises au 19ᵉ siècle*, edited by Jean-Paul Bernard, 127–49. Montreal: Boréal Express, 1973.
- "Rambau, Alfred-Xavier." www.biographi.ca.
- "La visite du prince Napoléon au Canada (1861)." *Proceedings of the Royal Society of Canada*, 4th series, 2, no. 1 (1964): 105–26.

Sylvain, Philippe, and Nive Voisine. *Histoire du catholicisme québécois*. Vol. 2, *1840–1898*. Montreal: Boréal, 1991.

Teyssier, Grégoire. "La distribution postale de la presse périodique québécoise (1851–1911)." MA thesis, Université Laval, QC, 1996.

Tousignant, Pierre. "*Appel à la justice de l'État*" [CIHM, nᵒ 3462]. In *Dictionnaire des œuvres littéraires du Québec*. Vol. I, edited by Maurice Lemire, 35–7. Montreal: Fides, 1978.
- "Les aspirations libérales des réformistes canadiens-français et la séduction du modèle constitutionnel britannique." In *La Révolution française au Canada français*, edited by Sylvain Simard, 229–38. Ottawa: Les Presses de l'Université d'Ottawa, 1991.

Tousignant, Pierre. "Les Canadiens et la réforme constitutionnelle, 1785–1791." Paper presented at the Canadian Historical Association, 1972.
- "*La Gazette de Montréal* de 1791 à 1796." MA thesis, Université de Montréal, QC, 1960.
- "La genèse et l'avènement de la Constitution de 1791." PhD diss., Université de Montréal, QC, 1971.
- "The Integration of the Province of Quebec into the British Empire, 1763–91." In *Dictionay of Canadian Biography*, IV, xxxii-xlix.
- "La première campagne électorale des Canadiens en 1792." *Histoire sociale/Social History* 15 (May 1975): 120–48.
- "Problématique pour une nouvelle approche de la Constitution de 1791." *Revue d'histoire de l'Amérique française* 27, no. 2 (1973): 181–234.

Tousignant, Pierre, and Madeleine Dionne-Tousignant. "Pierre du Calvet." www.biographi.ca.

Trépanier, Pierre. "Les influences leplaysiennes au Canada français, 1855–1888." *Journal of Canadian Studies/Revue d'études canadiennes* 22, no. 1 (1987): 66–83.
- "La Société canadienne d'économie sociale de Montréal, 1888–1911: sa fondation, ses buts et ses activités." *Canadian Historical Review* 67, no. 3 (1986): 343–62.
- "La Société canadienne d'économie sociale de Montréal, 1888–1911: ses membres, ses critiques et sa survie." *Histoire sociale/Social History* 19, no. 38 (1986): 299–322.

Triggs, Stanley, Brian Young, Conrad Graham, and Gilles Lauzon. *Le pont Victoria: Un lien vital/Victoria Bridge: The Vital Link*. Montreal: McCord Museum, 1992.

Trudel, Jean. "Aux origines du Musée des Beaux-Arts de Montréal. La fondation de l'Art Association of Montreal en 1860." *Journal of Canadian Art History / Annales d'histoire de l'art canadien* 15, no. 1 (1992): 31–60.

– "The Montreal Society of Artists. Une galerie d'art contemporain à Montréal en 1847." *Journal of Canadian Art History / Annales d'histoire de l'art canadien* 13, no. 1 (1990): 61–87.

– *La révolution américaine (1775–1783)*. Sillery, QC: Éditions du Boréal Express, 1976.

Tulchinsky, Gerald. *The River Barons: Montreal Businessmen and the Growth of Industry and Transportation, 1837–1853*. Toronto: University of Toronto Press, 1977.

Vaucamps, Françoise. "La France dans la presse canadienne-française de 1855 à 1880." PhD thesis, Université Laval, QC, 1978.

Verrette, Michel. "L'alphabétisation au Québec (1600–1900)." PhD thesis, Université Laval, QC, 1989.

Verrette, René. "Le libéralisme en région: le cas de Trois-Rivières (1850–1929)." In *Combats libéraux au tournant du siècle*, edited by Y. Lamonde, 185–212. Montreal: Fides, 1995.

Vigneault, Michel. "The Cultural Diffusion of Hockey in Montreal (1890–1910)." MA thesis, University of Windsor, Windsor, ON, 1985.

Vlach, Milada, and Yolande Buono. *Catalogue collectif des impressions québécoises (1764–1820)*. Montreal: Bibliothèque nationale du Québec, 1984.

Voisine, Nive. "Conroy, George." www.biographi.ca.

– *Les Frères des Écoles chrétiennes au Canada*. Vol. II. Quebec: Anne Sigier, 1987.

– "Laflèche, Louis-François." www.biographi.ca.

– *Louis-François Laflèche, deuxième évêque de Trois-Rivières*. Vol. I. Saint-Hyacinthe, QC: Edisem, 1980.

– "Pelletier, Alexis." www.biographi.ca.

– "Réticius, Brother." www.biographi.ca.

– "Taschereau, Alexandre-Elzéar." www.biographi.ca.

Wade, Mason. *The French Canadians 1760–1967*. Vol. I, *1760–1911*. Toronto: Macmillan Co. of Canada, 1968.

Wallot, Jean-Pierre. *Un Québec qui bougeait, trame socio-politique au tournant du xixe siècle*. Montreal: Éditions du Boréal Express, 1973.

Weill, Georges. *L'éveil des nationalités et le mouvement libéral (1815–1848)*. Paris: Alcan, 1930.

White, Ruth L. *Louis-Joseph Papineau et Lamennais. Le chef des Patriotes canadiens à Paris (1839–1845)*. Montreal: Hurtubise HMH, 1983.

Yon, Armand. *Le Canada français vu de France (1830–1914)*. Quebec: Presses de l'Université Laval, 1975.

Index